GENDER AND SEXUALITY IN SENEGALESE SOCIETIES

Crticial African Studies in Gender and Sexuality

Critical African Studies in Gender and Sexuality publishes innovative, interdisciplinary research on intersections of gender, sexuality, and other political, social, economic, cultural, and geographic identity markers. The series has particular interest in groundbreaking scholarship on herstories/histories, elements and politics of gender and sexuality that center critical African thought and philosophies within global contemporary theoretical debates across the disciplines. Thus, manuscripts exploring gender relationships, queer identities, sexualities, masculinities, and femininities within both Africa and its Diaspora in interdisciplinary contexts are highly encouraged.

Recent titles in the series:

Womanhood and Girlhoods in Twenty-First Century Middle Class Kenya: Disrupting Patri-centered Frameworks, by Besi Muhonja

Gender, Ethnicity, and Violence in Kenya's Transitions to Democracy: States of Violence, by Lyn Ossome

Gender and Development in Nigeria: One Hundred Years of Nationhood, edited by Funmi Soetan and Bola Akanji

Through the Gender Lens: A Century of Social and Political Development in Nigeria, editd by Funmi Soetan and Bola Akanji

Child Rape in Ghana: Lifting the Veil, by Matha Donkor

Gender and Sexuality in Senegalese Societies: Critical Perspectives and Methods, edited by Babacar M'Baye and Besi Brillian Muhonja

GENDER AND SEXUALITY IN SENEGALESE SOCIETIES

Critical Perspectives and Methods

edited by Babacar M'Baye and Besi Brillian Muhonja

LEXINGTON BOOKS
Lanham • Boulder • New York • London

Published by Lexington Books
An imprint of The Rowman & Littlefield Publishing Group, Inc.
4501 Forbes Boulevard, Suite 200, Lanham, Maryland 20706
www.rowman.com

6 Tinworth Street, London SE11 5AL

British Library Cataloguing in Publication Information Available

Library of Congress Cataloging-in-Publication Data

Names: M'Baye Babacar, editor | Muhonja, Besi Brillian, editor.
Title: Gender and sexuality in Senegalese societies : critical perspectives and methods / edited by Babacar M'Baye and Besi Brillian Muhonja.
Other titles: Critical African studies in gender and sexuality.
Description: Lanham, Maryland : Lexington Books, 2019. | Series: Critical African studies in gender and sexuality | Includes bibliographical references and index.
Identifiers: LCCN 2019019001| ISBN 9781793601124 (cloth) | ISBN 9781793601131 (electronic)
Subjects: LCSH: Women--Senegal--Social conditions. | Women's rights--Senegal. | Sex role--Senegal. | Gays--Legal status, laws, etc.--Senegal. | Gays--Senegal--Social conditions. | Gay rights--Senegal.
Classification: LCC HQ1236.S38 G46 2019 | DDC 305.309663--dc23
LC record available at https://lccn.loc.gov/2019019001

TABLE OF CONTENTS

INTRODUCTION

New Directions for Studies of Gender and Sexuality in Senegal

Babacar M'Baye

This book focuses on key aspects of gender and sexuality in Senegal, which are crucial themes that have been largely neglected in Africana studies.[1] The book is inspired by the conviction that a full understanding of the complexity of modern Senegalese society necessitates a reinterpretation of not just its precolonial and colonial history but also of its contemporary one as well in terms that recognize the importance of gender and sexuality in the history. We also need to explore Senegalese history, literature, culture, and other aspects in ways that center women's traumatic experiences with both patriarchal dominance and similar abuses that other marginalized groups face due to restrictive constructions of gender and sexual identities in Senegal. By focusing on these central and related dimensions, this volume hopes to pave the way for future scholarships that will recognize that a comprehensive study of gender in Senegal also requires a focus on how popular attitudes toward homosexuality, transgenderism, non-normative gender presentations, and other identities, are considered as transgressive, Western, colonialist, neocolonialist, or antinationalist. These types of inquiries will help to understand past and current constructions of womanhood and patriarchy in Senegal.

Another objective of this volume is to show that women have played a vital role in the development of the field of Senegalese studies. Among these women, one notes the strong presence of Ayo A. Coly and Marame Gueye, two Senegalese intellectuals who, among many other scholars, deserve recognition. For instance, Coly's 2010 book, *The Pull of Postcolonial Nationhood: Gender and Migration in Francophone African Literatures*, and Gueye's 2011 chapter, "Ode to Patriarchy: The Fine Line between Praise and Criticism in a Popular Senegalese Poem," deserve special mentions.[2] These two works have infused into Senegalese studies a new revolutionary focus on gender and (or) sexuality which has been largely missing from the field since the heydays of the 1970s when women pioneers established the intellectual tradition. Coly's contribution to Senegalese studies is enormous since it enables us to study nationalism without representing freedom struggle in postcolonial states as antithetical to valuations of gender equity and homeland. Building on a critical feminist tradition stretching back to Elleke Boehmer, Obioma Nnaemeka, and Carole Boyce Davies, Coly judiciously puts African patriarchy on trial. In *The Pull of Postcolonial Nationhood*, Coly writes: "[T]he choice by Francophone African migrant women to negotiate home in national narratives that most often than not subordinate women is important for what it reveals about the political and ideological resonance of postcolonial nationhood on the one hand, and, on the other, the weak appeal of postnationalism in the postcolonial context."[3] Thus, while it allows us to resist patriarchal dominance over Senegalese women, Coly's book warns us against replicating the binary which consists of representing these women as viscerally oppositional to home and nation.

This current project attempts to make a similar intervention by measurably putting Senegalese patriarchy on trial without essentializing it as an absolute structure in which women and other marginalized groups are unable to negotiate and obtain freedom. Our project seeks to do so by revealing the ways in which marginalization has historically allowed Senegalese women and other subaltern groups to employ any possible means to resist patriarchal and neocolonial dominations and create communities built on social solidarity, economic cooperation, political sagacity, and mental and artistic ingenuity. This reading of Senegalese women's position in the nation-state as a blend of both powerlessness and agency is evident in the phenomenal interpretation that Gueye makes in her study of a major Senegalese poem titled "Fatou Gaye." Discussing the poem, Gueye writes:

> Using an unfounded Islamic view on the relationship between men and women, Gaye represents husbands as "masters" and wives as "slaves" whose salvation depends on the formers' blessings. He validates his chauvinistic behavior and at the same time sings his own praises. For him, his creative work is a reward for Fatou and proof of his generosity. As her husband, he did not have to praise her for doing her "wifely job." However, although Gaye advocates male supremacy and represents Fatou as the subordinate, he continually contradicts himself throughout the poem. It is clear that Fatou was the pillar of his household and the one who "made" himself into who he was in the community. Thus his poem is convoluted and shows how complicated gender roles in Wolof society are. This text raises many questions that require further investigation.[4]

Like Gueye, the contributors of this volume seek to understand gender relations in Senegal beyond the Western either/or and us/them binaries which, so far, have prevented most scholars from addressing the complexity of male-female interactions and expectations in Africa. In this sense, Gueye's essay drives home an aspect that Western scholars may easily fail to notice, which is the complicated nature of the relations between men and women in Senegalese society that the common "top-down" approach to culture and people cannot comprehend. Yet, recognizing the danger of forcing Western scholarly interpretation of gender relations in Senegal does not preclude the need to make Senegalese patriarchy accountable for its historical and current abuses. Fortunately, Ivy Mills's dissertation, *Sutura: Gendered Honor, Social Death, and the Politics of Exposure in Senegalese Literature and Popular Culture* (2011), has made strong interventions in the study of this patriarchy. As a white American scholar who did fieldwork in Senegal, Mills participates in an increasing and very promising scholarship from women of diverse nations, background, and races on the complexities of gender and sexuality in Senegal. In this seminal scholarship, one also finds key contributions such as Erin Joanna Augis' article, "Aïcha's Sounith Hair Salon: Friendship, Profit, and Resistance in Dakar" (2014), Kelly M. Duke Bryant's book, *Education as Politics: Colonial Schooling and Po-*

litical Debate in Senegal, 1850s-1914 (2015), Hilary Jones's monograph, *The Métis of Senegal: Urban Life and Politics in French West Africa* (2013).[5] Among many other studies, these works have examined the agency that Senegalese women have demonstrated and exercised in either colonial or postcolonial times while suffering from injustices that put into question both European and African patriarchal dominance. Mills makes a very strong and brave contribution to this scholarship when she writes in her dissertation:

> While I was in Dakar, my exposure to the complex terrain of contemporary cultural politics also taught me that communal and familial *teraanga* has its limits. Popular debates around the exploitation of maids, the degradation of virtue embodied by prostitutes, the banishment of rogue Sufi wives from pious legibility, and the threat to communal life that *góor-jigéen* (gay/transgendered subjects) are purported to pose in the wake of a media-generated same-sex marriage scandal led me to a meditation on the terms of full inclusion into the normative honorable community, as well as of the care and protection that that inclusion guarantees.[6]

By drawing attention to the incongruency between Senegalese notion of "*teranga*" (a Wolof word for "hospitality") and the ostracization of "gay and transgendered subjects" in Dakar, Mills reflects the kind of deep schism that is preventing modern Senegalese society from extending the republican rights and benefits of liberty, equality, and fraternity to all its people. LGBTQI2-S (Lesbian, Gay, Bisexual, Transgender, Questioning, Intersex, or Two-Spirit) identified people are especially deprived of these privileges since they are victims of a fairly recent form of customary violence which, since its emergence in 2008, has rendered them strangers in their own land.

Unfortunately, the violence to which sexual minorities are subjected in Senegal is a serious problem that many African scholars are unwilling to address for reasons that deserve intellectual inquiry. On a personal note, I have been involved in the scholarship on LGBTQI2-S issues in Senegal for almost eight years now, because I have noticed that many black scholars, especially continental and male African intellectuals, tend to ignore them, preferring to discuss only racism, colonialism, neocolonialism, and other pertinent issues. Such problems should not be always explored in full isolation from those around gender and sexuality. The limited exploration of gender and sexuality in Africana studies has grave consequences since it is delaying a much-needed scholarship on the development of past and contemporary constructions of complex gender and sexual identities in African societies in which social, political, cultural, and spiritual forces cannot be explored in total isolations from one another.

Thus, while working on my second book, titled *Black Cosmopolitanism and Anticolonialism: Pivotal Moments*, I found in the archival materials that I perused numerous mentions of homosexuality in colonial Senegal and was flabbergasted by the absence of work about this topic. This oversight probably comes from a larger context in which African scholars, especially those who are men and heterosexual, are largely unwilling to study homosexuality in the continent or elsewhere. Such a situation has endured. Deborah P. Amory decried it in a 1997 article in which she found "In African Studies, the studied avoidance of research on homosexuality and the downright heterosexual panic concerning the issue."[7] Amory continues: "This tendency is perhaps best captured by the recurring and insistent refrain, 'There Is No Homosexuality in Africa!' This refrain is chanted like a mantra by politicians, scholars, and lay people alike, and is often accompanied by the similarly insidious accusation that homosexuality is a 'western perversion' imposed upon or adopted by African populations."[8]

Besides, there is the unjustified claim that people who study homosexuality in Africa are furthering the "gay agenda" or the influence of "the gay Western lobby" in the continent when nothing could be further from the truth. A case in point is that of the Ugandan activist scholar Stella Nyanzi, who, besides having lost her teaching position at the Makerere Institute, was smeared by the Ugandan Government for having allegedly committed crimes against the state and promoted feminism and queer ideology of the *Bazungu* (a Ugandan derogatory term for whites and foreigners), when all she did was stand up for women, sexual minorities, and other oppressed groups in her nation.[9]

Fear of a similar plight may be the reason why many African scholars easily ascribe to the unscientific attitude which consists of perceiving the study of homosexuality, transgenderism, and related topics as being unworthy of scholarly attention. But what is really driving these scholars to adopt these views is the fear of being associated with the lifestyles that the research on homosexuality or transgenderism examines. Discussing the ill-posed question of whether one should be "pour ou contre l'homosexualité" [for or against homosexuality] or not, an anonymous Senegalese blogger laments the binarity that shapes popular attitudes about this practice in his country. He writes: "Say that you are against and you are a model Senegalese, on the good side; say that you are for and you will be accused of being alienated, complexed, Western, atheist, homosexual" (translation by M'Baye).[10] Thus, fear of being maligned or associated with a lifestyle that is deemed as Western, uprooting, immoral, and decadent is preventing Senegalese scholars, especially men, to explore the issues of gender and sexuality in their country that they understand better than anybody else. By co-editing this book, I hope to give courage to other Senegalese male scholars to study topics which are as relevant as any others.

President Macky Sall often describes homosexuality and the attitudes against it in Senegal as "des problémes de société" [societal problems] that "chaque societé doit apprécier selon ses capacités" [each society must assess based on its abilities]."[11] If resolving the issues around homosexuality in Senegal requires the respect for every society's visions of its realities, then one needs to also consider all the angles through which these truths are known. In other words, scholars need to put aside their personal inclinations and preferences and conduct the needed scientific inquiries that will explicate homosexuality, transgenderism, and related controversial topics in all their complexities. As the anonymous blogger states: "Above all, this question, 'for or against homosexuality,' annihilates, by its very form, any kind of complexity; it hides the real stakes that the issue of homosexuality in Senegalese society questions" (translation by M'Baye).[12] In order to explore this complexity, Senegalese academics must recognize it and view research on homosexuality as well as on other LGBTQI2-S themes as a scientific and social exigency, like their contemporaries in many countries, such as South Africa, Uganda, Kenya, and other parts of Africa have done.[13]

A BRIEF REVIEW OF THE SCHOLARSHIP ON GENDER AND SEXUALITY IN SENEGAL

Scholarship on gender and sexuality in Senegal is necessary because the country could benefit from inquiries explaining the social causes of controversies around them. One of such controversies occurred on January 30, 2016, when Wally Ballago Seck, a major Senegalese singer, tore his handbag at the Grand Théâtre, a major concert hall in Dakar, Senegal, in front of his fans.[14] When Patrick Simonin, a French journalist, asked him, on the TV5 show called *Invité*, why he tore such a luxurious bag that many international stars carry? Seck, replied, "It's normal. Some people say it's a woman's bag. They do not understand. So, at one point, they hit a sore spot. My spiritual guide, my very dear marabout, cheikh Ahmad Bamba Khadim Rassoul, pushed me to tear the bag" (translation by M'Baye).[15] Seck also said, "I did it because I love my country. I do not like controversy and I love to please Senegalese" (translation by M'Baye).[16] Thus, Seck's religiosity and his loyalty to the Senegalese nation and people led him to succumb to the public representation of a man carrying a fancy bag deemed "female" as abominable. The pressure and bias of a public that he endearingly describes as the people "qui ne comprennent pas" [who do not understand] led an artist, who has not been given the full opportunity to express his creative Afropolitanism, to symbolically tear a bag in front of a defiant mob. Therefore, Seck surrendered to cultural vigilantism not because he personally believed that it was improper for a man to carry a woman's bag, but because he was afraid to be associated with a fashion choice that was perceived as a trait of homosexual culture. As was apparent in several journal front pages that were produced during the above controversy, Seck was so much ridiculed in Senegalese media that he ended up giving in to what amounted to no less than public or mob lynching.[17]

It was unfortunate to see how no commentator informed the Senegalese public that Seck's act of carrying fashionable bags could be experimental acts of Afropolitanism. His fashion choice registered his attempt to blend his creative modern African sensibilities with their world equivalents without losing his roots, communalism, and individuality. Seck is not alone in this development of a rich, yet unexplored, Afropolitanism in Senegal in which young people invent their unique sense of hybrid identities and popular culture with a blend of accouterments, sounds, feelings, and attitudes toward the past and the present. Describing Simon Gikandi's definition of the term "Afropolitanism," Jamin Ohwovoriole writes: "To be Afropolitan is to be connected to knowable African communities, nations, and traditions; . . . to live a life divided across cultures, languages, and states. It is to embrace and celebrate a state of cultural hybridity—to be of Africa and of other worlds at the same time."[18] This Afropolitanism transcends binaries and challenges intolerance, bigotry, and easy thinking.

Given its unique and rich multicultural and intellectual heritage, Senegal is a modern nation in which the influences of Afropolitanism on constructs such as gender, sexuality, religion, and politics should be studied. After all, Senegal was one of the former French African colonies that distinguished itself with an Afropolitan dandyism expressed in adorations of *savoir-vivre* and the art of smelling good and dressing, eating, and living well. Seck may be a modern example of this Afropolitan dandyism of which past and present histories remain unexplored. By dealing with transgressive gender and sexual identities in Senegalese culture, this volume hopes to open up new space through which these and other dimensions, which are thus far considered as taboo, may be examined.

Fortunately, model scholarships on sexuality in Africa have been produced within the past few years. These works have been made possible through edited volumes such as Signe Arnfred's *Re-Thinking Sexualities in Africa* (2006), Sylvia Tamale's *African Sexualities: A Reader* (2011), and Sokari Ekine and Hamika Abbas' volume, *Queer African Reader* (2013).[19] These books resist the myth of homogeneity which sanctions violence against sexual and gender nonconforming minorities in Africa. The studies confront the heteronormative essentializing of sexualities and demonization of nonconforming gender identities in contemporary Africa. A similar laudable effort is Anne Crémieux's edited volume, titled *Homosexualités en Afrique*, which was published as the ninety-sixth number of the cutting-edge journal *Africultures*.[20] It would be grave not to recognize the incredible contribution of the Senegalese woman scholar, Ndèye Gning, to this scholarship, especially through her article in this special issue of *africultures*. Entitled "Les motifs de l'illégitimité sociale de l'homosexualité au Sénégal" [The reasons for the social illegitimacy of homosexuality in Senegal], Gning's essay is crucial since it represents the term *goorjigeen* as not only a derogatory word but also an expression which can subsume a person to a low position. Gning explains: "Like equivalent terms in other languages, *goorjigeen* is an insult that humiliates the man by implicitly calling into question his status as a dominant, virile, and authoritarian male: the *goorjigeen* subordinates his status of man to that of the woman, placing the stigmatization of homosexuality in an essentialist vision of social relations of sex" (translation by Babacar M'Baye).[21] Gning is right because similar stigmatization processes have been historically deployed in other societies to relegate marginalized people to low and menial positions with the clear intent to maintain dogmatic worldviews.

Another major contribution to the study of non-binary gender and sexual identities in Senegal is Christophe Broqua's 2017 article titled "Góor-jigéen: la resignification négative d'une catégorie entre genre et sexualité (Sénégal)" [Góor-jigéen: the negative resignification of a category between gender and sexuality (Sénégal)]. Removing the term "*Góor-jigéen*" from the negative meaning in which it is confined, Broqua skillfully represents it as an expression of agency and resistance against oppression.[22] Broqua's article is crucial since it helps to bring forth the most important requirement in the study of variant gender and sexual cultures in Senegal. This precept is the fact that a *Góor-jigéen* is as human as anyone else. Zora Neale Hurston made a similar pronouncement in 1938 when she said that black people like to "love and hate and fight and play and strive and travel and have a thousand and one interests in life like other humans."[23] It is high time that Senegalese marginalized communities, such as the *Góor-jigéen* and other groups, are treated as equal humans in every sense of the word, and not as entities that should be brutalized and, then, made to feel lucky of being partially "tolerated" and "integrated" into a larger society or culture.

A TRIBUTE TO THE PIONEERS OF THE STUDY OF GENDER IN SENEGALESE CULTURE

Thirty-eight years after it was published, Mariama Bâ's *Song Long a Letter* remains central to the study of Senegalese culture, because it embodies many of the social and ideological challenges that thwart equal relationships between men and women in society. These obstacles are not particular to Senegal since they stem from a long history of gender relationships in Africa that was heavily transformed by the urgent nationalisms which compelled black male revolutionaries to postpone the needs of black women to the post-independence eras. It was thus with perplexity and disappointment that African women, who fought hard with their men during the pre-independence struggles, found their priorities brushed off or postponed. A good scholarly representation of these dynamics is the book, *Femme d'Afrique: La vie d'Aoua Kéita racontée par elle-même* [An African woman: The autobiography of Aoua Kéita told in her own words] (1975). This text reflects the type of chauvinism and stereotypes that a West African woman intellectual who wanted parity faced in the 1940s and '50s. Coupled with their disdain of the *autochtones*, the West African male elite that Keita met in Senegal and Mali during her early career also suffered from a dislike of educated black women, especially of those they viewed as threats to their political ambitions. This unjustified trepidation was apparent in the mid-1940s when Keita was a militant of the *Rassemblement Démocratique Africain* (RDA), a major political party in French Soudan (colonial Mali). Around that time, the head of the coalition of tailors in Tombouctou disparaged Keita and her female companion Bollo Yattara, who were both organizing Malian laborers for better work conditions.[24] Perceiving them as competitions, the West African man told the women, "You would better rest quietly in the shadow of your homes, instead of always being in the streets and in houses and bothering people all day and night. You are meddling with a man's work that no woman has ever done."[25] This prejudice from a privileged African man of the colonial period was not different from the bias of advantaged Europeans of the same epoch. Keita remembers a similar incident in which a European health inspector of the *Afrique Occidentale Française* (French West Africa) told her, during a meeting in colonial Sénégal, "I urge you, Madame, to stop your involvement in politics. You have a job that can help you serve your country, do a lot of good to your people, without being pursued by the government, which, no matter what is said, had done good things in Africa."[26] Thus, during the 1950s, both elite African and European men relegated West African women intellectuals and revolutionaries to margins, out of the privileged public and professional spheres, since they perceived their education as a limited opportunity that should serve for only the maintenance of patriarchal orders. Fortunately, in spite of the challenges against her attempts to organize French Soudan's workers and resist colonialism, Keita finally triumphed in her endeavors by becoming a major political figure in this region.

Though she hailed from Mali, Keita's resistant feminism inspires us to search for her equivalents in post-independence Senegal. In this context in which women's historical contributions to civil rights and independence struggles must be explored, Bâ's *So Long a Letter* is seminal because it challenges not only male patriarchy and chauvinism but also many interpretations of Islamic practices behind which Senegalese men often hide to craft ideologies that further alienate women and other marginalized groups. One of these practices is the institution of polygamy that Bâ vituperates through her depiction of Modou's disparate treatments of his numerous wives. Bâ dismantles not only the myth of the intrinsic virtues of polygamy but also the myriad of tensions that this practice creates in families that men can hardly treat humanely, fairly, and evenly as Islam recommends. Thus, a system that traditionally served to allow men to have multiple children who could till farms and enrich a community has ended up becoming a panacea to modernity when most husbands who are in polygamous unions are unable to take care of themselves, let alone feed, shelter, and care for their multiple wives and children. Consequently, Senegal has a very high number of children who are begging in the streets for means of survival when they are supposed to be nurtured by their parents of sent to proper schools for a prosperous future. Studying gender and sexuality in Senegal could help tackle these kinds of issues which hamper the country's development.

The essays in this volume build on Bâ's denunciations of polygamy since they look at the other domains in which women's conditions in Senegal reveal the enormous work that must be done before their country's dreams of national independence can be fully realized. Even if they do not quote her, these essays' authors would probably agree with the recommendations that the eminent Senegalese sociologist Fatou Sow Sarr made at a March 2013 convention at which she listed the five key elements that are required for the dismantlement of gender stereotypes and unequal relations between men and women in Senegal. These are:

- Harmonization of the law with commitments for the following points: granting of nationality, paternal power, choice of marital home;
- Media treatment of gender inequality issues;
- More commitment in terms of gender-sensitive budgeting;
- The autonomy of the ministry in charge of equality from the party in power; and
- Better involvement of men.[27]

While all the above points are crucial, the second one is highly important because gender inequality is such a neglected and lingering problem in Senegalese society that the media and, sometimes, many intellectuals avoid to tackle. The situation is so serious that archaic notions about women's status that one expects from the Middle Ages often emerge from the viewpoints of a number of modern Senegalese intellectuals who were trained in Western deductive reasoning and logic. Such was the case on March 9, 2018, when a philosophy professor called Songué Diouf, one of the regular guests of the *Jakaarlo* TV show of Télé Futurs Médias, blamed Senegalese women and girls who are raped for having asked for it due to the sexy ways they dress.[28] Diouf's statements that most Senegalese would simply brush off as the inappropriate assertations of a so-called philosopher are more dangerous than they appear. His declarations stem from a certain type of Senegalese male chauvinism which has been insufficiently confronted.

Diouf's prejudice stands on a long-held belief in the superiority of men over women that neither Christianity nor Islam have challenged enough in Africa. In fact, one may even argue that monotheistic religions in Africa have contributed to the reinforcement of kinds of male privilege that both European and Arab cultural imperialisms legitimized as divine and natural. It is therefore not a surprise that Senegalese women living in both their place of birth or the diaspora are sometimes victims of horrific gender-based crimes of unimaginable proportions due to the lingering archaic notion that a man is superior to a woman. It is probably a similar ideology that led Ahamdo Bubba M'Baye, a forty-one-year-old Senegalese man, to follow his estranged wife, Bigué Ndao, from her birth country to Southeast Edmonton, Canada, and stab her to death in her own apartment, on Monday, May 7, 2018.[29] The issue here is not just the universal threat to violence that wives who run from abusive partners face but also the baseless, antedated, discriminatory, and illegal view of men as more important than women that Senegalese culture accepts. Since the 1970s, key Senegalese's films and literary texts have addressed gender inequalities, but this important work remains insufficiently examined to provide a national framework and groundwork for tackling the disparities between men and women in the country.

In addition, this volume is inspired by the tremendous work that a few intellectuals of various backgrounds have produced since the 1980s to give voice to Senegalese women. A pioneering figure in this scholarship is Fatou Sow Sarr whose dissertation was one of the first scholarly texts to emphasize the centrality of women in Senegalese modern development. Building her own research on those of her predecessors, such as Marie-Angélique Savané, Ndèye Sow, and Fatou Sow, among others, Sarr laments the sustained ways in which the Senegalese state has not devoted full attention to women's conditions, preferring to only promote some idea of women's access to education, health, and employment.[30] According to Sarr, the Senegalese state ignores the aspect Ndèye Sow regards as the root cause of its unsuccessful policies toward women, namely, the fact that "the failure is due also to the erratic conceptual approaches to women's problems, to the prejudices against them, [and] to the type of development in which we wanted to integrate them" (translation by Babacar M'Baye).[31] The essays in our volume contribute to the seminal work that Sarr and her predecessors have done by focusing not only on the social and material conditions of Senegalese women but also on the psychological and cultural ones which have prevented their full emancipation. These women's fight for structural justice cannot be separated from their struggles for cultural freedom.

Sarr's contributions to the study of gender in Senegal cannot be underestimated since she was also one of the first African women intellectuals to pursue higher education in Sociology from the University of Dakar (Now Université Cheikh Anta Diop) in the 1960s before she later earned a doctoral degree in sociology at Université de Paris VIII, France, and a PhD in social work and social politics at the Université de Laval, Quebec. Yet, what makes Sarr unique is the ways in which she has almost single-handedly taken on male patriarchy in Senegal over the past decades by confronting lingering gender and sexual injustices that other pioneer feminists from various parts of the African continent have also resisted during the past few decades. Sarr's influence in this struggle is apparent in a November 2008 issue of the journal, *Travail, genre et sociétés*. In this interview done by Thérèse Locoh and Isabelle Puech, Sarr suggests the main challenges that one faces for being a feminist in Africa. Taking her own example, Sarr notes the reluctance of most Senegalese men to challenge male dominance in her native country.[32] Sarr states:

> [I cannot help recalling again, for I have done so many times since it was shocking, the commentary of a professor at the University of Dakar, during a debate on the radio. "Here you go back to a western feminist speech." And, doubtless, to better establish his argument, he said: "Islam allows a husband to correct his wife when she disobeys him." The commentary related to a miscellaneous incident in Kaolack, in 1993: Following an argument with her husband, a young woman was transported to the hospital where she was to die shortly after her admission. As the Muslim tradition wants, she was buried quickly (under the circumstances), without her husband being worried]. (translation by M'Baye)[33]

Therefore, a major issue women also face in Senegal is that one interpretation of Islam, Christianity, or any other faith is often used on ideological ground to delegate privilege to one group over another. The problem lies less with the religions themselves than with the fact that men often interpret their texts in terms that reinforce their dominance over women. Consequently, in Senegal, masculine interpretations of Islam often sanction or tolerate the kinds of daily violence that women may endure only to be told to bear the pain and wait for their salvation in the other world. Thus, the concept of *mugn* (bearing), that the Wolof people have used to convince or urge their women to tolerate the challenges of marriage with patience, courage, and perseverance, is pervasive in Senegal's moral conscience and folklore.[34] Fallou Ngom touches on this notion of *mugn*, that he spells as *muñ*, in his book, *Muslims Beyond the Arab World: The Odyssey of Ajami and the Muridiyya* (2016), in which he theorizes it as part of the larger concept that he calls *sanctified suffering*.[35] A similar concept is the idea that "*ku ndeyyam liggey du torox*" [the mother who served as a good wife protects her child from failure and social rejection].[36] These are very important concepts that can tell us much about Wolof and other Senegalese worldviews. But these beliefs sometimes obfuscate the fact that bearing pain should not prevent the victimized person from denouncing the abuse and its perpetrators and seeking justice.

Fortunately, Senegalese women are sometimes able to reject normative abuse that is imposed with masculinist and religiously manipulated notions about their roles. In this vein, Sarr lauds the bravery that a group of Senegalese women expressed in Kaolack after a 1993 incident by marching toward the governor's house to demand the arrest of a man who had killed his wife.[37] By praising these women for their bravery, Sarr suggests that feminism must not be considered as a dirty Western word in Senegal but, rather, as a progressist notion that invokes the importance of resisting oppression in radical ways. Feminism invokes the rightful stance against injustice that Senegalese women can demonstrate against all forms of subjugation.

Another reason why this volume is dedicated to Sarr is her status as one of the first Senegalese scholars to recognize the importance of studying the role of sexuality in her country. Sarr is part of a radical Senegalese women's intellectual tradition that places sexuality at the center of cultural debates with unflinching bravery. In the interview with Locoh and Puech, Sarr asserts:

> At the moment, the most difficult debate is about sexuality, that of body control and fertility. African women want contraception to decide on their number of children, but they are reluctant to talk about sexual freedom, sexual pleasure, or sexual orientation that is still very difficult to hold, as a public discourse defending women's rights. I know these difficulties since I coordinated, with Codou Bop, a collective work, *Notre corps, notre santé. La Santé et la sexualité des femmes en Afrique subsaharienne* [Our body, our health. Women's health and sexuality in sub-Saharan Africa] (2004]), from the initiative of the reproductive health Research Network in francophone Africa, which I chaired from 1992 to 1996. I am currently collaborating with the research group on women and laws in Senegal, coordinated by Codou Bop, to reflect on sexuality in Senegal. One of our members, the author of an article on female homosexuality, has encountered enormous difficulties in finding women who agree to speak to her. It is not yet in the public debate. (translation by M'Baye)[38]

Thus, in her interview, Sarr almost summarizes the major hurdles that one faces by studying gender relationships and (or) sexuality in Senegal. As the quotation suggests, the obstacles include the belief that women's emancipation has nothing to do with "sexual freedom, sexual pleasure or sexual orientation." These three concepts are so much taboo in Senegal that scholars from the country often avoid them for fear of controversies. This silencing of sexuality, sexual desire, and sexual preference, and other aspects, such as gender variance and play, reduces the scope and potentials of Senegalese studies scholarship. The avoidance of these themes encourages the lingering absence of more critical intellectual debates about them, leading one to wonder what the functions of university professors and students are when they do not entail examining the complex and taboo issues of the nations they serve. The contributions to this book attempt to end this unbearable silence and expand the intellectual and radical tradition that Sarr initiated by defiantly exploring issues of gender and sexuality in Senegal. In their unique ways, each author delves into special and relevant aspects of these themes, revealing the existence of a new critical mass that will hopefully invigorate the field of Senegalese studies.

M'Baye's chapter in the examination of the plight that gender-variant individuals have faced in Senegal within the past decade directs us to consider representations of queerness on record in literature and history. In so doing, M'Baye invites considerations of ignored histories, sources, and interpretations on the subject. Discussing texts such as Bâ's 1981 novel, *Un chant écarlate* [*Scarlet Song*], Aminata Sow Fall's 1982 novel, *Le Revenant* (The Revenant), and Ousmane Sembène's 1973 film *Xala* [*Xala*], M'Baye attempts to write Senegalese homosexual, transgender, and lesbian individuals back into their national history, culture, and literature in which they rightfully belong and are represented in ambiguous terms. Reading M'Baye's chapter, one notes how the portrayals of the *gôr djiguène* in post-independence Senegal somewhat mirror the depictions of these individuals in European colonial writings. In both kinds of accounts, the *gôr djiguène* appears as an anomaly in a society where deep-seated colonial, postcolonial, religious, and patriarchal norms contribute to their subjugations.

The collaborative essay written by Susan Telingator and Sindiso Mnisi Weeks enriches the collection due to the innovative ways in which its authors give considerable attention to the important "*Loi sur*

La Parité" [law of parity]. This 2012 law catapulted Senegal to the status of first Sub-Saharan African nation where women were the most highly represented at a national assembly that year. With a sophisticated level of details supported with analyses of pertinent facts and statistics about a number of Senegalese women parliamentarians, Telingator and Weeks demonstrate the gains that these female trailblazers have made in the struggle for gender equality not only in Africa but also around the world. At a time when women, including those living in Western democracies and in the Global South, have tremendous difficulties to be recognized and allowed to have and keep higher offices, it is refreshing to see that there are tangible examples of parity from Senegal that can be emulated to overcome numerous gender barriers to success. In addition, this chapter is special since it substantially draws from resources on gender parity in Senegal that Sarr made available to scholars.

Amy Porter's chapter is another crucial contribution because it focuses on the Entrepreneurship Training (ET) programs which have allowed many reasonably school-educated women of Dakar, Senegal, to gain substantial experiences and knowledge through networks allowing them to achieve both business skills and success. With appropriate details and sagacity, Porter shows that the gendered and typically Western ways of regarding African women as individuals who are mainly constricted by realities such as polygamy and the demands of motherhood and men's desires must be relativized, since there are under-studied groups of networks and women in Dakar whose economic success demonstrates otherwise. As Porter shows, these women are able to counter male dominance by taking advantage of educational programs and trainings that allow them to become professional adult workers rather than just domestic laborers, good spouses, and child bearers. What is also important in this chapter is how Porter suggests that these women still have challenges to face in Senegal where social and other responsibilities fall on members of their gender whether or not they are educated or choose not to be mothers or spouses.

Ruth Evans's chapter is equally deserving because it deals with the complicated issue of inheritance in the Serer community of Senegal through a qualitative methodology focusing on twenty families as well as on a number of religious leaders from this major ethnic group. Using data from the Fatick and Diourbel regions as well as from the capital city of Dakar, Evans shows the ways in which preserved traditions, enduring patrilineal power, and family conflicts end up impinging on the inheritance rights of Serer women and girls living in the three regions. These issues are all the more important because, as Evans suggests, they remain potent due to Serer customary laws and practices about gender, land, family relationships, and other aspects that altogether end up disfavoring women and girls in inheritance cases, especially after the decease of male heads of households.

Kadidia Sy's contribution is also vital since it examines the ways in which Bâ's classic novel, *So Long a Letter*, represents sisterhood both as an empowerment and an impairment of women in modern Senegalese society. Focusing on Ba's portrayals of female solidarity, Sy analyzes how the author perceives this bonding as a harbinger of both freedom and other liberating possibilities for Senegalese women while recognizing the limits of such advantages. As Sy also shows, Bâ reflects in her novel a number of factors such as polygamy, spousal desertion, caste prejudice, and neo-colonialism against which Senegalese women have to fight in order to achieve liberation from restrictive traditions. Also, as Sy reveals, Bâ depicts Senegalese women as sisters who must continually resist patriarchal dominance and other subjugations that contribute to their predicaments.

In her chapter, Beth Packer achieves something which has never been done before, which is to extensively study queer identity in Senegal in relationships with notions of Islamic religious morality. Specifically, Packer examines how the non-binary gender identity and undisclosed sexual orientation of a young female soccer player from Senegal do not conflict with this athlete's Islamic faith. Packer reveals the strong ways in which faith in Cheikh Ahmadou Bamba, who was the founder of the Murid Islamic Brotherhood of Senegal, allows the young Senegalese woman soccer player to endure the homophobic derisions and other abuses to which she is frequently subjected due to her queer identity. Beyond these elements, Packer's essay is also groundbreaking, since it focuses on women and sports in Senegal in juxtaposition with queerness and sexuality. This essay pushes the boundaries in which gender and sexuality can be theorized beyond the literal and narrow meanings that are often assigned to them.

Juliana Friend's essay is another groundbreaking contribution to this volume, because it may be one of the first scholarly studies of the numerous roles that social media such as Facebook and other online venues, including dating websites, serve as means of helping non-governmental organizations (NGOs) communicate with "men who have sex with Men" (MSM) in Senegal. The essay shows how the men who initiate conversations with other men to gauge their interests in sex are more interested in the value-neutral messages about HIV/AIDS and STDs that determine their pay. Yet, as Friend demonstrates, these workers of the E-Health Initiative go beyond their primary duties by also having web exchanges on social and human right issues facing the vulnerable populations they serve. Furthermore, at the center of Friend's article, one finds a compelling critique of how the NGOs, the state, and activists in Senegal tend to prioritize medical issues over human rights ones, weakening the constructive rapports and creative means that the E-Health workers develop in an attempt to effectively communicate with MSM living in the country.

The first and last chapter outside the editors' introduction and conclusion perfectly frame the ideas of the volume. Ayo Coly's chapter, the first in the anthology, stresses the humanity of same-gender-loving people in Senegal. Focusing on the emergence in Senegal of unprecedented forms of homophobia that she depicts as being "populist and quotidian," Coly reveals the ways in which the phenomenon has been appropriated as "a rhetorical category of geopolitical discourse." In an attempt to understand the roots of this use of homophobia as a "political currency" in Senegal, Coly provides us with a comprehensive history of the attitudes toward gender-variant individuals in Senegal before and after 2008. Moreover, the essay examines the various social, cultural, and political factors that contributed to the formation of a vigilantism against the *goordjiggen* in Senegal since that year. According to Coly, on February 1, 2008, "The publication of the photos and the discursive reframing of the *goordjiggen* as the homosexual by the magazine [called *Icône*] mediated the event of homosexuality in Senegal." In addition, Coly's essay suggests how the current discussions on homosexuality in Senegal favor the dramaturgy of the virile nation-state and the continuing circulation of heteropatriarchal masculinity as a political currency.

Cheikh Ibrahima Niang's critical thoughts on the politics of gender and sexuality and studies in critical African studies, in an interview with Ellen Foley, delivers an apropos final chapter to the deliberations of the anthology ahead of the conclusion. Conducted in 2017, this interview gives us rare insights on the history of activism and early scholarship on behalf of members of the lesbian, gay, bisexual, and transgender communities in Senegal. Niang's work is indispensable in the study of these communities since it was the first one to devote a strong and public attention to these groups. Moreover, Niang was the first Senegalese scholar to give scholarly attention to women prostitutes of Dakar who, along with homosexuals in the city, were, during the 1980s, the most vulnerable victims of HIV/AIDS in Senegal. Through Foley's interview with Niang, one also finds a crucial part of the unwritten history of not only sex workers and homosexuals in Senegal but also of those of *goorjigeen* who, as Niang points out, "have been completely left out." Being the first Senegalese intellectual to devote attention to the plight of Senegal's sex workers, homosexuals, and transgender communities, Niang deserves high praises. For this reason, this volume is also dedicated to him due to the courageous ways in which he has consistently valued the humanity of segments of Senegalese society that were and continue to be marginalized because of their gender appearances or sexual orientations.

By co-editing this current book, Besi Muhonja, who is a renowned Africanist scholar from Kenya, and I want to complement the extant scholarships on subversive gender and sexual identities in Senegal and help to inspire novel approaches to studies of Senegalese cultures. Our hope is to inspire other researchers to tackle the dissident identities in this and other African societies where gender and sexuality have crucial roles. Also, by co-editing this book, Muhonja and I want to encourage the kind of critical mass that is desperately needed in Africana studies where explorations of nonconforming and sub-cultural gender and sexual identities have been minimal. We unapologetically laud the scholars who have contributed to this volume for being brave enough to examine non-binary gender and sexual identities in Senegalese culture at a time when many other intellectuals shy away from these topics. Our concern is to show that this transgressive scholarship is central because it will reveal the complex ways in which Senegalese traditions can co-exist with masculinity, femininity, religiosity, and various social, political, and economic traditions, sensibilities, values, and dimensions. Given its complex colonial and postcolonial histories and the great caliber of its numerous intellectuals, Senegal deserves to be placed on the map of studies of gender and sexuality and this volume hopes to play a role in this endeavor.

BIBLIOGRAPHY

Amory, Deborah P. "Homosexuality in Africa: Issues and Debates." *I ssue: A Journal of Opinion* 25.1 (1997): 5–10

"Apologie du viol: Sur ce chapitre, Pr Songué a complètement déraillé." June 13, 2018. http:/ /www.seneweb.com/news/Societe/apologie-du-viol-sur-ce-chapitre-pr-song_n_240418. html.

Arnfred, Signe. *Re-Thinking Sexualities in Africa*. Stockholm, Sweden: Nordiska Afrikainstitutet, 2006.

"Art and Such," in "Excerpt from 'Hurston, Zora Neale, 1938-1939,'" Digital Public Library of America. June 13, 2018. http://dp.la/item/a8371e22c3eaa79f84383e80b40ee311.

Augis, Erin. "Aïcha's Sounith Hair Salon: Friendship, Profit, and Resistance in Dakar." *Islamic Africa* 5, no. 2 (2014): 199–224.

Broqua, Christophe. "Góor-jigéen : la resignification négative d'une catégorie entre genre et sexualité." *Socio* 9 décembre 2017. 163–83.

Bryant, Duke Kelly. *Education as Politics: Colonial Schooling and Political Debate in Senegal, 1850s-1914.* Madison: University of Wisconsin Press, 2015.

Camara, Mouminy. "Images et voix des minorités sexuelles dans les médias au Sénégal: Étude de contenu." Institut Panos Afrique de l'Ouest [Panos Institute West Africa]. September 19, 2017. http://panosmedia.org/sites/default/files/ressources/201711/documents/Etude%20de%20contenu%20me%CC%81diatique%20sur%20les%20minorite%CC%81s%20sexuelles%20au%20Se%CC%81ne%CC%81gal.pdf.

Coly, Ayo A. *The Pull of Postcolonial Nationhood: Gender and Migration in Francophone African Literatures*. Lanham, MD: Lexington Books, 2010.

Crémieux, Anne ed., Homosexualités en Afrique. *Africultures* 96, no. 6 (2013).

Ekine, Sokari and Hakima Abbas, eds. *Queer African Reader*. Nairobi, Dakar, and Oxford: Pambazuka Press, 2013.

Gueye, Marame. "Ode to Patriarchy: The Fine Line between Praise and Criticism in a Popular Senegalese Poem." In *Gender Epistemologies in Africa: Gendering Traditions, Spaces, Social Institutions, and Identities*, edited by Oyèrónké Oyewùmí, 64–83. New York: Palgrave, 2011.

Gning, Ndèye. "Les motifs de l'illégitimité sociale de l'homosexualité au Sénégal." *Africultures* 6. no 96 (2013): 22–39. Hereby Cited online. January 4, 2018. https://www.researchgate.net/publication/283018375.

Gueye, Marame. "Ode to Patriarchy: The Fine Line between Praise and Criticism in a Popular Senegalese Poem," in *Gender Epistemologies in Africa: Gendering Traditions, Spaces, Social Institutions, and Identities*, eds. Oyèrónké Oyewùmí (New York: Palgrave, 2011), 64–83.

Jones, Hilary. *The Métis of Senegal: Urban Life and Politics in French West Africa*. Bloomington: Indiana University Press, 2013.

Keita, Aoua. *Femme d'Afrique: La vie d'Aoua Kéita racontée par elle-même*. Paris: Presence Africaine, 1975.

Lecarme, Mireille. "La 'fatigue' des femmes, le 'travail' de la mère en milieu populaire dakarois." In *Femmes plurielles Les représentations des femmes discours, normes et* conduites, edited by Danielle jonckers, Renée Carré, and Marie-Claude Dupré, 255–71. Paris, Éditions de la Maison des sciences de l'homme, 199a.

"L'Invité." *TV5*. 8 Février 2016. https://www.youtube.com/watch?v=ncTMsCnMzdk.

Locoh, Thérèse and Isabelle Puech. "Fatou Sow. Les défis d'une féministe en Afrique," *Travail, genre et sociétés* 2, no. 20) (2008): 5–22.

Mbougar. "Opinion sur l'homosexualié au Senegal." July 31, 2018. http://chosesrevues.over-blog.com/2014/03/opinion-sur-l-homosexualite-au-senegal.html.

Mills, Ivy. "Sutura: Gendered Honor, Social Death and the Politics of Exposure in Senegalese Literature and Popular Culture." PhD diss., University of California, Berkeley, 2011.

Ngom, Fallou. *Muslims Beyond the Arab World: The Odyssey of Ajami and the Muridiyya*. New York and Oxford: Oxford University Press, 2016.

Nordling, Linda. "African Academics Challenge Homophobic Laws: Scientific Report Demolishes Assertions Used to Back Criminalization of Homosexuality." July 31, 2018. https://www.nature.com/news/african-academics-challenge-homophobic-laws-1.17720.
Nyanzi, Stella. "Here's how Trump undercuts anti-LGBT, anti-woman Africans." July 30, 2018. https://76crimes.com/2016/11/23/heres-how-trump-undercuts-anti-lgbt-anti-woman-africans/.
Ohler, Quinn. "Edmonton homicide victim fled Senegal with children; estranged husband charged." June 13, 2018. https://globalnews.ca/news/4198325/estranged-husband-charged-with-2nd-degree-murder-in-death-of-edmonton-woman/.
Ohwovoriole, Jamin. Review of *Negotiating Afropolitanism: Essays on Borders and Spaces in Contemporary African Literature and Folklore*, by Jennifer Wawrzinek and J. K. S. Makokha. *English Academy Review: Southern African Journal of English Studies* 28.2 (2011): 79–81.
Sarr, Fatou. *Études des Pratiques de Solidarité des Entrepreneures issues du Secteur informel au Sénégal: Quelles perspectives Pour les Politiques Sociales*? PhD diss., Université Laval, 1997.
Sow, Fatou Sarr. "Evolution des normes de genre et stéréotypes de genre au Sénégal et l'impact sur transformation des relations de pouvoir entre hommes et femmes au Sénégal." June 12, 2018. https://vdocuments.net/presentee-par-pr-fatou-sarr-sow-maitre-de-conferences-ifanuniversite.html.
Tamale, Sylvia, ed. *African Sexualities*. Dakar and Capetown: Pambazuka P, 2011.
"Waly Ballago Seck se Defends, Moi je suis Baye Fall." *La Tribune*. Samedi 23 et Dimanche 24 Janvier, 2016. 1, 4.
"Waly Seck vide son sac." *L'Observateur*. Samedi 23 et Dimanche 24 Janvier, 2016. 1.

NOTES

1. All individuals interviewed in this book have been given pseudonyms and have had identifying factors removed to protect their identity.

2. Ayo A. Coly, *The Pull of Postcolonial Nationhood: Gender and Migration in Francophone African Literatures* (Lanham: Lexington Books, 2010); Marame Gueye, "Ode to Patriarchy: The Fine Line between Praise and Criticism in a Popular Senegalese Poem," in *Gender Epistemologies in Africa: Gendering Traditions, Spaces, Social Institutions, and Identities*, eds. Oyèrónké Oyewùmí (New York: Palgrave, 2011), 64–83.

3. Coly, *The Pull of Postcolonial Nationhood*, xx.

4. Gueye, "Ode to Patriarchy: The Fine Line between Praise and Criticism in a Popular Senegalese Poem," 82.

5. Erin Augis, "Aïcha's Sounith Hair Salon: Friendship, Profit, and Resistance in Dakar," *Islamic Africa* 5, no. 2 (2014): 199–224; Duke Kelly Bryant, Education *as Politics: Colonial Schooling and Political Debate in Senegal, 1850s-1914* (Madison: University of Wisconsin Press, 2015); Hilary Jones, *The Métis of Senegal: Urban Life and Politics in French West Africa* (Bloomington: Indiana University Press, 2013).

6. Ivy Mills, "Sutura: Gendered Honor, Social Death, and the Politics of Exposure in Senegalese Literature and Popular Culture" (PhD diss., University of California, Berkeley, 2011), 1.

7. Deborah P. Amory, "Homosexuality in Africa: Issues and Debates," *Issue: A Journal of Opinion* 25.1 (1997): 5; 5–10.

8. Amory, "Homosexuality," 5.

9. Stella Nyanzi, "Here's How Trump Undercuts Anti-LGBT, Anti-woman Africans," July 30, 2018, https://76crimes.com/2016/11/23/heres-how-trump-undercuts-anti-lgbt-anti-woman-africans/.

10. The original quotation in French is: "Dites que vous êtes contre et vous êtes un Sénégalais modèle, du bon côté, dites que vous êtes pour, l'on vous accusera d'être aliéné, complexé, occidental, athée, homosexuel. Mais surtout, cette question, 'pour ou contre l'homosexualité', annihile, par sa forme même, toute forme de complexité; elle cache les enjeux véritables, de fond, que la question de l'homosexualité, dans la société sénégalaise, interroge."
See Mbougar, "Opinion sur l'homosexualite au Senegal," July 31, 2018, http://chosesrevues.over-blog.com/2014/03/opinion-sur-l-homosexualite-au-senegal.html.

11. See Mouminy Camara, "Images et voix des minorités sexuelles dans les médias au Sénégal: Étude de contenu," Institut Panos Afrique de l'Ouest [Panos Institute West Africa], September 19, 2017, http://panosmedia.org/sites/default/files/ressources/201711/documents/
Etude%20de%20contenu%20me%CC%81diatique%20sur%20les%20minorite%CC%81s%20sexuelles%20au%20Se%CC%81ne%CC%81gal.pdf.

12. The original quotation in French is: "Dites que vous êtes contre et vous êtes un Sénégalais modèle, du bon côté, dites que vous êtes pour, l'on vous accusera d'être aliéné, complexé, occidental, athée, homosexuel. Mais surtout, cette question, 'pour ou contre l'homosexualité', annihile, par sa forme même, toute forme de complexité; elle cache les enjeux véritables, de fond, que la question de l'homosexualité, dans la société sénégalaise, interroge."
See Mbougar. "Opinion sur l'homosexualite au Senegal," July 31, 2018, http://chosesrevues.over-blog.com/2014/03/opinion-sur-l-homosexualite-au-senegal.html.

13. See Linda Nordling, "African Academics Challenge Homophobic Laws: Scientific Report Demolishes Assertions Used to Back Criminalization of Homosexuality," July 31, 2018, https://www.nature.com/news/african-academics-challenge-homophobic-laws-1.17720.

14. See "L' Homophobie: le 'sac à main' de la star Wally Seck enflamme le Sénégal," 30 janvier 2016. http://www.leparisien.fr/international/le-sac-a-main-de-la-star-wally-seck-enflamme-le-senegal-30-01-2016-5500387.php.

15. The original quotation in French is: "C'est normal. Y'en a qui disent que c'est un sac de femme. C'est qu'ils ne comprennent pas. Donc, à un moment donné, ils ont touché un point sensible. Mon guide spiritual, mon très cher marabout, Cheikh Ahmad Bamba Khadim Rassoul, ce qui m'a poussé à déchirer le sac." See " L'Invité," *TV5*, 8 Février 2016, https://www.youtube.com/watch?v=ncTMsCnMzdk.

16. The original quotation in French is: "Je l'ai fait parce que j'aime mon pays. J'aime pas de polémique et j'adore faire plaisir aux sénégalais." See " L'Invité," *TV5*, 8 Février 2016, https://www.youtube.com/watch?v=ncTMsCnMzdk.

17. "Waly Seck vide son sac," *L'Observateur*, Samedi 23 et Dimanche 24 Janvier, 2016, 1; "Waly Ballago Seck se Defends, Moi je suis Baye Fall," *La Tribune*, Samedi 23 et Dimanche 24 Janvier, 2016, 1, 4.

18. Jamin Ohwovoriole, review of *Negotiating Afropolitanism: Essays on Borders and Spaces in Contemporary African Literature and Folklore*, by Jennifer Wawrzinek and J. K. S. Makokha, *English Academy Review: Southern African Journal of English Studies* 28.2 (2011): 79.

19. Signe Arnfred, *Re-Thinking Sexualities in Africa* (Stockholm, Sweden: Nordiska Afrikainstitutet, 2006); Sylvia Tamale, ed., *African Sexualities* (Dakar and Capetown: Pambazuka P., 2011); Sokari Ekine and Hakima Abbas, eds. *Queer African Reader* (Nairobi, Dakar, and Oxford: Pambazuka P, 2013).

20. Anne Crémieux, ed., *Homosexualités en Afrique*, *Africultures* 96, no. 6 (2013).

21. The original quotation is: "Tout comme les termes équivalents dans d'autres langues, goorjigeen est une insulte qui humilie l'homme en remettant implicitement en cause son statut de mâle dominant, viril et autoritaire13: le goorjigeen subordonne son statut d'homme à celui de la femme, plaçant la stigmatisation de l'homosexualité dans une vision essentialiste des rapports sociaux de sexe." Ndèye Gning, "Les motifs de l'illégitimité sociale de l'homosexualité au Sénégal," *Africultures* 6, no. 96 (2013): 22–39.

22. Christophe Broqua, "Góor-jigéen : la resignification négative d'une catégorie entre genre et sexualité," *Socio* 9 (décembre 2017): 163–83.

23. "Art and Such," in "Excerpt from 'Hurston, Zora Neale, 1938-1939,'" Digital Public Library of America, October 3, 2018, http://dp.la/item/a8371e22c3eaa79f84383e80b40ee311.

24. Aoua Keita, *Femme d'Afrique: La vie d'Aoua Kéita racontée par elle-même* (Paris: Presence Africaine, 1975), 112.

25. Keita, *Femme d'Afrique*, 112.

26. Keita, *Femme d'Afrique*, 191.

27. The original quotation in French is:

"Harmonisation de la loi avec les engagements pour les points suivant: l'octroi de la nationalité, la puissance paternelle, le choix du domicile conjugal; traitement par les médias des questions des inégalités de genre; davantage d'engagement en termes de budgétisation sensible au Genre; L'autonomie du Ministère en charge de l'égalité du parti au pouvoir; Une meilleure implication des hommes."

See Fatou Sarr Sow, "Evolution des normes de genre et stéréotypes de genre au Sénégal et l'impact sur transformation des relations de pouvoir entre hommes et femmes au Sénégal," June 12, 2018, https://vdocuments.net/presentee-par-pr-fatou-sarr-sow-maitre-de-conferences-ifanuniversite.html.

28. See "Apologie du viol: Sur ce chapitre, Pr Songué a complètement déraillé." http://www.seneweb.com/news/Societe/apologie-du-viol-sur-ce-chapitre-pr-song_n_240418.html, June 13, 2018; "Coumba Gawlo Seck L'habillement sexy d'une femme ne peut pas être une invite au viol," June 13, 2018. http://www.seneweb.com/news/Societe/coumba-gawlo-seck-laquo-l-rsquo-habillem_n_241580.html.

29. Quinn Ohler. "Edmonton homicide victim fled Senegal with children; estranged husband charged," June 13, 2018, https://globalnews.ca/news/4198325/estranged-husband-charged-with-2nd-degree-murder-in-death-of-edmonton-woman/.

30. Fatou Sarr, *Études des Pratiques de Solidarité des Entrepreneures issues du Secteur informel au Sénégal : Quelles perspectives Pour les Politiques Sociales*? (PhD diss., Université Laval, 1997), 13.

31. The original quotation in French is: "L'échec est dû aussi aux approches conceptuelles érronées des problèmes de femmes, aux préjugés envers elles, qu'au type de développement dans lequel on a voulu les intégrer" (13). Fatou Sarr, *Études des Pratiques de Solidarité des Entrepreneures issues du Secteur informel au Sénégal: Quelles perspectives Pour les Politiques Sociales*? (PhD diss., Université Laval, 1997), 13.

32. Thérèse Locoh and Isabelle Puech, "Fatou Sow. Les défis d'une féministe en Afrique," *Travail, genre et sociétés* 2, no. 20) (2008): 5–22.

33. The original statement in French is: Je ne peux m'empêcher d'évoquer à nouveau, car je l'ai fait à plusieurs reprises tant il était choquant, le commentaire d'un professeur de l'Université de Dakar, lors d'un débat à la radio. 'Voilà, vous reprenez un discours féministe occidental . . .' et, sans doute pour mieux asseoir son argumentaire, il avait affirmé: 'l'Islam permet de corriger sa femme lorsqu'elle désobéit à son époux.' Le commentaire se rapportait à un fait divers survenu à Kaolack, en 1993: à la suite d'une dispute avec son mari, une jeune femme était transportée à l'hôpital où elle devait décéder peu après son admission. Comme le veut la tradition musulmane, elle était enterrée rapidement (vu les circonstances), sans que son conjoint soit inquiété" (14).

Thérèse Locoh and Isabelle Puech, "Fatou Sow. Les défis d'une féministe en Afrique," *Travail, genre et sociétés* 2, no. 20 (2008): 14.

34. Mireille Lecarme, "La 'fatigue' des femmes, le 'travail' de la mère en milieu populaire dakarois," *Femmes plurielles Les représentations des femmes discours, normes et* conduites, eds., Danielle jonckers, Renée Carré, and Marie-Claude Dupré (Paris, Éditions de la Maison des sciences de l'homme, 1999), 263–64.

35. Fallou Ngom, *Muslims Beyond the Arab World: The Odyssey of Ajami and the Muridiyya* (New York and Oxford: Oxford University Press, 2016), 115, 116, 151, 209.

36. Lecarme translates "*ku ndeyyam liggey du torox*" into French as follows: [la femme-qui-a-bien-travaillé protège l'enfant de l'opprobre, du rejet social " (263). Mireille Lecarme, "La 'fatigue' des femmes, le 'travail' de la mère en milieu populaire dakarois," 263.

37. Thérèse Locoh and Isabelle Puech, "Fatou Sow. Les défis d'une féministe en Afrique," 14.

38. The original statement in French is: En ce moment, le débat le plus difficile est autour de la sexualité, celui du contrôle du corps et de la fécondité. Les Africaines veulent disposer de la contraception pour décider de leur nombre d'enfants mais elles répugnent au discours autour de la liberté sexuelle, du plaisir sexuel ou de l'orientation sexuelle qui reste très difficile à tenir, comme discours public de défense des droits des femmes. J'en sais les difficultés pour avoir coordonné, avec Codou Bop, un ouvrage collectif, *Notre corps, notre santé. La Santé et la sexualité des femmes en Afrique subsaharienne* [2004], à l'initiative du Réseau de recherche en santé de la reproduction en Afrique francophone, dont j'ai été la présidente de 1992 à 1996. Je collabore actuellement, avec le Groupe de recherche sur les femmes et les lois au Sénégal, à une réflexion sur la sexualité au Sénégal, coordonnée par Codou Bop. Une de nos membres, auteure d'un article sur l'homosexualité féminine, a rencontré d'énormes difficultés à trouver des femmes qui acceptent de lui parler. Ce n'est pas encore dans le débat public."
Thérèse Locoh and Isabelle Puech, "Fatou Sow. Les défis d'une féministe en Afrique," 21.

1

THE INVENTION OF THE HOMOSEXUAL

The Politics of Homophobia in Senegal

Ayo Coly

In May 2009, a mob in the Senegalese city of Thiès exhumed the body of a young Senegalese man alleged to be gay. The group dragged his remains across the city and to his parents' home. The media detailed the tedious quest of the family to find a new burial place for their son. This macabre development signaled a new era of antigay vigilantism in Senegal, a country formerly called "the gay capital of Francophone Africa" and host to social cultures of gender variance that also subsumed same-sex sexualities. While the 2009 event was unprecedented in terms of its macabre character, the foundational moment of antigay vigilantism in Senegal goes back a year earlier. In 2008, the publication of some photos of an alleged gay marriage between two Senegalese men in a suburb of Dakar launched a witch-hunt against gender-nonconforming men. These developments in Senegal signaled that the country was being swept in the massive wave of acute homophobia that had surged over the continent at the time, with unprecedented homophobic violence and criminal crackdowns on gender-nonconforming individuals in Kenya, Malawi, and Nigeria and a repressive antigay bill in the making in Uganda. The multiple surges are not coincidental. They are causally concurrent. Indeed, African homophobias are in conversation with each other, often borrowing from and competing against each other and, also, collectively enunciating an African moral superiority against the political and economic dominance of the West. There are clear political mechanics at play here. The character of homophobia as a rhetorical category of geopolitical discourse nuances culturalist readings of homophobia in Africa and balances out the bottom-up focus on populist and quotidian homophobia. This essay pursues such an alternative reading of homophobia by analyzing the causal relation between the circulation of homophobia as political currency in Senegal and the development of a social culture of quotidian homophobia. More specifically, quotidian homophobia here does not precede but instead follows political homophobia. The overnight presence of a zealous social culture of quotidian homophobia in Senegal, with a theatricality to match, indicates that the unfolding wave of homophobia in Senegal is a practice of social reform that is opportunistically spearheaded by political actors.

GENDER VARIANCE AND HOMOSEXUALITY IN SENEGAL BEFORE 2008

The media in Senegal draws a landscape of shifting attitudes toward gender variance and homosexuality in the country. Since 2008, following the alleged gay marriage, the topic of homosexuality, which is also made to incorrectly subsume gender variance, has been omnipresent in the media. Newspapers report on a regular basis on alleged homosexuality activities, out alleged gays, and publish the names of individuals who are arrested on presumption of homosexual activity. Additionally, news articles go beyond mere report of facts to egg on the populations, using alarmist titles like "Homosexualité au Sénégal: Alerte Danger au Président et au Peuple Sénégalais"[1] [Homosexuality in Senegal: A Danger Alert to the President and Senegalese Populations],[2] "La prostitution Gay Pollue Dakar"[3] [Gay Prostitution Is Polluting Dakar], or "Au Secours! L'Homosexualité Gagne du Terrain au Sénégal et notre Progéniture est Exposée"[4] [Help! Homosexuality Is Gaining Ground in Senegal and Our Offspring Are Exposed]. This pervasive and sustained stigmatization of gender variance and homosexuality in the media is a new development since 2008. In the 1980s, *Jamra Magazine*, a monthly publication of the Islamic NGO Jamra, tried in vain to force homosexuality into Senegalese public discourse. *Jamra Magazine* branded itself "the first Senegalese review on social issues" and targeted social ills associated with Westernization and secularism. As early as its second issue on "Prostitution, Débauche, Homosexualité au Sénégal"[5] [Prostitution, Debauchery, Homosexuality in Senegal], the magazine pinpointed homosexuality as a social evil that reflected the exposure of Senegalese youths to alien cultural frameworks and, concurrently, the failure of the secular Senegalese state to protect its youths. The relentless focus of *Jamra Magazine* on homosexuality, especially the magazine's framing of homosexuality as a byproduct of the cultural and moral laxity of the secular state, reflected the agenda of moral entrepreneurship that underpinned the work of the Islamic NGO Jamra and paved the way for the organization's claims to political leadership in the 1990s. But *Jamra Magazine*'s focus on homosexuality failed to sway the rest of the media in that direction. The failed attempts of the Islamic NGO and the magazine to mobilize public opinion around homosexuality pertain to the relatively liberal social, political, and religious landscape of Senegal in the 1980s and 1990s. Additionally, the behaviors that Jamra identified as homosexuality were tacitly understood as gender variance and not sexual variance. In pre-2008 Senegal, the term *goordjiggen*, used to describe gender-variant men, references gender nonconformity and leaves sexual orientation ambiguous, in conformity with the so-called "cultures of discretion" toward sexual matters that some African communities favored.[6] *Jamra Magazine* remained an outlier in the redefinition of gender variance as homosexuality. Up to 2008, the Senegalese media generally had a non-biased, sociological, and sexually discrete approach to gender variance, with newspapers occasionally devoting special dossiers to the subject.[7] The dossiers often featured interviews and pictures of men who talked about their gender variance. In 1999, when a group of gender-nonconforming Senegalese men organized a fashion show in the town of Saly Portudal, outside of Dakar, the press media covered the event.[8]

The media's casual treatment of gender variance corroborates the label of Senegal, at that time, as the "gay capital of Francophone Africa." Scholars have documented the existence of a culture of open gender variance in Senegal as far back as the precolonial era.[9] Despite the scapegoating of gender-nonconforming men by French colonials, this culture of open gender variance endured and made marks on the postcolonial urban Senegalese landscape through popular dances, known as *sabar goordjiggen*, and parties organized by gender-nonconforming men. All these events were well-attended by the community, including members of the Senegalese elite. The social elite sought out gender-nonconforming men for their flair in fashion and cuisine, and the latter officiated as social event organizers, masters of ceremony, cooks, make-up artists, confidants, and entourage members. Some gender-nonconforming men became well-known and much sought-out socialites. Senegalese writer Ken Bugul, whose novels often reference gender variance, describes her childhood in the 1960s, in the small Senegalese town of Guinguinéo accordingly:

> C'était la capitale des *goordjiggens*, mais pas en termes de mal. Dans toutes mes autobiographies, il n'y a pas un livre où je n'en parle pas, parce qu'ils faisaient partie de notre quotidien. Il y avait Samba Guissé Mabo qui était très connu, et il y avait au moins dix *goordjiggens* qui étaient avec lui. Je me rappelle qu'ils portaient un petit boubou, mettaient un peu de crayon et venaient même au marché faire leurs courses. Chaque année, Samba Guissé Mabo organisait l'une des plus grandes festivités à Guinguinéo. On demandait même à ceux qui avaient de la place dans leurs chambres de loger les *goordjiggens*. Tout le monde allait voir comment ils dansaient parce qu'ils étaient bons danseurs. Ce n'était même pas un problème de les intégrer parce que ça ne se posait pas.[10]
>
> [It was the capital of *goordjiggens*, but not in a wrong way. I mention the *goordjiggens* in all my autobiographies because they were part of our daily lives. There was Samba Guissé Mabo who was famous and who had an entourage of ten *goordjiggens*. I remember that they wore short boubous, applied a little bit of eyeliner and even went shopping at the market. Every year, Samba Guissé Mabo would throw one of the biggest parties in Guinguinéo. People who had spare rooms in their houses were asked to host some of the *goordjiggens*. Everyone went to see them dance because they were such good dancers. The question of their integration never arose.]

This culture of tolerance or, at best, indifference to gender variance, extended to religious circles. While Muslim religious dignitaries have spearheaded the unfolding antigay vigilantism in Senegal, Muslim leaders and clerics formerly displayed tolerance toward gender-variant individuals.[11]

Senegalese literatures provide a similar casual treatment of gender variance. Well into the 1990s, African literatures have generally championed the cultural nationalist statement that "homosexuality is un-African" by stigmatizing homosexuality and gender variance as foreign imports. However, already in the 1970s, Senegalese literatures offered representations of gender variance in such novels as *Le Revenant* [*The Revenant*] (1976) by Aminata Sow Fall, *Un Chant Écarlate* [*Scarlet Song*] (1980) by Mariama Bâ and *Le Baobab Fou* [*The Abandoned Baobab*] (1982) by Ken Bugul.[12] By using the Senegalese term *goor djiggen* to reference their gender variant characters, the writers give indigenous African anchors to gender variance. The novels also reference the *goordjiggens* in a matter-of-fact way, and this casual narration of gender variance normalizes the *goordjiggens* in the Senegalese context.

Still, Senegal has had legislation against homosexuality since 1965. Article 319.3 of Senegal's Criminal Code imposes a prison sentence of one to five years and a fine of $200 to $3,000 on people convicted of homosexual acts. The text refers to the latter acts as "acte impudique ou contre nature avec un individu de son sexe" [indecent or unnatural sexual acts with a person of the same sex]. Of note is that the law criminalizes acts and not identities. The Senegalese state has consistently insisted on that distinction when defending its human rights record before international human rights organization. For instance, in 2009[13] and 2013,[14] the Universal Periodic Review of the human rights situation in Senegal by the United Nations Human Rights Committee recommended that Senegal repeal Article 319. Senegal rejected these recommendations on the grounds that while homosexual practice is subject to legal sanctions, being homosexual is not a crime in Senegal. In 2009, Senegalese Minister of Foreign Affairs Madické Niang contended to the UN Human Rights Committee that:

> Senegal people are not prosecuted for their sexual orientation. Sexual orientation in Senegal is a purely private matter. It is a private matter, nothing more. For many years now, we have seen homosexuality in our country and that has never led to situations where homosexuals are harassed, persecuted, or prosecuted. What has happened is that there have been situations where shocking behavior which ran counter to our religious beliefs and morality which [unintelligible] punishes unnatural sexual relations. I would ask you to understand

> the social realities of our country. This is an issue which is very complex. It is a very complicated issue in Senegal. Let me say once again in Senegal homosexuals lead freely . . . we even had a federal republic to authorize a homosexual to have their name changed to a woman's name in order to emphasize their feminine side. No one was shocked when the president authorized the man to adopt the woman's name. But when homosexuality becomes blatantly public, it leads to embarrassing situations.[15]

Niang was invoking here the so-called "cultures of discretion" that I mentioned earlier. For Niang, Article 319 specifically criminalizes breaches of the rules of discretion. In his logic, Senegal does not discriminate against sexual minorities; instead Senegal exerts legal sanctions on individuals who violate cultural norms. In 2013, Senegalese Minister of Justice Sidiki Kaba also argued before the UN Human Rights Committee that "there is no criminalization of homosexuality in Senegal. Article 319 talks about acts contrary to nature. The fact of being homosexual in Senegal is not a crime, and there has been no prosecution or trial of persons who are homosexual under the Criminal Code."[16]

Between 1965 and 2008, Article 319 has had very sparse and uneven applications. Article 319 was almost dormant legislation and many people in Senegal ignored its existence until 2008, when the scandal over the gay marriage erupted. Case in point: in December 2003, Maniang Kassé, the most famous gender-nonconforming man in Senegal, was on trial in Dakar for attempted fraud against his French lover. A crowd of admirers and well-wishers, including gender-nonconforming men, filled the tribunal to capacity to support Kassé. The latter made a grand entrance, dressed in a white dress, face exquisitely made up and hands freshly manicured. He was greeted like a star. Kassé was sentenced to three months in prison for committing fraud and not for homosexual acts. That Kassé was a famous and self-proclaimed gender-nonconforming man who deliberately flaunted his gender variance in court was of no consequence to his supporters and the officiating judge. In the homophobic climate of post-2008 Senegal, Kassé nonetheless remains a sought-after socialite whose whereabouts and physical transformations continue to make the local headlines and spark curiosities. The continuing fascination with Kassé shows fissures in homophobic Senegalese discourses. In turn, these fissures speak to the fact that popular homophobia in Senegal is a recent phenomenon and is yet to stand on solid cultural ground, as also shown by the long-dormant legislation against homosexuality.

However, since 2008, the law is no longer dormant. People are regularly sentenced for homosexual acts. A high-profile case further confirmed that a new epoch of state-sponsored homophobia has dawned on the Senegalese gender-nonconforming community. Tamsir Jupiter N'diaye, a famous journalist, served a two-year sentence after being caught in the act in 2013. N'diaye was sentenced again in the summer of 2015, following allegations of soliciting a male minor for sex. In another case, much protested by human rights groups, five young men were sentenced after police found used condoms in their apartment. Neighbors have also started reporting or punishing alleged homosexual activity. This was the case in August 2015 when young people broke into a private residence and beat up its alleged gay occupants. The police intervened and the alleged gay men were sentenced to jail. Contrary to the declarations of Madické Niang and Sidiki Kaba that only homosexual acts are criminalized, perceived sexual orientation has become a criminal liability since 2008. According to a 2010 report from Human Rights Watch on antigay vigilantism in Senegal, homosexual activity is often inferred from physical appearance and gender nonconforming behavior.[17]

The notion of Senegal as a former gay capital may be useful in describing the absence of antigay vigilantism and the lack of a culture of public homophobia before 2008. But the notion is discursively inaccurate because the term gay simplifies and misrepresents forms of gender and sexual variance which are more fluid and slippery than the fixed sexual identities described by the term gay. There is now a substantial body of literature on the labor of mistranslation, stigmatization, and criminalization that the Western lexicon of sexual identifications has been performing in African contexts.[18] In the case of Senegal, Fatou Kiné Camara has noted that the Senegalese-Wolof term *goordjiggen*, used for gender-nonconforming men, originally lacked the connotations of perversity and sexual pathology embedded in the term homosexual.[19] *Goordjiggen* designates an effeminate man or a male crossdresser. The term is not linked to a sexual practice but often to a social role. Babacar M'Baye and Cheikh Niang have looked into the role of *goordjiggen* in cultural and religious rituals, one example being the Wolof Ndep ritual ceremony.[20] In that sense, Senegal could not be a gay or homosexual haven since there were discursively no homosexuals and gays in Senegal until 2008. Conversely, in the absence of homosexuals and gays, there could be no homophobia in the country since the notion "is ideationally and semantically attached to the modern term gay."[21]

THE 2008 INVENTION OF THE HOMOSEXUAL

Michael Bosia and Meredith Weiss describe how an invention of the homosexual occurs in some non-Western contexts when a "preemptive homophobia" imports its concepts of gender variance from Western LGBTQ paradigms and subsequently catalyzes the local development of collective LGBTQ identities:

> [P]olitical homophobia often takes root before a critical mass of sexual minorities even begins to think of itself as "lesbian," "gay," or "transgender," let alone to endow these identities with any collective, political significance or policy claims, threatening or otherwise. . . . In many cases, it is the homophobes who import a model of same-sex intimacy in terms of Western concepts of LGBT community. Theorising the spread and political nature of homophobia allows us to explore the implications of such preemptive homophobia—based as it is on borrowed images and rhetoric rather than local ones—on the subsequent development locally of the collective identities of emergent sexual minorities.[22]

Likewise, the authors of *More Than A Name: State-Sponsored Homophobia and its Consequences in Southern Africa* argue that gender-nonconforming individuals in Southern Africa "do not take the terms 'homosexual' or 'gay' or 'lesbian' from a foreign cadre of cultural corrupters; they take it from the words of their political leaders. In this sense, Mugabe and Nujoma are indeed 'promoters' of 'homosexuality' in their societies."[23]

The invention of the Senegalese homosexual entailed the sociocultural translation of the *goordjiggen* into the homosexual and the construction of the homosexual as disposable life. Christophe Broqua is thus correct that a "negative resignification" of the *goordjiggen* took place.[24] Before 2008, when the term homosexual was used in lieu of *goordjig-*

gen, the first term was made to bear the fluid cultural significations of the second. Post-2008, the term *goordjiggen* has now been made to absorb the semantic range and discursive baggage of the term homosexual. I trace the invention of the Senegalese homosexual to 2008, when homosexuality became an event, following the publication of the photos of an alleged Senegalese gay marriage. The ceremony took place in 2006 in the outskirts of Dakar. But it is only on February 1, 2008, that *Icône*, a Senegalese tabloid magazine, published the photos to accompany a special dossier on homosexuality. The publication of the photos and the discursive reframing of the *goordjiggen* as the homosexual by the magazine mediated the event of homosexuality in Senegal. In his editorial for the special issue, magazine editor Mansour Dieng castigates the fast spread of homosexuality in Senegal. While Dieng acknowledges the existence of gender variance in Senegal, he falsely argues that the culture of open gender variance is a new phenomenon that shows the country's increasing moral permissiveness. The interchangeable use of *goordjiggen* and homosexual in the article shows a semantic displacement at work.[25] In order to conflate the homosexual and the *goordjiggen*, Dieng has to first reinvent the *goordjiggen* as a marginalized and undesired body in yesteryear. To that end, he erases the previous history of tolerance toward gender-nonconforming men in Senegal and reinvents the *goordjiggen* as the homosexual, therefore, as a disposable and harmful body.

Following the publication of the photos, a group of Muslim religious leaders and organizations voiced their condemnations. As a result, the police arrested several of the men in the pictures. Yet the Senegalese penal code specifically criminalizes homosexual acts, of which there was no evidence in any of the photos that *Icône* published. The prompt police arrest of the men, just for being gender nonconforming, reified and legitimized the new discourse on gender variance that *Icône* was shepherding. In a bid to profit from the hot topic of the day, the media swiftly followed suit with daily updates on the case, sensationalist titles, and alarmist articles on an alleged homosexual menace.[26] In what appears as a feigned collective amnesia, there was no mention of the country's long history of open gender variance. Instead, there appeared to be an investment in constructing the *goordjiggen* as a harmful import. The men were released after four days in custody, following the protests of national and international human rights organizations. The intervention of international organizations fueled the thesis that the *goordjiggen*/homosexual was an import from the depraved West.[27] The release of the men intensified the indignation of the Muslim leaders. Relentless religious rallies and sermons over the next several weeks swayed the Senegalese populations into an unprecedented homophobic hysteria.[28] Then, in December 2008, police arrested nine members of an HIV/AIDS association who were doing outreach work among MSM (the acronym for men who have sex with men).[29] Under Articles 319.3 and 238 of the Criminal Code, the court charged the nine outreach workers with engaging in homosexual conduct and forming a criminal association. The nine men were not caught in the act, but the judge esteemed that the HIV/AIDS association was a cover to recruit and bring together homosexuals.[30] Each man received a sentence of eight years in prison, although all men were eventually released in April 2009.[31] This case prolonged the antigay hysteria started by the alleged gay marriage, consolidated homosexuality as a matter of public discourse in Senegal, and cemented the construction of the homosexual as disposable life. By the end of 2008, Senegal had definitely discarded its former label as the "gay capital of Francophone Africa" to reinvent itself as a homophobic enclave.

HOMOPHOBIA AND POLITICAL OPPORTUNISM

Patrick Awondo has correctly applied Gilbert Herdt's notion of "cultural anger" to the situation in Senegal.[32] According to Herdt, cultural anger may be engineered from an orchestrated moral sexual panic that usually constructs "monstrous enemies" and "sexual scapegoats" who are a threat to the well-being of the community.[33] Still, Awondo delivers a truncated analysis because he does not delve into the full politics of the cultural anger that scapegoated gender-nonconforming men. In other words, who created and marshaled that cultural anger? And for what purpose? Awondo does not take up Herdt's proposition that we look into how social or political agents engineer a cultural anger to serve their specific agendas. Instead, Awondo infers that Muslim religious leaders in Senegal tapped into a pre-existing cultural anger fermented by the economic recession in Senegal.

An important clue that Awondo did not pick up on is that the infamous gay wedding took place in 2006 and the pictures were only published in February 2008, a few months before the local elections of May 2008. Imam Mbaye Niang, a Muslim religious leader, used the pictures to orchestrate an intense alarmist moral crusade against gender-nonconforming men. Imam Niang also happened to be the leader of the Mouvement de la Réforme pour le Développement Social [Reform Movement for Social Development], a political party that he created just before the 2000 presidential elections in Senegal. The gay marriage affair was fodder for the Imam to rally fifteen Muslim organizations to form the Collective of Senegalese Islamic Associations. The Collective undertook a massive nationwide campaign of sermons at mosques and in the media. The gist of these moralizing discourses was that homosexuals were on the brink of destabilizing Senegalese society, corrupting moral values, and throwing the nation into total disarray. Subsequently, in April 2009, following the release of nine members of an HIV/AIDS association who were doing outreach work among MSM, several Islamic organizations formed the Front Islamique pour la Défense des Valeurs Ethiques [Islamic Front for the Defense of Ethical Values]. In its first official declaration, the Front accused homosexual lobbies of nurturing an evil plan to destabilize Senegalese society.[34]

The recourse by the Muslim religious leaders, in all their declarations, to the lexicon of impurity, foreignness, decay and maleficence to describe gender-nonconforming individuals is purposive. The lexicon is meant to trigger social fear and cultural anger followed by defensive and offensive political action to remedy the crisis. The Muslim leaders were able to provoke cultural anger by presenting people with a new sociocultural logic to reinterpret their environment and lived realities. The sermons of the religious leaders pinpointed the homosexual as the harbinger of all the ills of Senegalese society, including youth rebellion, changing gender roles and arrangements, drought, and natural catastrophes. The homosexual was a harmful and foreign element who had to be eliminated for Senegalese society to be functional again, for men to be men again and women to remain women. The new interpretative logic put forward by the religious leaders gained traction and generated cultural anger because the leaders offered up the homosexual as a much-needed placeholder for various anxieties relating to economic uncertainty and sociocultural transformations in 2000s Senegal. In the

1980s, Jamra failed to negatively resignify the *goordjiggen* as the homosexual. However, in 2008 that resignification gained traction as a result of a changed social and economic landscape and probably the *goordjiggens'* adoption of the social and cultural codes of LGBTQ communities in the West. Going back to Madické Niang's point about the rules of discretion that *goordjiggens* abided by, the 2008 gay wedding defied the rules of ambiguity and flaunted the same-sex practices that Senegalese society would rather not know about. The concept of *sutura*, which prescribes what belongs to private or public domain, captures the Senegalese notions of discretion described by Madické Niang.

However, *sutura* also pertains to the right to privacy. The expression *Niit deñu koy sutural* [you owe your fellow human being discretion] is commonly used in Senegal to stress the right to privacy and call people to order whenever they volunteer indiscreet disclosures about another person. Cheikh Niang is thus right to argue that in making the intimate lives of gender-nonconforming men a matter of public discourse, antigay vigilantes violated the important Senegalese cultural code of social discretion that *sutura* constitutes.[35] But the refusal to extend *sutura* to gender-nonconforming individuals speaks to the reinvention by the Muslim religious leaders of the *goordjiggen* as the homosexual, meaning barely a fellow human being. That redefinition comes forth in the declaration by Jamra Leader Abdoul Latif Coulibaly that "Le combat contre l'homosexualité et toutes les déviances qui déshumanisent l'individu est un combat légitime et moral, mais aussi hautement civique et patriotique. (. . .) Il est illusoire de construire un pays avec des désaxés, des détraqués, des déculturés et des lobbies aux desseins sordides" [The fight against homosexuality and all deviant behaviors that dehumanize individuals is a legitimate and moral crusade as well as a civic and patriotic one. (. . .) It is illusory to build a nation with people who are unhinged, unbalanced and culturally alienated on the one hand and, on the other, lobbies with sordid agendas].[36] The new cultural logic at work in the homophobia crisis in Senegal, that made *sutura* inapplicable to gender-nonconforming individuals, relates to Judith Butler's interrelated concepts of the socially unintelligible and unmournable, as laid out in *Precarious Life*.[37] That the socially unintelligible is also the unmournable, hence the sub-human, as Butler notes,[38] became the reality of Senegalese homosexuals as they were denied *su-*

tura and angry mobs barred the families of deceased homosexuals from burying, indeed mourning, their loved ones. Such gestures demarcated what counted as valid life in post-2008 Senegal.

This orchestrated reinvention of the Senegalese *goordjiggen* as a socially unintelligible figure shows that homophobia here does not stem from a deep-rooted religious or cultural sentiment. Homophobia in Senegal is a clever and purposive political strategy that creates and manipulates what S. N. Nyeck calls "erotic paranoid nationalism."[39] This form of paranoia feeds off "obsessive beliefs about sexual enemies" of the national community and hinges on the power of its orchestrators to "control public opinion, outlaw dissent, and obstruct critical thinking without which the sanity of the polity becomes questionable."[40] In Senegal, Muslim religious leaders triggered a cultural anger that subsequently became a ripe terrain to whip populations into an erotic paranoid nationalism. The leaders succeeded because they offered a very much socio-economically frazzled population the psychosocial comfort of a scapegoat and, most importantly, a respite in sight. In René Girard's theory of the sacrificial scapegoat, scapegoats bring the community together in solidarity while relieving social pressures.[41] In Nyeck's analysis of Cameroon, the scapegoating of the homosexual subject serves a political project, inasmuch as "the creation of the homosexual deviant subject, and subsequent attempts to fixate state institutions within the perspective of deviance, empower radical nationalists in all political circles with the mandate to exorcize state power."[42] As such, erotic paranoid nationalism anticipates a politico-moral model of governance. This form of nationalism saturates political discourse and mobilizes populations against the immoral state and existing political-governmental regime and toward a new leadership. It is no coincidence that Imam Niang used that moment of cultural anger and erotic paranoid nationalism that he helped create to announce that his party would participate in the upcoming local elections. Imam Niang positioned himself as the man of the situation, the much-needed moral leader who would turn the destiny of the embattled nation around. Cultural anger ferments erotic paranoid nationalism and henceforth creates a ripe terrain for a new political leadership and hegemony to stake claim to governance.

But it would be a mistake to reduce the rise of homophobia in Senegal to the political ambitions of just one man. The noted political ambitions speak to the new political lay of the land in Senegal, with the emergence of Islamic militancy and political parties.[43] Some scholars of Islam and politics in Senegal have argued that these new political parties pursue a project of reislamization, and an Islamic State may be in their agenda.[44] Such a plan of instituting an Islamic social and political order that would include Sharia law and Islamic family laws can only be achieved by taking hold of the state apparatus. A petition that the Collective of Senegalese Islamic Association sent out after a planned protest march was banned by the state provides insights into their political ambitions. The Collective called on "the active forces of the country to face what it considers to be the repeated assaults by the enemies of faith and morality, who unscrupulously attack those sacred values which constitute the very essence of the noblest virtues of our society."[45] In the petition, the Collective interpellates the proper citizen and patriotic subject of the nation as a heterosexual, an antigay vigilante and a Muslim. The embattled nation needs Muslims; to be Muslim means not only to be heterosexual but to be vehemently opposed to the homosexuality to the point of engaging in antigay vigilantism. Subsequently, to be Muslim means to be a proper and legitimate citizen of the nation since the practice of heterosexuality and homophobia that are constitutive of Muslim identity are designed to protect the nation. The Collective pursues in another declaration that eliminating homosexuals is a "religious and patriotic obligation that befalls any citizen who values peace and the well-being of the younger generations."[46] In that sense, the interlocking and mutual dependency of the identities of the homophobic heterosexual, the Muslim and the legitimate citizen of the nation binds Senegalese nationals to a new logic of identity and grammar of citizenship. Most importantly, this new logic and grammar leave room only for one type of political leadership and, of course, totally discounts the current state leadership.

Once homosexuality was made a matter of public and political discourse by the politically savvy Collective to the point where homosexuality later became a determining topic during the 2012 presidential campaign, the sitting state leadership was on the spot. On the one hand lied a population and electorate who had been whipped into an antigay fervor and, on the other hand, was the geopolitical necessity of not being labeled a violator of human rights. Kapya Kaoma has argued that Ugandan president Yoweri Museveni had to play good politics in a similar context, with respect to the infamous "kill the gays" bill.[47] Museveni's contradictory positions signaled his attempt to cater to national and international constituencies. In Senegal, President Abdoulaye Wade and Macky Sall, his successor, also had to play good politics.

Both Presidents Wade and Sall have been accused of flip-flopping on the subject of LGBTQ rights. Abdoulaye Wade and his government kept silent throughout the 2008-2009 witch-hunt against gender-nonconforming men, including the desecration of the tombs of alleged homosexuals. As Cheikh Niang writes, the Senegalese state tried to play the role of mediator between opponents and defenders of gay rights.[48] In fact, since 2008, the Senegalese state has been walking, in a zigzag fashion, a very fine line between state homophobia and state homoprotectionism. Both Human Rights Watch and Amnesty International have published detailed reports on homophobic violence in Senegal. The reports have repeatedly denounced the lethargy of the Senegalese state on homophobic violence. Conversely, the political opponents of Presidents Wade and Sall have pinpointed their lethargy when it comes to condemning and punishing homosexuality. The opponents of President Wade circulated rumors that the president had a gay entourage. During the 2012 presidential campaign, the camp of Abdoulaye Wade tried to position Macky Sall as the candidate of the homosexuals. After offering an ambiguous response to a question on the decriminalization of homosexuality, Macky Sall was confronted with the threat of a massive defection if he did not take a firm stand.[49]

Macky Sall's alleged laxity toward sexual minorities has become a political resource for his political foes. The subject is a recurrent theme in social media, online forums and daily conversations in Senegal. Senegalese newspapers regularly announce an impending decriminalization of homosexuality. The members of "Y'en a marre," a movement of young social activists who helped Macky Sall defeat former President Wade, have positioned themselves as defenders of morality and crusaders against the global gay agenda of Western neo-imperialism. They have repeatedly threatened to oust President Sall from power if he capitulates to international pressure and decriminalizes homosexuality. The visit of President Obama to Senegal in June 2013 was a turning moment for President Sall. Obama's visit intensified speculations that a decriminalization of homosexuality was in the works. The media fed the frenzy with sensationalist headlines like "Barack Obama Vient au Sénégal pour Déchirer une Page du Saint Coran"[50] [Barack Obama Is Coming to Senegal to Rip a Page out of the Holy Coran], "Barack Obama à Dakar pour Exiger à Macky Sall la Dépénalisation de l'Homosexualité"[51] [Barack Obama Will Order Macky Sall to Decriminalize Homosexuality] or again, "Le PDS-France Révèle de Deal Obama-Macky qui Va Dépénaliser l'Homosexualité"[52] [PDS-France Reveals a Deal between Macky and Obama to Decriminalize Homosexuality].

During his visit, President Obama forced President Sall to take a stand when Obama declared during a joint press conference with Sall his support of a decriminalization of homosexuality in Senegal. Sall responded unequivocally that homosexuality was at odds with the cultural values of the land. Judging from the media and online discussions, Sall redeemed himself with flying colors to many of his Senegalese constituencies. This was an instance of political homophobia as a state strategy and a tool of statecraft, mostly in response to the charges of homosexuality leveled by civil society against the state. Judging from the bombastic titles of newspapers the following day, this moment is best remembered as a lovefest between President Sall and his constituencies. Writing for *The New York Times*, Adam Nossiter cites the cheering headlines of Senegalese newspapers following Sall's retort: "Firm . . . and subtle," crowed *Sud Quotidien* on its front page, praising Mr. Sall for his response. "No, We Can't," trumpeted *Liberation*. "Macky Says No to Obama," said *Walfadjri* on its front page. "Obama Makes a Plea for the Homos, Macky Says No!" said *Le Pop*. "President Sall Has Closed the Debate on Homosexuality," read a headline in *L'Observateur*."[53]

The metaphor of the homosexual state in Senegal also pertained to changing gender legislation in the 2000s. In 2004, the Family Code, which guaranteed a number of rights to women, came under attack again when the Islamic Committee for the Reform of the Family Code in Senegal, a consortium of Islamic associations, tried to push for a new code that would conform to Sharia law.[54] The Gender Parity Law, adopted with much difficulty by the parliament in 2010, had been the subject of intense public debates and pushback since 2006 when President Wade appointed a national committee on gender parity. Afua

Hirsh reports that in some parts of rural Senegal, parity now means "I no longer accept my husband's authority" in the local Wolof language.[55] The unsuccessful attacks against the Family Code and the voting into law of the Gender Parity Law became fodder for patriarchal anxieties and heteropatriarchal panic. The perceived inability of the state leadership to protect so-called traditional Senegalese gender roles and arrangements called into question the ability of the state to represent and protect the nation. In lay terms, the current leaders of the nation were not true men and had failed in their patriarchal duties. Discourses of nationhood, gender and sexuality are interwoven, as Tamar Meyer notes:

> The nation is comprised of sexed subjects whose "performativity" constructs not only their own gender identity but the identity of the entire nation as well. Through repetition of accepted norms and behaviors—control over reproduction, militarism and heroism, and heterosexuality—members help to construct the privileged nation; equally the repetitive performance of these acts in the name of the nation helps to construct gender and sexuality.[56]

In Senegal, the perceived failure of the state to uphold gender norms helped the metaphor of the homosexual state gain traction in 2008. Conversely, the state became invested in contesting the metaphor in order to retain legitimacy. The state had to engage in a performance of homophobia.

Following Achille Mbembe's theorization of the link between politics and theatricality in the postcolony,[57] state homophobia in Senegal is an aesthetic and political accoutrement that complements the theatrics of the postcolonial state. These theatrics, per Mbembe, pertain to the state's dramaturgy of its omnipotent power and serve to "safeguard the official fictions that underwrite the apparatus of domination, since these are essential to keeping the people under the commandment's spell."[58] Thus, the state is invested in the protection, at any cost, of "the vocabulary used to denote or speak to the commandment."[59] The metaphor of the homosexual state sabotages the dramaturgy of the state in Senegal inasmuch as the performance of omnipotent power draws on the phallic symbolism of the state.

Beyond domestic politics, state homophobia in Senegal is also in conversation with African state homophobias. Kapia Kaoma astutely notes that the antigay bills in different African countries share the same language.[60] African states seem to be vying for the top spot in state homophobia. For instance, the escalating homophobic rhetoric of Gambian President Yahya Jammeh in 2008–2010[61] cannot be considered independently of the unfolding spectacle of homophobia in neighboring Senegal and the rivalry between the two nations. In fact, President Jammeh's first homophobic statements were made after the 2008 gay wedding scandal forced a number of Senegalese gender-nonconforming men to seek refuge in Gambia. Popular opinion in Senegal lauded President Jammeh for being a "real man," in contrast to President Sall who had not taken a firm stand on homosexuality at the time. When President Obama visited Senegal and pushed for a decriminalization of homosexuality, President Jammeh was quick to retort that Obama would not have dared make such a call in Gambia. President Jammeh implied that Senegal was a homosexual state. In rebuffing Obama's call for a decriminalization of homosexuality in Senegal, President Sall engaged in a performance of virile postcolonial African nationhood on the world stage. Indeed, African state homophobias are also in conversation with the (emasculating) metaphor of the "colonial penetration" of Africa. Metaphors of sexual domination and non-normative sexualities thus recur in analyses of the asymmetrical power relations between the West and African states and the minor position of African states in global geopolitics. Take for instance Achille Mbembe's recurrent metaphor of an "emasculation of the postcolonial state" or Malawi's Bishop Joseph Bvumbwe's statement that Western nations and international donor agencies use their "financial muscle to advance gay rights in Malawi."[62]

A recurrent argument in discussions of anti-gay legislations in Africa is the colonial origin of these laws. But in Senegal, legislation against same-sex sexuality was introduced in the wake of national independence from France. The significance of this criminalization of homosexuality by the newly formed postcolonial nation is twofold. First is the function of heterosexual masculine sexuality as an expression of virile nationhood and a performative symbol of phallic governance. Second is the intertwined constructions of proper national citizenship and heterosexuality. But until 2008, Senegal's legislation against same-sex sexuality remained dormant, with hardly anyone being prosecuted for homosexual activity. Since 2008, a new state-sponsored homophobia and a new culture of permissive violence toward gender-nonconforming men seem resolute to reinvent Senegal as a homophobic nation. The salience around homosexuality in electoral and party politics and the bearings of the homosexual question on statecraft and state governance map a political genealogy of homosexuality and homophobia in Senegal. But in Senegal, politicians have not limited themselves to using the figure of the homosexual. The political usability of the homosexual first necessitated a meticulous manufacturing of the homosexual, meaning a displacement of the indigenous figure of the *goordjiggen* by the homosexual. The category of the homosexual thus had to be invented. More specifically, the figure of the homosexual in Senegal is an invention while popular homophobia represents the politically engineered sociocultural response to this invented figure. The relative invisibility of women who have sex with women in homophobic discourses in Senegal suggests that what is also at stake here is the dramaturgy of the virile nation-state and the continuing circulation of heteropatriarchal masculinity as political currency.

BIBLIOGRAPHY

Agence de Presse Sénégalaise. "Sénégal: Les Journaux Commentent la Libération des Homosexuels." *Agence de Presse Sénégalaise*, April 21, 2009. http://aps.sn

Akara, Fatou. "La Prostitution Gay Pollue Dakar." *Rue Publique*, May 25, 2011. http://www.ruepublique.net

Arnfred, Signe, ed. *Rethinking Sexualities in Africa*. Uppsala: Nordiska Afrikainstitutet, 2004.

Awondo, Patrick. "Une Afrique Homophobe? Sur quelques Trajectoires de Politisation de l'Homosexualité: Cameroun, Ouganda, Sénégal et Afrique du Sud." *Raisons Politiques* 49 (2013): 95–118.

Bâ, Mariama. *Un Chant Ecarlate*. Dakar: Nouvelles Editions Africaines, 1981.

Bangré, Habibou. "Comnent les neuf Homosexuels ont été Libérés." *Jeune Afrique*, April 23, 2009. http://www.jeuneafrique.com

Basse, Arona. "Homosexualité et Médias." *Le Quotidien*, April 5, 2014. http://www.lequotidien.sn

Bop, Codou. "Senegal: Homophobia and Islamic Political Manipulation," 2008. http://www.wluml.org

Bosia, Michael J. and Meredith L. Weiss. "Political Homophobia in Comparative Perspective." In *Global Homophobia: States, Movements, and the Politics of Oppression*, edited by Weiss, Meredith L. and Michael J. Bosia, 1–29. Chicago: University of Illinois Press, 2013.

Broqua, Christophe. "Góor-jigéen: la Resignification Négative d'une Catégorie entre Genre et Sexualité." *Socio* 9 (2017): 163–83.

Bugul, Ken. *Le Baobab Fou*. Dakar: Nouvelles Editions Africaines, 1982.

Butler, Judith. *Precarious Life: The Powers of Mourning and Violence*. New York: Verso, 2004.

Camara, Fatou Kiné. "Ce Délit qui Nous Vient d'Ailleurs: l'Homosexualité dans le Code Pénal du Sénégal." *Psychopathologie Africaine* XXXIV.3 (2007–2008): 317–42.

Camara, Mamadou Lamine. 2011. "Au Secours! L'Homosexualité Gagne du Terrain au Sénégal et notre Progéniture est Exposée." *Seneweb News* May 18, 2011. http://www.seneweb.com

Coly, Ayo A. "Introduction: Homophobic Africa?" *African Studies Review* 56, no. 2 (2013): 21–30.

Crowder, Michael. *Pagans and Politicians*. London: Hutchinson, 1959.

Currier, Ashley. *Out in Africa: LGBT Organizing in Namibia and South Africa*. Minneapolis: University of Minnesota Press, 2012.

Dakar Actu. "Barack Obama à Dakar pour Exiger à Macky Sall la dépénalisation de l'Homosexualité." *Dakar Actu*, May 24, 2013. https://www.dakaractu.com

Epprecht, Marc. *Hungochani: The History of a Dissident Sexuality in Southern Africa*. Montreal and Kingston: McGill-Queen's University Press, 2004.

———. *Heterosexual Africa?: The History of an Idea from the Age of Exploration to the Age of AIDS*. Athens: Ohio University Press, 2008.

Fall, Aminata Sow. *Le Revenant*. Dakar: Nouvelles Editions Africaines, 1982.

Feder, J. Lester. 2014. "African Homophobes are Politicians, Not Lunatics, Writer Says." *BuzzFeed News*, May 21, 2014. https://www.buzzfeed.com

Girard, René. *The Scapegoat*. Baltimore, MD: John Hopkins University Press, 1986.

Gomez-Perez, Muriel. 1994. "L'Islamisme à Dakar: D'un Contrôle Social Total à une Culture du Pouvoir." *Afrika Spectrum* 29.1 (1994): 79–98.

Herdt, Gilbert. *Moral Panics, Sex Panics Fear and the Fight over Sexual Rights*. New York: New York University Press, 2009.

Hirsch, Afua. "Has Senegal's Gender Parity Law for MPs Helped Women?" *The Guardian*, November 15, 2012. https://www.theguardian.com

Hofnung, Thomas "Les Homosexuels Harcelés au Sénégal." *Libération*, January 16, 2009. http://www.liberation.fr

Huffington Post. "Senegal: 9 Men Jailed for Homosexual Acts." *Huffington Post*, January 8, 2009. https://www.huffingtonpost.com

Human Rights Watch. *Craindre pour sa Vie: Violences contre les Hommes Gays et Perçus comme tels au Sénégal*. New York: Human Rights Watch, 2010.

Jeune Afrique. 2009. "Sénégal: Création d'un Front Islamique pour la Défense des Valeurs Ethiques." *Jeune Afrique*, April 29, 2009. http://www.jeuneafrique.com

Kaoma, Kapya. *How the US Christian Right is Transforming Sexual Politics in Africa*. Somerville, MA: Political Research Associates, 2012.

———. "Uganda's New Anti-Gay Law A Copy of U.S. Right-Backed Laws in Russia/Nigeria." *Political Research Associates*, November 13, 2014. https://www.politicalresearch.org

Kassé, Mouhamadou Tidiane. "Mounting Homophobic Violence in Senegal." In *Queer African Reader*, edited by Ekine, Sokari and Hakima Abbas, 262–72. Dakar, Nairobi and Oxford: Pambazuka Press, 2013.

Korycki, Katarzyna and Abouzar Nasirzadeh. "Homophobia as a Tool of Statecraft: Iran and its Queers." In *Global Homophobia: States, Movements, and the Politics of Oppression*, edited by Weiss, Meredith L. and Michael J. Bosia, 174–95. Chicago: University of Illinois Press, 2013.

Long, Scott, et al. *More Than a Name: State-Sponsored Homophobia and its Consequences in Southern Africa*. New York: Human Rights Watch; San Francisco, CA: International Gay and Lesbian Human Rights Commission, 2003.

M'Baye, Babacar. 2013. "The Origins of Senegalese Homophobia: Discourses on Homosexuals and Transgender People in Colonial and Postcolonial Senegal." *African Studies Review* 56.2 (2013): 109–28.

Mbembe, Achille. *On the Postcolony*. Berkeley: University of California Press, 2001.

Meyer, Tamar. *Gender Ironies of Nationalism: Sexing the Nation*. London: Routledge, 2002.

Niang, Cheikh Ibrahima, et al. 2003. "'It's Raining Stones': Stigma, Violence and HIV Vulnerability among Men Who Have Sex with Men in Dakar, Senegal." *Culture, Health and Sexuality* 5.6 (2003): 499–512.

Nossiter, Adam. "Senegal Cheers its President for Standing Up on Same-Sex Marriage." *The New York Times*, June 28, 2013. https://www.nytimes.com

Nyanzi, Stella. "Rhetorical Analysis of President Jammeh's Threats to Behead Homosexuals." In *Sexual Diversity in Africa: Politics, Theory and Citizenship*, edited by Nyeck, S. N. and Marc Epprecht, 67–88. Montreal and Kingston: McGill-Queen's University Press, 2013.

Nyeck, S. N. "Mobilizing against the Invisible: Erotic Nationalism, Mass Media, and the 'Paranoid Style' in Cameroon." In *Sexual Diversity in Africa: Politics, Theory and Citizenship*, edited by Nyeck, S. N. and Marc Epprecht, 151–69. Montreal and Kingston: McGill-Queen's University Press, 2013.

Samson, Fabienne. "Islam, Protest, and Citizen Mobilization: New Sufi Movements." In *New Perspectives on Islam in Senegal: Conversion, Migration, Wealth, Power and Femininity*, edited by Diouf, Mamadou and Mara Leichtman, 257–72. New York: Palgrave MacMillan, 2009.

Sud Quotidien. "Pour Protester contre la Libération des Homosexuels: Marche de Protestation, Sermon des Imams au Menu." *Sud Quotidien*, February 8, 2008. http://ww1.sudonline.sn

Tall, Aliou. "Homosexualité au Sénégal: danger et alerte au president et au peuple Sénégalais." *Setal*, May 21, 2013. https://www.setal.net

Tamale, Sylvia. "Researching and Theorising Sexualities in Africa." In *African Sexualities: A Reader*, edited by Sylvia Tamale, 11–36. Cape Town: Pambazuka Press, 2011.

Teunis, Niels."Same-Sex Sexuality in Africa: A Case Study from Senegal." *Aids and Behavior* 5.2 (2001): 173–82.

Thiès Actu. "Barack Obama Vient au Sénégal pour Déchirer une Page du Saint Coran." *Thiès Actu*, June 25, 2013.http://www.thiesactu.com

UN Human Rights Council. "Draft Report of the Working Group on the Universal Periodic Review: Senegal."A/HRC/11/24. October 5, 2009.

———. A/HRC/WG.6/17/L.2. October 23, 2013.

———. UN Fourth Universal Periodic Review, 9th Plenary Meeting. "Comments and Answers by Senegal." February 6, 2009.

———. 17th Session of Universal Periodic Review. "Comments and Answers by Senegal." October 21, 2013.

Villalón, Leonardo A., and Kane, Ousmane. 1998. "Senegal: The Crisis of Democracy and the Emergence of an Islamic Opposition." In *The African State at a Critical Juncture: Between Disintegration and Reconfiguration*, edited by Villalón, Leonardo A. and Philip A. Huxtable, 143–66. Boulder: Lynne Rienner, 1998.

Xalima News. "Macky Sall sur l'Homosexualité: 'Nous la Gérerons de Façon Responsable.'" *Xalima News*, March 10, 2012. http://xalimasn.com

Xibar. "Abdou Latif Guèye, Président de Jamra: 'Nous Allons Poursuivre le Combat contre l'Homosexualité, sans Passion.'" *Xibar*, February 21, 2008. https://www.xibar.net

Xibar Tamba. *2013. "Le PDS-France Révèle de Deal Obama-Macky qui va Dépénaliser l'Homosexualité." Xibar Tamba, June 25, 2013. http://www.xibartamba.com*

NOTES

1. Aliou Tall, "Homosexualité au Sénégal: Danger et Alerte au Président et au Peuple Sénégalais," *Setal*, May 21, 2013.

2. All translations are mine, unless noted otherwise.

3. Fatou Akara, "La Prostitution Gay Pollue Dakar," *Rue Publique*, May 25, 2011.

4. Mamadou Lamine Camara, "Au secours! l'Homosexualité gagne du terrain au Sénégal et notre progéniture est exposée," *Seneweb News*, May 18, 2011.

5. "Prostitution, Débauche, Homosexualité au Sénégal," *Jamra Magazine* 2, no. 6, April 1984.

6. Signe Arnfred, ed., *Re-thinking Sexualities in Africa* (Uppsala: Nordiska Afrikainstitutet, 2004); Marc Epprecht, *Hungochani: The History of a Dissident Sexuality in Southern Africa* (Ithaca: McGill-Queen's University Press, 2004); Ibid., *Heterosexual Africa: The History of an Idea from the Age of Exploration to the Age of AIDS* (Athens: Ohio University Press, 2008); Sylvia Tamale, "Researching and Theorising Sexualities in Africa," in *African Sexualities: A Reader*, ed. Sylvia Tamale (Cape Town: Pambazuka Press, 2011), 11–36.

7. Mouhamadou Tidiane Kassé, "Mounting Homophobic Violence in Sénégal," in *Queer African Reader*, ed. Sokari Ekine and Hakima Abbas (Dakar, Nairobi and Oxford: Pambazuka Press, 2013), 262–72; Cheikh Ibrahima Niang, "It's Raining Stones: Stigma, Violence and HIV Vulnerability among Men Who Have Sex with Men in Dakar, Sénégal," *Culture, Health and Sexuality* 5, no. 6 (2003): 499–512.

8. Kassé, "Mounting Homophobic Violence," 269.

9. Michael Crowder, *Pagans and Politicians* (London: Hutchinson, 1959); Babacar M'Baye, "The Origins of Senegalese Homophobia: Discourses on Homosexuals and Transgender People in Colonial and Postcolonial Senegal," *African Studies Review* 56, no. 2 (2013): 109–28; Niels Teunis, "Same-Sex Sexuality in Africa: A Case Study from Senegal," *Aids and Behavior* 5, no. 2 (2001): 173–82.

10. Arona Basse, "Homosexualité et Médias," *Le Quotidien*, April 5, 2014.

11. Babacar M'Baye, "The Origins of Senegalese Homophobia;" Cheikh Ibrahima Niang, "It's Raining Stones."

12. Mariama Bâ, *Un Chant Écarlate* (Dakar: Nouvelles Editions Africaines, 1981); Ken Bugul, *Le Baobab Fou* (Dakar: Nouvelles Editions Africaines, 1982); Aminata Sow Fall, *Le Revenant* (Dakar: Nouvelles Editions Africaines, 1982).

13. "Draft Report of the Working Group on the Universal Periodic Review: Senegal," UN Human Rights Council, A/HRC/11/24, October 5, 2009: 20.

14. "Draft Report of the Working Group on the Universal Periodic Review: Senegal," UN Human Rights Council, A/HRC/WG.6/17/L.2, October 23, 2013: 20.

15. "Comments and Answers by Senegal," UN Human Rights Council, Fourth Universal Periodic Review, 9th Plenary Meeting, February 6, 2009.

16. "Comments and Answers by Senegal," UN Human Rights Council, 17th Session of Universal Periodic Review, October 21, 2013.

17. Human Rights Watch, *Craindre pour sa Vie: Violences contre les Hommes Gays et Perçus comme tels au Sénégal* (New York: Human Rights Watch, 2010), 2.

18. Ayo A. Coly, "Introduction: Homophobic Africa?" *African Studies Review* 56.2 (2013): 21–30; Ashley Currier, *Out in Africa: LGBT Organizing in Namibia and South Africa* (Minneapolis: University of Minnesota Press, 2012); Marc Epprecht, *Hungochani*; Ibid., *Heterosexual Africa*.

19. Fatou Kiné Camara, "Ce Délit qui nous Vient d'ailleurs: l'Homosexualité dans le Code Pénal du Sénégal," *Psychopathologie Africaine* XXXIV. 3 (2007–2008): 317–42.

20. Babacar M'Baye, "The Origins of Senegalese Homophobia;" Cheikh Ibrahima Niang, "It's Raining Stones."

21. Katarzyna Korycki and Abouzar Nasirzadeh, "Homophobia as a Tool of Statecraft: Iran and Its Queers," in *Global Homophobias: States, Movements, and the Politics of Oppression*, eds. Meredith L. Weiss and Michael J. Bosia (Chicago: University of Illinois Press, 2013), 175.

22. Michael J. Bosia and Meredith L. Weiss, "Political Homophobia in Comparative Perspective," in *Global Homophobias*, eds. Michael J. Bosia and Meredith L. Weiss, 16.

23. Scott Long, et al., *More than a Name: State-Sponsored Homophobia and its Consequences in Southern Africa* (New York: Human Rights Watch; San Francisco: International Gay and Lesbian Human Rights Commission, 2003), 8.

24. Christophe Broqua, "Góor-jigéen: la Resignification Négative d'une Catégorie entre Genre et Sexualité," *Socio* 9 (2017): 163–83.

25. Christophe Broqua also notes that in the back cover of Karim Deya's novel *J'attends mon Mari* (2014), the terms goordjiggen and homosexual are used interchangeably. The back cover explains that the protagonists of the novels are "goordjiggen, c'est-à-dire des homosexuels" [goordjiggen, meaning homosexuals].

26. Human Rights Watch, *Craindre pour sa Vie*.

27. "Sénégal: Les Journaux Commentent la Libération des Homosexuels," *Agence de Presse Sénégalaise*, April 21, 2009.

28. "Pour Protester contre la Libération des Homosexuels: Marche de Protestation, Sermon des Imams au Menu," *Sud Quotidien*, February 8, 2008.

29. "Senegal: 9 Men jailed for Homosexual Acts," *Huffington Post*, January 8, 2009.

30. Thomas Hofnung, "Les Homosexuels Harcelés au Sénégal," *Libération*, January 16, 2009.

31. Habibou Bangré, “Comnent les neuf Homosexuels ont été Libérés,” *Jeune Afrique*, April 23, 2009.

32. Patrick Awondo, “Une Afrique Homophobe? Sur quelques Trajectoires de Politisation de l'h Homosexualité: Cameroun, Ouganda, Sénégal et Afrique du Sud,” *Raisons Politiques* 49 (2013): 95–118.

33. Gilbert Herdt. *Moral Panics: Sex Panics Fear and the Fight over Sexual Rights* (New York: New York University Press, 2009).

34. “Création d'un Front Islamique pour la Défense des Valeurs Ethiques,” *Jeune Afrique*, April 29, 2009.

35. Cheikh Ibrahima Niang, “It's Raining Stones.”

36. “Abdou Latif Guèye, Président de Jamra: “Nous Allons Poursuivre le Combat contre l'Homosexualité, sans Passion,” *Xibar*, February 21, 2008.

37. Judith Butler, *Precarious Life: The Powers of Mourning and Violence* (New York: Routledge, 2006).

38. Ibid., 12.

39. S. N. Nyeck, “Mobilizing against the Invisible: Erotic Nationalism, Mass Media, and the “Paranoid Style” in Cameroon,” in *Sexual Diversity in Africa: Politics, Theory and Citizenship*, eds. S. N. Nyeck and Marc Epprecht (Montrealand Kingston: McGill-Queen's University Press, 2013), 151–69.

40. Ibid., 153.

41. René Girard,*The Scapegoat* (Baltimore: John Hopkins University Press, 1989).

42. S. N. Nyeck, “Mobilizing against the Invisible,” 169.

43. Muriel Gomez-Perez, “L'Islamisme à Dakar: d'un Contrôle Social Total à une Culture du Pouvoir,” *Afrika Spectrum* 29, no. 1 (1994): 79–98; Fabienne Samson, “Islam, Protest, and Citizen Mobilization: New Sufi Movements,” in *New Perspectives on Islam in Senegal: Conversion, Migration, Wealth, Power and Femininity*, eds. Mamadou Diouf and Mara Leichtman (New York: Palgrave Macmillan, 2009), 257–72; Leonardo A. Villalón and Ousmane Kane, “Senegal: The Crisis of Democracy and the Emergence of an Islamic Opposition,” in *The African State at a Critical Juncture: Between Disintegration and Reconfiguration*, eds. Leonardo A. Villalón and Philip A. Huxtable (Boulder: Lynne Rienner), 143–66.

44. Codou Bop, “Senegal: Homophobia and Islamic Political Manipulation,” *2008*. http://www.wluml.org; Fatou Kiné Camara, “Ce délit qui nous vient d'ailleurs.”

45. Codou Bop, “Senegal: Homophobia and Islamic Political Manipulation.”

46. Ibid.

47. Kapya Kaoma, "Uganda's New Anti-Gay Law a Copy of US Right-Backed Laws in Russia/Nigeria," *Political Research Associates*, November 13, 2014.

48. Cheikh Ibrahima Niang, "It's Raining Stones."

49. "Macky Sall sur l'Homosexualité: "Nous la Gérerons de Façon Responsable," *Xalima News*, March 10, 2012.

50. "Barack Obama vient au Sénégal pour Déchirer une Page du Saint Coran," *Thiès Actu*, June 25, 2013.

51. "Barack Obama à Dakar pour Exiger à Macky Sall la Dépénalisation de l'Homosexualité," *Dakar Actu*, May 24, 2013.

52. "Le PDS-France Révèle le Deal Obama-Macky qui va Dépénaliser l'Homosexualité," *Xibar Tamba*, June 25, 2013.

53. Adam Nossiter, "Senegal Cheers Its President for Standing up on Same-Sex Marriage," *The New York Times*, June 28, 2013.

54. Senegal's Family Code has been in place since 1972. At various points, Islamist tried to overturn it.

55. Afua Hirsh, "Has Senegal's Gender Parity Law for MP's Helped Women?" *The Guardian*, November 15, 2012.

56. Tamar Meyer, *Gender Ironies of Nationalism: Sexing the Nation* (London: Routledge, 2002), 5.

57. Achille Mbembe, *On The Postcolony* (Berkeley: University of California Press, 2001).

58. Ibid., 11.

59. Ibid.

60. J. Lester Feder, "African Homophobes Are Politicians, not Lunatics, Writer Says," *BuzzFeed* News, May 21, 2014.

61. Stella Nyanzi, "Rhetorical Analysis of President Jammeh's Threats to Behead Homosexuals," in *Sexual Diversity in Africa*, eds. S. N. Nyeck and Marc Epprecht, 67–88.

62. Kapya J. Kaoma, *How the US Christian Right Is Transforming Sexual Politics in Africa* (Somerville, MA: Political Research Associates, 2012), 8.

2

QUEERING THE "GREATER JIHAD"

Sufi Resistance and Disruptive Morality in Senegalese Women's Soccer

Beth Packer

After Friday's training, Fatou and I decided to go back to her house to watch television and make *attayah* [Senegalese tea]. As we walked out of the sandy lot next to an abandoned apartment structure, I noticed that everyone was watching her. She had a white muscle tank top and soccer shorts, which she wore very low on her hips so that her blue bunched-up boxer shorts were visible. Her head was completely shaved except for a bleach blonde tuft near her forehead; her only jewelry was her single diamond earring and amulet ring. As she walked, she would drag her feet on the ground in a relaxed and almost lazy manner, squaring her hips and shoulders and clenching her jaw in a frown. A group of young boys dressed in school uniforms passed us once we reached the paved street, shouting at her and laughing loudly. They cried out to her "Hey jigéen walla goor la? Dafa niaw" [it's a boy or a girl? It's ugly]. Fatou didn't respond. She kept her regard focused straight ahead. She straightened her shoulders; it seemed to me that the more the boys yelled at her mockingly, the taller she became.

A few minutes later, at the crossroads of the market, we met an elderly lady whose face was ravaged by the sun and wrinkled with age. She was dressed in a traditional boubou, the normative style for Friday, which is the day of prayer and tradition in Senegal. The elderly woman covered her head with a large yellow and orange scarf made from wax fabric, swinging her hips slowly from side to side as she passed us on the sidewalk. When she saw Fatou, she nearly stopped in her tracks; and then, because Fatou refused to make enough room to pass on the sidewalk, she scowled at us and mumbled something incomprehensible. When Fatou still didn't move, she shouted loudly "Baxhul affair goor, war nga solu ak yeere jigeen liiii bahxul kai" [It is not good to do boy's things, you should dress like a girl, this is not good indeed]. As we continued down the street, the elderly woman followed us with her eyes, and when I looked back in her direction even several minutes later, I saw her still gesturing with her hands and repeating "Baxul, affair goor, baxul" [Not good, doing boys' things, not good!] I looked at Fatou who kept a firm and steady gait, as she lifted her chin up and continued to walk straight ahead without responding. The elderly woman kept desperately attempting to shame and goad her into responding, but nothing could make Fatou crack and turn back.[1]

This interaction shook me to my core. The nastiness in the old woman's tone and the vitriol in her eyes made me feel so helpless for Fatou that I wanted to cry. However, Fatou explained that this type of situation happens all the time and that I should get used to it if I want to play soccer in Senegal as a woman. She explained that although this type of negative encounter is painful, it is part and parcel of the game. Fatou is a *footballeuse*—a Senegalese female soccer player who adopts a bodily performance that publicly blurs the lines between masculinity and femininity both on and off the pitch. The *footballeuse* represents the purposeful performance of a socially undesirable feminine masculinity, which disrupts how power operates through gender in Senegal. In fact, due to their disruptive gender performances in public space, these women are often exposed to physical abuse, social ostracism, and structural violence. When I asked Fatou how she dealt with this violence, she simply responded, "the pain, it's good, it makes me stronger than them. That old woman is not as strong as me."[2] Then in a very serious tone, she continued in her deep and raspy voice to explain through the story of Cheikh Amadon Bamba, founder of the Murids:

> You know, Beth, it's like Bamba. Do you know Bamba? Bah, Bamba, he resisted the whites; he was very strong, Bamba, he suffered a lot, greatly suffered for us. And it's God who helped him. This is the story of Bamba, quoi [what]. Well, there were French people, *toubabs* [French], you see who were there; they were with the *toubabs*,

> the soldiers, and there was his chief: a *toubab* [French] who told him, to Bamba, "'Now it's time to pray, what are you going to do? You are going to pray to your god, we say no you cannot.' It was forbidden, you see? The soldier told him, 'I tell you, you can not pray here, you have to go somewhere else; now, if you go to pray you will disobey me, if you do not pray you disobey your god, but if you go to pray, you disobey me. So what are you going to do?'" And there, he decided to pray what, in front of there . . . uh . . . in front of the *toubab* [French]. The *toubab* [French] was angry, *waaw waaw* [*yes, yes*].[3]

Then she gave me a huge smile and tapped me on the shoulder, nodding enthusiastically. Drawing a parallel between her social suffering because of her non-conforming gender performance and Bamba's suffering at the hands of the French administration, Faton said.

> Can you imagine? And the *toubab* [French] told him "Noooonn Bamba" you cannot do that, and he put Bamba in jail! And all this time, he did not have anything to eat, he had nothing, but nothing, the *toubabs*[French] they did not like him, and believe me, Beth, it was hard hard, for him; he suffered a lot Bamba; he was in pain, but he succeeded, thanks to God, who had helped him because he suffered a lot for God, and he came out and he helped us a lot; helped a lot. The *toubabs*[French], they could not stop Bamba; God was with Bamba. It's like us, Bamba shows that you have to suffer for god but that god is with us, you see?[4]

In this chapter, I argue that the Senegalese *footballeuses* challenge gender and sexuality norms prescribed by Islam from within a Sufi framework of resistance. I first show how the *footballeuses* voluntarily engage in confrontational practices of public gender-bending as a way to resist restrictive patriarchal heteronormative beliefs about the limits of femininity in Senegalese society, which leads to their stigmatization. I reveal how their embrace of the stigma symbols associated with these practices provoke further social exclusion, humiliation, and harassment. Yet, rather than distancing themselves from these negative reactions, the *footballeuses* embrace these encounters as tests of their faith which make them stronger than those who persecute them. Next, I discuss how their positive embrace of their suffering as a mode of resistance is shaped by Sufi beliefs about freedom and agency, in which the more one suffers, the closer he or she becomes to God. Where legitimate agency stems only from God, and all suffering is a test of one's faith, the Sufi subject's oppressors become mere vehicles for God's will and are thus void of their own freedom. This is a model of resistance that, I argue, is specific to Sufi spatialities. Finally, I suggest that the *footballeuses'* polemical adoptions of the stigma symbols associated with women's soccer are a mode of queering this model of resistance.

CONTEXT

In Senegal, women's sports such as basketball, handball, and judo are highly celebrated. As Martha Saavedra points out, for several years, women's basketball was even the third most watched sport in Dakar.[5] These sports flourish because they are considered both lucrative career paths and feminine, having evolved within a normative framework of femininity.[6] The media plays an important role in the popularity of these sports by portraying the women who participate in them as expressing an alternative, yet socially desirable femininity. This is in stark contrast with the media's treatment of women's soccer, which is often framed as a lesser version of the masculine sport, an activity that fosters a mode of deviant feminine masculinity. Coverage will often highlight the women's masculine appearance or discuss the sport in relation to the perceived problem of homosexuality. In light of popular religious and state discourses which frame homosexuality as a pressing menace to the moral fabric of Senegalese society, this depiction of women soccer players is highly ostracizing to the women involved in the sport. Such discourses judge the increased visibility of homosexuality in Senegal as a product of western corruption and denounce human rights discourses normalizing homosexuality as part of a larger imperialist project. Consequentially, being openly homosexual in public is dangerous from both a social and legal standpoint as homosexuality is not only punishable by law, but even casual interaction with openly homosexual individuals can result in social ostracism and community sanctions because of the political implications.

The women soccer players who participated in my study identify predominantly as Muslim (excluding three Christians) and range from the ages of seventeen to forty. They are mostly from *classes populaires* [working-class neighborhoods] in and around the urban areas of Dakar,

Saint Louis, or Thiès. A few of the women were from rural areas, having relocated to Dakar or Saint Louis for either soccer or employment opportunities. I should also note that a handful of women were from middle-class families and grew up in more privileged areas of these large cities, yet had some exposure to working-class neighborhoods prior to their involvement in women's soccer either through family or friends. Of the sixty women that I played with regularly, roughly 20 percent have an education of tenth grade or higher. Most are unmarried and publicly claim to be single. Three women are married with children but do not live with their husbands; two women are married with children and live with their partners. It is important to point out that the women in my study do not publicly identify as lesbians, yet they are stigmatized as such for their gender-bending style, which is perceived in popular opinion as a symbol of their homosexuality, which contaminates their social identity and jeopardizes their status as full citizens in the Senegalese polity.

METHODS

I was first made aware of the marginalized status of Senegalese women's soccer players while living and working in Dakar from 2008–2009, when I spent several months looking unsuccessfully to join pick-up games with other women near my neighborhood—there just simply weren't any women playing. I soon learned through preliminary research that there was in fact a small, yet vibrant soccer community. However, because women's soccer is highly stigmatized its players were largely hidden, relegated to a few working-class neighborhoods. This not only made it difficult for me to get in touch with other players but also to gather information about their lives and practices. In 2013, I began seriously conducting ethnographic fieldwork on the topic, playing on three different women's teams based in Dakar and Saint Louis. I spent nine months in Senegal in 2013, four months in 2014, and two months in 2016, playing and traveling with these teams as well as visiting with the women regularly in their homes or at social events and participating in family activities. Today I maintain regular contact with many of these women, whom I now call friends through Skype phone calls, WhatsApp messaging, and Facebook. I also conducted in-depth unstructured interviews with diverse social and political actors in Senegal. Without my prior experience playing soccer as a woman, it would have been impossible for me to gain entry into this closed social world. After several months proving myself on the field I was finally accepted first as a player, then as a researcher. Many of my teammates explicitly told me that the only reason why they were willing to discuss their experience openly with me was because they trusted me as one of them, knowing that I had developed an acute understanding of the effects of this stigma on their lives. I have thus taken great care to live up to this trust in protecting the identities of those involved in my research by changing the names and any descriptive information that could link individuals to my study. In line with this research philosophy, I also made an important ethical decision to not discuss the sexual preferences of the women who participated in my study since any information that could explicitly link them with homosexuality could place them in immediate danger. Although the Senegalese *footballeuses* publicly transgress the gender binary, none of them are openly lesbians. The focus of my study is neither to discuss their private lives nor to talk about their personal sexual preferences. I am interested in the question of sexuality as it is co-produced with that of gender transgression and the important role that sexuality plays in their stigmatization.

THEORETICAL FRAMEWORK

In this chapter, I draw on women's soccer as a lens to engage with scholarly debates about the politics of gender and sexuality in postcolonial Muslim worlds. My research builds on the work of transnational and postcolonial feminist scholars such as Saba Mahmood, Lila Abu-Lughod, Erin Augis, and Ivy Mills, who argue that secular understandings of the self, as shaped by liberal Western discourses which define agency as the ability to act without restraint, leave no room for alternative understandings of the practice of freedom.[7] Their research unveils how such narrow interpretations of agency deny the complex articulation of religion, power, and politics in many Muslim-majority contexts. For example, Mahmood[8] and Augis[9] understand Muslim women's exercise of Islamic piety in the context of the orthodox Egyptian and Senegalese revivalist movements as both a personal and political expression of agency. Their studies demonstrate how these women view their outward and inner adherence to this moral code of Islamic piety, "predicated upon, and transformative of, many aspects of social life,"[10] which demands that they conform to strict bodily rules about modesty and submit to masculine authority, not as a form of oppression but, rather an exercise in freedom. I find their assertion that what constitutes freedom is always already culturally and historically situated particularly germane to my study of Muslim women who desire to fashion themselves as both pious Muslims and Queer subjects. It is only by suspending the Western liberal secular lens, as Mahmood and Augis suggest, that we can explore the myriad ways to practice freedom.[11] In this regard, I join queer studies and transnational feminism scholars Paola Bacchetta and Ayo Coly, who push back against the claims that queer subjectivity and modes of power are extrinsic to postcolonial Muslim and African contexts.[12] Although I agree with Mahmood that we must be critical of the binary model of agency since actors do not only resist or submit to cultural norms, there are in fact many different ways of forming relationships to these norms. I use the term *resistance* as it is used by Paola Bacchetta[13] as a way of exercising power that creates the possibility of new subjectivities and practices within a particular social and historical space. Drawing on these groundbreaking feminist studies, I explore how the soccer players both challenge male domination and heteronormativity by what K. L. Broad describes as a mode of queer resistance or "gender transgression" asserting "sexual fluidity" and enacting "in your face presentations" of a "stigmatized self,"[14] thus exposing the "imitative structure of gender itself"[15] and fashioning themselves as pious Muslim subjects through their embrace of the suffering they experience because of this stigmatization.

GENDER UNAPOLOGETIC, STIGMA AND WOMEN'S SOCCER IN SENEGAL

> If you see us, you know that we are *footballeuses*. We don't need to scream it from the rooftops because our image, our look, does it already. It's about femininity. We aren't like other women. It's our style—as soon as we walk, you know what we are about, you know what activity we practice.[16]

In the above citation, Aicha, a *footballeuse* from a working-class suburb of Dakar in her early twenties, explains the embodied performance that differentiates her from other Senegalese women in public space, namely her unapologetic display of urban masculinity. This performance, characterized by the adoption of stigmatized objects and mannerisms associated with women's soccer in Senegal—dressing in typical men's athletic or hip-hop clothing and embracing masculine gestures and speech patterns—marks her as a *footballeuse*. At home, Aicha is just as likely to be found braiding her sister's hair and wearing a typical feminine *pagne* (skirt) as making *attayah* [Senegalese tea] with her brothers dressed in a muscle tank top and soccer shorts. Yet, when Aicha goes out into public space, she always dresses in men's athletic gear or a button-down long-sleeves tailored shirt, and is never without her silver chain and her baseball cap which she tilts nonchalantly to one side of her head to show off her tight cornrows. She sags her pants to show off her boxer shorts when she walks or sometimes, on Fridays, dresses in men's *boubou* [traditional Senegalese dress]. Outside of the home, her voice drops to a deep raspy tone when she talks to others and minimizes the movement in her hips, squaring her shoulders to de-emphasize her feminine "curves."

In addition, Aicha and the other *footballeuses* use their bodies to take over and assert themselves in public spaces, which has a marginalizing effect on their social lives, yet, also provides them with a sense of freedom and empowerment. For example, Aicha claims that by adopting this style she can circulate freely in the streets and public spaces without constantly subjecting herself to the male gaze: "Yeah, you see, I have less problems with boys when I am a *footballeuse*. They know what I am. It protects me because men are scared of me. Here we don't approach women who are, well, you know, who have this style."[17] Fatou, a *footballeuse* from Saint Louis, describes how adopting an aesthetic of female masculinity grants her access to male privilege: "Me, I love playing football. That's why I dress in my style. Because it shows me that, there you have it. I can do what men can do. I can be where men can be. You see. That is equality. My style shows this."[18] When asked about how they choose to become *footballeuses*, both Fatou and Aicha assert that their embrace of the stigma symbols associated with women's soccer in Senegal is a purposeful performance that challenges male authority and heteronormative gender ideology. Fatou states:

> Pshhhhhhh. You don't even know how hard it is to be a woman here in Senegal. We can't do anything. It is like my older sister. She is always telling me how to live my life. My whole family, they run my life. But, it is my life. Shit. It is not their life. Psshhhh. To be a woman in Senegal, it stinks. We can't do anything. Me, I want to show them that I can do what I want—I'll dress like I want. I'll be who I want. So it makes people mad? Good. I want people to be uncomfortable. It's my style. It's football.[19]

Aicha and Fatou are examples of how the *footballeuses* live between gender categories that organize Senegalese social, economic, and political life. In fact, every time they step into public space, they disrupt taken-for-granted assumptions about gender, subverting the "naturalness" of the power structures which define their place in society. Although Aicha and Fatou do not explicitly identify as lesbians, their refusal to apologize for their performance of masculinity and their confrontational adoption of stigma symbols openly challenge heteronormative gender hierarchies. K. L. Broad observed a similar phenomenon in the 1990s among US female rugby players who publicly challenged the limits of heteronormative gender categories through the voluntary adoption of stigma symbols associated with women's rugby. Similar to my research in Senegal, Broad observed that the female rugby players were "both 'out' and 'cocky' about their rugby playing and gender transgressions . . . in many ways enacting, confrontational, in your face tactics that embrace deviance and disrupt normative constructions."[20] Broad represents this refusal to distance themselves from the stigma attached to rugby by engaging in defensive practices as embracing a "gender unapologetic."[21]

In addition, according to Broad, adopting an attitude of "gender unapologetic" is a mode of *queer resistance*, meaning that it disrupts "stable sexual and gender identities through individualized acts of gender/sexual transgression."[22] Broad's research on the gender unapologetic and women's rugby informs my study in that it shows how women who integrate male dominated sports are finding new ways of existing in society outside this realm. Yet Broad's discussion of queer resistances is based on the assumption that the ultimate goal of these actions is the emancipation of the individual will. My research suggests that the mode of queer resistance exercised by female soccer players in Senegal is shaped rather by a religious-political subjectivity based on a Sufi model of resistance which frames emancipation as an inner moral power.

SUFI RESISTANCE AND POPULAR YOUTH CULTURE

During the late nineteenth and early twentieth centuries, popular discourses emerged among certain factions of Sufi brotherhoods in the Sahel. Critical of hierarchal power regimes, these discourses reframed victims of colonial oppression as agents of divine authority; their marginalization were seen as a test of faith for which they will be rewarded, if not in this life, then in the next. Spiritual guides such as Bamba built on the principles of what Bamba referred to as the "Sufi attitude," in delegitimizing colonial authority by emphasizing the moral power of the oppressed. From this perspective, legitimate authority, or the "belief by virtue of which persons exercising authority are lent prestige,"[23] stems not from a particular government or social position, but from one's proximity to God, proven by the trials endured in pursuit of salvation. Historian Sean Hanretta describes the Sufi ethos as

> this embrace of suffering by reference to . . . a "Sufi attitude" toward the physical world: the reconceptualization of pain and deprivation as a spiritual achievement that puts the self in a closer relation to the divine. In its simplest form, such an interpretation allows those who suffer as a result of their marginality and powerlessness to see themselves as agents in their own spiritual struggle.[24]

The idea that those suffering from conditions outside of their control can take charge of their destiny and reverse their fate through their ability to transform their suffering into moral power is a longstanding belief in Senegal. This belief is epitomized by the Wolof virtue of *muuñ*, which translates as "to endure; to support; to tolerate; to arm oneself with patience."[25] *Muuñ* is a virtue that is often evoked in discussions about the suffering of the weak or disadvantaged—those who can do little to change their outward experiences. *Muuñ* is the inner strength which allows the disadvantaged to endure hardships, with patience and grace, until they are rewarded in life in proportion to their suffering. In fact, according to the logic of *muuñ*, the more one suffers, the more virtuous he/she becomes. Joined with the Islamic virtue of *fitna*, which adds a salvific quality to the virtue of *muuñ*, the capacity to bear suffering becomes a mark of moral purity. *Muuñ* thus reverses feelings of shame and helplessness for those who would otherwise be considered victims of their material circumstances. This aspect of *muuñ*, which transforms the capacity to bear suffering into a form of moral power, underpins Sufi discourses of resistance which render agentive power to victims of oppression and nullify that of their oppressors.

Cheikh Amadou Bamba, founder of the Murid brotherhood, exemplifies this spirit of Sufi resistance. Although Bamba never intended to directly defy French colonial rule, his refusal to cease proselytizing after numerous and persistent attempts by the French administration to squelch his growing Murid movement put him in direct opposition with the colonial regime. Bamba framed this struggle with the colonial administration as part of a larger battle against the corruptive forces associated with the material world. Historian Cheikh Anta Babou adeptly describes Bamba's understanding of this struggle:

> [Amado Bamba] who conceived of the Muridiyya as a major weapon in the *jihad al-akbar* [greater jihad] he waged against the detrimental political and social forces of his time. This greater jihad was the jihad of nafs [the ego or carnal soul] which aimed at using tarbiyaa [the education of the soul] as a tool to instill Islamic values and shield people against the corrupting effects of negative traditional and French influences.[26]

Bamba perceived French colonial rule as Christian domination and implored his followers to resist French authority not through the *jihad* of the sword but through the *jihad* of the soul. In this respect, emancipation would come not from waging a physical war against abusive regimes, but from the spiritual transformation of individuals which would eventually touch all of society. As Cheikh Anta Babou notes, in his instructions to his followers on how to interact with colonial authority, Bamba advised Senegalese Muslims to treat

> the French the same way that the Prophet treated the Christians and unbelievers in Mecca, where he was also in a position of inferiority. He supported these recommendations by quoting from the Quran,

> citing passages in which Allah, addressing the Prophet, said, "be nobly armed with patience"; it is not to you to guide them (the unbelievers) in the right path. God guides whom he wishes.[27]

In this sense, Bamba, who suffered from years of persecution at the hands of colonial rule—having been twice exiled and, eventually, even imprisoned in his own home—conceived of resistance not as an external attempt to affect change, but, rather, as the process of societal transformation from the individual soul outward. Although Bamba eventually cooperated with the colonial administration, he remains in the Senegalese imaginary, as much a political hero who resisted colonial rule as a Sufi spiritual leader. Marginalized Senegalese youth like Fatou, a *footballeuse*, find inspiration in Bamba's story and his ability to transform his persecution into personal and moral strength through his faith in God. Discourses about Bamba's strength circulate widely today among Senegalese youth and portray him as a rebel and defender of his faith, a marginalized person, like them, who confronted seemingly unstoppable Western forces from a spiritual perspective and won on moral grounds. These discourses focus on how Bamba, despite his position of social inferiority in French colonial Senegal, or rather because of this marginalized status, rose above oppressive regimes to the highest throngs of the Senegalese moral hierarchy.

Today, Bamba has become a symbol of resistance for Senegal's marginalized youth that are pushing back against local and global regimes which cast them as victims rather than agents of their own destiny. Religiously and culturally based youth movements adopt a model of power inspired by a Sufi ethos that values suffering as an essential aspect of morality, where legitimate authority lies at the margins rather than the center of power regimes. Critical of the elite and ruling classes (including the State and gerontocracy), these actors flip the script of the established orders of governance. I found similar discourses of resistance among hip-hop artists, the hip-hop-inspired political movement of *Y'en a marre* [fed up], the new Sufi reform movements of *Dahirat al-Mustarshidin wal Mustarshidat* and *Le Mouvement Mondial pour l'unicité de dieu*, and, of course, the women's soccer community. Although these groups diverge in activity and form, they share the common theme of posturing their marginality as granting them moral legitimacy rather than disadvantage, spreading their message through popular cultural forms such as clothing styles, hip-hop, social media, and graffiti. The use of these popular cultural forms ensures that even those who do not directly partake in these organized movements are strongly influenced by the underlying shared ethos of resistance.

The youths' admiration for Bamba, who relied on spiritual rather than material weapons, makes sense when considering their dire material position in Senegalese society. Sufi discourses of moral resistance provide the youth with concrete solutions to the hardships, such as crushing unemployment rates, high levels of income inequality, and poor living conditions. These discourses enable the youth to fight back against what they view as the underlying culprit—the corruption of state power and new social norms imposed by Western regimes. This ethos is characterized by discourses that are critical of dominant power regimes, glorify the marginalized persons and void their oppressors' agency by framing oppressors as mere instruments of God's will which exist to guide them on their personal path to salvific emancipation.

For example, among the *Dahirat al-Mustarshidin wal Mustarshidat* and *Le Mouvement Mondial Pour l'Unicité De Dieu*, two Sufi reform movements that focus on re-islamicizing public space and purifying society from the ground up, followers emphasize their marginalized status among political regimes in order to gain legitimacy as public actors. Anthropologist Fabienne Samson, who conducted an ethnographic study of both movements, explains:

> [T]he disciples generally prefer to be perceived as disliked by a government that, according to them, acts against Muslims. This constant need to be seen as victims is precisely what allows the leaders and the disciples of both movements to justify their citizenship activities, which they present as the only answer to the state's mobility in the domains of education and social protection. If the politicians do nothing and leave society in a state of perdition that signals, in their eyes, the end of the world, they must act against the current to save humanity through Islam.[28]

We can surmise that their distrust of dominant power regimes stems heavily from Sufi teachings that emphasize the salvific power of suffering and God's supreme authority over matters in this life and the next. As Sean Hanretta notes, "such aloofness from power can be traced in the West African-Maghrebian ecumene at least as far back as al-Ghazali in the eleventh century among Sufis."[29] A disdain for regimes of power whose legitimacy is based on material wealth and earthly prowess is especially evident in the Murid tradition. Bamba dedicated his life to spreading the message that true emancipation arises through complete submission to God's will, which is achieved through the values of hard work, spiritual discipline, and humility. He promoted the renunciation of earthly pleasures among his followers and advocated for a more equitable distribution of wealth and power in his teachings.[30] Not surprisingly, his teachings attracted a large number of disciples from the margins of society.[31] A striking example of this philosophy is found in the preamble of his work *Massalik Al-Jinan*, written in response to his own discrimination by Sufi scholars in Mauritania because of the color of his skin, where he argues that "the best of man before God, without discrimination is the one who fears Him the most."[32]

Furthermore, Bamba taught that those who are furthest from the riches of this world are closest to God, an ideology that incited the Murids to "retain social and geographical distance from the centers of power."[33] This is why in *daaras Tarabiyaa* [Murid schools], *talibés* [students] were subjected to work and lived in difficult conditions.[34] In fact, Bamba was always critical of dominant power regimes in his teachings, be it toward the Wolofs, the Serers, or the French administration. His assertion that he was accountable only to the rule of God caused disruption in colonial Senegal. As historian David Robinson points out:

> Bamba developed a growing reputation as a teacher, and rallying point among a large number of displaced persons. That reputation included an attitude of opposition to the practices and agents of power, whether they were members of the old regimes of the Wolof and Serer states, or those who had attempted to put the Islamic governments in their place, or the emerging colonial order.[35]

We see the same disdain for dominant regimes of power and a tendency to venerate marginality in the hip-hop music produced in urban working-class neighborhoods of Senegal's largest cities. Hip-hop artists vie for the role of "sentinel of the people" by proving themselves as authentic marginal actors. For example, in an interview that I conducted with a well-known hip-hop artist from an underprivileged community in Dakar, the rapper spent thirty minutes explaining to me how his music truly represents the voice of the resistance, since he too has grown up in poverty. For this artist, legitimate authority lies not in the hands of the government which he deems as corrupt; it is in the streets, in the margins. In his words:

> The power is in the street, the power is with the people, don't you see? That's real power. They know suffering, they know God. We [hip-hop] are the voice of the people; they listen to us because we know suffering, we know God. The corrupt politicians and elite that run everything, they are scared, scared because they know that we are the ones who toppled the old government. We will keep coming. Us, the people.[36]

Anthropologist Sophie Moulard makes a similar observation from her research on hip-hop and slam movements of Dakar:

> Si l'on en croit les habitants du département de Pikine-Guédiawaye, eux seuls sont à même de produire une musique contestataire, jouissent d'une véritable légitimité pour se faire les porte-paroles de la rébellion.[37]
>
> [If we believe the inhabitants of the Pikine-Guédiawaye department, only they can produce music of dissent and enjoy the legitimacy derived from this position to become the spokespersons of the rebellion.]

For political youth movements like *Y'en a marre*, marginality not only grants cultural authenticity but also the right to act against established political and social regimes. For example, Senegal has a long tradition of gerontocracy that excludes younger generations from taking part in many public life activities. This is something that the rapper and political organizer Fou Malade claims must change in order for Senegal to become a fair and just society. According to Fou Malade, "the [problem] of older people in Senegal is that they believe the youth do not have the right to talk."[38] For him, it is precisely their marginal position in this power configuration that lends the Senegalese youth their political legitimacy.

Moreover, it may be their wariness of established power regimes that informs the youths' discourse on resistance, which is founded on an underlying belief that their oppression is part of a divine purpose which informs their actions. Instead of fighting with weapons, these actors wage a moral war, a combat that renders their oppressors powerless and delegitimizes their authority to act on society. Take the *Y'en a marre* movement for example, whose organizers reformulate their role of victims of the state into that of moral warriors. By turning threats of violence and suppression into opportunities to demonstrate their moral superiority, the Senegalese youth render themselves "good" and their opponents "evil." Once their political actions become a moral struggle of good vs. evil, and they are on the side of good, the youth are also understood implicitly to be on the side of God, and, thus, in the Senegalese imagination, as the winning side. If God has planned for them to take up this struggle, then their opponents are mere vehicles for them to realize their purpose. From this perspective, their opponents are completely void of agency. Anthropologist Abdoulaye Niang discusses an excellent example of this strategy:

> Le combat contre la modification constitutionnelle permet l'affirmation d'une dignité que la violence ne peut faire taire: 'Nous ne t'offrirons pas un centimètre de répit / Père, n'espère pas que l'on s'arrête / quitte à ce que les prisons soient pleines / tire, frappe, fais sortir l'armée et la police! / Nos corps sont là, transforme-les en steak![39]
>
> [The fight against the constitutional amendment allows the affirmation of dignity that violence cannot silence: 'We will not offer you a centimeter of respite / Father, do not hope that we stop / wait until the prisons are full / shoot, strike, get out the army and the police! / Our bodies are here, turn them into steak!]

While the members of *Y'en a marre* may not explicitly evoke their relationship to God, those of the *Mouvement Mondial Pour L'unicité de dieu* do. In a conversation with several students at Dakar, who claim to be a part of this movement, I discovered that they viewed the youths' struggle against Wade's government as a step in God's plan to build a new type of society. Unlike members of *Y'en a marre*, these ones did not believe that people should take to the streets and threaten the existing social order. Rather, they believed that they should endure the politics of Wade because his mandate was simply a test from God to make them stronger. Moustapha asserts:

> Well, it is really not good all these movements like *Y'en a marre*, and all that. It's not right to share secrets with the public like that, to manifest in the streets, to not respect others in doing it, to denounce people publicly, to show that you are angry, to fight against Wade like that in the streets. It's God that put Wade in power and it's God that will take it from him, that will judge him and will give us the power, we have to endure the test, but it always happens like this. Wade has no power; his power comes from God. Yes, we must vote, we must take part in society, but work on ourselves and let the government push us, God is with us.[40]

In both cases, we see echoes of Bamba's "greater *jihad*," the moral war he waged against what he perceived as destructive forces in Senegalese society in which his greatest weapon was his faith. In fact, Bamba interpreted his own deportation and persecution at the hands of the French colonial administration through this lens. The more he suffered at the hands of the French, the more his faith increased. Once he turned this into a war of good and evil against the non-believers who asked him to renounce his faith, he then positioned himself on the side of God. To strengthen his social and political authority, he often used Islamic grammar, likening his persecution to that of the prophet Muhammad. As Babou suggests:

> Bamba reported that the first verses he reminded himself of at the beginning of the conflict were excerpts from the sura "The Spoils of War" in which Allah addresses the Prophet in these terms: Remember when the infidels contrived to make you a prisoner or to murder and expel you, they plotted but God planned and God's plan is best.[41]

Thus, Bamba reformulated his suffering at the hands of the French as a test of his devotion to Allah which would purify his soul. In doing so, he denied the power from his oppressors by making their actions void of all agency. Babou notes:

> The French conceived of the arrest and deportation of Amadou Bamba as a simple routine operation for the maintenance of order in the colony . . . Bamba saw his plight in the hands of the colonial administration as a highly meaningful test of his faith. He likened his position to that of the Prophet Muhammed in Mecca and drew ex-

> tensively from Quranic idioms to rationalize his actions and strengthen his resolve . . . by placing the conflict in the broader context of the confrontation between good and evil, Amadou Bamba sought to deny agency to the colonial administration. From the outset, he depicted the French as mere instruments of God, who were acting as they were instructed by a higher power.[42]

If Bamba had not gone through all these extreme difficulties, he could not have claimed a position of moral superiority over the French to justify his right to act on the world. Similarly, the emancipation sought by Bamba was not a relief from all forms of material oppression depriving him of the exercise of his individual will, but the liberation of his soul from all human temptation through an entire dependence on the will of God. This reflects what Ivy Mills describes as the Murid ethos when she writes: "The Murid self is realized through its willful cleaving to a discipline dictated by an external superior power, not by casting off the external shackles that prevent an underlying, fully-present self from directing its own actions."[43]

In this sense, Mills aligns with Babou in emphasizing that by transforming the French administration into a simple instrument of God's plan, Bamba cast himself as being stronger than his oppressors. Mills argues:

> In Bamba's version of the story of his exile, the French are completely evacuated of independent agency, serving as mere vessels through which God tests and challenges him so that he can reach new levels of piety and faith. If all suffering, adversity, and hardship is sent by God (divine challenges called *nattu* in Wolof), and is therefore an opportunity for self-discipline and spiritual growth, then colonial and white supremacist oppression does not suppress or destroy the Murid self—as in the account of colonial alienation so ubiquitous in Francophone literature—but rather unintentionally enables its production.[44]

Whatever actions the French administration took to crush Bamba's social influence, they only strengthened his power in the eyes of God, and therefore, from his followers' viewpoint, his legitimacy. This is precisely the ethos that underlies the queer resistance of the *footballeuses*.

BAMBA REALLY IS FEPP: QUEERING THE "GREATER *JIHAD*"

After witnessing the alarming interaction between Fatou and the elderly woman who admonished her for dressing like a man, hurling insults at her as we passed, the two of us walked home in silence. Fatou only removed her large black DJ-type headphones when we were safely back in the familiar streets of her neighborhood. As we turned the corner toward her family compound, we saw a dozen young boys dressed in soiled rags carrying plastic tubs. A few of the boys were seated in the sand leaning against a concrete wall while the others were kicking a pebble as if it were a soccer ball, barefoot or in mismatched oversized sandals. One very young boy, dressed in a tattered green T-shirt and soiled shorts that were almost completely worn to shreds, was hiding his head in his hands and crying hysterically while an older boy, also dressed in rags and wearing two different shoes, had his arm around the younger boy and appeared to be comforting him. I recognized these young boys as *talibés*, street children that are sent to Koranic schools and forced to beg under the charge of a local marabout, or religious leader. Senegal's *talibés* are among the most marginalized in society, and these children are often quickly dismissed or treated harshly when they approach adults on the street. Much to my surprise, Fatou approached the little boy and knelt down beside him, putting her arm around him, asking him what was wrong. He explained that he hadn't earned his daily offering for his marabout, and so he wouldn't be allowed back, or he would receive a beating. Even though I know she struggles to make ends meet daily in providing for her family, Fatou reached into the outside of her sports bag and placed a 500 CFA coin in the little boy's hand, caressing his shoulder before standing up and telling me he would be ok and we should walk home. When I asked Fatou why she had been so kind, she explained:

> You know, here in Senegal, we say that those who have nothing, those who suffer the most in this life are closest to God. It is the people who are poor and have the most difficulty in life who God rewards. The boy suffers, but it's good; he will be stronger for it. I told you that those who suffer are the strongest, they are the most loved by God.[45]

Fatou and the other *footballeuses* are critical of social privilege, since, from their perspective, the privileged endure less hardship, which directly reflects their lack of proximity to God. In this understanding of social hierarchy, the wealthy and elite enjoy material power, yet are morally inferior to those who have little wealth but are rich in faith. Faced with intense discrimination due to the transgression of gender norms, the *footballeuses* frame their marginal relationship to society in terms of the moral power they derive from their social suffering. What is perceived by others as a dishonorable social distinction is understood by the *footballeuses* as a purifying source which brings them closer to God and makes them stronger than those who persecute them. Unlike other forms of power, theirs is sanctioned by God and, from their perspective, their devotion far outweighs their transgression. When I questioned her one evening while we were preparing *attayah* in her courtyard as to what God thought of her "*footballeuse* style," Seynabou, Fatou's teammate from the same working-class neighborhood in Saint Louis, said:

> Beth! Nobody can do everything God asks of us. We are only human, but God knows this, he forgives us when we turn to him. It is far worse to not have faith, to not pray, or to not fast during Ramadan than to be, well, to dress like a *footballeuse*, or to be like this. It's hard to be a *footballeuse*, but this pain it strengthens my faith in me because it is God who gave me this faith. For me it is only God who guides my life, who knows if what I do is good and who knows who I am. Many people, important people, say that we go against God, and they say they are so good, but they are corrupt, they take all for themselves. Whatever people say about football, we're not going to stop them, they are there to test us. But real strength comes from faith in God.[46]

By perceiving people who discriminate against them in their everyday lives as having a role in God's plan for them, the *footballeuses* reject their victim status and turn their stigma into a source of power. No matter how much they are persecuted or ostracized, the *footballeuses* refuse to back down. This demonstrates their high volume of the moral virtue of *muuñ*, and faith in God's plan. Since they have God in their camp, even their transgressive actions and desires become legitimate. Fatou observes:

> I like it when people talk about me, when they try to hurt me. You see, I don't care, it only makes me stronger, it's between me and Allah. You see I love football. I was born like this with a talent for football, and it is God who gave me this talent, it is God who decides my life, everything. If it is God's plan, it will only make me stronger.[47]

Fatou justifies her provocation in terms of the moral value that she perceives suffering to bestow upon her life. The more that she suffers, the more righteous and deserving of God's love she becomes. In this sense, Fatou frames her transgression of gender norms as a spiritually purifying process. As with the organizers and participants of *Y'en a marre*, the followers of *MMUD* and *Dahirat al-Mustarshidin wal Mustarshidat* and the hip-hop artists that make music for social change, the *footballeuses* reformulate their oppression in moral terms in which the faithful "oppressed" not only reverse their own feelings of helplessness associated with their marginalized status but also simultaneously void the power of their persecutors.

Despite their clear line of departure from Islamic gender ideology, the women who participated in my study did not consider their membership in the Muslim and football communities as incompatible, even if they often described this relationship as feeling like a contradiction. In fact, as I argued in this chapter, contrary to popular belief, most of the *footballeuses* express a deep faith in Islam, respecting Islamic rules of prayer and piety and drawing on Islamic idioms to make sense of their stigmatization. They believe in an inherent gender hierarchy which underlies Islam, in which women are subordinate to the authority of men and yet simultaneously seek to challenge this hierarchy. The *footballeuses* view their marginality as bringing them closer to a higher order, thus purifying their actions even as they unapologetically challenge gender and sexuality norms. When people admonish or shun them in public, as I showed with Fatou and the elderly woman who passed us in the street, the *footballeuses* are meant to feel ashamed and deprived of their social honor. However, even if these experiences deeply hurt them in the moment, the moral gains that these individuals experience because of their trials allow them to reframe themselves not as victims but as agents in God's plan. Thus, the women continue to seek out these moments and aggressively wield their stigma in public, an act which causes them even more suffering. It is this paradox—the fact that the *footballeuses* derive their moral agency in a struggle against oppression from a position of moral inferiority—that allows them to queer their path to salvation, bringing to light new forms of gendered subjectivities and Muslim spatialities.

BIBLIOGRAPHY

Abu-Lughod, Lila. *Do Muslim Women Need Saving*? Cambridge: Harvard University Press, 2013.

Augis, Erin. "Dakar's Sunnite Women: The Dialectic of Submission and Defiance in a Globalizing City." In *Tolerance, Democracy, and Sufis in Senegal*. New York: Columbia University Press, 2013.

Babou, Cheikh Anta Mbacké. *Fighting the Greater Jihad: Amadu Bamba and the Founding of the Muridiyya of Senegal*. Athens: Ohio University Press, 2007.

Bacchetta, Paola. "o-Formations: des spatialités de résistance décoloniales chez les lesbiennes 'of color' en France." *Genre, sexualité & société* 1, no. 1 (June 2009). September 16, 2018. https://journals.openedition.org/gss/810

Broad, K. L. "The Gendered Unapologetic: Queer Resistance in Women's Sport." *Sociology of Sport Journal* 18, no. 2 (2001), 181–204.

Butler, Judith. *Gender Trouble: Feminism and the Subversion of Identity*. New York: Routledge, 2011.

Coly, Ayo. "Carmen Goes Postcolonial, Carmen Goes Queer: Thinking the Postcolonial as Queer." *Culture, Theory, and Critique* 57, no. 3 (2016): 391–407.

Diouf, Jean Léopold. *Dictionnaire wolof-français et français-wolof*. Paris: KARTHALA Editions, 2003.

Gueye, Marame. "Urban Guerrilla Poetry: The Movement Y' En a Marre and the Socio-Political Influences of Hip Hop in Senegal." *Journal of Pan African Studies* 6, no. 3 (2013): 22–42.

Hanretta, Sean. *Islam and Social Change in French West Africa: History of an Emancipatory Community*. Cambridge: Cambridge University Press, 2009.

Mahmood, Saba. *Politics of Piety: The Islamic Revival and the Feminist Subject*. Princeton: Princeton University Press, 2004.

Mills, Ivy. "Sutura: Gendered Honor, Social Death and the Politics of Exposure in Senegalese Literature and Popular Culture." PhD diss., University of California, Berkeley, 2011.

Moulard, Sophie. "'Senegal yewuleen!' Analyse anthropologique du rap à Dakar: liminarité, contestation et culture populaire." PhD diss., Université Victor Segalen—Bordeaux II, 2008.

Niang, Abdoulaye. "Le rap prédicateur islamique au Sénégal: une musique 'missionnaire.'" *Volume! En Ligne* 10, no. 2 (2014): 69–86.

Packer, Beth. "Breaking the Rules: Politics, Piety and Resistance in Senegalese Women's Soccer." In *Women, Violence and Resistance*, edited by Hager Ben Driss and Meryem Sellami. Tunis: Editions Arabesques, 2017.

Robinson, David. "The Murids: Surveillance and Collaboration." *The Journal of African History* 40, no. 2 (1999): 193–213

Saavedra, Martha. "Sports: Sub-Saharan Africa." In *Encyclopedia of Women & Islamic Cultures: Family, Body, Sexuality And Health*. ed. Suad Joseph. Leiden: Brill, 2003. September 16, 2018, http://dx.doi.org/10.1163/1872-5309_ewic_EWICCOM_0207d.

Samson, Fabienne. "Islam, Protest and Citizen Mobilisation: New Sufi Movements." In *New Perspectives on Islam in Senegal: Conversion, Migration, Wealth, Power, and Femininity*, edited by Mamadou Diouf and Mara Leichtman. London: Palgrave Macmillan, 2009.

Weber, Max. *The Theory of Social and Economic Organization*. New York: Free Press, 1964.

NOTES

1. Extract from the author's field notes, May 2016.
2. "Fatou" (soccer player) in discussion with the author, May 2016.
3. "Fatou" (soccer player) in discussion with the author, May 2016.
4. "Fatou" (soccer player) in discussion with the author, May 2016.
5. Martha Saavedra, "Sports: Sub-Saharan Africa," in *Encyclopedia of Women & Islamic Cultures*, ed. Suad Joseph (Leiden: Brill, 2003) September 16, 2018, http://dx.doi.org/10.1163/1872-5309_ewic_EWICCOM_0207d.
6. Packer, Breaking the Rules, 2017.
7. Saba Mahmood, *Politics of Piety: The Islamic Revival and the Feminist Subject* (Princeton: Princeton University Press, 2004); Lila Abu-Lughod, *Do Muslim Women Need Saving?* (Cambridge: Harvard University Press, 2013); Erin Augis, "Dakar's Sunnite Women: The Dialectic of Submission and Defiance in a Globalizing City," in *Tolerance, Democracy, and Sufis in Senegal* (New York: Columbia University Press, 2013); Ivy Mills, "Sutura: Gendered Honor, Social Death, and the Politics of Exposure in Senegalese Literature and Popular Culture" (PhD diss., University of California, Berkeley, 2011).
8. Saba Mahmood, *Politics of Piety*.
9. Augis, "Dakar's Sunnite Women," 2013.
10. Mahmood, *Politics of Piety*, 4.
11. Mahmood, *Politics of Piety*; Augis, "Dakar's Sunnite Women," 2013.
12. Paola Bacchetta, "o-Formations: des spatialités de résistance décoloniales chez les lesbiennes 'of color' en France." *Genre, sexualité & société* 1, no. 1 (June 2009). September 16, 2018, https://journals.openedition.org/gss/810; Ayo Coly, "Carmen Goes Postcolonial, Carmen Goes Queer: Thinking the Postcolonial as Queer," *Culture, Theory and Critique* 57, no. 3 (2016): 391–407.
13. Paola Bacchetta, "o-Formations."
14. K. L. Broad, "The Gendered Unapologetic: Queer Resistance in Women's Sport," *Sociology of Sport Journal* 18, no. 2 (2001), 187.
15. Judith Butler, *Gender Trouble: Feminism and the Subversion of Identity* (New York: Routledge, 2011), 175.
16. "Aicha" (soccer player) in discussion with the author, June 2013.
17. "Aicha" (soccer player) in discussion with the author, June 2013.
18. "Fatou" (soccer player) in discussion with the author, February 2014.
19. "Fatou" (soccer player) in discussion with the author, February 2014.
20. Broad, "The Gendered Unapologetic," 195.
21. Broad, "The Gendered Unapologetic," 195.
22. Broad, "The Gendered Unapologetic," 187.
23. Max Weber, *The Theory of Social abd Economic Organization* (New York: Free Press, 1964), 382.

24. Sean Hanretta, *Islam and Social Change in French West Africa: History of an Emancipatory Community* (Cambridge: Cambridge University Press, 2009), 173.

25. Jean Léopold Diouf, *Dictionnaire wolof-français et français-wolof* (Paris: KARTHALA Editions, 2003), 229. Translated from French by the author.

26. Cheikh Anta Mbacké Babou, *Fighting the Greater Jihad: Amadu Bamba and the Founding of the Muridiyya of Senegal* (Athens: Ohio University Press, 2007), 123.

27. Babou, *Fighting the Greater Jihad*, 155.

28. Fabienne Samson, "Islam, Protest and Citizen Mobilisation: New Sufi Movements," in *New Perspectives on Islam in Senegal: Conversion, Migration, Wealth, Power, and Femininity*, ed. Mamadou Diouf and Mara Leichtman (London: Palgrave Macmillan, 2009), 256.

29. Hanretta, *Islam and Social Change in French West Africa*, 1541.

30. Babou, *Fighting the Greater Jihad.*

31. David Robinson, "The Murids: Surveillance and Collaboration," *The Journal of African History* 40, no. 2 (1999): 193–213; Babou, *Fighting the Greater Jihad*, 185.

32. Babou, *Fighting the Greater Jihad*, 62.

33. Robinson, "The Murids," 194.

34. Babou, *Fighting the Greater Jihad.*

35. Robinson, "The Murids," 194.

36. "Cheikh" (hip-hop Artist) in discussion with the author, March 2014.

37. Sophie Moulard, "'Senegal yewuleen!' Analyse anthropologique du rap à Dakar: liminarité, contestation et culture populaire." (PhD diss., Université Victor Segalen—Bordeaux II, 2008), 319.

38. Marame Gueye, "Urban Guerrilla Poetry: The Movement Y' En a Marre and the Socio-Political Influences of Hip Hop in Senegal," *Journal of Pan African Studies* 6, no. 3 (2013): 32.

39. Abdoulaye Niang, "Le rap prédicateur islamique au Sénégal: une musique 'missionnaire.'"*Volume! En Ligne* 10, no. 2 (2014): 80.

40. "Moustapha" (student member of MMUD Dakar) in discussion with the author, February 2014.

41. Babou, *Fighting the Greater Jihad*, 134.

42. Babou, *Fighting the Greater Jihad*, 134.

43. Mills, "Sutura," 25.

44. Mills, "Sutura."

45. "Fatou" (soccer player) in discussion with the author, May 2016.

46. "Seynabou" (soccer player) in discussion with the author, June 2016.

47. "Fatou" (soccer player) in discussion with the author, January 2014.

3

REPRESENTATIONS OF THE *GÔR DJIGUÈNE* [MAN WOMAN] IN SENEGALESE CULTURE, FILMS, AND LITERATURE

Babacar M'Baye

One of the major challenges in Africana studies is to recover African people's history from the remnants that their ancestors have left behind. In this endeavor, archives have proved to be useful since they allow scholars to validate the history of African communities (religious, political, ethnic, historical, and otherwise) in museums, books, coins, medals, flags, and other sites and objects. Sadly, the figure of the Senegalese male-to-female transgender person (hereafter referred as *gôr djiguène*) is absent in such memorials because they is perceived as a pariah and an antithesis to African development. Drawing from selected literary, cultural, and cinematographic texts, this chapter places the neglected figure of the *gôr djiguène* in the Senegalese history out of which they have been mostly removed. The texts that will be discussed include Mariama Bâ's 1981 novel, *Un chant écarlate* [*Scarlet Song*], Aminata Sow Fall's 1982 novel, *Le Revenant* (The Revenant), Ousmane Sembène's 1973 classic film *Xala* [Impotence], and Moussa Sène Absa's 2002 film, *Madame Brouette* [Wheelbarrow Lady]. Discussing these resources, this essay seeks to draw attention on the scholarly significance of studying the literary, cinematographic, and historical representations of the *gôr djiguène* in Senegalese culture. These texts show that the *gôr djiguène* is integral to Senegalese culture in which they have had a substantial level of acceptance despite the oppression they have faced within it.

While there has been an increasing attention to the *gôr djiguène*, most of this work focuses on the homophobic and transphobic attitudes toward these individuals rather than on these persons' resistances against the prejudices. A simple keyword search on Google exposes a reader to countless websites giving the impression that the *gôr djiguène* is a complete anathema in Senegalese society because the extant journalistic and informal reports about these individuals tend to have the unintentional effect of reinforcing the homophobic and transphobic reactions against them. Many Senegalese, especially uneducated youth, express fascist-like hatred toward *gôr djiguène* since they grew up in a society in which one easily develop negative opinions about another individual or group simply because of a mob's myths about the latter person or community, and not because of research grounded in historical or cultural evidence.

Yet, numerous scholars, including many Senegalese, have devoted serious research on the *gôr djiguène* over the past few years, paving ways for future scholarship on the subject. One of these scholars is Cheikh Niang whose much quoted 2003 collaborative article, "'It's Raining Stones': Stigma, Violence and HIV Vulnerability among Men Who Have Sex with Men in Dakar, Senegal," inspired a substantial global scholarly interest in the situation of the *gôr djiguène*. In his study, Niang includes the following words of an informant: "When someone says [*goor-jiggen*] in our presence, it makes us shiver. The term is like a siren sound that we expect to be followed by insults, blows, or stones thrown at us by out-of-control mobs."[1] Many subsequent studies such as those of Fatou Kiné Camara, Ndeye Gning, Christophe Broqua, Ayo Coly, as well as my own have expanded the scholarship that Niang initiated. In a 2008–2009 essay for *Psychopathologie Africaine*, Camara shows that homophobia in Senegal started to become an issue only in 2008 when in February of that year five men were arrested following the publication in a local magazine of a report denouncing homosexual marriages that supposedly took place in Mbao, a commune of Pikine, located in the South East of Dakar, Senegal.[2] Placing this reaction in a large context, Camara shows how it counters the ideals of human rights and justice to which Senegal ascribes in spite of its legal sanction of homosexuality.[3]

Placing the debate in other contexts, Babacar M'Baye has shown that homophobia has existed in both colonial and postcolonial Senegal despite the ephemeral freedom that individuals with sexual and gender variances have had in the country.[4] In a similar vein, Ndeye Gning has studied, in "Les motifs de l'illégitimité sociale de l'homosexualité au Sénégal" (2013), how the dismissal of homosexuality since 2008 stems from a context in which "it appears for the actors as necessary to the claim of a Senegalese national identity, in a context where the crisis that crosses Senegal seems to threaten the foundations."[5]

Other important works on homosexuality in Senegal include Christophe Broqua's "L'Émergence des Minorités Sexuelles dans l'Espace Public en Afrique" (2012) and "*Góor-jigéen*: la resignification négative d'une catégorie entre genre et sexualité" (2017) which, like Ayo Coly's "Carmen Goes Postcolonial, Carmen Goes Queer: Thinking the Postcolonial as Queer" (2016) and Cheryl Stobie's "'She Who Creates Havoc Is Here': A Queer Bisexual Reading of Sexuality, Dance, and Social Critique in Karmen Geï" (2016) and M'Baye's "Variant Sexualities and African Modernity in Joseph Gaye Ramaka's *Karmen Geï*" (2011), have helped to bring the study of homosexuality in Senegal to the forefront of cultural and anthropological studies. Broqua's 2012 essay suggests the danger of generalizing about homosexuality in Senegal since it reveals the extent to which the state has sometimes taken direct measures to curb the hostility that certain religious and public groups attempted to publicly express against it.[6] In his 2017 essay, Broqua focuses on the *Góor-jigéen* whose representations in Western ethnographic writings he summarizes in succinct ways somewhat similar to how M'Baye does it in his 2013 essay. Also, like M'Baye's 2013 article, Yet Broqua's 2017 essay suggests the importance of validating the *Góor-jigéen* in African studies. Yet Broqua's essay is unique because it argues that in Senegal, as is also the case in other African countries such as Ghana and Nigeria, "the current vocabulary used to describe homosexuals refers more to gender dimension than to sexual orientation."[7] In this sense, the term *Góor-jigéen* should not be always confined to sexual orientation since it can refers to variant gender expressions in clothing, speech patterns, mannerism, and presentations as well as to sexual preference.

Other groundbreaking studies of homosexuality in Senegal stemmed from film scholarship, especially from the essays about Joseph Gaye Ramaka's 2001 film *Karmen Geï*. According to M'Baye, Ramaka's film provides space for understanding and accepting the variegated identities, such as sexual and gender variances, which accompany African modernity. M'Baye writes:

> In opposition to narratives that emphasize the alien nature of alternative gender expressions and sexualities in African cultures, Ramaka denounces the hypocrisy of such facile assessments by representing Senegalese society as a community that both accommodates and rejects unconventional identities. Instead of perceiving these identities as either indigenous or foreign to Senegal, Ramaka suggests their undeniable contributions to an African modernity that seeks to be recognized and liberated from a web of intolerant conservative, political, or religious rhetoric against variant gender expressions and sexualities in Africa.[8]

Taking the discussion to different levels, Coly's article shows that the significance of Ramaka's film also lies in the movie's exploration of a "queerness" that "happens to be an intrinsic postcolonial modality of power relations."[9] Discussing the angry reaction that the movie received in some segments of Senegalese society, Coly suggests that the problem lied not in the existence of homophobia in Senegal but in the fact that there were strong religious sensibilities which might have interpreted associations between Islam, Catholicism, and lesbian identity as offensive.[10] Cheryl Stobie's essay seems to argue otherwise since it interprets the film as a transgression of heteronormative sexualities and gender expressions. Stobie writes: "Karmen Geï depicts bisexuality as a complex, queer site that destabilizes stereotyped gender roles and monosexuality and calls into question the mechanisms by which desire and appetite are regulated. Karmen's mesmerizing, seductive dancing proves irresistible to female and male characters, and the representation of her bisexual behavior implicitly criticizes narrow conceptions of sexuality, including homophobia, monosexism, and possessive monogamy."[11] By extending the discussions on homosexuality in Senegal to queerness and bisexuality, Coly and Stobie allow us to expand the scholarship on the *gôr djiguène*. This scholarship still needs to further explore the pivotal role of the *gôr djiguène* in Senegalese culture and history. This overdue exploration will help to fight the prejudice and fear that have led many scholars, especially those from Africa, to be reluctant to give to the *gôr djiguène* the human, intellectual, cultural, and historical values they deserve like anyone else.

First, there is the problem to define the term "*gôr djiguène*" beyond the narrow confines in which it has been historically understood. Thus far, the word has been mainly conceptualized in sexualized ways rather than in gendered ones, leading to the popular representation of the *gôr djiguène* only as a homosexual. This definition is limited because the words "*gôr*" [man] and "*djiguène*" [woman] can have a diversity of significations not restricted to sexual identity, acts, or orientation when they are combined. Confining the meaning of the word *gôr djiguène* to homosexuality prevents us from understanding and appreciating the whole range of cultural representations, play with identity, and performance that the concept invokes. Without denying that the word "*gôr djiguène*" can have sexual connotations, this essay primarily theorizes the concept as one referring to a nonbinary gender identity embracing both masculinity and femininity. From this perspective, a *gôr djiguène* would be the equivalent of what is known in gender and sexuality studies as a male-to-female or a female-to-male transgender person and, as is often the case, can be represented as a creative and artistic individual who can deftly adopt the behavior, clothing, mannerism, and fashion ascribed to members of an opposite gender or sex. Conceptualizing the word "*gôr djiguène*" in such a broad and flexible way allows us to uncover the performative and real processes of play with identity (whether gendered, sexual, social, political, cultural, or artistic) that it entails. Doing so allows us to remove the term "*gôr djiguène*" from the merely homophobic, controversial, polemical, and dismissive attitudes toward this important identity that many Senegalese scholars, especially men, are reluctant to study due to the stigmas attached to it. And, yet, understanding and appreciating the meanings of this concept of "*gôr djiguène*" could advance the study of Senegalese literature, films, and culture, especially the country's popular music which is permeated with non-binary gendered and sexualized play. Studying the representations of the *gôr djiguène* in such sources will allow us to see that sexual and gender variances have historically existed in Senegal. Whether they are open or closeted, such practices are integral to world cultures. To this effect, Rosalind Petchesky writes:

> Rather than contributing, however unintentionally, to the insidious process of producing categories of deviance, sexual and gender rights advocates need to seek language that illuminates the reality that all kinds of practices and pathways labelled "abnormal"—cross-dressing, male femininity, female masculinity, homoeroticism, sex for exchange, female lust—are prolific within and across societies in an infinite and ever-changing variety.[12]

Second, there is an ethical problematic that scholars have thus far not been able to transcend. This problem stems from the undeniable fact that the word "*gôr djiguène*" is a concept that Senegalese people, including individuals who are labelled as such, find truly offensive. A 2013 study of Fatou Maria Dramé and a group of collaborators suggests that "Gay men in Senegal tend to self-identify as branché, a French colloquial expression for a trendy person. The expression *goor jiggen*, meaning literally 'man-woman' is the term used by the general population as a derogatory term to describe men who have sex with men. And while these men sometimes have feminine characteristics, they often do not show this openly for justified fear of violence."[13] From a similar angle, Gning represents the term "*goorjigeen*" as a derogatory word, but one which serves to subsume a person to low positions. Gning writes: "Like equivalent terms in other languages, *goorjigeen* is an insult that humiliates the man by implicitly calling into question his status as a dominant, virile, and authoritarian male: the *goorjigeen* subordinate his status of man to that of the woman, placing the stigmatization of homosexuality in an essentialist vision of social relations of sex." (translation by Babacar Mbaye)[14] Gning is right because similar stigmatization processes have been historically deployed in other societies to relegate people to low and menial positions with the clear intent to maintain essentialist worldviews. Yet, beyond these essentialisms, the use of the term "*gôr djiguène*" is an insidious strategy that individuals or groups may use to represent political opponents as being weak and corrupting the nation's identity. Senegal, like the rest of the world, is not exempt of the kind of viral conception of ultramasculinity that men often deploy against "femininity" whenever they feel threatened within or out of their own skin.

DEPICTIONS OF THE *GÔR DJIGUÈNE* IN EUROPEAN WRITINGS

European scholars who visited Senegal between the late nineteenth century and the 1950s were divided on the question of whether homosexuality existed in colonial Senegal even though they almost all recognized the occurrence of transgressive forms of sexual and gender expression in the territory. While a few European scholars argued that male and female homosexualities existed at some level in Senegal, others tended to deny such occurrences in their narratives. Fortunately, there is strong evidence in Senegalese literature and cinema that suggests that variant sexualities and gender expressions, including homosexuality, bisexuality, and transgenderism have existed in Senegal since the 1970s and fulfill important roles despite the lingering prejudices that confront such practices.

A few European sources suggested that both male and female homosexualities were rare in colonial Senegal. Jacobus X (the pseudonym of Louis Jacolliot), who was a French Army-Surgeon, a sexologist, sociologist, and an anthropologist, argued in his 1893 book, *L'Amour aux colonies* (Love in the colonies), that "The free black is neither sodomite nor pederaste" (258; translation by Babacar M'Baye). Jacobus represented homosexuality as a practice that was more common among Europeans and other Africans than Senegalese people. In this sense, he described two Bambara *tirailleurs* (African colonial soldiers serving France) from Kita, Mali, who admitted to the prevalence of the practice among kidnapped and enslaved Africans, especially when "the feminine gender [understood here as women or girls] was missing" (translation by Babacar M'Baye).[15] According to Jacobus, the two Bambara men continued to indulge in the practice until the day when they married a common wife in Saint-Louis, Senegal.[16]

In a similar vein, Jacobus regarded lesbianism in colonial Senegal as a rare practice that Europeans might have encouraged. For instance, in *Untrodden Fields of Anthropology* (1898), Jacobus suggested the occurrence of lesbian relationships in colonial Saint-Louis where he argued that the "negress" woman in a polygamous relationship "seeks the satisfaction of her unsatiated longings . . . without compromising herself, among her friends or companions, already initiated into the Lesbian mysteries" although she has "nothing of the inertia and passiveness of the sad sequestered women of the harem."[17] Yet, in *L'Amour aux colonies*, Jacobus wrote: "The Negress is not Lesbian" (translation by Babacar M'Baye).[18]

Moreover, Jacobus's narratives made an association of homosexual sexual orientation with pederasty. In *Untrodden Fields of Anthropology*, Jacobus described "a rich Black merchant" in Saint-Louis that he called "my landlord" who had proposed to sell him a young "Negro boy, the colour of old bronze, a half-breed between a Moor and a Negress."[19] According to Jacobus, the black merchant "had brought [the boy] with him from the station of Podor, when he went to attend the gum market."[20] This boy was probably a sex slave since Jacobus argued previously that, despite the existence of French laws, there were in Saint-Louis girls disguised as "domestics" who were "servants for life" who were "made over" and offered to clients seeking "virgins." [21] The "Negro boy" described above had a similar status of sex-slave that these gilds had, since his master wanted to sell him for twelve pounds to Jacobus whom, he thought, "appeared interested a little in the creature."[22] This discussion suggests that a few black inhabitants or travelers in colonial Saint-Louis were somewhat familiar with the idea of pederasty even if they might have regarded European settlers as the people who practiced it. Such an association of pederasty with Europeans may be the origin of contemporary Senegalese's representations of homosexuality as both a form of pederasty and a Western practice.

While Jacobus suggests that homosexuality in colonial Senegal was an effect of enslavement, other early Western ethnographers suggested that the practice stemmed from urbanization. In *The Wolof of Senegambia: Together with Notes on the Lebu and the Serer* (1957), David P. Gamble, who was an American anthropologist of Northern Irish origin, states:

> Life in urban centres [of Senegal] is also associated with a decline in morals. The rising cost of living, high marriage expenses, and housing difficulties have meant later marriages for both men and women. Homosexuality, practically unknown in rural society, has become established in large towns. Prostitution exists in the ports and big trade centres. [23]

Gamble's account is important because it strongly suggests that homosexuality was prevalent in Senegalese cities during the mid-twentieth century, reinforcing a theory that Geoffrey Gorer, a British anthropologist, had already developed in his 1935 book, *Africa Dances: A Book about West African Negroes* (1935). Gorer states:

> It is said that homosexuality is recent among the Wolof, at any rate in any frequency; but it now receives, and has for some years received, such extremely august and almost publicly exhibited patronage that pathics are a common sight. They are called in Wolof men-women, gor-digen, and do their best to deserve the epithet by their mannerisms, their dress and their make-up; some even dress their hair like women. . . . This phase is usually transitory, finishing with the departure of the European who has been keeping the boy; but a certain number from taste, interest, or for economic reasons continue their practices and there is now quite a large pederastic society.[24]

This statement suggests the ways in which both the European travelers and the Senegalese societies they studied shared one thing: a homophobic and transphobic impulse that led them to deny the existence of homosexuality in colonial Senegal and identify the practice as a disease found among men they viewed as effeminate and pederasts. Fortunately, there is strong representation of *gôr djiguène* in works of Senegalese intellectuals themselves.

Un chant écarlate [Scarlet Song]

An early portrayal of *gôr djiguène* is in Bâ's *Un chant écarlate* in which one of the main characters, Yaye Khady, depicts one of her neighbor's sons as follows: "Nothing short of a miracle will stop that youngster turning into a *gôr djiguène*, a pansy destined to spend his life at the feet of a courtesan, doing all her dirty work. His job would be to procure generous lovers to keep that type of pricey household going. His would be the job of settling the accounts for the meals. And sometimes it might happen that the clients would fancy him rather than his mistress."[25] Beside suggesting how the word "*gôr djiguène*" (man-woman in Wolof language) is a derogatory term that Yaye Khady uses to denigrate boys and men who fulfill feminine roles in Senegalese society, the quotation shows that such individuals were part of the community in the

1970s despite the stereotypes against them. Discussing the long excerpt from which the above quotation comes, Jarrod Hayes writes: "On one level, this passage constitutes a description of the scorn with which the *gôr-djiguen* is sometimes viewed. Yet it must be said that, in a society in which the actions of any family member may dishonor the entire family (which may also depend on a son for assuring patrilineal descendants), a parent's reaction to a son's becoming a *gôr-djiguen* might be very different from that of society as a whole. On another level, this passage is an eloquent description of how, even in spite of parental violence, a boy affirms a gender identity, which seems to develop 'naturally,' far removed from any foreign influence."[26] In this sense, Bâ validate the historical existence and significance of the "*gôr djiguène*" even when she reflects the prejudices they faced in post-independent Senegal due to the strong influence of traditions that expected boys and men to perform only hyper-masculine roles, attitudes, and behaviors. By drawing attention to such prejudices, Bâ challenged heteronormative expectations in Senegal.

The prejudices against the *gôr djiguène* are further evident in the manner in which Ba reveals through Yaye Khady's stream of consciousness which lays bare the character's inner fear and repulsion of the young boy. Divulging Yaye Khady's inner-thoughts about the *gôr djiguène*, Bâ writes:

> In their new neighborhood the couple opposite had a son, a very queer youngster [un fils bien drôle]! This fifteen-year-old obstinately refused the company and games of boys of his own age and sought the company and games of little girls! A funny sort of boy this was, who modelled his bearing, drawling speech and activities on those of girls!
>
> When his father came upon him, gossiping away with the old women, or cooking up dishes in the gutter, he went wild with rage and took a whip to him. But to no avail.[27]

By describing the neighbor's son as "a very queer youngster" who preferred to hang out and play with girls and engage in the daily activities such as cooking instead of those expected from males, such as, for instance, playing soccer, throwing marbles, wrestling outside, and hunting for birds, Bâ reflects the boy's distinctive form of queer identity which can be best understood through local lenses. Possessing such lenses, both Bâ and Yaye Khady are instinctually inscribe the boy's gender identity into femaleness, since he is naturally and socially inclined to indulge in women's company and girls' activities which, for most Senegalese, are the markers of the *gôr djiguène*. By showing how the boy's father attempts to thwart his son's inclinations through violence "to no avail," Bâ is sympathetic to the *gôr djiguène* by acknowledging that his or her independent identity that is bound to develop no matter how much pressure society uses to stifle or control it. It is perhaps with such empathetic feelings that Bâ later suggests the important role that the *gôr djiguène* can have in Senegalese society when she writes. This affirmation of the *gôr djiguène* appears later in the novel when Bâ describes a *gôr djiguène*'s involvement in an important ritual of the baptism of a child of Yaye Khady's son, Ousmane, and his new wife, Ouleymatou. Bâ writes: "Marième, Coumba's daughter, carried the basket of gifts, as was the custom. A *gôr djiguène*, one of those persons of ambiguous sex, whose existence revolved around similar ceremonies, watched over the infant's hamper, in which were piled up baby clothes and toys and carefully folded pagnes which the child would eventually wear."[28] By representing this "*gôr djiguène*" as a person of "ambiguous sex" who is, however, given the important task of attending to "the infant's hamper" where important items are stacked, Bâ suggests the key social and cultural role that this individual has in Senegalese culture. Even if the portrayal of the "*gôr djiguène*" as a person with an "ambiguous sex" may register homophobia, transphobia, or other prejudice, his depiction as a figure with a communal and sacred role in the baptism shows presence and validation rather than absence and alienation of this character. Such a dignified representation of a *gôr djiguène* counters a critic's argument that Bâ's Scarlet Song "presents homosexuality as an unsatisfactory future for a child."[29] Certainly, despite the real risks that it constitute due to the stigmas that it invites, homosexuality, from Bâ's perspective, does not and should not lead to a life of doom and perdition when the society respects the *gôr djiguène* and values his or her role in community.

Xala

Another representation of sexual and gender variances in Senegalese cinema is in Ousmane Sembène's 1973 classic film *Xala* where there is a scene in which a male-to-female transgender person, who hands a cigar to a wealthy guest, replies "week end" when the latter asks her, "Friend, how do you say weekend in English?" As soon as they walk away, the transgender person says, "Shit!" This rare allusion to gender variance in Sembène's cinema reveals his silence about the subject and his association of male effeminacy with Western-influenced political and cultural impotence in postcolonial Senegal. Sembène spoofs the Western heritage by depicting assimilated and corrupt Senegalese leaders who indulge in reckless flirtations, adultery, alcoholism, and meaningless dialogue with a gender-variant person whose knowledge of English is limited to saying "weekend" and swearing in this language.

However, from a different angle, one may perceive Sembène's representation of the transgender person as a recognition of the fact that knowledge of foreign language and customs and the rest of the world, is found not just in the corrupt upper class, but also among the marginalized individuals such as the two "*gôr djiguène*" figures in the film who, like the "géwél" woman in the film, witness the political and social impotence of El-Hadj, who is the movie's male protagonist, without being able to prevent this character's downfall. From this standpoint, the "*gôr djiguène*" is also a figure that Sembène represents, like the "géwél" confidant in the film, as an anti-elitist witness of the vanity and foils of El-Hadj's superfluous and reckless political class that has abandoned its noble duties to help the poor and marginalized Senegalese masses that elected it to power when independence was achieved in 1960. Being from such masses, the two "*gôr djiguène*" figures in the film are afraid to openly resist the exploitation of El-Hadj's political class due to a fear of retribution and further marginalization.

Yet Xala counters its stereotypical representation of the *gôr djiguène* as a sign of decadence by revealing the role of this figure as a respected dandy who fulfills important social and cultural role in the community. Such a depiction of the *gôr djiguène* as a dandy in Xala is apparent in the scene in which a male-to-female transgender person is show conversing with La Badiene, whose niece Elhadj Married as a third wife without being able to consummate his first sexual relation with her due to his sudden physical impotence. Sitting with La Badiene and the lead griotte, the *gôr djiguène* epitomizes a perfect dandy through her accouterment, which consists of a lightly purple and patterned *grand boubou* (a long-sleeved gown). Through her disciplined posture and calculated mannerism, the *gôr djiguène* is a dandy figure who reflects the sense of measured hand movements, gaze, and conversational skills that have earned Senegalese women their reputed charm and elegance. Yet, this dandy figure is not a commodity since they convey Sembène's major critique of postcolonial Senegal. This critique centers the idea that the real corruption besieging the nation is not the *gôr djiguène* who is scapegoated as the cause and effect of moral degeneration in the country, but the political and economic leadership which is not male enough to lead the state to prosperity. Given the tense relations he had with the socialist government of then president Léopold Sédar Senghor, Sembène had to be careful to make such a direct criticism against his regime and, consequently, chose to convey the rebuttal through the voice of the dandy *gôr djiguène* character who says: "Ihhh! Gooru tayyi daal kenna ducci goor!" ("Ihhh! Today's men are less than men!") This assertation is Sembène's ironic use of a *gôr djiguène* character to represent vapid masculinity as trait that is found in the impotent postcolonial nation where men are less than their forebears and not necessarily in the persona of the much-loathed dandy figure. The *gôr djiguène*'s assertion may indicate Sembène's displacement of the root of the postcolonial dilemma in Africa from the segments of the society such as homosexuals, transgender, and disabled, and supposedly illiterate people to the elite which has replaced former colonials and created alien forms of masculinities based on bourgeois and capitalist exploitations. Ada Uzoamaka Azodo and Maureen Eke write:

> Historical, economic, and cultural developments do indeed affect and transform individual genders and sexualities. Excessive masculinity already evident in traditional Africa got out of hand as African elite men sought to surpass the past white masters in violence and masculinity. They kept strings of mistresses paid for with embezzled public funds, as seen for example in *Xala*. (21)[30]

For Sembène, this ultramasculinity which mirrors colonial plutocracy and violence is damaging to the postcolonial state since it reinstates the divisions and aggressions that European imperialists deployed to impose their hegemonies in Africa.

Madame Brouette

Madame Brouette is also an important film in the study of the portrayal of the *gôr djiguène* in Senegalese culture since it revisits the popular association of this transgender figure with either the police or bourgeoisie which are both portrayed as impotent. This frequent correspondence between the *gôr djiguène* and the police is apparent early in *Madame Brouette* when a group of children heckle Naago, a former police officer who has become a drug dealer. In the scene, the children mock at Naago, who is drunk and is dressed in full female attire. As soon as they see Naago in a taxi, the children run behind the vehicle that is taking him home to the district of Niaye Thiokeer, Dakar. Wearing a red dress, a necklace, a frizzled yellow wig, and gold-colored mules, Nagoo gets out of the cab in an inebriated state, insulting the kids and telling them, "Dégagez! Mal conscients! Imbéciles! C'est ma frite. J'en fais ce que je veux" ["Get out of here, Unconscious! Fools! It is my money and I can do whatever I want with it"].[31] Nagoo's verbal violence foreshadows the abuse that he perpetrates in Niaye Thiokeer, especially in the domestic sphere. This abuse is noticeable in the film's next scene which shows a tragic encounter in which Nagoo is shot by dead his wife, Mati, as he attempts to beat her again. As soon as they hear the deadly shot, a few community members rush to the tumult and see Naago lying on the ground, outside of Mati's room.

The rest of the film is a series of flashbacks showing Naago's transformation from a sweet and innocent police officer to a corrupt, vile, and brutal person who uses his ties to underground crime, fraud, and the drug world to exert his authority on the vulnerable populations of Niayes Thiokeert. Nagoo's easy targets include his wife, Mati, her daughter, and his son, whose lives he greatly endangers. In this sense, Naago's crossdressing transcends the popular conception of this activity as the physical or psychological metamorphosis of a person who adorns the clothing of the opposite gender or sex. Like Sembène, Absa represents crossdressing as a metaphor for socio-political and cultural decadence. Like his predecessor, Absa also depicts this activity as the epitome of moral, spiritual, economic, and legal decay in the Senegalese nation-state. This individual is associated with all the ills of the society, just like the corrupt economic class of con businessmen, legal advisors, and political councils who lure the frail and gullible individuals that Mati and her other abused friends represent in Niayes Thiokeert's community. Discussing *Madame Brouette*, Dennis Harvey states:

> Uncomplicated script makes its points without sermonizing, illustrating the struggles—legal and otherwise—most Senegalese endure while the government makes empty promises of economic improvement. Principal message, however, fingers the unreconstructed misogyny that allows women to be treated as male property.[32]

In this sense, Absa's depiction of Naago as a corrupt and former policeman who now crossdresses into female clothing during the Tajaboon ceremony resonates with the Senegalese's stereotypical association of the *gôr djiguène* with moral, political, and economic corruption. By representing Nagoo as a *gôr djiguène*, Absa captures the Senegalese people's perception of corrupt political leaders as emasculated men who claim to be defenders of social order and women only to abuse both entities. In this sense, the numerous anonymous insults against certain political leaders or artists (especially singers) as effeminate or franc-maçon (freemason) that permeate comments sections of numerous Senegalese news sites stem from this popular representation of corrupt leadership as an embodiment of *gôr djiguène*.[33] The goal, of course, is to weaken an adversary through character assassination by typecasting him or her as an emasculated person who serves Western and other imperialistic and capitalist exploitations. Thus, a part of the political leadership in Senegal faces a contradiction. On the one hand, this leadership is part of the local movement viewing homosexuality as an international conspiracy. "Indeed, influential Senegalese religious and political leaders seem to be convinced that an actual infiltration of homosexuality—as an imposition from outside—threatens the social order and the *intégrìté nationale*."[34] Yet, in Senegal, political leaders themselves are often typecast by rivals as freemasons or supporters of homosexuals, and therefore as infiltrators of Western decadence into Senegal.[35]

Therefore, as Patrick Awondo, Peter Geschiere and Graeme Reid as well as Broqua show in their articles, the demonization of homosexuality in Senegalese media and culture since 2008 have been the effect of the politicization of the image of the *gôr djiguène* more than anything else. Sadly, the body and soul of the *gôr djiguène* have become the parameters through which the Senegalese society is becoming aware of the contradictions within its identity. This is inexcusable injustice and violence since the larger causes of the paradoxes within modern Senegalese society must be found within the customs, desires, hopes, and conditions of all segments of the society and not just on an invented image of one single group. Besides, as Niang points out in his 2000 interview with *L'Observateur*,

> Senegal has enough problems and discussing who is homosexual and who is not is not one of them. We have other challenges to resolve, such as development challenges and the fight against poverty. And then we have this capacity that our ancestors, grandparents, and other forebears bequeathed to us, which is a capacity to have compassion translated into the concept of *Yeurmandé*. This consists of saying, for example, that it is God who settles his problem with the believer. This should not be as much a problem as people make it seem. One does not have the right to kill a person whom God has made (Babacar's translation).[36]

It should not be hard for the Senegalese to develop to type of *Yeurmandé* toward *gor djiguen* because the society tolerates androgyny in many cultural contexts. For instance, though they are not expressed in their fullness during this event, Senegalese men and woman are allowed to indulge in reversals of gender attributes and roles during the *taajaboon* celebration. During this day, crosssgenderism is allowed in Senegalese culture. Francoise Bouffault writes: "It is Tajaboon. On the day that marks the Muslim new year, men dress as women, women as men. It is an old tradition, harmless, festive, happy, meant to scare bad spirits away. I asked the Senegalese about Tajaboon and they all pointed to it as a fond memory of their adolescence."[37] Also spelled as *taajaboon*, *taajabone*, or *tajabone* (just like the title of Ismailo Lô's famous song, this word describe a Muslim festivity in Senegal marking the tenth day of the Islamic New Year known as Achoura (Tamxarit in Wolof). The song originally served as a verse that young Koranic students used to sing in Senegal to remind people of the dangers that a Muslim risked facing if they failed to worship the religion as is prescribed in the Holy Book. To scare believers, the song reminds them of how Abdu Jaambar, the much-feared angel of the Islamic religion, will descend upon Earth to ask everyone whether they fulfilled key duties such as praying, fasting, and giving zakat [charity].[38] Yet, according to an unnamed critic points out in the documentary titled *L'Authentique Taajaboon*, the celebration has been corrupted in contemporary Senegalese culture in which the crossdressing component of the *bawnaan* ceremonies, dancing, and other practices that did not belong to the original custom now prevail in the ritual.[39] In Wolof language, "*bawnaan*" means "streaming rain." According to this commentator, *bawnaan* occurred in traditional times, mostly in the Baol region of Senegal where, during the summer drought, men and women would wear the clothes of the opposite gender and dance so that rain would fall.

Yet, the term "*bawnaan*" has another origin. Two reporters, Mohamadou Sagne and Samba Oumar Fall, write: "The Serer Ol who lived in Sine came here and were faced with drought. They practiced the dance called the '*bawnaan*.' It was performed by griot women and male slaves under a tree frequented by some dignitaries . . . It was after dancing that heavy rain fell with a lot of water runoff. They said that "ndokhmi bawnaan na."[40] It is very interesting that the crossdressing of the *bawnaan* ritual has been preserved in the modern *taajaboon* in which boys and girls can wear the clothes of the opposite gender just as men and women can also do. They all can go from house to house singing and dancing in merriment and expect to receive compensation in the form of some rice, sugar, similar items or money. The songs usually go as follow:[41]

Taajaboon, àllay
de gnuy tajaboon, àllay!
Abdu Jambaar,
gniari malaykala
Chi kaw layy joggé,
daanu si séroo
Bo yewoo suba!
Muhnilla juli ngam?
ngané deedet!
Muhnila woor ngaam?

ngané deedet!

[Taajaboon, àllay!
Let's taajaboon, àllay
Abdu Jaambar
Is made of two angels!
He descends from above
and lands on a cloth
When he wakes up!
and ask you, have you prayed?
You say, no!
Have you fasted?
You say, no!]

This excerpt from the longer *taajaboon* song is highly important because it is regarded as a verse with traditional Muslim origins which, along the years, has been corrupted in modern Senegalese culture where it celebrates crossdressing and mere merriment while the initial and, sometimes, current message of the songs are about a believer's responsibility to fear God and follow the pillars of Islam. The song's repetition of how the angel Abdu Jambaar will appear on a day of judgement and inquire about whether every Muslim follows Islam's pillars is supposed to instill in the believers' reminiscence and fear of god and humility about life. Discussing the original message of the feast, Abdou Khadre Gueye states: "The choice of the word 'Tahjabuun' may have been motivated by this verse where Allah (peace be upon Him) marvels at the discrepancy between the gravity of the recall of the Quranic discourse and the distraction in which the recipients are plunged."[42] According to Gueye, in past times, people who participated in "Tahjabuun" were mostly young *talibés* (Koranic students) who wore rags and painted their faces in ashes, appearing like zombis and revealing their precarious lives. Thus, for a Senegalese Muslim who wants to preserve the original custom of *taajaboon*, the kinds of metamorphosis in which the current participants are indulged by crossdressing into the opposite gender becomes a distraction and a corruption of the original purpose. In this sense, *taajaboon*, as Ndeye Fatou Diouf points out, is a celebration in which tradition has taken over the religious.[43] Yet it may be more productive to say that tradition has blended with religion in a secular and hybrid manners that make Senegal be a nation that tolerates and accepts all forms of diversity, including the *gôr djiguène*, that Niang wants to see. By crossdressing and singing verses with Islamic message and words, the young Senegalese of both sexes who participate in the celebration reveal the creative balance that Senegalese have created between traditions and modernity. Both the crossdressing of the *baw-naan* and the warnings for those who fail to follow their Islamic duties are blended in this tradition which harmoniously coexists with modern times, showing, once again, how Senegalese people can epitomize the cosmopolitanism, universality, and openness to various cultures that have earned them the envy of many societies worldwide.

Le Revenant

Another representation of the "*gôr djiguène*" in Senegalese literature is in Aminata Sow Fall's 1982 novel, *Le Revenant* (the revenant), in which the figure is portrayed through the transgender character of Malobé Niang. This character serves as the transgender confidante and Mistress of Ceremony of Adja Yama Diop. The latter figure is a newly rich woman and a sister of the protagonist called Bakar. When she has festivities to which she invites her wealthy friends of Dakar, Yama puts the whole event's organization in the hands of Malobé due to the latter's fame in the community. Fall writes: "For this celebration, she [Yama] called for Malobé Niang, the fiercest and most feared and sought-after man-woman [*gôr djiguène*]. He was the one who handled the major events of the real 'diriyanké'" (40; translation by Babacar M'Baye). The Wolof term "*diriyanké*" refers to opulent Senegalese women who like to show off their beauty, social stature, and wealth sometimes in the company of the "*gôr djiguène*," who can freely speak and act in major gatherings such as weddings, birth ceremonies, and other events. In having such a role and freedom of expression, the "*gôr djiguène*" is like the traditional Senegalese storyteller, poet, healer, historian, and diplomat known as the "*géwél*." According to Ivy Mills, in Senegalese society, "the góor-jigéen takes on the géwél role of proxy communicator which marks the diriyaanke as elite and powerful."[44]

One portrayal of the *gôr djiguène* figure in *Le Revenant* is the passage where they appear as a person who is substantially integrated into Senegalese society. The *gôr djiguène*'s significance in Senegalese culture is revealed early in the novel through her or his representations as part of then *diriyanké*'s entourage in which Yama belongs. The narrator depicts Yama as "a beloved and fulfilled wife, a great 'diriyanké' . . . surrounded by a court of thurifers, men-women . . . and griots" (Babacar's translation).[45] The representation of the "men-women" as "thurifers" gives the *gôr djiguène* a spiritual quality that derives not only from their embodiment of a certain form of religiosity, but their personification of a new age in which modernity challenges the strictures of tradition.

Like Malobé, Yama also embodies a challenge of tradition, though in negative ways. Yama, like Malobé, also reflects a new area in which pride in one's royal caste is replaced by one's need to survive economically. Aminata Sow Fall describes the clash between tradition and modernity as a cultural war between two segments of Senegalese society:

> Some, retreating behind birth, glorious past and the historical role of ancestors, looked down upon those who owed their notoriety to money. These, however, saw themselves as the strongest, and Yama also believed it, she who lived with the paradox every day. Principles as hard as steel could be reduced to nothing, and previously forbidden and impassable walls could be straddled in the name of this material ideal that one pretended to despise (Babacar's translation).[46]

Fall's quotation provides the large context out of which most of the tensions in Senegalese postcolonial society evolved. In this social environment in which material expediency troubles past versions of nobility, both the *gôr djiguène*, griots, and other marginalized social classes thus far perceived as inferior to the royally blooded families create their own degree of freedom in the new nation-state. Like other marginalized groups, the *gôr djiguène* is compelled to be inventive and create new possibilities in the independent nation. Unfortunately, the so-called nobles and other individuals whose ancestors used to be the hegemony in Senegal are unwilling to allow formerly marginalized groups to shatter the inequities of tradition for the sake of modernity. Consequently, an unavoidable conflict between various notions of what constitutes real and fake culture has prevailed in Senegal since independence and has taken strong turns since the homophobia of 2008.

The inevitable clash between tradition and modernity is the roots of the culture wars in which the *gôr djiguène* has unfortunately been represented as one of the instigators, when this tension is part of the predictable course of a complex Senegalese society which is coming to terms with itself. In order to correct the scapegoating of the *gôr djiguène* as the source of decadence in the postcolonial state, Fall shows that the real source of discord in the country is about the worship of money. According to fall, greed, not moral corruption, is the root cause of the problems facing Senegalese society. The predicament stemmed from the excessive materialism that has increasingly disunited families and created a blind rush to riches in Senegal since the mid-1970s.

Fall laments the danger of materialism through Yama because this character will go to any extent to represent herself as a wealthy urban woman even if she came from very humble beginnings. Forgetting her roots, Yama has become a cold person who looks down upon the poor and creates a fantasy world in which she ruthlessly portrays herself as a woman to whom modernity has given power over those Senegalese, such as the "royally blooded" ones who, she believes, perceive themselves as better than the other members of society. For instance, when Bakar wants to marry Mame Aïssa, who is the daughter of a designated noble family of Dakar, that of Adja Dado Sarr and El Hadji Wellé Gueye, Yama uses the wedding as an opportunity to show off. The union becomes ill-fated since it triggers a series of competition of wealth display in which Yama and Malobé do their best to become infamously victorious. Thus, in *Being Black, Being Human: More Essays on Black Culture* (2004), Femi Ojo-Ade represents *Le Revenant* as a novel "depicting the laughable personality of Malobé and the ridiculous nature of Yama's actions . . . Indeed, Yama goes overboard in everything. Fall seems to enjoy detailing the materialistic woman's stupidity."[47]

However, resisting the homophobia and transphobia which consist of perceiving the *gôr djiguène* as an absolute representative of decadence in Senegal, Fall shows that the vices that are perceived in this individual are, in fact, societal since they are shared by a whole society in which wealth, grandeur, and cult of the personality are valued over other qualities. Fall does not exonerate the *gôr djiguène* from this blind materialism because she shows that this dandy figure mirrors the fascination with material and social aggrandizement and opulence that have displaced many traditional virtues such as restraint and humility in modern Senegal. In this sense, Malobé is a *gôr djiguène* who, like her patroness, represents the insatiable capitalism which, like those of the postcolonial leadership, threatens the livelihood of the nation-state. The lack of true sovereignty and good governance, which were later reinforced by the failures of structural adjustment policies, created in post-1970s Senegal a growing climate in which winning over others by any necessary means began to tear the society's fabric. This ruthless state of order in which both gendered and neocolonial capitalisms put tradition on its head is apparent when Fall depicts Yama and Malobé like two sides of the same bad coin. Fall writes:

> Yama had broken all records. Malobé exulted, the victory was his. and [sic] it is only in these overheated atmospheres, when he created the suspense and awed with the unusual, that he felt in his element, because for the great master of ceremonies he was, every encounter was a fight and it was not just a matter of winning it; it was necessary to defeat the antagonists; it was a moral duel, where decency and prudence demanded one to be victorious. And Malobé was always victorious because she was always above calculations and restraint (Babacar's translation).[48]

This quotation has a double meaning. On the one hand, it is a criticism against a post-1970s Senegalese society in which ruthlessness, competition, fantasy, and trickery replaced the traditional codes of mutual respect, humility, and truthfulness. To compound this new order, rivalry and vanity between families exacerbated by women such as Yama who used their new-gained wealth to win a false sense of popularity built on vanity. This vanity threatens the kinds of equity and balance that traditional and rural Senegalese societies had despite their imperfections. In this context, Malobé should not perceived as a pariah but just as a mirror image of Yama. Malobé is just another Senegalese who has fallen to the charm and mirage of quick capitalist success, showiness, and hedonism which have strongly influenced modern Senegalese society. In this sense, Fall's depiction of both Yama and Malobé is incriminatory since it vituperates a modern Senegalese society in which femininity is sometimes mistaken for mere spectacle and enmity rather than genuineness and friendship among women and families.

However, although she also represents Malobé as a ridiculous person, Fall does not express any transphobic or homophobic attitudes toward this transgender character. Therefore, Fall humanizes Malobé by portraying him with a substantial degree of acceptance of the identity they represent. In order to appreciate Fall's positive depictions of

Malobé, one must value the ways in which she reveals this character's integration into Yama's women's circle despite her or his blurred gender identity in a society in which the *gôr djiguène* was substantially marginalized. Countering this marginalization, Fall reveals the important role that the *gôr djiguène* often played in Senegalese women's gatherings and communal social events without facing overt denigration and malice. In this vein, Fall represents Malobé as an individual who has gained power in Yama's circle for many reasons including her oratory and leadership qualities. Malobé's important status and skills are apparent when Yama forms a delegation visiting Mame Aïssa's family during the birth ceremony of Bakar's child. Malobé is represented as a quintessential Mistress of Ceremony who commands high respect. Fall writes:

> For this ceremony, she [YAMA] had appealed to Malobé Niang, the most formidable, the most feared, but also the most sought-after man-woman. It was he who organized the ceremonies of the real 'diriyanké'; he was choosy; few were the ones to whom he agreed to offer his services because he was demanding. he [sic] saw things in a big way and did not suffer when others discussed his propositions. Every great lady sought her company; gaining his favors was a sure promise of celebrity entry (Babacar's translation).[49]

This quotation reflects the important role of communicator, counselor, and event planner that a transgender person such as Malobé is given in a modern Senegalese society where they are sought by the wealthy and respected women known as "diriyanké." In addition to her power to facilitate a woman's fame, Malobé's influential status in both Yama's circle and community shows that 1970s Senegalese society was not always aversive or intolerant toward the *gôr djiguène*.

Archival, literary, and cinematographic texts about the figure of the transgender person in Senegal are highly importance because they help to study the crucial role that the *gôr djiguène* has played in Senegalese culture. These narratives are central because they reflect complex images of the *gôr djiguène* which, when they are analyzed in objective and balanced terms, show that this individual was not as demonized and marginalized in Senegal as they have been since 2008. With the onset of rampant homophobia and transphobia in the country, the *gôr djiguène* has been depicted in Senegalese media as the cause and consequence of moral decadence and Western negative influence on Africa. The narratives discussed above counter such negative portrayals of the *gôr djiguène*. As the texts show, in the past, the *gôr djiguène* was revered and admired for her or his organizational, oratory, and ritualistic skills although they could also succumb to the same greed, vanity, and other weaknesses in which many fame-seeking and pretentious diriyanké women of Dakar indulged during the 1970s.

The literary and cinematographic depictions of sexual and gender variances in Senegal also serve as effective means to counter the homophobia and transphobia that have prevailed in postcolonial Senegal. For instance, a 2010 special report of Amnesty International documents serious attacks and human rights violations against homosexuals in Senegal. According to this report, most of the nine men who had been arrested in 2009 "had been tortured and subjected to homophobic attacks and remarks by the police officers that questioned them and by the prison officers where they were imprisoned" (19). The gruesome report suggests that homophobia in Senegal is a result of state-sanctioned policy and culturally dismissive, sexist, and masochistic notions of gender relationships and femininity. Moreover, since the late 2000s, homosexuality has been a major issue in Senegal that continues to capture the attention of the media. There rarely is a week or month during which a media story accusing a person of having indulged or condoned this practice does not appear. Yet most of the country remains underdeveloped, undereducated, and unemployed due to inadequate economic conditions. Instead of perceiving the *gôr djiguène* as part of the Senegalese people who are impacted by these situations, the media and certain political and religious demagogues use them as easy targets of public scapegoating and humiliation which divert attention from the country's plight.

BIBLIOGRAPHY

Absa, Moussa Sène. *Madame Brouette*. Paris: Productions de la lanterne, 2005.

Amnesty International. "Senegal: Land of Impunity." London, UK: Amnesty International Publications, 2010. http://www.amnesty.sn/IMG/pdf/Senegal_terre_d_impunite.pdf.

Awondo, Patrick, Peter Geschiere and Graeme Reid. "Homophobic Africa? Toward a More Nuanced View." *African Studies Review* 55, no. 3 (December 2012): 145–68

Azodo, Ada Uzoamaka and Maureen Eke, eds. *Gender and Sexuality in African Literature and Film*. Trenton, NJ: Africa World Press, 2007.

Bâ, Mariama. *Un chant écarlate.* 1981. Dakar: Les Nouvelles Éditions Africaines; trans. as *Scarlet Song*. Trans. Dorothy S. Blair. New York: Longman, 2000.
———. *Scarlet Song*. New York: Longman, 2000.
Bouffault, Francoise. "*Madame Brouette*: A Film by Moussa Sene Absa." 2004. http://www.africanfilmny.org/2004/%E2%80%9Cmadame-brouette%E2%80%9D-a-film-by-moussa-sene-absa/.
Broqua, Christophe. "Introduction au Thème L'Émergence des Minorités Sexuelles dans l'Espace Public en Afrique." *Politique africaine* no. 126 (juin 2012): 5–23.
———. "'Góor-jigéen': la resignification négative d'une catégorie entre genre et sexualité." *Socio* (9 décembre 2017): 163–83
Camara, Fatou Kiné. "Ce délit qui nous vient d'ailleurs: l'homosexualité dans le Code pénal du Sénégal." *Psychopathologie africaine* 34, no. 3 (2007–2008): 317–42.
"Cheikh Niang, Sociologue 'Nous Avons Besoin des Homosexuels.'" https://www.leral.net/CHEIKH-NIANG-SOCIOLOGUE-NOUS-AVONS-BESOIN-DES-HOMOSEXUELS_a4068.html. Lundi 20 Avril 2009. Accessed February 10, 2018.
Coly, Ayo. "Carmen Goes Postcolonial, Carmen Goes Queer: Thinking the Postcolonial as Queer." *Culture, Theory and Critique* 57, no. 3 (2016): 391–407
Dramé, Fatou Maria, Sarah Peitzmeier, Magda Lopes, Marième Ndaw, Abdoulaye Sow, Daouda Diouf, and Stefan Baral. "Gay Men and Other Men Who Have Sex with Men in West Africa: Evidence from the Field." *Culture, Health & Sexuality* 15, no. 1 (July 2013): S7–S21.
Fall, Aminata Sow. *Le Revenant*. Dakar: Les Nouvelles Editions Africaines, 1982.
Gamble, David P. *The Wolof of Senegambia: Together with Notes on the Lebu and the Serer.* London: International African Institute, 1957.
Gning, Ndèye. "Les motifs de l'illégitimité sociale de l'homosexualité au Sénégal." *Africultures* 6, no. 96 (2013): 22–39.
Gorer, Geoffrey. *Africa Dances: A Book about West African Negroes*. New York: Norton & Company, 1935.
Gueye, Abdou Khadre. "L'origine du 'Taajaboon' (Version Française)." January 24, 2013, http://akaademiwolof.seneweb.com/l-rsquo-origine-du-laquo-taajaboon-raquo-version-francaise_b_8.html. Site désactivé.
Harvey, Dennis. "Madame Brouette." January 1, 2018. Variety.com. http://variety.com/2002/film/markets-festivals/madame-brouette-1200546310/.
Hayes, Jarrod. *Queer Roots for the Diaspora: Ghosts in the Family Tree*. Ann Arbor: University of Michigan Press, 2016.
Jacobus X. *Untrodden Fields of Anthropology: Observations on the Esoteric Manners and Customs of Semi-Civilized People; Being a Record of Thirty Years' Experience in Asia, Africa, America and Oceana. Vol II.* Paris: Librairie de Médicine, Folklore et Anthropologie, 1898.
———. *L'Amour aux Colonies. singularités physiologiques et passionnelles, observées durant trente années de séjour dans les colonies françaises, Cochinchine, Tonkin et Cambodge, Guyane et Martinique, Sénégal et Rivières du Sud, Nouvelle-Calédonie, Nouvelle-Hébrides et Tahiti*. Paris: Isidore Liseux, 1893.
L'Authentique Taajaboon. Africa 7 TV. Aired October 22, 2015. https://www.youtube.com/watch?v=7Z-Fe27gNuY.
Martin, Marie-Claude. "Le Sénégal interdit les sacs à main pour un homme." February 11, 2016. https://www.letemps.ch/societe/senegal-interdit-sacs-main-un-homme.
M'baye, Babacar. "The Origins of Senegalese Homophobia : Discourses on Homosexuals and Transgender People in Colonial and Postcolonial Senegal," *African Studies Review* 56, no. 2 (2013): 109–28.
———. "Variant Sexualities and African Modernity in Joseph Gaye Ramaka's Karmen Geï." *Black Camera* 2, no. 2 (Spring 2011): 114–29.
Mills, Ivy. "Sutura: Gendered Honor, Social Death and the Politics of Exposure in Senegalese Literature and Popular Culture." PhD diss., University of California, Berkeley, 2011.

Niang, Cheikh Ibrahima, Placide Tapsoba, Ellen Weiss, Moustapha Diagne, Youssoupha Niang, Amadou Mody Moreau, Dominique Gomis, Abdoulaye Sidibé Wade, Karim Seck, and Chris Castle. "It's Raining Stones': Stigma, Violence and HIV Vulnerability among Men Who Have Sex with Men in Dakar, Senegal." *Culture, Health & Sexuality* 5, no. 6 (2003): 499–512.

Ojo-Ade, Femi. *Being Black, Being Human: More Essays on Black Culture*. Trenton: Africa World Press, 2004.

Petchesky, Rosalind, "The Language of 'Sexual Minorities' and the Politics of Identity: a Position Paper," *Reproductive Health Matters* 17, no. 33 (2009): 105–10.

Ridinger, Robert B. Marks, "African Literatures." In *Gay and Lesbian Literary Heritage*, edited by Claude J. Summers, 5–8. New York and London: Routledge, 2002.

Sagne, Mohamadou and Samba Oumar Fall. "Arts et traditions: Baol, un musée à ciel ouvert inexploité." January 16, 2018. http://seneweb.com/news/Culture/arts-et-traditions-baol-un-musee-a-ciel-_n_228428.html.

Sembène, Ousmane. *Xala*. Dakar, Filmi Domirew. New York: New Yorker Films, 2005.

Stobie, Cheryl. "'She Who Creates Havoc Is Here': A Queer Bisexual Reading of Sexuality, Dance, and Social Critique in Karmen Geï." *Research in African Literatures* 47, no. 2 (Summer 2016): 84–103.

"Ti-Bahou, le blog," January 16, 2018, http://tibahou.blogspot.com/2010/09/tajabone-chanson-du-monde-2.html.

NOTES

1. Cheikh Ibrahima Niang, Placide Tapsoba, Ellen Weiss, Moustapha Diagne, Youssoupha Niang, Amadou Mody Moreau, Dominique Gomis, Abdoulaye Sidibé Wade, Karim Seck, and Chris Castle, " 'It's Raining Stones': Stigma, Violence and HIV Vulnerability among Men Who Have Sex with Men in Dakar, Senegal," *Culture, Health and Sexuality* 5, no. 6 (2003): 505.

2. Fatou Kiné Camara, "Ce délit qui nous vient d'ailleurs : l'homosexualité dans le Code pénal du Sénégal," *Psychopathologie africaine* 34, no. 3 (2007–2008): 317–18.

3. Fatou Kiné Camara, "Ce délit qui nous vient d'ailleurs ," 320–21.

4. Babacar Mbaye, "The Origins of Senegalese Homophobia: Discourses on Homosexuals and Transgender People in Colonial and Postcolonial Senegal," *African Studies Review* 56, no. 2 (2013): 109–28.

5. The original statement is: "[I]l apparait pour les acteurs comme nécessaire à la revendication d'une identité nationale sénégalaise, dans un contexte ou la crise que traverse le Sénégal semble en menacer les fondements" (23).Ndèye Gning, "Les motifs de l'illégitimité sociale de l'homosexualité au Sénégal," *Africultures* 6, no 96 (2013): 23.

6. Christophe Broqua, "Introduction au Thème L'Émergence des Minorités Sexuelles dans l'Espace Public en Afrique," *Politique africaine* no. 126 (juin 2012): 12.

7. The original statement is: "[L]e vocabulaire désignant aujourd'hui les homosexuels renvoie à la dimension du genre plus qu' à celle de l'orientation sexuelle" (179). Christophe Broqua, "Góor-jigéen: la resignification négative d'une catégorie entre genre et sexualité," *Socio* 9 (décembre 2017): 179.

8. Babacar M'Baye, "Variant Sexualities and African Modernity in Joseph Gaye Ramaka's Karmen Geï," *Black Camera* 2, no. 2 (Spring 2011): 115.

9. Ayo Coly, "Carmen Goes Postcolonial, Carmen Goes Queer: Thinking the Postcolonial as Queer," *Culture, Theory and Critique* 57, no. 3 (2016): 391.

10. Coly writes: The contention then, is not the representation of non-heteronormative sexualities but rather what was perceived as an inappropriate use and blasphemous displacement of religious texts: the use of Moslem praise poems in a Catholic church, and to accompany the burial of a lesbian. Without this "misappropriation" of religious texts, Karmen Gei may have enjoyed a very smooth and uneventful run in Senegal (406).

Ayo Coly, "Carmen Goes Postcolonial, Carmen Goes Queer," 406.

11. Cheryl Stobie, "'She Who Creates Havoc Is Here': A Queer Bisexual Reading of Sexuality, Dance, and Social Critique in Karmen Geï," *Research in African Literatures* 47, no. 2 (Summer 2016): 84.

12. Rosalind Petchesky, "The Language of 'Sexual Minorities' and the Politics of Identity: a Position Paper," *Reproductive Health Matters* 17, no. 33 (2009): 106.

13. Fatou Maria Dramé, Sarah Peitzmeier, Magda Lopes, Marième Ndaw, Abdoulaye Sow, Daouda Diouf and Stefan Baral. "Gay Men and Other Men Who Have Sex with Men in West Africa: Evidence from the Field," *Culture, Health & Sexuality* 15, no. 1 (July 2013): S11.

14. The original quotation is: "Tout comme les termes équivalents dans d'autres langues, goorjigeen est une insulte qui humilie l'homme en remettant implicitement en cause son statut de mâle dominant, viril et autoritaire . . . le goorjigeen subordonne son statut d'homme à celui de la femme, plaçant la stigmatisation de l'homosexualité dans une vision essentialiste des rapports sociaux de sexe."

Ndèye Gning, "Les motifs de l'illégitimité sociale de l'homosexualité au Sénégal," *Africultures* 6, no. 96 (2013): 22–39.

15. Jacobus X, *L'Amour aux Colonies. singularités physiologiques et passionnelles, observées durant trente années de séjour dans les colonies françaises, Cochinchine, Tonkin et Cambodge, Guyane et Martinique, Sénégal et Rivières du Sud, Nouvelle-Calédonie, Nouvelle-Hébrides et Tahiti* (Paris: Isidore Liseux, 1893), 258.

16. Jacobus X, *L'Amour aux Colonies*, 258.

17. Jacobus X, *Untrodden Fields of Anthropology: Observations on the Esoteric Manners and Customs of Semi-Civilized People; Being a Record of Thirty Years' Experience in Asia, Africa, America and Oceana. Vol II* (Paris: Librairie de Médicine, Folklore et Anthropologie, 1898), 12–13.

18. Jacobus X, *L'Amour aux Colonies*, 257.

19. Jacobus X, *Untrodden Fields of Anthropology*, 43.

20. Jacobus X, *Untrodden Fields of Anthropology*, 43.

21. Jacobus X, *Untrodden Fields of Anthropology*, 43.

22. Jacobus X, *Untrodden Fields of Anthropology*, 43.

23. David P. Gamble, *The Wolof of Senegambia: Together with Notes on the Lebu and the Serer* (London: International African Institute, 1957), 80.

24. Geoffrey Gorer, *Africa Dances: A Book About West African Negroes* (New York: Norton & Company, 1935), 35.

25. Mariama Bâ, *Scarlet Song* (New York: Longman, 2000), 70.

26. Jarrod Hayes, *Queer Roots for the Diaspora: Ghosts in the Family Tree* (Ann Arbor: University of Michigan Press, 2016), 93.

27. Bâ, *Scarlet Song*, 69.

28. Mariama Bâ, *Scarlet Song* (New York: Longman, 2000), 131.

29. Robert B. Marks Ridinger, "African Literatures," in *Gay and Lesbian Literary Heritage*, edited by Claude J. Summers (New York and London: Routledge, 2002), 5–8.

30. Ada Uzoamaka Azodo and Maureen Eke, eds. *Gender and Sexuality in African Literature and Film* (Trenton, NJ: Africa World Press, 2007).

31. Moussa Sène Absa, *Madame Brouette* (Paris, France: Productions de la lanterne, 2005).

32. Dennis Harvey, "Madame Brouette," Variety.com, January 1, 2018, http://variety.com/2002/film/markets-festivals/madame-brouette-1200546310/.

33. To understand these issues, read the following web articles: Marie-Claude Martin, "Le Sénégal interdit les sacs à main pour un homme," February 11, 2016, https://www.letemps.ch/societe/senegal-interdit-sacs-main-un-homme.

34. Patrick Awondo, Peter Geschiere and Graeme Reid. "Homophobic Africa? Toward a More Nuanced View," *African Studies Review* 55, no. 3 (December 2012): 156.

35. See Broqua, "La question homosexuelle et transgenre," 14.

36. The original statement is here: "Le Sénégal a suffisamment de problèmes pour qu'on se mette à discuter sur qui est homosexuel, qui ne l'est pas. Nous avons d'autres défis à régler, qui sont des défis de développement et de lutte contre la pauvreté. Et puis nous avons cette capacité que nous ont léguée nos ancêtres, grands-parents etc, qui est une capacité de compassion traduit dans le concept de *Yeurmandé*. En disant par exemple que c'est Dieu

qui règle son problème avec le croyant, le problème ne se pose plus comme certains veulent le poser. On n'a pas le droit de tuer une personne que Dieu a faite."

"Cheikh Niang, Sociologue 'Nous Avons Besoin des Homosexuels,'" https://www.leral.net/CHEIKH-NIANG-SOCIOLOGUE-NOUS-AVONS-BESOIN-DES-HOMOSEXUELS_a4068.html. Lundi 20 Avril 2009. Accessed February 10, 2018.

37. Francoise Bouffault, "*Madame Brouette*: A Film by Moussa Sene Absa," 2004, http://www.africanfilmny.org/2004/%E2%80%9Cmadame-brouette%E2%80%9D-a-film-by-moussa-sene-absa/.

38. For a study of the original verses and meaning of Tajaboon, see "L'origine du 'Taajaboon' (Version Française)," June 24, 2013,http://akaademiwolof.seneweb.com/l-rsquo-origine-du-laquo-taajaboon-raquo-version-francaise_b_8.html.

39. *L'Authentique Taajaboon*. Africa 7 TV, Aired October 22, 2015, https://www.youtube.com/watch?v=7Z-Fe27gNuY.

40. The original statement is here: Les sérères Ol qui habitaient le Sine sont venus ici et sont tombés sur la sécheresse. Ils ont pratiqué la danse appelée le 'bawnaan.' Elle était exécutée par les femmes griottes et les esclaves hommes sous un arbre fréquentée par certains dignitaires . . . C'est après avoir dansé qu'une forte pluie est tombée avec beaucoup de ruissellement d'eau. Ils ont dit que 'ndokhmi bawnaan na.'"

See Mohamadou Sagne and Samba Oumar Fall, "Arts et traditions : Baol, un musée à ciel ouvert inexploité," January 16, 2018, http://seneweb.com/news/Culture/arts-et-traditions-baol-un-musee-a-ciel-_n_228428.html.

41. To provide quite an authentic version of this song, I used my own memories of my own participations in taajaboon celebrations and supplemented them with missing words from those from other accounts of the same song. Versions that I found useful was from these sites: Ti-Bahou, le blog," January 16, 2018, http://tibahou.blogspot.com/2010/09/tajabone-chanson-du-monde-2.html; Abdou Khadre Gueye. "L'origine du 'Taajaboon' (Version Française)," January 24, 2013, http://akaademiwolof.seneweb.com/l-rsquo-origine-du-laquo-taajaboon-raquo-version-francaise_b_8.html. Site désactivé.

42. The original statement is here: "Il se peut que le choix du mot 'Tahjabuun' ait été motivé par ce verset où Allah (swt) s'émerveille du décalage entre la gravité du rappel du discours coranique et la distraction dans laquelle les destinataires sont plongés." Abdou Khadre Gueye, "L'origine du 'Taajaboon.'"

43. See Ndèye Fatou Diouf. "Couscous, tajabone, keup, etc.—Quand la tradition l'emporte sur le religieux," November 24, 2012, https://fr.allafrica.com/stories/201211261015.html. Accessed January 19, 2018.

44. Ivy Mills, "Sutura: Gendered Honor, Social Death, and the Politics of Exposure in Senegalese Literature and Popular Culture" (PhD diss., University of California, Berkeley, 2011), 143.

45. The original statement in French is: "[U]ne épouse aimée et comblée, une grande 'diriyanké' . . . entourée d'une cour de thuriféraires, d'hommes-femmes . . . et de griots" (34).See Aminata Sow Fall, *Le Revenant* (Dakar: Les Nouvelles Editions Africaines, 1982), 34.

46. The original quotation is here: "Les uns, re retranchant derrière la naissance, le passé glorieux et le rôle historique des ancêtres, regardaient avec un certain mépris ceux qui ne devaient leur notoriété qu'à l'argent. Ceux-ci pourtant se croyaient les plus fortes, et Yama aussi le croyait, qui vivait chaque jour le paradoxe. Des principes aussi durs que l'acier pouvaient être réduits à néant, et des murailles naguères interdites et infranchissables pouvaient être enjambées au nom de cet idéal matériel qu'on faisait semblant de mépriser." (34–35) See Fall, *Le Revenant*, 34–35.

47. Femi Ojo-Ade, *Being Black, Being Human: More Essays on Black Culture* (Trenton: Africa World Press, 2004), 93.

48. The original quotation is here: "Yama avait battu tous les records. Malobé exultait, la victoire était sienne. et[sic] c'est seulement dans ces atmosphères surchauffées, lorsqu'il avait créé le suspense et fait éclater l'insolite, qu'il se sentait dans son élément, car pour le grand maitre de cérémonies qu'il était, chaque rencontre était un combat et il ne s'agissait pas seulement de le gagner, il fallait terrasser les antagonistes; c'était un duel moral ou la pudeur et la décence exigeaient que l'on fût vainqueur. Et Malobé était toujours vainqueur parce qu'étant au-dessus des calculs et de la mesure." (41–42)
See Fall, *Le Revenant*, 41–42.

49. The original translation is here: "Pour cette cérémonie, elle [Yama] avait fait appel à Malobé Niang, l'homme-femme le plus redoutable, le plus redouté, mais aussi le plus recherché. C'était lui qui agençait les cérémonies des vraies 'diriyanké'; il faisait la fine bouche; rares étaient celles à qui il acceptait d'offrir ses services, car il était exigeant. il[sic] voyait les choses en grand et ne souffrait pas que l'on discutât ses propositions. Toute grande dame cherchait sa compagnie; entrer dans ses faveurs était un gage sur de célébrité." (40)
See Fall, *Le Revenant*, 40.

4

SUCCESSFUL SCHOOLGIRLS

Maintaining Spatial Freedom and Personal Time in Dakar

Amy Porter

While marriage, household, and family management remain markers of adulthood for women in Senegal, young, urban, and school-educated women, who have spent the majority of their lives to date as students, see earning for their (future) children, husband, and mother as critical to their lives. In this study, I examine the lives of educated women, meaning those who have persisted in school, and tie this form of education to ideas of professionalism and potential for earning profit and economically providing for those around them. A central part of this chapter focuses on the ways in which women—particularly those still residing in their natal households—endeavor to maintain their spatial freedom and control of their time. These claims are critical to what the young school-educated women in this study believe they need to continue striving and establishing themselves as earners and to take up the adult roles that such earnings enable. One mechanism for making claims for mobility and time is by participating in non-formal education programs, such as entrepreneurship training (ET). Such ET programs promulgate self-led economic activities which are a means of translating educational attainment to economic prospects, particularly in cases when formal employment fails to materialize.

In this chapter, I examine the endeavors of a selection of young and school-educated women in Dakar, who are active in their pursuit of obtaining both earning and employment—as evidenced by their decision to enroll in an ET course. I specifically explore the unintended positive consequences of ET and how women understand these programs as useful in holding space and time to continue their professional pursuits. Trainees' motivation for, and reflection on, their ET experiences elucidate the economic and professional nature of these young women's desires for their future lives and how their motivations and realities differ from those of young male ET trainees. ET, and arguably similar adult non-formal training spaces—regardless of their curricula—serve an important role in holding space and time for young women. Time in the ET program in this study extended ten months, allowing trainees to pursue professional and earning-related goals in the liminal period before women enter their marital households, at which time they anticipate reduced freedoms of movement and additional domestic burdens.

Young women in the training were nearly all unmarried, without children to care for, and lived in their natal households. Women with these characteristics, who tend to be school-educated and have delayed marriage and childbirth, are held up as exemplars of "successful schoolgirls." Such young women are praised in development programming and policy such as, for example, The Girl Effect and Let Girls Learn, as keys to a multitude of metrics related to community, societal, and global economic and social well-being. However, policies and programs based on this developmental logic have been critiqued by feminist scholars.[1] Discourses that instrumentalize girls' and women's lives in these ways do not tell the stories of how young women themselves view their schooling and post-schooling lives. In this study, I endeavor to shift this perspective by contributing to literature[2] that demonstrates how schooling alters young women's perspectives of how they envision their responsibilities for providing for others, namely in financial ways. I argue that these young women's personal motivations and desires are divergent from gendered expectations that even young women who succeed in school still become adults exclusively through motherhood and managing domestic spaces.

The background and context for this study include both a focus on Dakar and a tracing of global discourses of girls' education, women's economic empowerment, and youth unemployment. Specifically, I examine how urban, school-educated young women embraced training programs. ET was frequently cited as one of many training opportunities pursued, because these programs enable women to maintain spatial freedom and personal time. I also reflect on young men's lives to illuminate the differences in the lives and choices available to them and to young women who train side-by-side in ET.[3]

In this study, I reframe global discourses focused on getting girls to take actions in ways that will serve others by examining how girls who have taken advantage of the growing opportunities to pursue formal and non-formal education reflect on and understand these experiences. Women's desires for their lives are not necessarily at odds with development objectives: higher educational attainment, more freedom of choice in when and whom to marry, and having the power to choose if and when to become mothers. Yet these often-mutual ideas should be understood through young women's lives and experiences, a few of which are elaborated in this chapter.

TIME, SPACE, AND ASKING PERMISSION IN NATAL HOUSEHOLDS

In order to understand young women's economic lives, it is necessary to examine the household structures within which economic rationalities are constructed. Patterns among women whose lives I examine in this research include lower socio-economic status women who reside in medium to large households in poor and middle- or working-class neighborhoods. Often households have at least one member whose regular wage is expected to contribute to monthly expenses. Women's varied situations within their natal or marital household structures influence their sense of self, their desires, and their livelihood considerations. Household structures are thus an important context through which to study women's understanding of their economic livelihoods. Rather than considering market places and household spheres in isolation, I explore how women's situations within their natal and maternal households plays a large role in determining the terms of women's economic participation.[4] Women in this study link spatial freedoms and securing time to participate in public spaces directly to their ability to pursue economic lives of their own design.

Women (and men) are also socially situated by their educational, training, internship, work, business, and commercial engagements; that is, in addition to the central focus on the household, there are several institutions that structure the women in this study's social networks and how their sense of belonging, adulthood, and future claims are understood. The centrality of different institutions, including schools, varies among women who are struggling to transition from being students to young adults who regularly engage in work or an economic activity.

Young men and women in this study are frequently excluded from formal employment in the public and private sectors. As an alternative, the young women in this study who are no longer in school seek permission from their fathers (or, in a few select cases, their husbands) for the space, time, and resources to regularly engage in a commercial activity. School-educated women without a job and who are not "known for" their engagement with a particular economic activity are commonly expected to remain in their households, the effect of which is a reduction in their ability to maintain school-based social networks. This is due to the preference among parents and husbands for women to remain in the household if they do not have specific reasons for being out. Often this translates to women who remain in the household being tasked with increased domestic labor.

Becoming "known for" an economic activity, that is, to become recognized by others as someone who does commerce is thus a pragmatic future outcome for school-educated young women and an important secondary aspiration for the young women in this study. It is important for several reasons, including that women who are "known for" an economic activity are more likely to sell beyond their close network, opening the possibility for more profitable sales, and that women "known for" an activity expect to receive permission to continue it in their marital household. For a young woman without a job, future chances of earning money are heavily dependent on if and how they present themselves as oriented toward becoming "known for" an activity, even if they cannot command the resources to fully take up the type of economic activity they desire.

Without regular and justified reasons to be out in the community, such as schooling, training, or an established economic activity for which they are known, women's social networks center strongly on their household, and they spend much of their time in domestic support roles. In positive natal household settings, women draw on supportive and nurturing household networks to partake in educational and training experiences, sell on behalf of others, take up internships, and search for employment. However, women recognized that moving to their marital household would likely disrupt these freedoms, especially for those who do not have regular personal activities. By taking advantage of their position above in-laws in natal household hierarchies, women strive to find regular occupations of their time, so that they might be "known for" an activity in their natal home that could then be continued into their marital home in order to provide a continued measure of financial independence.

Household socio-economic structures in Dakar are rarely limited to the nuclear family. Several family units might live within the same household. It is therefore possible to examine the varied experiences of unmarried women living with their parents, married women living with their in-laws, and the dynamics between these women. It is often the case that the young women with the most freedom to engage in their own activities are unmarried women who live with their parents, that is, most women in this study. This includes women who are never married, or otherwise live separate from their child or children's father(s), such as the case of women whose husbands live abroad. Women who join the household of their husband are generally responsible for more of the household labor and childcare, including time-intensive tasks such as cleaning and cooking. It is important to note this difference in household labor responsibilities for women who move into their husband's family versus women who still live in their parent's household. Unmarried women living with parents—even when they have a child—generally have lower household responsibilities and understand that they have more freedom to take up education, training, or economic activities in their natal household.

The amount of domestic labor that a woman is responsible for relates to her position in female household hierarchies. Extended family and fictive kinships add complexity to household relationships. Access to resources, such as time, space, and money, within household structures are often controlled by individuals through gender and age hierarchies, and depending on who has occupations that require (permit) them to divert attention from domestic tasks. Even without domestic labor demands, young women lack the freedom to pass time in the city like young men who are expected to go out to earn. Women understand that being perceived by others as staying occupied, or "not doing nothing" (NDN) within one's household, is desirable from a reputational standpoint. But women also want to have a measure of financial independence and therefore aim to be recognized as people who have a legitimate claim to partake in their own personal activities. Examining women's engagements in educational, training, and economic activities, as well as their situation within their households, gives us a window into what it means to apply the socio-economic logics of staying occupied, NDN, for the majority of women in this study who live in their natal households.

METHODS

In this study, I contextualize ideas about why and how critics, particularly Western scholars, have promoted expanding school-based educational opportunities, globally, to all girls. In Dakar, this was particularly salient in the 2000 World Economic Forum, centered on education for all (EFA), which further legitimized ongoing efforts to increase educational access and attainment for girls. Girls' education and the assumed economic empowerment that follows[5] are imperatives supported by international development actors and government ministries of education, including in Senegal. Many actors, especially those in the microfinance sector and supporters of youth entrepreneurship, are keen to support linkages between girls' education and their deepened participation in increasingly formalized economic spheres.[6]

I selected young women in this study based on their participation in an ET program. Entrepreneurship is presented to youths as a gender-neutral process to start an enterprise, which defaults to ideas about entrepreneurs that assume lessons can equally be applied by men and women. Women had moderate educational attainment levels, from some middle school to completing high school; however, few received passing marks on their Baccalaureate (BAC). In this study, I apply ET as a filter through which to identify young men and women in transition from being full-time students to attempting to claim adult spaces in their households and communities. I use ethnography and ethnographic methods to study various ET programs as points of entry to analyze the social construction of ideas about youths' economic livelihoods within and outside of their ET classrooms.

Rather than focusing mainly on economic factors, such as production of goods or monetary gain, I examine economic exchanges that are also valued for non-economically productive reasons. By focusing on what these transactions allow in terms of relationships and social meaning, I examine distributive values, taking up Mains's[7] claim that youths consider employment based on how different types of work shapes their social relationships with others. Jean Lave's[8] reflection on her studies of tailors in Sierra Leone from the 1970s is a good example of research that recognizes the need to situate ethnographic research relationally. She offers that one way to achieve this is by focusing on relationships of exchange in situated contexts, encouraging researchers to examine not only the methods but also how the epistemological foundations of their research can maintain or breakdown established categories. Doing so is a strength of ethnography, which can facilitate "productive disruptions" and "open[ed] a space in which I could produce new knowledge that was neither identical to theirs, nor was it limited by my initial categories and assumptions."[9] This is particularly important when investigating subjects as fluid and broadly conceptualized as entrepreneurship, youth, and gender.

A multifaceted approach was used to identify patterns and understand commonalities across young women's experiences of transitioning from school into their adult lives. Research in Dakar began in the fall of 2013 and extended a total of twenty months. During my first year of research in Senegal, I spent time with female-exclusive urban iterations of village savings and loan (VSL) programs that met weekly in two households in an economically poor suburb of Dakar. Households were women-run during the daytime hours, when men were frequently hustling around the city. Observations, interviews, and focus groups in these household settings later enabled me to ask directed questions to ET trainees about the impact of intra-female household dynamics on: a.

attitudes young women had toward the role of economic activities in their current and future lives, and b. the types of economic activities accessible to women.

In order to explicate various social and institutional relationships that structure individuals' actions and understandings, this research follows a multi-sited ethnographic approach.[10] Informal sector studies commonly reference Marcus's[11] multi-sited ethnographic work as a way to follow connections, associations, and relationships across research sites. Marcus argues that "the object of study is ultimately mobile and multiply situated, so any ethnography of such an object will have a comparative dimension that is integral to it."[12] The value of this type of multi-sited interpretive work is that it allows the researcher to connect what is articulated as significant in one setting with others, eventually situating a particular detail in context so that it can render a broad social pattern visible. This approach of deriving meaning across public and private spaces in the city is key to my analysis of the effects of gender and geography on young women's post-schooling lives.

GENDERED IDEAS ABOUT SCHOOLING AND WORK

A recent body of literature focuses on male experiences of being seemingly stuck in a state of perpetual youth and youthhood in which many young adults are unable to advance to adulthood due to an inability to secure employment.[13] Theories of youthhood connect to larger critiques of time and modernity.[14] The connection to employment is based on an understanding that being recognized as an adult depends largely on one's ability to materially provide for others.[15] Scholars proffering this view include Mains, who observes that "the movement from child to adult may be conceptualized in terms of a shift in one's position within relations of reciprocity,"[16] further arguing that money "shifts one's position within social relationships from one of dependence to offering support to others."[17] While linear progress to adulthood on these terms is unlikely for most, youth strategize ways to integrate themselves as providers, rather than dependents, to the extent they are able.

Fascinatingly, young, school-educated, urban women are relatively dismissed from the masculinized problematizations of youthhood; instead, from the time they are young girls, females are described, targeted, and associated with a mission to improve themselves in prescriptive ways (e.g., staying in school, delaying childbearing and marriage), which are assumed to lead to their economic empowerment, yielding individual and societal benefits. It is critical to note that the older female youth represented in this study have, for the most part, followed the prescriptive pathway to personal and societal change assumed of the contemporary "Third World girl."[18] These young women are grappling with how they can organize their lives around the central questions of what it means to and how they can move from youth to adult. Implicit in that desire is a shift to becoming a provider—materially, relationally, and reproductively—for others. It is tempting, but reductive, to assume that women will shift from youth to adult *on terms that they accept and desire*, only through marriage or childbearing: personal economic livelihoods are intrinsic to ideas of adulthood among the educated young women in this study.

Both young men and women globally, and especially in countries with significant youth demographics and where the availability of private-sector jobs cannot meet demand for employment, regularly face exclusion from formal work and, more broadly, from formal institutions and infrastructures. But, in developmental theorizing, young school-educated men face the problem of youth unemployment, while young women are being school-educated, in increasing numbers and to higher attainment levels[19] *because* their inclusion in school is expected to result in economic outputs that are conceptualized as instrumental to resolving poverty and other developmental ills.[20] Alongside these disparate gendered constructs of the value of schooling and economic empowerment, there is a reoccurring theme that if men's economic livelihoods are stabilized, women will naturally feel the benefit—of being married to these wage-earning or enterprise-owning men.[21]

Women's economic stability has long been assumed to be inherently tied to the men in their lives, in particular, to their father or husband. These lines of reasoning essentially question whether women even need the option of full economic inclusion, framing the current "masculinity crisis" such that improving young men's experiences will ripple to the proximate young women in their lives.[22] Schultz[23] points out the fallacy in this thinking: "A women's sense of economic and emotional instability does not stop with marriage. She rightly fears that her husband might take a second wife (in case he does not already have more than one wife) which would further diminish the resources on which one wife may lay claim."[24] Other scholars take a similar stance. Calvés and Depledge[25] and Honwana[26] agree that women's ability to attain full adult status depends on men moving beyond waithood, that is, dependent men being willing and financially able to marry them. More recently, Calvés[27] questions this link, noting how marriage in West Africa is undergoing significant change, particularly in urban areas where increasing numbers of men and women cohabitate without formally marrying. This potentially raises concerns over women's greater need for their own means to economic stability, as "a female cohabiter remains a 'stranger' to her partner's family and a single woman in the eyes of her own family."[28] Growth in women-headed households and ongoing economic insecurity that women often continue to face in marriage[29] disrupt claims that helping young men to attain economic security intrinsically helps young women.

While these studies do rightly confirm the real cultural significance of marriage and motherhood, they leave no room for women to even aspire to become adults in any independent or alternative ways, for example, in financially independent, childless, and non-heteronormative relationships, and so on. Men cannot be adults until they have a source of income, and build a household, initiate marriage, and so on. But women cannot be adults until they engage in roles of submitting themselves and their bodies to others. Given that perpetual youthhood reflects an increasingly extended phase, the social, cultural, and economic realities of women's everyday lives; that is, what women deem significant to their social and economic well-being, must be considered alongside, but not in subordination to, men's experiences of youthhood.

For women, reaching the status of adult has historically hinged on marriage and children, meaning that women, in theory, have alternative (non-economic) ways of shifting from being dependent to providing for others. In Senegal, married women's financial contributions to their household continue to be viewed as "helping husbands" rather than women "doing their share" to contribute to household expenses.[30] While women may have more avenues to non-financially providing for others, their ability to take on the status of provider is facilitated by discretion over financial spending, which makes youths' ability to earn important across genders. Young, educated women in Dakar have social and economic needs and desires, apart from those connected to men and marriage. Women's desire for personal economic livelihoods must be examined, because of, not despite, the common increase in domestic responsibilities expected of young women's post-schooling when they are unable to attain regular work or take up additional training opportunities.

Studies of youthhood assume (often correctly) that women do not experience the same boredom as men, since domestic responsibilities increase for young women who are no longer students. Women who leave school early in their lives (or never attended) often are tasked with heavy domestic workloads, and may also, or alternatively, accompany female relations in their daily social and economic labors. In these cases, women may learn to buy and sell, transform cereals, or other small-scale activity for which they might become known in their household and community. Women with higher levels of educational attainment should, in theory, be able to better execute the technical side of identifying and exploiting economic opportunities. However, women with higher scholastic achievement are in some ways at a disadvantage in starting up a small-scale economic opportunity because they lack social recognition as independent economic actors. They are known as school-educated women rather than as "vendors of X," which has implications for the domestic and economic labor they are expected to perform in their household and community. Shifting to become "known for" an economic activity became a preoccupation of these young (unmarried) women, as this reflected a path to a measure of economic independence apart from waiting to secure a job.

Literature on girls' experience in schools demonstrates that while in school, girls attribute a variety or meanings and expectations to their scholastic efforts and related expectations for their post-schooling lives.[31] Kendall and Kaunda[32] find that female primary school students "talked about experiencing what we might call the 'education double shift,'"[33] being tasked with domestic work in addition to schooling. However, older female elementary students and secondary school students reflect on how their student status plays a role in "providing protection from adult demands on their labor and their transition from 'childhood' to marriage and motherhood."[34] However, this protection afforded by school was "an extension, but not a transformation, of their post-schooling opportunities and life paths."[35] In other words, girls who persist; that is, successful schoolgirls, distance themselves from expectations of domestic work during the time they are students.

With increasingly higher levels of educational attainment, women tie their future hopes to their roles as earners rather than providing for others through domestic roles. In Dakar, young women in this study who advanced further in school shift how they talk about their current and expected future roles. They speak little of domestic responsibilities in their natal household, focusing instead on strategizing ways to maximize their spatial mobility in the city and methods to hold time to develop their professional and economic engagements. These women seek ways to become adults who can economically provide for others.

Women Desire to Take on Provider Roles

When talking with young people in Dakar, they often express a need to begin their working lives, to become responsible for themselves, to support their needs, and to assist with supporting the needs of others where they can. Many had begun to think about how they could support other family members, and especially their parents. For women with children, there is a particular concern with how they can support their children, notably in financing their children's education. Additionally, for the young women who are the primary research informants for this study, whether married, single, with or without children, all feel an obligation and desire to provide financial support to their own mothers and to financially provide for others more broadly. Men and women report that money that an adult son or daughter provides directly to their mother is especially critical in cases where a young adults' mother has experienced a loss or decrease in financial support from her husband. Youths' desire to financially support their mothers particularly arises in the case of their mother's divorce, their mother's husband taking on an additional wife, or other financial instability related to their mother's, or her husband's, socio-economic standing.[36]

However, across certain categories of young adults, specifically among unmarried women, attempts to hold or save money were often seen as acting against or delaying taking on the financial responsibilities of care for their mother, or, for unmarried men, care for their mother and female relations. They and their families recognize that beyond meeting one's basic needs, these relations should be the recipients of any financial or material resources they obtain. With the exception of one unusually independent woman who lived apart from her family, and who gave back to her household and community in many other ways, women directly described their desire and eagerness to contribute financially to others in their household. Because women's economic activities are most commonly initiated within or in close proximity to their household, their earnings are subject to greater surveillance than young men who often go out into the city to earn.

SCHOOLING, TRAINING, AND HOLDING SPACE

Despite their desire to be recognized as providers in their households and communities, the young women in this study have extremely limited financial resources which restrict their ability to materially contribute to household economic structures. However, women in their natal households leveraged their participation in educational experiences as a means of continuing to assert themselves within their households as socio-economically active individuals. In this, they added to their professional skill set and signaled that they were not yet ready for marriage. In doing so, these women demonstrated that they were productive and "not doing nothing" (NDN), laying the foundation to be seen as contributors to the household, and position themselves to make demands of others in their households.

Among women who sustain a trajectory through school, other training experiences, or internships, being female is not something they consider a major factor in whether (or not) they are able to advance to additional educational or economic opportunities. They feel that access is mainly dictated by who has grades that secure them a place at Université Cheikh Anta Diop (UCAD), who can secure monthly payments for advanced training, or who can network their connections to enroll in municipal training programs or work opportunities. Trainings, such as the ET program in this study, are important opportunities for women to spend time away from home and to, even if only temporarily, engage in expanded networks.

Women in this study who live in their natal homes speak of the relative ease of asking their father's or guardian's permission to engage in a project or activity outside their home. These women take advantage of their largely school-based social networks to claim a need for personal time and space, and ideally for a job, before they move into their marital household. Women with whom I engaged for this study express their preference for starting their own activity before marriage because negotiating for freedom of movement and time is more easily granted by a woman's parents. Fathers, whose permission is often required for women to engage in activities outside the home, are considered more apt (than husbands) to encourage their daughters to partake in educational or economic experiences. Receiving permission from a husband is less sure. Women understand that even if one's husband is very supportive, his family might influence him to be restrictive with his wife. Women in the husband's family have more say in the division of household labor than women who marry into the household. What this means in practice is that while it is not uncommon for a husband to support his wife's desire to partake in an economic opportunity, even by giving her money to start, this is never sure to be accepted by the other women in the household.

Women who are still in professional or tertiary school reflect on their families' investments in their education. One woman says, "All the time I have been at school! I will not leave it now! . . . with all my parents have invested in my studies, if someone comes from the other side that I don't know well, and tells me I must quit, I would not accept that." Additionally, she continued, in an exaggerated tone, "If I stop my studies my mother will kill me. . . . it's my grandmother that raised me. In the whole family no one has studied to this level, so each time they say I am the family intellectual, so if one day a husband says I have to stop. Oh, my mother will kill me!"

Another woman similarly speaks of the sacrifices made by her family to support her education, explaining that "my parents have not gone to school, my father is an electrician, my mother did not go to school, and each time they tell me the only thing they want is that I work to meet my own needs so that I am not like them, it's that which motivates me." Unlike the unknown character of one's future husband, parents are more likely to be permissive and encouraging of their school-educated daughter's aspirations, granting them relatively wider freedoms in order for them to move toward their goals. However, once the progression from school to an alternative activity that requires some level of movement in the city is broken, negotiation is required to take up a new opportunity. It also means that the question of marriage becomes a more immediate and logical next step for young women.

A common theme of uneven progress, of starting and stopping, marks the educational and economic experiences of many of the young people with whom I met in conducting this study. Men and women recounted the different economic activities and educational experiences they had undertaken, with high expectations, and described their serious efforts and sacrifices to succeed. But issues including monthly tuition payments and monthly business expenses force people to temporarily abandon their pursuit of various activities. And, despite a commonly expressed desire to pick back up at some time in the future, there is a pattern of varied circumstances that often force people to stop short of realizing their objectives. This sporadic nature of access to personal activities, earning, and having money, more gravely affected women, as restarting required re-negotiating permissions. But both men's and women's ability to make a straightforward movement toward goals is clearly affected by constant starting and stopping due largely to irregular flows of money, as well as other conditional impediments.

Leaving school does not necessarily signify an end to women's formal educational experiences. For those with access to money, one could still pursue private or public-private professional training programs. However, leaving school does mark a transition to a more unstable path through a combination of private, public, and non-governmental training experiences.

POSITION OF ET AND OTHER NON-FORMAL EDUCATION PROGRAMS

While literature is scarce on educated women in developing countries' motivation for post-schooling non-formal education, and training, the women in this study were clear in their desire to be recognized as students again. This desire was integral to their multiple reasons for participating in ET. It also reflects women's struggle to make sense of their economic exclusion after following the path of schooling that was supposed to lead to economic inclusion. Examples of women seeking to both extend their educational experiences and shield against economic exclusion can be found in apprenticeship programs that women might enter after formal schooling ends. Langevang and Gough[37] describe the aspirational goals of young women who reflect on their desire for professional work (e.g., secretary, journalist, newscaster) while they were in school, but after having left school, and being unsuccessful in securing work, come to conclude that there are many forms of good work (e.g., hairdressing, or less desirably, dressmaking). Notably, women in Langevang and Gough's study and the women on whose lives this study is based, enter apprenticeship programs after they leave school in order to keep them effectively away from home and in pursuit of economic opportunities. Langevang and Gough also find that women who are unable to establish themselves in these trades might then "leave the vocation in search of other income-generating opportunities, often in petty trading."[38] An important thread in these young women's lives, and the examples of training experiences below, are that women seek to maintain educational opportunities or income-generating work that can justify time spent away from their household.

Professional and Alternative Trainings

Trainings generally required small monthly payments, and many women reached a point at which they could not pay the monthly fee and left the training prior to completing it in full. Because trainings and education require monthly fees, they are not well-suited to common female-managed savings or rotating credit groups. In Senegal, there are several different types of women-organized rotating credit systems, which, in French, are called *tontines* (Wolof, *natt*). Each has multiple ways that money is collected and distributed. Commonly, money is pooled together, and then immediately redistributed according to the group's arrangements. While these useful systems of savings and credit are important, they do not facilitate monthly payments required for most trainings. This means that access to these opportunities usually depends on a woman being given money each month, often from a male relation.

Apprenticeships were another way to gain experience in a trade. This path is more common among women who leave school much earlier than women whom I met through their participation in an ET program. However, women noted the challenge in securing a non-exploitative apprenticeship. Those who did find reliable master teachers sometimes learned that their artisanal master had left the neighborhood or city unexpectedly, in which case the apprentice was unable to complete their training. Once an apprenticeship ended (before its scheduled completion), women tended to shift their focus to other, often reselling, opportunities.

Access to non-governmental trainings, such as the ET programs observed in this study, frequently depended on wide social networks or chance encounters. For some, ET represented a place to shift their focus after having left school. As one trainee reflected, "last year I took the test [BAC]; this year the results came out and I did not pass. I need to redo that year, but I decided that I will no longer go there to do it again. Now, I am focused on the training." Multiple trainees informed me that they had completed similar ET programs in the past. They believed that another (even repetitive) training might "complete" or deepen what they had already learned. It might also provide another credential that could advance their CV over that of another applicant when searching for a job. Another woman described her motivation to enroll in the ET program, saying that "studies never end. One must always restart, have other objectives, know other things, new things, meet with new people." There were many potential paths when one fell short of the future imagined during the years spent in school. Entrepreneurship was presented in trainings as ownership of a large enterprise that would meet a community need and employ others, thereby providing a service to society. Being an economically successful entrepreneur was another desirable future path. However, young women's multiple pathways became blocked after formal educational and training experiences ended. Women who completed an ET program were acutely aware of the time-sensitive nature of their desire to take up work or an activity for which they were known in their natal household and community.

Outside of official work and school structures, socio-cultural expectations rule over economic practices and most facets of women's lives. In general, studies of women's post-schooling lives demonstrate that "post-school lives became a signal of how little their efforts could accomplish in the face of deep structural constraints and inequities."[39] When school-educated women are compared to girls with low-educational attainment who are at the same age as the female ET participants in this study, often these women are known in their families and communities for their engagement in specific economic activities or for their domestic roles. School-educated women are seen as students or professionals, which challenges their ability to be recognized for their small-scale economic work. Efforts to expand educational opportunities to all women must recognize how this positive change will shift and complicate the lives and sense-making of many women who complete their education, sometimes with training and professional development, but are then excluded from economic opportunities.

WOMEN'S SPATIAL ARRANGEMENT IN THE CITY

Young women's formal schooling and post-school education and training experiences highlight that beyond earning, women first struggle to continue justifying their need for spatial mobility and time to take on professional and personal activities. Developmental efforts, such as those that suggest entrepreneurship is equally accessible to men and women, often fail to fully consider that women's lives remain ordered by their social situations. This includes both in the broader patriarchal society and in terms of female-hierarchies within their households. It is within these multiple contexts that young women's engagement with small-scale economic activities, the social expectations of these activities and how discourses around their work, space, and economic practices are constructed. These spaces also demonstrate that women's abilities to do things and be able to move through the city are often vastly different from those of young men. There are heavy social impositions on movement and visibility that restrict women's economic abilities, especially for educated women who are relatively unknown for small-scale economic work in their communities.

Those studying economic activities in gendered urban space commonly associate "going out" with men seeking employment, which, in practice, is often small-scale hustling or day labor,[40] and "staying home" with women in the domestic sphere. Jarvis, Cloke, and Kantor argue that inequitably gendered urban spaces are due to "the (false) separation of discrete functions of production, consumption and social reproduction . . . [arguing that] in the global south the household itself is a vital source of production and here there is a complete erosion of the boundaries between livelihood and household, spatially, physically, and economically."[41] Their claim is taken up in this study, as the household proved to be an important space for women's social, economic, and political lives.

Women experience significant restrictions on their movement in urban spaces, which undercuts their ability to access deeply desired work or other means of personal income. Drawing from his research in India, which is also resonant in Senegal, Craig Jeffrey states, "young women were typically unable to participate in the types of public timepass in which young men engaged . . . Parents, professors, and urban society at large considered it inappropriate for unmarried young women to 'hang out,' except in certain public spaces."[42] Restrictions on where and when women are socially sanctioned to spend time meant that "men often dominate commerce in public places. [Meanwhile,] Women tend to operate canteens in the home and conduct more invisible[43] businesses."[44]

The study of poverty and economic engagements of urban women must not be limited to public spaces. It must also investigate what happens in the private spaces. Women find their time highly constrained in their natal households, yet they also expect increased demands on their time in their marital household.[45] This means that the time available for women to seek employment is extremely limited. In contrast to young men, "young women who were expected to perform large amounts of housework never complained of excessive unstructured time."[46] For women in Dakar, who, at marriage, enter their husband's household, the dynamics and hierarchies among women in the household greatly impacted economic livelihoods. The household "can be a site of security and belonging as well as of violence, oppression, alienation and asymmetrical gender relations, perhaps especially where women are under the jurisdiction of extended families as well as husbands."[47] Inequities in city spaces, both public and private, in which women spend their time greatly impact women's "choice" to participate in economic and other accessible activities.

GENDER, EARNING, AND SOCIAL RESPECT

Visible striving to meet one's own needs is revered in the turbulent, challenging city of Dakar. Everyone who is able is expected to demonstrate that they are socio-economically active, and one means of demonstrating this is engaging in small-scale business and commerce opportunities. Even in cases where these activities are unsuccessful at generating profits, these efforts are still respected and ensure that individuals maintain positive ties to their households and communities. A woman describes her belief that even financially unsuccessful businesses are worth pursuing, noting that, "It's good for me. Because I say that in life you do not need to always depend on others. To know how to fight in order to have one's own activities [is good]. Even if you do not gain, to have a preoccupation allows you to free yourself from stress, solitude, from things like that." In essence, to fail to even be recognized as striving toward economic gains, and then ask others for assistance, was universally disrespected behavior.

Young people who are trying to support themselves and to begin aiding their maternal families, even if unsuccessfully, are well regarded in society. This community support, even for menial work, is demonstrated by displays of encouragement that young people receive from their neighbors. It is not uncommon for young men and women who are doing the difficult work of selling door-to-door to be invited into a potential customer's home, particularly in economically stable, middle-class households, and to be given food or drink and time to sit and rest. The efforts of these young men and women are generally highly respected by the communities where they sell. These types of door-to-door sales, visible and ambulant commerce, do not fit into idealized conceptions of work, but are respected in that they orient one toward NDN.

While these activities are respected, they seldom result in significant earnings. Men often state their belief that their earnings are more important (than women's earnings) to themselves, to their families, and to their communities—an attitude of greater importance that is not agreed on by young women. Men feel they need to earn more than could usually be accomplished with women's close-to-home activities; to them, it is critical that they go out into the city and "do business." The potential to earn money, and thus, respect, is the ubiquitous motivation driving how men perceive their need for engaging in varied economic activities. Men explain that their work is more important because it is vital that they meet their economic needs. For example, one man expressed his gendered vision of the significance of men's earnings saying, "in terms of women. There are those who work and those who do not work, it's the same. . . . But, because all men have needs, . . . and if you don't work you need to ask, or do other things [reference to particular types of illicit trade, e.g., drugs and alcohol]. Then you lose your respect." Men usually frame their responses as a question of respect. "If you work you will gain respect, [people] won't see you sitting there, asking to have your needs met. You are responsible for your own actions."

Women also connect respect to their own economic activities, but most women emphasize that what is important to maintain the respect of others is not being idle. Indeed, women tend to describe the significance of their being seen as economically active in relation to their lack of need to rely on others, for their personal satisfaction, and because of a desire to not appear idle. For women, this means that those who gain money from non-outwardly visible sources, often become targets of questioning about their morality, regardless of how they use their resources. Since men's economic exchanges are more often with those outside their close networks, if they gain from these exchanges in ways that benefit them over others, this was hidden from their close relations' view and possible scrutiny. However, women, who operate with greater visibility, and among close relations—people with whom they would likely have life-long ties, rationally factor the long-term reciprocal value of their relationship with a potential customer into their commercial exchanges. Women are less likely than men to say that they need to be able to make money to give to others, but they are much more likely to say that it matters that they become "known for" an activity. This sheds light on how gender relations impact the moral norms influencing women's and men's economic activities. Women's reputations rest in large part on the visibility of their activities. While men who go out and make money among loose ties are valued by those around them for the act of going out regardless of how these exchanges are enacted.

Youth value and measure their belonging in their households and communities by whether they can take on the adult roles of providing for those in their close networks. Since few youths are able to fully take up provider roles, these remain aspirational for young people. In practice, older youths contribute by redistributing from the little they gain in order to demonstrate their desire to provide for others. For example, one woman formerly had regular work assisting a woman in her neighborhood with her catering business. From her earnings, she had given generously to those in her relational network as well as neighbors in her community. She lost this job after a few years, but still regularly received demands from others who knew her as someone who worked. In addition to her earnings from work, she had always received a small remittance from a male family member living in France. Since losing her job, despite her reduced financial position, she divides the small amount of money she receives in remittances and gives what she can to those who ask. Although she has little to give, this woman's efforts to provide for others maintain her respected position in her household and community.

For women, the ability to earn respect is grounded in their household and extended family networks. Within these networks, women can be respected for their contributions to household labor or their engagement in their own economic activities. Describing a woman who occupies her time with household work, one female ET trainee explains that, "even if she doesn't do anything we should respect her for many things. Also, before I did commerce, people respected me." Often women's reselling efforts effectively subsidize goods to others within their networks, which brought its own form of respect. However, similar to Robertson's[48] findings in her study of dried staples (mainly bean) traders in Nairobi, women see value in the freedom and measured independence derived from their commerce activities, whereas men do not attribute these positive traits to their participation in trade.

While domestic labor, economic work, or a combination of paths can lead them to be respected in their family and community, women desire their own economic activities for the agency it gives them over some of their personal decisions. Having their own money also enables them to provide, even in small ways, for those around them. There is also a tangible need to acquire at least a small amount of money to support quotidian needs. One woman in this study explains that, for her, "with sales, the benefit is that I can meet my needs without demanding of others. It is a pleasure to be able to meet my own needs without asking from others." Whereas men also describe a similar desire to not rely on others, women express the need to be seen as economically active as an explicit means to acquire and maintain the respect of others.

Again, referencing the importance of orienting oneself as NDN, one woman advises other young women that "even if the sales don't have a benefit, the important thing is that you cannot sit and do nothing, to get up and do something; that is satisfying." Satisfying encompasses both meanings of pragmatic financial gain, as well as gaining respect from others. But, as one woman surmises, "in a world where everyone is occupied with their own problems, you need to find your own work to satisfy your own needs . . . go to market and sell veggies or fish, or work as domestic. At least that allows a gain."

When I asked female ET participants what advice they would give to other young women, having themselves participated in a training designed to promulgate the benefits of self-led economic activities, they encourage all young women to do something. That "something" is not predicated on planning and starting up a business, but rather on simply taking advantage of opportunities to NDN, which would ideally also allow for financial gain, whenever an honest means of making money is available.

Some men express negative opinions of what they feel is women's propensity to not be willing to take on small or menial work. For example, one man, whom I interviewed in French, switched into Wolof to say, "Because the women are lazy, in general they cannot have money. . . . they are easily discouraged if there is not money involved. Men, they say, 'I am a man I must have work,' but women they say, 'I prefer to wait.' Women are lazy . . . women have a complex against doing certain types of work." However, these peer-aged men are either unaware or unwilling to consider what might lead women to undertake various kinds of economic activities (or chose not to).

For women, being considered NDN is broader than how it is understood for men because their activities are valued even if not profitable. However, their activities are also narrower than men's because they need to be visible to others in their family and community. Women understand the multiple risks and opportunities of engaging in commerce within their relational networks and think a lot about their social and economic responsibilities to their families. All female participants, regardless of where they live and whether or not they have children, seek ways to become or remain economically active in their social, generally household-centered, relational networks. Men root their sense of NDN on whether they go "out" in search of work or other means of financial gain. Their activities are not necessarily visible, certainly not to their household networks, and therefore judgment and respect within men's households are based on whether or not they made efforts to bring money into their close networks.

BEING "KNOWN FOR" AN ACTIVITY

Young women aimed to develop an activity which they were "known for" in their community because this would provide them with a small source of income, integrate them into credit and debt (reciprocal) exchanges with others in their relational network, and give them the permission to continue an activity they are "known for" in their marital household. This study is different than the many studies that investigate the lives of women who have relatively stable micro or small-scale economic activities.[49] Studies focus on the types of activities women do, how they organize their activities, if and how women access microcredit, whether their activities are profitable if they employ others, and other operational characteristics. The intent here is a descriptive and analytical presentation of a different category of young, educated, urban women who are grappling with questions of who they are as adults, in many cases trying to define themselves in ways that allow them to continue to be recognized as NDN now that they are no longer positively revered as students.

Despite limited personal resources, women who do not have their own economic activity strategically integrate themselves within their household structures in order to support the social and economic well-being of their households. The above sections argue that women in their natal households strive to NDN by targeting multiple training, educative, and selling activities, as encouraged by others and based on their own interest, in order to ideally secure a job or become recognized for an occupation. All the while, women recognize that during post-education and after training, they are operating in a limited time window between completing their education and marriage. Women in this study express a strong desire to delay marriage until they secured a job, or, more likely, became "known for" an activity.

Negotiating an Activity into Marriage

Women recognized the importance of "what they carry" or claim ownership of when they enter into their marital homes, that is, existing work or self-led economic activities for which they are recognized in their community. This includes activities for which a woman is "known" as described above. For most women, the time they dedicate to labor in their natal household is significant but irregular. Women understand that they will most likely be required to take on more domestic work in their marital households. Therefore, having an economic activity that is recognized by others in the household makes it more certain that they will have the time and resources free from domestic work to continue their existing economic activity.

Pre-marital agreements made between a couple could be in perfect harmony, but what the couple decides is enacted in his family's household, whose influence affects the new wife's ability to draw on such an arrangement. In particular, women of the husband's family have real power over a woman who enters the household as wife of their son or brother. One woman articulates the power struggles within a household:

> The husband might accept, but sometimes there is a whole family behind him that influences him. The in-laws, "because in Senegal we say that women should stay at home," in the in-law family, family can say that a woman who only moves [works] spends all their time away from home, doesn't do housework, cooking, etc., your husband might understand, but at the level of the family, his mother or his sisters might influence your husband, to say that a woman who doesn't clean the house or cook doesn't care for you. A woman who is always on the move, that is not a good wife. Even if you husband understands, that could influence him or lead him to change his mind. At a certain time, he may be frustrated with you. But, a relationship must

> be based on confidence and comprehension. If you have good communication with your husband, that would have less risk. But really sometimes it is the family that causes problems.

Her statement speaks to the often-contested space of labor sharing arrangements in multiple-generation extended-family households where age, gender, and hierarchy factor into decisions regarding household work. Commonly, women mention that cooking schedules are divided among women in the household.[50] On days when a woman is responsible for the main midday meal, she does not have time for her own activities. Women explain their activities in terms of this schedule, saying, "if not my turn to cook, I might do other work, sell small things, and do hair braiding for people." Those who are involved in irregular buying and selling can sell from home, door-to-door, or possibly in the market on days when they are not responsible for cooking.

A woman whose economic activities require her to leave the household for long periods of time, or to work within the household, but toward the production of her own goods is naturally unable to contribute the same time to household labor. Women foresaw domestic complications with waiting to begin work until after marriage, as one woman expresses:

> We are in Africa and we have customs [values]. If you marry and stay at home, you do all the housework. If one day you find work and you start working your husband's family could see that you have changed, because you can no longer do the same work at home. So they could say that you changed, because you didn't have work and were doing housework, and now that you work you cannot do housework. To avoid that, I prefer to work and then get married.

The ability to claim time and space to engage in an economic activity is a contested space for women entering their conjugal family in the tight quarters of Dakar.

Women shared many examples that similarly highlight the intra-household balance of domestic work and freedom to engage in income-generating activities. One woman describes her ambition to work. "I say that I must work without fail to have my own business before marriage. If you marry there are the house activities. Could you realize that [your business] within the household? But if I start, for me, I think that I will continue [my business]; that [household demands] will not be a blockage."

The common objective of securing a regular occupation of one's time, as well as a source of income, is paramount to women as they describe the role of economic activities in their current and future lives. The scale or formality of such activity was less important. Reiterating the significance of NDN, women noted that "the essential is that it is an activity." And, that the activity begins "before the marriage, because . . . if your husband finds you doing any type of activity, they cannot prohibit that activity because they have found you doing it, whether it is formal or informal." Women who attain higher levels of education, and continue to NDN through trainings and other educational experiences particularly focus on legitimizing themselves economically and being sure "not to stay at the house doing nothing."

This research includes participants from a wide range of demographic backgrounds, and women at different life stages, however, what is common among female participants is the increased financial burdens women face when they have children. Women know that their need for money will become acute at the moment they become mothers, whether married or unmarried. Mothers need money for their children's upbringing and education as they are ultimately responsible for child-related costs. Husbands often aim to contribute to their children's education, however, changes in their circumstances, whether related to their earnings or other life changes, such as a second wife and her children, may disrupt a husband's contribution toward any of their children's education. One woman explains this saying:

> Because men cannot do everything, and they have the right to up to four wives, and if you are with a guy who already has two wives and with your children's education, you could want your child to do a training and you ask your husband to pay. That [request], he could refuse saying, "you are two [wives] in the household and I did not do for your co-wife's child, so I cannot do for your child." And, in that case if you work and have means you can just seek his authorization and pay for your child's education.

Similarly, women cannot assume stable household maintenance support even in the optimal case where a husband is wealthy. Enlisting moral language to argue the need for economic independence, women observe that, even if one's husband was wealthy, for a woman "to be there always waiting with your hand extended [for him to give to you], that is not good." Also, in part, women desire independent sources of income even within a marriage because often financial instability continues, and sometimes increases in marriage. Women desire, and often need, to attain financial independence even within marriage in order to ensure that their primarily cited concerns, their children's welfare, and education, as well as support for their mother's needs, are covered. Despite all women in this study expressing an absolute desire to marry, and marriage remaining an important marker of adulthood, many women have a strong underlying distrust of placing their financial security in the hands of their husband. Money held by one's husband could go toward a second wife, his mother, sisters, or be spent on his own needs, women feel that the only way to ensure that their own needs are met is to depend on themselves and manage their own money. Aminata, a woman who is among the most independent of those in this study, lives apart from her family in a shared room with a female colleague. She explains:

> I can say that I am not a dependent woman, I will not depend on my parents or my husband. It's been a long time since I was dependent on my family, maybe one of my brothers helps me a little from time to time, but otherwise I do my own business to satisfy my needs. And I say that even after marriage, if I have a husband I will not depend on him. If he wants to help me he can help me with my own project, ok, but in another case, I will do my own work if I need to. . . . Here, men do not know how to share, they don't even tell their wife their salary, they say that once they tell their wife their salary their wife will claim control of it all. It's rare to see men who say to their wife "at the end of the month I have this much money."

Women who are not yet married are passionate in their explanations of why they feel it is so important for them to have their own work before marriage. One woman explains her desire to have her own work, saying:

> With work you have your money and you do not have to have confidence in him. He has his work and you have your work. You do not ask him for anything. You are married but you do not ask for anything, you manage your children because the guys in Senegal here, when they know that you do not have work, in one year of marriage, they will have a second wife and after they will give you nothing at all, it's you who needs to start out. Manage your home and your children. It's for that that I want to have my own work and manage my house and my mother when I have a husband.

She continues, saying that it is important that her work begins before she marries because one's husband could equally accept or refuse his wife's request to start an economic activity. However, if a woman is already actively engaged in a particular economic activity, she "carried" this activity with her into marriage. Another woman articulates this point noting, "I want it to be before the marriage, because there it's forced that he cannot, even if he wants to he cannot come and say to stop because he found you in the midst of doing that, so it's easier. . . . you have power to say you found me sitting [economically active], so I prefer you let me continue like that." An existing activity, or a job, which one is "known for," is considered a valuable negotiation piece toward a women's economic independence within her marriage. All husbands (or their families) will not accept their wives to start up a new activity.

Although young unmarried women widely recognize that securing permission from their fathers to engage in training, other educational experiences, or an economic activity is much more assured, fathers are unwilling to wait indeterminately for their daughters to find work before marriage. Specifically, once a daughter's education, including schooling and any professional training, was complete, there is a limited period in which it is considered reasonable for daughters to put off marriage in order to search for work or to start up their own activities. Continuous demonstration of NDN, whether through an activity, or ET, is important to women's ongoing extra-household associations. Yet, some women consider the unlikely nature of starting a regular economic activity or finding stable work, and are themselves only willing to put off marriage for a short while.

Women realize that there are multiple paths to meeting the goal of securing some level of financial independence and their ability to provide for others. Some women note that a husband could be the key to networks or financial resources that might enable a woman to start up an activity. "There are husbands who help. That if you have nothing [no activity] they will give you something [to help you start]." While most women agree that they face mounting pressure from their families to marry even before they are able to find a regular source of income, they are variously optimistic that the right marriage could mean finding a husband who would help them to start up an activity.

What is evident in young people's strategies and practices is that individuals, especially women, often consider their options for economic activities in the context of their social networks, which heavily center on extended family relationships, and their situation within their household. Women learn from their initial commerce experiences, which begin little by little, as they start to identify and strategize how to take up regular activities that they can become "known for."

Despite vastly different socio-economic statuses among research participants, the types of self-led economic activities performed by female participants are very similar. While in school, progress toward imagined futures seems possible. Yet, within households post-schooling, it seemed that some women had spent many years in school while others became "known for" their regular engagement in various economic activities. As soon as women are out of school, if they do not remain NDN by taking up "tangential trajectories"—that is, additional educational or training opportunities, internships, a job, or a self-led economic activity—they are perceived by their household as "doing nothing" and tasked with more domestic labor, or otherwise expected to remain within the household. While women are respected for their household labor, they are not recognized as someone who is NDN. This means that subsequent opportunities to attend trainings, start an activity, and even their visibility in a variety of community spaces diminish. School-educated women are often less known for an activity than is someone less educated who has, for years, been regularly engaged in an economic activity.

Given women's greater challenge versus men in taking up new opportunities once their schooling is completed, when expectations of marriage and children become more immediate, the pattern of starting and stopping trainings or small-scale economic activities, is particularly problematic. For men, taking large risks was more acceptable, as they were more readily able to stop, regroup, and restart an activity in the future. For most women, with the exception of those whose households are unusually permissive, being regularly engaged in an activity or experience outside the household is far more important to secure the chance to continue to take new opportunities—be it schooling, training, economic activities, and so on. In natal households, the question of marriage came up when a woman transitioned from personal activities to greater domestic responsibilities (or time otherwise spent in the household). Women in their natal households are especially keen to take advantage of all potential opportunities as they recognize that they currently had fewer domestic responsibilities and financial burdens than their married female friends and relations have. For young, educated, urban women in their natal households, this liminal stage was one in which they sought to become "known for" self-led economically generative work, all the while maintaining aspirations to secure formal sector work before marriage.

The assumption that education will necessarily lead to economic outcomes for women, and that economic earnings necessarily indicate economic empowerment, must be continually challenged. It is not enough to see that women achieve higher educational outcomes, without bridges to earning opportunities and recognize how this alters dynamics among women within households. Many women within a household are, in essence, competing for space and time to enact economic activities. Increasing women's freedom to move in the city must be paired with men's recognition and willingness to take up household responsibilities in order to give women more opportunity to make choices about how they manage their economic lives. The dynamic of women "staying in" and men "going out" limits the possible arrangements that would better serve young men and women in their social and economic pursuits along more equitable terms.

Non-formal educational opportunities, such as ET, help young educated women to maintain space to exercise economic roles—which is important in these women's lives. Research on economic activities often centers on economic outcomes, but closer investigation elucidates that for women, household negotiations are conducted alongside technical business decisions. One must first understand the context in which negotiations are undertaken within women's social lives that impact who can start a business, how they can do so, and under what geographic and material restrictions. Non-formal adult education programs, such as ET, provide spaces in which young women have space to strategize and navigate the social permissions which will then allow space for them to become "known for" an activity, and to have a measure of technical training with which to operate when these hard-earned economic spaces materialize.

Education, even when technical and pragmatic in nature, does not necessarily link to economic outcomes; however, it does change the way that young people see themselves—increasing the desirability and acceptability of earning and providing for others. For women whose educational access and attainment has expanded greatly following nearly two decades of focused global efforts to expand access to girls' education, the shift to educated women defining their adult lives not only as domestic laborers, good wives, and mothers, but also as educated, professional, adults who provide for others, is an expanding category affecting gender dynamics between men and women in Senegal and beyond. Education, with the goal of economic empowerment, raises questions of what is socially and culturally considered to be "appropriately desirable" for young women in terms of economic independence? How can female intra-household dynamics and the limited urban spaces women currently occupy be reconstructed to support young and educated women to achieve socio-economic success on their own terms? And, in what ways can non-formal educational spaces play a role in enabling women to achieve what they desire in their economic and social lives?

BIBLIOGRAPHY

Appadurai, A. *Modernity at Large: Cultural Dimensions of Globalization*. Minneapolis and London: University of Minnesota Press, 1996.

Bâ, Mariama. *So Long a Letter [Une Si Longue Lettre]*. Translated by Modupe Bode-Thomas. Long Grove, IL: Waveland Press, Inc, 1981 [1980].

Banet-Weiser, Sarah. "'Confidence You Can Carry!': Girls in Crisis and the Market for Girls' Empowerment Organizations." *Continuum: Journal of Media and Cultural Studies* 29, no. 2 (2015): 182–93.

Bedford, Kate and Shirin M. Rai, "Feminists Theorize International Political Economy." *Signs* 36, no. 1 (2010): 1–18.

Bourdieu, P. *Distinction: A Social Critique of the Judgement of Taste*. Cambridge, MA: Harvard University Press, 1984.

Calvès, Anne-Emmanuèle. "First Union Formation in Urban Burkina Faso: Competing Relationship Transitions to Marriage or Cohabitation." *Demographic Research* 34, no. 15 (2016), 421–50.
Calvès, Anne-Emmanuèle and Roger Depledge. "Too Poor to Marry? Urban Employment Crisis and Men's First Entry into Union in Burkina Faso." *Population* 62, no. 2 (2007): 293–311.
Chant, Sylvia. and Cathy McIlwaine. *Cities, Slums and Gender in the Global South: Towards a Feminized Urban Future.* London and New York: Routledge, 2016.
Cole, Jennifer. "Fashioning distinction: Youth and Consumerism in Urban Madagascar." In *Figuring the Future: Globalization and the Temporalities of Children and Youth*, edited by Jennifer Cole and Deborah Lynn Durham, 99–124. Santa Fe, NM: School for Advanced Research Press, 2008.
Cole, Jennifer and Deborah Lynn Durham, eds., *Figuring the Future: Globalization and the Temporalities of Children and Youth.* Santa Fe, NM: School for Advanced Research Press, 2008.
Drolet, Julie. Feminist Perspectives in Development: Implication for Women and Microcredit. *Journal of Women and Social Work* 25, no. 3 (2010), 212–23.
Duffy-Tumasz, Amelia. Paying Back Comes First: Why Repayment Means More Than Business in Rural Senegal. *Gender and Development*, 17, no.2, (2009), 243–54.
Ferguson, James. *Expectations of Modernity: Myths and Meanings of Urban Life on the Zambian Copperbelt.* Los Angeles and Berkeley: University of Berkeley Press, 1999.
Frye, Margaret. "Bright Futures in Malawi's New Dawn: Educational Aspirations as Assertions of Identity." *American Journal of Sociology* 117, no. 6 (2012), 1565–624.
Hannaford, Dinah. "Intimate Remittances: Marriage, Migration, and MoneyGram in Senegal." *Africa Today*, 62 no. 3, (2016), 93–109.
Hanson, Susan. "Changing Places through Women's Entrepreneurship." *Economic Geography*, 85, no. 3 (2009): 245–67.
Honwana, Alcinda. *The Time of Youth: Work, Social Change and Politics in Africa.* Sterling, VA: Kumarian Press, 2012.
Isserles, Robin G. "The Rhetoric of Empowerment, the Reality of "Development as Usual." *Women's Studies Quarterly* 31, no. 3/4 (2003): 38–57.
Jeffrey, Craig. "Timepass: Youth, Class, and Time Among Unemployed Young Men in India." *American Ethnologist* 37, no. 3 (2010), 465–81.
Kane, Abdoulaye. "Financial Arrangements Across Borders: Women's Predominant Participation in Popular Finance, from Thilogne and Dakar to Paris: A Senegalese Case Study." In *Women and Credit: Researching the Past, Refiguring the Future*, edited by Gail Grace Campbell, Ruth Pearson, and Beverly Lemire, 295–317. New York and Oxford: Berg, 2002.
Keating, Christine, Claire Rasmussen, and Pooja Rishi. "The Rationality of Empowerment: Microcredit, Accumulation by Dispossession, and the Gendered Economy." *Signs* 36, no. 1 (2010): 153–76.
Kendall, Nancy. and Kaunda, Zikani. "Transitions: Girls, Schooling, and Reproductive Realities in Malawi." In *Educating Adolescent Girls Around the Globe: Challenges and Opportunities*, edited by Sandra L. Stacki and Supriya Baily, 23–39. New York and Abingdon, Oxon: Routledge, 2015.
Langevang, Thilde and Katherine V. Gough. Diverging Pathways: Young Female Employment and Entrepreneurship in Sub-Saharan Africa. *The Geographical Journal*, 178 no. 3, (2012), 1–11.
Lave, Jean. *Apprenticeship in Critical Ethnographic Practice.* Chicago and London: University of Chicago Press, 2011.
Li, Tania Murray. *Land's End: Capitalist Relations on an Indigenous Frontier.* Durham and London: Duke University Press, 2014.
Madsen, U. A. "Towards Eduscapes: Youth and Schooling in a Global World." In *Youth and the City in the Global South*, edited by K. T. Hansen, 151–74. Bloomington and Indianapolis: Indiana University Press, 2008.

Mains, Daniel. *Hope is Cut: Youth, Unemployment, and the Future in Urban Ethiopia.* Philadelphia, PA: Temple University Press, 2012.

Marcus, George E. "Ethnography In/Of the World System: The Emergence of Multi-Sited Ethnography." *Annual Reviews in Anthropology* 24 (1995): 95–117.

Moeller, Kathryn. Proving "the Girl Effect": Corporate Knowledge Production and Educational Intervention. *International Journal of Educational Development* 33 (2013): 612–21.

Murphy-Graham, Erin. *Opening Minds, Improving Lives: Education and Women's Empowerment in Honduras.* Nashville: Vanderbilt University Press, 2012.

Perry, Donna. "Microcredit and Women Moneylenders: The Shifting Terrain of Credit in Rural Senegal." *Human Organization* 61, no. 1 (2002): 30–40.

Rankin, Katherine N. Social Capital, Microfinance, and the Politics of Development. *Feminist Economics* 8, no. 1 (2002): 1–24.

Robertson, Claire C. *Trouble Showed the Way: Women, Men, and Trade in the Nairobi Area, 1890–1990.* Bloomington and Indianapolis: Indiana University Press, 1997.

Roy, Ananya. *Poverty Capital: Microfinance and the Making of Development.* New York and London: Routledge, 2010.

Scheld, Suzanne. "Youth Cosmopolitanism: Clothing, the City and Globalization in Dakar, Senegal." *City and Society* 19, no. 2 (2007), 232–53.

Schulz, Dorothea Elisabeth. "Love Potions and Money Machines: Commercial Occultism and the Reworking of Social Relations in Urban Mali." In *Wari Matters: Ethnographic Explorations of Money in the Mande World,* edited by Stephen Wooten, 93–115. New Brunswick and London: Transaction Publishers, 2005.

Simeen, Mahmud. "Actually How Empowering Is Microcredit?" *Development and Change* 34, no. 4 (2003): 577–605.

Singerman, Diane. "The Economic Imperatives of Marriage: Emerging Practices and Identities among Youth in the Middle East." *The Middle East Youth Initiative Working Paper* 6 (September 2007). Washington DC, and Dubai: *Wolfensohn Centre for Development and Dubai School of Government,* 2007. 1–51.

Sommers, Marc. *Stuck: Rwandan Youth and the Struggle for Adulthood.* Athens and London: The University of Georgia Press, 2012.

Stambach, Amy. *Lessons from Mount Kilimanjaro: Schooling, Community and Gender in East Africa.* New York: Routledge, 2000.

Whitehouse, Bruce. *Migrants and Strangers in an African City: Exile, Dignity and Belonging.* Bloomington: Indiana University Press, 2012.

NOTES

1. Sarah Banet-Weiser, "'Confidence you can carry!': Girls in crisis and the market for girls' empowerment organizations," *Continuum: Journal of Media and Cultural Studies* 29, no. 2 (2015): 182–93; Kathryn Moeller, "Proving "the Girl Effect": Corporate Knowledge Production and Educational Intervention," *International Journal of Educational Development* 33 (2013): 612–21.

2. Amy Stambach's *Lessons from Mount Kilimanjaro* (2000) examines "city women" whose ideas about their careers are shaped by their school experiences. See Amy Stambach, *Lessons from Mount Kilimanjaro: Schooling, Community and Gender in East Africa* (New York: Routledge, 2000).

3. One ET program in this study was female only, while a second training program was mixed gender.

4. Sylvia Chant and Cathy McIlwaine, C. *Cities, Slums and Gender in the Global South: Towards a Feminized Urban Future* (London and New York: Routledge, 2016).

5. Erin Murphy-Graham, *Opening Minds, Improving Lives: Education and Women's Empowerment in Honduras* (Nashville: Vanderbilt University Press, 2012).

6. Julie Drolet, "Feminist perspectives in development: Implication for women and microcredit," *Journal of Women and Social Work* 25, no. 3 (2010): 212–23; Amelia Duffy-Tumasz, "Paying Back Comes First: Why Repayment Means More Than Business in Rural Senegal," *Gender and Development* 17, no. 2 (2009): 243–54; Christine Keating, Claire Rasmussen, Pooja Rishi, "The Rationality of Empowerment: Microcredit, Accumulation by Dispossession, and the Gendered Economy," *Signs* 36, no. 1 (2010): 153–76.

7. Daniel Mains, *Hope Is Cut: Youth, Unemployment, and the Future in Urban Ethiopia* (Philadelphia, PA: Temple University Press, 2012).

8. Jean Lave, *Apprenticeship in Critical Ethnographic Practice* (Chicago and London: University of Chicago Press, 2011).

9. Tania Murray Li, *Land's End: Capitalist Relations on an Indigenous Frontier* (Durham and London: Duke University Press, 2014).

10. George E. Marcus, "Ethnography In/Of the World System: The Emergence of Multi-Sited Ethnography," *Annual Reviews in Anthropology* 24 (1995): 95–117.

11. Marcus, "Ethnography In/Of the World System."

12. Marcus, "Ethnography In/Of the World System," 102.

13. Diane Singerman, "The Economic Imperatives of Marriage: Emerging Practices and Identities among Youth in the Middle East," *The Middle East Youth Initiative Working Paper* 6 (September 2007) (Washington DC, and Dubai: *Wolfensohn Centre for Development and Dubai School of Government*, 2007): 1–51; Jennifer Cole, "Fashioning Distinction: Youth and Consumerism in Urban Madagascar," in *Figuring the Future: Globalization and the Temporalities of Children and Youth*, edited by Jennifer Cole and Deborah Lynn Durham (Santa Fe, NM: School for Advanced Research Press, 2008), 99–124; Jennifer Cole and Deborah Lynn Durham, eds., *Figuring the Future: Globalization and the Temporalities of Children and Youth*; Marc Sommers, *Stuck: Rwandan Youth and the Struggle for Adulthood* (Athens and London: The University of Georgia Press, 2012).

14. Arjun Appadurai, *Modernity at Large: Cultural Dimensions of Globalization* (Minneapolis and London: University of Minnesota Press, 1996); Ferguson, James, *Expectations of Modernity: Myths and Meanings of Urban Life on the Zambian Copperbelt* (Los Angeles and Berkeley: University of Berkeley Press, 1999).

15. Mains, *Hope Is Cut.*
16. Mains, *Hope Is Cut*, 68.
17. Mains, *Hope Is Cut*, 114.
18. Moeller, "*Proving 'the Girl Effect.'*"
19. Kendall, Nancy. and Kaunda, Zikani, "Transitions: Girls, Schooling, and Reproductive Realities in Malawi," in *Educating Adolescent Girls Around the Globe: Challenges and Opportunities*, Sandra L. Stacki and Supriya Baily, eds., (New York and Abingdon, Oxon: Routledge, 2015), 23–39.
20. Chant describes how women are instrumentalized toward particular developmental objectives. See Chant and McIlwaine, *Cities, Slums and Gender in the Global South*.
21. Sommers, M. *Stuck: Rwandan Youth and the Struggle for Adulthood.*
22. Sommers, M. *Stuck: Rwandan Youth and the Struggle for Adulthood.*
23. Dorothea Elisabeth Schulz, "Love Potions and Money Machines: Commercial Occultism and the Reworking of Social Relations in Urban Mali," in *Wari Matters: Ethnographic Explorations of Money in the Mande World*, edited by Stephen Wooten, 93–115. New Brunswick and London: Transaction Publishers, 2005.
24. Schulz, "Love Potions and Money Machines," 104.
25. Anne-Emmanuèle Calvés and Roger Depledge, "Too Poor to Marry? Urban Employment Crisis and Men's First Entry into Union in Burkina Faso," *Population* 62, no. 2 (2007): 293–311.
26. Alcinda Honwana, *The Time of Youth: Work, Social Change and Politics in Africa* (Sterling, VA: Kumarian Press, 2012).
27. Calvés, "First Union Formation in Urban Burkina Faso: Competing Relationship Transitions to Marriage or Cohabitation," *Demographic Research* 34, no. 15 (2016): 421–50.
28. Calvés, "First Union Formation in Urban Burkina Faso," 424–245.
29. Schulz, "Love Potions and Money, Machines."
30. Dinah Hannaford, "Intimate Remittances: Marriage, Migration, and MoneyGram in Senegal," *Africa Today* 62, no. 3 (2016), 93–109.
31. Margaret Frye, "Bright Futures in Malawi's New Dawn: Educational Aspirations as Assertions of Identity" *American Journal of Sociology* 117, no. 6 (2012), 1565–624.
32. Kendall and Kaunda, "Transitions."
33. Kendall and Kaunda, "Transitions," 32.
34. Kendall and Kaunda, "Transitions," 30.
35. Kendall and Kaunda, "Transitions," 32.

36. The best-known female Senegalese writer, Mariama Bâ, explores the potential for socio-economic instability in polygamous marriage in her short novel, *Une Si Longue Lettre*. See Mariama Bâ, *So Long a Letter*, trans. Modupe Bode-Thomas (Long Grove, IL: Waveland Press, 1980).

37. Thilde Langevang and Katherine V. Gough, "Diverging Pathways: Young Female Employment and Entrepreneurship in Sub-Saharan Africa," *The Geographical Journal* 178, no. 3 (2012), 1–11.

38. Langevang and Gough, "Diverging Pathways," 7.

39. Kendall and Kaunda, "Transitions," 33.

40. Craig Jeffrey, "Timepass: Youth, Class, and Time Among Unemployed Young Men in India." *American Ethnologist* 37, no. 3 (2010), 465–81; Mains, *Hope Is Cut.*

41. Chant and McIlwaine, *Cities, Slums and Gender in the Global South*, 51–52.

42. Jeffrey, "Timepass."

43. I take invisible to mean that trade often occurs among relations, and is often conducted in their or their relations households; that is, not in public view. In this study visibility of earnings was important to women in order to maintain one's moral reputation.

44. Suzanne Scheld, "Youth Cosmopolitanism: Clothing, the City and Globalization in Dakar, Senegal," *City and Society* 19, no. 2 (2007), 241; Whitehouse (2012) similarly finds that in Brazzaville trade and shops were male spaces. See Bruce Whitehouse, *Migrants and Strangers in an African City: Exile, Dignity and Belonging* (Bloomington: Indiana University Press, 2012).

45. Schultz, D. Love Potions and Money Machines."

46. Mains, *Hope Is Cut: Youth.* 47.

47. Chant and McIlwaine, *Cities, Slums and Gender in the Global South*, 41.

48. Claire C. Robertson, Robertson, *Trouble Showed the Way: Women, Men, and Trade in the Nairobi Area, 1890- 1990* (Bloomington and Indianapolis: Indiana University Press, 1997).

49. Kate Bedford and Shirin M. Rai, "Feminists Theorize International Political Economy," *Signs* 36, no. 1 (2010): 1–18; Drolet, "Feminist Perspectives in Development"; Susan Hanson, "Changing Places through Women's Entrepreneurship." *Economic Geography*, 85, no. 3 (2009): 245–67; Robin G. Isserles, "The Rhetoric of Empowerment, the Reality of "Development as Usual," *Women's Studies Quarterly* 31, no. 3/4 (2003): 38–57; Abdoulaye Kane, "Financial Arrangements Across Borders: Women's Predominant Participation in Popular Finance, from Thilogne and Dakar to Paris: A Senegalese Case Study," in *Women and Credit: Researching the Past, Refiguring the Future*, Gail Grace Campbell, Ruth Pearson, and Beverly Lemire eds. (New York and

Oxford: Berg, 2002), 295–317. Keating, Rasmussen, and Rishi, "The Rationality of Empowerment," Donna Perry, "Microcredit and Women Moneylenders: The Shifting Terrain of Credit in Rural Senegal," *Human Organization* 61, no. 1 (2002): 30–40; Katherine N. Rankin, "Social Capital, Microfinance, and the Politics of Development. *Feminist Economics* 8, no. 1 (2002): 1–24; Ananya Roy, *Poverty Capital: Microfinance and the Making of Development* (New York and London: Routledge, 2010); Mahmud Simeen, "Actually How Empowering is Microcredit?" *Development and Change* 34, no. 4 (2003): 577–605.

50. A wife's cooking is a sign of love and hospitality in Wolof culture. See Hannaford, "Intimate Remittances."

5

WIDOWHOOD AND ASSET INHERITANCE AMONG THE SERER IN SENEGAL

Ruth Evans

Senegalese families are often characterized by large multi-generational households, extensive kinship ties, and considerable mobility between rural and urban areas.[1] In this context, the death of a male head of household, who provided financial support to close and extended family members, may lead to significant economic and emotional insecurity for widows and children. Greater vulnerability to chronic poverty results from the loss of the main income earner and changes in livelihoods, domestic and caring responsibilities during the period of widowhood-mourning and thereafter delays, and sometimes disputes, over asset inheritance.[2]

Drawing on feminist qualitative research with twenty Serer families living in Greater Dakar and rural communities in Fatick and Diourbel regions of Senegal, this chapter[3] explores the relationship between gender norms, religious and cultural practices of widowhood, and asset inheritance. I first highlight key themes from the literature on gendered inheritance practices, legal pluralism, and widowhood in the Senegalese context and outline the research methods used in this study. After a brief discussion of widows' and widowers' experiences of the death of a spouse and mourning rituals, I explore how Serer[4] inheritance practices are influenced by religion, customary law, and gender norms in contrasting rural and urban environments. The chapter then explores participants' perceptions and experiences of inheritance disputes, which appeared more likely to occur in urban areas. Finally, the chapter discusses the economic security of widows and their children and identifies some of the challenges posed by legal pluralism in efforts to support women's inheritance rights in Senegal.

GENDERED INHERITANCE PRACTICES AND LEGAL PLURALISM

Inheritance represents a critical mode for the transfer of land, property, and other material assets between generations.[5] However, customary and religious inheritance practices often reinforce existing social inequalities and perpetuate hierarchies of gender, age, class, caste, and ethnicity. In many Sub-Saharan African countries, customary law often excludes women from owning and inheriting assets.[6] Recent legal reforms and development initiatives in many African countries have sought to promote women's equal access to land and property ownership as a means of alleviating poverty and reducing gender inequalities.[7] Increased control of land, property, and other assets and resources by women and other marginalized groups is thought to break poverty cycles and interrupt the intergenerational transmission of poverty.[8] Assets controlled by women, for example, often result in increased investments in the next generation's health, nutrition, and schooling.[9] Few studies to date have explored how widows and other family members negotiate statutory, religious, and customary laws surrounding the inheritance of land, housing, and other assets in Senegal and considered the implications for women's economic and emotional security.

The contradictions of legal pluralism and the "triple heritage" of African, Islamic, and colonial influences[10] are particularly evident in relation to family law and inheritance in Senegal. Although the majority of the population practice Sufi Islam, Senegal is a secular state. Islamic and Christian practices have become syncretized with traditional practices.[11] The Constitution, reformed most recently in 2001, provides many formal rights for women, including equality with men before the law and the right for women to control their own property.[12] Senegal is also a signatory to the UN Convention on the Elimination of All Forms of Discrimination against Women (CEDAW) and other international human rights conventions. However, Senegal has often failed to harmonize its national laws with the provisions mandated in international conventions.[13]

The statutory Family Code in Senegal, based on French law, has been the subject of much debate, criticism, and lobbying for reform from religious leaders and women's rights proponents alike.[14] Camara argues that although it was dubbed the "Women's Code" and hailed as a "triumph of modernity" over traditional custom, the law "substitutes African matriarchy-based laws for patriarchal rules taken from French Civil Law and Islamic law."[15] The reality is more complex; the Family Code contains elements of French Civil Law which reflects the patriarchal origins of French law and retains provisions important in Muslim traditions which are also patriarchal in nature. In contrast, the Senegalese customs which existed before colonialism (and which have evolved and are still practiced today to some extent) vary according to ethnic group and reflect both patrilineal and matrilineal inheritance systems.[16]

While the Family Code does not eliminate polygamy, it requires men to choose between monogamy, polygamy with two, or polygamy with more than two wives, with a default rule whereby the marriage is considered polygamous if a husband fails to make a choice.[17] Furthermore, in relation to succession, the Family Code includes special provision for Muslims to opt for Islamic law regarding the division of inherited assets, while common law based on French law provides for the spouse and his/her male and female children to inherit equal shares of the inheritance. According to Islamic law, in the case of a death of a household head, Muslim daughters are entitled to only half of the estate that their brothers receive, and widows are only entitled to one-eight of their husband's estate. Other family members are also entitled to shares of the inheritance.

Similar contradictions posed by legal pluralism are evident in many other post-colonial African countries. Cooper's policy overview of Ghana, Kenya, Mozambique, Rwanda, and Uganda suggests that statutory inheritance laws do not make adequate provision for wives in polygamous unions in these countries.[18] Miles argues that Shari'a law, as a reflection of the Islamic faith, is likely to continue to grow and develop its position in Africa, while customary law faces an uncertain future, save in South Africa, where there has been considerable attention and codification.[19]

RESEARCH CONTEXT IN SENEGAL

The vast majority of the population of Senegal are Muslim (94 percent), while a minority are Christian (4 percent) and animist and other religions (2 percent).[20] The majority of marriages in Senegal are monogamous, but almost 30 percent of household heads are married in polygamous unions and almost 12 percent are widows.[21] Despite the gender discriminatory nature of religious and customary inheritance practices, analysis of Demographic and Health Surveys reveals that such practices may be more favorable for women in Senegal than in many other African countries. Indeed, 57 percent of widows in Senegal reported inheriting assets compared to an average of 47 percent across fifteen sub-Saharan African countries.[22] In Senegal, widows and/or their children inherited the majority of the assets, while on average in sub-Saharan Africa, the spouse's children/family inherited the majority of assets. Women's inheritance and ownership of property and financial assets thus may play an important role in alleviating poverty among widows and children. However, 14 percent of widows in Senegal reported that the deceased husband had no property to inherit, which is almost double the average (8 percent) for the fifteen sub-Saharan African countries.[23]

Studies of family and household relations in Senegal to date have tended to focus on the Wolof, the largest ethnic group.[24] Yet Fall et al. suggest that socio-economic status differs significantly according to ethnicity.[25] This research focuses on the Serer ethnic group who represent 15 percent of the Senegalese population and are significantly more likely to experience poverty (83 percent greater risk of living in poverty) than the Wolof.[26] The Serer adopted Islam and Catholicism during the twentieth century, later than most other ethnic groups in Senegal.[27] Polygamy is slightly less common among the Serer than other ethnic groups (38 percent of marriages are polygamous compared to 44–50 percent among other ethnicities).[28] Levirate marriage, whereby a younger brother or other paternal relative may remarry the widow of his deceased brother, is commonly practiced. Traditionally, the Serer observe aspects of both patrilineal and matrilineal inheritance systems for the transfer of wealth, values, and knowledge between generations.[29]

A quarter of the population of Senegal and over half of all urban residents live in Dakar and its surrounding suburbs.[30] In Dakar, there is a higher percentage of widows (15 percent) heading households and a lower percentage of household heads living in polygamous unions (23 percent) compared to the national average.[31] Although the incidence of poverty is lower in Dakar compared to other cities and rural areas in Senegal, comparison by the marital status of household heads shows that the largest proportion of households affected by poverty in Dakar (31 percent) are those headed by widows.[32] Dakar's low-income inner-city neighborhoods and peripheral suburbs provide an interesting contrast to Serer rural communities in Diourbel and Fatick regions. Together, they form the geographical focus of this research.

RESEARCH METHODS

This exploratory study aimed to investigate inheritance, access to resources and the intergenerational transmission of poverty among Serer families in Senegal.[33] A feminist qualitative methodology informed by a lifecourse perspective was considered most appropriate. Using key gatekeepers such as local facilitators, religious and community leaders, NGO contacts, and snowballing techniques, a purposive sample of twenty families of Serer ethnicity who had experienced an adult relative's death in recent years was identified. Two research locations traditionally inhabited by the Serer ethnic group in the groundnut growing area in Senegal were selected to provide a contrast of rural livelihood opportunities and access to natural resources: small villages in the rural community of Tocky Gare, Diourbel region, where livelihoods are predominantly focused on groundnut and millet production and livestock rearing; and villages and islands in Fimela rural community, in Sine Saloum, Fatick region, where livelihood opportunities exist in artisanal fishing and tourism, in addition to groundnut, millet, and rice cultivation and livestock rearing. For the urban research locations, working-class districts and suburbs of Greater Dakar were selected, including Médina, Guèdiawaye, Keur Massar, and Yeumbeul.

In-depth semi-structured interviews were conducted with a total of fifty-one participants: twelve widows and six widowers; ten young people (aged fifteen to twenty-seven) whose mother/father or both had died; six adult relatives; seven religious and community leaders (three imams, one Catholic priest, two village *notables*/nobles and one *chef du quartier*/head of district in Guèdiawaye), and eleven professionals working on poverty alleviation, women's and children's rights, and development in Senegal. The majority of families (seventeen out of twenty) were Muslim; three Roman Catholic families also participated. A focus group was conducted with four Serer women who were members of a women's group in Tocky Gare and with four Muslim widows (of Serer, Wolof, and Toucouleur ethnicity) who were members of a widows' association in Médina, Dakar. This chapter mainly draws on the interviews with widows, religious leaders, and professionals and on focus group discussions. Pseudonyms have been used to protect participants' anonymity.

French-Serer and -Wolof interpretation was provided by a research assistant during interviews with family and community members, while interviews with professionals were conducted directly in French. All audio-recordings were transcribed into French with research assistance. I acknowledge that the nuances of language and culturally specific meanings may have been lost in the double translation of information from Serer or Wolof to French to English.[34] Given the interpreters' and translators' fluency in French and relative ease in interpreting from Serer or Wolof into French compared to English, it was most appropriate for me to work with them in French. The French transcripts of Serer audio-recordings were transcribed and translated in full by a different Serer research assistant than my interpreter and French and Wolof audio-recordings were transcribed and translated in full by a Wolof research assistant, which provided a degree of rigour and verification of understandings generated both in the research settings and in the transcription process. The translators provided further elaboration of Serer cultural terms and practices where appropriate. Any errors in translating quotations used in this chapter from French to English are my own.

Thematic analysis of the French transcriptions was undertaken and an analytic summary of each transcript was written to assist in the interpretation of the data, which was informed by theoretical concepts of gender and intergenerational relations, asset inheritance, and the intergenerational transmission of poverty. Following preliminary analysis, participatory feedback workshops were conducted with participants in

Guédiawaye, Dakar, and in Fimela and Tocky Gare rural communities to identify key messages for a short digital video that was discussed with policymakers, practitioners, participants, and researchers in a seminar in Dakar. This exploratory study does not aim to be representative of widows' and widowers' experiences, but rather provides qualitative insights into inheritance practices, access to assets and the diverse experiences of Serer families who have lost a close relative in rural and urban locations in Senegal.

RESEARCH FINDINGS

Mourning and bereavement

Over a third (four out of eleven) of the Serer women interviewed had been recently widowed and were observing widowhood mourning rituals at the time of the interview, which sometimes restricted the discussion about inheritance. A further three women had lost their husband within the previous year; two women had been widowed two years previously, and three women had lost their husband in the last five to ten years. The women all confirmed that they had observed widowhood mourning practices in the months following their husband's death. The Serer word *ñaawax* and the Wolof word *téndeu* were translated into French by the word *veuvage*, or *widowhood* in English. Yet these words in Serer and Wolof refer specifically to the widowhood mourning period in the weeks and months after the husband's death and the words for widow, *o ñaaw oxe*, in Serer and *dieutour*, in Wolof, refer to a widow in mourning, rather than referring to any woman whose husband has died, as would usually be understood by the term *widow* in English or *veuve* in French; a woman is no longer referred to by these terms among the Serer and the Wolof once the specific mourning period has come to an end. The lack of a precise equivalent term in English to refer to widows' mourning practices has meant that in this chapter, and in our larger study of bereavement in urban Senegal, we opted to use the hyphenated phrase "widowhood-mourning" to denote this particular period and the practices observed.[35]

For Muslim women, these practices comprised a number of restrictions from their usual activities for a period of four months and ten days. Deguène, an older widow living in Guédiawaye, explained that the widowhood-mourning period was characterized by segregation from everyday routines in the household, as well as from the neighborhood: "When you do the widowhood-mourning [French: *le veuvage*], you don't go outside, you do nothing. [. . .] You have to stay in your room. Even if you want to go to the toilet, you must cover yourself with a veil."

For Catholic women living in Fimela rural community, the mourning period lasted for six months to one year. Coumba, a Catholic widow explained:

> if you are in widowhood-mourning, you can't go anywhere, you always stay at home until the end of the mourning and in the evening you are in your room or you go to church to pray and then come straight back to the house and change clothes and always stay in your room until the next day and then you go to church to learn.

With the exception of the length of the mourning period, and the custom of wearing a black veil and going to church among Catholics, the similarity in Muslim and Catholic widows' experiences of withdrawing from everyday family and community life during this special period of widowhood-mourning suggests a syncretism between Serer customary practices, religious traditions, and dominant gender norms, as Galvan has observed of Serer practices more generally.[36] Most participants did not mention any particular mourning rituals that men practiced, although some said that Serer widowers were expected to observe a period of contemplation and sexual restraint for forty to forty-five days following the death of their wife.

Many widows said that they found the widowhood-mourning period "very hard" (French: *très dur*), a recurring phrase in the interviews, which seems to convey both economic and emotional hardship, as we also found in our larger study of bereavement in urban Senegal.[37] Women who lived alone with their children in urban areas found the mourning period particularly restrictive, since they were unable to work, which put increased pressure on their older children to work to support the family. For example, Gnilane, a widow who relied on an irregular income from selling fish at the market to support her five children, commented: "I was no longer selling. One of my daughters used to go to sell at the market, but after less than two months, she said that she could no longer tolerate the hard work, so we just stayed like that."

For most families, the death of a close relative represented a "critical moment" in their lives,[38] in terms of both emotional and economic impacts. Many women and men talked about the profound sense of loss, sorrow, and loneliness they experienced following their spouse's death, in addition to their concerns about the effects of bereavement on their children. In rural areas, widows and orphaned youths did not cultivate the deceased husband/father's fields the year of their loss, which perpetuated the poverty they experienced. The loss of the male head of household usually led to increased responsibility for widows and young people to provide for the family and pushed several families into situations of chronic poverty. The death of a wife/mother often led to increased domestic and childcare responsibilities for girls and young women living in the household, in addition to increased pressure on the widower, older children, and other relatives to support the family.[39] The death in the family could also result in moving home and changes in household composition, such as the dispersal of co-wives, remarriage and levirate practices, decisions to migrate to urban areas, emigrate to Europe, and/or to entrust a child to relatives as part of kinship care/child fosterage practices.

Many of those who later died had chronic illnesses which required expensive medical treatment and hospital care, which had a detrimental impact on families' economic security. Married couples struggled to pay high medical costs and drew on extended family support for financial assistance. According to Serer customs, maternal relatives were usually seen as responsible for providing care for the ill person and meeting medical costs. In Dakar, however, participants also drew on social networks with neighbors and friends for support when they faced such financial pressures. For example, Ousmane, a widower who worked as a mechanic and rented a room in Dakar, was still paying off the debts he owed to a friend from his wife's medical care several months after her death. In Gnilane's case, the high costs of medical treatment had forced her husband to sell the family house in Guèdiawaye, and after his death, Gnilane and her children relocated to a suburb of Dakar where housing costs were lower. The building work on the new house was not yet finished at the time of interview, the house was not furnished and was much further away from where she needed to go to purchase fish to sell at the market. This meant that she incurred significant transport costs each day, which reduced considerably her already low, irregular income. She was constantly worried about money and how to "get by" and manage:

> We live in poverty, having to get by [French: la débrouillardise] and other things, when you are responsible for providing for the children, there are problems feeding them and so on, still another difficulty is that we've only just started living in this district, we don't know anyone here yet.

Following this overview of how widowhood-mourning, illness, and bereavement impacted on the economic and emotional wellbeing of family members, the next section discusses in more depth the relationship between gender, religion, and customary inheritance practices among the Serer.

Asset Inheritance

The dynamics of asset inheritance contrast in urban and rural areas of Senegal, largely due to differences in the types of assets that are passed on to family members. This section discusses how religious and customary practices among the Serer are entwined and intersect with wider gender and generational relations.

As in many other African countries and in common with other ethnic groups in Senegal, the Serer very rarely expressed their wishes for inheritance in a written or verbal will. The inheritance of land, property, and other assets was usually settled within the extended family after the intestate's death. According to traditional inheritance practices in rural areas, the Serer transferred land, livestock, and other assets to the next generation through the maternal lineage; maternal nephews would inherit their uncle's assets. Male elders and imams in the rural communities commented that traditionally, rather than building up financial assets, the Serer tended to invest money in livestock (bullocks, cows, sheep, goats, etc.) which they could sell during periods of financial pressure, or use for bride-price or for family ceremonies such as marriages, baptisms or funerals. Thus, wealth was transferred to the next generation predominantly through the inheritance of land and livestock from maternal uncles, although *inter-vivos* transfers of cattle, for example, on the occasion of a maternal nephew's marriage or for funeral ceremonies, could also be significant.

Increasing adherence to Islam since the 1970s, however, had resulted in Serer families in the rural locations shifting predominantly to patrilineal inheritance practices. A similar shift from matrilineal to patrilineal inheritance has been witnessed in recent decades in Ghana, albeit within a different socio-ecological and religious context.[40] In general, in Serer rural communities, brothers tended to live together with their wives and children in the family home, considered an "undividable asset" in rural areas. Hence, when the eldest son and head of the household died, another brother would usually become head of the household. In such circumstances, land and other heritable assets were often not divided among family members for several years, until the deceased's sons had matured and were able to manage the inherited assets.

Sons usually inherited land and the family home from their fathers, while other assets (such as livestock, horse and cart, agricultural machines, a house, savings, furniture, and other personal belongings) were usually divided among male and female children. Women did not generally inherit land or the family home in rural areas. According to Islamic law, daughters are expected to receive half of the share of inherited assets that their brothers receive, but the research found that this did not usually include land. This was justified by the fact that daughters would marry and leave the household; according to patrilocal marriage practices, daughters usually moved to their husband's home when they married and gained secondary use rights to cultivate land there.[41]

Many participants in Tocky Gare and Fimela rural communities stated that matrilineal inheritance practices no longer existed among the Serer and thought that the division of assets according to Islamic law ensured a fairer (although still gender discriminatory) means of transfer of wealth between generations. An imam explained that in Serer rural communities, practicing Muslims usually divided the deceased person's assets among the heirs according to the recommendations of Islamic law, but many families adapted this to follow some Serer customs and came to an agreement within the family. This suggests that religious and customary inheritance practices were characterized by a degree of flexibility and negotiability which could work in women's favor.[42] Indeed, bilineal inheritance of land continued in some villages in Fimela rural community, especially in those inhabited by Roman Catholics and Muslims; some agricultural land and rice paddies were regarded as belonging to the maternal lineage, and their use was controlled by male members of the maternal lineage.[43] A priest in this community reported that Catholic families usually followed traditional (Serer) inheritance practices and the church was not usually involved in inheritance.[44]

Given the importance of social capital in negotiating inheritance, a widow's former status as a wife (including as a co-wife in polygamous unions), her role as a mother, and social relations with her in-laws' family significantly influenced her position, as other studies have shown.[45] Sons enhanced widows' status, due to patrilineal inheritance practices, and were key to safeguarding widows' continued access to land in rural areas; if widows did not have children, they usually returned to their natal families or remarried. Three widows living in the rural communities who had remarried gained secondary use rights to land through their new husband's family. However, if children were young when their father died and moved with their mother to her new husband's family in a different locality, the children's inheritance claims to their father's land and other assets might be jeopardized when they came of age.[46]

Imams were sometimes called to advise Muslim family members about the division of the assets according to Islamic law. They confirmed that compared to the sons' and daughters' shares, the widow was allocated a smaller share of the inheritance (the *soumoul* in Wolof), which was divided among co-wives in polygamous families. An imam justified the fact that women and girls received half the share of men and boys in similar positions by referring to other aspects of Islamic law that specified that a wife is entitled to maintenance from her husband, in terms of shelter, clothing, food, and medical care:[47]

> in Sharia [law], the girl will not take care of a family, but she is taken care of, in contrast to the boy who will maintain the family with this money. As for the girl, she will keep her money even if she is married, she will leave with her money to do what she wants with it because it's up to her husband to pay for everything for her in the household. So with the division [French: *partage*, that is the sharing

> out of the inheritance], you see that the girl profits more than the boy because the girl will keep her money, while the boy is constrained by having to maintain his family.

Although women may contribute to the costs of supporting the family, the imam emphasized that a wife was not obliged to provide financial support under Islamic law. Camara argues that customary practices train women to be economically independent of their husbands and consequently they often have their own financial resources and property such as furniture and jewellery.[48] The statutory Family Code directly contradicts such religious and customary practices, since it mandates that women have a duty to provide for their siblings and parents in need and to contribute to the home and family maintenance.[49]

In urban areas of Dakar, a regular income and the inheritance and ownership of housing were identified by widows and widowers as the key means of ensuring economic security. In Dakar, most of the widows interviewed (four out of six) and their children had inherited housing or a financial share of their deceased husband's property, which helped to reduce the economic pressures on the household following their husband's death. Widowers reported that their wives had few, if any, heritable assets.

The inheritance of housing and other assets in urban areas was usually settled within families, sometimes with reference to imams and other religious leaders, according to Islamic law (in Muslim families) and customary practices, with little, if any, reference to the Family Code. In two polygamous households in Dakar, the value of the property was divided between co-wives and their children. In Mariama's case, the maternal uncle of each co-wife sought advice from the local imam about how to proceed with the division of assets according to Islamic law and discussed this with the widows, who were observing mourning rituals at the time. Through this process, it was agreed that Mariama, the widow interviewed, could remain in the inherited house since she had eight children, while her co-wife left with her child to live with her mother in another city. Mariama and her children were under considerable economic pressure, however, and she was only able to pay off the debt (574,000 CFA, equivalent to approximately £767) owed to her co-wife for her inherited share of the house gradually over several years: "Sometimes, if I have 10,000 CFA from the rental payment [she rented out a room in the house as a source of income], I keep it, if I have 5,000 CFA, I keep it, so if it's a substantial amount, then I pay her back." When asked what changes she had noticed in her life since her husband's death, Mariama said:

> I am worn out. Sometimes we don't have any lunch, another day, we don't have any dinner. . . . Sometimes, we do laundry work for people who pay us 2,000 CFA, and if we don't have any laundry to do, we are worried. With the money they pay us, we buy food to eat.

Despite these financial pressures, which caused considerable anxiety, Mariama was pleased that an amicable agreement about the inheritance had been reached with her co-wife, who was understanding of her situation: "When we spoke to her about it, she knew that she could go to her mother's place, she wouldn't pay any rent, but me, I had lots of children, so she accepted." The application of Islamic law thus was flexible enough to recognize the circumstances of widows who may only be able to pay back a co-wife's share of the inherited property over an extended time period. Such practices, however, depended on goodwill, understanding, and amicable relations between different co-wives and the relatives of each family.[50] In contrast to this example of an amicable relationship between co-wives and consensual negotiation of inheritance within the family, a small number of participants had experienced family conflicts and disputes surrounding asset inheritance, as the next section discusses.

Family Conflicts and Disputes over Asset Inheritance

Many family members, community and religious leaders, and professionals perceived inheritance disputes as more likely to occur in urban areas of Senegal. Participants also thought that disputes were more common in polygamous unions, particularly when the husband had significant assets to be divided between co-wives and their children. Indeed, some professionals felt that polygamous households were increasingly incompatible with urban lifestyles and that jealousies between co-wives were becoming more evident as Dakar became more urbanized.

A representative of the Association of Senegalese Women Lawyers (*Association des Juristes Sénégalaises*, AJS) explained that in polygamous Muslim families, co-wives with the largest number of adult sons would generally gain most from the division of inherited assets under Islamic law, while co-wives with daughters or fewer or no children might lose out. Younger co-wives could also be disadvantaged compared to older co-wives, especially if they were the same age or younger than the eldest children of the first wife. These differential positions of co-wives could lead to disagreements about whether Islamic law or common law should be applied. In disputed inheritance cases of a deceased Muslim, the judge decided whether Islamic or common law should be applied, on the basis of whether the deceased had been a practising Muslim, while also taking into account the heirs' wishes.

Imams and NGO staff providing legal advice commented, however, that in their experience, inheritance disputes were not confined to polygamous unions and were found in Catholic as well as Muslim families. Inheritance disputes sometimes emerged when a brother or sister of the deceased wanted to appropriate all of their relative's property to the exclusion of other heirs. These perspectives were supported by the experiences of widows and their children.

Some widows living in Dakar had experienced tensions and disputes with co-wives and their children over property and other assets that they had expected to inherit from their husbands. Yacine was an older Muslim widow living in Dakar whose husband had three other wives, two of whom lived in his natal village. Yacine's co-wives and their children had tried to force her to sell the house where she lived with her children in Dakar and divide the proceeds, despite the fact that she owned the house in her own right. The house had formerly belonged to her husband and the couple had lived there for many years. When he retired to live in the village with his other wives and wanted to sell the house, Yacine's younger brother bought the house for her, so that she could continue living there with her children. The co-wives and children's inheritance claim to the house was therefore unfounded.

Furthermore, co-wives living in urban areas, such as Yacine, were regarded as having little claim to any of their deceased husband's assets owned in the village. Yacine thought that she and her children should have inherited a share of the value of her husband's horse, agricultural equipment, and the groundnut and millet harvest. She explained, however, that the eldest son of one of her co-wives had "made out" that her husband had, "bought all these assets for them and so everything now belonged to him. We received nothing." In common with the other widow in a similar situation, Yacine did not want to cause further family conflict by trying to claim their share of the inheritance: "For us, it's not worth the trouble."

The most notable inheritance dispute among interviewees, however, concerned the inheritance of property among non-cohabiting co-wives and their children. Coudou, a Roman Catholic widow and her children had been forced to resort to the law courts to secure their share of the deceased husband's property and financial assets from her co-wife and children. Codou was the second wife and had lived with her nine children in rented accommodation, paid for by her husband, while the first wife lived in the conjugal house with her adult children. Following her husband's death, Codou had to rely on her eldest son's student bursary, her work at the market, and occasional donations from members of her faith community to pay the rent and other basic needs. Although Codou and her children tried to settle the dispute amicably by calling family meetings with the first wife and her children, they were forced to seek legal redress to settle the dispute:

> They lived in the house that my husband had left, and they didn't want to do the inheritance. I stayed three years like that, when it was my husband who used to pay my rent. . . . It's my co-wife who wore me out the most. She should have organised her children, since my husband had left a house. . . . That really aggravated me, I thought I would go mad. Finally, I went to court because I could no longer tolerate it. I said to the children that this house was for your father, we have to share it out equally, they have monopolised it, they don't want us to live there and they don't want to rent it out and share the rent money, now I can't take it anymore.

The judge ruled that the house should be sold and the proceeds divided, or if the first wife wanted to continue living there with her children, it should be valued and the share of the second wife's and her children's inheritance should be paid to them. After a long legal process, Coudou and her children received a lump sum payment for part of the inheritance, but the co-wife's adult children often paid the annual installments for the rest of the money several months late. Coudou did not want to have to take legal action again to force them to pay the remaining amount. In her view, inheritance disputes were often linked to conflictual relations between co-wives in polygamous unions, and as in her case, the first wife often refused to accept that the second wife and her children were entitled to a share of the husband's inheritance.

An imam explained that under Islamic law, women in polygamous unions inherited less than those in monogamous marriages, since the eighth share allocated to a widow was divided among the wives. In addition, the shares allocated to children were divided among all the children of the deceased. In the focus group in Médina, Dakar, widows highlighted the fact that it was usually the deceased's children rather than widows who directly inherited property, and hence it was difficult for widows in polygamous unions who did not have children to secure their share of the inheritance. They also commented that wealthier members of the family sometimes bended the rules of Islamic inheritance to their own ends: "It [inheritance] is based on religion, but sometimes people modify the procedure. They don't do things normally or they even block some shares and the well off will distribute the assets among themselves and the weakest will lose out." A community worker also commented that the brother of the deceased or other male relatives responsible for dividing inherited assets sometimes forged or modified paperwork such as title deeds to their own benefit. Women with low levels of literacy were particularly vulnerable to this form of exploitation.

Participants living in the rural locations confirmed that inheritance disputes were very rare in their communities. Nevertheless, tensions were apparent within some families, regarding delays in the division of assets and the potential diversion of financial assets, which disadvantaged women and children. Women's low levels of literacy, limited experience of negotiating administrative procedures, and dominant gender norms meant that widows in rural areas were often reliant on their deceased husband's male relatives to access inherited financial assets. For example, Coumba was a Roman Catholic widow living in Fimela rural community, whose husband had worked for a company in Dakar. Coumba expected to receive his pension but was still waiting for her husband's brother to sort out the paperwork six months after her husband's death: "The salary [pension] that he would have received, in truth, that should be returned to me, but his younger brother came and took the children's papers to sort it out, but up to now, I haven't seen anything."[51]

In another family in Fimela rural community, delays in asset inheritance had resulted in considerable economic and emotional insecurity. Yangoor was an older widow who lived with her granddaughter, Khady (aged twenty) and cared for her five other grandchildren following both the deaths of both of their parents within a short time period. Yangoor was angry with the children's paternal uncle because, three years after the parents' deaths, he had still not divided the deceased's herd of cattle which the children should have inherited, under Islamic law:

> If he noticed that the family is living in poverty, he should order that the sharing of assets be done and that the children have their share and others too [. . .]. In this case, if they sold their share of the cattle, they would have something to live on for months and months, but he hasn't done it, he doesn't feel any pity for the children.

Such delays in the division of the deceased's assets could be particularly detrimental to widows and orphaned children experiencing chronic poverty. The next section focuses on widows' economic security and legal support available to them, primarily in urban areas.

Economic Security and Legal Support for Widows

While this research suggests that inheritance was the main means of the intergenerational transfer of wealth in Serer families, *inter-vivos* transfers of property could be significant in securing widows' control of property and in preventing potential conflicts over inheritance between family members. In Dakar, two widows owned their house in their own right and enjoyed greater economic security than the other widows interviewed. As discussed earlier, in Yacine's case, her brother bought the house from her husband and gave it to her, when she and her children were at risk of losing their home.

In another case, Deguène, an older widow, lived with her sons and daughters-in-law and their children at the time of the interview. She described how she had moved to Dakar when she married at a young age. She worked in the fish market and bought a *baraque* [shack] in central Dakar, where she used to live with her husband. When the government cleared the city center of informal housing in the late 1970s, they were relocated to a house in Guédiawaye, on the outskirts of Dakar, which was now much more densely populated. When her husband took second and third wives, the co-wives stayed in his family home in the village. In widowhood, Deguène was able to continue living in the house she owned with her sons and daughters-in-law in Guédiawaye without the risk of her co-wives demanding a share of the house.

Thus, widows' inheritance and ownership of property helped to provide economic security. For some widows, such as Mariama (discussed earlier), property also provided an important source of income through renting out rooms, which helped to meet the high living costs in Dakar. Furthermore, many participants in urban areas suggested that they were expected to accommodate extended family members, neighbors, and children from their natal village for sometimes several months or years in order to enable them to access work, education, or medical care in Dakar. Serer men and women have long engaged in circular, seasonal, as well as more permanent migration to Dakar as an important survival strategy.[52] Serer women traditionally work in low-income jobs in the informal sector as millet pounders, *laveuses* [laundry women], and as *bonnes* [maids/domestic workers] in the city.[53] This research found that Serer young women often sought domestic work in the city during school vacations to pay for clothing and school expenses. Some young women had continued with full-time work in the city when they left school, sending remittances to rural family members when they were able.[54]

Widows with young children living in rented accommodation in Dakar without access to inherited property or financial assets faced the most precarious economic circumstances, which as Coudou's experience shows, also impacted on their emotional well-being and security. Almost half of Dakar's residents (44.9 percent) were tenants living in rented accommodation, over a third (36 percent) had a land title and own their own homes, 11.3 percent owned their property but lack a title, while 4.5 percent were accommodated by a relative or friend free of charge.[55] In the short video summarizing key messages for policy and practice produced with participants, widows in Dakar emphasized how important the inheritance and ownership of property was for women in alleviating the financial pressures they faced. Widows emphasized that if their housing costs were taken care of, they could meet their remaining living costs, such as food, clothing, water and electricity bills, children's schooling and healthcare, and so on by themselves through their income-generation activities. Good quality housing for poor widows with children was identified as their key priority. As noted earlier, the family home was not usually inherited by women in rural areas and the costs of living were generally much lower in rural communities, thus equal access to land, rather than housing, was the priority for women in rural communities.

None of the widows or widowers interviewed in rural or urban areas had benefited from governmental or NGO support following the death of their spouse. While some financial assistance was available to the poorest families through the Ministry of Social Action, professionals commented that the support provided was often minimal, only available as a one-off grant and could be delayed or diverted. As one professional commented: "It's just one-off assistance. You eat that, and it's finished." Widows participating in the focus group in Dakar had received some assistance through the local Centre de Promotion et de Réinsertion Sociale under the Ministry of Social Action, which they valued. The short-term nature of the support, however, had led to the widows' decision to organize themselves into an association that operated a rotating credit and savings scheme. Some participants commented that any support available usually only benefited those who had connections to local officials in positions of power.

While the Constitution of Senegal guarantees equal rights to women and men before the law, national laws based on French civil law, such as the Family Code, include options for Muslims to follow Islamic law regarding inheritance and often contradict customary practices, the Constitution and international UN conventions such as CEDAW. The research suggests that women's property rights are both constrained and enabled by this plural legal framework. Some women's rights organizations provided free legal advice, support, and advocacy for women and young people in pursuing inheritance claims in urban areas. Listening centres or law shops [*boutiques de droit*] in low-income neighbourhoods of Dakar and Kaolack enabled widows and others to access legal consultations and assistance with inheritance disputes, gender-based violence,ur and other discriminatory practices.

While professionals generally considered that the Family Code was appropriate in protecting widows and orphans in Senegal, they highlighted the fact that laws were often not applied. Low levels of education and literacy and a lack of knowledge about women's rights and how to claim these were identified as major barriers by several professionals. One professional, for example, commented that a widow needed to be educated and aware of her rights, and the legal system needed to function to her advantage, to be able to seek legal redress:

> The problem is the education of women, of the population who don't know what their rights are and how to claim them. The state has made provisions for possible claims and perhaps the state has not made services available to facilitate these claims.

Adult literacy rates are only 40 percent among women compared to 66 percent for men nationally, although rates are considerably higher in urban areas of Dakar, for example, 59 percent for women and 80 percent for men.[56]

Other barriers to pursuing legal inheritance claims included: a lack of money to pay for legal services—for example, a lawyer's fees are often in excess of 200,000 CFA, equivalent to £240, beyond the means of many; a lack of documents needed to pursue cases through the courts, such as marriage certificates, property deeds, and land use titles; and a reluctance for a widow to take her in-law's family or other relatives to court due to a fear of social condemnation and causing conflict. A leader of one women's organization explained:

> Here, you should not, for example, drag your husband, the family of your in-laws to court, it's seen badly [. . .] it's paradoxical, since there is a law which protects everyone, I believe that women should not stay bound. At the moment, they are fearful, so it's a situation of last resort, if you talk about the law, it's because there's no other solution, no possibility and you appeal to the law, but as long as there is a possibility of reconciliation, of negotiation, it's much better to do it within the family, negotiate so that you don't have to take legal action.

Camara argues that going to court to settle a marital dispute is regarded as an unforgivable offence and completely contrary to customary practices in Senegal, which, rather than an adversarial legal system, are based on a process of mediation, negotiation, and counseling, led by family elders.[57]

This chapter has highlighted the complex interactions between gender norms and religious and cultural practices that shape women's experiences of widowhood and asset inheritance in Senegal. Among Serer families in rural and urban areas, the inheritance of land, housing, financial assets, and other resources was usually based on a syncretism of religious and customary practices, underpinned by patrilineal rules that often disadvantaged women and girls. Widowhood-mourning practices reveal gendered dimensions of bereavement, which entail a withdrawal from household and community life for several months and potentially exacerbate poverty. Furthermore, the emotional impacts of bereavement were bound up with the economic insecurity and hardship that widows and their children often faced following the death of a male head of household.[58] Such emotional and economic insecurity was particularly evident among widows with young children living in urban areas, when the deceased husband lacked property and other assets, when widows and children were unable to access their inherited share of property and any other assets, or when they were in debt or needed to repay co-wives' inherited shares of property.[59]

In Serer rural communities in Fatick and Diourbel regions, land was usually inherited by the eldest son and other male relatives according to customary practices, and the family home was not divided, valued ,or sold, but passed on to brothers and sons where they lived with their wives and children. Cattle and other livestock, farm equipment, and financial assets were usually divided among sons, daughters, and widows according to Islamic law (in Muslim families) and customary practices (in Catholic families), or a mixture of both. Delays in the inheritance of these assets, however, could be particularly detrimental to widows and orphaned young people experiencing poverty in rural areas. Furthermore, women with low levels of literacy could lose out if male family members, who were responsible for completing paperwork for the transfer of pensions and other financial assets, were unscrupulous. Despite evidence of such tensions within some families, inheritance disputes appeared to be rare in rural areas. This is likely to be linked to the strong sense of familial duty and the high level of social cohesion and conformity in Serer rural communities, where marital disputes and family conflicts are usually settled through mediation with family and lineage elders and imams.

The research suggests that inheritance disputes were more likely in urban areas, especially between co-wives in polygamous unions and their children. One Roman Catholic widow's experience of disputed inheritance with her husband's first wife and children that she was forced to pursue through the law courts was the exception rather than the norm. In Serer Muslim families in Dakar, the inheritance of housing, financial assets and other resources was usually settled in accordance with Islamic law. Most widows and their children had inherited a share of their deceased husband's property (in the case of polygamous marriages)b or owned property in their own right. The process of sharing out the inheritance within families was, however, often characterized by flexibility, which provided space for widows, co-wives, and their children to negotiate when inheritance shares were paid back, taking account of their differing circumstances.

Thus, widows occupied differential legal and social positions in asset inheritance, depending on whether they were married in polygamous or monogamous unions and on their religion, ethnicity, education and literacy, the gender of their children, relations with co-wives and in-laws, and other social ties and support networks they were able to draw on. This reveals the importance of an intersectional analysis of widows' social location, which pays attention to their differing access to, and inheritance of, land, property, financial, and other assets in diverse urban and rural environments, within a wider context of legal pluralism.[60]

BIBLIOGRAPHY

Agence Nationale de Statistique et de la Démographie (ANSD). 2013a. *Enquête Démographique et de Santé Continue au Sénégal (EDS-Continue) 2012–2013, Rapport final lère année.* Dakar: ANSD, Calverton, Maryland: MEASURE DHS, ICF International. September 17, 2018. https://dhsprogram.com/pubs/pdf/fr288/fr288.pdf.

ANSD. 2013b. *Deuxième Enquête de la Suivi de la Pauvreté au Sénégal (ESPS II 2011). Rapport Définitif.* Dakar: Ministère de l'Economie et des Finances, République du Sénégal. September 17, 2018. http://anads.ansd.sn/index.php/catalog/17.

Bass, Loretta and Fatou Sow. "Senegalese Families: The Confluence of Ethnicity, History and Social Change." In *African Families at the Turn of the 21st Century* edited by Yaw Oheneba-Sakyi and Baffour K. Takyi, 83–102. Westport: Praeger Publishers, 2006.

Bird, Kate. 2011 "Land Inheritance: A Gendered Analysis of Factors Influencing the Intergenerational Transmission of Poverty." *Chronic Poverty Research Centre (CPRC) Working Paper No. 181* (2011). May 1, 2011. www.chronicpoverty.org.

Budlender, Debbie and Eileen Alma. *Women and Land. Securing Rights for Better Lives*. International Development Research Centre (IDRC) in Focus, Ottawa, 2011. April 24, 2012, https://www.idrc.ca/en/book/infocus-women-and-land-securing-rights-better-lives.

Camara, Fatou Kiné. "Women and the Law: A Critique of Senegalese Family Law." *Social Identities* 13, no. 6 (2007), 787–800.

Cooper, Elizabeth. "Women and Inheritance in Sub-Saharan Africa: What Can Change?" *Development Policy Review* 30, no. 5 (2012): 641–57.

Deere, Carmen Diana and Cheryl R. Doss. *Gender and the Distribution of Wealth in Developing Countries*. Research Paper No 2006/115. United Nations University World Institute for Development Economics Research (UNU-WIDER), Helsinki. October 2006. http://ucanr.edu/blogs/food2025/blogfiles/14584.pdf.

Delaunay, Valérie and Catherine Enel. "Les migrations saisonnières féminines: le cas des jeunes bonnes à Dakar." In J. Vallin, ed. *Du Genre et de l'Afrique*, 389–402. Paris: INED, 2009.

Diop, Abdoulaye-Bara. *La Famille Wolof*. Paris: Karthala, 1985.

Evans, Ruth. "Parental Death as a Vital Conjuncture? Intergenerational Care and Responsibility Following Bereavement in Senegal." *Social & Cultural Geography* 15, no. 5 (2014): 547–70.

———. "Working with Legal Pluralism: Widowhood, Property Inheritance and Poverty Alleviation in Urban Senegal." *Gender and Development* 23, no. 1 (2015): 77–94.

———. "Gendered Struggles over Land: Shifting Inheritance Practices among the Serer in Rural Senegal." *Gender, Place and Culture* 23, no. 9 (2016): 1360–75.

Evans, Ruth, Mariwah, Simon. and Barima Antwi, Kwabena. "Struggles Over Family Land? Tree Crops, Land and Labour in Ghana's Brong-Ahafo Region." *Geoforum* 67 (2015): 24–35.

Evans, Ruth, Ribbens McCarthy, Jane, Bowlby, Sophia, Wouango, Joséphine and Kébé, Fatou. *Responses to Death, Care and Family Relations in Urban Senegal*, Research Report 1, Human Geography Research Cluster, University of Reading. 2016. January 2, 2018. http://blogs.reading.ac.uk/deathinthefamilyinsenegal/report-key-finding/.

Evans, Ruth, Ribbens McCarthy, Jane, Bowlby, Sophia, Wouango, Joséphine and Kébé, Fatou. "Producing Emotionally Sensed Knowledge? Reflexivity and Emotions in Researching Responses to Death." *International Journal of Social Research Methodology* 20, no. 6 (2017a) 585–98.

Evans, Ruth, Jane Ribbens McCarthy, Fatou Kébé, Sophie Bowlby, and Joséphine Wouango. "Interpreting 'Grief' in Senegal: Language, Emotions and Cross-Cultural Translation in a Francophone African Context." *Mortality* 22, no. 2 (2017b), 118–35.

Fall, Abdou Salam, Philippe Antoine, Rokhaya Cissé, Latif Dramani, Mohamadou Sall, Tidiane Ndoye, Mody Diop, Bakary Doucouré, Momar Ballé Sylla, Papa Ngom, Abdoulaye Faye 2011. *The Dynamics of Poverty in Senegal: Chronic Poverty, Transitional Poverty and Vulnerabilities*. Policy Brief, LARTES National Studies. Dakar. no. 27 (2011). September 17, 2018. http://hal.ird.fr/ird-01145054/document.

Gadio, Coumba Mar and Cathy Rakowski. "Survival or Empowerment? Crisis and Temporary Migration among the Serer Millet Pounders of Senegal." *Women's Studies International Forum* 18, no. 4 (1995): 431–43.

Galvan, Dennis. *The State Must Be Our Master of Fire. How Peasants Craft Culturally Sustainable Development in Senegal*. Berkeley & Los Angeles: University of California Press, 2004.

Miles, John. "Customary and Islamic Law and Its Development in Africa." *Law for Development Review* 1, no. 1 (2006): 99–154.

Peterman, Amber. "Widowhood and Asset Inheritance in Sub-Saharan Africa: Empirical Evidence from 15 Countries." *Development Policy Review* 30, no. 5 (2012): 543–71.

Peters, Pauline E. "Challenges in Land Tenure and Land Reform in Africa: Anthropological Contributions." *World Development* 37, no. 8 (2009): 1317–25.

Quisumbing, Agnes. "Investments, Bequests and Public Policy: Intergenerational Transfers and the Escape from Poverty." *Chronic Poverty Research Centre* (CPRC) *Working Paper* 98 (October 2007). September 17, 2018. http://www.chronicpoverty.org/publications/details/investments-bequests-and-public-policy-intergenerational-transfers-and-the-escape-from-poverty.

Scales-Trent, Judy. "Women Lawyers, Women's Rights in Senegal: The Association of Senegalese Women Lawyers." *Human Rights Quarterly* 32, no. 1 (2010), 115–43.

Sow, Fatou. "Fundamentalisms, Globalisation and Women's Human Rights in Senegal." *Gender and Development* 11, no. 1 (2003): 69–76.

Thomson, Rachel, Robert Bell, Janet Holland, Sheila Henderson, Sheena McGrellis and Sue Sharpe. "Critical Moments: Choice, Chance and Opportunity in Young People's Narratives of Transition." *Sociology* 36, no. 2 (2002): 335–54.

UN-Habitat, *Paper 6: Islamic Inheritance Laws and Systems. Islam, Land and Property Research Series*. Nairobi: United Nations Human Settlements Programme, 2015. September 17, 2018. mirror.unhabitat.org/downloads/docs/3546_3490_ILP%206.doc.

NOTES

1. Loretta Bass and Fatou Sow, "Senegalese Families: The Confluence of Ethnicity, History and Social Change," in *African Families at the Turn of the 21st Century*, ed. Yaw Oheneba-Sakyi and Baffour K. Takyi (Westport: Praeger Publishers, 2006), 83–102; Ruth Evans, Jane Ribbens McCarthy, Fatou Kébé,Sophie Bowlby, and Joséphine Wouango, "Interpreting 'Grief' in Senegal: Language, Emotions and Cross-Cultural Translation in a Francophone African Context," *Mortality* 22, no. 2 (2017b), 118–35.

2. Ruth Evans, "Parental Death as a Vital Conjuncture? Intergenerational Care and Responsibility Following Bereavement in Senegal," *Social & Cultural Geography* 15, no. 5 (2014): 547–70; Ruth Evans, "Working with Legal Pluralism: Widowhood, Property Inheritance and Poverty Alleviation in Urban Senegal," *Gender and Development* 23, no. 1 (2015): 77–94.

3. This chapter is a synthesis and revised version of the material and arguments developed in relation to inheritance in urban areas in "Working with Legal Pluralism: Widowhood, Property Inheritance and Poverty Alleviation in Urban Senegal," Ruth Evans, 2015, in *Gender and Development*, copyright © Oxfam GB, reprinted by permission of Taylor & Francis Ltd, http://www.tandfonline.com on behalf of Oxfam GB. See Evans, "Working with Legal Pluralism." The arguments regarding rural areas are derived to some extent from Evans' 2016 article published in *Gender Place and Culture*, available online: www.tandfonline.com/10.1080/0966369X.2016.1160872. See Ruth Evans, "Gendered Struggles over Land: Shifting Inheritance Practices among the Serer in Rural Senegal," *Gender, Place and Culture* 23, no. 9 (2016): 1360–75.

4. I recognize that the ethnic category "Serer" is an umbrella term employed since the colonial era that groups together heterogeneous populations from seven major sub-groups: Galvan, 2004. Participants in this research identified with the term "Serer" and did not specify a sub-grouping. Dennis Galvan, *The State Must Be Our Master of Fire. How Peasants Craft Culturally Sustainable Development in Senegal* (Berkeley & Los Angeles: University of California Press, 2004).

5. Elizabeth Cooper, "Women and Inheritance in Sub-Saharan Africa: What Can Change?" *Development Policy Review* 30, no. 5 (2012), 641–57.

6. Carmen Diana Deere and Cheryl R. Doss, *Gender and the Distribution of Wealth in Developing Countries,* Research Paper No 2006/115, United Nations University World Institute for Development Economics Research (UNU-WIDER), Helsinki, October 2006, http://ucanr.edu/blogs/food2025/blogfiles/14584.pdf.

7. Debbie Budlender and Eileen Alma, 2011. Women and Land. Securing Rights for Better Lives. International Development Research Centre (IDRC) in Focus, Ottawa, 2011. April 24, 2012, https://www.idrc.ca/en/book/infocus-women-and-land-securing-rights-better-lives.

8. Cooper, "Women and Inheritance in Sub-Saharan Africa;" Kate Bird, "Land Inheritance: A Gendered Analysis of Factors Influencing the Intergenerational Transmission of Poverty," Chronic Poverty Research Centre (CPRC) Working Paper no. 181 (2011), http://www.chronicpoverty.org/publications/details/land-inheritance.

9. Agnes Quisumbing, "Investments, Bequests and Public Policy: Intergenerational Transfers and the Escape from Poverty," *Chronic Poverty Research Centre* (CPRC) *Working Paper 98* (October 2007), September 17, 2018, http://www.chronicpoverty.org/publications/details/investments-bequests-and-public-policy-intergenerational-transfers-and-the-escape-from-poverty.

10. Bass and Sow, "Senegalese Families."

11. Fatou Sow, "Fundamentalisms, Globalisation and Women's Human Rights in Senegal," *Gender and Development* 11, no. 1 (2003): 69–76.

12. Judy Scales-Trent, "Women Lawyers, Women's Rights in Senegal: The Association Nof Senegalese Women Lawyers," *Human Rights Quarterly* 32, no. 1 (2010), 115–43.

13. Judy Scales-Trent, "Women Lawyers, Women's Rights in Senegal."

14. Fatou Kiné Camara. "Women and the Law: A Critique of Senegalese Family Law." *Social Identities* 13, no. 6 (2007), 787–800; Judy Scales-Trent, "Women Lawyers, Women's Rights in Senegal."

15. Camara. "Women and the Law," 789.

16. Bass and Sow, "Senegalese Families."

17. Sow, "Fundamentalisms, Globalisation and Women's Human Rights in Senegal." Sow, 2003; Scales-Trent, "Women Lawyers, Women's Rights in Senegal."

18. Cooper, "Women and Inheritance in Sub-Saharan Africa."

19. John Miles, "Customary and Islamic Law and Its Development in Africa," *Law for Development Review* 1, no. 1 (2006): 99–154.

20. Agence Nationale de Statistique et de la Démographie (ANSD). 2013a, *Enquête Démographique et de Santé Continue au Sénégal (EDS-Continue) 2012-2013, Rapport final 1ère année.* Dakar: ANSD, Calverton, Maryland: MEASURE DHS, ICF International. September 17, 2018, https://dhsprogram.com/pubs/pdf/fr288/fr288.pdf.

21. Agence Nationale de Statistique et de la Démographie (ANSD). 2013a,

22. Amber Peterman, "Widowhood and Asset Inheritance in Sub-Saharan Africa: Empirical Evidence from 15 Countries," *Development Policy Review* 30, no. 5 (2012): 550.

23. Amber Peterman, "Widowhood and Asset Inheritance in Sub-Saharan Africa," 550

24. Abdoulaye-Bara Diop, *La Famille Wolof* (Paris: Karthala, 1985); Bass and Sow, "Senegalese Families."

25. Abdou Salam Fall, Philippe Antoine, Rokhaya Cissé, Latif Dramani, Mohamadou Sall, Tidiane Ndoye, Mody Diop, Bakary Doucouré, Momar Ballé Sylla, Papa Ngom, Abdoulaye Faye, *The Dynamics of Poverty in Senegal: Chronic Poverty, Transitional Poverty and Vulnerabilities,* Policy Brief, LARTES National Studies, Dakar. no. 27 (2011), September 17, 2018, http://hal.ird.fr/ird-01145054/document.

26. Fall et al, *The Dynamics of Poverty in Senegal.*

27. Bass and Sow, "Senegalese Families."

28. Bass and Sow, "Senegalese Families."

29. Dennis Galvan, *The State Must Be Our Master of Fire.*

30. ANSD. 2013b. *Deuxième Enquête de la Suivi de la Pauvreté au Sénégal (ESPS II 2011). Rapport Définitif.* Dakar: Ministère de l'Economie et des Finances, République du Sénégal. September 17, 2018. http://anads.ansd.sn/index.php/catalog/17.

31. ANSD. 2013b. *Deuxième Enquête de la Suivi de la Pauvreté au Sénégal (ESPS II 2011). Rapport Définitif.*

32. ANSD. 2013b. *Deuxième Enquête de la Suivi de la Pauvreté au Sénégal (ESPS II 2011). Rapport Définitif.*

33. Ethical approval for the research was granted by the University of Reading 2011–2012.

34. Ruth Evans, Jane Ribbens McCarthy, Fatou Kébé, Sophie Bowlby, and Joséphine Wouango, "Interpreting 'Grief' in Senegal: Language, Emotions and Cross-Cultural Translation in a Francophone African Context," *Mortality* 22, no. 2 (2017b), 118–35.

35. See Evans et al. "Interpreting 'Grief' in Senegal," for further discussion of the cross-cultural interpretation of grief and cultural nuances of language within Wolof, French and English.

36. Dennis Galvan, *The State Must Be Our Master of Fire.*

37. Evans et al, "Interpreting 'Grief' in Senegal."

38. Thomson, Rachel, Robert Bell, Janet Holland, Sheila Henderson, Sheena McGrellis and Sue Sharpe, "Critical Moments: Choice, Chance and Opportunity in Young People's Narratives of Transition," 2002.

39. Evans, "Parental Death as a Vital Conjuncture?"; Evans, "Working with Legal Pluralism."

40. Evans, Ruth, Mariwah, Simon. and Barima Antwi, Kwabena, "Struggles over Family Land? Tree Crops, Land and Labour in Ghana's Brong-Ahafo Region," 2015.

41. Evans, "Gendered Struggles over Land: Shifting Inheritance Practices among the Serer in Rural Senegal," *Gender, Place and Culture* 23, no. 9 (2016): 1360–375.

42. Pauline E. Peters, "Challenges in Land Tenure and Land Reform in Africa: Anthropological Contributions," *World Development* 37, no. 8 (2009): 1317–25.

43. Evans, "Gendered Struggles over Land."

44. See Evans 2016 for more in-depth discussion of land inheritance practices in the Serer rural locations.

45. Peterman, "Widowhood and Asset Inheritance in Sub-Saharan Africa."

46. Evans, "Gendered Struggles over Land."

47. UN-Habitat, *Paper 6: Islamic Inheritance Laws and Systems. Islam, land and property research* series (Nairobi: United Nations Human Settlements Programme, 2005), September 17, 2018, mirror.unhabitat.org/downloads/docs/3546_3490_ILP%206.doc.

48. Camara, "Women and the Law."

49. Camara, "Women and the Law."

50. Evans, "Working with Legal Pluralism."

51. Evans, "Gendered Struggles over Land."

52. Coumba Mar Gadio and Cathy Rakowski, "Survival or Empowerment? Crisis and Temporary Migration among the Serer Millet Pounders of Senegal," *Women's Studies International Forum* 18, no. 4 (1995): 431–43.

53. Gadio and Rakowski, "Survival or Empowerment?" 1995; Valérie Delaunay and Catherine Enel, "Les migrations saisonnières féminines: le cas des jeunes bonnes à Dakar," in J. Vallin, ed. *Du Genre et de l'Afrique* (Paris: INED, 2009), 389–402.

54. Evans, "Parental Death as a Vital Conjuncture?"

55. ANSD. 2013b. *Deuxième Enquête de la Suivi de la Pauvreté au Sénégal (ESPS II 2011). Rapport Définitif*, 17.

56. ANSD. 2013b. *Deuxième Enquête de la Suivi de la Pauvreté au Sénégal (ESPS II 2011). Rapport Définitif*, 46.

57. Camara, "Women and the Law."

58. Evans, Ruth, Ribbens McCarthy, Jane, Bowlby, Sophia, Wouango, Joséphine and Kébé, Fatou. *Responses to Death, Care and Family Relations in Urban Senegal*, Research Report 1, Human Geography Research Cluster, University of Reading. 2016. January 2, 2018. http://blogs.reading.ac.uk/deathinthefamilyinsenegal/report-key-finding/; Evans et al, "Interpreting 'grief' in Senegal."

59. See Evans, "Gendered Struggles over Land," on responses to death, care and family relations in urban Senegal for more in-depth discussion of bereavement in urban contexts.

60. I wish to thank all the family members, religious and community leaders and professionals who so willingly shared their experiences and views. I am very grateful to Baba Sarr, Fatou Kébé, Prosper Diene Faye, and Laurie Marie for their research and translation assistance and to Khady Sarr, Yacine Diagne, Prof. Abdou Salam Fall, and Ian Hopwood for facilitating access to participants. I am also grateful to the University of Reading and Walker Institute for funding the research. I thank Babacar M'baye and Besi Muhonja, editors of this collection, for their helpful feedback and assistance.

6

SISTERHOOD IN MARIAMA BÂ'S *SO LONG A LETTER*

Kadidia Sy

Mariama Bâ was a Senegalese female writer who made a great contribution to African literature, mainly through *So Long a Letter*, a contemporary novel that drew the attention of many critics. The book has received international recognition because of the way it foregrounds female subjugation in Senegalese society. As stated below, "the novel has been thematically and critically analyzed in numerous ways to applaud its thought-provoking perspectives on the condition of women, patriarchy, African politics, the institution of marriage, polygamy, education, and Islam."[1] Through this portrayal, Bâ brings awareness to the plight of women who face patriarchal constraints and struggle to overcome these challenges. Belonging to the first generation of African women who benefited from Western education, she had the privilege of receiving an education during an era in which boys were encouraged to attend school whereas girls were expected to stay home, help their mothers in the kitchen, and remain illiterate. Bâ and many other intellectuals took charge and participated in the effort of nation-building, each in his or her field of activity. As a teacher, she trained Senegalese youths and prepared them for a better future. In addition, her commitment to women's organizations such as *Les Soeurs Optimistes Internationales* demonstrated how she cared about women.[2] Through these associations, Bâ constantly fought for the improvement of women's conditions and against the injustices daily perpetrated on women, the same pain and suffering she describes in *So Long a Letter*.

Senegal, where the novel is set, became independent from French colonial rule in 1960. Split between tradition and modernity, the country strives to preserve its cultural values, which are deeply threatened by the intrusion of Western culture. Long before the arrival of white colonialists on the coast of Africa, Senegal had undergone an Arab invasion that brought Islam in the country. Indeed, 95 percent of the Senegalese population is Muslim, and that explains the predominance of polygamy, a practice that allows men the right to have up to four wives, if they can treat them all equally. Although it is believed that polygamy existed in traditional Africa before the Arab invasion, Islam makes it more conventional through its law.[3] This situation explains the expansion of polygamy in Senegal, where the need to have many children that can help work the land finds an approval among men who take advantage of this opportunity to keep multiple wives. Polygamy as a patriarchal institution oppresses women and causes much pain and suffering, a reality Bâ portrays through the experiences of Ramatoulaye and Aissatou, the protagonists. However, although polygamy is still rampant in Senegal, more women have started to challenge the system by questioning its foundation. In fact, some educated women denounce the injustice and oppression that polygamy imposes on women and reject the practice.

First, *So Long a Letter* offers a representation of the Senegalese society in which Bâ (1980) describes the plight of women through both the content and form of the novel. The book constitutes an epistolary novel that presents a letter that Ramatoulaye is writing to her friend Aissatou. Through this epistolary form of the novel, Bâ foregrounds female friendship, since the correspondence between the two women and the issue of female empowerment it reveals attest to the closeness of the protagonists' relationship. Mary Jane Androne (2003) asserts:

> [I]n her letter—the most intimate and personal form of correspondence—to her closest friend, Ramatoulaye bares her soul and divulges her innermost concerns, worries and beliefs. The confiding tone in many instances in this letter suggests the trust that exists between writer and recipient and this carries over to the reader who often feels as if she is overhearing a private monologue.[4]

The letter's form also reinforces the confusion about its actual addressee. Some critics argue that Ramatoulaye may be writing to herself in order to alleviate the loneliness and pain of her seclusion, especially since the letter will not be mailed. Ramatoulaye spent the whole period of her widowhood writing a letter to her friend, in which she describes the joys and sorrows of their lives. In fact, talking to Aissatou, the narrator seems to be addressing herself not only because they share the same memories and experiences but also because she feels the need to reflect on the issues bothering them. This epistolary form serves to express their bonding and reveals the intensity of the relationship. The recollection of their shared memories makes it easier for Ramatoulaye to overcome the four months and ten days of seclusion Islam requires of widows. Ramatoulaye's husband dies and, according to Islamic rule, she has to remain in seclusion for a period of four months and ten days. Although she can run errands inside and outside the house, she has to cover her whole body and lower her voice.

The narration of both stories keeps Ramatoulaye busy and gives her an opportunity to address her friend as if she were talking to her physically. The letter reduces the distance between them and establishes communication. Christina Abuk (2003) writes: "Whilst the act of communication reveals the personal changes and experiential gaps that result from the two friends' separation, the effect of the long-letter structure is to convey a sense of unbroken unity and communication between them."[5] The composition of this letter gives the narrator an opportunity to share the story about her ordeals with her friend. An epistolary form requires a confidant, and Ramatoulaye finds one in Aissatou. According to Coulis (2003), "The question of genre might be explained by double coding or, in Bâ's work, multi-or plural coding. While Ramatoulaye speaks ostensibly to Aissatou, her narrative includes messages to her Senegalese sisters, brothers, children, other postcolonial societies, former imperial powers, not to mention the chapter which speaks directly to Modou, her late husband."[6] The question surrounding the genre of Bâ's book gives way to many speculations. Whether regarded as a letter, a diary, or an autobiography, the form draws much attention. Because the narrative does neither match the author's life nor record the events daily, it seems to be a letter even though it will not be mailed. Whatever genre you choose to name this narrative, it conveys Bâ's message properly and allows her to highlight female solidarity.

The main points Bâ describes in *So Long a Letter* foreground the healing powers of female friendship. Women's relationships allow the protagonists to fight polygamy, colonialism, the caste system, and any form of prejudice. Indeed, Bâ emphasizes the way female friendship, through mutual support and sincere commitment, helps women overcome any attempt at subjugation and heals the pain resulting from oppression. As this example shows, "fiction such as Bâ's can be read variously, for instance as an embodiment of feminist or womanist principles, as a portrait of postcolonial conflicts, or as a coming to consciousness and writing."[7] Consequently, Aissatou and Ramatoulaye succeed in extending their bonds into a type of female solidarity that reaches more women and that even contributes to nation-building. Bâ's protagonists also gain female empowerment and build new identities that allow them to survive their respective husband's betrayal and assume their new lives as single mothers. Their belief in education grants them the status of professional women in a context where most women remain at home, and their struggle over women's liberation secures their own freedom and that of their community as well.

In the process, Bâ clearly reveals the pain and suffering women experience through polygamy in *So Long a Letter*. She portrays polygamy as an agent of patriarchy that keeps women oppressed through the daily injustices perpetrated on them. The two friends and protagonists of the novel, Ramatoulaye and Aissatou, have both known the discomfort of polygamy and undergone its dire consequences. Indeed, after many years of happy marriage and the birth of three sons, Aissatou's husband, Mawdo Bâ, takes a second wife to honor his mother's demand. Unhappy with the social background of her daughter-in-law, Aunty Nabou, Mawdo's mother, urges her son to marry a woman of his own class. Aissatou refuses to share her husband with another woman and condemns Mawdo for his weakness toward his mother, who urges him to marry his cousin. She chooses divorce over polygamy and writes in a note she leaves for Mawdo, "I am stripping myself of your love, your name. Clothed in my dignity, the only worthy garment, I go my way."[8] Her difficult decision to leave and start a new life results from her determination to fight polygamy in all its forms and a desire to claim her independence. She considers her husband's acceptance of Young Nabou, as a second wife, to be a denial of the commitment they made to each other many years ago. Feeling betrayed, she refuses to get involved in polygamy and prefers divorce, despite the difficulty of single parenting. Her friend, Ramatoulaye, understands and accepts her decision and even encourages Aissatou to assume her new responsibility. This support has been very important to Aissatou, who finds the courage and strength to face the challenges. She, in fact, needs all the assistance she can get to face this patriarchal institution that breaks her marriage and transforms her into a single parent.

Aissatou's choice to leave her husband and raise her three children alone conflicts with Senegalese custom and tradition that require women to be obedient and be ready to welcome co-wives openly. Bâ foregrounds the Senegalese custom that urges its citizens to share almost everything, which applies even to the conjugal life, since women learn very early all the aspects of polygamy and know that they may have to share their husband with another wife or more. Aissatou's decision is unique, and she faces severe criticism and judgment from the community, which does not approve of her stand. Western education plays a key role in her choice and offers her the opportunity to embrace the concept of monogamy and, therefore, reject culturally accepted polygamy. Addressing educated women, Abuk (2003) asserts, "Their rejection of polygamy is based on the enduring Western ideal that the only acceptable marriage is monogamous marriage for true love. They are the first generation of Muslim Senegalese women for whom such a rationale would be imaginable."[9] As an educated woman, Aissatou dares to challenge institutionalized polygamy and finds her way through the painful experience of single parenting.

Although her mentoring and counseling help her friend Aissatou recover from her predicament, Ramatoulaye finds herself in need of support when she goes through an experience that is almost the same or even worse. Aissatou also shows compassion and dependability when Ramatoulaye's husband, Modou Fall, takes a second wife, who happens to be the friend and classmate of their daughter, Daba. Ramatoulaye complains, "Binetou, a child the same age as my daughter Daba, promoted to the rank of my co-wife, whom I must face up to."[10] Unlike his friend, Mawdo, who wanted to accommodate both of his wives had Aissatou accepted his second marriage, Modou makes the dramatic decision to leave Ramatoulaye and her twelve children behind, after twenty-five years of marriage. This move severely affects the latter, who feels betrayed and abandoned. Surprised by Modou's attitude, she does not understand his decision to marry a second wife, especially, Binetou, her daughter's classmate. The betrayal and deception grow considerably when Ramatoulaye gradually realizes that her husband is not even coming back to give her an explanation. The following statement translates her dramatic situation, "Yet social restrictions steered many talented women into the silent roles of the everyday, where they made their lives, and those of their households, into a species of poetry."[11] Then, her anger becomes bitterness because after the frustration of the beginning, as a devout Muslim, she is prepared to accept polygamy according to the precepts of Islam only to discover that Modou does not even give her a choice. Ramatoulaye reflects: "I lived in a vacuum. And Modou avoided me. Attempts by friends and family to bring him back to the fold proved futile. [. . .] He never came again; his new found happiness gradually swallowed up his memory of us. He forgot about us."[12] His decision to abandon Ramatoulaye and her children altogether for the sake of a new and younger wife saddens the first and transforms her into a head of household and a single mother overnight. Unlike Aissatou, she did not choose such status and would, indeed, have tolerated polygamy had her husband decided to stay with her. Ramatoulaye reflects, "I had the solution my children wanted—the break without having taken the initiative."[13] Modou's departure urges Ramatoulaye to take charge since she has to fill in the gap he left.

As Ramatoulaye helps Aissatou go through her painful experience, the latter also shows a tremendous support to her friend throughout her ordeal, even though they have different answers to the question of polygamy. Because she understands her friend's predicament, Aissatou completely empathizes with her situation, thereby, helping her overcome this challenge. The narrator sums up the events as follows, "Your disappointment was mine, as my rejection was yours."[14] The two friends have both suffered deception and betrayal from husbands to whom they were married for a long time. However, they adopt different attitudes toward their misfortunes. While Aissatou moves forward and starts a new life as a single mother, Ramatoulaye prepares herself to accept polygamy. Coulis (2003) observes, "Aissatou has known the same betrayal as her friend. And yet, she, unlike Ramatoulaye who chose to stay and remain a co-wife, refuses to accept the situation and leaves. She will not accept the othering by her husband, or his attempt at colonizing her and their children."[15] Aissatou takes Mawdo's betrayal seriously and refuses to forgive or forget; she prefers divorce and takes full responsibility for herself and her children. This decision is very courageous and actually rare in a society where polygamy constitutes the rule and not the exception. Ramatoulaye's decision to stay comes from her beliefs in marriage. She deeply believes that a woman needs a man in order to be accomplished. She says, "I am one of those who can realize themselves fully and bloom only when they form part of a couple. Even though I understand your stand, even though I respect the choice of liberated women, I have never conceived of happiness outside marriage."[16] She insists on the complementarity between men and women. Her ideals about marriage have been shattered by her husband's decision to leave her, but she would not have taken the first step, despite her children's wishes. Furthermore, even though Ramatoulaye accepts a co-wife, she refuses to become a second wife of Daouda Dieng, a former suitor, who renews his marriage proposal to her, after the death of her husband, partly because she does not want to harm his wife. She says: "Abandoned yesterday because of a woman, I cannot lightly bring myself between you and your family."[17] Ramatoulaye refuses because she understands the pain and suffering associated with polygamy and does not wish to impose such a plight on anybody.

Through the different approaches that Ramatoulaye and Aissatou have toward polygamy, Bâ demonstrates that women's differences should not be an obstacle to female friendship. She invites women to consider their differences as positive elements that call more for unity than division. The close friendship between Aissatou and Ramatoulaye allows them to tolerate differences. These situations have never endangered their relationship because what unites them is stronger than those clashes of opinion. The mutual respect they have for one another and their open-mindedness allow them to support each other under whatever circumstances. Coulis (2003) writes:

> Even though Ramatoulaye and Aissatou choose different responses to the attempt to subjugate them, they retain a friendship and respect that endures. Their bond transcends distance and all differences and is the core of the narrative. Being unclassified or unclassifiable by genre, *So Long a Letter* seems a metaphor for the sisterhood Ramatoulaye and Aissatou forged in childhood, modified throughout many years together and apart, and continues to offer sustenance and support to them both.[18]

Their different answers to polygamy only reflect their different stands on women's issues; while Aissatou regards polygamy as an injustice to fight, Ramatoulaye sees it as a burden society imposes on her, with which she has to cope. However, their ability to handle this divergence of opinion demonstrates the strength of their friendship. This situation shows that differences do not always destroy female bonding; they can be cleared and, sometimes, they are not even an issue.

Commenting on Buchi Emecheta and Bâ, Dubek (2001) states:

> Both these novelists persuasively argue against the belief that such differences between women's experiences constitute overwhelming, insurmountable obstacles to building female bonds. Their novels make clear that the physical and psychic survival of individual women depends on our ability to foster supportive female communities that find strength in cultural difference while working actively to eradicate the differences in power that separate one woman from another.[19]

Emecheta's (1979) *Joys of Motherhood* also raises the issue of female friendship and asserts how building communities can be vital to women's survival.

Class division may also explain the different choices the friends make. Aware of the status the society reserves for her as a goldsmith's daughter, Aissatou rebels against polygamy in the same way she rejects social classification.[20] Through her marriage with the prince Mawdo, she challenges the system that prevents unions between men and women of different castes. But when she thinks she has overcome the obstacle of class, another challenge surges and urges her to divorce her husband after many years. However, even the divorce is a form of revolt against not only the institution of polygamy but also against the society that advocates it. Ramatoulaye does not face the same caste problem, which may explain her stand about polygamy. Abuk (2003) asserts: "The different responses of the friends to marital betrayal are largely determined by contrasts in their social position. It is significant that Aissatou, of working-class origins, is not constrained as Ramatoulaye is: when she strips herself of a betrayed commitment, her choice of naked vulnerability is in striking contrast to Ramatoulaye's enclosed view."[21] Aissatou has nothing to lose in leaving Mawdo since the community does not tolerate a marriage between a—noble—and a goldsmith and, therefore, expects a failure. This makes her choice easier. Ramatoulaye does not follow her friend's example, which may prove to be more challenging to her, not only because of her social status but also because of her twelve children. Aissatou's three children are far easier to handle, and for once her low-class status participates in her liberation.

Besides, Aissatou's expatriation to the U.S. helps her escape the caste system in Senegal because she becomes less exposed to the community's demands. Ramatoulaye's ability to treat Aissatou equally despite her low-class status makes their bonding possible and keeps it alive. She refuses to adhere to the community's class division that assigns people ranks according to their lineage and dictates who is noble and who is not, regardless of their achievement in the society. Ramatoulaye's acceptance of Aissatou reinforces the latter and restores her dignity after Aunty Nabou's open rejection. The friendship heals this painful and humiliating experience and arms Aissatou with courage that allows her to face her destiny. Bâ criticizes the Senegalese caste system that causes much division and weakens the country because those whom society considers—noble—refuse to bond with or marry members of the less fortunate low caste. This unjust and belittling categorization frustrates and revolts Aissatou, who finds herself a victim of the situation. Writing to Mawdo, she complains, "Princes master their feelings to fulfill their duties. Others bend their heads and, in silence, accept a destiny that oppresses them."[22] In accepting the marriage orchestrated by his mother, Mawdo indirectly joins her in an attempt to purify himself from the humiliation of marrying a low caste goldsmith. Aissatou manages to live through Aunty Nabou's rejection and scorn of her, but she will not allow Mawdo to violate her dignity and minimize her.

Despite these challenges, the support and comfort Aissatou and Ramatoulaye provide each other help them overcome and demonstrate the healing powers of female friendship. The two protagonists devote themselves entirely to each other, nurture, and care for one another, and succeed in keeping their relationship strong. Their commitment to each other and their refusal to be subjugated help them escape the patriarchal structures that attempt to oppress them. A critic writes: "The heroines in *Une Si Longue Lettre,* Rama, Aissatou, and Jacqueline, are a living testimony to the positive transformative capabilities of a negative experience born of the problematic of abandonment."[23]

Through the portrayal of this strong form of female bonding, Bâ exposes the advantages of female friendship that helps overcome difficulties, and she invites women to follow the example of Ramatoulaye and Aissatou. Each of them survives the painful experiences she has been through and, therefore, becomes an inspiration to other women who may go through similar situations. Their achievement may have an impact on entire communities and spread the word about female solidarity. Each accepts the other's decisions and endeavors as they build a strong sisterhood. Bâ's novel shows the impact of female bonding in women's lives and how it brings positive changes in their attitude and environment.

The two friends in *So Long a Letter* give a perfect example of what female friendship should be; their relationship defies time as their bonding starts in their childhood and becomes deeper and stronger in their middle age life. The narrator states,

> Your presence in my life is by no means fortuitous. Our grandmothers in their compounds were separated by a fence and would exchange messages daily. Our mothers used to argue over who would look after our uncles and aunts. As for us, we wore out wrappers and sandals on the same stony road to the Koranic school; we buried our milk teeth in the same holes and begged our fairy godmothers to restore them to us, more splendid than before.[24]

Their reliance on each other, their mutual trust and dependability nourish their friendship. This multi-generational relationship—their grandmothers and aunts were friends before them—has been preserved because of their respect for the basic principles of friendship. Through this bonding, Bâ's novel gives hope to those who believe in the necessity of female solidarity and work hard in their attempts to build a strong sisterhood. It argues against those who think women incapable of building serious friendship and see female solidarity as utopia or as a highly feminist project. Hudson-Weems (2004) sees *So Long a Letter* as an embodiment of her theory on womanism mainly because of the novel's focus on female friendship. Aissatou and Ramatoulaye's struggle to define and develop new selves makes them stronger and allows them to survive their predicaments. Ann McElanie-Johnson (1999) notes: "Both the closeness of this relationship and its healing powers become basic to the thematic texture of this novel of female friendship."[25] Ramatoulaye and Aissatou's empowering relationship is an inspiring example that may impact the lives of many people.

Besides highlighting female solidarity, Bâ also uses the examples of Aissatou and Ramatoulaye to show that women can fight and even overcome patriarchal oppression through material independence. Her novel encourages women to find ways and means to free themselves from financial dependence that keeps them in formal bondage. The protagonists' move to get remunerated jobs contrasts with the reality of the Senegalese society where men are encouraged to seek professional success whereas women expect to get husbands and raise families. They both become teachers, professional women with salaries who can take care of themselves. Aissatou succeeds as a single mother because she strives to reach a stable financial situation that allows her to provide for herself and her children without expecting any external help. Her divorce prompts her to choose another career as a translator, which provides her with a better opportunity to cover her expenses compared to her former job as an elementary school teacher. This critic acknowledges the challenges: "The women in Bâ's novels need not be reduced to naive converts of assimilation or to superwomen battling the forces of patriarchy. They are simply human beings who are as flawed as they are triumphant. Attributing to them heroic feats without acknowledging their pain and weaknesses is as oppressive as portraying them as male bashers or self- righteous victims."[26] Realizing the difficulty of her task, Aissatou, very soon, starts looking for a suitable solution that may allow her to meet her expectations. Similarly, Ramatoulaye's salary as a schoolteacher sustains her twelve children when her husband abandons her and then dies. The economic freedom of the friends saves them from humiliation and more suffering when they face situations that require self-sufficiency. Abuk writes: "By rooting her text in the artifacts, routines and material concerns of a world of women, Bâ implies that their material dependence or independence is the key determinant of the social justice and equality they are accorded."[27] Bâ's novel offers professionalism and paid labor as solutions to women's oppression and abuse because they bring material freedom; however, the first step is education, which leads to that opportunity.

As pioneers of educated African women, Ramatoulaye and Aissatou set a strong example for their generation and those that will follow by showing that women can be both providers for their family and mothers. There is no contradiction between the two roles; they actually complement each other because the working mother can secure the material needs of her children and, at the same time, offer emotional and nurturing support. As Dubek (2001) observes, "Education's effect of raising female expectations has been critical to the subject formation of Ramatoulaye and Aissatou. Their hopes have been shaped by ideologies of individualism and romanticism. Both are acting in self interest in seeking this social model, which promises them comparative wealth and power."[28] Neither Ramatoulaye nor Aissatou hesitates to take advantage of such opportunity, which liberates them from financial dependence. They, thus, set another example of empowerment which provides women with economic freedom.

Through education, colonialism has another impact on Aissatou and Ramatoulaye. They both go to colonial school and abandon the Koranic school they used to attend. Although both schools are foreign to Senegalese culture, the second one is deeply embedded in the tradition because Senegal had embraced Islam for many centuries before the beginning of colonialism. School gives the protagonists an opportunity to consolidate their friendship which started long before they attended Koranic school. Although Western education is a way toward women's liberation, it also creates ideological changes that make it hard for the friends to cope with their traditional values. Aissatou's rejection of polygamy and caste system, for example, is caused by the influence of her Western education. Abuk states: "Colonial education has revolutionized the lives and minds of *SLAL*'s two friends, turning them into upper-class matrons—professional, widely read."[29] Western education interferes with the class system in Senegal and grants the educated male elites a middle-class status. In fact, both Aissatou and Ramatoulaye and their respective husbands, Mawdo and Modou, belong to the middle class regardless of their rank in the society. However, the conservatives in the novel like Aunt Nabou do not acknowledge this new social stratification and still cling to the old rules. Abuk writes: "Actually, despite Aissatou's lower class status in the Senegalese caste system, education promulgates her to the middle class; in the same way, Ramatoulaye enjoys a bourgeois life with servants and outings."[30] Thus, despite the patriarchal attempts to subjugate them, women are able to use education as an opportunity to liberate themselves.

Ramatoulaye pays tribute to a headmistress for introducing Aissatou and her to school and encouraging them to stay. A form of sisterhood grows between the girls and their headmistress who cares about their future and teaches them how to be independent. This white woman cares more for female solidarity and the need to emancipate these girls than the concerns of colonialism. Ramatoulaye also remembers the multitude of girls, from different countries, that used to attend school in Dakar, and she praises the solidarity between them. She describes it as "a fruitful blend of different intellectuals, characters, manners and customs," saying, "Friendships were made that have endured the test of time and distance. We were true sisters, destined for the same mission of emancipation."[31] This assertion refers to colonization, when Dakar was the capital of the West African colonies ruled by the French system. The schools of the administration were located in Dakar, which explains why the girls attend school in Dakar and not in their countries. Reminiscing this history, the headmistress trains many African women to liberate themselves from the burden of patriarchal oppression and nourish the dream of sisterhood. All these girls have the same goals: to make changes for themselves and their society through education. Their success will not only empower them but also contribute to nation building because their achievement also has an impact on the development of their countries. The headmistress' goal goes beyond female friendship and reaches female solidarity since these girls represent different nations and cultures, but they all enjoy the same seeds of liberation. The female friendship between Aissatou and Ramatoulaye expands into female solidarity that goes beyond national boundaries. As their example illustrates, education can not only provide freedom but also offer a good opportunity for female solidarity. Ramatoulaye and Aissatou's experiences through colonization, independence and neocolonialism teach them how to cope with the various changes going on in Senegal as the country attempts to stand on its feet. As patriarchal structures, the above-mentioned agents participate in keeping women in bondage. After many centuries of colonization, Africa gets its emancipation from colonial rule. This liberation parallels the protagonists' struggle for emancipation.

However, independence does not liberate Senegalese women from the various forms of oppression they are experiencing. Indeed, neocolonialism creates new challenges for Ramatoulaye and Aissatou, who face new realities. Obviously, these transformations impact their lives since they face the daily struggle between traditional beliefs and modern Western values. Aissatou and Ramatoulaye have challenged some aspects of their traditions like polygamy and caste prejudice, but they have also refused to be alienated from their community through the influence of colonialism. As Patricia Sehulster (2004) indicates, "While *So Long a Letter* focuses specifically on Senegalese society and on the Islamic patriarchy that controls women's lives, by extension, it also makes a statement about the movement from colonization to independence that all of Africa has faced because of imperialism."[32] Bâ's novel does not call for a total rejection of traditional values but invites women to make careful choices and question some aspects that may oppress them. Facing the double burden of colonialism and traditional rules, Ramatoulaye and Aissatou survive because their friendship helps them face various challenges. Coulis observes,

> While the other female characters are hurt and perplexed by their seemingly powerless situations and remain ignorant of the causes, Ramatoulaye and Aissatou are particularly wounded: they are both fully aware of the workings of double colonization. They have been educated in the French rule and recognize that they have again been colonized, this time by patriarchal authority in the guise of religious custom.[33]

Although colonialism offers the friends the opportunity to challenge patriarchal oppression because their education brings an awareness that encourages them to fight back, it also keeps them in bondage. Indeed, colonialism calls for a rejection of traditional values, posing the threat of cultural alienation. One critic observes: "It is evident that the distorted view of African traditions, marriage, and sexuality in Bâ's novels is rooted in colonial assimilation, but few critics have furnished details of who, when, why, or how it functioned."[34]

Aissatou and Ramatoulaye, indeed, put some of their traditional beliefs aside and embrace some Western values. This clash between modernity and tradition draws the attention of Bâ, who encourages African people in general and Senegalese in particular to find the right balance between the two cultures. Coulis claims, "Aissatou's stance sums up her refusal to be personally colonized by patriarchal ideology through Muslim custom."[35] Ramatoulaye and Aissatou seem to have found the appropriate solution, which allows them to benefit from both cultures equally, but most importantly they succeed in keeping their friendship that strengthens them throughout the years.

Moreover, although both Ramatoulaye and Aissatou have experienced the impact of colonialism, Ramatoulaye is still more traditional because she lives within the Senegalese society the rules of which dictate her daily conduct, whereas Aissatou's displacement exposes her more to Western culture. Keith L. Walker (2003) asserts: "The move to colonial independence also involves a shift in the identity of the colonized subject."[36] This shift in identity explains how far the subject is willing to embrace the culture of the colonizer. Ramatoulaye's deep respect for African traditional values makes her tolerate polygamy even though she realizes the difficulty of such sacrifice. She chooses to suffer personally rather than reject a profoundly rooted custom. Living in New York, Aissatou has no direct contact with the Senegalese community and has the freedom to choose more independent principles. Dubek writes: "The enduring friendship between the Westernized Aissatou and the traditional Ramatoulaye affirms that different cultural mores can co-exist. The challenge facing a modernizing Senegal is exactly how to negotiate a union of two such diverse cultures without destroying the integrity of either one."[37] Neither distance nor the different cultures endanger the friendship which keeps growing. The displacement does not totally transform Aissatou, who still does not forget her friend or her identity even though she has embraced some aspects of modernity. Aissatou's displacement results from her constant fight against patriarchal oppression. Both Aissatou and Ramatoulaye strive hard to build themselves new identities. They challenge traditional barriers, Islamic rules and colonial chains, and they define themselves according to their own understanding. Sehulster observes,

> Although Aissatou left and discovered her own, very different life, she had to step outside of her environment, her family, and her traditional roles to do so. She became a sort of exile. On the other hand, Ramatoulaye remained a sort of outcast in her own home [. . .] Ramatoulaye and Aissatou, like the colonized of the many countries of Africa, have found freedom by remembering, finding, and devel-

oping their true selves. They have broken the fetters of oppression and falsehood to emerge in a new day fashioned entirely on their own terms.[38]

Through Aissatou and Ramatoulaye's friendship, Bâ shows that differences can be positive and actually contribute to the success of relationships because each part brings something, thereby, calling for the complementary nature of the bonding. Through this conflict, Bâ's novel foregrounds the complex dilemma of colonized people. Torn between the desire to preserve their culture and the temptation to adopt modernity, African people in general and Senegalese in particular have a difficult choice to make. As Aissatou and Ramatoulaye develop and transform their friendship into female solidarity, their relationship reaches a new stage that allows them to survive.

So Long a Letter describes not only the oppression of Ramatoulaye and Aissatou, but also that of the Senegalese women in general who face various challenges related to neocolonialism, tradition, or religion. The portrayal goes beyond the boundaries of Senegal and extends to women all over the world. Indeed, the pain described in the novel concerns all women who live a similar situation in Africa and elsewhere. Referring to Bâ, Sehulster states: "Her tale does much more than narrate the story of oppression of a few female characters or of the African female race; it reveals instead the process of colonization and the move toward independence of all of the African nations once subjected to colonial rule."[39] Indeed, almost all African countries have experienced colonialism and neo-colonialism, and women mainly suffer from the same patriarchal constraints. Thus, through *So Long a Letter*, Bâ denounces the injustice perpetrated against women everywhere. This situation shows the precarious conditions of women who still have to fight to liberate themselves from subjugation. As female friendship extends to female solidarity, the suffering of Senegalese women reflects the pain of all women regardless of national origin. In an interview, Bâ explains:

> Naturally, because this book often described as a—cry from the heart, is indeed a cry from the heart of all women everywhere. It is first a cry from the heart of the Senegalese women, because it talks about the problems of Senegalese women, of Muslim women, wom-

en constrained by religion and other social constraints that weigh them down. But, it is also a cry that can symbolize the cry of woman everywhere.[40]

Despite the different experiences and the forms of oppression under which they suffer, women have a status of victims which puts them in the same category: "Instruments for some, baits for others, respected or despised, often muzzled, all women have almost the same fate, which religions or unjust legislation have sealed" (Bâ 1980, 88). The commonality of different forms of injustice in different parts of the world calls attention to women's condition. The similarity in women's experiences require measures that are likely to fight any form of injustice from which women are suffering. Bâ's novel advocates female friendship as a solution to the plight of the Islamic and postcolonial woman. Ada Uzoamaka Azodo (2003) observes, "We may lose sight of Bâ's recordings of her cultural understanding of what it means to be a woman in Senegal, specifically a woman in the Islamic-African home space. Still, there is a need in contemporary society to understand why so many women, beyond the boundaries of race and ethnicity continue to be victims of societal and/or male subordination, exclusion and marginalization."[41] The two friends and protagonists fight alone against their predicaments whereas the whole society sides with their husbands who are responsible for their oppression.

Despite their friendship and the experiences they have been through, Ramatoulaye and Aissatou do not embrace the same form of feminism. Even though Ramatoulaye is an emancipated woman, she does not believe in an extreme form of feminism. Her view of feminism is somewhat conservative since it takes into consideration African realities and her own conception of the relationships between men and women. Omofolabo Ajayi-Soyinka (2003) writes:

> *So Long a Letter* advocates feminism without dismissing the specificity of the African experience or the different aspects that constitute a people's culture. It is a feminism that combines the quest for African identity with personal independence, a responsible individualism committed to a responsive collectivity. It supports self-fulfillment but not self-centeredness; celebrates motherhood, but not as the flag of identity.[42]

In spite of her education and her awareness about the different trends, Ramatoulaye adopts a form of feminism that does not alienate her from her culture. Although she believes in women's liberation, she also understands that some feminists' principles do challenge African traditional beliefs. Her views qualify her as an Africana woman who, according to Hudson-Weems, strongly believes in the peaceful cohabitation of men and women. Ramatoulaye sees men and women as partners in the general struggle for survival rather than as enemies. Azodo writes: "What Ramatoulaye spells out in rehearsing the events, decisions, crises and joys of her life is what it means to live a feminist life that can tolerate contradictions, overcome challenges, endure loss and find fulfillment in the interstices of an imperfect society as she struggles to raise her children, work at her profession and participate in the life of the community."[43] Her respect for traditional values and her views about men and women's relationships make her special. Sehulster states: "Though Ramatoulaye seeks within a framework of new rules and new self-concept, she maintains her traditional belief in motherhood, in marriage, and in love, though she views marriage without love as impossible."[44] In contrast, Aissatou is a fully liberated woman who does not need a man at her side and prepares herself to face all challenges, whereas Ramatoulaye advocates another form of liberation which requires men and women to work together. Ramatoulaye does not believe in a feminism that advocates animosity between men and women. She calls for a good understanding between men and women for the benefit of the community as a whole.

Although Ramatoulaye seeks the collaboration between men and women, the attempt does not work well in the novel. Indeed, the seeming harmony between the couples breaks and leaves an emptiness that fails to be filled. This failure of marriage is reflected in Bâ's own life even though the book is not an autobiography. Answering a question about not being married, Bâ states: "No, although I am divorced, I *wish* I were married. Men and women are complementary. I know many women who prefer to divorce and remain single because their interests do not always work out within a marriage. I am not married, but that is not because I would not prefer to be married."[45] Bâ's view differs considerably from those of some feminists who see marriage as an obstacle to their professional growth. In the neocolonial context of *So Long a Letter*, more issues are at stake than a gender conflict. The struggle for liberation and economic freedom represents a real challenge in Senegal and requires the joined efforts of men and women altogether. Despite the betrayal she suffers from her husband and her friend's bitter experience, Ramatoulaye asserts: "I remain persuaded of the inevitable and necessary complementarity of man and woman / Love, imperfect as it may be in its content and expression, remains the natural link between these two beings."[46] However, Ramatoulaye's widowhood brings a new perspective in her life because through the rejection of all her suitors, she also rejects marriage and takes full responsibility for herself and her children as a single mother. She wins a great battle with the patriarchs by refusing to marry Modou's brother, Tamsir, who attempts to make use of an orchestrated leviratic system in which men can inherit their brother's wife after their death. Addressing Tamsir, she complains, "You forget that I have a heart, a mind, that I am not an object to be passed from hand to hand."[47] Ramatoulaye openly challenges patriarchy by rejecting Tamsir because the community expects her to accept the proposal. This new status leads her to join Aissatou in her newfound field. The narrator observes: "I am not indifferent to the irreversible currents of women's liberation that are lashing the world. This commotion that is shaking up every aspect of our lives reveals and illustrates our abilities."[48] Thus, Ramatoulaye's different form of feminism does not exclude her from the movement. She actually identifies herself with the women's liberation group and is committed to the struggle to free women from oppression. Brandy Hayslett (2003) notes:

> Ramatoulaye's decision to choose sisterhood as a way of expressing her concept of feminism is one that gains her respect as well as freedom from the orders of any man. Her assurance that knowledge, femininity, and power would gain her the freedom she desires is her own brand of feminism in a country full of women like her, who may have only a slight difference in their own definitions of feminism.[49]

Despite the various attempts to subjugate her, Ramatoulaye finally overcomes and succeeds in liberating herself. She becomes a liberated woman like Aissatou and assumes her new identity as a single mother who does not need a husband in order to be complete.

Although Bâ presents the healing powers of female friendship in *So Long a Letter*, she also shows that some women are a threat to others. The novel presents this aspect of women's relationships as a challenge to female solidarity because, instead of joining hands in bonding, women fight for personal interests. A critic states: "The phenomenon of women deliberately and maliciously sabotaging the happiness of other women in a male-dominated society is one that has come to be a major focal point in the work of Mariama Ba."[50] This statement denounces the fact that some women use others as tools in order to accomplish their own goals and harm other women equally. Thus, the novel also reveals that not all women are willing to cultivate female friendship, and that some may even cause pain to others for their own empowerment or for the sake of patriarchy. Those women used as tools are victims of a situation in which they have no control and cannot liberate themselves. Neither Binetou nor Nabou have chosen to become co-wives respectively to Ramatoulaye and Aissatou. The women who command the plot, Aunt Nabou and Binetou's mother, Lady Mother-in-Law, manipulate and exploit them without caring for their well-being.[51] Azodo (2003) writes: "The Binetous and the Nabous in general represent young girls sacrificed at the altar of materialism in modern Senegal by rapacious mothers and mother figures, who crave the good life at the expense of their wards."[52] Both Binetou and Nabou have been led to marry older men for their mother's and aunt's respective personal gratification. While Binetou marries Modou in order to provide her mother with a chance to enjoy a middle-class status, Nabou allows her aunt to regain her lost nobility and take revenge on Aissatou. The older women do not care about these children's happiness; they put forward their own goals and engage the girls in polygamous marriages in which they will end up as victims. Azodo (2003) adds:

> Though the actions of Bâ's heroines represent ways in which women claim constructive power, which affirms women's positive roles in society and frees them from the constraints demanded by patriarchal tradition, some of the women who have access to power use it destructively. These women cause various problems for the heroines, whom they see as threats to the fulfillment of their own agendas.[53]

Sacrificing the girls' happiness at the expense of the adults creates much harm in causing the breakdown of other women's marriages. While Nabou causes Aissatou's divorce, Binetou constitutes the main reason why Modou leaves Ramatoulaye and her twelve children. Rebecca Wilcox (2003) observes: "Many of Bâ's women find their happiness and independence thwarted by overbearing parents, as in the case of Binetou, or by negligent and deceptive husbands."[54] While the heroines struggle against patriarchal domination, other women endanger the process and serve as agents to motivate and facilitate the oppression. Modou's and Mawdo's plans would not work if Nabou and Binetou did not accept to be the scapegoats for Aunty Nabou and Lady Mother-in-Law.

Overall, *So Long a Letter* presents a strong form of female friendship that ultimately extends to female solidarity as Aissatou and Ramatoulaye not only empower each other but also participate in nation-building. The sisterhood they build and maintain secures their survival against the constraints of patriarchy, tradition, polygamy, colonialism and other forms of oppression. Garoiu (2014) supports this view in the representation of the challenges women face. In a similar vein, Bâ advocates female empowerment that outweighs any other relationship, stating: "Friendship has splendours that love knows not. It grows stronger when crossed, whereas obstacles kill love. Friendship resists time, which wearies and severs couples. It has heights unknown to love."[55] This novel mainly foregrounds the way the sisterhood between Ramatoulaye and Aissatou reaches out to other women and then becomes female solidarity which, in return, impacts whole nations. Therefore, Wilcox (2003) comments, "Bâ provides her reader with two models for female empowerment: the woman who empowers herself at the expense of other women contrasted with the woman who empowers herself by working, however, subtly, to empower all women."[56] Their bonding not only benefits the people around *them* but also through the experience at the girls' school, female solidarity becomes a reality that involves women from different nationalities, who acquire their own emancipation and provide a great contribution to their countries. Through this example, Bâ demonstrates that female solidarity goes beyond national boundaries and that female empowerment may also contribute to nation building.

BIBLIOGRAPHY

Abuk, Christina. "Urbanisation's Long Shadows: Mariama Bâ's *So Long a Letter*." *Journal of Ethic and Migration Studies* 29, (2003): 723–40.

Ajayi-Soyinka, Omofolabo. "Negritude, Feminism, and the Quest for Identity: Re-Reading Mariama Bâ's *So Long a Letter*." In *Emerging Perspectives on Mariama Bâ: Postcolonialism, Feminism, and Postmodernism*, edited by Ada Uzoamaka Azodo, 153–74. Trenton: Africa World Press, 2003.

Androne, Mary Jane. "The Collective Spirit of Mariama Bâ's *So Long a Letter*." In *Emerging Perspectives on Mariama Bâ: Postcolonialism, Feminism, and Postmodernism*, edited by Ada Uzoamaka Azodo, 37–50. Trenton: Africa World Press, 2003.

Azodo, Ada Uzoamaka. "Theorizing the Personal in Mariama Bâ's Novels: Narration as Configuration of Knowledge." In *Emerging Perspectives on Mariama Bâ: Postcolonialism, Feminism, and Postmodernism*, edited by Ada Uzoamaka Azodo, 51–69. Trenton: Africa World Press, 2003.

Bâ, Mariama. *So Long a Letter [Une Si Longue Lettre]*. Translated by Modupe Bode-Thomas. Oxford: Heinemann, 1980.

Celarent, Barbara. "So Long a Letter by Mariama Bâ and Modupe Bode-Thomas." *The American Journal of Sociology* 116, no. 4 (2011): 1391–96.

Cham, Mbye Baboucar. "The Female Condition in Africa: A Literary Exploration by Mariama Ba." *A Current Bibliography on African Affairs* 17, no. 1 (1984–1985): 29–41.

Coulis, Shari. "The Impossibility of Choice: Gender and Genre in Mariama Bâ's *So Long a Letter*." In *Emerging Perspectives on Mariama Bâ: Postcolonialism, Feminism, and Postmodernism*, edited by Ada Uzoamaka Azodo. Trenton: Africa World Press, 2003.

Dubek, Laura. "Lessons in Solidarity: Buchi Emecheta and Mariama Bâ on Female Victim(izer)s." *Women's Studies* 30 (2001): 199–224.

Edwin, Shirin. "Subverting Social Customs: The Representation of Food in Three West African Francophone Novels." *Research in African Literatures* 39, no. 3 (2008): 39–50.

Emecheta, Buchi. *The Joys of Motherhood*. New York: George Braziller, 1979.

Garoiu, Monica. "Ecrire la Femme Africaine: Le Discours Feminin dans Une Si Longue Lettre de Mariama Ba et *Tu T'Appelleras Tanga* de Calixthe Beyala." *Journal of Research in Gender Studies* 4, no. 2 (2014): 313–24.

Harrell-Bond, Barbara. "An Interview with Mariama Bâ." In *Emerging Perspectives on Mariama Bâ: Postcolonialism, Feminism, and Postmodernis*, edited by Ada Uzoamaka Azodo, 383–402. Trenton: Africa World Press, 2003.

Hayslett, Brandy. "Sisterhood, Knowledge, Feminism, and Power in Mariama Bâ's *So Long a Letter*." In *Emerging Perspectives on Mariama Bâ: Postcolonialism, Feminism, and Postmodernism*, edited by Ada Uzoamaka Azodo, 142–50. Trenton: Africa World Press, 2003.

Hudson-Weems, Clenora. *Africana Womanist Literary Theory: A sequel to Africana Womanism: Reclaiming Ourselves*. Trenton: Africa World Press, 2004.

———. *Africana Womanism: Reclaiming Ourselves*. Troy: Bedford, 1998.

McElaney-Johnson, Ann. "Epistolary Friendship: La Prise de Parole in Mariama Bâ's *Une Si Longue Lettre*." *Research in African Literatures* 30 (1999): 110–21.

Njoya, Wandia. "On Mariama Bâ's Novels, Stereotypes, and Silence." *Comparative Studies of South Asia, Africa and the Middle East* .27, no. 2 (2007): 450–62.

O'Keefe, Charles. "Sinking One's Teeth into Mariama Bâ's *So Long a Letter*: Lessons of Cadmus." *Research in African Literatures* 40, no.2 (2009): 63–81.

Sehulster, Patricia. "*So Long a Letter*: Finding Self and Independence in Africa." *The Western Journal of Black Studies* 28 (2004): 365–71.

Walker, Keith L. "Postscripts: Mariama Bâ, Menopause, Epistolarity, and Postcolonialism." In *Emerging Perspectives on Mariama Bâ: Postcolonialism, Feminism, and Postmodernism*, edited by Ada Uzoamaka Azodo, 247–74. Trenton: Africa World Press, 2003.

Wilcox, Rebecca. "Women and Power in Mariama Bâ's Novels." In *Emerging Perspectives on Mariama Bâ: Postcolonialism, Feminism, and Postmodernism*, edited by Ada Uzoamaka Azodo, 121–42. Trenton: Africa World Press, 2003.

NOTES

1. Shirin Edwin, "Subverting Social Customs: The Representation of Food in Three West African Francophone Novels," *Research in African literatures* 39, no. 3 (2008): 45.

2. Associations like this one work to promote women and help them acquire financial freedom.

3. Arabs invaded many African countries long before white colonialism and converted most people to Islam.

4. Mary Jane Androne, "The Collective Spirit of Mariama Bâ's *So Long a Letter*," in *Emerging Perspectives on Mariama Bâ: Postcolonialism, Feminism, and Postmodernism*, ed. Ada Uzoamaka Azodo (Trenton: Africa World Press, 2003), 38.

5. Christina Abuk, "Urbanisation's Long Shadows: Mariama Bâ's *So Long a Letter*," *Journal of Ethic and Migration Studies* 29 (2003): 727.

6. Coulis, Shari. "The Impossibility of Choice: Gender and Genre in Mariama Bâ's *So Long a Letter*," in *Emerging Perspectives on Mariama Bâ: Postcolonialism, Feminism, and Postmodernism*, ed. Ada Uzoamaka Azodo (Trenton: Africa World Press, 2003), 28.

7. Charles O'Keefe, "Sinking One's Teeth into Mariama Bâ's *So Long a Letter*: Lessons of Cadmus," *Research in African Literatures* 40, no. 2 (2009): 69.

8. Mariama Bâ, *So Long a Letter*, 2.

9. Christina Abuk, "Urbanisation's Long Shadows," 735.

10. Mariama Bâ, *So Long a Letter*, trans. Modupe Bode-Thomas (Oxford: Heinemann, 1980), 9.

11. Barbara Celarent, "So Long a Letter by Mariama Bâ and Modupé Bodé-Thomas," *The American Journal of Sociology* 116, no. 4 (2011): 1395.

12. Mariama Bâ, *So Long a Letter*, 6.

13. Mariama Bâ, *So Long a Letter*, 52.

14. Mariama Bâ, *So Long a Letter*, 55.

15. Coulis, Shari. "The Impossibility of Choice," 31.

16. Mariama Bâ, *So Long a Letter*, 56.

17. Mariama Bâ, *So Long a Letter*, 68.

18. Coulis, "The Impossibility of Choice," 32.

19. Laura Dubek, "Lessons in Solidarity: Buchi Emecheta and Mariama Bâ on Female Victim(izer)s," *Women's Studies* 30 (2001): 218.

20. Goldsmiths belong to the lowest class according to the Senegalese caste system. This situation explains Aissatou's predicament when she marries a prince—her mother-in-law rejects her and finds her a co-wife.

21. Christina Abuk, "Urbanisation's Long Shadows: Mariama Bâ's *So Long a Letter*," *Journal of Ethic and Migration Studies* 29 (2003): 736.

22. Mariama Bâ, *So Long a Letter*, 31.

23. Mbye Baboucar Cham, "The Female Condition in Africa: A Literary Exploration by Mariama Ba," *A Current Bibliography on African Affairs* 17, no. 1 (1984–1985): 31.

24. Mariama Bâ, *So Long a Letter*, 1.

25. McElaney-Johnson, Ann. "Epistolary Friendship: La Prise de Parole in Mariama Bâ's *Une Si Longue Lettre*." *Research in African Literatures* 30 (1999): 114–15.

26. Wandia Njoya, "On Mariama Bâ's Novels, Stereotypes, and Silence." *Comparative Studies of South Asia, Africa and the Middle East* .27, no. 2 (2007): 462.

27. Christina Abuk, "Urbanisation's Long Shadows," 727.

28. Laura Dubek, "Lessons in Solidarity: Buchi Emecheta and Mariama Bâ on Female Victim(izer)s," *Women's Studies* 30 (2001): 211.

29. Christina Abuk, "Urbanisation's Long Shadows," 730.

30. Christina Abuk, "Urbanisation's Long Shadows," 731.

31. Mariama Bâ, *So Long a Letter*, 15.

32. Patricia Sehulster, "*So Long a Letter*: Finding Self and Independence in Africa." *The Western Journal of Black Studies* 28 (2004): 366.

33. Coulis, "The Impossibility of Choice: Gender and Genre in Mariama Bâ's *So Long a Letter*," 32.

34. Wandia Njoya, "On Mariama Bâ's Novels, Stereotypes, and Silence." *Comparative Studies of South Asia, Africa and the Middle East* .27, no. 2 (2007): 457.

35. Coulis, "The Impossibility of Choice," 31.

36. Keith L. Walker, "Postscripts: Mariama Bâ, Menopause, Epistolarity, and Postcolonialism," in *Emerging Perspectives on Mariama Bâ: Postcolonialism, Feminism, and Postmodernism*, ed. Ada Uzoamaka Azodo (Trenton: Africa World Press, 2003), 251.

37. Laura Dubek, "Lessons in Solidarity: Buchi Emecheta and Mariama Bâ on Female Victim(izer)s," *Women's Studies* 30 (2001): 212.

38. Patricia Sehulster, "*So Long a Letter*: Finding Self and Independence in Africa." *The Western Journal of Black Studies* 28 (2004): 369–70.

39. Patricia Sehulster, "*So Long a Letter*," 367.

40. Barbara Harrell-Bond, "An Interview with Mariama Bâ," in *Emerging Perspectives on Mariama Bâ: Postcolonialism, Feminism, and Postmodernis*, ed. Ada Uzoamaka Azodo (Trenton: Africa World Press, 2003), 396–97.

41. Ada Uzoamaka Azodo, "Theorizing the Personal in Mariama Bâ's Novels: Narration as Configuration of Knowledge," in *Emerging Perspectives on Mariama Bâ: Postcolonialism, Feminism, and Postmodernism*, ed. Ada Uzoamaka Azodo (Trenton: Africa World Press, 2003), 52.

42. Omofolabo Ajayi-Soyinka, "Negritude, Feminism, and the Quest for Identity: Re-Reading Mariama Bâ's *So Long a Letter*," in *Emerging Perspectives on Mariama Bâ: Postcolonialism, Feminism, and Postmodernism*, ed. Ada Uzoamaka Azodo (Trenton: Africa World Press, 2003), 169.

43. Ada Uzoamaka Azodo, "Theorizing the Personal in Mariama Bâ's Novels," 47.

44. Patricia Sehulster, "*So Long a Letter*: Finding Self and Independence in Africa." *The Western Journal of Black Studies* 28 (2004): 369–70.

45. Barbara Harrell-Bond, "An Interview with Mariama Bâ," in *Emerging Perspectives on Mariama Bâ: Postcolonialism, Feminism, and Postmodernis*, ed. Ada Uzoamaka Azodo (Trenton: Africa World Press, 2003), 383.

46. Mariama Bâ, *So Long a Letter*, 88.

47. Mariama Bâ, *So Long a Letter*, 88.

48. Mariama Bâ, *So Long a Letter*, 88.

49. Brandy Hayslett, "Sisterhood, Knowledge, Feminism, and Power in Mariama Bâ's *So Long a Letter*," in *Emerging Perspectives on Mariama Bâ: Postcolonialism, Feminism, and Postmodernism*, ed. Ada Uzoamaka Azodo (Trenton: Africa World Press, 2003), 149.

50. Mbye Baboucar Cham, "The Female Condition in Africa: A Literary Exploration by Mariama Ba," *A Current Bibliography on African Affairs* 17, no. 1 (1984–1985): 47.

51. The narrator does not give Binetou's mother a name. Ramatoulaye ironically calls her Lady Mother-in-Law because of her affiliation with Modou.

52. Ada Uzoamaka Azodo, "Theorizing the Personal in Mariama Bâ's Novels," 57.

53. Ada Uzoamaka Azodo, "Theorizing the Personal in Mariama Bâ's Novels," 57.

54. Rebecca Wilcox, "Women and Power in Mariama Bâ's Novels," in *Emerging Perspectives on Mariama Bâ: Postcolonialism, Feminism, and Postmodernism*, ed. Ada Uzoamaka Azodo (Trenton: Africa World Press, 2003), 122.

55. Mariama Bâ, *So Long a Letter*, 54.

56. Rebecca Wilcox, "Women and Power in Mariama Bâ's Novels," 121.

7

"HOW CAN YOU PROMOTE HEALTH WITHOUT PROMOTING FREEDOM?"

Reasserting Social Personhood for "Men Who Have Sex with Men" in Senegalese E-Health

Juliana Friend

For five years, Mohammed[1] and seven other "men who have sex with men" (MSM)[2] were employed by a Senegalese health NGO[3] to disseminate HIV/AIDS prevention messages to their peers through Facebook and dating websites. This local NGO focuses on using digital technologies to promote health and has received financial and strategic support from the Centre National de Lutte Contre le SIDA (CNLS), a Senegalese state agency, the US Agency for International Development (USAID), and Family Health International (FHI 360). One of the NGO's stipulations for its MSM activists is this: Only those conversations addressing sexual health will count toward each activist's "quota." Financial compensation depends upon reaching a given number of digital conversations and a given number of conversations with new individuals each month. According to the NGO's rubric, to count toward the quota, messages must convey purportedly value-neutral, scientifically accurate information about HIV/AIDS and sexually transmitted diseases (STDs). The valence of "information" in this and many other public health contexts is value-free, objective, and affectively neutral.[4] If a conversation treats a number of human rights issues like housing and legal representation, but does not mention HIV specifically, it will not count toward the activists' quota.

The peer educators have different strategies of hooking people's interests online. Some divulge their role as sex educators at the start. Others hide their role for most or all of the conversation. Common strategies for catching interlocutors' attention include flirting, sexual banter, and intimating, if not explicitly promising a future offline sexual encounter.

Mohammed is known among his peer educator colleagues for conducting with online interlocutors long-term conversations carried out over weeks or even months. The conversations have a decidedly flirtatious tone. Mohammed's favorite phrases before signing off include "You're beautiful, baby," "You excite me," or simply, "I love you, baby." As is typical on the website www.planeteromeo.com, he often shares his height, weight, and sexual preferences. He also invites his interlocutors for an offline sexual encounter. If an interlocutor accepts the invitation, he then copies and pastes a paragraph of information about HIV: modes of transmission, the importance of testing, and how to protect oneself and one's partners. It should be added that the NGO prohibits sexual relationships between peer educators and online interlocutors. Accordingly, Mohammed says that he never had an offline sexual relationship with someone he met online through his sexual health education work.

What is the role of erotic seduction in a public health initiative portraying sexual health education as value-neutral and informational? As reflections by state and NGO officials working in tandem with these e-health projects indicate, the "informational" character of the activists' work is a key defense against critiques that engagement with or care for LGBT+ Senegalese "promotes homosexuality." If information is defined as value-less, these programs cannot be accused of promoting so-called "homosexual values." Regardless of the intentions of the NGO workers administrating the e-health program, activists like Mohammed experience these stipulations and requirements as reductionistic and dehumanizing, as if the activists were only important as purveyors of information, and as if their bodies only mattered for the diseases they did or did not carry. This feeling is compounded by the privileging of health over other human rights within the program. Even if online interlocutors face challenges of discrimination or social isolation, due to the quota requirement, the activists are often forced to cut the interaction short if sexual health is not the issue at hand.

Activists' ability to emotionally and erotically connect with others online subverts the reduction of their bodies to information or to their HIV status. Furthermore, their online conversations suggest a key irony; their "informational" communication harnesses affective intensities and erotic charge that subvert the underlying assumption that health information is value-free and affectively neutral. Information must be affectively potent to be convincing. In the hands of skilled activists, the erotic force of online bodies-qua-information becomes impossible to ignore. This chapter is an exploratory effort to unpack the significance of this subversion for the politics of dissident sexualities and public health in contemporary Senegal.

The chapter has three central claims. First, it argues that the e-health project discussed in this study reduces the complexity of the lives it aims to protect due to the way in which it functions. The project recognizes the importance of disease prevention and the preservation of biological life. It receives resources from the Senegalese state—the same state whose constitution makes homosexuality illegal—to prevent the spread of HIV/AIDS. Indeed, prevalence rates among men who have sex with men (estimated between 21.7 percent and 41 percent) are disproportionately higher than prevalence rates for the Senegalese population as a whole (<1 percent).[5] However, in spite of the wider reaching aspirations of individual NGO actors, many of whom have been involved in human rights work, the policies for which they work place sexual health front and center, such that many dimensions of life that are crucial to socially recognized personhood are rendered illegible within regimes of care. Policies and funding priorities also narrowly define "health" as infectious disease prevention. Regardless of NGO and state personnel's intentions, many activists experience the prioritization and narrow definition of health as dehumanizing.

Second, I build on the work of Ivy Mills to show the historicity of this reductionism. While shaped by legal realities of contemporary Senegal and part of a transnational heteronormative discourse linking homosexuality to AIDS, the failure to recognize the full social personhood of e-health activists also invokes deeply rooted narratives about queer(ed) subjects who are perceived as biologically impure contamination risks to the "general population."

Third, the experiences of Mamadou and his activist colleagues illustrate the contradictions that emerge when policies implicitly reduce dynamic and politically conscious young people to bare life. These contradictions are imminent in regimes of care themselves. The communicational dynamics of online queer activism—together with the commitment of activists themselves to address a broad range of human rights *in addition* to the right to health—makes these contradictions visible. For it is precisely the activists' ability to create erotic charge and/or emotional connection within the "informational" context that makes them valuable assets to public health projects. The activists' online conversations and alternative vision of advocacy highlights the interrelationship between pedagogy and erotics. These interrelationships frustrate attempts to reduce bodies to purportedly neutral "information" or confine complex individuals to their disease profiles. Activists' own vision of care and advocacy reasserts their social personhood. It reaffirms their right to pursue the full breadth of their aspirations for a better life, including, but not limited to, HIV negative status.

THE E-HEALTH INITIATIVE

The e-health initiative that employed Mohammed proposed digital media as a crucial tool for sexual health education, considering that many LGBT+ Senegalese fear stigmatization, intimidation, exposure, or violence if they seek health or other resources in-person at a hospital or clinic.[6] The e-health initiative used online communication to conduct outreach and convey the importance of using condoms and water-based lubricants to prevent HIV and sexually transmitted infections (STIs). They also provided the number of an anonymous hotline, confirmed that HIV testing is free, voluntary, and accessible to all, and informed people online of the availability of anti-retroviral drugs (ARVs).

I first made contact with these activists in 2013 after meeting the director of the Technology for Development (T4D) organization with which the eight activists collaborated most directly and to whom they turned in their conversations every month for review. The peer educators told me that the sole focus on health, namely sexual health, was too limiting. The people they spoke with on Facebook or dating sites often shared significant challenges in their life, after getting past initial flirtation and/or awkwardness at hearing that their potential date was actually a sexual health advisor from an NGO. They spoke of discrimination at their place of employment. They also spoke of rejection from family members and housing applications, expulsion by landlords, and the inability to hire a lawyer to prosecute those discriminatory property-owners.

The men had different strategies for addressing concerns that exceeded infectious disease prevention. As will be discussed further below, some would stop their interlocutors before they had the chance to delve into these problems, stating that their job was to discuss health only; thus, they could not address other concerns. Others would discuss all concerns facing interlocutors and decide later whether or not to submit the conversation for the quota.

Regardless of their particular strategy, activists envisioned what they called a "human rights approach." They believed in the power of online outreach to contact those unable or to join Dakar-based gay associations. However, they wanted financial compensation for online outreach addressing the full range of issues facing interlocutors, including but not limited to HIV/AIDS, STIs, and sexual health. In order to one day petition aid agencies for independent funding, they commissioned my help in combing through their archive of online messages to select the ones which most convincingly showed the importance of these diverse concerns to their interlocutors. In the messages themselves, we thought, we would find concrete evidence that one cannot reduce complex individuals to their disease profiles. As one's ability to take medications depends upon stable housing and mental health, one cannot "keep one alive" biologically without recognizing a broader set of needs. Biological life is inextricably tied to socially recognized personhood. If we could find messages displaying the intersection between needs for health and housing, or between health and legal representation, we could show aid agencies that keeping someone alive is not simply a biomedical matter and could not be ensured with condoms alone.

The e-health project has links to both the Senegalese state and international donors. It was funded by USAID but drew some of its e-health personnel from those trained in sexual health outreach by CNLS, the Senegalese state's AIDS agency. And the parent organization continues to partner with the Senegalese Ministry of Health's AIDS agency. Therefore, it is one of many programs marked by intertwined histories of state and NGO engagement. This makes it a useful site for understanding the frictions that emerge when activists who are criminalized by the state work in an aid environment in which state and NGO projects are closely connected.

THE HISTORICITY OF REDUCING QUEER LIFE TO BARE LIFE

Engaging MSM as digital safe sex experts resonates with attempts to exert social control on purportedly dangerous sexual subjects during the peak of the AIDS epidemic in the 1980s and 1990s, during which time heteronormative discourses linked gender non-normativity to disease.[7] While I position this e-health initiative in this transnational legacy, I suggest that Mohammed's activism and challenges must also be contextualized within the historically persistent yet highly contingent Senegalese ethic of *sutura*. Mills has pointed to the interanimation of the transhistorical Wolof value of *sutura*—a complex ethical value in which discretion and privacy are gendered forms of honor—and contemporary moral panics about homosexuality in Senegal. Queer subjects, according to Mills, are portrayed as presenting a dual risk of contamination to the higher status, honorable "community" at large: the threat of biological contamination and communicative excess. Mills argues that media portrayals of homosexuality during moral panics convey gay Senegalese to be impure and biologically contaminated, a threat to be physically contained. At the same time, they are accused of communicative excess and violating *sutura* by purportedly making their sexual practices and/or identities visible in the public sphere.[8]

Mills further traces the genealogy of this "illusion of containment" to the role of the *géwél* in precolonial Wolof caste systems.[9] Underlying logics linking gender non-normativity to contamination animate social life in new ways. The *géwél*, or griots, were a biological threat to be contained. They were buried outside the community or not buried at all for fear of contaminating noble Senegalese blood.[10] They were also considered as loud, brash, and ignoble. Nobles were confined to speak with restraint, discretion, and *sutura* and used *géwél* as spokespeople to communicate what they could not say. This chapter will focus on the impetus toward biological containment. Interrelated conceptions of discursive contagion and bodily contagion will be discussed in a future study.

Mills analyzes the *géwél* as a queer figure. She notes that Senegalese literature and popular culture often depict the *géwél* as illegibly gendered—using words and bodies in ways inconsistent with proper gender roles—and, in this sense, queer.[11] Within this framework, one who has no gender has no legible social role. An illegibly gendered person is not a person at all. Drawing upon the work of Georgio Agamben, Mills further argues that *géwél* occupy the space of bare life, one between life and death, and can be killed but not murdered.[12] Both *géwél* in Wolof caste systems and gay Senegalese in recent moral panics occupy a space between life and death. Their right to biological life is recognized; but they are not socially recognized persons within the Wolof social order. Illegible gender makes them illegible as social persons. Queer life is reduced to bare life.

Notable too is the link between vulnerability and dishonor. The fact that *géwél* needed *géer/noble* protection reflected and performed their dishonor, even as it deepened links of interdependence between dishonorable and honorable Senegalese.[13] The gender-queer figure in social imaginaries presents a threat of contamination to the same normative community from which it receives protection and patronage.

PRESERVING (BARE) QUEER LIFE IN SENEGAL'S STATE-NGO HEALTH NEXUS

State-NGO regimes of care must be situated within this broader history of reducing queer life to bare life. This is not a causal argument. I do not wish to suggest any linear teleology linking precolonial protection and abjection of queer(ed) subjects to the complexities of health NGOs. Nevertheless, resonances between these discourses are analytically informative. In resonance with Mills' account of *sutura* and gender nonnormativity, protection, and abjection converge in e-health initiatives. The reduction of health to disease containment relies upon a familiar contagion logic. It implicitly endorses the separation of MSM from the "general population." This marginalizes the very individuals the initiative is committed to protect.

I do not, in any way, wish to diminish the aspirations of NGO and state program officers[14] to better the lives of their compatriots. Indeed, the aspirations of many individuals working in these programs reach far beyond HIV/AIDS initiatives. Many envision a more egalitarian social order as articulated within idioms of universal human rights. Civil society and state officials have participated in training programs on human rights. A task force working on MSM health includes NGO, religious, and state actors. This task force has identified LGBT+ friendly lawyers. Moreover, it has organized trainings for both police officers (to reduce harassment of LGBT+ people) and journalists (to decrease sensationalism in the reporting of events or issues involving LGBT+ individuals). In one exciting step, an employee of Centre National de Lutte contre le SIDA (CNLS)—that is, someone on the state's payroll—conducts outreach with the police force to prevent violence against and intimidation of MSM.

However, these aspirations and nascent movements are constrained by policies and programs that 1) elevate sexual health over other priorities and 2) narrowly define "health" as disease prevention/containment. Health interventions, and specifically HIV/AIDS interventions form the crux of state/NGO engagement with MSM. The Senegalese state finances research and HIV/AIDS prevention services for MSM. Currently, the main agency for doing so is CNLS, which partners with a range of local, national, and international NGOs. Estimates for HIV prevalence among MSM ranges between 21.7 percent and 41 percent, compared to the <1 percent of the total Senegalese population.[15] Following arrests of HIV/AIDS activists in 2008, a "crisis committee" was formed first to liberate the activists who were charged and, then, to fight more broadly for an environment of acceptance by reaching out to religious leaders, police, journalists, and members of civil society to discuss just treatment of LGBT+ Senegalese. While their hopes and goals for tolerance are wide-ranging, their approach explicitly targets HIV/AIDS work as the portal through which better conditions for MSM will eventually be reached. As journalist and scholar Mouhamadou Tidiane Kassé writes,

> The approach adopted by the crisis committee is not to frame the debate about homosexuality in terms of human rights or to advocate for the decriminalization of homosexuality. The emphasis, rather, is on issues of public health: the safeguarding of the achievements of

> the fight against AIDS; respect of the right to treatment services and prevention. It is in this dimension of public health that the committee seeks to promote religious and cultural discourses of tolerance and non-violence.[16]

While aspirations of many key players reach further, health is the least common denominator, the common ground on which different actors—state, NGO, religious—can come together.

Among health officials in both state and NGO sectors, two key justifications emerge for why state resources should be allocated to groups that the state has criminalized. First, the criminalized groups must be contained from infecting the "general population." Second, MSM are humans too. They have a right to stay alive. Regarding the first, in public health documents, MSM are labeled both as "vulnerable populations" to be protected and "key populations" augmenting heterosexual Senegalese's risks to contract HIV. Both terms are telling. The category of vulnerable populations sometimes applies to young unmarried women / "jeunes filles"—unmarried and presumed pure and, therefore, honorable—in the southern region of the Casamance. But "key populations" are a special subset of "*couches vulnérables*" [vulnerable populations]. The term "Key populations" designates the socially marginalized and/or morally tainted. Namely, three groups: drug users, sex workers, and "MSM." The slippage between the two terms, "key" and "vulnerable," indicates MSM's double status in public health programs. They deserve care because they are vulnerable, at risk, and affected. Yet they require care because they are the "key" to containing the spread of HIV/AIDS.

Public health discourse employs a contagion/containment logic that resonates with *sutura.*[17] Many health officials assert that stigmatization leads some MSM to enter into heterosexual marriages.[18] The assumption is that if these individuals are HIV positive, they would transmit the virus to a woman who is otherwise a member of the "general population," making her linked to the "key population" without her knowledge. As one CNLS official put it, "we know that many marry women out of obligation, or they are bisexual. We know that MSM enter so-called 'stable relationships' with women."[19] Here, MSM are analytically separable from the "general population," which is rendered de facto heterosexual. Yet their sexual contact with the general population through heterosexual marriage raises the stakes of disease containment. As the CNLS official reiterated, we must "break the chain of transmission so it does not affect the general population."

Gay and straight Senegalese cannot be spatially separated. According to these NGO and public health logics, disease containment must be done through the adoption of "*comportements responsibles*" [responsible behaviors], which can only happen when MSM have "scientific, unbiased information" and share that knowledge with others.[20] As MSM intermarry with "general population," information becomes the means of disease containment. Armed with information, the potential contaminant (the MSM body) becomes a tool of containment. The goal of training MSM as peer educators is to make the dishonored subject productive, rather than harmful, to the social body as a whole: productive to the "community," in Mills' terms, to the "population," in Foucault's terms,[21] and to the "general population," in public health parlance.

Health officials are prepared to answer accusations from religious representatives and others that they are "promoting homosexuality" with the retort that they are simply trying to reduce infection rates through scientific information and, furthermore, that they have the interests of the Senegalese population as a whole at heart. As articulated by one doctor who had been trained by a civil society AIDS organization, "We are saving lives by providing reliable and accurate information. We have no agenda. Information is crucial to protecting the general population."[22] The defense is twofold: 1) our work helps (honorable) heterosexual Senegalese in addition to MSM and 2) our engagement with the (dishonored) gender non-normative Senegalese is the distribution of information, which stands outside culture and thus cannot be seen as promoting a particular value system. The purported value-free, neutral scientific "information" neutralizes disease without legitimating the sexual practices or identities of information purveyors (MSM). It is their heteronormative sexual behavior that makes care a top priority. Here, then, we see a clear analogy to the "illusion of containment" that Mills identifies in the moral panic around gender-queerness in Senegal's not-so-distant Senegalese.[23] Furthermore, the aspect of biological contamination through blood[24] is mirrored by the exchange of fluids that is necessary for the transmission of the HIV virus. The condom—the centerpiece of all awareness-raising initiatives for MSM—provides a physical barrier.[25]

One of the striking results of Mills's analysis is the pairing of protection and abjection of *géwél* subjects. The need for and reception of the nobles' protection is at once a sign of disgrace and a mark of subjection to a relationship of interdependence between honored and always-already dishonored subjects.[26] This relationship mirrors how forms of NGO protection—in this case, the provision of care—can implicitly reflect or reinforce exclusion. The perceived impurity of griot bodies and the queer bodies with whom they are discursively linked is reenacted by efforts to contain the perceived threat that the MSM poses to the "general population." Though the means and motives are radically different, a parallel impetus to containment echoes through both NGO regimes of care and the protection/abjection of queer(ed) *géwél* subjects.

The first explanation of the reason why MSM deserve government funds—which is that MSM are humans too—is, in some ways, more ambiguous and complex than it seems. On one level, it suggests an inclusive humanism. But health interventions focus on disease prevention and containment, rather than on a broader recognition of MSM's rights to flourish in all dimensions of life—social, political, and economic. One state agency official said that he helped members of the peer educator cohort in the past by even accompanying them to court. However, the official affirmed that CNLS is, first and foremost, an HIV/AIDS organization. Moreover, one CNLS official stated that he collaborated with human rights efforts to assist MSM who had been arrested. However, regardless of his personal aspirations, the organization for which he works focuses on HIV/AIDS and is accountable to all Senegalese people.

Other practitioners—including the individual heading the local NGO to which the e-health activists must submit their quota of messages each month—stress the importance of universal human rights regardless of sexual orientation, but place the greatest responsibility of securing those rights on individual LGBT+ people themselves. They cite the notion of "self-stigmatization." As the local NGO head stated, enacting a conversation she said she repeatedly had with her MSM activist employees, "it's you who are scared. No one is preventing you from having your rights. You must have self-esteem. . . . Since the law is against you, educate yourself and use the laws that are for you."[27]

It is worth underscoring the prevalence of the term "information" in constructions of the e-health program. The local NGO's project leader asserts the necessity to train e-health activists to be "serious" about transmitting "objective scientific information." To do so, it is critical to differentiate e-health work from everyday online chats that focus on erotic or sexual connection. The NGO staff would often remind the activists that they must be "professional," that their work should be separated from their personal use of the targeted websites, and that they are not here for *draguer*, or hitting on people. In a sense, the containment of dangerous gay bodies to protect the "general population" requires producing "bodies in-formation," that is, bodies that circulate in informational form.[28] The main feature of queer bodies becomes the information they convey, not the erotic affects they exude. When transmitted as information, gay bodies go from being sexually dangerous to being salutary. They become safe. Not only this, they become *instruments* of safety for others. This outcome requires a model of health communication in which information and embodiment do not meet, nor do information and affect. When queer bodies are *informationalized,* they indeed provide the "key" to solving the problem of disease infection and spread. (Though as Carlo Caduff points out, and the activists described below rightly show, informationalized bodies have their own modes of embodiment.)

Similar logics of containment vs. contamination operate within regimes of care designed to save lives, as in precolonial caste systems in which queer(ed) subjects can be killed but not sacrificed. This e-health program for saving lives deploys historically embedded logics of dishonor and honor, but adapts and reformulates them into a regime of care. To do so, it draws upon dominant constructions of information and science as outside culture and politics. Whether one reads this as the redemptive dimension of dishonoring LGBT+ subjects, or the insidious remnants of discrimination haunting a purportedly progressive program, it is vital to situate healthcare for non-normative sexualities within a broad historical landscape in order to understand its messages and social effects.

PEER EDUCATOR RESPONSES TO NGO REDUCTIONISM

Casting broader human rights as a distant goal, or a matter of personal responsibility of the marginalized group, can feel to MSM peer educators like a failure to prioritize their well-being and a denial of their full humanity. One's potential positive contribution to society may one day be honored; for now, the point of consensus is the negative gesture of *not* transmitting an infection. As one member of the online health project articulated in an interview, "how can you promote health without promoting freedom?"[29] He went on to describe the sole focus on sexual health as a complete contradiction with his NGO contacts' stated objective of improving LGBT+ lives. "They say they want to help us, but they don't work on human rights." I responded by noting a recent discussion in which the head of the local NGO administrating the project talked about legal recourse in the case of housing discrimination. The online activist responded, "but that was a conversation over lunch! Why isn't that in our grant?" Indeed, all the e-health activists have participated in human rights trainings, learning what their rights *are*. However, a common refrain among activists is that they have had plenty of training. What they need is funding to put that training into practice. According to the MSM activists, NGO and state commitments to human rights besides health remain insufficient and have yet to congeal in concrete policies or programs.

Certain e-health activists write conversations that accede to the sharp distinction between health and other rights, staying close to their mission of providing accurate information. Otherwise put, their digital conversations comply with the reduction of queer life to bare life. Whatever the intentions and long-term goals of NGO and state actors are, policy limitations remain acutely felt and may hinder e-health activists' ability to help and support their peers. In the message below, an interlocutor approaches the e-health activist (not yet identified as such) for help with his boyfriend who is not receiving the social support he needs. The interlocutor has suffered physical violence and intimidation. The activist responds:[30]

> On diré kil respecte pas c droit d s soigné mais a notre niveau on peu pas faire gran chose car on slimite sur les ist kil essaye d'aproché les association gay 785938550 Je m'en duter. mais je suis la pour vous

orienter et vous informé sur tous les forme de dépistage au vih du sida et les lieux adéquat pour un meilleur déroulement dans la confidentialité, l'anonymat et discrétion si intéressé laissé votre message ou bipé le 77 4409287.

One could say that he does not respect the right to health but in our capacity we cannot do very much because we are limited to STDs he should try to get in touch with the gay associations 785938550 I doubt it. But I am here to guide and inform you about everything related to HIV/AIDS testing and the suitable places for an experience of confidentiality, anonymity and discretion if interested leave your message or beep 77 4409287.

The e-health activist notes that their role is to "guide and inform" their peers, but they cannot intercede directly, or even protect the "right to health" (droit de se soigner), which are human rights that are linked most directly to the informational labor for which they are employed. This message directly suggests that conveying information is not, in and of itself, sufficient to secure one's right to health. As the activist who wrote this message observed, "That's the reality with [name of e-health program]. You just have to send the information and move on."[31] In concrete, personal ways, limiting engagement to the dissemination of "information" curtails the reach of online activism. The activist chafes against the limited definition of "health" as disease containment and the extraction of "health" from a broader matrix of social, economic, and political relations.

In another conversation, an e-health activist registers the breadth of the interlocutor's concerns, but pivots to a health-only message:

10. meissawally709621418 16. Oct. 2014—17:43
ok bb; on c déja parlé. C moi ki avait eut des probléme avec les jeunes de mon quartier qui se battait avec moi a cause de mon orientation sexuel et tu mavait dit d aller a la pólice pour porté plainte je les fait finalment jai démanager au banlieu maintenant
11. craigprevent 16. Oct. 2014—17:51
Ok mon amis je te conseil de rester discret maintenant comme on est ds un pays ou il ya des homophobe le mieux c de rester discret ; bon je te conseil aussi de tjrs bien se protger et de protéger aussi tes partenaires avec du préservatif afin d éviter le virus du vih sida et les ist

> 12. meissawally709621418 16. Oct. 2014—18:31
> ok
>
> 10. meissawally709621418 16. Oct. 2014—17:43
> ok bb; we've already talked. It's me who had the problems with kids in my neighborhood who fought with me because of my sexual orientation and you'd told me to go to the police to register a complaint I did it in the end I moved to the suburbs now
> 11. craigprevent 16. Oct. 2014—17:51
> Ok my friend i advise you to be discrete now since we're in a country with a lot of homophobes the best is to stay discrete ; well i advise you to always protect yourself and also your partners with condoms to avoid the hiv aids virus and stds
> 12. meissawally709621418 16. Oct. 2014—18:31
> ok

The interlocutor recounts an experience of physical harassment based on sexual orientation, referencing a past conversation in which the e-health activist had recommended a course of action. In a previous exchange, the e-health activist had given advice about how to respond to harassment. In a current one, while registering the personal gravity of this concern and situating his advice in a broader sociopolitical context of homophobia in contemporary Senegal, he quickly pivots to the importance of using condoms. The conversation terminates shortly thereafter.

Another e-health activist takes a starkly different approach. He sometimes spends up to an hour on a single conversation, exploring all concerns that the interlocutor may have, even if they already possess necessary health information. Such a conversation may include all manners of personal experiences, positive and negative, such as difficulties with workplace harassment, police abuse, family issues, and more issues. However, the activist noted that this kind of message would not count toward his quota. He does not regret spending time on it, however, because he knows that even if one already knows how to use a condom and water-based lubricant, "You have other things going on in your life which you want to talk about. Even just daily life. And you still may need a friend which you can't have face to face because you are afraid people will discover your [sexual] orientation."[32]

This assertion poignantly reflects the reductionism involved in health-only (or health-mostly) programs. The activist feels that the focus on sexual health does not reflect the fullness of an individual's concerns, interests, and needs for connection. The broad range of human needs and desires is rendered illegible in this framework. Furthermore, attending to these needs is disincentivized within the e-health program. In a world with limited resources, addressing the breadth of an interlocutor's concerns presents a financial burden. It is not just the online interlocutor but the activist himself who feels undervalued. Concerns of "daily life," the activist suggests, do not matter to health regimes as much as disease susceptibility. As a result, social isolation may increase as someone may not receive the support, connection, or solidarity they seek online. In focusing on risk, disease, and death, this e-health program fails to recognize the fullness of their employees' social personhood. This particular activist defies this reductionism by maintaining long conversations on every topic, in addition to his e-health work. In the end, the activist's self-conscious defiance of NGO restrictions draw those limitations into relief.

The key difference from the two cases is that e-health is explicitly designed to *benefit* queer Senegalese. Another difference is the emphasis by many NGO and state personnel that gay activists become autonomous and independent actors who no longer need training, support, or "capacity building" from trainers. However, activists themselves are skeptical of this apparent push toward autonomy. As one put it, "it's like, we need them to help us be independent. Needing someone else is not independent." Indeed, many activists already performed informal HIV/AIDS education online before they received NGO funding to do so. The local NGO personnel's story of the origins of MSM e-health, however, does not reflect this timeline. Ironically, by claiming that, one day, with enough training and—to use a loaded term reminiscent of Mills—economic "patronage," MSM will be self-sufficient, NGO calls for autonomy actually reinscribe MSM dependence on NGO programs. Real autonomy, activists assert, would be receiving funding that is provided directly to gay associations, without having to work with local NGO intermediaries and submit monthly reports. Real autonomy does not require proving one's self-sufficiency to anyone else.

Another key difference is that, on the biological level, gay bodies are not always-already contaminated in contemporary Senegalese society, whereas *géwél* subjects were always already impure in precolonial Wolof caste systems.[33] Some MSM are HIV positive and others are not. Prevention is one of the primary goals of NGO and state initiatives. But the fact that they are more "at risk" brings two dimensions of vulnerability—need for protection and susceptibility to contamination—into an uncomfortable proximity.

INFORMATIONAL EROTICS: THE FULLNESS OF BARE LIFE

Reducing queer life to bare life—biologically human, but socially disavowed—is a fragile and contradictory project. The peer educators' e-health conversations make this fragility visible by revealing the inextricable connection between information and erotics. This interconnection illustrates the tenuousness of any project reducing a "target population" to their biological humanness. The eroticism and emotional connections that emerge within pedagogical interactions defy reductionism of bodies to information and of selves to disease profiles. In other words, activists' online sociality reasserts social personhood. NGO policies that implicitly reduce gay selves to bare life rub up against the intractable fullness and richness of these activists' online sociality.

In fact, e-health initiatives *depend* on this fullness for their efficacy. Mohammed, the peer educator mentioned at the beginning of this chapter, not only seduces his interlocutors but also listens to their concerns, long after he sends his safe sex message. For Mohammed, information hit its mark within a broader relationship of erotic attachment and emotional intimacy. The use of new media—namely, social networks and dating websites—for HIV/AIDS prevention reminds us that disease *containment* depends upon emotional (and often erotic) connectivity.

While NGO logics *informationalize bodies*, the online communicative tactics of the activists they employ *embody information* through what I call "informational erotics." Mohammed and his activist colleagues seduce, play, and flirt to get and hold interlocutors' attention; only then can they effectively inform and teach the required information points. They intimate, if not promise, the possibility of a sexual encounter. As one colleague noted, the "flirting approach"—which involves giving your height and weight, divulging sexual preferences, and bragging about sexual prowess—is more effective than the "direct approach," as the latter one often leads the annoyed interlocutor to quickly sign off.[34] If effectively transmitting information requires describing one's body and its capacities in precise detail, informational labor is hardly disembodied labor.

An adequate discussion of how the technical affordances of particular digital infrastructures shape the activists' political and ethical projects goes beyond this chapter's scope. For now, we can simply observe that the peer educators use online fora in order to seduce and flirt in an attempt to attract and hold interest long enough to enable exchange of health information. This affectively charged and often explicitly sexual connection seems to undercut the "scientific" impetus of the program; if "science" is imputed to be affectively neutral and value-free,[35] personnel can use this other viewpoint to persuade skeptics that they are not promoting homosexual "values." Yet, seduction is actually what makes information transfer possible. The local NGO program officer herself acknowledged this symbiosis, albeit ambivalently. While she recalled instructing the e-health activists clearly that their purpose is not "*draguer*" (to flirt), she also confessed that "everyone has their own way" of engaging in conversation. As her personnel review all conversations to determine whether each activist reaches his quota, the NGO is well aware that sexually explicit talk or flirting sometimes precedes and/or facilitates a message about the modes of transmission of HIV. Here, what I am calling 'informational erotics' is harnessed to meet NGO ends. By extension, it helps fulfill the requirements of the state policy with which NGOs are entwined.

A "HUMAN RIGHTS APPROACH" AS A REASSERTION OF SOCIAL PERSONHOOD

Although activists' conversation tactics implicitly reveal the contradictions undergirding NGO reductionism, these activists' organizing confronts this reductionism head on. By promoting a "human rights approach," they contest the confinement of queer life to bare life. Such an approach, as envisioned by the activists, would value—and financially compensate—online discussions of issues like discrimination and housing. This strategy counters the extraction of "health" from social and political processes with which it is intertwined and disrupts the reduction of "health" to disease containment. "Human rights" signifies an acknowledgment of the social personhood of MSM even if they remain criminalized by Senegalese law.

The activists link their proposed "human rights approach" to recognition and self-acceptance. As an activist who was elected treasurer explained, "when a man doesn't know he has human rights, he doesn't accept himself. Then one day he will have an opportunity to have sex. And he will act on impulse. He will not use a condom."[36] Here, "knowing one's rights" facilitates self-acceptance and self-care. This scenario suggests that sexual health cannot be separated from recognition of social personhood which, in turn, cannot be removed from self-acceptance. This view contrasts sharply with the discursive isolation of health from other dimensions of life. It should be noted that this activist does not advocate directly petitioning for decriminalizing homosexuality in Senegal. Legal recognition is not the recognition he seeks—at least not for now. Recognition can come from peers like the activists themselves. He sees the e-health activists as providing a vital form of validation and social connection. It is within this context that one can read the activist's provocative declaration mentioned earlier: "how can you promote health without promoting freedom?"

When the USAID funding cycle ended, so too did funding for the e-health program for MSM. This termination of financial support provided an (imposed) occasion for the activists to review their strategy. The activists decided to form their own non-profit organization and apply for grants directly, without an administrative intermediary. Once NGO funding was removed, the activists saw no reason to fit their approach of online engagement into pre-existing NGO e-health frameworks. In a strategy meeting, the activists stated that while HIV/AIDS prevention would always play a major role in their work, they no longer wanted to apply for health-only grants. Now, health was to stand as one of *many* human rights. The activists currently intend to apply for grants from human rights agencies and/or LGBTQ+ foundations.

Many important critiques have been made about liberal-secular human rights discourses, and their potential to constrain, rather than promote, alternative ethical projects.[37] A full exploration of these critiques and their relation to e-health goes beyond this chapter's purview. What I wish to highlight here is the fullness of social personhood that the term "human rights" indexes within activists' own visions of care. Put simply, I want to show what the term means and does for them. A "human rights approach" stands as the opposite of a health-only approach; it recognizes and cares for socially recognized persons and bodies, not just for bare biological life. In doing so, it contests heteronormative systems of protection/abjection.

The central case study of this chapter attempts to clarify how e-health can, on the one hand, acknowledge the wide-ranging needs of gay men, and yet—within the logics of their regimes of care—reduce humans to bare life. Activists feel like they are used as beings to keep alive, but not as persons to nurture or allow to flourish.

Activists confront persistent legacies of protecting and abjecting queer(ed) subjects at the same time. They disrupt the reduction of bodies to information, of queer life to bare life. They do so through an alternative vision of care which is articulated through the language of human rights. They also do so more implicitly, through online conversations whose pedagogical impact depends upon erotic and emotional connections. The activists re-embed information into a relational matrix: both through erotically charged conversations and their gestures to the larger issues that interlocutors face in their lives, such as discrimination, intimidation and violence. Scientific "information" is not a magic bullet, they suggest. Transmitting facts about how to prevent HIV is absolutely essential. But it is part of a larger project of conveying to peers that they have value, not just as solutions to a problem, but as socially recognized persons with needs, desires, and rights. If MSM Senegalese believe this, the activist suggests, they will protect themselves and their partners. Forming interpersonal connections and reducing feelings of isolation are co-constitutive of not just communicating information, but ensuring that this knowledge is actually put into practice when and where it counts. When an interlocutor states that they are in conflict with their landlord and that "this is not something I can talk about with just anybody," they need not just information, but support and reassurance.

Moreover, the activists re-embody information. They accept and embrace the different communicative strategies which are necessary to attract and hold interlocutors' interest and develop a connection. This refuses the discursive desexualization and disembodiment of information implicit in NGO demands. Here, informing and flirting may go together. Sex educators can be sexy; and, indeed, they often *need* to be sexy to communicate information about sex. In this way, activists shift from a notion of *informationalized bodies* to *embodied information* and what I might call "informational erotics." However, to enact this alternative ethics of care, the first step to implementing "human rights" grants is to form a non-profit, non-governmental agency. In a double contradiction, those whose sexualities are criminalized by the Senegalese state will need to depose their application for "non-governmental" status at the appropriate bureaus of the Senegalese state.

BIBLIOGRAPHY

Adams, Vincanne and Stacey Leigh Pigg. "Introduction: The Moral Object of Sex," in *Sex in Development: Science, Sexuality and Morality in Global Perspective*, edited by Vincanne Adams and Stacey Leigh Pigg, 1–38. Durham: Duke University Press, 2005.

Agamben, Giorgio. *Homo Sacer. Sovereign Power and Bare Life*. Stanford: Stanford University Press, 1998.

Boellstorff, Tom. "But Do Not Identify as Gay: A Proleptic Genealogy of the MSM Category." *Journal of Cultural Anthropology* 26, no. 2 (May 2016): 287–312.

Caduff, Carlo. "The Semiotics of Security: Infectious Disease Research and the Biopolitics of Informational Bodies in the United States." *Cultural Anthropology* 27, no. 2 (May 2012): 333–57.

Dearham, Kaitlin. "NGOs and Queer Women's Activism in Nairobi," in *Queer African Reader*, edited by Sokari Ekine and Hakima Abbas, 186–202. Dakar, Nairobi and Oxford: Pambazuka Press, 2013.

Englund, Harri. *Prisoners of Freedom: Human Rights and the African Poor* Berkeley: University of California Press, 2006.

Foucault, Michel. *Security, Territory, Population: Lectures at the Collège de France, 1977-78,* edited by Michel Senellart. Translated by Graham Burchell. London: Palgrave Macmillan, 2007.

Kassé, Mouhamadou Tidiane. "Mounting Homophobic Violence in Senegal." In *Queer African Reader*, edited by Sokari Ekine and Hakima Abbas, 262–77. Dakar, Nairobi and Oxford: Pambazuka Press, 2013.

"Key Populations Atlas," UN AIDS. April 7, 2018. http://www.aidsinfoonline.org/kpatlas/#/home.

Mills, Ivy. "Sutura: Gendered Honor, Social Death and the Politics of Exposure in Senegalese Literature and Popular Culture." PhD diss., University of California, Berkeley, 2011.

Nguyen, Vinh-Kim. *The Republic of Therapy: Triage and Sovereignty in West Africa's Time of AIDS*. Durham: Duke University Press, 2010.

Payne, Robert. *The* Promiscuity of Network *Culture: Queer Theory and Digital Media*. New York: Routledge, 2014.

Pigg, Stacey Leigh. "Languages of Sex and AIDS in Nepal: Notes on the Social Production of Commensurability." *Cultural Anthropology* 16, no. 4 (November 2001): 481–s541.
Respondent A, Interview.
Respondent B, Interview.
Respondent C, Interview.
Respondent D, Interview.
Respondent E, Interview.
Respondent F, Interview.
Respondent G, Interview.
UN AIDS. "Key Populations Atlas." April 7, 2018, http://www.aidsinfoonline.org/kpatlas/#/home
Watney, Simon. "The Spectacle of AIDS." *AIDS: Cultural Analysis/Cultural Activism.* 43 (October 1987): 71–86.

NOTES

1. For the purposes of this chapter, one of my main informants will be called Mohammed. Anonymity is at the heart of these activists' work. It is therefore an ethical precondition for this chapter.

2. To reference their sexual orientations and practices, the activists use both the NGO parlance—men who have sex with men (MSM)—and the terms "gay," "bisexual," and "LGBTQ." I will follow their usage, moving between terminologies. For a fuller discussion of the unusual emergence of the term "MSM," its imbrication with forms of social control, and the binary it invokes between "behavior" and "identity," see Tom Boellstorff, "But Do Not Identify as Gay: A Proleptic Genealogy of the MSM Category," *Journal of Cultural Anthropology* 26, no. 2 (May 2016): 291.

3. I have chosen not to give the name of the organization working most directly with the activists. Identifying this small organization could facilitate identification of the activists. Indeed, throughout this chapter, I seek to balance my ethical commitment to protect interlocutors from harm with values of transparency and academic norms of citation. Therefore, I protect the anonymity of key organizations, as well as those of officials who work with MSM, in ways not explicitly condoned or publicly advertised by their organizations. I do not identify the name or organization of a doctor known by MSM as non-stigmatizing and welcoming to LGBT+ people. Otherwise, association with this doctor could become a means for identifying one's sexual orientation, endangering the privacy and safety of my interlocutors. However, I do identify larger sponsoring organizations that work with both queer and heteronormative populations. The risks posed by identification are minimal in this case, and their work with "vulnerable populations" is publicly accessible information.

4. Stacey Leigh Pigg, "Languages of Sex and AIDS in Nepal: Notes on the Social Production of Commensurability," *Cultural Anthropology* 16, no. 4 (November 2001): 489.

5. "Key Populations Atlas," UN AIDS, Accessed April 7, 2018, http://www.aidsinfoonline.org/kpatlas/#/home.

6. 7 There is a tension between discretion (one of the many valences of "sutura") and exposure. The digital peer educator program is premised on the importance of discretion and anonymity. Program officers and MSM alike suggest that gender nonconforming Senegalese are more willing to ask questions related to sexuality if they feel they are protected from exposure of their sexual orientation or practices. However, MSM constantly fear the exposure that the internet makes possible, such as data breaches or "traps": almost every MSM activist in the program has a story of someone posing as another MSM and, in fact, flipping a switch to troll the activist. Cases include physical meetups when the person posing as an MSM threatened physical violence.

7. See Robert Payne, *The Promiscuity of Network Culture: Queer Theory and Digital Media* (New York: Routledge, 2014), 24 and Simon Watney, "The Spectacle of AIDS," *AIDS: Cultural Analysis/Cultural Activism* 43 (October 1987): 72-73.Carlo Caduff, "The Semiotics of Security: Infectious Disease Research and the Biopolitics of Informational Bodies in the United States," *Cultural Anthropology* 27, no. 2 (May 2012): 343.

8. Mills rightly notes that it is in fact the Senegalese press outlets that violate *sutura* insofar as they invasively expose the private lives—and in one case, the physical remains—of gay Senegalese to public scrutiny. See Ivy Mills, "Sutura: Gendered Honor, Social Death, and the Politics of Exposure in Senegalese Literature and Popular Culture" (PhD diss., University of California, Berkeley, 2011), 119.

9. Mills, "Sutura," 120

10. Mills, "Sutura,"119.

11. Mills, "Sutura,"119.

12. Mills, "Sutura," 121.

13. Mills, "Sutura," 2.

14. NGO actors are presumed a priori by both colleagues and beneficiaries to be heterosexual unless they state otherwise, and thus part of the "general population."

15. "Key Populations Atlas," UN AIDS, April 7, 2018, http://www.aidsinfoonline.org/kpatlas/#/home

16. Mouhamadou Tidiane Kassé, "Mounting Homophobic Violence in Senegal," in *Queer African Reader,* ed. Sokari Ekine and Hakima Abbas (Dakar, Nairobi and Oxford: Pambazuka Press, 2013), 266.

17. Vinh-Kim Nguyen has explored the ways in which colonial power in West Africa deployed mechanisms of containment in the name of "hygiene." Indeed, contemporary e-health could be contextualized within broader historical legacies of colonialism and containment.

18. Kassé, "Mounting Homophobic Violence," 262–77.

19. Respondent B, Interview by Juliana Friend, June 28, 2016

20. Respondent B, Interview by Juliana Friend, June 28, 2016

21. Michel Foucault. *Security, Territory, Population: Lectures at the Collège de France, 1977-78,* ed. Michel Senellart, trans. Graham Burchell (London: Palgrave Macmillan, 2007), 285.

22. Respondent C, Interview by Juliana Friend, February 2, 2018.

23. Mills, "Sutura," 120

24. Mills, "Sutura," 123

25. This containment logic has strong echoes to homophobic discourses during the '80s and '90s in the United States, which used heteronormative moralizing frameworks to link gay men with HIV/AIDS and gay sex with contagion (See Watney, "AIDS," 1987). In addition to invoking particularly Senegalese gender logics, e-health initiatives resonate with transnational discourses that gender discourses of containment and contagion and use them to justify heteronormative projects of exclusion.

26. Mills, "Sutura," 2.

27. Respondent F, Interview by Juliana Friend, January 29, 2018.

28. Carlo Caduff, "The Semiotics of Security: Infectious Disease Research and the Biopolitics of Informational Bodies in the United States," *Cultural Anthropology* 27, no. 2 (May 2012): 343.

29. Respondent G, Interview by Juliana Friend, January 30, 2018.

30. For the translation of online messages, I decided not to mirror the abbreviations used in the original French versions, except those abbreviations in English. This means that the translation will not capture the texture, mood, and rhythm of the original words. However, this decision was made with the advice of the activists themselves, who agreed that they have a system of abbreviations unto themselves and preferred that their words be translated into "standard English" for fear that, otherwise, the semantic meaning of the text would be lost. I include the original versions so that readers with facility in French can get a sense of the rhythms of e-health internet talk.

31. Respondent H, Interview by Juliana Friend, June 29, 2016

32. Respondent I, Interview by Juliana Friend, July 2, 2016.

33. Mills, "Sutura," 9.

34. Respondent G, Interview by Juliana Friend, January 30, 2018.

35. Vincanne Adams and Stacey Leigh Pigg, "Introduction: The Moral Object of Sex," *in Sex in Development: Science, Sexuality and Morality in Global Perspective*, eds. Vincanne Adams and Stacey Leigh Pigg (Durham: Duke University Press, 2005), 1–2.

36. Respondent G, Interview by Juliana Friend, January 30, 2018.

37. Kaitlin Dearham, "NGOs and Queer Women's Activism in Nairobi," in *Queer African Reader*, eds. Sokari Ekine and Hakima Abbas (Dakar, Nairobi and Oxford: Pambazuka Press, 2013). Harri Englund, *Prisoners of Freedom: Human Rights and the African Poor* (Berkeley: University of California Press, 2006).

8

CATALYZING STAGNANT NORMS

Female Parliamentarians' Creative Impact on Weary Public Institutions

Susan Telingator and Sindiso Mnisi Weeks

Research on women's increased participation in governments has largely focused in recent years on the impact of quota systems as a mechanism for transforming predominantly male governments into bodies with greater gender equality.[1] On the African continent, in particular, where Rwanda consistently holds the highest ranking in the world for the number of women in its parliament[2] and thirty-two countries overall have some form of a gender quota,[3] it is worthwhile to explore how increasing diversity within such institutions can increase the creativity of the institutions.

From 2012 to 2017, Senegal had the second highest percentage of female parliamentarians in Africa due to the passage of the electoral law of parity in 2012.[4] Parity is the legal requirement in a parliamentary system of proportional representation that each party list alternate between male and female candidates. There has not been a great deal of literature highlighting Senegal's momentous achievement, nor has there been much exploring what effect this uncommon solution to the need for increased representation of women[5]—namely, parity—has had on the country's legislature. This chapter therefore seeks to address this vacuum of knowledge by analyzing the perspectives of female parliamentarians in Senegal regarding their first five years in government after the passage of the law of parity.

More broadly, the chapter argues that female parliamentarians catalyze stagnant norms and have a creative impact on weary public institutions. It demonstrates the potential resilience of African institutions, evidencing that women's participation is instrumental in realizing that potential. The authors suggest that this evidence shows why it is important to increase women's participation in governments worldwide.

We conducted our empirical research in Senegal in two phases. The first phase was in August 2017, the day after the 2017 Parliamentary elections. We conducted one-on-one elite interviews with three female parliamentarians over the course of a few days. We used purposive sampling to identify parliamentarians and determine who was available to be interviewed. We interviewed one female parliamentarian in her office and the two others at their homes. The second set of interviews was conducted mid-September 2017. We identified four parliamentarians, based on their experience working on women's issues.[6] The initial interviews suggested that those parliamentarians unfamiliar with the concept of gender required that more time be spent explaining the research to them. Interviewing those parliamentarians with a basic understanding and awareness of gender allowed more time for the interviews and richer examples from which to develop research. We interviewed two at their homes and two at the National Assembly itself. All interviews were semi-structured. The emphasis was on probing the experience of female parliamentarians and how they navigated male-dominated institutions. With the exception of one parliamentarian, none of the others went on to serve in the 13th legislature, for various reasons, whether they chose not to or their parties were not successful. The interviews were conducted in French by the first author, and were tape recorded. A local female interpretation student fluent in French and Wolof (the local language) transcribed them and returned them to the first author who translated the transcriptions into English. Finally, we coded the interviews thematically.[7]

In addition to the interviews, several secondary source materials related to the female parliamentarians of the 12th legislature and the vote on parity were donated by the Director of the Laboratoire Genre et Recherche scientifique de l'IFAN/UCAD (Laboratory for Gender and Scientific Research of IFAN/UCAD), Mme. Fatou Sarr Sow, and by the *Conseil Sénégalais des Femmes* (Senegalese Women's Council).[8]

Furthermore, from the archivist of the National Assembly we received copies of membership lists of all the previous legislatures since Parliament was first established in 1960, as well as the parity law itself.

Theoretically, the study draws upon a relatively new body of research known as feminist institutionalism, which explores traditional understandings of institutional systems using a gender lens.[9] This form of analysis helps to conceptualize theories of change by identifying patterns of behavior related to gender and determining if altering the institutional system by varying its actors can make it more inclusive and resilient. The questions for our survey were developed with this theory in mind. However, once we began to code the responses, we found that the answers given required an additional form of analysis to incorporate the complexity and nuance of the responses. Therefore, we also relied upon grounded theory to gain additional insights from the phenomena we were exploring. Thus, using both feminist institutionalism and grounded theory, the chapter examines the impact of women's increased political participation in transforming stagnant political institutions such as the hybrid (both colonially inherited and locally shaped) institutions that are African parliaments. How do women play a role in maintaining the status quo versus changing established norms? Do women see themselves as change makers? If so, what sorts of creative approaches do they use to challenge established norms?

The chapter is divided into three sections. The first provides a brief overview of feminist institutionalism (FI), showing how using FI as a theoretical framework for analysis can potentially help to better understand women's impact on existing institutional norms. The second section provides an historical background of the role of women in government in Senegal, up to and including the landmark passage of the parity law. Finally, the third section applies a combination of the FI framework and grounded theory-based analysis to research on seven female parliamentarians conducted in Dakar, Senegal, in July and September, 2017, after the completion of the 12th legislature—the first to apply the parity law in its elections.

UNDERSTANDING FEMINIST INSTITUTIONALISM

To examine whether female parliamentarians change institutional norms and the creative approaches they use to do so, we positioned this research within the theoretical framework of feminist institutionalism (FI). Feminist institutionalism uses a gendered approach to institutional analysis to illuminate how the different characteristics and behaviors of men and women influence the formation of institutional norms and how they function. For the purposes of this discussion, "institutions" and "institutional norms" refer to rules, policies, and norms that are discussed within the context of institutionalism, while "organizations" refers to a political body of actors who construct and implement the policies of these institutions, namely parliaments.

Feminist institutionalism has grown out of feminist research on organizations and combines the concepts of feminist political science with new institutionalism. Feminist political science addresses behaviors, attitudes and actions that take place within the political arena, particularly within the organizations existing in the state and in society. As politics is conducted by its actors, namely men and women,[10] the relationship between men and women becomes central to better understand what takes place within politics. Feminist scholarship includes an awareness of gender, or socially constructed roles that men and women play within society that can dictate their social access. For example, feminist scholars have shown that within society, these gender roles are unequal, with men holding the preponderance of positions of decision-making power. Therefore, feminist political scientists began to study how gender inequality impacts political actors within their workplace.[11]

As gender scholars began to examine gender inequality within political organizations, such as parliaments, they theorized that these organizations were predominantly patriarchal, as most were formed by those societal actors who were historically in positions of power—men. However, they also found that there was no such thing as a unique understanding of patriarchal organizations. Instead, while these organizations generally tend to perpetuate unequal social relationships, they also vary based on their specific origins, histories and actors and therefore can be changed.[12]

At this point, feminist political science shifted from a focus on individual actors to institutional analysis, including how one's gender creates or impedes opportunities within an organization.[13] For example, if men are more comfortable working with other men, or seeing other men, as opposed to women, in positions of leadership, they are more likely to support putting a man in a position of authority. This "norm" is then informally adopted throughout the organization, and it becomes difficult to alter. The theory holds that organizations are constructed through the practices of the actors who inhabit them. Feminist political science has demonstrated that this gender difference is what leads to inequality within these organizations.[14] Researchers identified institutional "masculinities" and "femininities," as more and more women participated within previously all-male governments.[15]

Researchers therefore reoriented from gender inequality in politics to an examination of "the multiple ways in which gendered power relations and inequality are constructed, shaped, and maintained through institutional processes, practices and rules."[16] Yet, feminist political science acknowledges that there is a dynamic interchange between the gendered power relations and processes that take place within organizations and gender dynamics in broader society. Therefore, by changing what takes place within organizations, there is an opportunity to affect change on a societal level as well.

New institutionalism (NI) is not oriented around gender but emphasizes the general importance of institutions within society and the ways in which their organization impacts political life.[17] NI research is organized around four approaches: rational choice institutionalism, historical institutionalism, organizational or sociological institutionalism, and discursive institutionalism[18]—each approach making a unique set of assumptions in order to develop political theories around the creation, development and operation of institutional norms. Though NI does not focus on gendered power dynamics, it is useful for understanding institutions in a broader sense. Moreover, through its use of the unique frameworks of analysis named, NI often incorporates a vocabulary similar to that of feminist political science. This shared approach to exploring the endogenous and exogenous structures of institutional norms is what led to the development of feminist institutionalism, a combination of the two theories that enables theorists to better understand gender both within an institutional context and in society at large.[19]

When examining the gendered effects of institutions, one must consider how actors within these political organizations navigate such institutional norms to achieve their interests. An institutional norm that has otherwise reproduced itself with each new cohort that passes through its halls demonstrates "institutional resistance" and forms a "weary institution."[20] However, with the introduction of women into such weary institutions, previously established norms and practices must now exist within a gendered structure. Fiona Mackay, Meryl Kenny, and Louise Chappell discuss how certain actors deploy agency within government organizations, which involves "strategic, creative and intuitive action as well as calculating self-interest. Strategic actors initiate change within a context of opportunities and constraints."[21] It is this creative action that can then infuse energy into a stagnant organization and make the organization more resilient. Women who enter a previously andronormative organization and merely perpetuate these existing masculine institutional norms maintain the status quo. However, if instead of tolerating existing norms, they attempt to defy or change them, they then make a creative change to this institution.

Examining an organization from both a horizontal and vertical perspective using an FI approach can reveal the gender dynamics of institutional norms and provide greater insight into the level of change or stasis that has taken place since the introduction of female political actors. Horizontally, one might examine rules of behavior, whether formal or informal, and the use of resources. Vertically, one might review structures of hierarchy and the power relations that continue to define relationships between men and women. As our analysis centers on whether female parliamentarians in Senegal play a role in maintaining the status quo versus using creative approaches to change institutional norms, we will examine not only the institutions which affect the behavior of these political actors but other factors that constrain or inspire their participation in a previously male-dominant organization.

WOMEN'S POLITICAL PARTICIPATION IN SENEGAL

To better understand women's participation in Senegal's Parliament, it is important to understand the historical context of women's relationship to the state. When the West African country of Senegal became independent from its colonial ruler—France—in 1960, it inherited a legacy of governance systems that were a complex mixture of African and European traditions of power and influence. Patronage networks perpetuated a male majority in the political power structure.[22] Senegalese women, who had had marginal formal political participation in institutions immediately preceding colonialism, continued to remain in the background after independence, supporting those in positions of power through marital or relational connections. It was not until the mid-1980s that women began to participate more significantly within government institutions and until the 2000s that things started to shift in terms of the unequal gendered division of power within the country. How did the numbers of women participating at the highest level of government, the Senegalese Parliament (known as the *Assemblée Nationale*, or National Assembly), increase from one female in 1963 to sixty-four females nearly fifty years later in 2012? The change did not occur until fairly recently in Senegalese history and could be partially attributed to the significant increase in the agency and persistence of women.

Background on the Parity Law in Senegal

Parity is a quota system that sets targets for women's participation. It can be reserved for seats in the legislature or as a percentage of party candidates and is usually defined by political party, constitution, or legislation.[23] Political quota systems have been adopted in more than 100 countries.[24] The difference between using a "quota system" to increase women's representation versus a "parity" system is that parity means equality, or 50 percent female representation, while quotas are usually for significantly less than 50 percent female representation.

Senegal's electoral system uses proportional representation. Parties make candidate lists, and depending on what proportion of the vote a party has won, winning parties then send the corresponding number of candidates from the list to the National Assembly. Therefore, the order of names on these lists is highly significant. Before 2010, women's names on these lists, if they occurred at all, tended to be toward the bottom of the lists.

Senegal's successful adoption of the parity law can be attributed to many factors, including a vibrant civil society of women's NGOs,[25] the strength of the international conferences on women by the United Nations in the 1990s,[26] and the right political leadership at a specific moment in history.[27] While many civil society actors and political leaders at the grassroots, municipal, and national levels helped to play a role in the law's passage, the *Conseil Sénégalais des Femmes,* (COSEF) [Senegalese Women's Council], was one of the most prominent organizations at the forefront of the campaign for parity in Senegal. Through its extensive documentation of its advocacy efforts, one can better understand how women's agency and leadership played a significant role in shaping the current dynamics within the National Assembly.

COSEF was created in 1994, after a two-day public meeting to reflect on the theme of "Women and Democracy in Senegal" (*Femmes en Démocratie au Sénégal*). An NGO comprising women from all walks of society, including political actors, union members, and attorneys, COSEF was "a space of engagement, a crucible where questions about the evolution of women's position in decision-making circles are posed and debated."[28] Its focus was to discuss the role women should play within the Senegalese democracy. The following year, in 1995, the UN Fourth World Conference on Women was held in Beijing. The COSEF contingent who attended the conference was particularly intrigued with Point 7 of the Beijing Platform for Action (PFA) that focused on equal participation of women and men in decision-making and began a series of strategic activities to create awareness around this issue.[29]

Meanwhile, in 2000, Senegal adopted a new Constitution that explicitly affirmed its adhesion to international treaties in its preamble, including CEDAW. The president at the time, Abdoulaye Wade, seemed to be open to the notion of parity; when asked by a women's NGO in 2002 at an African Union conference to introduce the idea of a 30 percent quota for women, he demanded parity for women instead. In April 2005, South African President Thabo Mbeki awarded Wade the "African Gender Award" and Wade expressed his desire to apply parity in Senegal.[30] Thus, there was a convergence of international activity, presidential interest, and civil society engagement.

After several years of continued discussions, mobilization, and raising awareness by COSEF and other female leaders, organizations, and activists, the "Law of Absolute Parity between Man and Woman, 10/

2010" passed; it applied not only to the National Assembly but to the Senate (no longer in existence), regional councils, municipal councils, and rural councils. It stated that two candidates of the same sex could not follow each other on the party list. It also stated that in case of a vacancy, the elected member shall be replaced by a member of the same sex.[31] If an odd number of seats is sent to the Assembly, the even number below them must alternate between male and female candidates. For example, if a party wins five seats, four of them must alternate between men and women.[32] (This provision, along with the fact that those parties with single member representation tend to send male representatives, has resulted in less than 50 percent female representation in the National Assembly.) To ensure that the parity law continues to be respected, as well as to continue to promote gender parity, the government established an independent body known as the *l'Observatoire national de la parité* (ONP) or National Observatory of Parity.[33]

The elections after the passage of the parity law show its enormous impact on women's participation in government. Alternating women's names on party lists resulted in sixty-four female parliamentarians out of 150 members or 42.67 percent, making Senegal the second African country with the most female representation in Parliament from 2012 to 2016.[34] In the elections held in July 2017, that percentage dipped slightly: there were sixty-nine women elected out of 165 positions, or 41.8 percent.[35] Senegal fell just below Namibia and South Africa as the fourth African country with the most women in Parliament.[36]

WOMEN'S IMPACT ON WEARY INSTITUTIONS

Drivers of Change

When examining how the National Assembly changed after the parity law, it is important to understand the demographic makeup of the women elected to the 12th legislature. In her work, *Les premières héritières de la loi sur la parité*, (The First Heirs of the Law on Parity), Fatou Sarr conducted a demographic profile of the 12th legislature.[37] Her findings show that ethnically, female parliamentarians have at least one representative from nine different ethnic groups of Senegal, the majority being Wolof at 48.4 percent with Toucouleur (15.63 percent), Sérère (10.94 percent), and Peuhl (9.38 percent) closely following.[38] The average age of the parliamentarians is fifty-two, with the youngest aged thirty-two and the oldest being eighty years old. Nearly 69 percent are married, and two-thirds are in polygamous relationships.[39]

The levels of education for female parliamentarians range from none (12.5 percent), to religious education solely (9.4 percent), primary school (14.1 percent), secondary/technical school (26.5 percent), and finally baccalaureate degree and beyond (37.5 percent). Although only twenty-seven out of sixty-four are literate, of the twenty-seven, many speak more than one language with French at 75 percent and Wolof at 70.37 percent being the most common. Professionally, the women have backgrounds in the public, private, and informal sectors, with the majority coming from business (20) and teaching (13). Additionally, they are active in civil society organizations—nearly 72 percent have participated in women's associations, women's economic groups and other non-governmental organizations. As for political experience, 70 percent have at least ten years' experience, with the majority (32.8 percent) having more than thirty years' experience.[40] This understanding of women's educational, professional, and political experience helps to inform an understanding of the complex mix of opportunities and barriers they faced during their service in government, which are outlined below.

Female parliamentarians acknowledged several factors that significantly influenced their work—what we refer to as "drivers of change." One driver of change is that of women's agency and leadership. It is women's agency and leadership that created the social and political movement resulting in the passage of Senegal's parity law in 2012. This agency and leadership are also responsible for the struggles and achievements of these women during their time in government. The second driver of change is the parity law itself. It is due to the passage of this legislation that women gained greater access to a previously and predominantly male institution and began to implement their agendas. Finally, due to their unique perspectives based on their sex and gender, women brought their own attitudes, approaches and behaviors to Parliament, introducing new and creative solutions to the daunting challenges they faced.

Women's Agency and the Parity Law

If one considers the advocacy efforts of COSEF in 1995 as its beginning, then the struggle for the passage of the parity law took seventeen years to achieve. This work to establish equal representation was not lost on the first cohort of female parliamentarians. As Aminata[41] stated, "the women of Senegal have stood upright, they have been in solidarity. They have united in order to be able to vote the law and to be able to apply it. So, it's a fight, a long battle . . . we always struggled for the advancement of women and it is this struggle that brought us here today."

Many of the women interviewed were well aware of the history of the law, its implications, and their own roles within this history. Female parliamentarians consistently expressed that they wanted to make the most of their public service because they felt a sense of purpose, a responsibility to represent not only their constituents, but most particularly those who fought for greater equality. As Khady put it, "We were fortunate to be part of this legislature, a really enriching experience—we learned a lot—we also tried to give what we could and so, for me, it's an unforgettable experience that I do not regret."

The constant reference to a unique moment in Senegalese history, and to themselves as part of the tide of change, suggests that female parliamentarians are driven to do their part by their sense of purpose. This "agency" is reminiscent of the vibrant women's movement that propelled these women into their new roles. For these parliamentarians, there is a reciprocal effect that takes place between the society, which has been sensitized to the value of bringing more women into government, and the government, particularly female parliamentarians, that feels compelled to do its best for a newly aware female citizenry. As Fatou described after losing in the 13th legislature: "Today my maid said 'but Madame, in the Assembly, there has not been parity. You were not there. Nobody said anything. You would be there. You would have spoken." Her statement reflects how women's obligation to those who sent them there incentivizes them to continue their agency and leadership. In turn, women in society who see the achievements of female representatives are more inspired to engage as citizens and help to energize the public sector.

Women's Unique Perspective

In addition to women's agency and leadership and the importance of the parity law, women bring a unique perspective to their work primarily because they navigate the world differently due to socially and culturally constructed gender roles as well as differences related to their sex. It is this perspective, which is different from men's perspective, that helps to shape women's work within institutions and potentially drives those institutions to become more flexible and creative to accommodate their specific approach. As feminist institutionalism suggests, women demonstrate distinct differences from men based on their gender and these experiences can shape "ways of valuing things, ways of behaving and ways of being."[42]

Ways of being acknowledges the biological sexual differences between men and women and informs their ways of valuing things and behaving, which might be interpreted to mean the traits and behaviors that are typically ascribed to men and women, or what Joni Lovenduski calls "codes of masculinity" and "codes of femininity."[43] Political scientists have linked these concepts to women's governance through "substantive representation," meaning that female parliamentarians will introduce policies that originate from women's exclusive experience, through their "feminine" traits and behaviors which might include more socially conscious sensitivities or through their biological experiences such as those related to childbirth or female genital mutilation, for example.[44] Awa explained it this way:

> Things have changed, on all sides, in all ways, because yes or no, the future of Africa is in the hands of women. We have already seen all the institutions that are not dominant, but very strong in terms of women, even more so, especially in terms of gender sensitive budgeting. Women take control. We read the budget wearing glasses, the glasses of gender. So, compared to men, they are gender-sensitive but not the same with women. That is why it is important to be able to help each other, not only for parity, but I would like to see 80 percent of women in Parliament because women are workers and are almost always looking at the other side. If we say gender budgeting, we do not say women, we do not say girls, but we say gender. To the villagers, to the handicapped, then, the neediest, the most vulnerable . . . I think when we talk about gender, we are targeting them. When we build schools, we think of handicapped people who cannot

> walk, we think of disabled people who do not see. Is that in the other villages? Are there hospitals, healthcare? Do they take care of women who give birth? . . . There are plenty of things that one still thinks of as a female parliamentarian compared to men, who do not think so because they do not even know.

According to Awa, women will organically transform a political institution by the presence of their bodies and the perspectives they offer. Women's distinctly embodied viewpoint then helps to catalyze institutions, depending on the level of engagement and access afforded to women. Thus, the combination of all three elements—agency, access through parity, and perspective—is what has laid the foundation for Senegalese women to manifest change in the National Assembly.

Barriers to Success

Within the National Assembly, women have faced challenges that have forced them to develop certain strategies and tactics in order to be effective. These challenges are described as "barriers to success" and the strategies and tactics women use as "pathways to navigating the institution." Barriers to success can be divided into three categories: (1) barriers created when men reject parity, (2) barriers due to lack of training and language skills, and, finally, (3) barriers common to both women and men related to resources and party politics.

Men Reject Parity

Many barriers that female parliamentarians have faced reflect traditional norms related to the formal authority of men within the institution and their perceived failure to accept parity and its implications. Awa noted that having to make lists that now included women frustrated men. Binta said she felt men worried that women have taken their place. She stated: "It's always an internal fight . . . we have just set up 11 committees and there are only two headed by women . . . and the men are not even glad women have these two. Yesterday, when I was asked to read, I said I do not read as long as there are no women." Another noted that the patriarchal norms reflected the family code where the man is still head of the family.

Lack of Training and Language

Women confronted two institutional norms upon their increased participation in government: knowledge of parliamentary matters and the official language of government—French. These institutional norms become highly relevant when new actors with less training and language skills are introduced into Parliament. Both of these barriers are situated within the broader socio-cultural implications of what it means to be female in Senegal. As noted earlier, 36 percent of female parliamentarians have no more than a primary level of education, with only 42 percent who are literate. While Senegal's level of primary education for girls is notable, when it comes to the mean years in school, according to the Human Development Index, girls rate 2.1, while boys rate 3.6.[45] Generally, education equality is difficult to attain as more families place a greater emphasis on educating boys, because they are more likely to work and bring income to the family. Girls are more likely to marry and leave the family, or perhaps are sent to find domestic work so that they can help their families financially.[46]

Several women remarked that the fact that their fellow parliamentarians did not speak French or understand what was being said in the assembly had posed a significant problem in their ability to perform their work. In a previously and predominantly male institution, men with more training and greater literacy would have less difficulty participating in daily tasks required of their positions. It was only after the adoption of the simultaneous translation system, discussed in greater detail below, that they realized what formidable women were working with them. The inability to write creates a further institutional barrier for those women who lack literacy skills.

Women revealed lack of training as the source of their struggle to make informed decisions regarding legislation. Without subject matter expertise, parliamentarians are unable to make thoughtful choices on behalf of their constituents. Some women also felt uncertain about how to conduct themselves in their new position. "First, there must be literacy, then training, knowing what the members of the institution should do, how they should speak, how they should act, what is their role, there is all that . . . in order to be able to achieve convincing results," Fatou stated. Ultimately, women recognize the limits of their education, once in office. As Binta said, "I have served three terms, but I know that it takes a certain level of education to be a good parliamentarian."

Barriers Common to Both Men and Women

Finally, women mentioned institutional norms that they had been unprepared to address—norms that both men and women face, although women might experience them differently. Those include a lack of adequate resources in Parliament and the pull of allegiance to party over conscience when voting on legislation. Lack of resources includes human resources such as assistants or secretaries who can help in researching issues and managing documentation or correspondence. However, female parliamentarians also complained about a lack of financial resources, especially in comparison to their ministerial counterparts who receive cars with drivers or payment for housing. As Oumou said, "The issue of parliamentarians is a problem of means because we are politicians, politicians who live with their policy base and do not have the means. Like me, I live in . . . the poorest community, the most vulnerable of . . . Dakar . . . it's not easy." This concern was exacerbated by the social expectations that parliamentarians provide material support to needy constituents, a duty that female representatives experience as more onerous because they are also expected to be caregivers and sympathetic listeners, due to their gender.

Allegiance to party created frustration for many women. Some noted that political calculation won out over competence, when it came to making appointments on committees, for example. Others were well aware that party leaders had chosen them to appear on party lists and felt an obligation to abide by their wishes. Aminata commented that she believed there was no change in parliament after parity due to the obligations elected leaders held to their political parties. As she stated,

> So, it's for you to say that the freedom that people think we have, we don't. We have the freedom to speak. But for . . . the vote in general, people have constraints. Because, for example, a person who is in power hesitates to vote against a bill coming from power . . . there are, of course, changes but . . . at the level of numbers of women. But on the job, there has not been much change.

This obligation to vote along the party line is arguably one of the main reasons why women maintain the status quo. Oumou observed that "since the party is there, and it has 'gendarmes' who are there and who check what is done, often they vote in the direction that their party orders and not in the interests of the people." Women wanting to introduce representational legislation or legislation that reflects the lived experiences unique to women, for example, could be hesitant to do so, as they would have to persuade not only their fellow parliamentarians, but their political parties.

Pathways to Navigating the Institution

While female parliamentarians face certain institutional norms that frustrate their ability to participate on equal footing with men, they have also actively created methods to achieve their objectives. These methods or "pathways" have been produced by (1) developing informal institutional approaches, (2) creating innovative methods to resolve problems, or (3) by exhibiting conscientious behavior so as to maintain their non-dominant member standing within the institution. In all cases, the research suggests that these pathways were the result of being new and different from the traditional male actors in parliament. As we will discuss below, oftentimes, the behavior was either in direct response to the barriers faced by the parliamentarian or indirectly linked to the need to prove their value and justify their newly won status.

Informal Institutional Approaches

As mentioned, within institutional structures, there are "formal" rules and "informal rules." Informal rules can best be described as "socially shared rules, usually unwritten, that are created, communicated, and enforced outside of officially sanctioned channels."[47] Such informal approaches are a backlash to the formal barriers that actors face within institutions. For women, the "shared sense of identity and experiences manifested through friendship [which] can . . . enable female representatives to negotiate gendered political institutions" facilitate these informal approaches.[48] In the case of Senegal, these relationships were a necessary relief for women who were forced to participate in sometimes unexpected partisan politics. Women took great pride in their ability to form relationships with other women, at times across party lines, particularly when compared with men's relationships. Said Awa: "Women do it better than men, because you're not going to wait for the day you're going to need a person to tell him 'I need you.' She must feel that you are carrying an interest that is not a calculated interest. . . . And when you need the person, automatically, she answers 'yes.'" Binta talked about serving as a resource for those women who were illiterate and could not write correspondence, for example. She also mentioned that she communicated weekly by text with a group of women, asking about their health, family news, or sharing prayers, as a way to maintain close contact.

As strategic actors, women tried to capitalize on these relationships when it came to passing legislation, although, at times, they were not successful. In one instance, female parliamentarians suggested that when choosing actors for the Economic, Social, and Environmental Council, the Assembly could elect representatives by using the same process as the parity law, that is, man, woman, man, woman. The representative, Binta, texted her fellow female parliamentarians, as well as others, to vote on the amendment. While the proposed amendment passed in the first round, with the additional help of a few men, in the second round, it was rejected. She explained that "The amendment almost came to pass, but because they felt they owed their political party . . . they felt indebted, they were afraid of being punished, they rejected [it]. And we were beaten perhaps by two votes."

This comradery among female parliamentarians is significant, not only in creating built-in support for the passage of legislation, but also support for proposing legislation. In another example, Oumou mentioned her efforts to reject legislation related to creating 100 percent smoke-free public spaces, such as restaurants, hotels, and so on. The legislation dealt with the "smokehouses" where people who wanted to smoke could go do so freely. The research had shown smokehouses to be inefficient and expensive, and that workers who cleaned up afterwards faced significant health threats themselves, up to as much as four hours after smokers had left. Oumou fought against this amendment in plenary and stated that she felt supported by the female chair of the health committee, in spite of potential political consequences for her support. "My chair got along well with the Minister, but it was me she followed, it was me she supported, and it gave me great pleasure . . . we were hand in hand until the end of the voting process . . . it amazed me."

What these experiences show is that, as Sarah Childs proves, women's friendships become a highly valued resource that "helped them negotiate and challenge Parliament's masculinized institutional norms and practices."[49] Women used their relationships with other female parliamentarians to address personal challenges, in the case of literacy, as well as professional challenges, in the case of legislation. And while their efforts were not always successful, using their informal networks based on gendered alliances was an efficient and valuable process for addressing their vulnerabilities and engaging with like-minded actors across the political spectrum.

Innovative Methods for Solving Problems

Faced with barriers due to lack of training and language skills, female parliamentarians found ways to address these obstacles in a creative manner. Feminist institutionalism suggests that men are able to perpetuate their power over women through the culture they have developed as a result of their longstanding presence. From this perspective, "men's domination of political institutions has been their ability to set the rules of the game . . . enabling them to structure institutions . . . legitimize particular knowledge . . . and shape culture in ways that perpetuate their power over women."[50] Those women who enter previously male-dominated institutions must either find ways to penetrate these elite cliques of knowledge or be forced to remain in subservient positions within government. Those women who had limited capacity to address relevant issues that were debated and voted upon in the legislature turned to external resources that were available to them.

Among the trainings available to them, the Women Lawyers' Association (*Association des juristes Séné galaises*), which helped improve women's understanding of Parliamentary processes, was mentioned. Other organizations that were mentioned, both local and international, included COSEF, *Association Séné galaise pour le Bien-Être Familiale* (ASBEF) [the Senegalese Association for Family Welfare], UN Women, and the Open Society Institute of West Africa (OSIWA). While these trainings were also open to men, they reported that it was primarily women who attended them.

In addition, understanding the benefits of capacity building, female parliamentarians used this approach to their own advantage when seeking ways to persuade colleagues to pass relevant legislation. Oumou, who led the vote against the smokehouse amendment, for example, mentioned that she had held training sessions "for 100 deputies out of 150" and stated: "We did three successive workshops to inform people. So, all those who came to these workshops were sensitized and ready to vote all the amendments." Capacity building of female parliamentarians not only served to inform those who may not have had experience in the institution, but to refine the knowledge of those with some past exposure to parliamentary procedures and issues. One could certainly argue that such trainings helped to infuse the institution with fresh ideas and a higher level of competence than perhaps it had previously contained.

Another innovation is the installation of a simultaneous translation system after the start of the 12th legislature. The system was actually arranged during the 11th legislature in a deal with the European Union, but it was not implemented at that time. After President Macky Sall came to power, he personally went before the leaders of the EU and received a donation of translation equipment, including headphones, and training for simultaneous translators.[51]

The implementation of simultaneous translation—perhaps catalyzed due to the increased number of members, predominantly female, who did not speak French—created a palpable effect on the institution's efficacy and efficiency. Heartily endorsing its introduction, Aisha stated: "So, when the minister comes, they pose their problems in their language. The minister understands because there is translation. He answers; it is translated and they have the answer. And when one is in the plenary, when one speaks in their language, it is diffused to the population who follows it. It is a very good system." Khady noted: "The exchanges were more fluid, easier."

In fact, the simultaneous translation system acted as a unique form of empowerment, particularly for women, who suddenly gained recognition for their leadership, and in turn, felt encouraged to increase their participation even more. Aisha described the experience:

> When we started the retransmission in the languages, we noticed that people were more comfortable, especially women. And there is a woman I noticed who is . . . from within the country, she must be from Bakel or something like that, but it is from the simultaneous translation that I realized that she was really a woman leader. Because she does not speak our national language, Wolof, she does not speak French, either, we did not know what she was saying. But when we started the translation, I said, "Attention, here is a woman leader." . . . And I could have left the assembly without knowing her leadership.

Building this level of inclusion within the parliamentary system, not only through gender parity but through increased engagement from multiple ethnicities, is a remarkable achievement for a government institution that, only a few years earlier, could not support those outside the dominant male and French-speaking majority. Translation generated greater participation from all members of parliament, ideally allowing Senegal's citizens to receive a more effective level of representation from their elected officials. In terms of women's agency, translation helped women bypass a traditional norm that otherwise might have taken years to overcome.

A third innovation that women brought into the institution, which has helped both sexes, is the *tontine*. A tontine is a savings program where members contribute a defined amount of money on a monthly basis. Each month, one member receives the total amount, which allows the member to buy more expensive goods that are not generally affordable. In the case of parliament, the savings program was targeted for religious pilgrimages—Mecca for Muslims and Rome for Christians.

Women in parliament, before the 12th legislature, had started a tontine as a way to address their lack of financial resources. However, with increased female participation during the 12th legislature, the tontine not only boosted its female membership, but attracted men in parliament, allegedly because they were jealous of their female colleagues. This innovation increased collaboration within the institution by providing women and men a platform to work toward mutual goals and benefits.

All three innovations are not only opportunities for women to increase their professional and personal standing but also to engage both men *and* women in their roles as government representatives, ultimately allowing the politics of Parliament to be "regendered." As Mackay (original emphasis) notes, "the everyday acting out of gender relations in institutions, coupled with institutional innovation and strategic action by actors such as feminist norm entrepreneurs *may* lead to the regendering of politics to one degree or another."[52] Dynamic Senegalese women who helped reform the institution through a substantial increase in female participation, it can be argued, have also impacted the institution through their innovative and collaborative approaches.

Conscientious Behavior to Maintain Standing

When interviewed, female parliamentarians consistently stressed persistence and spending long hours at the Assembly as critical to their effectiveness. Feminist political science focuses on the ties between gender and power, suggesting that power held by the dominant gender creates a stability that, when threatened, can lead to a reinterpretation of this power.[53] Introducing a significant number of women into the National Assembly can threaten this stability. The research also suggests that, due to vertical power dynamics at constant play, women must continue to strategize and overcompensate to maintain their own relevance and their newly contested positions within the government. As Khady said:

> But I'm telling you, for example, that attendance in parliament today was women. . . . They were more assiduous. . . . This is the truth. They were there at the most advanced hours of the night, for you know that the parliament works until almost midnight. Many men slipped in and left. In the technical commissions, you heard some [men] even tell you "ah, but I went back to my second wife," for example, and then the women were there until the end.

The irony about the exemplary attendance that women demonstrate is that, according to FI theorists, the gendered effects of formal rules, such as meeting times and hours of operation, would normally prevent women from participation, due to their responsibilities for care within the household.[54] Yet, women often stated that they and their colleagues would stay far longer than male counterparts in the office, so that they could work—in spite of the fact that they faced additional responsibilities at home. Some observed that they made these trade-offs at great cost to themselves and their families.

In this instance, formal rules do not prevent women from the opportunity to work. Instead, the institutional culture leads women to face a double-bind of proving themselves at work and at home. Yet, their behavior seems to be self-imposed, due to the fear of losing their perceived authority rather than any overtly imposed demand on their time. In fact, some women said this behavior was the result of a newly elected group of representatives who do not want to let down their constituents; others felt this was typically gendered behavior. Perhaps it is a combination of the two. As Aminata said: "Well . . . women, they always want to prove themselves and, also, for them it was a chance. It was a first and they had to deserve it." Binta mentioned, when describing the women that "they are more conscientious . . . she does not want anyone to say that she does not work, she safeguards her dignity. That's the difference."

This issue needs further investigation to truly understand women's motivations to maintain this level of effort in their work. The risk for these women is that by trying to prove themselves, they will burn out or become demotivated to pursue further responsibilities within the government.

Those who care about greater equality between men and women see political power as crucial to achieving that dream. Sharing decision-making in the political arena, while often messy, allows for greater opportunities for inclusiveness and diversity within political leadership so that resources within societies can benefit a broader share of the population. The combination of women's agency, the passage of the parity law, and the biological, cultural and societal forces that impact the way Senegalese women view the world differently from Senegalese men have all contributed to the development of the National Assembly as a government institution that is very different than it was at its inception in 1960, and even than it was during the 11th legislature.

Feminist political scientists examine the links between women's descriptive representation and women's substantive representation to determine whether women's increased presence in government will lead to more legislation that reflects women's lived experience. Using a narrower lens, our research was situated around whether women's increased participation changes stagnant institutional norms. As we have demonstrated, while increased participation of women in a previously and predominantly male institution can initially produce barriers to women's full participation, the same agency that propelled them into these positions of power helped them to create pathways to effectiveness rather than maintain the status quo. This is not to suggest that the National Assembly is now permanently changed through these efforts, although many of their innovations, such as capacity building, translation services, or the tontine are potentially sustainable initiatives in the future. Nor is it to suggest that there is no further work to be done. Remaining barriers related to women's participation within vertical power structures, such as committee leadership, will require greater advocacy and strategic efforts on the part of female parliamentarians to increase their numbers in these positions. Indeed, at the conclusion of our interviews, women were in the midst of fighting for greater internal parity in all departments within the institution.

Parity is the first step in a long process to achieve greater inclusion and diverse representation within the political system. As the research showed, while women are buoyed by their newly won political power, they are still constrained by the double-bind of responsibilities they face within their home and work lives. As these dilemmas are negotiated, women will continue to find creative solutions either within or outside the systems they navigate. Some researchers have found fault with quota systems and point to a lack of substantive change for women as a reason to reject their implementation.[55] The Senegal case, contrary to such contestations, shows a more nuanced impact as a result of parity laws. It illuminates how women bring new approaches, new resources and new definitions to the role of parliamentarian. It defines their struggles which not only have to do with gender, but with the pressures of party politics which can undermine their abilities to successfully introduce legislation that represents women's interests. In these instances, women may be forced to collaborate more fully with male actors to seek political solutions that empower their positions and inform their agency.

To maintain their authority among their constituents, government institutions must be relevant to the populations they govern. This means they must be flexible enough to embrace new actors and resilient enough to adapt to new behaviors and approaches. This research shows that infusing homogenous institutions with more diverse populations can serve to revitalize reified systems of governance and potentially bring greater energy to an otherwise apathetic citizenry.

Table 8.1. Senegal—Number of Women in the National Assembly by Year

Legislature		*Sex of Members*		*Total*	*% Women*
Mandate	*Year*	*Male*	*Female*		
1	1960-1963	80	0	80	0.00
2	1963-1968	79	1	80	1.25
3	1968-1973	79	1	80	1.25
4	1973-1978	76	4	80	5.00
5	1978-1983	93	7	100	7.00
6	1983-1988	105	15	120	12.50
7	1988-1993	105	15	120	12.50
8	1993-1998	106	14	120	11.67
9	1998-2001	119	21	140	15.00
10	2001-2007	101	27	120	22.50
11	2007-2012	117	33	150	22.00
12	2012-2017	86	64	150	42.67
13	2017-2021	96	69	165	41.80

Source: Archives of the National Assembly, Dakar, Senegal; *Les Premières Heritières de la Loi Sur La Parité*, Fatou Sarr (2013)

BIBLIOGRAPHY

Arendt, Christie Marie. "From Critical Mass to Critical Leaders: Unpacking the Political Conditions behind Gender Quotas in Africa." *Politics & Gender* 14, no. 3, 2018, 295–322. https://doi.org/10.1017/S1743923X17000502.

Assemblée Nationale. "Douzième Legislature (2012–2017): Liste de Deputés." Dakar, 2012.

———. "Triezième Legislature (2017–2022): Liste de Deputés." Dakar, 2017.

Ballington, Julie. "The Implementation of Quotas: African Experiences, Quota Report Series," 2004.

Bauer, Gretchen. "'A Lot of Head Wraps': African Contributions to the Third Wave of Electoral Gender Quotas." *Politics, Groups, and Identities* 4, no. 2 (2016): 196–213. https://doi.org/10.1080/21565503.2015.1112293.

Beck, Linda. "Democratization and the Hidden Public: The Impact of Patronage Networks on Senegalese Women." *Comparative Politics* 35, no. 2 (2003): 147–69.

Chappell, Louise, and Georgina Waylen. "Gender and the Hidden Life of Institutions." *Public Administration* 91, no. 3 (2013): 599–615. https://doi.org/10.1111/j.1467-9299.2012.02104.x.

Charmaz, Kathy. *Constructing Grounded Theory: A Practical Guide through Qualitative Research*. London: Sage Publications, 2006.

Childs, Sarah. "Negotiating Gendered Institutions: Women's Parliamentary Friendships." *Politics & Gender* 9, no. 2 (2013): 127–51. https://doi.org/10.1017/S1743923X13000019.

Corbin, Juliet M., and Anselm Strauss. "Grounded Theory Research: Procedures, Canons, and Evaluative Criteria." *Qualitative Sociology* 13, no. 1 (1990): 3–21.

COSEF. *Combats pour la parité: Actes du Séminaire d'élaboration d'un modèle de loi sur la parité*. Dakar: COSEF, 2011.

COSEF and AECID. *Combats pour la parité, "La loi sur la parité absolue au Sénégal."* Dakar, 2011.

Duerst-Lahti, Georgia, and Rita Mae Kelly, eds. *Gender, Power, Leadership and Governance*. Ann Arbor: University of Michigan Press, 1995.

Ertan, Senem. "Gender Quotas and Women's Representation in Muslim Countries," *2nd European Conference on Politics and Gender*, (January 2011): 1–23.

Fifth Regional Conference on Women. African Platform for Action (1994).

Franceschet, Susan. "Gendered Institutions and Women's Substantive Representation: Female Legislators in Argentina and Chile." In *Gender, Politics, and Institutions: Towards a Feminist Institutionalism*, edited by Mona Lena Krook and Fiona Mackay, 58–78. London : Palgrave MacMillan, 2011. https://doi.org/10.1057/9780230303911.

Glaser, Barney, Anselm Strauss, and Elizabeth Strutzel. "The Discovery of Grounded Theory: Strategies for Qualitative Research," *Nursing Research* 17, no. 4 (1968): 364.

Helmke, Gretchen, and Steven Levitsky. *Informal Institutions and Democracy: Lessons from Latin America*. Johns Hopkins Universtiy Press, 2006.

IDEA, Inter-Parliamentary Union, and Stockholm University. "QuotaProject: Global Database of Quotas for Women: Senegal." Accessed December 5, 2017. http://www.quotaproject.org/country/?ul=undefined&country=205.

Inter-Parliamentary Union. "Women in National Parliaments, World Classification," 2017. http://archive.ipu.org/wmn-e/classif.htm.

Kenny, Meryl. *Gender and Political Recruitment: Theorizing Institutional Change*. New York: Springer, 2013.

Krook, Mona Lena, and Fiona Mackay. "Introduction: Gender, Politics and Institutions." In *Gender, Politics and Institutions: Towards a Feminist Institutionalism*, edited by Mona Lena Krook and Fiona Mackay, 1–19. London: Palgrave MacMillan, 2011.

Lovenduski, Joni. "Gendering Research in Political Science," *Annual Review of Political Science* 1, no. 1 (1998): 333–56. https://doi.org/10.1146/annurev.polisci.1.1.333.

Mackay, Fiona. "Thick Conceptions of Substantive Representation: Women, Gender and Political Institutions." *Representation* 44, no. 2 (2008): 125–39. https://doi.org/10.1080/00344890802079607.

———. "Nested Newness, Institutional Innovation, and the Gendered Limits of Change." *Politics and Gender* 10, no. 4 (December 2014): 549–71. https://doi.org/10.1017/S1743923X14000415.

Mackay, Fiona, Kenny, Meryl and, Chappell, Louise. "New Institutionalism through a Gender Lens: Towards a Feminist Institutionalism?" *International Political Science Review* 31, no. 5 (2010): 573–88. https://doi.org/10.1177/0192512110388788.

République du Sénégal. Loi instituant la parité absolue Homme-Femme (2010).

Sarr, Fatou. *Les premières heritières de la loi sur la parité*. Dakar: Fondation Friedrich Ebert, 2013.

Shyrock, Ricci. "Senegalese Girls Forced to Drop out of School and Work as Domestic Help." UNICEF Senegal, 2010. https://www.unicef.org/protection/senegal_56856.html.

Tøraasen, Marianne. "Gender Parity and the Symbolic Representation of Women in Senegal" Master's thesis, University of Bergen, 2016).

Tripp, Aili Mari. "Legislative Quotas for Women: Implications for Governance in Africa." In *African Parliaments: Between Governance and Government*, edited by M. A. Mohamed Salih, 48–60. New York: Palgrave MacMillan, 2005. https://doi.org/10.1057/9781403979308

Tripp, Aili Mari, Isabel Casimiro, Joy Kwesiga, and Alice Mungwa. *African Women's Movements: Changing Political Landscapes*. Cambridge: Cambridge University Press, 2008.

———. *African Women's Movements: Transforming Political Landscapes*. Cambridge: Cambridge University Press, 2009.
United Nations Development Programme. "Human Development Reports - Senegal Country Profile," 2016. http://hdr.undp.org/en/countries/profiles/SEN.

NOTES

1. See, for example, Christie Marie Arendt, "From Critical Mass to Critical Leaders: Unpacking the Political Conditions behind Gender Quotas in Africa," *Politics & Gender* 14, no. 3 (2018): 295–322, https://doi.org/10.1017/S1743923X17000502; Aili Mari Tripp, Isabel Casimiro, Joy Kwesiga, and Alice Mungwa, *African Women's Movements: Transforming Political Landscapes* (Cambridge, Cambridge University Press, 2009); IDEA, Inter-Parliamentary Union, and Stockholm University, "QuotaProject: Global Database of Quotas for Women: Senegal," December 5, 2017, http://www.quotaproject.org/country/?ul=undefined&country=205.

2. Inter-Parliamentary Union, "Women in National Parliaments, World Classification," 2017, http://archive.ipu.org/wmn-e/classif.htm.

3. IDEA, Inter-Parliamentary Union, and Stockholm University, "QuotaProject: Global Database of Quotas for Women: Senegal."

4. Inter-Parliamentary Union, "Women in National Parliaments, World Classification."

5. Quotas stem from transnational women's movements. In many African countries, quota systems have been adopted up to 35 percent with the hope that this level of participation by women will inspire greater advocacy to achieve parity. There have been a multitude of "50-50 campaigns" to create parity in Africa (see the 2008 SADC Protocol on Gender and Development) and elsewhere (such as the European Women's Lobby 50/50 Campaign for democracy). For more information on women's quotas, see Aili Mari Tripp et al., *African Women's Movements: Changing Political Landscapes*.

6. Based on information found in individual biographies of the first mandate of female Parliamentarians, as presented in Fatou Sarr, *Les premières heritières de la loi sur la parité* (Dakar: Fondation Friedrich Ebert, 2013), we identified women who had worked for Senegalese women's organizations.

7. "Glaser, Barney, Anselm Strauss, and Elizabeth Strutzel, "The Discovery of Grounded Theory: Strategies for Qualitative Research," *Nursing Research* 17, no. 4 (1968)" 364; Juliet M. Corbin and Anselm Strauss, "Grounded Theory Research: Procedures, Canons, and Evaluative Criteria," *Qualitative Sociology* 13, no. 1 (1990): 3–21; Kathy Charmaz, *Constructing Grounded Theory: A Practical Guide through Qualitative Research* (London: Sage Publications, 2006).

8. Unless otherwise noted, all translations were done by the authors.

9. Lovenduski (1998) traces the history of feminist political science to the 1970s in describing the shift of the usage of the term "sex" into "gender." She shows that the discussion of gendered institutions began in the late 1980s to mid-1990s. Mackay, Kenny and Chappell (2010) identify a seminal article by March and Olson (1984) as the introduction of new institutionalism. *See* Joni Lovenduski, "Gendering Research in Political Science," *Annual Review of Political Science* 1, no. 1 (1998): 333–56, https://doi.org/10.1146/annurev.polisci.1.1.333.

10. In this study, we have applied a binary construct of gender primarily because those are the terms in which the parity law was passed and the terms in which interviewees discussed the gender dynamics within parliament and their society.

11. Joni Lovenduski, "Gendering Research in Political Science."

12. Mona Lena Krook and Fiona Mackay, "Introduction: Gender, Politics and Institutions," in *Gender, Politics and Institutions: Towards a Feminist Institutionalism*, ed. Mona Lena Krook and Fiona Mackay (London: Palgrave MacMillan, 2011), 1–19.

13. Georgia Duerst-Lahti and Rita Mae Kelly, eds., *Gender, Power, Leadership and Governance* (Ann Arbor: University of Michigan Press, 1995).

14. Lovenduski, "Gendering Research in Political Science;" Fiona MacKay, "Nested Newness, Institutional Innovation, and the Gendered Limits of Change," *Politics and Gender* 10, no. 4 (2014), 549–71, https://doi.org/10.1017/S1743923X14000415; in Krook and Mackay, "Introduction: Gender, Politics and Institutions," 3.

15. Duerst-Lahti and Kelly, *Gender, Power, Leadership and Governance*; Lovenduski, "Gendering Research in Political Science."

16. Krook and Mackay, "Introduction: Gender, Politics and Institutions," 4.

17. Lovenduski, "Gendering Research in Political Science."

18. Fiona Mackay, Meryl Kenny, and Louise Chappell, "New Institutionalism through a Gender Lens: Towards a Feminist Institutionalism?," *International Political Science Review* 31, no. 5 (2010): 573–88, https://doi.org/10.1177/0192512110388788.

19. Krook and Mackay, "Introduction: Gender, Politics and Institutions"; Mackay, Kenny and Chappell, "New Institutionalism through a Gender Lens: Towards a Feminist Institutionalism?"; Louise Chappell and Georgina Waylen, "Gender and the Hidden Life of Institutions," *Public Administration* 91, no. 3 (2013): 599–615, https://doi.org/10.1111/j.1467-9299.2012.02104.x.

20. Mackay, Kenny, and Chappell, "New Institutionalism through a Gender Lens: Towards a Feminist Institutionalism?"

21. Mackay, Kenny, and Chappell, "New Institutionalism through a Gender Lens: Towards a Feminist Institutionalism?", 583.

22. Linda Beck, "Democratization and the Hidden Public : The Impact of Patronage Networks on Senegalese Women," *Comparative Politics* 35, no. 2 (2003): 147–69.

23. IDEA, Inter-Parliamentary Union, and Stockholm University, "Quota-Project: Global Database of Quotas for Women: Senegal."

24. IDEA, Inter-Parliamentary Union, and Stockholm University.

25. Organizations such as the Association of African Women for Research and Development (AAWORD or in French AFARD) and Akina Mama wa Afrika (London Women's Center) were part of a broad network of civil society groups that participated in an NGO forum organized by the African Women's Communication and Development Network (FEMNET) and the UNECA prior to the Fourth UN World Conference on Women and the Fifth Regional Conference on Women in Dakar. Tripp et al., "African Women's Movements" highlights the importance of African-based women's NGOs in creating the foundation for many of the platforms leading up to the women's conferences and also emphasizes the participation of key representatives from the civil society arena.

26. At the time, Dakar hosted the Fifth Regional Conference on Women (from November 16-23, 1994), where it created an African Platform for Action, (APFA) in preparation for the Fourth UN World Conference on Women in Beijing. The APFA highlighted many areas where women's concerns regarding development were not taken into consideration at the national, regional and subregional levels, including the "Political Empowerment of Women" and proposed many actions that could be taken at all levels to increase women's political participation. See Fifth Regional Conference on Women, "African Platform for Action" (1994).

27. Marianne Tøraasen, "Gender Parity and the Symbolic Representation of Women in Senegal" (Master's thesis, University of Bergen, 2016).

28. The original French words of this translation are: "*Il aété conçu comme un espace d'engagement, un creuset où sont posées et débattues les questions relatives à l'évolution de la position des femmes dans les sphéres de décisions.* See COSEF, *Combats pour la parité: Actes du Séminaire d'élaboration d'un modèle de loi sur la parité*" (Dakar: COSEF, 2011), 3.

29. COSEF and AECID, "Combats pour la parité, 'la loi sur la parité absolue au Sénégal'" (Dakar, 2011).

30. COSEF and AECID.

31. COSEF and AECID; République du Sénégal, "Loi instituant la parité absolue Homme-Femme" (2010).

32. République du Sénégal; IDEA, Inter-Parliamentary Union, and Stockholm University, "QuotaProject: Global Database of Quotas for Women: Senegal."

33. Gretchen Bauer, "'A Lot of Head Wraps': African Contributions to the Third Wave of Electoral Gender Quotas," *Politics, Groups, and Identities* 4, no. 2 (2016): 196–213, https://doi.org/10.1080/21565503.2015.1112293; Inter-Parliamentary Union, "Women in National Parliaments, World Classification."

34. Inter-Parliamentary Union; Assemblée Nationale, "Douzième Legislature (2012–2017): Liste de Deputés" (Dakar, 2012).

35. Assemblée Nationale, "Treizième Legislature (2017-2022): Liste de Deputés" (Dakar, 2017).

36. Inter-Parliamentary Union, "Women in National Parliaments, World Classification."

37. Sarr, *Les premières heritières de la loi sur la parité*.

38. While Senegal is a predominantly Muslim country, we chose not to analyze the research from a religious perspective. Some may argue that precepts in Islam reinforce women in a dependent position in relation to men and discourage leadership in public spaces, but clearly that has not been an impediment for these parliamentarians.

39. Sarr, *Les premières heritières de la loi sur la parité*.

40. Sarr, *Les premières heritières de la loi sur la parité*.

41. For the purposes of clarity, we have chosen fictitious names for those persons quoted in the chapter, who choose to remain anonymous.

42. Duerst-Lahti and Kelly, *Gender, Power, Leadership and Governance,* in Mackay, Kenny, and Chappell, "New Institutionalism through a Gender Lens: Towards a Feminist Institutionalism?," 582.

43. Lovenduski, "Gendering Research in Political Science," 339.

44. Tøraasen, "Gender Parity and the Symbolic Representation of Women in Senegal."

45. United Nations Development Programme, "Human Development Reports - Senegal Country Profile," 2016, http://hdr.undp.org/en/countries/profiles/SEN

46. Ricci Shyrock, "Senegalese Girls Forced to Drop out of School and Work as Domestic Help," UNICEF Senegal, 2010, https://www.unicef.org/protection/senegal_56856.html.

47. Gretchen Helmke and Steven Levitsky, *Informal Institutions and Democracy: Lessons from Latin America* (Johns Hopkins University Press, 2006) in Chappell and Waylen, "Gender and the Hidden Life of Institutions," 605.

48. Sarah Childs, "Negotiating Gendered Institutions: Women's Parliamentary Friendships," *Politics & Gender* 9, no. 2 (2013), 129, https://doi.org/10.1017/S1743923X13000019.

49. Childs, "Negotiating Gendered Institutions," 146.

50. Duerst-Lahti and Kelly, *Gender, Power, Leadership and Governance*; Meryl Kenny, *Gender and Political Recruitment: Theorizing Institutional Change* (Springer, 2013), 20.

51. Mr. Coumba Diouf, Archivist, *Assemblée Nationale*, Personal Communication, September 20, 2017.

52. Fiona Mackay, "Thick Conceptions of Substantive Representation: Women, Gender and Political Institutions," *Representation* 44, no. 2 (2008): 125–39, in Kenny, *Gender and Political Recruitment: Theorizing Institutional Change,* 48.

53. Lovenduski, "Gendering Research in Political Science."

54. Chappell and Waylen, "Gender and the Hidden Life of Institutions."

55. Mackay, "Thick Conceptions of Substantive Representation: Women, Gender and Political Institutions;" Aili Mari Tripp, "Legislative Quotas for Women: Implications for Governance in Africa," in *African Parliaments: Between Governance and Government*, ed. M. A. Mohamed Salih (Palgrave MacMillan, 2005), 48–60, https://doi.org/10.1057/9781403979308; Senem Ertan, "Gender Quotas and Women's Representation in Muslim Countries," *2nd European Conference on Politics and Gender*, January (2011): 1–23.

9

RADICAL INCLUSION AND THE LIFE OF A PUBLIC INTELLECTUAL

A Conversation with Cheikh Ibrahima Niang

Ellen Foley and Cheikh Ibrahima Niang

Cheikh Ibrahima Niang is a unique figure among Senegalese social scientists whose work falls within the broad field of gender and sexuality studies. Currently a professor at Institut des Sciences de l'Environnement at Université Cheikh Anta Diop, Niang has conducted research in socio-cultural anthropology in Senegal for over forty years. Initially trained in applied environmental science, Niang quickly came to appreciate that environmental vulnerability, particularly food insecurity, intersected with gender hierarchies, and other social inequalities. This finding launched Niang's subsequent work on marginal populations and gendered vulnerability to HIV/AIDS. Though he is best known for his research on sexual minorities, particularly sex workers and LGBTQ communities in Senegal, all of Niang's research addresses the core themes of social hierarchies, gender dynamics, the social construction of gender and sexual orientation, and the social dangers of stigma and exclusion.

The corpus of Niang's work, much of which remains unpublished, documents the rich local cultures of gender, sex, sexuality, marriage, motherhood, in/fertility, masculinities, and femininities in Senegalese societies. Niang's detailed ethnographies of sexual culture offer students of Senegal access to foundational (and often forgotten) cultural frameworks that shape social relations. In addition to this primary research, Niang has played a significant role in reimagining how public health interventions, from HIV prevention and treatment to the Ebola response, might operate within and build upon local cultural frameworks. Long before decolonial approaches of analysis and knowledge production became mainstream in the Western academy, Niang positioned himself as a co-producer of knowledge with the various communities among whom he conducted research. In his own words, "the first test of validity always comes from the research participants."

Throughout the 2000s Niang worked closely with a wide range of LGBTQ networks in Senegal to combat stigma and social exclusion, to end health disparities, and to improve Senegal's AIDS response. In the midst of the 2008 and 2009 sex panic over homosexuality in Senegal, Niang, his students, and his research participants in the gay community were at the center of a violent and explosive backlash. In the midst of death threats, religious condemnation (including a fatwa against him), and being ostracized by many of his university colleagues, Niang became a lone public voice defending the civil rights of LGBTQ people in the Senegalese media. His courage, intellectual integrity, and deep-seated commitment to challenging injustice and social exclusion are nothing short of remarkable. With limited resources and minimal institutional support, Niang has continued his work in spite of daunting challenges to his academic freedom and personal safety.

In this interview, Ellen Foley, a long-time colleague and collaborator of Cheikh Niang, invites him to reflect on his academic career and the myriad influences on his intellectual development. His biography reveals a childhood marked by gender nonconforming women, an adolescence fueled by global liberation movements and anti-colonial activism in Senegal, and a university career focused on privileging local knowledge and cultural traditions. A bibliography of Niang's publications appears at the end of the interview.

Ellen Foley: Let's start from the very beginning in order to have some background on your life. When and where were you born?

Cheikh Niang: I was born in Kolda, and my mother and I are very close, in fact, she is my role model, and she helped me a lot in my research. I can argue that she is my first thesis advisor, because in formulating questions, determining where to find key sources of information, how to address people, how to avoid upsetting questions, my mother played a crucial role in my research. Even when I was writing up, she validated, confirmed, researched, and so on.

My mother taught me interculturalism, because her own mother is Joola and her father Cape Verdean, she was born in Ziguinchor, while her mother, my grandmother (who also had a huge impact on me) was from Bignona. On her father's side they are Carvalho. So Carvalho is related to Portugal and to Judaism. My mother tended to bring up Judaism, and she identified somewhere somehow with a Jewish past. She ended up becoming Muslim, and her mother was of traditional religion and occupied a priestly status in society. I think it is this mixture that played a major role in preventing me from being closed-minded.

I was born in Kolda in 1953, and Kolda is a combination of Manding, Peul, Joola, Wolof, Balanta, and Mancagne populations. It is this melting pot where you speak Manding and Peul, you go home and speak Wolof, go back to school and speak French; that helped me out. Behind all this, there is a spiritual heritage. My grandmother, Liis Badji Bagnotoon, was always barefoot; she never wore shoes. She could be very nicely dressed with a very decorated boubou and jewelry and everything, but no shoes. It was much later that I realized that for her the earth was sacred, [she was barefoot to be] in contact with the power of the Earth, to convey it to the community, as well as to convey the sacrifice to the community. It took me a long time to understand that.

Badji was her last name. She was Joola. She settled in Kolda in a region with very few Joola. However, her ancestors were Baynunk. The very first people who populated the region. The Baynunk know the secret of the forest and cure the sick with plants and prayers. I guess, my early interest in ecology comes from my grandmother.[1, 2] It was as though she was exiled. In Joola society, men do the plowing as the masculine work in farms, not women. Women do the planting and the harvest. So when she labored by herself using the Kajandu,[3] a very heavy instrument, difficult to manipulate, which stands as a masculine symbol, a manly job, she was very strong, and doing a manly job.

Ellen Foley: So she was man and woman at the same time?

Cheikh Niang: She was, and you see how early I was confronted with this question. What is masculine, what is feminine, what is man, what is woman, those are all relative and socially constructed ideas. She incarnated both masculinity, femininity, and priesthood. So I lived like that until I came here [Dakar].

During my childhood, my mother, Elie Carvalho, created what she called a university, where all the children in the community came home and at night, they studied, and she made sure that they memorized their class notes. That's all she could make sure of, so if you recited with hesitation, she would send you back to restart and the oldest took charge of the youngest in terms of education. Eventually many people succeeded in their studies, went to university, and so on. She started making an impact as if she were taking over her mother's role, because when her mother harvested crops, she would stock a portion in our house, and I saw her helping people around her.

My mother took over that practice, especially by listening, to people who were stigmatized as being crazy, rebellious, abused women. . . . She would summon women that claimed to be abused and their husbands, and she would listen to them. When I went there on holidays, she recurrently went in and out with women that came to her, one group after the other, dancing and singing, jumping from one language to the other, and each time, there was a stress release, joyfulness was restored, and there was empowerment for women to face situations of violence and crisis. So I was greatly influenced by her.

Ellen Foley: When did you come to Dakar?

Cheikh Niang: Approximately in 1966. My father was in Kolda, and at some point, he went to do an internship in France, because he was a veterinary nurse, and upon his return, we left Kolda to come to Dakar, and he died some time after that in Dakar. At that point, I stayed in Dakar with my uncles, because there was no high school in Kolda at the time. It was the first separation from my family.

While I was in Dakar, I immediately engaged with Leftist movements, and we followed a lot of liberation movements from abroad.[4] We were very passionate about the idea of freedom. In school, we dealt with colonial situations. Independence was very colonial, with French ideology, so the school climate was always very tense. We went through dramatic situations of injustice at school. For example, I was very talented in mathematics. We had a teacher from France who seated students in alphabetical order and then had the list, so that if you made noise in class, she sanctioned you by identifying where you were located in the classroom. It was already a very terrifying climate. I was not doing poorly because I sat in the front in order to stay focused, but with her class, she sent me to the back of the classroom. From the back I could not see much, which I told her, but she asked me to tell my parents to buy me a pair of glasses. Meanwhile, it was the year my father had died and we had no money at home. She was very rigid and as a result, I came in last in my class because I missed all the instruction.

We had another teacher who said, "You Negroes have never invented anything. You need to get civilized." The atmosphere of racial and colonial superiority was omnipresent. We dreamt of undoing the world and putting it back together, so I became very implicated in movements for such causes. We also went through periods of intense dictatorship, and we didn't feel free at all. I started being involved in student movements, and when a teacher made a racist statement, I organized a movement. A professor removed me from his class and told me he would make sure I was blacklisted from all schools within the week. Thankfully, I came across a principal who took my side, which prevented me from being expelled. When the teacher wrote his report, the principal just archived it and told me he would deal with him. The teacher panicked and then took me back into his class, without which I would have halted my studies, because I would not have been authorized to take any exams. This gave me great conviction about battling against injustice, domination, humiliation, and so on. In my final year in school, there was a Senegalese philosopher who died in jail, which created a lot of turmoil, and the following year I organized a movement to denounce the absence of democratic freedom. For us, democratic freedom was essential and worth gold. It was not poverty that motivated us, but the fact that we were ostracized by the secret police, we could not speak, and so on, which made us very uncomfortable. I was arrested and went to jail for a year, where I took my high school graduation exam (Baccalaureate).

Ellen Foley: What year was that?

Cheikh Niang: This was in 1974. It is important to have context. The context in this case was that of a dictatorship. It wasn't as strong as in many other African countries, but it was the regime nonetheless. We were in a country with one political party: the ruling party. All the members of the Parliament served the ruling party, there was only one radio station, and in school we suffered most. We had French professors who maintained the colonial ideology, who were not in touch with the new realities. It was also a period of liberation movements. There were movements in Angola, Guinea Bissau, Mozambique; South Africa with Mandela; and in the United States, civil rights movements for blacks; so it was in this context. At the same time, my mother was thinking about it, she was very fond of Martin Luther King and John Kennedy. Although we only had radio as media, people were connected and knew what was happening. Kennedy for us was the non-colonial America that supported human rights, generosity, and most of all, who was not a friend to colonial powers. That is how we saw it, and when he died people cried like it was their relative. It was very moving, and I remember my mom crying like she knew him well.

So this was in the '60s and '70s. You see the contradiction between what was going on in the world and the dictatorship that we were facing, which gave people the feeling of being imprisoned. There was a strong quest for freedom. There were a lot of movements that I couldn't take part in because I was too young, but I remember my father going to join labor unions with my older brother, because everyone was fed up. I once saw the French army go with their tanks to occupy downtown Dakar in order to protect the regime. That's an image I can't forget.

In the '70s, I heard of a philosopher who was trying to free his brother sentenced for life in prison for political reasons and was working on a plan to kidnap the French ambassador in Mali, and he was caught, sentenced, and ended up dying in jail. The year after that, I began to organize all the high schoolers in the country to commemorate his death so that he would not be forgotten. Meanwhile, I had written a leaflet talking about the colonial regime, the right to democracy, racism, inequalities, a little flyer with all that. The regime's police started to think it could not be a child that had written it, and if it was an adult then it has to be someone from the Communist opposition. Therefore, when they arrested me, they thought the Communist movement was supporting me; meanwhile I had no idea who they were.

I organized a lot of protests, so they arrested some of my friends and they started to hunt me down. I lived with a friend at the time because my uncles had completely shunned me. The police approached a friend of my mother, so I had to surrender and take responsibility for the accusations. That's how I found myself as the "wanted man" they were looking for. There were nine of us, one woman, who unfortunately is no longer with us. So that's the context and story of the arrest.

When I was in jail, they kept telling me to ask for a pardon from the president of the Republic because I was still young. He would give me a scholarship and I would go abroad to finish my studies in France. I said no, because I would ask for forgiveness if I was in the wrong, but they were the ones in the wrong, so I would not ask them for forgiveness. As for their scholarship, they could keep it, because I would stay here and see what I could do. In jail, it is very physically violent, practically close to torture, because you are beaten consistently and broken down. At that age you're even more vulnerable.

Ellen Foley: How did your uncles and your mother react to this?

Cheikh Niang: After my father's death, there was a strong retreat from solidarity in my family, especially on my father's side, where few people even tried to understand me. They were convinced I deserved what I was getting because it was too risky to challenge the state, and I think they were afraid for themselves too.

My mother came to see me in jail, and she told me that politicians had handed her a letter for me and that all I needed to do was to sign it in order to be free, that they would give me a scholarship and I would go and study in France. She asked me what I thought of the proposal, and I said I was not interested. She asked me the same question three times, and I said no each time. After that, she said, "I wanted you to confirm this three times. Don't sign it, and wherever you die, I will die there with you." It was very powerful and I will never forget it.

Then she said, "Take responsibility for your decision, and I will support you." This is how she started to embrace many ideas, that people could fight for their convictions, and she developed some for herself and saw how a woman could stand tall where many men fell. All these concepts helped me very early on to develop my own ideas about gender. So this was in the '70s, and after I came out of jail, I met Cheikh Anta Diop who also had a profound influence on me and co-directed my first doctoral thesis. What I recall of him is that he read a lot; he was a great African scholar. My friends and I read Marx, Marcus, Fanon, Che [Guevara], Reich, Nietzsche, Simone de Beauvoir, anarchists, we were thirsty for everything that was close to atypical literature, literature for contestation, but Cheikh Antra Diop constantly reminded us we still did not know the realities.

Ellen Foley: Realities such as?

Cheikh Niang: Realities on the ground, local realities in the villages.

Ellen Foley: So it was the "big Literature," literature with capital "L."

Cheikh Niang: Yes, big Literature. So I met with Cheikh Anta Diop. My friends and I we were in a hurry to get to the revolution. When I passed my Baccalaureate exam in jail, which I passed with honors, the prosecutor at the time who was a part of a special court which they called "The State Security Court" accused us of all you can think of. They said we were being manipulated by the Cubans, by the Chinese, meanwhile I could not even locate Cuba on a map. We couldn't care less about any of that, we were just pissed-off youths. It was blown out of proportion just to give us ridiculous sentences. When he saw that I passed my exam, he said that it was evidence I was the leader, because I was more intelligent than the others. Instead of congratulating a child's endurance in the midst of struggle, he did quite the contrary.

We insisted on this revolution, and Cheikh Anta Diop insisted on leading peaceful revolutions because Gandhi was a role model for him, so this was important to us. "You are right, but you cannot use violence. It is even easier to use weapons than a peaceful protest, because fighting with arms is the easy way out." That was his philosophy, listening to the other, empathy. He would often say, "Try to find out if your enemy is not right. Is there an area where they can be right?" He pushed us to put things in perspective, and most of all, to hear local languages. He said that we couldn't work for the people without being able to express ourselves in the languages that they speak, or living in the conditions that they live in. Then he sent us off and said, "What if you tried to understand your people a little?" and we were excited at the idea of liberating our villages.

That is how I organized a student movement of about 200 to 300 students for the first time to go and sleep in the villages. So we slept on mats, we ate what they ate, in the morning we went to the farms, and so on, and it was a tremendous experience. In the beginning, I enrolled in philosophy for a master's degree, but one step closer to it and I thought it seemed too speculative and theoretical and that it wouldn't be relevant to us, which led me to do anthropology and sociology, so social science. As much as philosophy made me critical of political discourse, anthropology made me adamant about helping people and communities. That's how I enrolled and got a degree in it. In the third year of my doctoral studies I became more familiar with the cultural and social aspects, as well as gender relations and so on. And I applied it to environmental factors, because it was a period of intense drought and the Institute of Environmental Science was working on environmental issues, desertification and climate change in the north of Senegal, although these were not the terms used at the time.

Ellen Foley: Did the peasant farmers figure out early on that the climate was changing?

Cheikh Niang: Yes they did and interestingly, Cheikh Anta Diop in the '60s when he returned here, he held a first press conference at the chamber of commerce at the time, to talk about deforestation, and in the 1980s, he was the first to talk to us about climate change, saying to change our fossil fuel consumption. He had ideas very ahead of his time. He was among the people who influenced me greatly to get interested in issues pertaining to the environment.

But what I noticed the most was that sexuality itself was changing. Women carried the burden of what we would eat at the campsites. So the daily bread was women's responsibility in our camp. They took milk that they curdled and, in the morning, they went to exchange it for rice or millet to feed everyone. The nutritional survival of the group was managed by the women.

For this reason, they were very vulnerable sexually, because they were under the pressure of economic inequalities and men wanting to have sexual relations with them. They were exposed to all sorts of sexual assault, and as a result, sexual transactions took place to address nutritional needs for survival. That is what led me to AIDS.

At the time we started to talk about risky sexual behaviors, AIDS prevention, and people immediately started to see that there is community, there are structures and there are gender relations and other elements within. At the time, we were very frustrated by the KAP (knowledge, attitudes, and practices) surveys, and we were challenged by questions that we couldn't answer using the classic measures. It was not possible.

At that point, also, we were addressing questions surrounding stigmatization head on, beginning with prostitutes, sex workers, and after the sex workers, we discovered the link with homosexuals. Let's just say they are old questions, always in the background, but one needs to have the ability to sense it. What helped us was our capacity to put ourselves in people's shoes and feel their sufferings and translate that into research questions and build theories and methodologies, because sometimes we felt like what we were feeling wasn't what we were being told officially. You should feel it in the heart, before all else, because if the heart is not able to feel, you will not succeed in finding answers, so empathy was a key element in the fight against AIDS.

Ellen Foley: So that is how environmental challenges ended up raising important questions for you about the structures in society, gender, sexuality, and so on. And after completing your PhD research on environmental issues, you started to teach in ISE and you continued with research?

Cheikh Niang: Right. After the PhD I was part of the ISE staff, but at the time, the challenge and the catastrophe was AIDS and I needed tools and knowledge to address what people called "the challenges of the current times." I went to the Sociology Department and I started to work on a PhD in sociology on the topic of sexuality. I was in between the two. On the one hand, I continued teaching on environmental issues, and on the other hand, I was working on issues related to sexuality and AIDS. That was a significant workload, but it was necessary and fortunately, I realize today that those topics are intertwined once more. Environmental issues have become central and issues of gender, violence, exclusion, stigma, and sexual minorities have also become very central. Finally, everything is working as if the harmony that one must create with the environment and with nature must also be created with humans. Domination, exclusion, and violence against humans, whatever they might be, is the same as that imposed upon nature. I find this connection between environmental issues and social questions of gender and inequality.

Ellen Foley: What was your research project in sociology? I remember the first research of yours that I came across was on the Laobé and the transmission of sexual knowledge in Kolda. Was that it?

Cheikh Niang: Yes! My problem was that at the time, people using KAP investigations concluded that people did not talk about sexuality. Meanwhile, I knew that they talked about sex in their own way. So how could we close the communication gap to prevent HIV using existing cultural ideas? To reflect on old ideas and give them contemporary meaning? That was it. Even problems of modernity or post-modernity and all that can be explained using ideas that are ancient. People will understand. You can take an old idea and give it a new content. It was in that sense that I asked myself how to revisit the Laobé and Dimba discourses. The Dimba take care of fertility and maternity, and the Laobé sexuality. I wanted to use their practices to demonstrate that in fact protecting oneself against AIDS is not a sad idea and it can be fun.

Ellen Foley: So this is how you developed a research project?

Cheikh Niang: Yes, in order to see what we could learn from traditional groups and organizations that had developed knowledge on sexuality, on the body and on maternity, and it was at that time that I started to work. I got networked with Laobé women. The Laobé women used local proverbs, songs, dances, and small gathering to converse about their sexual life, to eroticize male and female condom, to share preventive messages against HIV, to develop self-esteem and the power to have their dignity and their rights recognized in contexts of patriarchal societies.

Ellen Foley: Did you mother help you get started in Kolda? What exactly did you do?

Cheikh Niang: In the beginning, I explained it to my mother, and she agreed to help me. She had a very good Laobé friend who went from house to house selling beads, and she managed the traditional activities of Laobé women in Kolda. My mother introduced us, and we discussed methodology, research questions, and so on, and I began my first focus groups with the Laobé women of Kolda.

After I developed a project and received some funding from ICRW (International Center for Research on Women), and I was able to recruit some student assistants. So that is how it began. I hung out in bars and nightclubs in Kolda following the Laobé group of women that was very mobile and I was in their milieu. People started telling my mother that her son ran with a bad crowd, and you know right away you begin to live the stigma, exclusion, because people don't only exclude the group, but the friends of the group. All those who get close to the group are seen negatively. My mother confronted the community saying that I was doing AIDS research; she defended me.

From time to time, it was difficult to organize focus groups, because a meeting of Laobé prostitutes in your house does not fit with social norms. My mother took on the challenge and organized the first meetings in her house, making them comfortable and so on. Bit by bit, the Laobé started to share the secrets and knowledge that they had. They put me in contact with Laobé from Kaolack, and I started to know the networks, all the way to Dakar. We were able to obtain a lot of poems, *taasu*,[5] hundreds of *taasu*, and we had to decipher them together with the group, because they were coded messages, so to be sure that you had the code and the right interpretation, we created validation groups. Finally, Laobé groups were like scientific institutions.

Ellen Foley: Yes, like community laboratories.

Cheikh Niang: The first validation [of the research] is not the academic validation, it was not the university. It was validation by the community that held this traditional know-how. From that moment, I started to see how they lived their sexuality. They were not passive. There was an aspect of an active person who takes responsibility for her sexuality and her desires, which was not the perspective of the mainstream literature. So I said to myself, in order to challenge inequalities, violence, and exclusion, what are the existing local resources, before looking for answers outside? How are those answers sufficient or insufficient? How can they be improved? We had to start from there. That is, if women are victims of domination, which women resist? There must be at least one woman who resists, so how do you side with this woman so that other women will be able to resist, without making them feel like Western ideologies are being imposed on them? Because they rejected that, they insisted on not wanting to be European. We explained that they could be African and feminist, or African and still rebel against such inequalities without fear, because their culture allows it. As much as there are sexist concepts in the culture, there are concepts that question those norms, so take those. Then, we did a large project on how women value their bodies for themselves, the role of orgasm, how they achieve orgasm, how they send signals to say that they are not satisfied with their partners and so on. The idea was self-esteem, to make them feel that they are stronger than they think and they can face the situation. The Laobé were very helpful in this. And the Dimba.

Ellen Foley: Who exactly are Dimba?

Cheikh Niang: They are groups of women whom I also met through my mother. They are initiation groups for ceremonies and rituals that address a specific group of women, the ones that have never had children, those whose children die at young ages or those that have adopted children that have lost their mothers and those that have given birth to twins. So you see all these four groups have struggles with motherhood, childbearing. . . .[6]

Ellen Foley: Yes, and stigma as well, vulnerability.

Cheikh Niang: So they form solidarity groups and perform fertility rituals, and when there are long periods of drought, they dance for the rain, they dress up and so on. In my opinion, they are interlocutors, but in the official discourse they are primitive, savage, and so on, which made it impossible for me to carry out the official AIDS response with these women. But I was able to continue working with them and obtain great amounts of ethnographic data on coaching during pregnancy, nutrition, their fight against inequality and gender violence.

Ellen Foley: We haven't touched on the topic of LGBT communities or MSM yet. Your research has always explored questions of gender, power, and violence. By the late 1980s the main topic of discussion was HIV/AIDS. So you started with women, who were actually very vulnerable, but how did this research lead you to working with other sexual minorities?

Cheikh Niang: Actually, I had just completed a research project with UNAIDS on migration and HIV and in that project I did a lot of work with sex workers. When we were finished, they said, "You shouldn't stop with us, there are also homosexuals." At the time, the official literature asserted that there were no gay men in Africa. But due to their insistence, I told them we could try. So I began. They introduced me.

Ellen Foley: Here in Dakar?

Cheikh Niang: Yes, here in Dakar, The sex workers would show up at my office 6 or 7 p.m. We would eat dinner, and then I would accompany them. We went to bars, nightclubs, we went around, and they introduced me to gay men.

Ellen Foley: So it turns out that they frequented the same spots?

Cheikh Niang: They shared the same spots. And they told me that *goorjigeen* or transgender women and homosexual men were even more vulnerable than they were, and they had been completely left out.

Ellen Foley: Around what year was this?

Cheikh Niang: It was in the late 1990s. The first cases of AIDS in Senegal were registered in 1986. Meaning that from 1986 to 2003, homosexuals were not in the official discourse. Quite the contrary. People said it [homosexuality] was a thing of the Western world that did not exist in Africa. That was the discourse at the time. So by the end of the '90s, I began to look into it a little, to take notes, and try to understand, consult existing literature. I started to get interested. Then there was someone from the Population Council who was visiting to look into AIDS. He came by my office and we shared our observations. Then I told him that we were missing a very vulnerable group. He asked me which one, and I said "Homosexuals." He asked, "Homosexuals?" and I said, "Yes." He then asked, "What do you think about it?" and I replied, "It is an emergency. It is absolutely crucial that we start addressing this question." He then asked, "Do you have anything on it yet? A protocol or anything of the like?" and I said, "Yes, I have something prepared." He replied, "Send it to me."

I sent it to him, and the Population Council office in Dakar was also involved. I had Placide Tapsoba, a doctor who was also a member of the Council, shared a lot with me. He was working on it. He said to me, "Now, the only problem is to get the project validated by the National AIDS Council (NAC) and your official response by authorities, because for them, it is not reasonable. So, Placide gets the idea of hosting a meeting of researchers in social science on the topic of HIV, sexuality, and homosexuality, or something like that. And just this way, all the researchers who were summoned reckoned that it was a pertinent topic. So, the Ministry and the NAC yielded to the idea as well. In the beginning, the NAC did not want to be associated with the LGBT communities.

Ellen Foley: The NAC?

Cheikh Niang: Yes the NAC. Whenever a meeting was organized with homosexuals, they made sure to sit as far away from them as possible. Even regarding physical contact. . . .

Ellen Foley: So there was always a huge distance?

Cheikh Niang: A huge distancing that was blatant with regards to body posture or physical posture.

So I began, and I was lucky, to have the opportunity to meet with gay leaders and leaders of LGBT communities. So, very active and very popular people, and I began with them. I had some support from the Population Council to perform an investigation through a survey. So the topic was how to recruit them, the champions. . . .

Ellen Foley: This was mostly in Dakar or . . . ?

Cheikh Niang: Mostly in Dakar and then in St Louis. From key informant interviews, we know whom to approach, how to address them, and so on. That's how we began and we had long sessions of just listening with the sole aim of winning their trust. How to win the trust of homosexual communities that are being stigmatized, assaulted, etc. That was the main challenge. It was necessary to create some time to listen. The first focus group meetings in my office lasted from 2 a.m. to 5 a.m. It was the only time and space that was convenient for them, otherwise, they wouldn't trust any other space. Seeing three to four homosexuals gathered together, neighbors would knock on the door, the police would come over.

Ellen Foley: Already? Because this is before the events in 2008 and 2009. There was already a feeling of fear and insecurity?

Cheikh Niang: Because there is a political context. In the 1960s, homosexuals were traumatized by the government. Prostitutes were chased down, jailed, and married off by compulsion. Michelle Lewis (1997) covers some of this in her book. It seemed like they tried to purify society by ridding it of anything that appeared to be immoral. It was the first backlash against homosexuals. There was violent repression. It was a time of disillusion following independence, disagreements among leaders, democratic leaders. In short, it was a transition phase where several political parties were shrinking down to one party, to a regime of one-party rule. So there was a need to create a scapegoat somewhere and I think prostitutes and homosexuals paid the price. I was told that it was during that phase that the word *ibbi* came into play, to replace *goorjigeen*, which was too dangerous. There was no form of defense within the community to protect them, because women in leadership no longer had any political weight, since there was no more competition in the electoral realm they were no longer needed. Clearly, we have a very powerful patriarchal, masculine and sexist state government that changed the status of homosexuals.

So they were traumatized by this, and it dwelled in their memory, such that in the beginning of the research when we talked about forming groups, the first thing that came to their mind was that if people saw them in groups it could be dangerous. All this had to be negotiated. We had to convince some of the leaders that they could work with us, and even then, the ones that agreed had to convince and negotiate with the others. It was pretty hectic. The first group that came to participate inspected my entire office. They suspected that I had hidden cameras and that I was going to hand them over to the authorities. I had to prove maximum transparency. I also needed to train the students who were working with me. Because while you might think that you are the observer, they are also observing you.

Ellen Foley: Was there some reticence from the students?

Cheikh Niang: Yes. They asked me why I was getting involved. There was a lot of resistance based on religion, morality, ethics, and similar arguments. The rejection was very strong from students. So for some, I didn't push it. Others came, and you could tell they were scared. For example, if a homosexual was sitting somewhere, they would sit three chairs away. But it was clear to the homosexual man that he was being rejected, he wasn't daft. It became very important to create an atmosphere of trust.

After that, the groups would spontaneously organize activities, dinners, and they'd invite us and some of the students. We came, we ate with them and joked around and left. On one occasion, they invited us for dinner, but I could not go. That evening the neighborhood caught wind that there was a group of gay men socializing together and the neighborhood rose against them and started stoning them. This was before 2008. Ndack (then, a PhD student) called me in the middle of the night because she was there. She told me they were running for their lives, it was an emergency. So I jumped into my car, and on the way there I came across police officers and I asked them for help.

Ellen Foley: Do you remember what neighborhood it was?

Cheikh Niang: It was in Yoff. I told the police I needed their help and told them there would be killings if they didn't come. They came to help scatter the crowd. There was a homosexual man who fell and broke his skull and died fifteen days later. Unfortunately, he was one of the leaders who was very faithful to the cause and who had helped me travel to Gambia in order to meet other people and prepare a document for the World Bank. It was through the homosexual network here in Senegal that we were able to produce working documents based on participatory research to benefit other countries such as Burkina Faso and Gambia, since the World Bank supported this program with a stipend.

Our research explored this fear of violence and stigma, but at the same time, we started searching for the cultural factors that protected homosexuals. We were able to find that there were instances where there was a lot of violence against them and others where there was none. So how to use one against the other? The men started to gain confidence as we helped them organize themselves. They created small organizations and associations, acquired some farmland. In other words, we helped them to act on their own behalf for disease prevention, treatment of ill members, getting in contact with partners, landlords, and so on.

Finally, an entire dynamic was created out of this so that the outcome of the research was exactly as intended. From small groups, associations were formed that become very active, with great collaboration among each other. The various leaders were always in my office, and you could tell that they could joke together, plan together, and exchange amicably, and sometimes when I went to conferences they were invited to make presentation and contribute to the debates. When they came back, they told their groups what they had experienced. It was a very interesting dynamic. The two leaders with whom I worked the most have died, a woman six months ago and the man one or two years ago. The rest are still here, and I still work with them. They gained confidence, took some initiatives . . . they worked hard!

Ellen Foley: But of course, things got more complicated.

Cheikh Niang: Progressively there was hostility, violence, and then in 2008 and 2009 there's this huge cataclysm that came as a surprise to everyone. In fact, we all knew, but we weren't completely sure and we didn't think it would have this magnitude.

We had succeeded in locating almost all the gay networks in Saint Louis, Kaolack, actually almost the entire country, and we tried to work with the health system in order to find doctors that could work with them without stigmatizing them. This is how we collaborated until 2008. But at a certain point, I was becoming known and targeted by religious students and certain religious leaders.

Ellen Foley: How did you become known? One of your major articles came out in 2003, but at that time you were not a public figure.[7]

Cheikh Niang: In the beginning, we didn't really want to put our research out in the media, in order to avoid antagonism. At the same time, we wanted to accomplish as much as possible. We progressed as such and had a lot of success with all the endeavors we had initiated. Things were going well until the activities became visible at a large scale. After that, there was a massive hunt for homosexuals, violence, death threats, exhumation, in fact, the level of violence was at a record high.

I felt responsible for all this. I thought to myself, if we hadn't worked with them [gay men and MSM] they would not have been exposed. A lot of people had worked with them, but perhaps I was one of the first people that exposed them to that extent. It actually depends on the context, because it turns out that they are visible in certain communities. So seeing what they were going through, I called the United Nations and said we can't just abandon them. We have to do something and take responsibility. They decided to take part in this and help figure out an adequate response.

I went to visit some of the men who had been jailed with Ndack, so that they wouldn't feel alone. I have been to jail, I know what it is like. Sometimes it is just to give a bag of tea or coffee which seems like gold, or a piece of bread or a croissant which is like giving someone a tray of diamonds. I said to myself that I needed to raise the stakes. We had to start fighting openly.

Ellen Foley: Since some people were already exposed, it became difficult to defend them behind the curtain.

Cheikh Niang: I called the most virulent media sources and let them interview me.[8] I told them everything. I defended human rights, civil rights, our history, our culture, and so on. I even used religious concepts to say, "Listen, this is not how things ought to be." This was a turning point. People were coming to tell me that I was being talked about in mosques, in their neighborhoods, all the way to Saint Louis. People were saying, "There are academics, university professors protecting homosexuals. It is their fault if homosexuals feel so empowered. They are themselves influenced by Western ideals." Some said, "He must be a homosexual himself, and even if he isn't, he is worse because he protects them." Those are some of the things that were being said. Lots of people were talking about killing gay men, and some said they should start with me because I protect them.

At a certain point one becomes scared of physical violence. I often work [in my campus office] in the middle of the night, until 3 a.m. or so. The work was completely disrupted. Students and assistants working with me were upset. Fortunately, they didn't give up, they were consistent, and everyone was faithful. They worked as if nothing bothered them. Sometimes mosque leaders would come as a group to curse me. You realize that there is only one small step between demonstrating outside my office building and coming upstairs to break everything. Some threatened to kill me. I told the person that if they mentioned my name in her mosque, to tell her leaders that they can't kill me, only God can. If I die today in their hands it is God who allowed it.

They realized that they had a stubborn adversary, and they were calling me of all sorts of names. I thought it was time for the university to step up, because we couldn't continue with the killings. It was only a matter of time before it could turn into a mass killing of different group. It was homosexuals first, but then it was going to be prostitutes and other groups and so on and so forth. The door was open to everything. The media played a critical role in the Rwandan genocide. The university needed to step up in the midst of this to provide a rigorous scientific point of view.

Fortunately, I got some support from the university. I went to the dean saying we need an auditorium to meet with the homosexuals. He agreed and proposed the biggest auditorium in the department. They were afraid nonetheless. We then met with the director of the doctoral department to organize a roundtable. We had to make sure that people could come and be comfortable and safe without fear of being lynched afterward. Gary Engelberg (ACI) summoned all these people who showed up, with NGOs and international organizations and I invited the groups to speak up. The media showed up as well.

Ellen Foley: What year was that?

Cheikh Niang: It was in 2009, March or April. The most interesting part was that several media sources did not cover the symposium. Which was fine, because we were afraid they would talk about it negatively. I met with journalists later who admitted that they couldn't cover it, but they knew that the researchers had completely silenced the fundamentalists. Because we called out the religious institutions. We opened up to all of them, but we made sure it was a safe space for peaceful discussion. I think it was the BBC that covered it afterward, but the general atmosphere remained tense.

A little before the symposium, Ndack suggested that I visit the number two person in the religious hierarchy of the Tijaniyya, the person closest to the Khalife. He was actually the one in charge because the Khalife was already old. I went to see him with a delegation of people who we were working with, and I went with a presentation. But when we arrived there was no electricity. I went ahead anyway, saying that we had come soliciting his advice, because there had been violence and threats of more violence. I started by saying that there are verses in the Koran or the Bible, or any other religion, if you understand those passages you will not choose violence. Whereas in the media, people were citing other verses to promote killing. And I added that I personally don't think that we should kill. All things aside, there is a public health issue at hand, and if we continue this way, AIDS will proliferate in the country, and it will not stop with just gay men. I added that since I am not knowledgeable when it comes to religious matters, I came to ask for his advice.

He said, "You are right. All the things they are saying on TV shows they understand nothing about religion. You cannot say that you are a man of God and encourage violence. It is absurd." He added, "Every verse that they have cited to curse you will become positive energy for you. Don't fear anything. What you are currently doing is a mission we should undertake. It is a holy mission. You are in the place where I should have been."

Of course, I was very happy. So I told him we would be on our way. He asked me to wait. He went to his room and picked up 500,000 FCFA (approximately $1,000 USD) and handed it to me. Before I could refuse, he said, "It's not for you. It's so you can accomplish the research and work that you have started. To keep fighting." He continued, "If you are going through so much violence that you can't continue the work, come with your staff and I will give you an office. Don't give up the good work, keep it up. It is my religious duty to support you."

Thousands of people were standing outside the place where we were meeting, and he escorted me out and held my hand all the way to the exit to show that he supported me. And I said goodbye. In our traditional understanding, once you go to the marabout for protection, anyone who shakes your hand afterward takes a bit of the power that was given to you. So I became selective with the people whose hands I shook. Some professors had refused to have anything to do with me or shake my hand after I spoke with the media, claiming that I was staining the university's honor for the sake of money. Some colleagues told me that I was making a huge mistake. I had no support until I met with the marabout. People who had turned their backs on me came back to my office to congratulate me and encourage me, which of course was irrelevant to me. But this gave me hope and the insight that that there is never a desperate situation. If you dig deep enough, you will find strength to harness. I also had other meetings with imams who confided that they had grandsons or nephews who were homosexuals. It seemed like they were rediscovering something that they had always lived with, but were afraid to associate with or talk about.

Ellen Foley: In the 1990s and 2000s you were working a lot with SAHARA.[9] Can you talk a bit about this part of your career?

Cheikh Niang: A colleague in the United States put me in contact with the South Africans that were at the head of the SAHARA project. This was in the early '90s. At the time, I had just had some issues with the French regarding the organization of a conference on HIV. I told them we needed Anglophones, and they told me that we could not afford the translation. I wanted to find the funds. It made no sense to reinforce an anglophone and francophone dichotomy. AIDS was a prominent threat to the African people.

At the time we were being clobbered by the negative portrayal of Africa in the international media, and the stigma and guilt being placed on Africa with regards to AIDS. For me, this was a time to unite Africa. There was no way individual countries could manage it on their own, because the stigma was collective. Mutual accusation among African nations was only going to weaken us and create further division. SAHARA had some financial resources to organize conferences and we took advantage of those. This allowed us to plan the 2005 conference on "bridging the gap" between intervention, research and communities. It was very successful and we were able convene about 600 participating delegates.

Ellen Foley: In Dakar ?

Cheikh Niang: Yes, it was here in Dakar. The first one was hosted in Kenya, the second was in South Africa, and the third one was in Dakar. I wanted to change the concept. I didn't want for it to be the classic conference as performed in a developed country, with presentations in French and English, with very sophisticated speeches and absent communities. We wanted to recreate the concept, such that right from the first day of the conference, we communicated in Wolof and translations were done in French and English. This made it possible for community leaders battling against AIDS on a daily basis [to participate]. We invited a woman who had done a lot of work in her community in spite of a male-dominated environment, and we invited traditional healers, because they are the hosts in traditional settings. They are the welcomers and spokespersons and they communicate in Wolof. We invited people infected with HIV, as well as sex workers and homosexuals and made them the focus. This was one of the first times that these groups of people were given symbolic power. This was very empowering for them and it gave them a sense of pride and confidence, which explains why later they became more visible (sadly to their detriment).

Ellen Foley: So for you, 2005 stands as a landmark in this trajectory.

Cheikh Niang: Yes. The community leaders took leadership of the conference, which was what we had hoped. We also wanted to share how women and the Laobé understood sexuality. They took control of the meeting and brought it to life. We brought a traditional "Bombolong" drum (in Balanta language) from Guinea Bissau, because the Bombolong sound is a message that announces death. Death from AIDS needed to be addressed at the conference, which means that when they played the drums, those who knew the language understood why we did that. We needed to touch people's hearts. It was a point at which scientific information was known, people knew the means of transmission, and they were pretty advanced on this point. But if from a social and community standpoint we do not have a significant response, it is because people have not been moved, they don't relate to our cause. SAHARA helped us do that.

Before getting to that point, we had held several workshops and the homosexuals we knew put us in contact with other homosexuals, and there were homosexuals from places like Ivory Coast, Burkina Faso, Mali, and Guinea at the workshops. We were able to place them in workshops for two to three weeks, in order to reduce their fear and restore their self-esteem. It was less about scientific knowledge and more about empowering individuals to face adversity. We put pressure on the university administration to secure meeting space. We were able to obtain meeting rooms from some departments, and dorm rooms to host homosexuals during the meetings. We were able to hold our workshops and invite officials from the National AIDS program (CNLS) to showcase what we had been working on and generate institutional support.

I was also able to visit other countries such as Ghana to prepare for the conference, to meet with people, and I did the same in Mauritania, Mali, Burkina Faso, and so on. We were able to spread the notion that stigmatized and marginalized groups should be put in leadership positions, which is the best way to fight stigmatization. This is the theory of the circle, where in a dance, the shyest person, the one that does not want to dance either because they don't know the steps or they are afraid, whatever the reason might be, that's the person we pick and put at the center. That was my initiative. I had also realized that the Dimba picked the disabled, the ones labeled as crazy or mentally ill, and put them at the center of the dance. So that was the metaphor I adopted as a radical inclusion strategy. There was also a risk associated with that, because in some sessions when we put homosexuals at the center, we invited imams, and in the beginning, they didn't want to come in when they saw homosexuals. So we had people tell them that if they are Muslim, the Koran says to love your neighbor, which convinced them to stay, but they would often get offended by the discourses with the prostitutes and leave again,and we would have to bring them back.

Ellen Foley: So it was like dance steps, right? Forward and then backward.

Cheikh Niang: In the end, when all was said and done, we would laugh and find similarities and affinities. We did the same with unions and employers. There was a lot of contestation and questioning, but that is what we were aiming for. Areas of confrontation, because it allowed for communication and, if well moderated, people leave with something.

The last thing to add here is that with this approach, the idea was mostly to undo guilt, because there was a strong sentiment of self-guilt and self-stigmatization. Doing the research allowed us to tell people that they could be Senegalese and homosexual, which was fine. They could be African and homosexual, have a religious or spiritual life and be homosexual, and it was fine too. It was their story and they did not have to feel guilty about anything. From that point, they started to design action plans, which we were able to push to the national council and obtain funding, which had a snowball effect. People organized themselves in associations.

There was capacity building from NGOs. We tried to do the same in Senegal and other African countries, to finally get social momentum to face AIDS. It wasn't about the medical information, but to know whether people were prepared to fight for themselves, and if so, with what resources, from a local community level and so on. The fundamental question was to change self-image, and I think SAHARA was very helpful in doing that and bridging gaps for all of Africa. We also didn't want homosexuals to feel isolated in their battle. That is why we worked with women, given that the issue of homosexuality could be traced back to issues of gender, and that everywhere people are stigmatized they have to be united and support one another. This was witnessed at the leadership level from both sides and every time there was conference, I made sure that they were part of the Senegalese delegation. We had a leader representing each group, PLWA, homosexuals, sex workers, and so on. SAHARA helped us at that level and I traveled around with them to South Africa and so on. They had an international experience. They were not necessarily literate, but they were leaders. They could not necessarily speak polished French or English, but it was not important. They spoke their language and we translated, so that was our philosophy. At the end of the SAHARA conference, I was approached by Professor Mboup who asked me to help to make the voices of MSM heard at the ICASA conference in 2008. I worked with the ICASA organizing committee, and we managed to get the LGBT communities to take the floor and animate debates on HIV/AIDS prevention and human rights issues. ICASA was a success in this regard. It came with more visibility. Then the new religious parties took advantage of this event to circulate hate speech.

The end of 2008 and 2009 was the catastrophe. They became visible, people knew them and they became targets for violence. This is why at some point I slowed things down, which is part of the responsibility of the researcher. When researchers, especially in social sciences, do certain work, they take risks, like in all the jobs. So at some point, we were at the front line, because there was a front line and we were there. But if what you say is pertinent, other people will join you and your presence might no longer be necessary because others will take over your battle. At that point, it was as if the world was falling apart. I agreed to take responsibility, but I knew it was fine because at some point I would not be alone. There were limits nonetheless. The limit was that even a well-organized civil society was not enough when it came to ending stigma.

We continued to work on violence, homophobia, and after that Ebola. it was exactly the same thing. It was a social issue. Then for non-communicable diseases, we also discovered that it was society, it was inequalities and all that we saw with AIDS. . . . Social exclusion leads to silence and so does gender exclusion. When you are excluded, you are not free. So it brings me back to the old battles of my childhood. I think the human being is not only a social animal but one that also always seeks freedom. If he can't be free physically, he will otherwise, in either dreams or metaphors. I think the quest for freedom is consubstantial to life itself.

Ellen Foley: Let's talk about the university environment from 2005 to date. You said that among your colleagues there was not really support until you met with the Khalife in 2009. How was your university life after the crisis in 2008 and 2009?

Cheikh Niang: During the crisis, many of my colleagues in the University were scared, including being scared to be seen with me. Luckily not all of them, for instance, the director of the Institute that accompanied me to Tivouane. He actually comes from the Casamance.

Ellen Foley: Bienvenu Sambou?

Cheikh Niang: Yes. He knows the significance of going into the sacred woods, going there does not require any social or ethnic distinction. All the members of neighboring communities, whatever their status or culture or language, may be at some point provided assistance with circumcision and initiation to youths. I think this somehow gives an international reflex. It is not based on the discourse of rights, but on a culture of inclusion.

The fact remains that he fully supported me, without reserve. Not only that but he mobilized his cousin, who was older than me and a deputy in the National Assembly, to push the battle forward. Seeing it as a human rights issue was my point of view, but the way he perceived it was that we couldn't keep excluding people. Bienvenu was very active. The support from him was priceless and counterbalanced the ostracism of my colleagues. They were discrediting the messenger to prevent the message from being heard. This is the entire period of 2008 and after the [intervention of the] Khalife we had people affiliated with him or respectful of him change because of his influence. And because of heated international debates, people began to realize a lot of things.

Ellen Foley: And after things calmed down?

Cheikh Niang: I continued to meet with the homosexual networks and be active. The CNLS progressed a lot. The last time they invited me to take part in a workshop where there were a lot of sex workers and homosexuals I repeated the same discourse, to renounce guilt, feel strong, and engage in battles, not only for you but also for society.

I encountered this question of social exclusion everywhere when working on Ebola, as well as the question of homosexuality, the question of women, gender relations. . . . These are permanent questions that we encounter. It is a part of social reality. In the early 1980s, people sought out women's perspectives since the dominant scientific and academic discourse was a patriarchal one, all about men. From the '70s and '80s, there were feminist movements that claimed there were other voices to consider. In universities, however, the discourse remained predominantly heterosexual, but all social realities have dimensions that go beyond binary gender and sexuality. Speaking about gender is also talking about sexual minorities and gender conceptions and what goes beyond binary sexuality. I think that's how we need to start thinking about realities and how to plan interventions, which is what we are working on. We have hope, although I have lost a lot of leaders, there are others that come around, which is why my office is always functional.

Ellen Foley: Do you still feel targeted by the fundamentalist students and the media?

Cheikh Niang: I think that for now the hostility is not open. There are no explicit calls for violence toward me. It's different from when my name was mentioned in mosques and I had a death sentence hovering over my head.

Ellen Foley: Where do you find the strength to continue? At first glance, you appear to be a quiet and reserved person, at the base you have a strong character. I wonder how you maintain your courage and strong will. Where does that strength come from?

Cheikh Niang: It comes from my mother and my grandmother. When I was in elementary school, I remember a scene. I was ill and even when I got very ill, my grandmother came to pick me up to take me to school. On the way she asked me what I wanted to eat, and I said very adamantly I wanted a guava. She knew I was frustrated and ill, so around 10 a.m. she suddenly shows up at the gate to tell the teacher that she wanted him to make me smile. He tried to explain that I was in class, but she insisted, saying a guava was all that I needed at the moment. She made so much noise at the gate until I came out and she was able to hand me the guava. She was not afraid to create turmoil in the school, because she knew that is what I needed at that time.

Ellen Foley: So the influence from those two powerful women must have really marked you.

Cheikh Niang: Yes. For my grandmother, it was her generosity and her courage to face adversity and not to be intimidated nor to conform. In fact, they were two nonconformists, which really helped me.

Secondly my mom was initially a Catholic and then converted to Islam, but she reminded me of her Jewish origins, saying that Carvalhos were initially Jewish. I don't even know how she managed to know that. She said they were the Jews of Spain and Portugal who at some point were victims of genocide and who were converted by force and so on. So she was attached to this myth. Now, from my own investigations, I know that so far in Portugal, the family name Carvalho commonly passes for descendants of Jews who were forcibly baptized (cristãos novos) at the end of the fifteenth century or persecuted during the period of the Inquisition Tribunal from the sixteenth century. It is associated with Judaism in American Jewish Archives, and in research studies on the history of graves of cemeteries in the islands of Cape Verde where my mother's father was from. I have a very diverse background.

Ellen Foley: In your generation, many Senegalese intellectuals left the country to go either to France or to the United States You could have had a more prominent career with fewer problems, but you never left, why?

Cheikh Niang: I have confronted a kind of glass ceiling for much of my career, and yet I have stayed. In the time that I was preparing my dossier to defend my dissertation d'état, a professor at University Cheikh Anta Diop told the head of sociology that the university would never permit the defense of my thesis [implying that gender and sexuality were not worthwhile academic studies]. It took a legal battle before my defense was authorized. For that, US-based professors Collins Airhihenbuwa of Penn State University and you (Ellen Foley) had to be solicited and to give assessments of my work.

The first time I had the opportunity to go to France was related to my jail time. I could have asked for forgiveness and received a scholarship. People older than me had done that. For me, it [studying in France] was not the be all and end all. What mattered to me was justice. Secondly, I could study here. I didn't see why I needed to go to France when you have the same thing here, and I didn't want to ask. That comes from my mother, the pride of not begging and staying content. Sometimes it was when we were poorest that she seemed most joyful. I refused to be in such situations. I continued my studies and I started to go to the United States, but my first trip was to Belgium.

Ellen Foley: What year was that?

Cheikh Niang: It was in 1982. I had a scholarship for a few months every year, but I knew that I couldn't stay. It was as if I was paranoid.I felt the look of superiority, paternalism, racism at times. For the first time I discovered that I was black, that race was an issue. From the airport to the city, I was the Congolese or the African. You could not be more than that box you were locked in. That is when I knew I could not stay. People try to convince me that I would make more money and be successful, but I didn't see it that way. This struck me in France, because I was not convinced that the French would ever see beyond the color of my skin, and I had done work on brain drain, so I knew I didn't want to find myself in that situation. My society invested a lot in me and there was a lot I wanted to give back. The intellectual training I had received had to serve people.

After that, I went to the United States for a short stay, where I had a Fulbright scholarship. The atmosphere there was very stimulating for me. On the one hand, I met other Africans, Senegalese, and so on who urged me to stay. The first time I went to Portland, Oregon, to visit a colleague with whom I got along well, when it was time to leave he said, "Make sure you stay, don't be crazy and return." He asked me whether I had a car in Dakar, and I said no, I took the bus. He was shocked to hear that I couldn't afford a car. Then he asked me if I had a house, and I said no. Then he asked me why I would want to go back and suffer. I had to explain all the activities awaiting me, my students and so on. He told me I'd regret my decision and probably die miserable, because what I was doing was suicidal.

After my Fulbright, I came back occasionally, and it would have been easy for me to stay, but I didn't want to because I had just started to work on AIDS. There were a lot of things that I was eager to understand and I didn't think I could understand them at a distance. If I managed to collect enough valid information, the beneficiaries will not only be my society, but the world. The sure thing was that I was not ready to leave my country. I had African American friends who invited me for meals, and one day an older man asked me why I wanted to leave, and I told him there was a lot I needed to do back home. He replied, "I have never seen an African as foolish as you. There are a lot of Africans here. Apparently you like to suffer."

That's the only image they have of Africa—misery, violence—but what I told them was that there was more to it than what they saw. Also, if Africans don't stay to fix it, who will? There were many opportunities for partnership, but in exchange you had to give up the strong beliefs for which you were fighting. They would give you a new paradigm or a framework that suits them, which I didn't agree with. So I asked myself what I would gain from staying there. . . . Probably comfort and quality of life, but in terms of ideas, not much. Also, if I was there I would not have been able to do my research.

Ellen Foley: Thank you so much for sharing your story.

Cheikh Niang: It was a pleasure.

Acknowledgments: Special thanks to Claire Doualla Bija who helped with the translation and transcription of our conversation.

BIBLIOGRAPHY

Bathily, Abdoulaye. *Mai 68 à Dakar ou la révolte universitaire et la démocratie*. Paris: Chaka [Afrique contemporaine], 15, no. 186 (1992).

"CHEIKH NIANG, SOCIOLOGUE NOUS AVONS BESOIN DES HOMOSEXUELS." April 20, 2009. https://www.leral.net/CHEIKH-NIANG-SOCIOLOGUE-NOUS-AVONS-BESOIN-DES-HOMOSEXUELS_a4068.html.

Coulon, Christian. "Senegal: Development and Fragility of Semi-Democracy." In *Democracy in Developing Countries: Africa*, edited by Larry Diamond, Jonathan Hartlyn, and Juan J. Linz, 141–77, Boulder: Lynne Rienner, 1989.

Diop, Momar Coumba et Mamadou Diouf, *Le Sénégal sous Abdou Diouf*. Présence Africaine, Paris, 1990.

McKnee, Lisa. *Selfish Gifts: Senegalese Women's Autobiographical Discourses*. Albany: SUNY Press, 2000.

Niang, Cheikh Ibrahima. "Approche historique et socio-anthropologique des constructions de genre autour de la sexualité." Institut Panos Afrique de l'Ouest, 2016.

———. Ebola: une épidémie postcoloniale. *Politique étrangère* 4 (hiver 2014): 97–109.

———. *Anthropologie de la sexualité. Philosophie, Culture et Construction sociale du Sexe au Sénégal*. Thèse de Doctorat d'Etat-es Lettres, Université Cheikh Anta Diop, Dakar, Sénégal, 2013.

———. 2010. "The Social Environment of Homosexual Men: The Effect of Homophobia Violence in the Prevention of HIV and Care of AIDS." Report funded by the NGO ANCS.

———. "Understanding Sex Between Men and Men: Beyond Current Linguistic and Discursive Categories." In *Routledge Handbook of Sexuality, Health and Rights*, edited by Peter Aggleton and Richard Parker, 116–24. London and New York, 2010.

———. "Analyse de contenu des medias sénégalais sur le traitement de la question de l'homosexualité et de l'homophobie," Institut Panos Afrique de l'Ouest, avril 2009.

———. "The Dimba of Senegal: A Support Group for Women," *Reproductive Health Matters* 2 no. 4 (1994): 39–45.

Niang, Cheikh Ibrahima and Hamadou Boiro. 2007. "You Can Also Cut My Finger!": Social Construction of Male Circumcision in West Africa, A Case Study of Senegal and Guinea-Bissau. *Reproductive Health Matters* 15, no. 29 (2007): 22–32.

Niang, Cheikh Ibrahima, Olive Shisana, G. Andrews, Dan Kaseje Leickness Simbayi, Karl Peltzer, and Yoesrie Toefy. 2006. "Innovations dans les approches, activités et résultats des conférences internationales sur le VIH/SIDA en Afrique—Le cas de la 3ème conférence africaine sur les aspects sociaux du VIH/SIDA, Dakar, 10–14 octobre 2005" *SAHARA-J: Journal of Social Aspects of HIV/AIDS* 3, no. 2 (2006): 436–49.

Niang, Cheikh Ibrahima, Placide Tapsoba, Ellen Weiss, Moustapha Diagne, Youssoupha Niang, Amadou Mody Moreau, Dominique Gomis, Abdoulaye Sidibé Wade, Karim Seck, and Chris Castle. "It's Raining Stones': Stigma, Violence and HIV Vulnerability among Men Who Have Sex with Men in Dakar, Senegal." *Culture, Health & Sexuality* 5, no. 6 (2003): 499–512.

O'Brien, Donald Cruise. "Political Opposition in Senegal: 1960–1967." *Government and Opposition* 2, no. 3 (1967): 557–66.

Palmeri, Paolo. *Retour dans un village diola de Casamance. Chronique d'une recherche anthropologique au Sénégal.* Paris: L'Harmattan, Connaissance des hommes, 1995.

Pélissier, Paul. *Les paysans du Sénégal. Les civilisations agraires du Cayor à la Casamance.* Saint-Yrieix [Haute-Vienne]: Imprimerie Fabrègue, 1966, 708.

"Social Aspects of HIV/AIDS Research Alliance (SAHARA)," October 1, 2018, http://www.hsrc.ac.za/en/departments/hiv-aids-stis-and-tb/SAHARA.

Vincent, Thomas Louis. *Les Diola. Essai d'analyse fonctionnelle sur une population de Basse Casamance.* Dakar: IFAN, 1958.

NOTES

1. Paolo Palmeri, *Retour dans un village diola de Casamance. Chronique d'une recherche anthropologique au Sénégal* (Paris: L'Harmattan, Connaissance des hommes, 1995).

2. Thomas Louis Vincent, *Les Diola. Essai d'analyse fonctionnelle sur une population de Basse Casamance* (Dakar: IFAN, 1958).

3. Paul Pélissier, *Les paysans du Sénégal. Les civilisations agraires du Cayor à la Casamance* (Saint-Yrieix [Haute-Vienne]: Imprimerie Fabrègue, 1966), 708.

4. For more on Leftist organizing in Senegal during this period see: Abdoulaye Bathily, *Mai 68 à Dakar ou la révolte universitaire et la démocratie* (Paris : Chaka [Afrique contemporaine], 15, no. 186 (1992)Christian Coulon, "Senegal: Development and fragility of semi-democracy," in *Democracy in Developing Countries: Africa*, eds. Larry Diamond, Jonathan Hartlyn, and Juan J. Linz (Boulder, CO: Lynne Rienner, 1989), 141–77.
Donald Cruise O'Brien, "Political Opposition in Senegal: 1960-1967," *Government and Opposition* 2, no. 3 (1967): 557–66.
Momar Coumba Diop et Mamadou Diouf, *Le Sénégal sous Abdou Diouf* (Présence Africaine, Paris, 1990).

5. *Taasu* are a form of women's poetry and coded knowledge. For more on *taasu* see Lisa McKnee, *Selfish Gifts: Senegalese Women's Autobiographical Discourses* (Albany: SUNY Press, 2000).

6. For some of the published results of this work, see Cheikh Ibrahima Niang, "The Dimba of Senegal: A Support Group for Women," *Reproductive Health Matters*, 2 no. 4 (1994): 39–45.

7. Cheikh Ibrahima Niang, Placide Tapsoba, Ellen Weiss, Moustapha Diagne, Youssoupha Niang, Amadou Mody Moreau, Dominique Gomis, Abdoulaye Sidibé Wade, Karim Seck, and Chris Castle, "'It's Raining Stones': Stigma, Violence and HIV Vulnerability among Men Who Have Sex with Men in Dakar, Senegal," *Culture, Health and Sexuality* 5, no. 6 (2003): 499–512.

8. See "CHEIKH NIANG, SOCIOLOGUE NOUS AVONS BESOIN DES HOMOSEXUELS," April 20, 2009, https://www.leral.net/CHEIKH-NIANG-SOCIOLOGUE-NOUS-AVONS-BESOIN-DES-HOMOSEXUELS_a4068.html.

9. SAHARA stands for the Social Aspects of HIV/AIDS Research Alliance. It is a HIV Prevention Research and Policy center based in South Africa, October 1, 2018, http://www.hsrc.ac.za/en/departments/hiv-aids-stis-and-tb/SAHARA.

CONCLUSION

Identities, Text, and Texts

Besi Brillian Muhonja

The project of instituting a robust and responsive critical African gender and sexuality studies presents challenges related to defining a language and approaches for scholarship on what are, in fact, thousands of communities with unique mores, values, practices, and even legalities, in relation to gendered spaces. Babacar M'Baye, in the introduction, outlines some of these challenges, specifically focalizing studies on Senegalese societies. He historicizes Senegalese gender and sexuality studies and underlines the necessary work in the field, cautioning that failure to invest boldly in this area of scholarship is injurious to Africana studies across the disciplines. This work he locates as urgent and demanding critical lenses and approaches.

I reflect, in this conclusion, on the responses to the charge M'Baye poses to the authors of the chapters in this volume, examining how their inquiries into the pasts and presents of Senegalese societies imagine future directions in research. I kick off this rumination by acknowledging studies, elsewhere, which affirm that indigenous Senegalese societies have historically and traditionally embraced differences and diversity.[1] In some ways this remains so today, with Senegal recognized as a model for religious and cultural tolerance.[2] These inclusive ways of knowing, being, and doing are grounded in performances of humanness, a concept the Wolof reference as *nite*. *Nit* translates to human.

Scholar Cheikh Thiam defines *nite* as that which makes a human being human. He illustrates this using the Wolof proverb, "*nit niteey garabam*," meaning, "to be human is the remedy of the human being."[3]

This indigenous philosophy of Senegalese societies, which encapsulates the performance of humanness, informed values and practices of acceptance and respect at all levels of society. It helped characterize communities as all-embracing, except in the face of negative transgression. However, even with such contravention, the presence of processes of restorative justice allowed for re-entry into the fold. The scholars contributing to this volume grapple primarily with questions of variance and exclusion and ways in which othering female and queer bodies and identities is a departure from this tradition of inclusiveness and leads to the emergence of new ways of being—a new Africanness and a new Senegalese-ness. In the two sections that follow, I contemplate these dynamics, and the contributors' investigations into the identification, handling, and study of certain bodies and their performances within Africanness. I tease out the core ideas the contributors offer on circumscribing distinct histories, languages, and approaches through critical African studies lenses for studies in gender and sexuality.

ON THE INVENTIONS OF DIFFERENCES

To study constructed "dissimilarity" that undergirds othering practices, the contributors offer that it is necessary to uncover the origin of divergence as an end point in research. Such an exposition also serves as a foundation and conduit to establishing proper histories and appropriate methodologies and languages for the necessary academic work on gender and sexuality in Africa. The scholars float the idea that difference and differences construct and are constructed by new forms of Africanness, in this case, a new Senegalese-ness. I borrow Ayo Coly's use of the term "invention" to capture the fashioning of particular emerging performances of being Senegalese as engaged by the authors. In speaking about the rise of vigilante homophobes and other manifestations of new homophobia, Coly explains: "I trace the invention of the Senegalese homosexual to 2008, when homosexuality became an event, following the publication of the photos of an alleged Senegalese gay marriage." With this statement, Coly pushes us to ponder over a number of things including what it means to be Senegalese, African, and queer, and what represents Senegalese sensibilities on particular productions of othering. Her declaration also leads us to cogitate on the origin of identities, languages, ideas, even communities in the study of "the African," and in this scenario, of that which is or is not Senegalese. This is one of the core principles the chapters in the book exemplify as necessary to critical African gender and sexuality studies, and which this section of the chapter explores.

Coly advises, in the study of identities, consideration of the multiple-sided production of identities. Scholars often make explorations into the othering of queer and female bodies as if the resulting experiences of identity performance and recreation happen only to these particular bodies, ignoring effects on the other players in the practice of bias. In itself, this kind of reading is also a practice of othering. What Coly presents as an alternative is a multi-pronged observation or study of the invention of identities that considers all players as well as the particularization of players occupying different queer and female bodies and identities. She illustrates the latter point by first historicizing the invention of the homosexual, not as an invention of queerness but indeed the invention of a particular othered homosexual within Senegal. Coly, Niang, and M'Baye make the case for the existence of queer people in Senegalese societies before the invention of this contested homosexual identity. By making this distinction, Coly delineates two different queer identities, so to speak. One is the accepted and respected queer identity reading where different queer bodies and identities are discerned, while the second is the one whose invention she tenders as emerging in 2008.

Having characterized these two dynamics, Coly then submits the invention of other identities attached to the creation of the contested homosexual, primarily, the invention of the homophobe. The homophobe represents an invention of multiple identities manifesting in various characters and spaces from the media to political worlds to personal spaces. M'Baye, Coly, and Niang highlight the political opportunism attached to media and politicians' use of queer populations' experiences. M'Baye explicates: "The media and certain political and religious demagogues use them as easy targets of public scapegoating and humiliation which divert attention from the country's plight." Thus, the birthings of the "contested homosexual" and homophobia happen in tandem, and this delivers a new Africanness and Senegalese-ness in the performance, while being of differently situated homophobes—individuals not guided by *nite*. Furthermore, as M'Baye's statement directs, there are other creations of Senegalese-ness that emerge from this process including manipulative personalities in the media, politics, and religious arena; and on the other side of that equation, duped masses not paying attention to failures of the state and development in the nation. This bids a new performance of Senegalese citizenship—that is citizens failing at active citizenship. These inventions of identities and values on multiple levels, which produce new performances of Senegalese-ness refabricate societies and communities, that is, what Senegal is, what Senegalese people are, and what being African is.

Before these regenerations that Packer, Niang, M'Baye, and Coly uphold in their chapters cultures that considered and accepted gender variance. They clarify that what were once acceptable gender variant identities have now come to be defined monolithically as contested homosexuality. This, Coly highlights as one of the key characteristics of the invented homosexual. The constructed reality, where all identities and spaces of queerness or gender nonconformity are denigrated, can be observed in Packer's exposition of the masculinization of soccer, which draws negative attention to nonconforming female soccer players. While female players are expected, just like their male counterparts, to excel on the soccer field, a further expectation is that they maintain performances of patriarchally defined femininity. Porter presents the same treatment of successful female students, who must also exist as conforming to specific family values. These are the nuanced rewritings of society and community that can go unnoticed and so unstudied. Consider the interrogations raised in Packer's chapter, directly focussing the definition of what represents Senegalese-ness, including the question of why soccer, a sport that is foreign to the community, should be used as a descriptor for Senegalese masculinity or femininity? The argument that this question could be raised about any aspect of modern-day living in any society holds water. However, that very argument also underlines the great motivation for engaging the invention and construction of things, in this case, identities, and expectations placed on them.

Packer, in her study of *footballeuse,* uses the narratives of Fatou and Aicha, who allow their bodies to reflect different performances of gender, sometimes presenting themselves androgynously or performing what the scholar calls "female masculinity." Fatou and Aicha perform their selves as resistance to oppression when attacked by other society members, which only enhances the vitriol against the two and others like them. Engaging the Sufi principles of freedom and agency that inform these soccer players' performances of the self, Packer advances a third factor influencing being Senegalese, namely, religion and how they contribute to inventions of new identities and partialities. Religious tolerance is a key value among communities in Senegal; therefore, the influence of religions on different ways of being Senegalese is significant, as drawn out by Ruth Evans and Khadidia Sy. People employ religion and ritual in performing different selves and registering agency, and this raises a number of points and questions. First, if religious entities preach tolerance, why is this acceptance dished out selectively? Second, if the nonconforming persons consider their practices as grounded in their religious values, who gets to contest this and use it to other them? Between the people employing religion as a tool for resistance and self-actualization and those using it as a defense for homophobia, which group is practicing apropos Senegalese-ness? What is clear is that religions influence the invention of at least two other performances of Senegalese-ness, as illustrated in the foregoing, further complicating the landscape of identifying.

Religion-invented Senegalese-ness is not the only one defended while using virtue as a principle. As part of the refashioning and invention of post-colonial Senegalese identities, for political and social reasons, the homosexual was invented, and women reconstructed as the weaker sex. Niang, Porter, Coly, Telingator and Weeks, and M'Baye deconstruct this other invention of Africanness and Senegalese-ness. Coly, M'Baye, and Niang explain that the antigay and anti-woman rhetoric and actions attached to these processes were purposed to serve the definition of a virtuous postcolonial Africanness, femininity, and masculinity. Coly affirms this idea in arguing that the invented contested homosexuality is a post-colonial event since the delegitimizing of homosexual acts through the law of the land was a post-independence happening dated 1965. Niang supports this observation, elucidating that even in the 1980s and early '90s, "homosexuals were not in official discourse." He explains that, at the time, homosexuality was presented simply as un-African, thus mostly ignored as a reality in Senegal. M'Baye determines that these assessments contributed to the emergence of ultramasculinity. In defining this "virtue" of a postcolonial African identity, the human rights of some members of society have been compromised, placing the very societal virtue desired in question, and also unfairly questioning the uprightness of those who were now easily demonized by these new invented values and parameters of gender and sexuality. This postcolonial ultramasculinity, which delivers a new kind of African or Senegalese man, can be observed as present at the individual level, but also as part of the general public psyche and institutions. This kind of masculinity then effects new expectations and socializations of African and Senegalese boyhoods, girlhoods, womanhoods, and queerness.

The postcolonial erasures of certain ways of performing Africanness or Senegalese-ness are sustained in other more nuanced ways in every day practice and in scholarship, policy, and activism. Juliana Friend initiates debate on another aspect of creating new Africanness and Senegalese-ness when she outlines the practice of erasing parts of people's identities in order to study or serve them as a rewriting of their persons, bodies, and identities. Friend questions the effectiveness of this practice and underlines the dangers of promoting health without fostering freedom. The e-health program she studies looks at queer customers as biomedical entities, for convenience's sake, without recognizing their other selves and lives including social, political, and personal lives, struggles, and capacities, or even their self-identifying. This magnifies the danger of homogenizing all queer people and so the continued invention of the contested homosexual that Coly defines. In relation to queer people, as with the example of Friend's study, directing all services to a group of people toward preventing and managing diseases also pathologizes them, further characterizing the invented homosexual and heightening their marginalization. In such a reality, disease is imagined as consistent with queer lives.

Friend's observation is more disturbing than one might imagine at first reading. If, in fact, only medical intervention programs erased parts of queer people, that would be dangerous enough. The challenge and damage, however, materializes as bigger when one considers that in almost every area of their encounters with life, for the sake of convenience, different sets of people rewrite or erase the narratives and experiences of queer people. They imagine queer people in ways that are expedient for their own purposes, and not in ways that represent how diverse queer people experience life or self-identify. Academics are not immune to this either. Thus, the contributor contends that effective studies, policies, and interventions must be more holistic. Ideally, to even adequately address health or other concerns requires understanding the realities of people's lives. Holistic approaches to not just treating and advocating for but also studying queer experiences and people, is an application of the indigenous African philosophy of *nite*. Friend's work reminds us of these indigenous philosophies of holistic existence and *nite* when she determines that "Casting broader human rights as a distant goal, or a matter of personal responsibility of the marginalized group, can feel to MSM like a failure to prioritize their well-being and a denial of their full humanity."

Against these inventions of identities, Niang challenges deliberation on what represents Senegalese masculinity or femininity. Both Niang and Packer raise questions on what makes up a female or male African body and identity. Niang's grandmother, in performing as an African male and female, and his mother stepping in to take over the grandmother's duties, would constitute nonconforming female bodies. He however cautions that such an appraisal is only made possible by standards mostly introduced from outside cultures. The scholar celebrates the transgressing bodies of his mother and grandmother as having been his inspiration, contesting the use of Western lenses and other limiting readings on what constitutes being woman or being man. He focusses, instead, his grandmother's bounteousness and fearlessness and celebrates the fact that these two women were nonconformists. He engages their bodies, as well as bodies of queer people as performing in different cultural, social, religious, and political milieus, in which different values and strengths are required of said bodies. What he directs us to ponder is the irrationality of placing judgment on bodies performing adequately, naturally, and appropriately within contexts. Packer entreats the same contemplation with her presentation of the female soccer players. The scholars highlight the need to reorient the framing we use to study bodies performing gender and sexuality but also reconsider that marginalized bodies performing within spaces that do not support them require unique attentions in scholarship.

Offering such attention engenders appreciation for what the authors posit as reading these gender-disrupting bodies as bodies in deliberate resistance to the very limiting readings of Eurocentric lenses—in effect, the bodies endorse Africanness. M'Baye, Niang, Packer, and Coly invite new nuanced interpretations of difference that study nonconforming individuals as bodies in resistance to Eurocentric imaginings. The suggestion here is that imagining these bodies simply as different or othered, and taking the analysis no further, diminishes them, the attached identities, and their societal impact. This reduction preserves and supplements the invention of differences and erasures, specifically of certain values celebrated about human bodies, regardless of their gender or sexual location in indigenous and some present-day Senegalese societies.

Niang expands this argument to application, using the example of the inventions of new womanhoods and femininities. He highlights the sophistication of communities in Senegal and their capacity to contest Eurocentrism averring. He states: "There must be at least one woman who resists, so how do you side with this woman so that other women will be able to resist, without making them feel like Western ideologies are being imposed on them? Because they rejected that, because they insisted on not wanting to be European. [We explained] that they could be African and feminist, or African and still rebel against such inequalities without fear, because their culture allows it." In this quotation, Niang calls attention to the colonial and postcolonial molding of women as the weaker sex, and then locates nonconforming bodies and identities, which he imagines as reproducing indigenous ways of being, as a location of resistance. These bodies reaffirm different ways of being African and Senegalese. Accordingly, nonconforming bodies represent a Senegalese-ness that contests much of what is presented as mainstream Senegalese sensibilities and performances of gender and sexuality.

By locating the narratives of queerness and gender within the history of Senegal as a macro-nation, the contributors reveal state responsibility in sustaining gender differences and othering practices. Appreciating this state-sponsored construction of identities highlights the folly of considering a generalized Senegalese idea of femininity, masculinity, or homosexuality. Laying out these differences as inventions of the politics of the times, allows us to reimagine the past and consider a future where the politics of the time affect encounters with difference and variance, as illustrated by Telingator and Weeks and Porter. In a similar vein, Niang, Packer, M'Baye, Friend, Porter, and Coly suggest that we must consider the fluidity of identities, as well as the reading of identities as influenced by different temporal, societal, political, and historical factors. Understanding the inventions of identities and societal views and practices toward those identities makes it possible to imagine new multi-directed and multi-pronged lenses for the exploration of identities and bodies, which, the contributors argue, demands new text and texts.

TEXT AND TEXTS

The task of creating new critical texts for the study of gender and sexuality in Africa requires closer investigations into old oral and written text and texts, and the establishment of new text and texts. The contributors to this volume show that this demands a reading of not just text but contextualized cultural subtexts. The driving question is: What text and texts are relevant and appropriate for the critical study of gender and sexuality in African societies? The authors' findings suggest that this query should inform deliberations on the following questions: What is studied? Who studies it? Whose voice reports it? How, when and where it is reported? What language is used? What words are used? What sources are considered? Who is studied? Where those studied are located in the process? I explore their postulations in this section.

What is advocated is not just establishing the right text and texts to be studied but also the right text to use for interpreting and delivering the findings of research. The scholars' analyses suggest going beyond the simple word and published texts including historical records, religious texts, literatures, news reports, and academic works to investigate cultural texts and subtexts of verbal and non-verbal languages, as well as performance and performativity of identities and bodies as text. To effectively identify and engage these texts they suggest two approaches which I explore in this section of the chapter. These are: Centering the informational authority of Africans whose experiences are studied and respecting and creating space for the moral authority of oppressed identities and bodies under study.

Promoting informational authority of persons and communities within African queer and gender studies, M'Baye, Niang, and Coly note that research, analysis, and reporting on African entities through Eurocentric lenses and text is characterized by focus on the voice of the scholar. This has contributed to the marginalization of the voices and ideas of Africans. Often, this is exacerbated by the application of Eurocentrically tinged paradigms. To counter such objectification, M'Baye and Niang suggest a centering of African voices, and particularly those of the specific demographic under study. Niang shares his work on sexualities and public health and reports having had to go the extra mile to adequately include the voices of the queer communities. Secondly, the scholars propose a focus on layered texts of resistance. M'Baye tenders that habitually "work focuses on the homophobic and transphobic attitudes toward these individuals rather than these persons' resistances against the prejudices." Such concentration on voices and texts of resistance, also captured in Sy's chapter, addresses other challenges related to erasure, by recording the agency of the oppressed. At the same time, it logs critical thoughts of the people and their communities. Niang recommends questions that can guide scholarship that pivots around the informational authority of the people. He proposes deliberating, as a starting point, "in order to challenge inequalities, violence and exclusion, what are the existing local resources, before looking for answers outside? How are those answers sufficient or insufficient? How can they be improved?" He suggests directing attention to the people by posing, out of his practice, the question, "if women are victims of domination, which women resist?"

Such questioning teases out different texts and subtexts, which heightens attention on not just what one says but also the nuances of languages and frameworks used. Text is inseparable from language, whether that language is written, verbal, or non-verbal. To truly benefit from the informational authority of communities, it is necessary to learn to "read" their text and texts in ways that honor the interpretations that they give those texts, as Ruth Evans does with her chapter's considerations of widowhood among the Serer people. The guiding principle, then, would be: how do the queer people and women studied use and interpret their verbal and non-verbal text, texts, and performativity within different realities? Packer, Niang, M'Baye, Porter, and Coly introduce us to individuals who position and read the performances of their bodies in ways that are dissimilar from the way the public reads them. This is especially significant when considering contested identities. In relation to non-verbal text, communicating with and understanding physical language becomes especially important in spaces where people are afraid to speak or cannot freely express themselves and their identities. Thus, Niang, Coly, Friend, Packer, Telingator and Weeks, Coly, and M'Baye's work points us toward reviewing bodily performances and interactions, along with oral and written sources in search of the right text and texts to study and record findings in the area of gender and sexuality.

Supplementing informational authority of individuals and communities, this second subsection delivers thoughts on what Packer refers to as the moral authority of the oppressed. Defining suitable text, texts and approaches for the study of gender and sexuality, as well as studies related to other forms of marginalization within African contexts, requires respect for what the oppressed know, value, and experience. Niang and Packer propose two applications of the same idea. In the following statement, Niang articulates experiences from his involvement with this kind of community-engaged scholarship, which I deliberately quote in its entirety: "The first validation [of the research] is not the academic validation, it was not the university. It was validation by the community that held this traditional know-how. From that moment, I started to see how they lived their sexuality. They were not passive. There was an aspect of an active person who takes responsibility for her sexuality and her desires, which was not the perspective of the mainstream literature."

Packer recommends bearing in mind, in privileging moral authority of the oppressed, how the people use their cultural practices and belief systems. She theorizes religion as a site of resistance, locating the *footballeuse* as performing a queer resistance that claims, "a religious-political subjectivity based on a Sufi model of resistance which frames emancipation as an inner moral power." She proposes new conceptions of the space where queerness encounters religious human rights discourses as disruption of the societal patriarchal standards and modes of feminizing and masculinizing. She states, referring to Fatou, that the soccer player "frames her transgression of gender norms as a spiritually purifying process." The *footballeuses*, at once, play under the principle that there is a gender hierarchy built into the practices of Islam while also challenging it. In this way, they "derive their moral agency in a struggle against oppression from a position of moral inferiority—that allows them to queer their path to salvation, bringing to light new forms of gendered subjectivities and Muslim spatialities."

Niang captures the same idea of spiritually grounded moral authority and resistance by defining what he calls sacred transgression. He speaks of his grandmother as embodying "both masculinity, femininity, and priesthood." In addition, Niang urges *nite*-grounded scholarship and activism as another path to recognizing and employing the moral authority of the oppressed. He shares experiential illustrations of what such scholarship would look like. It would involve walking in the shoes of the communities, societies, and individuals one studies or works among to "feel their sufferings and translate that into research questions and build theories and methodologies." He explains that from his experience there can sometimes be a sense that what scholars or researchers feel may not be an accurate translation of what the people or communities they study are experiencing or saying. Thus, the researchers or scholars have to care about the topics studied as much as the people they study do. To reach that level of consciousness, especially when working with stigmatized and traumatized populations, Niang indicates the importance of extended and in-depth listening and courting of trust. He proposes meeting them in spaces where they feel safe physically, intellectually, emotionally, mentally, and spiritually. The scholar draws from his experiences to underscore the importance of scholars being activists and locating their bodies and voices in confrontational spaces where the marginalized cannot afford to stand for fear of victimization. In this way, scholar-activists practice *nite* in defending the rights of marginalized populations in Senegal and elsewhere as "human rights, civil rights, our history, our culture," (Niang) even invoking religion.

Paying attention to proper text and texts can buttress intellectual access to these values Niang and the other scholars proffer and guide a better appreciation for how indigenous Africans conceptualized queer and gendered relationships and identities through the philosophy of *nite*. M'Baye and Coly point us toward an inquiry into the meaning of words, like *gôr djiguène,* which disrupt Western conceptualizations of gender and constructions of the homophobe. M'Baye, on the texts he analyzes concludes, "the *gôr djiguène* is integral to Senegalese cultures in which they have had substantial level of acceptance despite the oppression they have faced within them." According to M'Baye, such critical engagement with knowledge compels recovery of histories of African peoples and their languages. On the value of indigenous texts to the exercise of critically studying African spaces, Niang suggests that to truly resolve gender-related issues, applying cultural ideas and philosophies can help bridge the gap between where people are, what they know and what they have access to. He proposes reflecting "on old ideas and giv[ing] them contemporary meaning? [. . .] Even problems of modernity or post-modernity and all that can be explained using ideas that are ancient." Niang continues: "People will understand. You can take an old idea and give it a new content."

Arguments presented in the chapters of this volume, which force us to interrogate the names, texts, and parameters we apply in engaging African identities and bodies as gendered and sexual entities in aesthetics and performance, have implications for critical African studies, and not just Senegalese studies. The multicultural nature of African communities, as well as the continent's histories and encounters with other cultures, inadvertently means that various forces have impacted any one phenomenon. These scholars suggest that engaging proper histories, as well as consulting the informational and moral authority of the demographics under study, provides a good foundation for defining languages and methods for critical African studies in gender and sexuality.

BIBLIOGRAPHY

Bop, Codou, and Jane Pincus. "Senegal: 'Homophobia and Islamic Political Manipulation.'" *Occasional Paper* 1, no. 08 (2008). September 22, 2018. http://www.arsrc.org/downloads/others/codou.pdf.

Coly, Ayo A. "Carmen Goes Postcolonial, Carmen Goes Queer: Thinking the Postcolonial as Queer." *Culture, Theory and Critique* 57, no. 3 (2016): 391–407.

Riccio, Bruno. "Talkin' about Migration- Some Ethnographic Notes on the Ambivalent Representation of Migrants in Contemporary Senegal." *Stichproben. Wiener Zeitschrift für kritische Afrikastudien* 8, no. 5 (2005): 99–118.

Smith, Ettiene. "Religious and Cultural Pluralism in Senegal: Accommodation through 'Proportional Equidistance.'" In *Tolerance, Democracy, and Sufis in Senegal*, edited by Mamadou Diouf, 147–79. New York: Columbia University Press, 2013.

Thiam, Cheikh. Interview with the author. August 15, 2018.

NOTES

1. Mamadou Diouf, ed., *Tolerance, Democracy, and Sufis in Senegal* (New York: Columbia University Press, 2013) 147–79; Codou Bop and Jane Pincus, "Senegal: 'Homophobia and Islamic Political Manipulation,'" *Occasional Paper* 1, no. 08 (2008): 5. September 22, 2018.http://www.arsrc.org/downloads/others/codou.pdf; Bruno Riccio, "Talkin' about Migration- Some Ethnographic Notes on the Ambivalent Representation of Migrants in Contemporary Senegal," *Stichproben. Wiener Zeitschrift für kritische Afrikastudien* 8, no. 5 (2005): 99; Ettiene Smith, "Religious and Cultural Pluralism in Senegal: Accommodation through 'Proportional Equidistance,'" in *Tolerance, Democracy, and Sufis in Senegal*, Mamadou Diouf, ed., (New York: Columbia University Press, 2013), 147–48, 153; Ayo A. Coly, "Carmen Goes Postcolonial, Carmen Goes Queer: Thinking the Postcolonial as Queer," *Culture, Theory and Critique* 57, no. 3 (2016): 391–407.
2. Ettiene Smith, "Religious and Cultural Pluralism in Senegal," 156.
3. Cheikh Thiam, interview with the author, August 15, 2018.

INDEX

ABOUT THE CONTRIBUTORS

Dr. Babacar M'Baye is professor of English and Pan-African studies at Kent State University. A native of Senegal, Dr. M'Baye received his PhD in American studies from Bowling Green State University in Ohio. His research varies from Pan-African literatures, films, music, race, sexualities, and gender expressions to black postcolonial and transnational cultures. Dr. M'Baye is the author of *Black Cosmopolitanism and Anticolonialism: Pivotal Moments* (2017); *The Trickster Comes West: Pan-African Influence in Early Black Diasporan Narratives* (2009); and a co-editor of *Crossing Traditions: American Popular Music in Local and Global Contexts* (2013). He is also the co-editor of Lexington Books's *Critical African Studies in Gender and Sexuality* series and has written essays for various journals and volumes.

Dr. Besi Brillian Muhonja is associate professor of African, African American, and diaspora studies, and women's, gender and sexuality studies in the Department of English at James Madison University. Her work is extensively published in academic peer-reviewed journals and edited volumes. She is author of the book *Womanhood and Girlhood in Twenty-First Century Middle Class Kenya: Disrupting Patri-centered Frameworks* (2018); co-editor of the volume *Mothers and Sons: Centering Mother Knowledge* (2016); and editor of three peer-reviewed journal issues. She is co-editor of the *Critical African Studies in Gender and Sexuality* series with Lexington Books and serves on the board for

Michigan State University Press Ruth Simms Hamilton African Diaspora Series, as well as the advisory and editorial boards of various academic journals.

Dr. Ayo A. Coly is associate professor of comparative literature at Dartmouth College. Her research focuses on colonial and postcolonial discourses about Africa and gender and sexuality in Africa. She is the author of *Postcolonial Hauntologies: African Women's Discourses of the Female Body* (2019) and *The Pull of Postcolonial Nationhood: Gender and Migration in Francophone African Literatures* (Lexington Books, 2010). She has guest-edited special issues of *The African Studies Review* on "Homophobic Africa?" and *Callaloo* on "The Cultures and Letters of the Black Diaspora."

Dr. Ruth Evans is associate professor in human geography at the University of Reading, UK. She received her PhD from the University of Hull, UK. Her research focuses on family geographies, care, bereavement, and inheritance. She led the research project, *Death in the Family in Urban Senegal* (funded by The Leverhulme Trust). Her recent articles discuss women's and young people's land rights and inheritance in Senegal (*Gender, Place & Culture*) and Ghana (*Geoforum*). She is an editorial board member of the journals, *Gender, Place & Culture* and *Social & Cultural Geography*.

Dr. Ellen E. Foley is associate professor in the Department of International Development, Community, and Environment (IDCE) at Clark University. She is a medical anthropologist who focuses on sexual and reproductive health. Her research addresses the social production of disease and health disparities, including how place, race, age, class, and gender shape vulnerability to disease and access to care. Her primary field site is francophone West Africa, with a focus on three areas: the shifting dynamics of urban sexual culture; the global and regional politics of sexual and reproductive health; and the influence of space and place on urban health.

Juliana Friend is PhD candidate in anthropology at the University of California, Berkeley. Focusing on digital media and sexuality in West Africa, her research has been supported by the Wenner-Gren Foundation and the Social Science Research Council (SSRC). She is also the founder of www.many-to-many.net, an experimental ethnographic archive that aims to promote reflection on the ethics and politics of digital circulation in archival practice.

Dr. Cheikh Ibrahima Niang studied at Cheikh Anta Diop University, Dakar, Senegal, where he currently teaches social science research methods and medical and social anthropology. He obtained a bachelor's degree in philosophy before earning two master's degrees, respectively in anthropology and in environmental sciences. Then, he completed a doctoral thesis (Doctorat de 3ème cycle) in environmental sciences and a Doctorat d'Etat es-Lettres in sociology. He benefited from a Fulbright scholarship (1991–1992) to do training in the United States. His main works were primarily on sexuality, LGBT studies, homophobia, gender, and gender-based violence. He is known as advocating for the protection of sexual diversities and human rights. He has also conducted studies in several countries in West and Central Africa on social aspects of HIV/AIDS, youth and adolescent reproductive health, child and maternal health, and non-communicable diseases. During the last Ebola outbreak in West Africa, he pointed out the health crisis as a postcolonial epidemic. Recently, he was involved in the response to Ebola in the north of Kivu (DRC) and analyzed the situation as a crisis of multilateral responses, a deficit of global empathy, and a continuation of women's and communities' marginalization.

Beth D. Packer is PhD candidate in sociology at the École Des Hautes Études en Sciences Sociales in the Department of Geography, Society and Development and was a visiting graduate student researcher at the University of California Berkeley from 2013 to 2017. Beth's research explores the articulation of gender, Islam, and sexuality in urban Senegal through the lens of women's soccer as a site of transformational politics. She is the author of the essay, "Breaking the Rules: Politics, Piety and Resistance in Senegalese Women's Soccer," published in Hager Ben Driss and Meryem Sellami's book, *Women, Violence, and Resistance* (2017).

Dr. Amy Porter is senior program manager at Social Impact, where she leads evaluations of international development projects related to education policy, school-to-work transitions, youth leadership, and other topics. Amy received her doctorate in educational policy studies from the University of Wisconsin, Madison. Her dissertation examined contemporary understandings of gender and entrepreneurship and included research conducted over two years in Dakar, Senegal.

Dr. Kadidia Sy is part-time instructor of English at Georgia State University Perimeter College and a freelance writer. After her master's degree, earned at the University of Saint-Louis in Senegal, Dr. Sy received a Fulbright Scholar grant to pursue doctoral studies at Georgia State University in Atlanta. She was awarded a PhD in English in 2008. Her research interests are gender studies and the African Diaspora literature and culture. She is the author of *Women's Relationships: Female Friendship in Toni Morrison's* Sula and Love, *Mariama Ba's* So Long a Letter *and Sefi Atta's* Everything Good Will Come (2009).

Susan Telingator is a doctoral student in the School for Global Inclusion and Social Development at the University of Massachusetts, Boston. Previously, she spent more than thirty years as a writer, editor, journalist, and gender specialist in international development. Most recently, she lived and worked for six years in Dakar, Senegal, for USAID, UNICEF, and the TrustAfrica Foundation. She was also a Peace Corps volunteer in Namibia, focusing on girls' education in the rural north. She received a double master's degree in international relations and public service at DePaul University and a bachelor's degree at Barnard College, Columbia University.

Dr. Sindiso Mnisi Weeks is assistant professor of public policy of excluded populations, in the School for Global Inclusion and Social Development at the University of Massachusetts Boston, and adjunct associate professor in the Department of Public Law at the University of Cape Town (UCT), where she was previously a senior researcher in the Rural Women's Action Research Programme, combining research, advocacy and policy work on women, property, governance and participation under customary law and the South African Constitution. Dr. Mnisi Weeks received her DPhil in law from the University of Oxford, where she was a Rhodes Scholar based at the Centre for Socio-Legal Studies. Prior to Oxford, she clerked for then Deputy Chief Justice of the Constitutional Court of South Africa, Dikgang Moseneke. She is the author of *Access to Justice and Human Security: Cultural Contradictions in Rural South Africa* (2018) and co-author of *African Customary Law in South Africa: Post-Apartheid and Living Law Perspectives* (2015).

www.ingramcontent.com/pod-product-compliance
Lightning Source LLC
Chambersburg PA
CBHW051254200926
51612CB00001B/38
* 9 7 8 1 7 9 3 6 0 1 1 2 4 *

Table of Contents

Preface

This book is the result of a year-long ethnographic exploration of a modern scientific laboratory in which rats and mice are utilised as experimental animals by a range of scientific researchers, including the virologists, immunologists, and neuroscientists who participated in my study. In my ethnographic examination of the laboratory, I took for analysis the locations of mouse and rat animals in polar positions; as 'animals' to the humans in the lab, for instance, and the ways in which these animals were equally located as ambiguous and ambivalent sites of slippage and indistinction between many polar categories. The capacity of rodent research animals to simultaneously embody more than one meaning as well as to embody competing or opposed meanings in the laboratory presents the possibility that researchers and rodents may not simply relate to one another from either side of the 'Great Divide' that separates humans from animals, and which would see humans operate on prone mice and rats in an entirely hierarchical arrangement of differently constituted speci-al (i.e., of species) bodies. I found other possibilities for relating in the laboratory, many of which crossed the Great

Divide that, in Cartesian terms, has separated humans and animals from one another—a separation that has been emphasised in many academic and popular understandings of laboratory spaces.

I have described many of these possibilities in terms of kinship, as many of the scientists in this study also did. The term occurs in the book not only as an analytic frame I utilise to describe relatedness, but it also appeared in the words of scientists, who invoked it to describe the qualities and characteristics of their relationships with rodent research animals.

When I invoke the term 'kinship' to describe the relationships I found operating across the human-animal divide, I speak to a number of different registers of relatedness that persisted between humans and animals in the laboratory. These registers speak to the biological relatedness of rats and mice to humans that makes animal research valid and valuable in the lab. They also recognise the simultaneous giveness of animality and humanity that results in intercommunicative exchanges between humans and animals in the lab, to the extent that some researchers said they felt they could speak 'fluent rat'. In addition, they recognise the speci-al differences that resulted in the provision of care to laboratory animals through the relations of what, following Haraway (2008), I have called 'mundane' kinship. This is a kind of kinship that is based on the recognition of the specifics of specie membership and the ways in which other speci-al being might be understood to be equally important as human being. Each of these kinships were recognised as operational by the scientists in the laboratory where I undertook my ethnographic study, and they necessitated the crossing of the Great Divide between humans and animals that is often assumed to be rigidly in place in the laboratory. Such crossings were regarded by the scientists in this study as critical to the production of 'good science'.

In the text that follows, then, I question key assumptions that have been made about the ways in which animals are located in the laboratory—firmly on one side of the hierarchically arrayed human-animal divide. Although rodent research animals did occupy polar positions in the laboratory context, these were not the only positions they inhabited. They also inhabited ambiguous positions that gave rise to a series of relationships and kinships between rodents and research scientists that were regarded by the latter as being key to the production of good science. I equally speak back, on the basis of rich ethnographic data, to the assumptions that are frequently made in academic work and in public opinion about the ways in which relatedness between researchers and laboratory animals does not—and cannot—occur in the laboratory context. This is a task that entails speculating on the grip of instrumental reason on modern laboratories and whether or not they are immune to contemporary ideas about nature and animals—ideas to which they instrumentally contribute.

Acknowledgments

I am grateful to many people for their contributions to the shape of this book, and I take the opportunity here to offer them my sincere thanks.

As always, I offer my thanks to everyone at Cambria Press. This is my third book with Cambria; in the production of each book, I have been offered excellent editing, encouragement, and assistance in a range of ways. I am very grateful.

I want to thank my anthropology colleagues, located in different institutions across the country, for their generous input. Megan Warin and Rod Lucas from the University of Adelaide read early drafts and made helpful, insightful comments that pushed and refined my thinking. Colleagues at the University of Melbourne, particularly Mary Patterson, gave helpful feedback on spoken, seminar versions of the work. I am very grateful to all of my colleagues at the Australian National University, my home institution, who gave me such positive feedback during seminar presentations of this work and who frequently asked after its development while I was penning it. Likewise, I offer my thanks to the animal studies scholars who attended the presentation of this work at the Animal Movements, Moving Animals conference held at the University of Uppsala, Sweden, during 2010. I am particularly grateful to Tora Holmberg and Jacob Bull, who gave detailed and thoughtful feedback on particular elements of my paper. Thank you for being generous with your time and considered in your suggestions.

I also want to make special mention of those people who read drafts of the work to ensure its clarity and its appeal to an audience beyond an anthropological readership. In this regard, I thank Dianne for the excellence of her editing and Don for his patience and honesty. I also want to thank Keaka for sharing with me his impressive knowledge of the presence of rats and mice in materials of popular culture—film, television, and books.

I also offer my sincere thanks to the research scientists who granted me access to their laboratories and allowed me to question them closely about their practices, relationships, and engagements with laboratory animals. I hope the book does justice to the richness of their offerings. Access to the laboratories would not have been possible without the help of Simon Bain, who took an early interest in my research and took it upon himself to connect me with the network of scientists in which he was embedded. I thank him for making my task easier and for smoothing the path into a world I was unfamiliar with and am the richer for having visited.

Finally, I want to acknowledge the rats and mice. I do not speak rat or mouse, as some of my informants did, and so I did not 'talk' with them in the ways that many of the research scientists who were interviewed for this book did. Therefore, I cannot thank them for their conversations. But I—as do all humans—owe them a debt of gratitude for standing in for humans, for bearing humans' pain, and for dying in humans' stead. The scientists in this study did not take them for granted, and I hope this book reveals the depth of their care for these animals to whom all people owe something.

FOR THE LOVE OF LAB RATS

Chapter 1

An Introduction to Polarity, Ambiguity, and Kinship

This book is concerned with exploring rodent-human relationships, particularly in the modern scientific research laboratory. I am particularly interested in the ways in which mice and rats are involved in the expression of opposites and the ways in which they also express vagueness, uncertainty, and the mixing or reconciliation of meanings—or, in other words, the ways in which they are expressive of polarities, ambiguities, and ambivalences. Rats and mice occupy opposing reaches of people's imaginations in the West. Although they are similar to humans in terms of their sociality, their habits of domestic occupation and food consumption, and in that they serve as homologies for humans' minds and genes in laboratory settings, they are also feared, demonised, and separated from people as the destroyers of human bodies and of material and technological worlds. Both rats and mice occur simultaneously in Western contexts as house pests and house pets; they are the filthy bearers of diseases that are harmful to people and, when they are located in the modern research laboratory, they occupy positions as weapons in the fight against human diseases.

Their capacity to occur simultaneously in more than one category of meaning means that mice and rats not only occur at the polar reaches of people's imaginations, but they can also be the loci of slippages and indistinction between many polar categories. Polarity, ambiguity, and ambivalence set up a number of possibilities for rat/mouse-human relations generally and also mark the relationships between scientists and rodent research animals that occur within the confines of the research laboratory, where they embody directly opposing positions and meanings, *and* present simultaneous and conflicting meanings, which are sometimes reconciled. This is an ethnographically based examination of some of the possibilities that arise for rodent-human relationships in the context of the modern scientific research laboratory.

My ethnographic examination of polarity, ambiguity, and ambivalence stands in stark contrast to recent examinations of rodent-human relationships in the context of the modern laboratory. Acampora, for example, in his recent book-length treatment of the topic, *Corporal Compassion* (2006), insisted that humans and animals occupy fixed, polar positions relative to each other in the modern research laboratory; his book calls for the radicalisation of such relations. In Acampora's estimation, the detached scientific practitioner operates from her position on the powerful human side of the Great Divide while the animal suffers her pursuit of data in its position as wholly subjected to scientific inquiry.

Where Acampora recognised the possibilities for kinship and relatedness between human and nonhuman animals in other contexts outside the lab, he characterised the domain of science as one in which these possibilities do not emerge; indeed, his book is offered as an antidote to this situation. Acampora is an accomplished theoretician in the area of human-animal relatedness and is most adept in his use of phenomenological works to elucidate the area of animal-human relatedness. However, his willingness to treat science that is concerned with animal research as a bounded domain in which animal-human relatedness does not operate is problematic. His equal willingness to suggest that scientists are not aware of and do not act upon the anti-Cartesian understandings of animals that have been explored in other disciplines is also problematic, at least in respect to the ethnographic exploration I made of laboratories that undertake animal research. As I will suggest throughout this book, practice in the laboratory context I explored did not pivot on detachment, even when rodent research animals were being regarded in the laboratory as units of analytic research equipment. I here explore the variety of attachments that connected rodent research animals with scientific investigators in different ways, which were critical to the practice of science—and, as the informants in my study insisted—to the practice of good science.

Particular relationships between rodent research animals and scientists arose out of the polar, ambiguous, and ambivalent locations of rats and mice in the context of a suite of modern research laboratories in which I undertook ethnographic research over a period of 1 year. The research participants included 31 scientists—immunologists, virologists, and neuroscientists—who were working with either rats or mice. In this book, I examine the ways in which mice and rats occupied polar positions as both 'animals' compared to the humans in the lab and as inanimate equipment, in contrast to the animate status of the humans therein. I also examine the ways in which rats and mice occupy ambiguous and ambivalent positions between the polar opposites of humanity and animality and between disposable laboratory equipment and animate beings capable of making relationships with people in the laboratory. Mice and rats were understood by scientists to have more than one meaning, and they simultaneously represented opposed and conflicting characteristics and values. The movement of research animals across the divides that have separated scientist investigators and research animals as Baconian dominators and research equipment, respectively (see Acampora, 2006), might well give one cause to reflect about what one thinks one knows about scientists and animals and how they relate to and with one another within the scientific coordinates of the modern research laboratory.

The speci-al and mammalian qualities of rat and mouse research animals were drawn out by the scientists in this study to indicate and describe both movements across animal-human and animate-inanimate divides and situations in which research animals remained firmly on one side or the other of a division. The invocation of these terms and the positions they referenced had particular consequences for the research animals, the scientists, and scientific practice.

I use the language of kinship to examine the ambiguities, ambivalences, and polarities I found in operation in the laboratory. As Latour (2004), Haraway (1997), and S. Franklin (2001) have each suggested, the strict (modernist) divide has been challenged by biotechnology. It can be useful to employ the language of kinship to explore the ways in which modernist divisions between humans and animals have been destabilised by biotechnology and its practices. In the examination I make of laboratory-based human-animal relationships, I seek to examine the fruits of such destabilisation. Anthropologists have, at least to some extent, reconsidered the scope for the study of kinship in post-Schneiderian terms (see, for example, Feeley-Harnik, 2001). Although for the most part these revisitations make comparisons between humans and animals on the basis of familial relationships, I seek to do something slightly different when I make recourse to kinship. Specifically, I use it first to demonstrate the ways in which animals and humans are considered to be biologically and genetically related to one another, which effects a crossing of the human-animal divide in the laboratory. Second, I use it to speak to a fleshy and indistinctive relatedness that rodent research animals and human scientists made with one another in their interactions in the laboratory space.

Between Human and Animal

I first apply the language of kinship (as, indeed, the scientists in this study did) to examine the location of rats and mice in relation to the poles of humanity and animality. I explore the ways in which the scientists in this study linked humans and rat and mouse research animals in terms of their shared biological and genetic kinship. Shared kinship in these terms links humans and animals as like beings and diminishes their speci-al differences, constituting a crossing of the human-animal and speci-al borders that is crucial to the practice of science dealing with the ways in which animals can contribute to human health. Because they are included in the laboratory context on the basis of their mammalian similarity with humans and because their bodies are operated upon in the stead of human bodies to create knowledge that is applicable to human bodies, rats and mice appear in the laboratory as human homologues—human biokin (i.e., mice and rats and humans can be regarded as closely related at the level of their biology) and genekin (i.e, scientists considered rats and mice and people to be closely considered in terms of gene homology). Humans and animals are blurred in the establishment of pan-mammalian genes and biological collinearity in the lab, but the establishment of animals and humans as genekin and biokin produces another division, between animate beings and inanimate equipment.

Speci-al ratness and mouseness are subsumed under the generic position of mammalian membership and genetic and biological relatedness to diminish the human-animal division as well as to yield a hierarchy of bodies wherein one mammalian embodiment is in the service of another. The subsumption of speci-ality and the marking of devalued mammalian being is accomplished in the making of the analytic animal, in which all elements of speci-ality are removed from the way the animal is understood in the laboratory. As much as mammalian membership is the bridge by which rodents and humans are connected (in their similar bodies, their equivalent DNA structures, their gene similarity, and the ease with which rodents might be engrafted with human substance to yield humanised animals), it is equally the ground upon which rodents' difference from humans is hierarchically presented. Acampora (2006) argued that the location of rats and mice as nonspeci-al, purely mammalian equipment in the laboratory indicates the firm maintenance of the human-animal divide. The location of the mouse or rat in the position of mammalian equipment means that the mouse is understood not as a 'mouse' but as a mammalian biological unit—genetic equipment.

Mammalian membership not only situates rats and mice as human kin and as mammalian units of equipment, but it also qualifies them for entry into the laboratory's sacrificial economy. In this laboratory context, as would be in the case in other laboratories, 'sacrifice' assumes particular meaning; it is used specifically to reference an exchange economy of equally mammalian, but substantively unequal, human and nonhuman bodies. This ambiguity is a key ambiguity for the practice of science: The slippage and ambiguity that are created by the dual affinity/dissimilarity of rodents and persons can be controlled and made productive in the lab in the very doing of science. The biological and genetic affinity between humans and rodents allows for human-meaningful, human-applicable data to be gathered, and the dissimilarity between rodents and humans allows rodent bodies to be regarded as productive and fully dispensable equipment. This crucial ambiguity in the practice of science—the subject of my third chapter—is manipulated to generate data that are highly relevant to the human body without injurious consequences for the human body.

FLESHY AND INDISTINCTIVE KINSHIPS

Recognising only the polar locations in the lab, Acampora (2006), in an invocation of Heideggerian language, claimed that rodent animals in the lab are not only physically restrained but are also ontologically reduced to the status of ready-to-hand tools, objects for investigation and examination. In the event that a research animal presents itself as unsatisfactory for a particular scientific use, it might be regarded as faulty equipment. I think it is very difficult to decide that the ontological status of the rat is the same as that of other, inanimate laboratory equipment. In my study, the scientists did regard animals as equipment, but this was not a fixed position of rodent research animals for the scientific practitioners in the laboratory. Instead, rodent research animals were ambiguously positioned between research equipment and beings with which scientists could and did make relationships that were founded on interpeci-al transivity. I argue herein that rat and mouse research animals very often occupy rather more ambiguous positions in the laboratory than Acampora's assessment permits. Just as they often occupy polar positions, rat and mouse research animals very often occupy ambiguous positions in the laboratory, and they often slip across the apparently firm boundaries that separate apparently irreconcilable domains, including the boundary between the detached Baconian God-scientists[1] of Acampora's imagination.

I have hinted so far at the ways in which it is critical for scientists who use rats and mice to make insights into the human body to establish relatedness across the human/animal border. The scientists in this study recognised that they shared other registers of relatedness with rodent research animals that did not derive from biological kinship or genetic connections. The scientific researchers reported a variety of interspecies communications and relations between themselves and their research animals, particularly rats. As a result, rats came to be ambiguously located between their place in the laboratory as research animals—live equipment—and as animals which could involve themselves with scientists in interspecies communication. This interspecies communication manifested in the form of communicative exchanges between rodent animal models and the scientists who were working with them. For example, the scientists drew on their abilities to 'speak fluent rat'. Similarly, the rodents would make themselves understandable to the scientists when they 'refused' contact with them, such as when they made their tails unavailable to a scientist's grasp when she was trying to pick them up in the correct way. They also 'understood' what particular approaches on the part of a scientist meant and 'responded' to the scientist's communications, such as when they jumped into buckets because a scientist 'asked them to'.

In the rodents' bucket-jumping, tail-refusing responses to people as well as in the ways in which people who are fluent in rodent in the lab 'ask for' rats and mice to bucket-jump or interpret what rats mean by refusing their tails to a human who is grasping for them, rats and people appear to be communicative, expressive, understandable, understood, and reponse-able (i.e., able to produce a response). Moreover, this communicative capacity crosses the Great Divide that appears in the laboratory to locate research animals and humans on the opposite sides of an ostensibly thick ontological divide. I argue in this book that a variety of kinship persists in the thick of interspecies communication, where it is possible for scientists to 'speak fluent rat' and for rats to communicate in terms that are readily understandable to humans. In the thickness of the interaction that flows across human/animal and speci-al borders persists a relatedness that has been of interest to phenomenologists such as Merleau-Ponty (1963, 1964, 1968, 1994), whose insights I use in order to analyse the fleshy register of relatedness I encountered in the lab. As Merleau-Ponty observed in his 1964 work, a fleshy unspecificity (i.e., the way in which bodies in general 'share a world') already persists between humans and animals in the sense that the world is shared among and generally available to the species, despite their evident differences, in the weight of their bodies and the fleshiness of their existence. Merleau-Ponty (1994) described this fleshy sharing of the world as 'strange kinship'. In such a kinship persists a 'we'—not the 'double we' that Despret (2008, p. 123) despaired over that separates animals from humans, but a unitary one, one that roots fleshy experience in a singular and universal common ground and posits animals and humans as 'variants' of the same sensible-sensing corporeality as humans.

I also turn to some ostensibly unlikely sources to explore this register of kinship, such as Agamben's *The Open* of 2002. In *The Open*, Agamben hinted—perhaps not intentionally (see Calarco, 2008)—at the undoing of the Great Divide between humans and animals when he suggested that the zone of indistinction of his original conception of bare life (1998) might be reconceptualised as a zone of possibility, within which the relations between humans and animals might be reworked. In a zone where humans and animals become biopolitically and discursively indistinct from one another, there might persist a kinship of indistinction, born not of the biological likeness of bodies but rather in the persistence of ambiguous unspecificity (i.e., not in a species category, moreover, not in hierarchical relation to one another) where, as Haraway (2008) suggested, 'no one gets to be Man' (p. 82). These fleshy and indistinctive registers of kinship were also recognised by the scientists in this study, and they served to connect the scientists with those rodent research animals which would otherwise be regarded as research equipment from which the scientific researcher might be completely detached.

Mundane Kinship, Caring, and Killing

I also invoke the language of kinship to explore the ways in which rodent research animals were included in the laboratory as equipment which would be dispensed with at the end of their research lives and as speci-al animals which required care. In this examination, I make recourse to the idea of mundane kinship, a kinship that is born in the attendance to the minutiae of specifically speci-al lives, which are valued not in hierarchical terms against human lives but rather in and on their own speci-al terms. In cases of both killing and caring, rodent research animals emerged as particularly speci-al animals. Many of those scholars who have analysed the situatedness of laboratory rodents in these terms, such as Reinert (2007), have taken the equipment status and high necroavailability (i.e., availablity for killing) of laboratory animals as evidence of the worst kind of humanist scientific practice and as evidence of the maintenance of the human-animal divide in the laboratory.

In the laboratory context I examined, it was certainly the case that rats and mice were regarded as equipment, and they were certainly destined for death and, in some cases, suffering. Even though they were involved in the laboratory in these terms, the animals were cared for. This caring was offered to the rats and mice out of a deep and nuanced understanding of what mice and rats like; how they responded better or worse to particular accommodations; how they liked to be touched, picked up, and engaged with; and what things they liked to eat and play with. Mice and rats emerged as mouse animals and rat animals; their generalised status as mammalian units of equipment was, in the thick of caring, diminished. This speci-al caring indicated that although the rats and mice would certainly die, they were not made 'killable', as Haraway has defined.

Haraway also deployed the term 'killable' in her *When Species Meet* (2008). When she did, she used it to refer to the way in which entire species (e.g., meat or research animals) have been relegated to a category in which they may be unceremoniously and even disrespectfully killed. This is a consequence of the fantasy of human exceptionalism. Without advocating for the undoing of the relationships of 'use' (i.e., for meat or for research) in which humans and animals are entailed, and without arguing for the fundamental wrongness of killing (as some feminists, animal rights activists, and vegans do; see also J. Franklin, 2007), Haraway argued that animals should not be made killable—that they should instead be killed with responsibility and respect. Such a demand neither undermines the relations of use nor renders killing undoable; indeed, Haraway argued that species that are currently kept for the express purpose of food would become extinct if killing were disallowed. In this way, she suggested, the relationships of use, and animals themselves, flourish.

I have come at unkillability in my examination of the practices of care that scientists do relationally to (and for) animals in the laboratory. Therein I show that animals are not rendered killable in the sense that they do not live a 'bare life'. Under Agamben's original conceptualisation of bare life, as he described it in his *Homo Sacer* (1998), a human being is given the status of the living dead—it is biologically living but does not have human rights. Lacking these, it cannot be sacrificed, it is necroavailable (to the state), and can be killed without the charge of murder being brought. Many theoreticians of animal rights (including Singer, 1975) have argued that animals that are located within the industrial coordinates of the slaughterhouse or the scientific coordinates of the laboratory can be understood as living a bare life. Although Singer's veal calf certainly fits this bill, I am not sure that lab rats and mice fit it so snugly. They would fit well if there were no substantive difference between the lives of all of the animals that are lived under conditions of certain death (as battery chickens, veal calves, and laboratory rats and mice all indubitably do). But it is my view that laboratory rodents, though they are certainly subject to death as a condition of their lives in the laboratory, do not live a life in which they are made killable or in which they are wholly reduced to the conditions of bare life.

What I mean to suggest is that there is a substantive difference between intending to kill an animal and treating that animal during its life as killable. It is tempting to use the example of the life of a battery hen against that of a free-range bird to get an idea of the difference: Each will die within the industrial coordinates of meat or egg production, but only the former will live a bare life and be treated accordingly—as killable. But, the example itself brings its own complications. In Australia, real questions have begun to emerge about what 'free-range' really means and if consumers can be assured that the eggs or meat they are purchasing really comes to them after the bird has lived well. The consumer affairs reporter for a major Australian metropolitan daily newspaper *The Sydney Morning Herald*, Kelly Burke, reported in 2009 that the supermarket giant retailer Woolworths had recorded a significant increase in consumer demand for both free-range eggs and free-range chicken meat. In good faith, consumers assume they are purchasing the meat and egg products of birds which have had access to open spaces and the opportunity to graze and predate on insects. However, Burke broke the story in the *Sydney Morning Herald* about the discrepancy between the amount of free-range eggs that were produced in Australia and the amount that supermarket retailers were selling—many more were being sold than it was possible for the small amount of accredited free-range producers to place into the market. This led Burke to detail in the *Herald* the differences between the categories of free-range, which are not generally known to consumers, who are presented with carton images of freely grazing, unrestrained birds. The 'cage' classification pertains to shed-housed birds with a minimum of 550 square centimetres per bird, and 'barn' describes birds who are also wholly contained indoors, with 14 birds per square meter (1,500 per hectare). 'Free-range' has two classifications within it. In the first, the only difference from the 'barn' category is that the birds have access to an outdoor area (which may not always be available to them). In the second—which is endorsed by the Free Range Egg and Poultry Association of Australia (FREPAA), a group that producers can join voluntarily in order to receive its endorsement when its conditions are met—only 750 birds are permitted per hectare, birds have unrestricted access to the outdoors during daylight hours, and beak trimming, which is present in all other classifications, is prohibited, because the birds are not so crowded that cannibalism and competitive behaviour will cause deaths in the flock (Burke, 2009). In Australia, clearly not all poultry products that claim to be free-range can be safely assumed to have come from birds that have been raised outside the industrial coordinates that give rise to bare life. Equally clearly, the term 'free-range' has value in the marketplace that departs from the value that FREPAA accords to the life of the chicken.[2]

Here emerge values of free-range that speak to both the life of the bird and the financial gain that is extracted by producers and retailers from appearing to speak to and privilege the valuing of the bird's life. It appears that it is easier to kill animals when one can be assured that one has recognised their right to live and be according to their natures—chickens, cows, pigs, and rats. Evidently, it is also easier for producers to kill on people's behalf when the value of life coincides with the monetary value that can be drawn from such a product. In this book, and particularly in chapter 5, I examine the practices of care that I saw appearing in the lab and the values that are given to them. These included the value that was accorded to the good rat or mouse life, the value such a life offers to the practice of 'good science' in terms of the validity of data and the reliability of results, and the value that scientists might draw from appearing to be good, responsible killers.

In attending to these values and ways of valuing, calculi emerge. In the practices of caring that persisted in the recognition of mundane kinship, a calculus of caring became evident. Even in the shadow of the calculus of death that persists in the laboratory, wherein mice and rats are valued in hierarchical relation to humans and can be killed to benefit them, rats and mice yet presented to science a cost for their sacrifice—a cost that was recognised and met in the laboratory by the provision of speci-ally specific caring regimes in the relations of mundane kinship.

If human-animal relationships are contingent upon the practices in laboratory labour, the relationships I found therein are those that slip across or underneath the hierarchically arranged human-animal divide that would insist on Baconian scientist operators and entirely subject animals from which the scientists are wholly detached. I think it is more complicated than that, and that it is because of the movements that scientists and research animals make relationally to one another and across the Great Divide.

Kinship

In my attention to kinship, I raise and, by recourse to ethnographic data, in some respects respond to, questions about the bounds of kinship itself. The idea of biological animal kin, for instance, may be difficult to reconcile with an essentially humanist anthropological foundation of biological relatedness, because anthropology has not yet found a way of effectively speaking to the flows across the human-animal divide—at least, not in the West. What is perhaps more difficult to think about within the current anthropological kinship parameters is another register of kinship with laboratory animals—a fleshy one that is made outside the parameters of biological relatedness, which the scientists in my study recognised. In ways that suggested that scientists themselves recognise and act upon the idea that animals cannot be excluded from kinship and that the privileging of shared biogenetic substance is not the only way to define relatedness (something I take up for investigation throughout this book), biological and nonbiological registers of kinship emerge from science to trouble the present, humanist, categories of kinship.

In anthropological circles, kinship has been recently reexamined, with interesting results and outcomes which have been applied to new contexts as well as to reflections upon what have appeared to be solid disciplinary foundations. For instance, S. Franklin and McKinnon (2001) and Carsten (2000) argued that renewed anthropological interest in kinship often begins with the figure of a superseded 'nature.' Strong's (2001) reflections on Judith Butler's contribution to reworking kinship gives a present state of play and then asks how far more elastic conceptualizations of kinship can stretch and what they might stretch to cover. Strong considered new contexts and challenges for kinship studies that present the opportunity to put terms such as 'kinship' and 'nature' under erasure (i.e., to erase the current assumptions about these terms) but he concluded that these very opportunities seem to reassert their force. Finkler (2000) wrote, in the context of genetic testing and risk counselling, that 'people are compelled to recognize consanguinity even when in the lived world they define family by a sense of sameness that may be grounded in friendship or sharing of affect and interest rather than in genes' (p. 238). Drawing on this, Strong (2001) argued compellingly that people should examine just how much ground has actually been covered in this regard. Strong noted in particular these new contexts and the challenges they present to kinship studies:

> Schneider's critique of early- to mid-twentieth century kinship studies as exporting Euro-American notions of natural relatedness to cultures that divide up the world differently appears to have presaged the dissolution *within* Euro-American culture of the foundational status of 'nature' as the ground on which human enterprise is both reflected and constructed. Thus, Marilyn Strathern's creative dialogue with Schneider in *After Nature* (1992a) is something like a key text for the new studies. 'Nature' now seems, in an often-quoted phrase, 'enterprised-up' (Strathern 1992b), a notion that Paul Rabinow captures in the term 'biosociality' (Rabinow 1992). This means two things: it will not be obvious what 'kinship' is, for it will vary contextually, and, for that reason, there can probably be no universal theory of it. The new kinship studies apparently reflect this uncertainty and provisional particularity. Indeed, although all of them still deploy the term 'kinship,' they differently modify it. Kinship is now 'postmodern' (Finkler 2000) or 'nonmodern' (Carsten 2000:31—after Latour). Is it also 'flexible' (Martin 1994)? (pp. 403–404)

In this book, I turn to insights made by Haraway to begin to think through just how flexible kinship can be in the context of the laboratory. The ways in which Haraway asked questions about nature are helpful in this endeavour. In her *Simians, Cyborgs and Women* (1991), Haraway's chapter 'A Cyborg Manifesto: Science, Technology, and Socialist-Feminism in the Late Twentieth Century' appears. In it, Haraway created 'an ironic political myth' (p. 149) which combines postmodernism with socialist feminism. The cyborg, 'a cybernetic organism, a hybrid of machine and organism, a creature of social reality as well as a creature of fiction' (p. 149), undergirds this myth. Haraway said of this metaphor for the postmodernist, this political play of identity, this lived reality of new technology, 'I am making an argument for the cyborg as a fiction mapping our social and bodily reality and as an imaginative resource suggesting some very fruitful couplings' (p. 150). Her intention was to unsettle her readers; she claimed, 'acknowledging the agency of the world in knowledge makes room for some unsettling possibilities … [and it] makes room for surprises and ironies at the heart of all knowledge production' (p. 199). This means that the cyborg, of course, thoroughly questions what is 'natural', for in Haraway's paradigm, nature melds with technology and muddles the ostensibly firm borders between them.

Although Haraway's intention was to point to the ambiguity that undoes long-standing nature-culture binaries, she also pointed to the ways in which these might be called into question prior to the age of the cyborg. She specifically called into question those 'comfortable old hierarchical dominations' by contrasting some of these 'comfortable' things against 'scary new networks' (p. 161). One assumes organisms, physiology, and sex to be natural because they are embedded so thoroughly into the Western cultural consciousness. Things such as biotic components, communications engineering, and genetic engineering cannot be coded as natural in such a consciousness, but the fact that they cannot calls into question the naturalness of those comfortable categories of organisms, physiology, and sex. Such comfortable categories cannot be 'returned to':

> [The] objects on the right-hand side ['biotic component', 'communications engineering', and 'genetic engineering'] cannot be coded as 'natural', a realization which subverts naturalistic coding for the left-hand side as well. People cannot go back ideologically or materially. It's not just that 'god' is dead; so is the 'goddess'. (p. 162)

The 'goddess' is dead, too, because Haraway's insight here is a critique of the false organic self which some radical feminists use as a basis for affinity and identity. Feminists cannot use an imagined organic ontology as a point of politics because there simply is no such 'natural' self.

The cyborg has important implications for kinship and the ways people think about and conduct it, and it has particularly significant implications for human-animal kinship. Haraway detailed three major boundary breakdowns in the formation of the cyborg, including those between an organism and a machine (i.e., those between the human and the pacemaker or the dialysis machine) and those between organic matter and inorganic matter (i.e., the rise of 'ethereal machines', such as the tiny chip, which can carry an almost infinite amount of information and is more about consciousness than it is about grinding gears and heavy machinery). But the first boundary deconstruction she turned her attention to is the one between humans and animals. She noted that

> biological and evolutionary theory over the past two centuries have simultaneously produced modern organisms as objects of knowledge and reduced the line between humans and animals to a faint trace re-etched in ideological struggle or professional disputes between life and social science. (p. 152)

And, the development of transgenic organisms of course calls the whole idea of the genetic integrity of the single organism thoroughly into question. Haraway used her cyborg to represent 'lived social and bodily realities in which people are not afraid of their joint kinship with animals and machines, not afraid of permanently partial identities and contradictory standpoints' (p. 154). Such a view of kinship is not based on descent or relatedness by blood, and it is not limited to the world of humans; it is more encompassing of the ways in which relatedness is made and experienced in a more-than-human world.

Butler (2000) asked how flexible kinship can be, too, by looking into the ways in which incest taboos have been conceptualised in anthropology. Kinship has been reckoned in ways that are outside of the generational, too; Butler, for example, in her *Antigone's Claim* (2000), reconceptualised the incest taboo in relation to kinship and opened up the concept to cultural change. Such a view is not based primarily on generation, descent, and shared DNA but instead in repeated proclamations of kinship through actions, gestures, claims, and words. I add to this insight that it is equally present in a constant unfolding of gestural interplay. I turn to examine this way of seeing kinship by making recourse to the insights Merleau-Ponty made into the relations between animals and humans. In this book, then, I examine forms of kinship that rely on biological relatedness and forms of kinship that depend on transivity and contingency between different species, which were manifested in the fleshy relationships that rodent research animals and human scientists made with one another in their interactions in the laboratory space.

Even when theoreticians point to the distance between animals and humans, the language of kinship is not absent. From Heidegger's suggestion that animals may seem like kin but in terms of world formation could not be less related to humans emerged his abyssal kinship (1998). This is a concept which (although he intentionally undermined it) he used to point to the ways in which humans and animals (only) appear to be related to one another, as kin:

> Living creatures are as they are without standing outside of their being as such and within the truth of being, preserving in such standing the essential nature of their being. Of all the beings that are, presumably the most difficult to think about are living creatures, because on the one hand they are in a certain way most closely akin to us, and on the other they are at the same time separated from our ek-sistent essence by an abyss. (p. 248)

It was against this abyssal kinship that Merleau-Ponty (1994) argued that the 'thickness' of flesh, which constitutes and is constituted by the world people share, ensures kin-like relations. The differences in style of encountering and engaging with the world (e.g., rat style, mouse style, human style) distinguish our different experiences. Flesh makes communication possible because it is reversible, in that all beings are sensing and sensible—this enables intercorporeal being and founds transivity between bodies, including between animal and human bodies.

This kinship erases neither difference nor similarity and makes animals and people neither identical nor separate; for Merleau-Ponty, animals and people are at once strangers and kin (see Oliver, 2007, p. 18). Alongside this fleshy kinship persists a mundane kinship, which is evident in the relations of caring in the laboratory. Mundane kinship, in Haraway's (2008) language, is a kind of kinship that is forged in the recognition of speci-al difference and made evident in the care that is provided to species in the laboratory. It is based in nonanthropomorphic respect for animals and an attendance to the smallest details that make up specifically speci-al lives—this is a kinship that is forged between different species and arrayed in, at least in some ways, a nonhierarchical pattern.

Though I do attend to the kinship that manifests between humans and research animals in terms of substantive biogenetic relatedness, kinship is equally to be found in the way it is effectively lived in daily activity, and it is this 'livedness' (i.e., the act of living an experience that is largely unreflected upon) that also blurs those categorical divides between human and nonhuman in the laboratory setting. I look in this book at the everyday 'livedness' with animals that occurs in the lab as well as at the blurriness of and slippages across the divide that is ostensibly upheld in popular understandings of science involving animal subjects but not nearly so much in the living. How this 'living' is done in the future, within and between the categories of human and animal being, may be usefully speculated upon by turning, as I do in chapter 4 of this book, to the ways in which Agamben conceived of the world on the last day, in the messianic banquet of the righteous on the last day. Perhaps one will not have to wait quite so long as the end of the world for animals and humans to slip across the boundaries that even now might not separate them so firmly as some people believe, even (or perhaps especially) in the lab.

Speci-al and Mammalian Membership

The astute reader will probably have guessed that the categories of 'mammal' and 'species' are crucial to the ways in which rodent research animals are situated in the laboratory context. Speci-al and mammalian qualities of rat and mouse research animals were drawn out by the scientists in this study to indicate and describe both movements across animal-human and animate-inanimate divides and situations in which research animals remained firmly on or returned to one side of a division. The invocation of these terms and the positions they referenced had particular consequences for the research animals, the scientists, and scientific practice.

Although yeasts, worms, and flies are all suitable models for studying the cell cycle (and some developmental processes as well), mice in particular are far superior tools for exploring the complex physiological systems (immune, endocrine, nervous, cardiovascular, skeletal, and other) that mammals share. The category of 'mammal' is critical, therefore, in the diminishment of the border that separates animals and humans in the laboratory. As mammals, rats and mice come to be recognised as being much more similar to humans than they are different, and they come to be located as humans' biological and genetic kin. It is the mammalian membership of rodent research animals, and not their speci-al classifications, that renders rats and mice useful research equipment—in this sense, the category 'mammal' is invoked to situate rats and mice in a mammalian hierarchical arrangement relative to humans.

Speci-al classifications are very often invoked in the laboratory to situate rats and mice as fundamentally different from humans—for example, when animals are entered into the laboratory's sacrificial economy at the end of their research lives, it is 'only mice' that are disposed of—and in this, the limits of human-animal, scientist-rodent kinship are revealed. Though rats and mice are sacrificed precisely because they are rats and mice and not humans, speci-al categorisations often emerged in the laboratory context to locate these animals as living animals, not mammalian units of research equipment, with which researchers could develop a mundane register of kinship. Even as the animals were cared for through attendance to their specific speci-al needs, they were equally located as mammals who would feel in their bodies that which humans would feel when it came to assumptions about and assessments of pain.

Rats and mice were both speci-al and mammal in the relations of laboratory-administered caring. Speci-al differences between humans and rodent research animals were diminished in the operation of fleshy kinship to yield the grounds upon which rats and people could communicate. Mammalian and speci-al qualities of rodent research animals were, therefore, privileged at different times, and they yielded different possibilities for the recognition of different registers of kinship and human-animal relatedness. Throughout this book, I examine the ways in which classifications of 'mammal' and 'specie' are entailed in both crossings and undergirdings of human-animal, nature-culture, animate-inanimate (or equipment), and other divisions in the laboratory context.

POLAR, AMBIGUOUS, AND AMBIVALENT RAT/MOUSE/HUMAN RELATIONSHIPS IN THE WESTERN IMAGINATION: PET AND PEST

Let me start off by saying something briefly about rodent polarity, ambiguity, and ambivalence in the broader Western context. Of course, it is not only the West that might be discussed here. Drawing on the insights of Douglas (1966) and Leach (1964), Tambiah (1969), for instance, noted the ambiguous location of rats in the Thai context:

> Creatures like the … house rat (*nuu sing*) are not placed in any major class. Villagers say that these animals are found in the house and therefore resemble *sad baan* (domestic animals) but that they are not reared by people, so they are not *sad baan*. Thus, they are penumbral to *sad baan*, with which they share one property (location) but not the other (human care). (p. 449)

It is perfectly true that rats, and to a lesser extent mice, have long borne upon their small bodies the weight of deep, enduring, bitterly hateful human antipathy in the West (see Birke, 2003, pp. 207–208). However, one need only think of the popular movie-mouse Stuart Little or go to the nearest city pet store to be made aware that revulsion is not the universal human response to rodents, even when that universe is taken to be the West and even when it is (in this ethnographic circumstance) taken to be Australia. As I discovered after numerous visits to pet stores across two Australian states, it is not unusual for little children to coo over the rats that are displayed in glass cases in city pet stores the way they do over puppies and kittens, and it is not unusual for them to make pleas to their parents to take one special individual home. It is not unusual, either, based on my observations over the last 12 months, for the parents of these pleading children to in fact agree to take home a carefully chosen individual from the glass case. Equally prominent in my observations, though, were expressions of disgust from visitors to the pet store about the presence of 'vermin' there. 'Rats and mice belong in traps', suggested one outraged visitor.

The comment I overheard in the pet store, that 'rats and mice belong in traps', was very interesting to me, primarily because I overheard it in the pet store, a place in which humans seek on many occasions to begin a close relationship with an animal.[3] Alongside the domestic elimination of rats and mice and the big business of rodent extermination persists the practice of keeping pet mice and rats, which can be taught to perch aloft a shoulder or even to recognise their own names being called. As I will show in the second chapter, the inquisitive and charming pet rat which answers its owner's summons or which takes its place in an exhibition of fancy animals is the same species that spreads fearsome disease in the dark places of the house. The little mouse, too, running around a wheel in a pet cage, is essentially the same mouse that is flung unceremoniously out of a trap, having finally been caught and dispensed with.

The dual location of rats and mice as pets and pests generates a generalised situation in which there might occur around rats and mice the simultaneous existence of opposed and conflicting attitudes (ambiguity) and/or a situation in which rats and mice embody vague or uncertain meanings (ambivalence). Both are yielded from the capacity of these animals to simultaneously occupy polar reaches of the Western imagination. This imagination can be traced back at least as far as Victorian times, when the monarch herself kept a piebald rat in a delicate gilded cage, as did the ladies of her court, at the very same time that she kept in her permanent employ the royal rat-catcher Jack Black. Black provided

Queen Victoria and the ladies of her court with their spoiled and pampered pets from stock constituted of rats he collected in the course of his extermination work.[4] The Western affection for rats and mice, then, was present in the very same historical moment as the hatred for them and the determination to eliminate them was at fever pitch, when Jack Black made a very handsome return every year for eliminating them in the thousands. This same duality persists in the outraged comments that are made in the modern pet store, wherein rats are dually locatable as 'pets' and as 'vermin' which 'belong in traps'. Further, affection and loathing were and continue to be directed towards essentially the same rat or mouse body; nothing, besides the appealing piebald colours of Queen Victoria's companion, distinguished her pet rat from the vermin she ordered eliminated from London's sewers.

OLD FOES, MODERN MICE

Vermin mice and rats are also temporally ambiguous, despite Western attempts to locate their impact on humankind firmly in the past.[5] Ellmann (2004) has argued that rats are particularly threatening to modernism because they come to 'stand for the resurgence of the undead past' (p. 60). Where, for example, Ellmann noted that Joyce's *Ulysses* rat is an 'obese grey grandfather chewing on corpses' (p. 60; Joyce, 1922), the modern rat is hardly less impactful, chewing and nibbling as it does on the cables, wires, and pipes of the contemporary world. One might have thought—mistakenly, as it turns out—that the old rat persisted only because in the past, people exercised a lesser control over the sewers, pipes, and drains, the areas below the waist of the Victorian streetscape. The location of rats and mice in these dirty places spoke both to their capacity to spread diseases and to the dirtiness of their animal sexuality, conducted as it was to the extent that plague proportions of rats resulted under the London streets upon which ladies and gentlemen promenaded in all their finery (see Edelman, 2002, pp. 5–6). Fissell (1999) noted that vermin animals, including rats and mice, also occupied other ambiguous domains in Restoration England. Although Fissell did not cast vermin as boundary problems in the way that structuralists such as Douglas (1966) did, she did argue that vermin animals are often located at the cusp of boundaries that trouble the material conditions of life. Fissell (1999) noted in particular that at this time,

> vermin threatened the always tenuous balance between ease and hardship, satiety and starvation, enough and not-enough. At the same time, they were imagined as animals who sometimes displayed a mastery of certain human forms and customs, a mastery which made humans uneasy. (p. 2)

But rats and mice also bear a much more modern menace; they have not been banished to the sewers and the drains of the past. They infiltrate people's material and technological worlds, threatening the ease with which people communicate. With their penchant for chewing, rats and mice nibble and gnaw at the cords and cables that link modern technologies, disabling modern machines and modern e-mail and telephone communication systems. And, 'vermin' mice are, of course, now material technological mice; they have penetrated the worlds of people's desks, where they sit in the midst of people's technological mastery of modern machines. Their metaphorical and actual—and often destructive—intertwinement with modern communications technologies has also meant that despite the best efforts of humans to relegate rats and mice to the past through a variety of exterminatory methods (exercised largely in the shadow of the spectre of the plague that was unfairly blamed on rats), they have kept pace with humans and undermine the advances the 'modern' species has accomplished (Ellmann, 2004). Mice and rats, as much as they are associated with the old panics of plague and disease, are equally thoroughly modern animals. As much as they are modern, they persist in the historically loaded category of 'vermin'. Whereas other animals that were once classified as such, including the heron, the kingfisher, the otter, and the osprey, have all been transferred to more positive categories (see Fissell, 1999, p. 1), humans have continued to array the animal world in such a way as to leave mice and rats where they are—as vermin. Such historical determination on the part of humans has not meant that rats have stayed put, however.

DIRTY BLACK SEWER RAT, CLEAN WHITE LAB RAT

The ambiguous location of rats and mice between the past and the present is also a characteristic of another ambiguity, which manifests in the simultaneous location of rats and mice as at once vermin and laboratory animals. As vermin, rats and mice are an old foe, the dirty, black- or grey-furred, disease-bearing animals of ancient sewers, drains, and dark places. As laboratory animals, rats and mice are the (usually) white, clean animals that are located at the forefront of the new—the modern biotechnical fight against disease. Partly by recourse to the racial connotations that are embedded in dirty, diseased blackness and clean, germ-free whiteness, science has had its work cut out for it, locating disease-bearing rats and mice at a position at the forefront of the fight against disease. Rats and mice have had to be transfigured from their status as the bearers of disease and their location right in the thick of filth to the hygienic representatives of medical progress, where they are stationed as icons of biomedicine's struggle to conquer disease. Rats and mice very often appear as sacrificial, Christlike figures in this domain; the assignation of a crown of thorns and other Christian iconography to Oncomouse, the breast cancer mouse model in Lyn Randolph's painting that graces the cover of Haraway's *Modest_Witness* (1997), indicates that only the power of Christian salvation stories, 'steeped in transubstantiation of debased flesh into divine glory, has the gospel magic to perform such a feat of essentially soma-ontological conversion' (Acampora, 2006, p. 102).

The fact that rats and mice can stand in for humans and can be submitted to pain and death in their stead speaks directly to the biological and genetic similarities between humans and rodents. As abject as rats and mice are, as far as they are thrust from humans by means of traps or bait, they are included in the laboratory because they are so very like humans: rats and mice are people's genetic and biological homologues. Rats and mice share a high degree of genetic homology with humans. In genetics, homology refers to a similarity of DNA sequences; DNA codes with similar sequences are presumed to have a common ancestry. The mouse genome has been fully sequenced (the rat genome partially so), and virtually all mouse genes have human homologues. This homology has led to the involvement and now high participation of rodent animals in the laboratory, wherein rats and mice act as stand-ins for human bodies. At the level of basic biology, rats, mice, and humans are all mammals. Each gives birth to living young and eats similar foods—and even tends to access these foods in the same domains, because rats and mice dwell wherever humans are to be found, and in people's domestic dwellings and food production and storage facilities, rats and mice frequently access their foodstuffs. Resultant of our homologous basic physiology, similar organs, and similar body plans, we suffer from the same diseases. We each control our body chemistry using similar hormones, we each have nervous systems that work in the same way, and we all react similarly to infection and injury.

Rats, particularly, are also homologues for human minds. Rats, like humans, seem to have the capacity to carefully weigh the costs and benefits of making decisions. A 2006 study published by van den Bos, van der Harst, Jonkman, Schilders, and Spruijt in *Behavioural Brain Research* was the first to demonstrate this behaviour in nonhuman animals. The study found that rats weighed the benefits of obtaining a food treat against the effort that was required to obtain it. After a certain point, rats recognised that the treat was not worth the effort, and they satisfied themselves with a smaller, easier-to-obtain treat. The study found that the laboratory rats seemed to behave according to an internal constant standard, a relative ratio for each situation by which choices are measured. Because the standard varied depending on the situation, it was at least partly created by individual rats as they experienced various situations. Behavioural neuroscientist John Salamone also found in his studies of effort-related processes, such as how much energy an individual will put out to obtain a reward, that expending high effort for a low or negligible reward could be linked to depression—and that rats and people share the capacity to suffer from depression. It is even possible that rats share with humans a capacity for metacognition, a capacity that was once thought to be unique to humans and higher primates (Salamone, Correa, Mingote, Weber, & Farrar, 2006).

Beyond basic genetic and biological similarity, mice and rats share with people a capacity and, indeed, a need for sociality. They are, like people, profoundly social animals; they form cohesive social groups and cohabitate, and if they are isolated from their social networks, they can become anxious and stressed. Recent studies by neuroscientists Knutson, Burgdorf, and Panksepp (1998) suggest that, like people, rats have a marvellous sense of fun. The researchers noted that rats 'have fun' by seeking out social and physical stimulation from one another or from humans they are familiar with. Knutson, Burgdorf, and Panksepp discovered that rats emit short, high-frequency, ultrasonic, socially induced vocalization during play. When they experience physical stimuli, such as a tickle stimulus, rats, like people, have 'tickle skin' that when stimulated generates a sound that the authors called rat 'laughter'. The vocalization, which is made at a frequency beyond the range of human hearing, is described as a distinctive chirping. This chirping laughter is associated with positive emotional feelings. Stimulating it is one ground for social bonding between rats and humans and among rats themselves: The tickled animal seeks out more tickling from the tickler. The initial goal of Knutson, Burgdorf, and Panksepp's research was to track the biological origins of the joyful and social processes of the brain by comparing laughter among groups of rats with laughter commonly experienced by children in social play. Although the research was unable to prove that rats have a sense of humour, it did indicate that rats can laugh and express something that looks very much like enjoyment, and it did show a degree of brain similarity (i.e, even though their study could not prove 'sense of humour', it still showed that human and rat brains are similar as both brains allow both animals to express similar emotions) (Knutson, Panksepp, & Burgdorf, 1998).[6]

Rats and mice share other social processes with humans; like human learning, rat and mouse learning is social. Both rodents learn a range of behaviours from one another—rats, for instance, learn about the safety of new food sources by observing the foods that pioneering animals consume and observing the health of the animal while the new food is being digested.

And, of course, rat and mouse history is inextricably intertwined with human history; both animals live wherever people live, and they conduct their social lives in people's midst. Fissell (1999) noted that humans' long-standing relationships with rat and mouse vermin have always recognised our similarities. She characterised early modern English imaginaries of these animals around three characteristics: 'They ate human food, they were cunning; and they understood symbols. Each of these three, of course, was characteristic of humans' (p. 21; see also Hendrickson, 1983; Matthews, 1898). For Fissell, this symbolic capacity manifested in Restoration England in vermins' ability to understand and deploy language or to read signs, allowing them to trick, outwit, and outsmart (humans and other animals). Such a capacity, in common with humans, persists in the crafty modern rat who recognises the human-set trap or who is too smart and too wily to take the bait. But, as much as rats and mice are intertwined with humankind in historical, genetic, biological, habitation, and social terms and even in terms of having a shared capacity for crafty intelligence, rats and mice are equally feared, demonised, and made utterly distinctive from humans; they are creatures of ambivalence, embodying opposed and conflicting meanings. I provide a more fulsome discussion of the ambiguous location of rats and mice between those categories that generally appear to be dichotomies in the next chapter. I turn now to the area of cultural life that is of interest to me in this book: the scientific research laboratory and the ambiguities, ambivalences, and polarities that are to be found therein.

The Ambiguous Positions of Rats and Mice in the Laboratory: The Human-Animal Divide and the Dangers of Transgenic Implosion

The 31 scientists participating in my study all worked with rodent animal models. An animal model represents some, most, or all aspects of a normal or abnormal condition in human beings. The opportunity presented by mouse and rat bodies to study human diseases has spawned a great variety of rat and mouse models. Abnormal model conditions may be inherited, spontaneous, or experimentally induced.[7] Many rodent strains (or groups in which all members are genetically identical) have been bred expressly for the scientific experimentation on and investigation of human problems.[8] When a random population that has genetic diversity is required, a rat stock or group of animals (or 'outbred strain') that do not have identical genotypes is drawn upon. Inbred strains[9] are also used, as are various mutant strains of mice and rats. Where a model does not exist, it might be created. Researchers also may wish to learn about a gene that has been sequenced but which has an unknown or incompletely known function. In this circumstance, a genetic technique called gene knockout may be used to engineer an animal that carries genes that have been made inoperative (i.e., that have been 'knocked out' of the organism).

Where the knockout animal has deleted or inoperable genes, 'knock-in' rodents are those with foreign genes inserted into their genome. Some examples include abnormally large mice, with an inserted rat growth hormone gene; Oncomice, with an activated oncogene that significantly increases the incidence of cancer; and Doogie mice, with enhanced NMDA receptor function, resulting in improved memory and learning. Knock-in technology involves the insertion of a gene into a specific locus; it is a 'targeted' insertion, and it yields one variety of the transgenic animal.

Transgenic animals are contentious beings, and they are so because they are ambiguous. By definition, they bring together elements that would not otherwise occur together. In doing so, they become both powerful and dangerous beings which are not easily classifiable under regimes which understand and connote full beingness in terms of singular essence. Marcuse (1964) spoke to the danger of eliminating the boundaries between singular essences:

> In this universe, there are modes of being in which men and things are 'by themselves' and 'as themselves', and modes in which they are not—that is, in which they exist in distortion, limitation or denial of their nature (essence). (p. 125)

At the very heart of Marcuse's lament, Weisberg (2009) found the idea that when one animal is spliced with (a gene from) another, (another) qualitatively different reality is cut through, and therefore humans lose (yet another) contradiction by which to cultivate critical thought (p. 55). Marcuse drew attention to the consequences of dissolving the boundaries between singular essences, warning that dissolution may result in the collapsing of categories and the smoothing out of the contradictions that are at the heart of critical thought.This is particularly evident in the production of transgenic animals, because God-scientists claim to have not only omniscience but the ultimate creative power. As Bacon (1620/1999) wrote, 'On a given body to generate and superinduce a new nature, is the work and aim of human power' (p. 148).

Marcuse's is not necessarily a moral objection to the perceived cruelty or abusiveness of the procedures that have ushered Oncomouse and her purpose-built kin into existence. Instead, it is a protest that is directed toward the propensity of technological rationality to dissolve areas of contradiction. For Marcuse, the ontological consequences of breaking down boundaries include distortion, limitation, and denial; the restoration of a single essence that might constitute resistance is excluded, and one enters a dangerous territory in which everything collapses into everything else. In the scientific laboratory context, technological rationality favours boundary dissolution between animal bodies and human bodies and yields beings that would not otherwise exist. These beings are highly valued because their real, physical existence allows the ontological exploration of the breakdown of boundaries that would otherwise prevent certain kinds of knowing. But their ambiguity raises questions: What are they? What is their essence? Is the essence of mouse or the essence of rat recognized in the laboratory?

Crist (2004) drew attention to other dangers, particularly those issuing from the human dominance over nature and the animal. She warned specifically that humans must take great care with boundary dissolution and its meaning, because it is often symptomatic of a kind of colonialism. Crist offered the caution on the grounds that postmodernist constructivist views of nature relegate the animal to something indeterminate, something that is waiting for the human assignation of meaning. Waiting, they are ontologically indeterminate. Located in this zone of human supremacy, the transgenic animal languishes in the position of the ontologically indeterminate until it is assigned meaning in terms of a human (technoscientific) discourse about the nonhuman. Such a position is virtually indistinguishable from the Judeo-Christian heritage of human supremacy. Crist and Marcuse each drew attention to the consequences of dissolving the boundaries between singular essences; both saw the location of transgenic animals as a danger that has emerged as a result of a complex process of a merger between illusion and reality, science and magic, and imagination and progress. Animals are the unwilling and dominated victims of these processes. They languish in a humanist world in which they have no formative role; they instead await the assignment of their names and natures that the mergers they are involved in yield for them. In a similar vein, Weisberg (2009) argued that in these transgenic operations that undermine essence, one variety of essence is yet retained. She noted in particular that 'if transgenic animals have any essence at all it is to be dominated' (p. 55). Adorno and Horkheimer (2002) took a similar view, arguing that 'in their transformation the essence of things is revealed as always the same, a substrate of domination' (p. 6).

IMPLOSION AND RESISTANCE

Where Marcuse drew attention to the dangers that transgenic operations present to essence, Haraway drew attention to the powers that such hybridity might present for resistance. For Haraway (2004), the laboratory's power to create, in this case, animals of nonsingular essence, is one that has the capacity to render the 'normal' dubious. This power—already harnessed as resistance by feminists and antiracists,[10] who each have axes to grind against 'essence'—has the capacity to situate animals quite differently from beings which are either wholly reducible to essence or wholly dominated. Indeed, it has the capacity to trouble the categories of nature and culture.

Using as her example Oncomouse, the mouse used as a breast cancer model, Haraway (2004) argued that transgenic animals are the symbolic and organic sites for the implosion of cultural and natural categories 'for members of technoscientific cultures' (p. 273). Materially, Oncomouse and her transgenic cousins are the physical sites for the collapsing of the humanist binary between culture (humans) and nature (animals). As Haraway argued, Oncomouse is, at her essence, a 'natureculture' (p. 89) a hybrid. Oncomouse's essence, in common with humans, is 'to be mammal, a bearer by definition of mammary glands, and a site for the operation of a transplanted, human, tumour producing gene' (p. 89). In their duality, Oncomouse and her cousins challenge the anthropocentric dualism of the modern sadohumanist position. Haraway submitted that transgenic animals can be understood in terms of kinship, arguing that the power and hybrid agency that are present in (non-'essential') recombinant DNA life forms allows for the 'reconfiguration of the kinship between different orders of life' (as cited in S. Franklin, 2001, pp. 313–314).

The duality brought about by gene splicing that Haraway drew attention to is, crucially, a feature of all rodent animal models in the laboratory, transgenic or otherwise. Duality emerges in the situation of laboratory animal models as a consequence of their close relatedness to people in mammalian, biological, and genetic terms as well as in their position as specific (rat or mouse) species. As I have already suggested, speci-al heterogeneity and mammalian homogeneity are privileged at different times in the laboratory. These characteristics of the animal's being locate the rat and the mouse as at once human kin and unrelated to humans in the laboratory, as both a particular species and an inanimate piece of equipment, and move it across the human-animal divide within its scientific coordinates. Sometimes, these characteristics cement the rat or mouse's place in a human-animal, nature-culture, animate-inanimate hierarchy. The actual reengineering that can now be applied to animal bodies (and to plants), along with the understanding that rats and mice are closely related biokin to humans, troubles the biological discreteness of 'the human' on one side of the Great Divide and 'the animal' on the other. This leads me to question the strength of human exceptionalism and how its endurance may be called into question in the laboratory through the slippages that animals and humans make from their divided moorings.

The capacity of laboratory mice and rats to trouble the divisions between animals and humans and between nature and culture does not mean that these animals occupy a position as equal partners with humans in the laboratory, largely because the inequality between humans and animals in a laboratory (and other contexts) is not wholly reducible to the endurance (or the transcendent validity) of the human culture–animal nature divide. Human-animal inequality in the lab is, rather, contingent upon the practices in laboratory labour and the relationships that emerge from that contingency between animals and humans in the laboratory context.[11] In my study, these contingencies took particular forms in which human-animal relationships operated across the animal-human divide.

SCIENTIFIC RATIONALITY VERSUS KINSHIP AND EMOTIONAL ATTACHMENT

Descola (2005) pointed to the ways in which Western modern naturalism divides the human from the nonhuman, arguing that the nonhuman world is singularly knowable through science, whereas the human herself is embedded in a world of cultural meaning; in this regard, nature is knowable through empirical science. Humans are exempted from being understood in these terms; as cultural beings, people are unique in being consciously intended, deliberative, and the holders of agency through which intention and deliberation are enacted. As Despret (2008) argued, such an appreciation of difference generates a 'double we'; this imposes itself in the assertion of difference, in humans' knowledge that 'we' are different (p. 123).

As Milton (2002) suggested, a special irony is embedded in what humans know of scientific enquiry, which relates directly to animals and to kinship with them. Milton observed that humans are 'increasingly aware of nature's responsive relatedness to our actions' (p. 51). Further, 'it is science … that has created this awareness' (p. 51) through its public participation in, for example, the debates about genetically modified food in the United Kingdom and the United States and in other areas where the transformation of ecological systems has some sort of scientific input. This is an even more present sense of the awareness that Milton speaks of in the context of climate change, in which humans are becoming cognisant of the idea that they are the holders of geological agency—the capacity to actively influence the planet. In specific respect to animals, Shanor and Kanwal, in their 2009 offering *Bats Sing, Mice Giggle*, also noted that 'science is beginning to take us back to nature, providing a window into the minds of other species' (p. 1). There is an irony in their offering, and even in the title of the book, in the sense that it claims to demonstrate how much alike humans and animals are—and indeed, it does so in many regards. However, it also places a boundary between 'us' and 'them' in demonstrating the extraordinary capacities of animals beyond those of humans. By doing so, it concretises the division between animal nature and human culture—especially in the sense that humans have, as cultural creatures of the technological age, detached themselves from natural animal worlds.

Within the domain of scientific practice, here represented ethnographically in my analysis of the lab, another irony is in place. It was the case that the scientists participating in this study referenced what Milton (2002) called 'the myth of capitalism' which undergirds the opposition between emotion and scientific rationality and which promotes the treatment of nature, including animals, as resources—or, in my study, as 'equipment' that is critical to the doing of science with applicability to humans. However, they often engaged in practices that undermined such a myth, such treatment, such rigidly structural positioning of kinds—animal equipment here, human scientific investigator there. That scientists did so is surprising only if one subscribes to the notion that scientists are devoid of the habitus of other human beings when it comes to developing relationships with animals (Descola, 2005). If scientists say, as they told me in the course of this ethnographic study, that they have feelings for animals, that their relations with them in the laboratory are very often not impersonal, and that they, like most people, experience animals in, with, and through emotional connections, then why should scientists be wholly excluded from being able to establish connections with animals, even in the scientific context of the laboratory? Why should it be impossible that scientists compartmentalise their interactions with animals in that context, to the extent that emotional connections and interactions do not appear, as Acampora (2006) reported that they do not? Why should science continue to be treated as a domain in which animals and humans are held as separates, a domain that is still in the fast grip of instrumental reason?

The scientists in this study questioned the relevance of Cartesian thinking and Baconian practice. They indicated that a variety of connections with animals emerged in the course of scientific interactions with them. I am interested in demonstrating that these connections are present and that they trouble strict human-animal, nature-culture, and emotional-scientific divides. I hope that they will mitigate the view that scientists are wholly detached from animals in the context of the laboratory. I also hope that this work will go some way in diminishing the assumption that scientists have somehow been dispossessed of the interested, caring, and emotional habitus towards animals that other people seem to be granted. I am equally interested in showing that the connections scientists reported having with research animals are not in the least antithetical to science. It should not be overly surprising that the lab, home as it is to a recognised fundamental kinship between animals and people based on our genetic and biological homology, is also home to a series of animal-human kinships that are operated across the animal-human divide. Some of these are articulated in emotional connections with animals—something that Darwin recognised long ago in his 1871 work, *The Descent of Man and Selection in Relation to Sex*.

APPROACH

The examination of polarities, ambivalences, and ambiguities obviously calls for a close examination of the human-animal divide beyond the particular shapes it takes in the laboratory. In the lab, the human-animal divide is rigorously maintained in those practices that hierarchically array human-animal relationships and that locate the human and the animal on either side of a thick ontological divide. At the same time, it is undermined by the actual engagements that scientists and animal technicians have with animals in the lab. In the lab, there are deep divisions between animals and humans as well as equally deep kinships, communications, and relations that span the gulf, as I have discussed in the foregoing text. In fleshing them out in this book, I make recourse to theoreticians who have considered the animal-human divide.

The Animal-Human Question in Anthropology

The question of the animal-human divide has an obvious home in the multidisciplinary (yet semiautonomous) field of animal studies, whose members agree that the question of the animal is one of the most important questions in contemporary critical discourse (Calarco, 2008, p. 1). The animal-human divide, however, has a longer history in the disciplines of social science, humanities, and science, which have considered humans and their difference from animals in terms of the uniqueness of humans. Although animal studies is a fairly recent arrival to the 'studies[12]' that have attracted (and to some extent repelled) anthropologists, animals have long been central to anthropological inquiry.

I do not intend to have a fulsome discussion here of anthropology's engagement with animals—that itself would require a dedicated volume. In any case, it has been done before (see Ingold, 1988; Ingold, 1994, pp. 14–32; Mullin, 1999; and in animal studies, see Lloyd & Mulcock, 2007). I have in the past, in undergraduate teaching, used the sustained historical position of the animal in the discipline to examine the history of anthropology and to pay close attention to the most significant conceptual shifts it has undergone. Some of the features of this terrain are worth mentioning given my own intention here to perhaps support more elastic anthropological recognitions of kinship between humans and animals and given anthropology's intention to use research on human-animal relationships to make insights into human lives, as opposed to kinnings between them.

Even from a very cursory glance at the history of the discipline, looking from the window that animals offer into it, it is evident that animals have been generally perceived in anthropology as useful vehicles with which to explore human lives. In that animals have been used in the discipline to improve the understanding of the human condition, one might say that anthropology's use of animals is not that different from the scientific use of animals—it too uses animals to make insights into a range of human conditions. Shanklin's (1985) review of animals in anthropology, published in the *Annual Review of Anthropology*, tracked the variety of ways anthropologists had been thinking and writing about animals, 'from studies of domestication and cultural ecology to those focused on such topics as sacrifice, myth, and metaphor' (Mullin, 1999, p. 207). Shanklin (1985) concluded that there was a far greater emphasis and body of writing on animals as food and a lesser one on animals as symbols. She called for the integration of 'different dimensions in a non-determinist approach' (p. 398). The determinist approach is exemplified by Harris (1974), who explained the sacredness of Indian cattle in their worth as working animals. Nondeterminist approaches include symbolic and structuralist approaches, represented by Douglas in her analysis of dietary codes which avoid liminal animals (e.g., Douglas, 1957, 1990).

The next review of the terrain of human-animal relationships was conducted by Mullin in 1999. In her estimation, animal-human relationships have undergone considerable re-examination,

> reflecting key trends in the history of social analysis, including concerns with connections between anthropology and colonialism and with the construction of race, class, and gender identities. There have been many attempts to integrate structuralist or symbolic approaches with those focused on environmental, political, and economic dimensions. Human-animal relationships are now much more likely to be considered in dynamic terms. … Some research directly engages moral and political concerns about animals, but it is likely that sociocultural research on human-animal relationships will continue to be as much, if not more, about humans. (1999, p. 201; for the ways in which animal studies has provided anthropology with food for thought regarding animals, see Mullin, 2002)

Recent (i.e., post-1990) developments in social theory (including in the disciplines of sociology, technology, and anthropology) have shown increasing interest in questioning Cartesian binaries—those 'Great Divides', as Latour and Weibel (2005) called them, between nature and culture and animals and humans (among others) that anthropology, as a humanist pursuit, yet calls upon (see Latour & Weibel, 2005). As a result, new questions have been posed about the validity of those divisions in ethical as well as theoretical and practical (lived) terms. Posthumanism has arisen as a responsive stance; herein, the firm boundaries between humans and nonhumans, particularly, have been shaken to accommodate the view that beings of all fleshy manifestation are interconnected in a series of overlapping 'webs' or 'networks' of activity (Instone, 1998).

The grounds that were previously taken as unique to and characteristic of human beings have consequently been called into question. Arluke and Sanders (1996), Haraway (2003), Philo and Wilbert (2000), Whatmore (2002), and Wolch and Emel (1998) each challenged the ideas that agency, intentionality, and response-ability are human—and only human—domains. Despite the tremors that might be recorded in the Great Divide which have unsettled the certainty of the human abiding and enduring claims of certainty persist, in that the certainty of humanity practically informs everyday assumptions about people, animals, and their relationships. In this regard, C. Wolfe (2003) noted that it is not really known yet how these posthuman ideas will be played out yet, because few studies have grounded posthuman ideas in the practical terrain of everyday living. Castree (2003) advised that people should 'move beyond suggestive metaphors in order to properly flesh out what an amodern politics of socionatural hybridity is all about' (p. 209). Haraway was far more positive about the crumbling of the Great Divide in everyday life, suggesting in her *Simians, Cyborgs and Women* (1991) that by the late twentieth century,

> the boundary between human and animal is thoroughly breached. The last beachheads of uniqueness have been polluted if not turned into amusement parks—language, tool use, social behaviour, mental events, nothing really convincingly settles the separation of human and animal. And many people no longer feel the need for such a separation. (pp. 151–152)

One attempt to engage with the practicalities of relationships as they occur in everyday reality has revealed a tendency towards neo-Cartesianism, in which the category of personhood is expanded to encompass those animals (such as dogs and monkeys) that exhibit the key criteria for inclusion in the category 'human'. The extension of personhood to these animals leaves out in the cold those animals which do not exhibit such qualities. In the case at hand, these animals might well be the rats and mice of the lab, which could be understood to be relegated to the category of a terminable resource. However, there are enduring relationships between rats and mice and people that do not have their basis in likeness.

The Animal-Human Question in Phenomenology

As a phenomenologically interested anthropologist, and because phenomenological insights, though largely originating in anthropocentric concerns, offer tools, concepts, and theoretical frameworks that are particularly useful to the study of animal-human relationships, I am drawn to what phenomenologists have had to say about the human-animal question. This, of course, leads me back to the (continental) philosophers and what they have written about it. For the most part, classical philosophers have been consistently reductive and essentialist in their thinking about 'the animal', and 'the animal' has been equally consistently thought of as a homogenous category. The centrepiece of Heidegger's (1962) analysis of nonhuman animals, for instance, concerns their 'world poverty'; whereas animals are deprived of qualities such as 'mood' and 'attunement', humans are defined precisely in these terms. For Heidegger, the animal world is 'closed' and the human world is 'open'. Where animals experience a mindless captivation in the world, sufficient that a bee in the act of drinking honey can have its abdomen removed without noticing, humans have the unique capacity to distance themselves from their environments to create new possibilities. Humans can become bored, and this boredom leads them to find new ways to engage, whereas animals remain captivated by drive and instinct in a closed circuit between body and environment.

Heidegger's (1962) well-known position—that the stone is wordless, the animal is poor in the world, and the human being is world forming—is not based on a hierarchical organization of humans and animals (or, for that matter, stones). Indeed, Heidegger rejected the philosophical tradition that preceded him that insisted upon straightforward distinctions between humans and animals and between living and nonliving beings. Further, his position on understanding being and the sorts of worlds and world relations that are lived by nonhumans is firmly based on the rejection of anthropomorphic common sense and scientific approaches (see Calarco, 2008, p. 21). In part, this rejection is posed against the idea that humans and nonhumans can be understood in terms of differences of degree—for example, in degrees of richness, in degrees of complexity, in degrees of broadness, and in degrees of experience and availability. Such an understanding would imply that human and nonhuman lives could be compared on the grounds of those things we each share and the grounds on which we differ. It also undermines the evident richness and complexity of the nonhuman animal world—which Heidegger took to be replete with such qualities, and which allowed him to analyze the specific mode of animal being in and on its own terms rather than in hierarchically comparative ones, against the conditions of human being. This examination, of course, was an examination of what world poorness means on the animal's terms (Calarco, 2008, p. 22).

Instead of degrees of difference, Heidegger proposed that 'there is no difference in *degree* or quantity between human and animal … but rather a difference in *kind*, and this difference is meant to be understood in the most fundamental and radical way possible' (Calarco, 2008 p.22). Here, then, emerges the abyssal difference between human and animal in Heidegger's phenomenology.

Agamben's 1998 work draws heavily on Heideggerian notions of human-animal differences to understand what is essential about humans. In his 2002 *The Open*, Agamben abandoned his search for a postmetaphysical definition of the human, and 'the reliance on the human-animal distinction that serves as the foundation for Western political and metaphysical thought becomes, on Agamben's reading, the chief obstacle for a postmetaphysical concept of relation and community' (Calarco, 2008, p. 79). Agamben's abandonment of the human-animal distinction offers up possibilities for the relationships between beings, especially when his abandonment of the distinction is compared with his earlier work, which draws extensively upon that distinction. These possibilities spring from Agamben's reconceptualisation of bare life from a zone of 'indistinction' to a zone of 'possibility' within which the relation between humans and animals might be reworked. As Calarco noted, Agamben may have meant in so doing to point to a transmutation in the relations between human beings and animals. Agamben's view is that animals are caught up in a world that is wholly closed to them. Disinhibitors in the animal's environment initiate its actions and responses; these captivate it into interaction with the world. Human beings, in contrast, are able to separate from this sort of intensity of experience with the world. Humans can recognise that gap between the experience of captivation with the world and reflection on that captivation—and this is manifested in the human capacity for boredom with the world. Whereas animals lack an openness to the world, humans lack the interaction with the world of the ecstatic animal variety. The boredom that arises from this lack of ecstatic interaction drives humans to approximate the intensity of animal captivation. The things that humans do in this respect, which are produced as historical missions to keep peoples 'awake' 'have long since been transformed into cultural spectacles and private experiences, and have lost all historical efficacy' (Wolf-Meyer, 2006). For Agamben, it is humanism that has exhausted these historical potentialities.[13] As Wolf-Meyer (2006) put it,

> the modern world is one which is profoundly devoid of experience, it is, in light of *The Open*, eminently boring, and, as such, providing humanity with ample opportunities to experience being-captivated. What Agamben finds in boredom—following Heidegger—is the relationship between the boredom of man and the captivity of the animal. In both cases, the individual (man or animal) is being-held-in-suspense—it is in this moment in the full presence of Dasein: 'Dasein is simply an animal that has learned to become bored; it has awakened *from* its own captivation *to* its own captivation. This awakening of the living being to its own being-captivated, this anxious and resolute opening to a not-open, is the human.

Wolf-Meyer argued that here is potential

> for the animal and man to bleed into one another (and the metaphor of the flesh is important, for we share in the bodily experience of being) … the lesson Agamben draws from Heidegger is one of 'letting be,' of allowing the anthropological machine to idle, and for the posthuman to become a-human, for in this a-humanity is an infancy, a not-yet, a 'zone of indifference' within which there is no need for animal rights, nor human rights, but rather only the right to bare life. (n.p.)

Might we regard the zone of indifference as an opportunity to decouple the common binaries as they shape up with respect to the distance between animals and humans? As Wolf-Meyer (2006) suggested, with any of the binaries that are used to determine the realm of the human, 'it is in the double-articulation that the overdetermination of the terms as such is destructive' (n.p.). This does not lend itself to hybrid thought, after Haraway, who was critical of those people who are 'pure of heart' or 'romantic' as a result of their antihybridization stances; it steers away from linking nature-society or human-animal to make new beings which might raise questions about essence. Instead, as Wolf-Meyer pointed out, the zone of indifference offers up the possibility for 'anti-hybrids, Un-Natures, Un-Animals'—not essences, but absences. It is possible that this space of the 'un' and the not-yet characterises the technoscientific space of the laboratory, in which, rather than hybridity, a kind of bare life—a kind of a-human, a-animal—emerges.

Merleau-Ponty, who actually remained largely silent on the animal question, also responded to Heidegger's reflections on the human-animal distinction. Merleau-Ponty's (1994) response included the notion of 'strange kinship', with which he meant to point to the weighty, fleshy ways in which the world is shared among and generally available to the species, despite their evident differences, in the weight of their bodies and the fleshiness of their existence. In his later work, Merleau-Ponty attempted to overcome the ontological distinctions pertaining to human-animal separation; he even tried to 'disconnect reflection from exclusive humanness, thereby reintegrating the concept of reflection into being itself' (Painter & Lotz, 2007, p. 7).[14] No part of Merleau-Ponty's (1994) contribution suggests that animal-human relations are characterized by equality or organised symmetrically. But they are lateral in that there is 'an overcoming that does not abolish kinship' (p. 335). I am particularly interested in the ways in which these 'kinships' emerge in the context of the scientific laboratory, underneath or alongside the biological kinship that allows humans to treat animals in the laboratory as dispensable equipment.

Where Merleau-Ponty maintained a generic 'animality' which he deployed in his arguments about the strange kinship between animals and humans, Derrida was scathing of it. Derrida offered critical responses to essentialist and generalist discourse on 'the animal', dismissing the notion that on the 'other side' of the human animal divide, one might find a group of beings which share a common animality. His work is therefore critical of both the human-animal divide and the reduction of animals to the generic 'animal'. These two elements are drawn together in a logic that includes humans as a part of the multiplicity of being that is to be found among animals. If there is heterogeneous multiplicity to be found there, there would be no reason to assume that humans do not also belong, as one variety of this multiplicity. Derrida was particularly critical of Heidegger's views on human-animal difference, on the basis that Heidegger denied 'world' to the animal. Derrida (2004) began a critique that insisted that the reductive binary oppositions in Heidegger's work failed to do justice to the multiplicity of animals. One way in which he expressed his dissatisfaction with the binary opposition that is so present in Heidegger's work is in the notion that there are many divisions:

> If I am unsatisfied with the notion of a border between two homogenous species, man on one side and the animal on the other, it is not in order to claim, stupidly, that there is no limit between 'animals' and 'man'; it is because I maintain that there is more than one limit, that there are many limits. ... The gap between the 'higher primates' and man is in any case abyssal, but this is also true for the gap between the 'higher primates' and other animals. (p. 66)

Derrida's project is also predicated on his assumption (in his critical adaptation of Levinas's human-bound notion) that animals 'have face'—the face of an 'other' cannot be delimited to the domain of the human (and furthermore, contra Levinas, animal face presents itself with just as much ethical force as human face; see Levinas, 1969, 2004, and for a work that seems to undermine Levinas's own insistence on human face, see his *The Name of a Dog*, 1990). One cannot assume, in other words, that animals react and do not respond; instead, 'animals might call upon me and obligate me' (Calarco, 2008, p. 5). Derrida insisted that there is no clear separation between humans and animals 'inasmuch as both "kinds" of beings are irreducibly caught up in the "same" networks of differential forces that constitute their modes of existence' (as cited in Calarco, 2008, p. 106). Following Haraway's (2008) consideration of scientists and their relationships with animals, in her *When Species Meet,* I am particularly interested in Derrida's application of face to nonhuman animals and the way in which the recognition of animal response-ability—a condition of having face—offers up to scientists in this study the obligations of caring for and providing care to speci-al animals that appear in the lab. At first glance, these animals may seem to be nothing more than mammalian units of equipment from which scientists are wholly detached.

In the sense that it pulls away from reductive conceptualizations of animality and the division of humans and animals into a binary opposition, Derrida's work is aligned with that undertaken by Haraway. I also draw on Haraway's 2008 work, *When Species Meet*, to explore the ambiguous locations from which human-rat/mouse kinships emerge. Haraway (2008) argued that humans are ' "always-already" multispecies entities' (p. 5) and that they are the result of constant processes of being with and becoming with other species. This happens, Haraway explained, at the microlevel, where human bodies teem with a multitude of other species; in the processes of coevolution that embed ostensibly separate species, such as chickens and people, within one another's development; and in the being of companions to one another. In her own words,

> *When species meet* strives to build attachment sites and tie sticky knots to bind intra-acting critters, including people, together in a kind of response and regard that change the subject—and

> the object. Encounterings do not precede harmonious wholes, and smoothly preconstituted entities do not ever meet in the first place. (p. 287)

When Species Meet continues Haraway's objections, as she made them in *The Companion Species Manifesto* (2003), to the separation of human and nonhuman animals in theoretical terms. It asks 'what happens when people understand the degree to which they are always living with and "becoming with" other species' (Heinricy, 2009, p. 287). I use Haraway's insights to explore the ways in which scientists 'become with' rodent species and how their meetings change scientist subject and rat research objects in the laboratory context (see also Dillard-Wright, 2009).

METHODOLOGY

This book is based on 12 months of ethnographic fieldwork that was carried out between 2009 and 2010, which I completed in research laboratories in the Australian Capital Territory (ACT). The laboratories I studied dealt with, among other animals, rabbits, cats, lizards, frogs, birds, and sheep as well as the most common experimental animals, rats and mice. These rodents are included in these labs and others throughout the world on the basis of their biological and genetic homology with humans.

Over the course of this study, I had access to scientific researchers, neuroscientists, immunologists, and virologists, who ranged in age from around 35 years to around 65, as well as a small number of lab technicians and veterinarians. The bulk of the data for this book was collected in semistructured interviews with those research scientists. I secured 31 ethnographic interviews with 16 men and 15 women from across the three scientific disciplinary areas. I conducted semistructured ethnographic interviews with 5 animal technicians, all female, who were charged with caring for many of the laboratory's rats, mice, and rabbits. This study is much more concerned with the kinds of relationships that are created between animals and scientific researchers, and this is reflected in the relatively high number of interviews I conducted with research scientists, as compared to animal technicians. There are, however, some specific instances in which I discuss the particular experiences of animal technicians and veterinarians. I also engaged with the head of the animal ethics committee and reviewed the ethics documents and guidelines produced by his department that set out the legislative and institutional requirements for people working with animals at the university where the labs are located. Finally, I spent a goodly amount of time hanging around in local pet stores, observing the ways in which their visitors responded to the rats and mice that were located there as pets for sale.

My privileging of scientific research positions in this work responds to the idea that is present in much of the contemporary and historical literature dealing with animal inclusions in research laboratories—that is, that animal technicians are likely to have deeper, richer engagements with animals based on the greater time they spend caring for them relative to scientific researchers, who spend more time experimenting upon and disposing of animal models. Although this also seemed to be the case in my own exploration of the laboratory, the different locations of researchers and technicians to animal subjects does not mean that researchers cannot and do not care for animals or engage with them in emotional and other terms that speak across the human-animal divide. Indeed, as I have also already suggested, in much of the work that is produced about laboratories in which research on animals is conducted, it seems that researchers are denied the habitus that other people seem to have acknowledged when it comes to engagement with animals. I have been unwilling to deny research scientists this habitus, and though I did not set about this research with the express intention of uncovering it, the ethnographic information I collected over the course of my engagement with the laboratory has confirmed that research scientists are indeed capable of conducting and do conduct nuanced, rich, and oftentimes emotional relationships with animal subjects.

The information research scientists provided to me about their work on, about, and in the presence of rodent animal bodies was given in the course of semistructured ethnographic interviews which took place both within and outside of the confines of the research laboratory. This ethnographic work was not undertaken solely in the laboratory space. Indeed, I was very often unable to access laboratory spaces, particularly virology and immunology areas, because of the fear of contamination. I was frequently allowed to visit the neuroscience area's rats, and I conducted ethnographic interviews on occasion in the full view of these laboratory animals. This meant that for the most part I spent a good deal of my ethnographic time in semistructured interviews with research scientists outside of the lab.

Just as they do outside the laboratory, rats and mice appear in the laboratory as animals for which people feel affection and with which they might establish emotional connections. They also appear as animals that require disposal. One manifestation of the laboratory mouse as a site for the development of emotional and affective connections—which was more prominent among laboratory-based animal technicians than among scientific researchers—took the form of companionship. Mouse pets, drawn from the population of research animals, were sometimes brought into office spaces as pets to allow for the development of emotional and communicative relationships, largely between animal technicians and animals that they might be required to dispose of. This was initially done to minimise the stress that animal technicians sometimes felt about subjecting large numbers of rats and mice to death, which sometimes involved bloody operations, such as disposing of newborn rat and mouse pups which were not required for research—a practice which often fell to junior technicians rather than to senior research staff. Laboratory mouse pets were talked about with great affection by their animal technician owners and with reference to their different personalities, habits, appearances, and relations with a human handler.

In this context, mice appeared as companion animals. It was unsurprising from this perspective that on many occasions, they were discussed as one might discuss a dog; these mouse pets were significant to the people who kept them as much more than biological and genetic human proxies or as animals which had a function and a natural place in the laboratory. As Fox (2006) argued, companion animals often occupy ambiguous (and precarious) positions on the boundaries between human and animal domains; whereas they might be treated as being capable of feeling 'human' emotions, such as affection, they are equally objects that can be discarded if and when they fail to comply with human expectations of them. In the laboratory context, the failure to comply with the human technoscientific standards of animal models also results in the discarding of mice. Pet mice had quite a different set of standards with which to comply. In some cases, this set of standards represented the polar opposite set to that with which laboratory mice were expected to comply. Laboratory mice are required to be standardised in order to produce reliability of data. Often, pet mice were selected on the basis of their deviance from standardisation—Michael, for instance, kept 'Spot', who appeared to him as a mouse which was distinctive in appearance and different from Spot's other, monochromic cage companions.

The practice of keeping pet mice in the laboratory needs to be closely considered from the perspective of what their appearance in the laboratory means for the human-animal divide. The posthumanist Sanders noted in his 1993 work that pet owners—a category which here includes the laboratory technician members of the scientific community in the laboratories here under study—are themselves active in the practice of contesting Cartesian animal-human divides. Among other things, Sanders pointed out that pet owners have long recognized those elements considered to be characteristic of humans, such as individuality and subjectivity, as being present in their animals. These observations led him to conclude that dogs in particular are constructed in the human-pet relationship as fully minded social actors with personhood—something that is accorded to pet dogs on the basis of their evident 'personalities', their apparent capacity to engage in subjective thought, their personal likes and dislikes, their capacity to have and show emotions, and their ability to be reciprocal partners in social relationships. Similar qualities were understood by animal technician pet owners to be present in their mice. Flip, who was brought into the laboratory from the general cage population, came to be understood by his owner, Michelle, as 'particularly affectionate, cute, and tame'. She also felt she had a good sense of Flip's favourite foods and the way he liked to be petted.

It might also be argued that pet keeping reinforces human-animal divisions in some ways. For instance, the basis of Sanders's argument is, perhaps, a kind of neo-Cartesianism, in which what is understood to be constitutive and characteristic of the human person is extended to the dog, who is then, in conforming to the key criteria in the category 'human', afforded entry into the category. In this sense, Sanders's arguments intersect with those arguments that are generated from traditional animal rights theory (Regan 1983; Singer 1975). These call for the extension of moral consideration to animals on the basis of their similarities to humans—such as their abilities to act on intelligence rather than instinct; the extent to which they can demonstrate cognitive skills, curiosity, problem solving, and social awareness; and their ability to feel or express abstract emotions such as loss and deprivation. Plumwood (2002) and Seager (2003) have argued that the elevation of dogs (and other animals who demonstrate the capacity to conform to the category of 'human', including primates and some birds, such as the African Grey parrot), though it erases key differences between the forms of (some manifestations of) being, also rigorously maintains other divides that continue the Cartesian dualism between humans and animals. Plumwood and Seager both pointed out, for instance, that one consequence of the selective elimination of difference is that 'lower' animals that do not display such a capacity are relegated to the category of a resource for human exploitation.[15]

It would be easy to assume that rats and mice which are not located as pets in the laboratory assume the position of a resource for human exploitation. However, in both the context of pet keeping and in the context of research on humans' biokin, the human 'seeks to inhabit an intersubjective world that is about meeting the other in all the fleshy detail of a mortal relationship with all its inevitable comic and tragic mistakes in the permanent search for knowledge of the intimate other' (Haraway, 2003, p. 34)—whatever form that quest for knowledge might take. This relentless and permanent search has the capacity to 'make a mess out of categories in the making of kin and kind' (Haraway, 2003, p. 34). This mess is made in the creation of and entering into interspecies relationships across the Great Divide, across mouseness and humanness—whether in the quest to find knowledge of the human body in the rat or to find out about the possibilities of being affectionate with a mouse—which unravel the relentlessly particular, the especially specific, that might otherwise keep rats and humans within their places in the laboratory and in their places as 'owners' among their pets. Such crossings trouble the categories of kind that usually take, on the surface, a very particular form in the lab—the scientist is here and the rat is very firmly there, in a long-standing hierarchy of scientific practice. This 'here' and 'there', which emerge most evidently when the rat is biokin to be terminated, offer certain grounds for the searching out of knowledge about the rat or mouse other. Such a search proceeds along the lines of enquiry which yields information about the human, for the benefit of the human and not, specifically, for the research animal. Yet, the animal's position is one that is known in terms of its shared fleshiness and worldness with human investigators.

Pet or companion animals offer up quite different possibilities in this search. As Haraway noted, humans and their companions—dogs, cats, or mice—despite our speci-al differences, sort things out. We each bear our positions in our flesh—the research scientist, the laboratory rat, and the consequences of those positions are borne out relationally—and lab rats and research scientists have a particular and hierarchical relation to one another. How could lab rats or mice and the people who are related to them in strict hierarchical terms in the lab, given these discourses and their historical, contemporary, and ethical consequences, ever be companions? Haraway's answer in *When Species Meet* is that we make each other up; we constitute one another in the flesh in the immediacy of being together. In the pursuit of this other possibility, mouse flesh or rat flesh is encountered in another way—pet mice are not reduced to their biological mammalian flesh that is so like that of a human. Instead, possibilities for 'sorting things out' between our different speci-al bodies are pursued, wherein rats and mice and people can relate across the species boundary. This relating occurs in the ambiguous zone between the speci-al positions of 'human' and 'mouse', which emerges in both pet-like and scientific knowledge of the animal's body. As Birke (2003, p. 216) observed, both kinds of knowledge are possible in the lab, owing to the rodent's ambiguous status; it is this ambiguity that raises multiple possibilities for relating.

OUTLINE OF THE BOOK

I begin this book by sketching out more fulsomely than I already have some of the many ambiguities which characterize (Western) human relationships with rats and mice—and their relationships with humans. In the third, fourth, and fifth chapters, I seek to draw the reader into the world I considered ethnographically for the better part of a year through an exploration of the ways in which the scientists in this study interpreted animals as beings with which they were connected in the course of scientific practice, while simultaneously describing research rodents as detached objects. In the third chapter, I describe the biological and genetic kinship between humans and rodents that is privileged in the laboratory context. This kinship, born of our shared mammalian membership, is not only one which allows the articulation of that similarity. In becoming mammalian units of study that stand in for the human body in the laboratory context, rodent mammals are rendered equipment and qualified for entry into the sacrificial economy of the laboratory in order that human mammals might live. Mammalian membership is a central element in both the erosion of the division between humans and animals in the laboratory and in the erection of the division between animate being and inanimate status, human and animal. It is the case, though, that speci-ality emerges as an equally key element in establishing the division between humans and animals. Speci-ality emerged at key moments of laboratory practice to recognise this division, one being at the moment of termination. It is, as one of my informants told me, 'only mice' that are terminated—'only mice', or in other words, no big deal.

I begin the fourth chapter with the ways in which mice and rats cross the animate-inanimate, human-animal division—subtle ways that call into question notions of detachment and distance. A close examination of laboratory practice reveals that these ostensible cornerstones of scientific practice, as Acampora observed them, are not adhered to with quite the rigidity that is often claimed for them (see Acampora, 2006). Far from undermining scientific practice, the attachment and closeness that characterise many scientific engagements with research animals serve to undergird what counts as 'good science'. I go further in the fourth chapter, concerning myself with those kinships between humans and animals that are recognized as emotional and communicative and which further unsettle the divisions between animals and humans and render them indistinct in some significant ways. In this chapter, I move into an examination of several of these indistinct points in which rodents and humans meet, in which they are recognized as biokin, and in which they also recognize one another as companions and as nonbiological, strangely related kin.

In the fifth (and final) chapter, I turn to explore the ambiguous terrain in which animals are located as subject to both regimes of caring and of death, scientists are located as both carers and killers, and unkillability and killing coexist in the complex ethical terrain of the modern scientific laboratory. In ethical terms, particular notions of animal welfare are legislatively and institutionally required. These notions, which are given institutional life as principles and protocols, provide a framework of ambivalence for human conduct relationally to rats and mice in that they both privilege rats and mice as bodies which require speci-ally specific care and nourishment and situate them as equipment that will be entered into the sacrificial economy of the laboratory. This might appear on the surface as an interest in animal welfare in order that a healthy animal model might be generated to protect the integrity of data; images of state care and the rehabilitation of prisoners who are bound for the electric chair crowd the mind here. With those images in mind, I examine in this chapter the elements of ethical principle and practice that provide the parameters for animals living in the laboratory, and I ask whether or not they provide the conditions for a bare life for animals in the lab context. Even as I pose such a question, I also question whether the scientific coordinates of the lab are perfectly parallel with other contexts in which bare life might be lived, such as the modern industrial abattoir, and the camps of the Holocaust.

Taken together, these ethnographic chapters reveal a pattern of ambiguity, ambivalence, and polarity that is central to the doing and the knowing of science, its production of data, and its complex relationships with research rodents. These relationships are not the result of a straightforward humanist scientific approach. Rather, they are conducted in complex relationships that themselves arise out of ambivalence and ambiguity—a combination that troubles the veneer of the human-animal division that is only ostensibly and partially characteristic of scientific modes and methods of knowing.

Endnotes

1. Bacon positioned scientists as priestly, presiding over the manipulation of Nature, superindiucing a new nature onto bodies in its purview, thus, in his view, fulfilling the aim of human power.
2. And there are yet more, environmental, complications: The free-range classification is often accompanied by an organic one in the case of both chicken meat and eggs. Consumers who are attempting to attend to and support animal welfare in their purchases might also assume that 'free-range' and 'organic' equate to lower emissions. Organic poultry requires more energy than battery farming, because more inputs are required. This is a consequence of the fact that organic and free-range birds will take longer to develop; under intensive farming conditions, a meat chicken will live less than 6 weeks before slaughter, free-range birds will reach 8 weeks, and organic chickens need to reach 12 weeks of age to be at market weight. From the perspective of the well-meaning consumer, it may be very surprising to find out that when one ostensibly attends to animal welfare, one may also be contributing to environmental problems. In 2007, the U.K. newspaper *The Independent Sunday* reported that academics at the Manchester Business School had conducted the first comprehensive study on the environmental impact of food production and had found organic foods such as milk, tomatoes, and chicken to be significantly less energy efficient and more polluting than their intensively farmed equivalents. They also generally generated more carbon dioxide than did conventional methods (Milmo, 2007).
3. It is not always the case that people arrive at the pet store with the intention of beginning a close relationship with an animal—one of my colleagues shared with me a story of the time some of her South American friends came to stay with her and attempted to buy guinea pigs from the local pet store, which they intended to eat for their evening meal. They were asked to leave the store by a worker, who had suspicions the animals were intended for consumption on the basis that the guinea pigs were being selected not on the basis of their 'personalities' but instead for their girth measurements. This, of course, also speaks to the different locations animals occupy in different cultural contexts.
4. It is likely that laboratory rats came from the same source.
5. Both vermin and pet rats persist in modernity and are inextricably intertwined with modern life. Pet animals are involved in particular regimes

of care and companionship, and many of these are described and engaged with in peculiarly modern forms, including on the Internet in specialised forums dedicated to the care of the pet rat or mouse. Vermin versions of these animals are equally modern.

6. Knutson, Panksepp, and Burgdorf found that those rats which laughed the most played the most, and those that laughed the most sought out and preferred to spend more time with other laughing rats, suggesting a social preference for other rats exhibiting similar responses.
7. Some of the major inherited diseases of rats have analogous conditions in people, including hypertension, diabetes insipidus, retinal degeneration, and audiogenic seizures.
8. Accomplished by means of inbreeding, the existence of a genetically identical population allows the researcher to exclude variations in genetics as a factor.
9. One of their number is the biobreeding diabetes-prone rat which spontaneously develops autoimmune Type 1 diabetes.
10. See, for example, Rackham, 2001.
11. Haraway (2008) pointed to the historical and changing qualities of these contingencies and to the ways they might proceed in a variety of animal-human interactive contexts, including the laboratory.
12. This refers to the category of scholarly work which does not proceed from within the academic disciplines, although scholars with disciplinary backgrounds may participate in them. These scholars are drawn together by an interest in a particular thing or aspect of life (e.g., animals, films, etc.) rather than through a disciplinary (e.g., anthropological) relationship with one another.
13. Yet, it is under capitalism that spectacle and private experience replace the search for historical meaning. People become captivated, like animals, by the spectacles of consumer culture; no longer actively seeking meaning for their lives, they passively await the stimulation of their human-made disinhibitors (see Hudson, 2008).
14. Smyth (2007) noted that as far as Merleau-Ponty was concerned, such statements come from the human desire for a singular and universal world. They come from an ontological faith, a primordial and cognitive belief in the worldliness of human's experiences—that they are 'rooted in a singular and universal common ground' (p. 172).
15. Both argued, too, that the valuing of animals should not proceed against the animal's capacity (or not) to be human, but instead ought to proceed on the grounds of intrinsic value—an approach that would value autonomy

and difference over similarity (with human beings). From the perspective that Cartesian divisions might be at work in the practice of pet keeping, the keeping of pet mice in the laboratory may not appear to be at odds with the broader situation of laboratory mice and rats. Both animals are required to demonstrate a kind of kinship with humans—either biological/genetic or affective. Each is chosen on the basis of its capacity to demonstrate, and each is unsuitable and disposable if it fails. But, peculiar reachings across and breaches of what appear to be strict divides occur frequently.

Chapter 2

Meaningful Rodents

Introduction

In this chapter, I explore some of the meanings that are attached to the designations of 'rat' and 'mouse'. 'Rat' and 'mouse' are not interchangeable descriptions; in genetic, biological, cultural or symbolic, and meaningful terms, rats and mice differ. Even in the terms of metaphoric parlance, it is quite a different thing to be called a mouse than it is to be insulted with the term 'rat'.[1] It is not my intention here to systematically set out the diversity of ways in which mice and rats differ in these and other terms; rather, I follow the lead of the ancient Romans in that it is my intention to highlight that which rats and mice share. Where the ancient Romans did not differentiate rats and mice from one another in any terms except for their size difference, I seek to demonstrate that they are each understood primarily in terms of ambiguity and ambivalence. In their pest, pet, and laboratory manifestations, rats and mice bear the weight of a multiplicity of meanings, with the net result that ambiguity and ambivalence emerge as the dominant meanings. Ambiguity and ambivalence manifest in the terms, for example, of taboo, as well as in the investment of their bodies with the simultaneous capacities to spread filth and to hold and bear great power.

Edelman (2002) argued that the ambiguity of rats and mice is elaborated in three main (meta) cultural forms in the West. Following Morris (2000), who described this threefold complementarity in respect to Malawian attitudes towards animals, Edelman explored the ways in which rats are involved in Western experiences as pets, pests, and experimental animals. It is certainly the case that rats, particularly, are increasingly popular domesticated pet animals in the West, even while the rodent eradication industry grows. The practice of keeping rats as companion animals occurs simultaneously with the determined extermination of essentially the same animal: the Brown rat.

These polar positions of pet and pest have merged to yield a peculiar ambivalence because rats revealed themselves to be capable of embodying contradictory meanings simultaneously. As I sat in the hair salon one afternoon, Helena, the stylist, asked that I excuse her as she turned her attention to a man in overalls who had just walked in. He informed her that he had called in to finalize the date of the rodent control service her landlord had organised for her domestic residence. He suggested the next day, to which Helena replied, 'Oh, no, that's not going to work. That won't give me enough time to organise someone to have Leon'. The exterminator told her there was no need to organise overnight accommodation for her son because the service would consist mainly of laying low-toxicity baits. 'Leon's not my son', Helena returned. 'He's my rat'.

If pet and pest rats are the same animal, and if this holds in the case of mice, the same can be said of laboratory animals, which I examine specifically in this book. It is probably not widely appreciated that pest rats, pet rats, and lab rats on the one hand and pest mice, pet mice, and lab mice on the other are essentially the same animal—the Brown rat in the first case and the domestic mouse in the second. In the lab, though, the laboratory rat and the laboratory mouse are undone from their associations with the domestic mouse and the rat that dwells in the sewer by means of the moral, chromatic, ontological, and other situations of their bodies in the laboratory space. Once the lab body is hived off from the wild animal body—a movement that in itself yields the conceptual category of the analytic animal or the animal-as-tool—yet more ambiguities and ambivalences are drawn from rat and mouse bodies. These ambiguities and ambivalences concern the merging of humans and animals.

Rats figure prominently in my analysis of how mice and rats are included in the cultural life of the West in this chapter—largely because rats more effectively threaten the borders that contain the unique domain of the human. Mice, as the most common experimental animal model, dominate the technoscientific contextual, ontological, and physical spaces of the laboratory in chapter 3. Therein, I narrow my analysis of rats and mice to the ways in which both animals, but mice particularly, are frequently and fruitfully exploited for their occupation of a liminal conceptual, physical, and meaningful space in the technoscientific context of the laboratory. It may even be said that ambiguity and ambivalence are necessary to the production of scientific yields when they involve rat and mouse models as human homologues.

In this chapter, I follow Morris (2000) in pursuing the idea that ambiguity and ambivalence very often cloud those relationships which seem to be straightforwardly antagonistic or polarised, such as those which are conducted between humans and rats. There is an abundance of material drawn from popular culture that evidences the ambiguous and/or ambivalent place that is afforded the rat. In the ambiguous category belongs E. B. White's *Charlotte's Web's* Templeton, a rat whose actions save the main character's life—but only because he will eventually benefit from his actions, which will mean more food for him (White, 1952). Similarly, the cellar rat of John Masefield's *The Midnight Folk* (1927) requires bribery to be of any assistance. These rats can be helpful, but their selfish natures mar what would otherwise be the goodness of the act. There are positive popular culture representations of rats and mice, such as the main characters in the children's films *Ratatouille* (Disney Pictures/Pixar, 2007) and *Stuart Little* (Columbia Pictures, 1999) (based on E. B. White's 1945 book of the same name). However, these exist cheek by jowl with the far more common negative depictions that are to be found, for example, in the horror genre (examples include Lovecraft's *The Rats in the Walls* [1924] and Poe's *The Gift* [1842], in which *The Pit and the Pendulum* appears). This contrast serves to further illustrate the ambiguous/ambivalent place of the rat in particular, which I turn now to explore.

RAT KIND, MOUSE KIND, HUMAN KIND

Rats are medium-sized rodents belonging to the superfamily Muroidea. The muroid family is very large, being classified into 6 families, 19 subfamilies, 280 genera, and more than 1,300 species—over 50 of which are rats. Mice also belong to the Muroidea superfamily. The true, or Old World, rats, including the best-known species the Black rat and the Brown rat, are members of genus *Rattus*. Both the Black and Brown Old World species originated in Asia, spreading from the grasslands of China into Europe and arriving in the New World sometime after 1775. The Brown rat, the most common vermin species in Australia and the one from which both pet and laboratory rats have descended, has spread to all continents except Antarctica. These rats are so common because of their excellent survival skills, which are based in part on their opportunistic behaviours. They occur where human beings do—as a result of their long and intertwined history with humans, rats have cosmopolitan sympathies. Ellmann (2004) noted that 'the rat shares these sympathies with modernists and Jews, the exiles and émigrés attracted to the cosmopolitanism of the capital, with its porous boundaries of ethnicity, morality, and language' (p. 62).

For their presence in human habitations, Brown rats are also known in ecology as one variety of the commensal rats.[2] In ecology, commensalism is a class of relationship between two organisms wherein one organism benefits but the other does not. In an ecological context, Brown rats continue to be viewed commensally rather than parasitically (a relationship in which one organism benefits and the other is harmed)—even though the tunnelling activity alone of Brown rats causes structural damage to buildings to the tune of billions of dollars a year worldwide. Mice, too, are considered to be destructive pests. Their success in establishing themselves alongside human populations is reflected in the origin of their species name, 'mouse', which derives from the Sanskrit *mush*, meaning 'to steal'. Mice have lived alongside people since humans made the move from hunter gatherers to farmers and created for themselves—and for the mice—a stable food supply. Mice have been with people ever since.

Of course, the direction of harm is not one way; humans, for their part, have wrought very great devastation on rat- and mousekind. Traps are commonly available to the householder in the quest to keep rodents at bay. Because rats and mice have acute hearing, ultrasonic devices that emit a frequency that is distressing to rats and mice have also been brought onto the market to deter them from entering houses. Single-dose poison baits, which were traditionally popular in rodent control, are now in decline owing to the appearance on the market of the much lower toxicity anticoagulant rodenticides. In some instances, humans have directed harmful action towards rats sufficient to eliminate entire populations of the animal; an eradication program that was begun in 2007 on Alaska's Rat Island, for example, resulted in the island being declared rat free in June 2009. Determined governmental action taken in Alberta, Canada, has also led to the virtual elimination of the once-plentiful Brown rat population there. In the early 1950s, the government introduced a program that included poisoning rats (first by means of arsenic trioxide and thereafter with the more effective but less toxic Warfarin) and destroying (by means of explosion) buildings that were infested. Under supporting legislation that was introduced at the same time, householders and municipal authorities too were required to take lethal action against any rat they happened across and to take action to prevent rats from taking up residence in their properties.

The term 'commensal' is partly appropriate, though, if its Latin root, *cum mensa* ('to share a table') is foregrounded; in common with human mammals, rats consume a wide range of substances, including meat, fish, and cereals. The simultaneity of consumption suggested by the term 'share' is generally not appropriate in the West, however; the opportunity for the wild rat to share the spoils of human labour is wholly dependent on its opportunistic nature and not on the generosity of its generally unwilling human benefactors. Indeed, as Serres's (1982) lamentations suggest, the commensal rat-human relationship is frequently regarded in the terms of battle: 'the battle against rats is already lost; there is no house, ship, or palace that does not have its share' (p. 12). Their presence alongside humans is *unheimlich* (uncanny) in the double sense that Freud (1919/2003) employed the term: rats and mice are at once unhomely and homely, foreign and contemptibly familiar. Serres's language of war and the direction of violence towards the enemy which dwells within the walls, under floors, and in the unfamiliar places of the otherwise well-known homescape echoes Zinsser's wording in his *Rats, Lice and History* (1934/1963). In it, Zinsser employed the language of perpetual war to suggest that humans and rats have kept pace with one another but cannot seem to wholly destroy one another (p. 208).

In terms of its physical dimensions, the Brown rat (also known as the Norwegian rat[3]) does not appear at first glance to be much of an enemy. At 46 cm long from nose to tail and weighing between 300 and 500 grams, it is certainly the largest of the commensal rats, as well as the most common in terms of its association with people. The species has a blunt snout, small ears and eyes, a thick, heavyset body, and a scaly, hairless tail that is shorter than the overall body length. In its wild manifestation, the animal's coat is red-brown, gray-brown, or almost black, and its underside is anywhere from gray to cream to tan in colour. The Brown rat is a dichromate, and it perceives colour as a human with red-green colour blindness would and in quite low chromatic saturation. A non-pigmented animal's vision is very poor indeed (at around 20/1200, with very high interruptive light scatter). A pigmented animal fares slightly better (at around 20/600). Though their vision is poor, their hearing is relatively good; it exceeds the range of human hearing. Mice possess similar sensory capacities, being able to perceive ultrasound up to 100 kHz, but they have poor colour vision. Mice use pheromones for social communication, which they detect with the Jacobson's organ. Rats, more so than mice, are social animals, and as such, they exhibit co-sleeping arrangements and a hierarchical pack order. Their high-frequency, ultrasonic vocalizations, which occur in response to pleasurable stimuli such as sex and play, also seem to be socially motivated.

The mouse does not seem to be particularly menacing either; an adult house mouse, which may vary in fur colour anywhere from white to light brown to black, measures between 7.5 and 10 cm, of which the tail makes up around half. They rarely weigh more than 25 g in the wild. As they are very commonly predated, mice typically live for less than about a year in the wild.

Rats and mice (along with people) devise social solutions to survival problems. All three animals—mice, rats and humans—are willing to try a range of new foods; indeed, this is part of the reason that all three species are so successful. But, this willingness is also tempered by a high degree of caution—also a part of the success of rats and mice. Both show a conflict of motivation when it comes to new foods, with rats being somewhat more neophobic than are mice; rats will maintain known routes to food and shelter sources for as long as possible, whereas mice investigate new food sources very soon after they have appeared. In rats, this omnivore's paradox is solved by complex and highly developed social means; rats share with humans the capacity to learn from one another. When a brave and pioneering rat eats a new food source, other rats smell her breath and coat and follow suit if the pioneer seems to be well and unaffected by her new culinary adventure. If she is not well, rats learn from this 'poisoned partner effect' and avoid that food. Also in common with humans, rats can make the connection between eating and how they feel after eating, even hours after food has been consumed.

The capacity to develop social solutions is not the only thing that rats share with people. Both mice and rats have high genetic and biological homology with people—this is what makes them such appropriate animal models for the laboratory. Mice, for example, share 99% gene homology with humans. Further, it seems that rats also share some cognitive capacities with humans. The ability to reflect on one's own mental processes (metacognition) is a defining feature of human existence, and prior to 2007, it was considered to be a capacity that was limited to humans and some nonhuman primates. In 2007, Foote and Crystal published the results of their study on metacognition in rats, which revealed that rats had a working knowledge of their own cognitive states, evidenced when they showed that they knew when they did not know the answer in a duration-discrimination test (see Foote & Crystal, 2007).[4]

Such qualities as I have described hardly seem to be the stuff of the nightmarish scenarios in which rats, particularly, frequently feature. Clearly, the rat bears the weight of reputation upon its small body. And an uncannily familiar body it is, too—perhaps not in its physical appearance, but certainly in terms of its social bearing towards other bodies of its own kind and humankind as well as in that it is cognitively homologous with a human body. In the very recognition of the similarly between humans and rats in these and other terms, however, lies one of the foundations of the human enmity towards rats (and, as I will elaborate later, to a far lesser extent, mice). This enmity issues precisely from the extent to which humans and rats share substance, motivation, habitation, sociality, and apparently, some cognitive capacity. As Kristeva (1982) argued, when the boundary between self and other slips, the abject is produced, indicating that the horror in the abject is to be found not in that which is wholly beyond compare with the self but precisely in that which all too easily becomes the self. Following Douglas's insights in *Purity and Danger* (1966), Kristeva described abjection as an operation of the psyche through which subjective and group identities are constituted by excluding that which threatens borders. In this context, the concept of the abject exists in between the concept of an object and the concept of the subject. Given that the abject is situated outside the symbolic order, being forced to face it is an inherently traumatic experience. Facing it with repulsion, as humans consistently do where rats are concerned, is subject-affirming, even subject-constituting, because such a reaction confirms the repulsed individual as a properly located being in the symbolic order.

This repulsion often manifests in the relegation of the abject to the situation of the filthy. The repulsion with which humans reject rats and other identity disturbers can be readily evidenced in their relegation to the position of the foul and dirty other. Both rats and mice are associated—if not always demonstrably, then conceptually, morally, and frequently—with filth and disease. Rats, for their part, have inspired fear and loathing in the West since the occurrence in the 14th century of the Black Death.[5] Brown rats, in common with dogs, humans, and cats, can become infected with and die from bubonic plague. They are not the reservoirs of the responsible bacterium, *Yersinia pestis*, as they are often thought to be; the bacterium is, in fact, transmitted zoonotically[6] by the rat flea. Similarly, house mice are not directly responsible for causing all of the diseases they are considered to bear. Rickettsialpox, a febrile disease that clinically resembles chicken pox, is frequently thought to be caused by mice, but in fact, it is caused by *Rickettsia akari* and is transmitted from mice by mites. Mites feeding on mice become infected, and humans will become infected if they are bitten by an infected mite (rather than by the mouse itself).

This is not to say that mice and rats do not carry or spread diseases. Owing to the fact that mice and rats share the spoils of humans' tables, the contamination of food, food utensils, and storage containers with rodent urine and or feces is a frightening spectre, if the amount of advertising for rodent extermination is to be taken as a guide. Many rodent exterminator websites comprehensively list the ills that can be expected from contact with rats and mice, including information that alerts the reader to the fact that mice and rats carry the salmonella bacteria that causes food poisoning in humans, as well as Weil's disease, tapeworm, and jaundice. Mice also carry chloriomeningitis, a variety of the meningitis virus. Whereas bubonic plague is transmitted via fleas, Weil's disease is spread by direct contact with murine urine or feces, when bacteria are able to enter the skin through scratches or lesions. Worldwide, very significant losses are caused annually in animal and human food stocks by rat and mouse contamination. In Australia, the Brown rat is widely considered to be the most economically detrimental pest in the country as a result of its propensity to infest grain stores, flour mills, supermarkets, domestic houses, and anywhere else that offers shelter and a stable food supply.[7]

The assignation of filth to rat and mouse kind extends beyond their immediate capacity to transmit disease; in everyday metaphoric parlance, the rat is the bad other, the figure which contaminates and ruptures social solidarity (as in to 'rat' on someone or to be a 'union rat'). Mice and rats are also the common subjects of food prohibitions: In Leviticus (11:29), rats, along with lizards and weasels, are prohibited as food. In her examination of abominations in Leviticus, Douglas (1966) described how versions of the bad other—including mixed substances, defiled flesh, and unclean animals such as the rat—have the potential to merge with the human body, which then requires purification. Douglas noted in respect to animals that in general, the underlying principle of cleanness for animals that are to be consumed 'is that they shall conform fully to their class. Those species that are unclean are imperfect members of their class, or whose class itself confounds the general scheme of the world' (p. 69). She noted that rats are anomalous in their class—as four-legged animals, and in common with mice, rats perversely use their 'hands' for walking. Indeed, rats are extremely dexterous with their front paws and often use them as 'hands'—another indication of the ways in which rats might be understood to be similar to humans in terms of their bodily capacities, not least, as Fissell (1999, p. 2) suggested, in their imagined capacity to display a mastery of particular human capacities. This mastery of handedness, along with the other ways in which rats might slip across the bounded areas of human taxonomies, can make humans uneasy. Such unease is often reflected in the construction of the rat as a filthy other to the human self, but the assignation of such terms to the rat is not to be taken at face value.

In a passage that undermines the importance of filth in the construction of the rat as the problematically dirty and utterly different (from the self) other, Kristeva (1982) noted, 'It is not lack of cleanliness or health that causes abjection but what disturbs identity, system, order. What does not respect borders, positions, rules. The in-between, the ambiguous, the composite' (p. 4).

In 1996, the televised emergence of the Vacanti mouse, which produced reactions of horror and generalised outrage among the television-viewing public, drove home Kristeva's point. One year earlier, in 1995, Charles Vacanti, an anaesthesiologist at the University of Massachusetts, and Linda Griffith-Cima, an assistant professor of chemical engineering at the Massachusetts Institute of Technology (MIT), created the creature that is now colloquially known as 'ear mouse'. Ear mouse was developed for the purposes of demonstrating a method of creating cartilage structures that is suitable for transplantation into human patients. A biodegradable polyester fabric shaped into an ear mould and instilled with bovine cartilage cells was implanted onto the back of a hairless mouse. The genetic mutation that caused baldness in the mouse also inhibited the mouse's immune system, thereby reducing the chances of rejection of the implant. The bovine cells would be nourished from the mouse's blood supply and would eventually replace the biodegradable fibres to create an 'ear' for use in plastic surgery procedures for humans.

The first pictures of ear mouse were released following a 1996 BBC TV broadcast, 'Test Tube Bodies', produced by the British science show *Tomorrow's World*. The images were quickly grabbed and broadcast widely—the Jay Leno program screened the pictures, and they then flooded the Internet, where they were routinely and incorrectly regarded as the bringing together of a human ear and a mouse body. This misinformation was used to great effect by animal rights and advocacy groups, which protested the use of the mouse for the order of experimentation that would not only corrupt the mouse's corporeal integrity in attaching a foreign (human) body to it but would also regard the mouse's body as disposable once the all-important human ends had been met. It was used to greater effect by antigenetics groups. In 1999, Turning Point Project, a prominent American antigenetics group, placed a full-page picture advertisement in the *New York Times* with a caption reading, 'This is an actual photo of a genetically engineered mouse with a human ear on its back'. The advertisement brought about all the horror that might be expected at the prospect of bringing an (only) apparently human ear together with the body of the mouse—all the horror of abjection.

Ear mouse perhaps most dramatically illustrates the ease with which rats and mice—in this case, a mouse—can slip into the only ostensibly bounded domain of the human self. But, all told, rats appear to be greater threats to the self than do mice. Regarded in folklore as uncannily intelligent, they are supposed to be able to foresee the destruction of any house or ship they are living in and to abandon it just prior to a devastating event. Rats have long been warily regarded for their intuitive intelligences. Where mice share a high genetic affinity with people, rats share social capacities for learning, intelligence, and metacognition; their capacities to cross boundaries, to infest the place of the self, makes them all the more poised to disrupt the boundaries that separate the human self from the rat other. Ellmann (2004) argued that the capacity for rats to cross borders of many kinds and to invoke human disgust and fear also has a temporal quality. She noted that 'the fact that rats date back to the origins of human history makes [rats] particularly threatening to modernism, because they come to stand for the resurgence of the undead past' (p. 60). All of humans' modern equipment—such as the Internet and telephone cabling—are designed to differentiate humans' social and physical worlds from those which preceded them. However, they can be easily gnawed at by sharp little teeth—of course, not all of them belonging to rats, although they are frequently blamed if rodent extermination advertising is anything to go by—thusly materially destroying the differentiation between history and modernity. Rats have been with humans all along, and they gnaw at the material and knowledge boundaries that compartmentalise and safely contain humans' past.[8]

If one key element of the human antipathy for rats (and to a lesser extent, mice) lies precisely in their uncanny similarity with people, then certainly another issues from their apparent proclivity for sex. Indeed, their reproductive rate is very high, although the infant survival rate depends ultimately on the availability and quality of food, the population density in the area, and the age of the female rat.[9] Rats can breed at any time of the year providing conditions are suitable, but they are most active in the spring and autumn. The gestation period is very short—typically only some 21 days. The litter is usually comprised of between 6 and 12 infants (or pups), and up to 5 litters a year can be produced. Pups cease nursing at 4 to 5 weeks of age and reach breeding age at 12 weeks.

Like rats, mice are capable of increasing their populations very quickly. One of the most numerous of the genus *Mus*, the house mouse *Mus musculus*, has a gestation period of 19 to 21 days and can have between 5 and 10 litters per year comprising an average of 7 pups. Like rats, they continue to breed year round if conditions are favourable. Female and male animals are capable of breeding as early as 5 weeks of age. Such figures inspire all the horror that is associated with the filth of rats and mice and the filth of constant sex that begets images of plague proportions of rats and mice overrunning human settlements.

Pet Rats, Pest Rats

The recent history of the Brown rat is inextricably intertwined with the lives of two Victorian London men, Jack Black and Jimmy Shaw. Jack Black rose to prominence in the business of rat killing; he was so effective at it that he was appointed Her Majesty's rat catcher. By all accounts, he was a charismatic figure, sporting a homemade uniform comprising a top hat, bright-red waistcoat, and a leather sash featuring two cast-iron rats he had made himself from plaster casts of dead rats. His bright-red wagon decorated with white silhouettes of rats boasted a small stage and several large cages of rats (see Golding, 1990, pp. 30–32; Herbert, 1988; Mayhew, 1851, pp. 11–20). The rats were used to demonstrate Black's fearlessness because he handled them with great confidence. They were also used to prove the efficacy of his potions; he routinely carried out a live poisoning before his fascinated public. For Herbert, such a display evidences the 'cult of rat-worship' that was then operative—the cult being one expression of the equivalency of the sanctified and the unclean that characterised Victorian London at the time. Herbert (1988) suggested that Black's very ability to handle the rats with impunity was appreciated by the crowd, who knew that it 'is the sign of mystic affinity with them: they are his (and the queen's) totem in the primitive, magical sense of the term, and he performs the priestly rites of sacrifice almost in their full-blown cultic form' (p. 21).

Black obtained the post of Her Majesty's rat catcher sometime around 1835, when he learned that the queen's retained rat catcher, Mr. Newton, was ill. Having been adept at catching rats since he was 9 years old, when he used to do so to rid farmers of infestations and also to supply them to dog owners who were involved in rat-baiting, Black was initially retained at 6 pounds a year, but the rate was then changed to 3 pence per rat. At this rate, Black made good money. He also continued to sell rats in large numbers to rat-pit owners, including one Jimmy Shaw. Although the parliament of the United Kingdom implemented the Cruelty to Animals Act in 1835, which spelled the end of bull and bear baiting, rat baiting continued and, in the absence of the other baiting sports, became increasingly popular. Black sold large quantities of rats to Shaw, which were then sold on to 'pit-dog' owners. Shaw's pit was stocked with 100 rats, and then the pit dog, usually one of the terrier varieties, was introduced, with the aim of killing as many rats in as short a time as possible.

Although both men were involved in the business of rat killing, each was also involved in the breeding and supply of pet rats.[10] Their access to large numbers of rats gave them the opportunity to seek out those rats with unusual markings and colourings, including the albino rat, which Shaw described as 'a freak of nature' (see Golding, 1990, pp. 30–32). About his pet rat sideline, Black recalled to the chronicler and self-proclaimed anthropologist Henry Mayhew,

> I've bred the finest collection of pied rats which has ever been knowed in the world. I had above eleven hundred of them all wariegated [*sic*] rats, and of a different specie and colour, and all of them in the first instance bred from the Norwegian … I've sold many to ladies for keeping in squirrel cages. Years ago I sold 'em for five and ten shillings a-piece, but towards the end of my breeding them, I let 'em go for two-and-six. (as cited in Mayhew, 1851, p. 11)

It is supposed that Black supplied Beatrix Potter with the white rat upon which she based her whimsical character 'Samuel Whiskers' (see Ellmann, 2004, p. 64). It is known that he presented Queen Victoria and the ladies of her court with tamed pet rats that were kept in delicate gilded cages (Golding, 1990, pp. 30–32). Here again arises the cult of the rat, in which the reverence for the Queen and the abhorrence for rats evidence the equivalency of the sanctified and the unclean. The rats were bodies of ambivalence, not only because their bodies were vested with the capacity to be mystically powerful in spreading the filth of sex and the filth of other pollution, but also because their pollutive powers rendered them just as untouchable and powerful as the Queen herself. The power of the Queen and the power of the rat were intertwined in the oral histories of London sewer workers in the 19th century. The character of the Queen Rat, it was said, could turn into an attractive girl and seduce any tosher[11] she fancied. If the tosher satisfied the queen, she would see to it that he had good luck and found money and other valuables that had been lost down the gratings. This was under the condition that he never spoke of meeting her; if he did so, drowning was the likely punishment. Usually the man did not guess who she was, for she looked quite human, except that her eyes caught the light like an animal's and she had claws instead of toenails. Another telltale sign could be that she might leave upon his body a rat-like love-bite. Any children the man's wife bore after his liaison with the Rat Queen would have one blue eye and one grey—grey being the colour of the river, the domain of the Rat Queen (see Westwood & Simpson, 2005). An underlying logic of power here allows the queen and the rat to fantastically imply one another.

Though Mayhew's insights are usually dismissed out of hand as anthropologically irrelevant, or at least underdeveloped (see, for example, Yeo, 1971), Herbert (1988) noted that Mayhew's anthropological insights into uncleanness, contagion, and the forbidden are central not only to the argument he mounted in *London Labour*, in which Black's comments quoted earlier appear, but are also anthropologically significant. They are so in Herbert's view because in his investigation of aberrant phenomena (the lot of the urban poor), Mayhew touched on an important (or rather, later to be important) anthropological theme: the interrelation of the civilized and the primitive. This theme is pursued in several ways, including in and through the paradoxical character of the savage's taboo, later to be codified by James Frazer in his *The Golden Bough* (1951 [1919]), wherein the conceptions of holiness and pollution remain undifferentiated; in Mayhew's recognition of his own positionedness as a Bourgeois figure undertaking an examination of the wretched proletariat, which would later come to be known as reflexivity; and in his attention to Mayhew's own aversion in looking closely at the poor which, as Herbert noted, is an inversion of the Foucauldian appreciation of the disempowerment that can be caused by looking—Mayhew felt that to look away was far more damaging (Herbert, 1988:2). In his pursuit of the themes that articulated the nexus between primitive and civilized life, and of specific interest to my purposes here, though, is the role Mayhew assigned to the rat. In his pursuit of the themes that articulated the nexus between primitive and civilized life—and that are of specific interest to my purposes here—is the role Mayhew assigned to the rat.

Herbert argued that in his fascination with the creature and his refusal to make direct expressions concerning the threatening nature of the rat, Mayhew treated the rat as a symbol of profound ambivalence. *London Labour* is indeed strewn with figurative and pictorial images of rats which serve to index Mayhew's unspoken contention that just beneath the surface of the civilized lay the spectre of the primitive. Such an insight is borne out in the very physicality of the city of London, a physicality in which rats and people were inextricably intertwined. The well-documented Victorian divide between the dualisms of the upper and lower classes as well as clean and dirty places and notions merged with the physicality of major cities (London, Paris) and, in true Douglasian style, with corporeality. As for the body, the city's 'below-the-waist' ablutions were considered disgusting and were cleansed or hidden—a new habit of city design and maintenance that extended to the en masse bodies of its lowly inhabitants, the 'great unwashed'. Rats, too, were easily relegated to the position of filthy vermin, owing to their habit of dwelling in lower places, the sewers. As Herbert (1988) noted of the 19th-century social commentator Henry Mayhew's observations of rats, in its apparently rampant sexuality, the rat came to embody the dirty bodily drives that the Victorians strove, in their human civility, to suppress. The human capacity to suppress came to mark a key difference not only between humans and animals but also, according to Herbert, between Victorian Londoners and primitive others (including the urban poor). The apparent capacity of the animal to contaminate correlated closely with the moral values of the time. Moreover, in their imagined capacity to, according to Mayhew's informants, inflict a poisonous bite, magically communicate uncleanliness to things and persons, and inflict cancer in the mouths of dogs, as well as in their possession of a profligate libidinal drive, rats took on supernatural qualities or, as Herbert (1988) put it, came to embody the 'uncanny life that filth always possesses' (p. 14). The sexual drives and the pollutive associations of rats are here revealed to have passed into the realm of the magical: 'In rats, the state of being saturated with uncleanness and that of possessing frightening quasi-electrical force are identical—this identity being the crux of taboo thinking' (Herbert, 1988, p. 15). The rat is revealed to be an ambiguously located creature, as taboo animals invariably are; rats are both the embodiment of biblical injunctions against the unclean and, simultaneously, the holders of supernatural powers.[12, 13]

Mice, too, have been the subject of a similar taboo; the clergy of the Middle Ages connected their filthy demeanour with their 'lustfulness' to yield the mouse-instrument of the devil. Charlotte Latham referenced the association of the rat, particularly, with the devil—an association that is bound up with the rat's sexuality, because in the stories she recounted the rats appear in plague proportions or, in other words, in the physical outcome of their lustfulness (see Latham, 1878, p. 23). Charles Dickens's recollection of a terrifying tale his nurse used to tell him about a carpenter who 'sold himself to the Devil for an iron pot and a bushel of ten-penny nails and half a ton of copper and a rat that could speak'(Dickens, 1860, p.151) is also characterised by the appearance of rats in numbers; the carpenter is so tormented by the speaking rat that he tries to kill it, only to find himself haunted by dozens of them. He flees to a ship that is infested with rats—led, of course, by the speaking rat—who are busy gnawing the ship to pieces. The carpenter's warnings to the crew go unheeded, and all on board are drowned (Dickens, 1860).

Although the place of the rat might seem to have been securely tethered to the sewers, the human image of them was clearly sufficient to allow them to dwell simultaneously in a delicate gilded cage in the residence of the monarch herself.[14] However, as Kristeva (1982) noted, the abject is that which a culture casts out from itself in order to determine what is not itself, the casting out being accomplished through the ritual acts of burning, burial, and exorcism. The rat continues to emerge from the ashes, 'for the abject always pops back up' (Ellmann, 2004, p. 62). Indeed, as Derrida observed civilisation is founded on that which it excludes: on excess, excrement, and exteriority. Rats and mice, having demonstrated the failure of these rituals across time, can be, as Birke suggested, more than one thing at once. Nowhere is this more evident than in the simultaneous location of the house rat or mouse as the bearer of dirt and disease and the lab rat or mouse as being the forefront of the fight against disease, as I turn to discuss in the following section.

FROM THE SEWER TO THE LABORATORY

As early as the 17th century, mice were utilised in studies of anatomy and respiration. The first use of the Brown rat in laboratories occurred in 1828, when the animals were brought into laboratories for physiological studies (including a study on fasting). Crampe performed the first breeding experiments in the 1870s and 1880s. In the late 1800s, Swiss neuropathologist Adolf Meyer brought representatives of the recessive stocks that were developed by Crampe and other researchers in Europe to America. These animals became the foundation stock of American laboratory rats (see Porter, 2000).[15] In the 1890s, rats were used in neuroanatomical studies at the University of Chicago. From there, rats were sent to the Wistar Institute of Anatomy and Biology in Philadelphia. These animals established the Wistar stock of *Rattus norvegicus*. By 1906, Henry H. Donaldson began the process of standardizing albino rat strains, represented by the Wistar-derived rat. He initiated an important multidisciplinary research program that, in its earliest manifestation, utilised rats to explore nutrition, behaviour, and inheritance. By the 1930s, *Rattus norvegicus* had become a very common experimental animal that was utilised in many types of research (see Porter, 2000).[16]

The origins of laboratory mice can be traced to the breeders and fanciers of 19th-century Europe, who developed the albino and colour mutants. These provided stocks for later research. In 1907, a Harvard undergraduate named Clarence Cook Little began investigating the inheritance of coat colour in mice. Two years later, he began inbreeding mice. His interest in neoplastic diseases led him to recognise that inbreeding mice eliminated the genetic diversity in unrelated animals and facilitated his study of tumours. Within 15 years, many of the strains of mice that are used in research today were established (see Porter, 2000, p. 5).[17] Presently, rats and mice are the most commonly used vertebrate animals in research and testing. In the United States, they account for approximately 90% of all mammals used in scientific endeavours. Indeed, these two rodent species account for almost 14 times all other species combined. But it is the laboratory mouse that is the most important model organism in biology and medicine and is by far the most commonly used genetically altered laboratory mammal.[18] Mice are more frequently employed in the laboratory than rats because the genetic manipulation that is necessary to produce standard animals for specific studies is far more difficult to accomplish in rats. Specifically, rat strains are generally not transgenic or genetically modified because the gene knockout and embryonic stem cell techniques that work very easily in mice are relatively difficult to perform in rats. This means that rats and mice are good for different things in the lab. Because rats are intelligent (in terms that humans recognise) and demonstrate a psychology that is in many respects similar to that of humans, they are frequently involved in research related to intelligence, learning, and drug abuse. Rats are important in behavioural research because of their docility, adaptability to new surroundings, tendency to explore, ease of training, and responsiveness to reward-punishment and a variety of sensory cues. Mice are not as adept in these ways, and so they are used less in these types of research.[19, 20] Rats are considered to be a better 'model' than mice for studying certain human diseases and conditions, including memory loss, muscular dystrophy, cystic fibrosis, AIDS, substance abuse, genetic disease, spinal cord injuries, and heart disease. However, mice continue to be more prominent models in many of these investigations owing to the difficulties of producing transgenic rat bodies. Mice, for their part, are especially useful in cancer research because of their high tumour incidence and the association of specific types of tumours with certain inbred strains.[21] Because they are highly susceptible to many viruses, especially when they are injected as newborns, mice are used widely in virology research. Because they do not live very long, they are excellent experimental subjects for aging research. Mice are the primary mammal used in genetics research because of their high reproductive potential and short generation time. They are also used widely in drug testing and radiobiology research because they are economical to use in large numbers.

Despite the prevalence of mice in the laboratory for many kinds of research operations calling for animal models of human diseases, rats and mice are both the bearers of several attributes that make them popular research animals. Both animals are well understood anatomically, physiologically, and genetically. Rats and mice are generally hardy, very adaptable, easy to care for, and inexpensive. Their small size means they can be accommodated cheaply and in large numbers, and their short generation time and high reproductive potential contributes to the economy of their production. Rats and mice tolerate handling well and remain docile if they are handled frequently and gently, which means there is a high degree of safety in working with them. Mice are particularly safe to work with because their small incisor teeth do not allow them to inflict a serious bite. Both animals have high inbreeding tolerance, which means that there can be good assurance that laboratory animals are genetically identical where that is required. Many mutant stocks that are models of human disease have also been established. Both are amenable to germ-free and pathogen-free production techniques, thereby greatly reducing intercurrent disease as a variable.

Though the very body of the rat or the mouse is sufficiently nebulous to locate it simultaneously in the sewer and the scientific laboratory—lab and sewer rats and lab and house mice are, after all, essentially the same species—key meaningful elements of its body are highlighted in each space to locate the animal as one that is thoroughly integrated with one kind of space (i.e., sewer, domestic house) or another (laboratory, laboratory cage). Conceptual work is done on the body of the lab rat to separate it from its conjoined twin, the sewer-dwelling rat—even though many scientists in this study frequently joined them when they had to make responses about animal rights. As one scientist, Paul, said, 'People don't care much for rats—they eradicate them in their own homes—so they don't care much if a rat is killed in the lab'. Conceptual boundaries are drawn around the ambiguous body of the animal that manifest, in many actual cases and certainly in the public imagination, in terms of colour (or its absence). The typical lab rat derives from the brown *Rattus norvegicus* species,[22] yet in the laboratory, it typically appears as white as purely driven snow, as do laboratory mice. The visual differentiation of these animals marks them as qualitatively different from their sewer and house cousins. Although they are not all white—laboratory mice and rats come in a variety of coat colours and might be black, black and white, or brown as well as albino—I use the characteristic and publicly imagined whiteness of these animals in the laboratory setting to draw attention to the symbolic dimensions that are summonsed by their colour or lack of it. In her examination of the meaning of the laboratory rat, which she eventually declared to be 'neutral', Edelman (2002) summarily dismissed the whiteness of laboratory rats and mice as anthropologically unimportant because she believed their colour to be scientifically unimportant. She argued that the albino variety was chosen 'because it was "experiment friendly" and not because its colour matched the laboratory environment' (p. 5). This may well be so, but it has no bearing on the culturally driven conceptual domains into which animals, colours, and values fall. The public image of lab rats and mice is typically white, and so whiteness is key to understanding the cultural, if not always the scientific, place of rats and mice in the lab and in the gutter. Symbolically (and biologically, if Edelman is right[23]), whiteness marks the distance(s) that mice and rats have travelled from the gutter. It is, after all, sufficient to cause them to be considered different animals: The ambiguity which might otherwise conjoin sewer rats with laboratory rats in conceptual terms is cut into by whiteness to create racial distinctions and moral dimensions of rat and mouse positionedness. As Haraway (1997) showed in her analyses of some of the conceptual work of separating laboratory and wild rats, white rats have been used to imply race dominance in some biolaboratory advertising.[24] In the course of journeying from the gutter to the institution, rats and mice have lost their blackness and brownness, from which a similar insight into race and class hierarchy might be made; rats and mice have made a movement from the ranks of the unclean to the cutting edge and the hygienic. This movement is certainly embedded in the historical form of pet rat breeding. Like cat and dog breeding, it conformed to certain standards that were inspired by the eugenic movement, which was committed to improving human 'stock'. This inspiration was put to specific and very sinister use when specific strains were bred in the 1960s to prove the intellectual inferiority of African Americans. In these experiments, as the title of Guthrie's (1976) well-known text about this and other indicators of cultural attitudes that were present in scientific motivations at the time indicates, 'even the rat was white'.

Whiteness is also associated in Western cultures with goodness, purity, and cleanliness. In her attention to the conceptual work of separation, Haraway (1997) noted of biolaboratory advertising that laboratory rats and mice are frequently placed in the symbolic service of ideas of good and worthy 'battles', 'wars', 'struggles', and 'fights' against disease, a category that was once (and is presently) occupied by the Brown rats and mice (see also Arluke, 1994; Michael & Birke, 1998; Paigen, 1995). White rats and mice are at the frontline of the battle against disease, a position that is visually signalled in biolaboratory advertising by their sparkling, clean, germ-free whiteness. In this position, rats and mice are also the sacrificial victims in the fight against disease, just as brown rats remain the deserving victims in the purifying work of casting out the sullying evil that their low-dwelling bodies represent. Even as they remain fair game for exterminators, who actively raise their villain status, rats and mice are the tiny heroes of the laboratory, bearing the suffering of research into a range of human ailments so that humans will not have to.

As Haraway (2008) noted of the mouse model that is routinely used in research on breast cancer, 's/he suffers, physically, repeatedly and profoundly, that I and my sisters might live' (p. 76). Just as this mouse, Oncomouse, has been produced to bear a cancer gene, she also bears the weight of humans' suffering. The allocation of suffering to this Christ-like figure occurs in the context of a salvation metanarrative in which, at least in the humanist view, the (humanist) God-scientist inflicts suffering on one body in order to ultimately save the rest of humankind. As the dominant laboratory models of human disease frames, mouse and rat bodies are just such bodies.

Oncomouse is but one of the many rodent models that are used to study human diseases.[25, 26] The opportunity presented by mouse and rat bodies to study human diseases has quite evidently spawned a great variety of rat and mouse models that mark lab mice and rats as phenomenologically distinctive from sewer-dwelling rats and house mice in genetic and symbolic—not to mention chromatic—terms. Many rodent strains (or groups in which all members are genetically identical) have been bred for the scientific experimentation on and investigation of human problems. Accomplished by means of inbreeding, the existence of a genetically identical population allows the researcher to exclude variations in genetics as a factor. When a random population that has genetic diversity is required, a rat stock or group of animals (or 'outbred strain') that do not have identical genotypes is drawn upon. Most outbred strains are derived from the albino Wistar rat. Other common strains are the Sprague-Dawley, Fischer 344, Holtzman albino strains, the Long-Evans, and Lister black-hooded rats. Inbred strains are also available but are not as commonly used as inbred mice. One of their number is the biobreeding diabetes-prone rat, which spontaneously develops autoimmune Type 1 diabetes. These rats are used as an animal model for Type 1 diabetes. Various mutant strains of mice and rats that are useful as animal models for a variety of human problems have been created by a number of methods. Mutant mice resulting from ordinary breeding include NOD mice, which develop diabetes mellitus type 1; 'Waltzing' mice, which walk in a circular pattern due to a mutation adversely affecting their inner ear;

and immunodeficient nude mice, which lack hair and a thymus. These mice do not produce T lymphocytes (and therefore do not mount cellular immune responses), and they are consequently useful animal models for immunology and transplantation research, as ear mouse demonstrated in his very public television debut on the Jay Leno show.

Where a model does not exist, it might be created. Mice, in common with humans, naturally develop diseases including cancer, atherosclerosis, hypertension, diabetes, osteoporosis, and glaucoma. However, a normal mouse, although it has a high degree of homology with humans, cannot be infected with the polio virus that devastates human health. A normal, unaltered mouse[27] lacks the cell-surface molecule that serves as the receptor for the virus in humans. In such a case, a transgenic animal—one that carries a foreign gene that has been deliberately inserted into its genome—might be created to enable research in an animal model.[28, 29] Transgenic mice[30] expressing the human gene for the polio virus receptor can be infected by the polio virus and can express the pathological changes that are characteristic of the disease in humans. Other diseases that afflict humans but normally do not strike mice (including cystic fibrosis, for example) can be induced by manipulating the mouse genome.

Whereas in the early days of biomedical research, scientists developed mouse models by selecting and breeding mice to produce offspring with the desired traits, more recently researchers have utilized innovative genetic technologies to produce custom-made mouse models for a wide array of specific diseases, as well as to study the function of targeted genes. Certainly, one of the most important advances has been the ability to create transgenic mice, in which a new gene is inserted into the animal's germline. As the (U.S.) National Human Genome Research Institute Web site notes,

> Even more powerful approaches, dependent on homologous recombination, have permitted the development of tools to 'knock out' genes, which involves replacing existing genes with altered versions; or to 'knock in' genes, which involves altering a mouse gene in its natural location. To preserve these extremely valuable

> strains of mice and to assist in the propagation of strains with poor reproduction, researchers have taken advantage of state-of-the-art reproductive technologies, including cryopreservation of embryos, *in vitro* fertilization and ovary transplantation.

The selective breeding and genetic manipulation of laboratory rats and mice has produced animals that are evidently a long way from their wild counterparts in the sewer, and even from those which inhabited the gilded cage. Although they retain the filthy and diseased status of the villains of the dark sewer, mice and rats are now also the clean, white standardised tools of the laboratory and the heroes in the fight against disease. Where they bore the metaphorical weight of deep human antipathy, now, at least in the laboratory, it is possible to regard Oncomouse as the creature who bore humans' cancer and who was central in the development of a cure.[31] Their position in the lab has inevitably changed rat/mouse-human animal relations, and it has changed the way that they might be understood relative to other 'wild' animals. Thus, as Birke (2003) pointed out, lab rats and mice are 'doubly othered'—first in their location relative to humans and secondly in their conceptual relation to other animals (p. 207). What are lab rats to sewer rats? What are human homologues to humans themselves? What are humans and animals to one another, and under what conditions is the human-animal divide crossed in the research laboratory?

ENDNOTES

1. Some of the differences reference gender—women can be described as 'mousy', whereas men are not often described in such terms.
2. In ecology, there are three other types of association: mutualism (where both organisms benefit), competition (where both organisms are harmed), and parasitism (where one organism benefits and the other one is harmed). Commensalism is inherently more difficult to demonstrate compared with parasitism and mutualism, because it is easier to show a single instance whereby the host is affected than it is to prove or disprove that possibility. Frequently, a detailed investigation will show that the host indeed has become affected by the relationship.
3. The Brown rat did not, in fact, originate in Norway; rather, the species came from central Asia and (likely) China. Early assumptions concerning its origin are responsible for the assignation of the common name of 'Norway rat', which is still in use.
4. The rats were given the opportunity to decline the test before taking it. Declining a test yielded a small but guaranteed reward, accurate performance on the duration test yielded a large reward, and inaccurate performance resulted in no reward at all. The rats declined difficult tests, indicating that they had knowledge of their own cognitive states.
5. Brown rats are, however, responsible for carrying a variety of other dangerous pathogens that cause serious diseases, such as Weil's disease and viral hemorrhagic fever.
6. The term indicates viruses that naturally reside in an animal reservoir host or arthropod vector.
7. Many Web sites also list a range of material damages: The constant gnawing of rodents can be the cause of serious damage to a range of materials. Typically, they may damage doors, skirtings, and other parts of buildings; upholstery; books; food containers or packaging; and parts of equipment or machinery. The gnawing of wires and cables has caused the failure of telephone systems and short circuiting, which may result in equipment breakdown and fires. On occasion, fire damage has even resulted from the gnawing of matches that have been collected in the nest.
8. Ellmann (2004) also noted the spatial distinctions that are made indistinct by rat travel: 'Associated with migration, it eats away the bounds of countries and cultural traditions with the rapacity of a multinational company' (p. 62).

9. When she is pregnant or in her maternal role, the female rat is called a 'dam'; prior to becoming pregnant, she is known as a 'doe'. The male is known throughout his lifespan as a 'buck'.
10. In a wonderful quirk, a woman named Mary Douglas was responsible for introducing rats into the American National Mouse Fancier Society. Douglas did not think rats should be excluded on the basis that they were not as appealing as mice.
11. Tosher was the name for London sewer workers during the period of the 19th century.
12. However powerful they are as a result of their location as taboo animals (at least in Victorian London), rats live brief lives—usually no more than a year or two at best in the wild. Because many animals predate on rats, and because there is a good deal of interspecies conflict, an annual mortality rate of 95% is generally assumed. A similar rate is assumed for mice.
13. Rats are not universally abominated. In the Chinese zodiac, for instance, people born in the Year of the Rat are thought to be, as Ellmann (2004) noted, 'charming, ambitious, successful, acquisitive, gossipacious, and short-tempered—by no means an abhorrent combination' (p. 62). Rats have places of high importance in Hindu iconography, appearing as mounts and companions to Ganesha and in varying roles to other deities. The temple of Karni Mata, the Hindu goddess of war, is consecrated to the rat and is populated by thousands of protected animals that are believed to be reincarnations of the dead. As Ellmann further noted, Western depictions of the rat in positive roles are scant: 'No Brancusi has attempted to idealise the locomotion of the rat, despite its nimbleness, contractibility, and lightness on its feet. Van Gogh is exceptional for treating the animal with some respect: in his 1884 painting *Two Rats*, the eponymous rodents huddle close together in the dark, nibbling a crust of bread, and watch the viewer with as much suspicion as the viewer watches them, their stealthy feast a mockery of greedy eyes' (p. 63).
14. And, although the ban on rat baiting that took effect in 1870 (and saw the last public competition held in Leicester in 1912 and the rat pit owner fined) seemed to have more to do with the welfare of the rat-pit dogs than of the rats themselves, the rat ceased to be a pitiless victim, at least in the pit. As Queen Victoria's love of animals was widely understood to have helped the ban through, her own love of pet rats may well have also contributed to the ban.
15. The reason for the choice of albino rats and mice as the preferred animal for scientific study remains unclear. Occurring in many mammal populations, albinism is a common mutation that impacts the affected animal's capacity to survive, particularly if the animal is a common prey animal. These mutants

were marketable curiosities as pets for Jimmy Shaw and Jack Black, and it may be that their location as such marked them as animals of a docile nature, suitable for frequent handling by people. The breeders of pet or fancy mice of the *Mus musculus* species were invited to supply laboratories in the late 19th century—one Massachusetts breeder supplied the animals that led to the creation of the c57 and DBA lines of mice in the early C20. The oldest strain of inbred rats dates from 1856, when the Jardin des Plantes reported a feeder colony of black hooded rats. That colony was still in existence 132 years later in 1988, and it gave rise to a strain of inbred rats. The oldest purpose-bred strain of inbred rats, the PA strain, was created by Helen Dean King at the Wistar Institute in Philadelphia by 1909. The Wistar rat, and to a lesser extent the Sprague-Dawley rat, gradually became the most popular rat strains for laboratory research (see Porter, 2000).

16. Other strains of rats were developed, including the Osborne-Mendel rat in 1909 at Yale; the Long-Evans, or hooded, rat varieties during 1915 through 1920 at the University of California-Berkeley; and the Sprague-Dawley rat by 1925 in Madison, Wisconsin (see Porter, 2000).
17. In 1926, Clara Lynch of the Rockefeller Institute obtained two male and seven female albino mice from a colleague in Switzerland. These were the ancestors of the 'Swiss mice' that are widely used today in research. Swiss mice from different sources may differ extensively. This is due to the long separation from the non-inbred original stock, which was genetically heterogeneous. Another factor complicates the use of the term 'Swiss mice': Any white mouse may be referred to erroneously as Swiss, even if it does not originate from true Swiss stock (see Porter, 2000).
18. This has disadvantaged many investigators, who regard many aspects of behaviour and physiology in rats as being more relevant to humans and easier to observe than they are in mice, and who wish to trace their observations to underlying genes. As a result, many researchers have been forced to study questions in mice that might be better pursued in rats. In October 2003, however, researchers succeeded in cloning two laboratory rats by nuclear transfer. So, rats may begin to see more use as genetic research subjects.
19. However, mice are used in some behavioural studies, especially those that are focused on pheromone research.
20. Rats are also frequently used in toxicity testing; the LD50 test, for example, is used to determine what amount of a chemical will kill 50% of a group of animals.
21. In addition, histocompatibility within inbred strains facilitates tumour transplantation.

22. Another species, *Rattus rattus* (the black, or roof, rat) is also used as an experimental model, but it has not contributed to the common laboratory rat strains.
23. Indeed, in respect to pet rats and mice, the process of domestication has had some impact on their physiology and personality. As Barnett (2002) pointed out, domestic rats are calmer and less likely to bite than their wild counterparts, they can tolerate greater crowding, they breed earlier, and they tend to produce more offspring. Their brains, livers, kidneys, adrenal glands, and hearts are smaller than those of wild rats. Selection for coat colour also has (largely unintended) consequences for personality. It may well be that pet and pest rats are significantly physiologically and psychologically different from one another because of the human intervention of domestication, but they are also considered differently from one another as a result of their conceptual location in the human image of rats and mice. The first pet rats that were delivered by Jack Black to the ladies of London for 'two and six' were drawn from the ranks of wild rats, and very little domestication interference had been done to them. But still, by dint of their location in the gilded cage and in the imaginations of their owners, these rats were substantively different from those that were exterminated in the thousands and hidden from a lady's view below the covered sewers.
24. They have also been used to indicate a Western dominance in medical and scientific knowledge (Haraway, 1997).
25. An animal model represents some, most, or all aspects of a normal or abnormal condition in another animal or human being. Abnormal model conditions may be inherited, spontaneous, or experimentally induced. Some of the major inherited diseases of rats have analogous conditions in people; these include hypertension, diabetes insipidus, retinal degeneration, and audiogenic seizures. Less common examples include hydrocephalus, deafness, microphthalmia, cataracts, pituitary dwarfism, noneruption of teeth, acholuric jaundice, and obesity.
26. This can be a double-edged sword: The small size of rats and mice makes them suitable for handling, restraint, and injections. However, their small size makes them difficult subjects for surgery or obtaining measurements and volume samples.
27. Mice are ideal for transgenic use due to their pronuclei, which are suitable for manipulation.
28. 'The foreign gene is constructed using recombinant DNA methodology. In addition to a structural gene, the DNA usually includes other sequences to enable it to be incorporated into the DNA of the host and to be expressed

correctly by the cells of the host. Mice are currently the most closely related laboratory animal species to humans for which the knockout technique can easily be applied. They are widely used in knockout experiments, especially those investigating genetic questions that relate to human physiology. Gene knockout in rats is much harder and has only been possible since 2003' (see http://users.rcn.com/jkimball.ma.ultranet/BiologyPages/T/TransgenicAnimals.html)

29. Mice are more frequently employed in the laboratory than rats because the genetic manipulation that is necessary to produce standard animals for specific studies is far more difficult in rats. Specifically, rat strains are generally not transgenic, or genetically modified, because the gene knockout and embryonic stem cell techniques that work very easily in mice are relatively difficult to perform in rats. This is why mice are the most common animal to work with, rather than rats.
30. These are also known as 'knock-in mice'. Transgenic mice, with foreign genes inserted into their genome, include abnormally large mice, with an inserted rat growth hormone gene; Oncomice, with an activated oncogene, so as to significantly increase the incidence of cancer; and Doogie mice, with enhanced NMDA receptor function, resulting in improved memory and learning. The difference between knock-in technology and transgenic technology is that a knock-in involves a gene inserted into a specific locus and is a 'targeted' insertion. A knockout mouse is a genetically engineered mouse in which one or more genes have been turned off through a gene knockout. Knockout mice are important animal models for studying the role of genes which have been sequenced but have unknown functions. By causing a specific gene to be inactive in the mouse and observing any differences from normal behaviour or condition, researchers can infer its probable function.
31. Birke (2003) described the two phases that are necessary to separate wild rodents from laboratory rodents for research purposes, which have together resulted in the simultaneous location of the 'clean' and 'dirty' rats and mice in the lab and the house, respectively. She noted that the first phase entailed the transference of rodents from 'wild' to 'lab' space (via the fancier's breeding room). The second she referred to as 'a process of greater industrialisation', in which lab rodents 'became standardised and, increasingly, "a part of the apparatus of science"' (p. 217). Lynch (1988) suggested that it is in the scientific research community's interest that members of the public connect lab mice with wild mice, because the deep antipathy towards wild mice helps to stave off the potentially outraged attentions of animal rights activists.

Chapter 3

Between Human and Nonhuman

Crossing the Great Divide in the Laboratory

Introduction

One crossing of the human-animal divide is immediately evident in the laboratory in the incorporation of mice and rats into biological and genetic kinship with humans. This crossing is fundamental to the very doing of science that is concerned with the application of research derived from nonhuman animal bodies; nonhuman animal bodies must be sufficiently similar to human bodies for the yield of experimentation to be applicable to human bodies. This crossing is accomplished through the subsumption of the speci-al differences of rats, mice, and humans to a shared mammalian membership. This subsumption does not make for a straightforward crossing of the human-animal divide, however, because the mammalian classification of rats and mice is equally used to locate them as equipment—and moreover, as disposable units of mammalian equipment. In this sense, the membership of rats and mice in the classification of mammal effects a reestablishment of the divide; rodent animals are lesser mammals than humans. This mammalian hierarchy is often indicated by the emergence of speci-al terms to describe rats and mice as 'only' rats or 'only' mice, particularly when they are on their way to the laboratory's gas chamber. Rats and mice are thus ambiguously located as both human homologues and human heterogenes in the laboratory as a result of their classification as mammals.

The ways in which the mammalian characteristics of rats and mice were drawn out by the scientists in this study indicates that rats and mice are not straightforwardly located on one side of the human-animal divide or the other as a result of their shared mammalian membership with humans; mice and rats are located ambiguously, as both fundamentally similar to and profoundly different from humans. The consequences of mammalian membership are also not straightforward. One consequence of the location of rats and mice as mammals whose bodies could be used to make insight into human bodies that was recognised by the scientists in this study was the way in which the laboratory environment could repress behaviours that are specific to rat and mouse species. In efforts to diminish this possibility, attendance to speci-al differences was made to meet the needs and comforts of laboratory rats and mice that might suffer for their subsumption under the category 'mammal', to occupy the position of generic, mammalian laboratory equipment. Here, the specific speci-al needs of research rodents were considered against the idea that rats and mice might be mistreated if they were considered to be only mammalian units of experimentation rather than 'natural', speci-al animals which, despite their lifetime location in the laboratory accommodations, still had needs that were specific to their kind. Attendance to the needs of 'natural' animals through consideration of their speci-al requirements in some ways mitigated the impacts of generic mammalian location. It was used to address some of the consequences rats and mice might suffer as a result of being located as animals for human scientific consumption, as I discuss in chapter 5.

Recognition of laboratory rodents as particular (rat or mouse) species was not always used to undo some of the consequences of human dominance in the laboratory; the speci-al differences between rodents and humans were also commonly invoked at the terminus of a research rodent's life to indicate the firmness of the human-animal division. As Alan, an immunologist who contributed to this study, commented as he submitted his research animals to the laboratory's sacrificial economy, 'They're only mice'. Yet, although they were involved in his study, the mice were located as human similars and stood in for human bodies in Alan's research. At specific times, speci-al differences were highlighted to indicate the location of the mammalian mouse as an animal, not a human, which can validly be killed within the laboratory's scientific coordinates.

In this chapter, I look closely at the ways in which rats and mice are located as human similars and human heterogenes through the invocation of their mammalian and speci-al characteristics; I also consider the consequences of these locations. Herein, I show that the human-animal divide is routinely and necessarily traversed through the kinning (the making of kinship) of rodents and people in biological and genetic terms. It is equally maintained as a division when rodent research animals occur in the laboratory as units of mammalian research equipment and when they occur as 'only mice' that can be unceremoniously dispensed with.

Crossing the Human-Animal Divide in the Laboratory: 'We Are All Mammals'

As I suggested in the introduction to this chapter, crossing the human-animal border is fundamental to those scientific enquiries that are concerned with deriving data from nonhuman animal models for application to the human body. For scientific research that is guided by this intention, nonhuman animal bodies must be sufficiently similar to human bodies for the outcomes of experimentation to have application to human bodies. The required sameness of nonhuman animal bodies and human bodies is accomplished through the subsumption of the speci-al differences of, in this case, rodent research animals and humans to a shared mammalian membership. A crossing of the human-animal divide is then accomplished in the sense that rats, mice, and people are aligned in their mammalian biology and genetic makeup and are much more similar than they are different. The diminishment of human-animal differences is present whether or not 'close' mammalian relatives to humans are the animal research subjects; in the case of fruit flies, for instance, genetic similarity between these animals and humans builds the bridge across the divide.

In the laboratory that I studied, the human-animal divide was bridged on the strength of the close biological and genetic relatedness of humans to rats and mice. These animals appear in the laboratory as human genekin and biokin. The location is made of rat and mouse bodies in the laboratory to recognise that the data yielded of rat and mouse bodies has a primarily human application. The Jackson laboratory's Leonard Schultz indicated on the lab's Web site that mice, on the basis of their close biological and genetic relatedness to humans, are

> critical models for experimental investigation of human immune diseases without putting [human] individuals at risk. Our recent research has leveraged these mouse models for studies on diabetes, bone development, autoimmunity, malignancy, anemia, thrombocytopenia, infectious diseases, transplantation tolerance and asthma.[1] (http://research.jax.org/faculty/leonard_shultz.html)

Outside the confines of the laboratory, it is not often that rats and mice are understood as human similars; it is far more common for rodents to be cast out from the realm of human similarity. As I have suggested throughout the previous chapters, this casting out is made by recourse to images and sentiments of contagion and competition which together give rise to that panoply of fears that frequently articulate rodent unrelatedness to people. As I have also suggested, and as Kristeva (1982) argued, such robust insistence on profound difference often reveals the extent to which the other might resemble one and the ease with which it might become one. Having said this, it was with some excitement that the *San Francisco Chronicle*'s medical writer,

Sabin Russell, reported the following in 2002, under the title 'Of Mice and Men':

> Matching newly minted genetic blueprints of mice and men, scientists have found a wealth of common chemistry between human beings and our tiny, four-legged ancestors. In a series of publications today in the British scientific journal *Nature*, international teams of researchers published a nearly complete sequence of the genetic instructions of 'Black 6,' the most common breed of laboratory mouse, and matched its traits with the recently decoded human genome. The genetic code of the mouse, published on a public website (www.ensembl.org), is expected to speed the work of laboratory scientists studying human diseases around the globe. Dr. Francis Collins, director of the National Human Genome Research Institute, called the feat 'a tremendously exciting and defining moment for biomedical research'

In the laboratory, the rodent 'becoming' of humans was deliberately accomplished in the purposeful recognition of mice and rats as commensurate with humans in biological and genetic terms. Added to the advantages of working with small, inexpensive, rapidly reproducing, and easily handled animals are the biological similarities between rats, mice, and people. As one scientist, Paul, explained it to me,

> Mice are much more like us than people [outside the lab] think they are. As mammals, as people are, of course, they have pretty much the same basic body plan, they get the same diseases, they suffer in similar ways to us. For instance, we use the same analgesics to relieve pain in mice that you yourself would have access to in the hospital. Their similarity [to humans] is why we use them.

Melissa, a virologist, explained it this way:

> Mice and rats have the same organs as human beings do. Though they are, of course, smaller mammals than humans, and their organs are different in size, they occur in the same positions as humans have them. As mammals, they also share a remarkable degree of genetic similarity with humans.

These explanations pertain to unaltered mice, which are described as human homologues in terms of their mammalian classification. In them, one finds the diminishment of speci-al difference and the privileging of the mammalian similarities that make humans and rodents more similar than they are different. This view is also to be found in the Web site of the U.S. Department of Energy Office of Science, Office of Biological and Environmental Research Human Genome Program (http://www.ornl.gov/hgmis). The content of the site indicates that the cases in which a mouse counterpart cannot be found for a particular human gene are few and far between—the number of human genes without a clear mouse counterpart, and vice versa, is estimated to be no larger than 1% of the total.[2] Essentially, there is a one-to-one correspondence between the genes of the two species; gene for gene, then, humans are very similar to mice.[3, 4]

The diminishment of speci-al characteristics is even more pronounced in mice and rats which have been engrafted with human stem cells. These animals are routinely referred to as 'humanised' animals. This is a particularly common descriptor for mice that have been developed to bear human attributes, including, for example, hybrid humanised mice that are used in the search for an AIDS vaccine—these animals are engineered to have a human immune system.[5] As Bhan, Singer, and Daar (2010) argued, the development and use of humanised animals has been controversial and has attracted much philosophical, ethical, and political criticism. In these controversial terms—and even when they are not humanised animals in the technical production sense of the term—mice and rats are human genekin and biokin, sharing mammalian bodily and genetic membership with 'us'.

The deployment of the term 'humanised mice', and the characterisation by scientists in this study of mice and rats as human similars even when they had not been modified, indicates that the speci-al differences of mice (and rats) from humans are readily subsumed under their mammalian membership with humans for the purposes of cross-special applicability. Their membership in this category privileges rodent-human collinearity, in which genetic and biological lines continue across and diminish the human/rat/mouse speci-al border, so that rats and mice are related to humans sufficient to draw out data of human significance. Mouse and rat bodies were considered by researchers in this study as 'ideal models' and perfect 'equipment' for the yielding of data that are meaningful to human bodies in precisely these collinear terms.

Collinearity is expressed in the way in which the largest European supplier of genetically modified mouse and rat models, GenOway, describes the benefits of using humanised rodents (which it describes as the results of classical transgenesis or homologous recombination). Its Web site points directly to the ways in which the results that are obtained from humanised mice provide insight into human health, noting that researchers who utilise them

> try to predict the answers they would obtain directly if they could perform the experiments in humans. These models are key components of any R&D project, because the quality of the results that are obtained relies mainly on the intrinsic ability of the model to predict the human response accurately. In recent years, genetically manipulated animals, like humanized mouse, have proved hugely promising tools to decipher physiological processes … humanized mouse is a powerful research tool to in-vivo decipher [human] physiology.

As GenOway's website blurb indicates, collinearity is at the heart of scientific experimentation on animals: The commensurability of rodents with humans is critical to the application of rat-yielded and mouse-yielded data to human bodies, which will ultimately reap the benefits of animal experimentation. In the very breaking down of the human-animal divide, sufficient that rats, mice, and humans might be considered kin, are to be found the conditions under which humans' close kin are positioned as mammalian units of equipment.

The Making of Mammalian Units of Equipment in the Lab

Rodent speci-ality is subsumed through collinearity in the terms I have described, via the articulation of human-rodent mammalian similarity to yield a mammalian bridge across the human-animal divide by way of biological and gene kinship. It is also subsumed in the positioning of the research rat or mouse as a single mammalian unit of experimentation and analysis, whose data will be directly applicable to the human mammal. Lynch (1988) indicated the ways in which speci-al ratness and mouseness are subsumed under the generic position of mammalian membership to yield a hierarchy of bodies, wherein one mammalian embodiment is in the service of another, more valuable embodiment. The subsumption of speci-ality and the marking of a devalued mammalian being is accomplished through what Lynch referred to as the making of the analytic animal, in which all elements of speci-ality are removed from the way the animal is viewed in the laboratory.

Here, qualities of inanimateness are assigned to the analytic animal, effectively muting its ratness or mouseness and relocating it as an object/apparatus, a nonspecific mammalian unit of investigation (Arluke, 1988; Lynch, 1988; Paton, 1993). Where the 'naturalistic' animal is the creature Birke (2003) described as the animal that bites and has anthropomorphic associations (p. 207), the analytic animal is deanthropomorphised, despecial-ised, and exists in a scientific system of knowledge as the 'real' animal (see Lynch, 1988). The position of laboratory rats and mice as analytic animals or as equipment is one that has become cemented in the increasing industrialisation of science; under these conditions, laboratory rodents become standardised and increasingly, as Birke put it, 'part of the apparatus of science' (see also Arluke, 1988; Bowd, 1980; Reinhardt, 1996). This mammalian analytic unit was referred to as 'equipment' in the laboratories in which I carried out my fieldwork.

The location of rats and mice as mammalian analytic units of equipment is a consequence of their membership in the category 'mammal' that rats, mice, and humans share. As much as mammalian membership is the bridge by which rodents and humans are connected (in their similar bodies, their equivalent DNA structures, their gene similarity, and the ease with which rodents might be engrafted with human substances to yield humanised animals), mammalian membership is equally the grounds upon which rodent difference from humans is hierarchically presented. Acampora (2006)argued that the location of rats and mice as nonspeci-al, purely mammalian equipment in the laboratory indicates the firm maintenance of the human-animal divide. The location of the mouse or rat in the position of mammalian equipment occasions and entails the detachment of the scientist from the animal, which is itself understood not as 'mouse' but as a mammalian biounit (biological unit) gene equipment. The position of the animal body as 'equipment' is made manifest in a series of processes. These include deindividualising the animals and locating, speaking of, and writing about them as supplies—for example, in grant applications and laboratory order sheets—as well as representing animals as data in scientific papers. Other methods include the nullification of the moral constraints that bind people to other (naturalistic) animals, such as pets, and the routinized extermination of research animal units (see Birke, 2003). These processes assure the removal of the characteristics of the naturalistic animal, including, at the conclusion of the research, the removal of its natural life. They also indicate the intertwinement of the rodent body with the scientific context in which it is located.

The intertwinement of laboratory rodent bodies as equipment with the requirements of science is also evidenced by what happens to 'natural' animal bodies, which are marked in terms of their disintegration with the category 'equipment' and the laboratory's goal to extract data of human relevance from this equipment. 'Pinkie pup' is a specific term used by laboratory staff to describe mouse and rat pups younger than 5 days of age. They are so called because they have no fur on their bodies, which are baby pink. In circumstances of unauthorised breeding or where the progeny are not required, pinkie pups' bodies, though they are produced by lab animals in the laboratory setting, are not equipment. Because there is no possibility for extracting data from them, they are considered a by-product, not a piece of mammalian equipment, that requires immediate disposal. This is done at the labs under study in this book by means of decapitation with a sharp pair of scissors and a bucket. As naturalistic animals, pinkie pups are anomalies in the lab, and they indicate that unless a laboratory mouse or rat enters the space of the laboratory as a thoroughly integrated piece of scientific apparatus or as a thoroughly integrated 'analytic animal', its presence therein cannot be tolerated, and it is summarily removed.

In Acampora's (2006) estimation, the processes that yield the analytic mammalian unit of analysis also yield the detached scientific practitioner, operating from her position on the human side of the Great Divide while the animal suffers her pursuit of data in its position as wholly subjected to scientific inquiry. The analytic, nonspeci-al mammalian unit and the detached, enquiring scientist ostensibly appear here in the classic Baconian configuration of the strict human-animal divide.

THE ENTRY OF LESSER MAMMALS INTO THE SACRIFICIAL ECONOMY

Mammalian membership also qualifies rodent research animals for entry into the laboratory's sacrificial economy. As Haraway (1997) noted, the mammalian homology between the transgenic breast cancer animal model Oncomouse and people is based on 'Oncomouse's essence, which, in common with humans, is "to be mammal, a bearer by definition of mammary glands, and a site for the operation of a transplanted, human, tumor producing gene" ' (p. 79). In this situation, mammalian homology is the basis upon which the mouse must be sacrificed, in order 'that I and my sisters [the human mammals in the equation] might live' (p. 79). Calculations are possible on the basis of the animal's reactivity to the procedures that are brought to bear on it by the God-scientist. The amount of mouse bodies that are pained and rat lives that are lost yields good for humans—maybe the cure for cancer, or perhaps advances in obesity and diabetes treatments. On the basis of such calculations are yielded sacrificial animals. This definition of sacrifice belongs with Foucault's (2004) calculus of war: the relationship between my life and the death of the other, which enables and justifies the sovereign—and in this case, the scientific—exercise of killing. Such a calculus is developed in line with the thanatophobia—the fear of death—that is fundamental, in Heideggerian terms, to human existence. As a cultural practice, scientific quests to stave off death may be understood to fit with Becker's (1973) arguments that human desires to defy mortality manifest in the defiance of the cycles of nature; science seeks to submit natural animal vitality to this defiant cultural quest, making the animal-human and nature-culture divisions key divisions in scientific endeavours.

Referencing the key frames of nature and culture, human and animal, and life and death, the 17th-century French transfusionist Jean Denis believed that the blood of animals was infused with a kind of robustness that went beyond the properties of human sanguinary substance. He thought that the animals were gravid with vitality and that the lives of animals were closer to the cosmic fountainhead of death and regeneration than were those of people (see Guerrini, 1989). Theoreticians such as Christman (2008) have taken modern scientific practices involving animals to be concerned with the same ideas of the transfer of vitality from the animal to the human domain. Drawing further on Heideggerian notions of the arrogated place of science in modernity, Christman drew out the desire to secure the vitality of nature that is the genesis for the calculus of war, foregrounding the human desire to push back the boundaries of life via fortification with the vital, natural life-force that is understood to dwell in humans' animal kin (p. 307). Here, the profound nexus between thanatophobia and zooicide speaks to both the primal, human need for death transcendence and to the vitality of animal life that succours it. For Christman (2008),

> that the white-coated priests of science themselves resort to the term 'sacrifice' reveals more than fondness for euphemism: it exhumes the sacrificial principle of metemphsychosis by proxy, of the divinely-mediated migration of the life-force of animals into the sanctum of the human body.[6] (p. 307)

Christman's claims undermine the pragmatics of a sacrificial economy that is reckoned on a straightforward exchange of inferior animal lives for superior human lives. It speaks instead to the mysticism of animal vitality and the epic stakes of staving off the reaper of human lives—who, it seems, is impervious to all other human attacks but the scientific.

Rats and mice appeared in the laboratory that is under study here as disposable mammalian equipment that was to be entered into the sacrificial economy by recourse to legislatively and institutionally endorsed methods, including carbon dioxide poisoning and isoflurane poisoning. When her mice were scheduled for termination, Leisel, a virologist, said that it meant disposing of 'research equipment' that could no longer produce useful data for her study. As Leisel put it,

> These mice die so that I can find out how to address a problem that is devastating to human health. And definitely a lot of mice die, but it is worth it—imagine if we did no animal research. We would still be beset by polio, for instance, along with a whole raft of other diseases that impact *human* mammals. [italics added]

Other examples were given. The head of the animal ethics committee gave his in the form of questions:

> Would you inject human semen into dogs? Would you allow viper toxin to be injected into cats? Would you allow the injection into rodents of mould originally found growing on unwashed lab glassware? If you said no, you would have aborted the discovery of prostaglandins; the discovery of safe, effective antihypertensive acetylcholinesterase inhibitors; the antibacterial properties of penicillin. And you would have denied work that gained two Nobel prizes.

In such cases, mammalian laboratory animals such as the cats, dogs, and rodents that were described by the head and by Leisel are killed by routinized processes of death that marks their presence in the laboratory as 'disposable' tools and lower members of the mammalian hierarchy which locates humans at its summit. This disposability can also be conceptualised by recourse to Deleuze and Guattari's (1987) contrast between minority and majority identities. Deleuze and Guattari argued that those (political) connections that are excluded in identity formation are consequences of (social and political) power. Majority here is not a question of numbers but a question of relative social power; it is 'the determination of a state or standard in relation to which larger quantities, as well as the smallest, can be said to be minoritorian: white-man, adult-male, etc. (Deleuze & Guattari, 1987, p. 291). This can be expanded to encompass not only those (humans) who are articulated against the (white-adult-male 'normal') majority, but also those animals which are articulated against the human.[7] As Vint (2005) argued, this human majority, as Deleuze and Guattari described it, 'assumes as pregiven the right and power of [hu]man' (Vint, 2005, p. 294). It is possible to apply Deleuze and Guattari's (1987) notion of majority to mammalian membership as it is hierarchically conceived of in the confines of the laboratory; a 'majority' mammalian membership is claimed over animals (which, of course, are in the vast majority in the numerical sense in the lab) by humans.

In his examination of the location of meat animals in relationship to their human killers, Reinert (2007) drew attention to the ways in which humans and animals in such contexts are understood to be unrelated to one another. This lack of relation, in his view, permits the quotidian routinisation of killing that is required in the slaughterhouse and in the laboratory. Reinert argued that the banality of such frequently repeated actions of death in both of these contexts effectively turns 'the humane act' of violence, the terminal act, into a socially invisible form of everyday violence that is visible only to laboratory staff. He located this situation as 'the exact antithesis—a reverse, or negative correlate—to the extraordinary and socially marked violence of the sacrifice'(n.p.). Comparing the affinity—of personhood and other qualities—that is more usually present in human-animal relationships of sacrifice, Reinert (2007) took the relations of these transferences as

> a measure of the growing 'abyss of essence' that separates the human from the non-human, and across which the act of killing now takes place: an ontological gulf that reconstitutes the sacrificant, not as a killer but as a *technician* conducting routine manual labour, and transforms the victim into mere meat, stripped of agency, personhood and other qualities that it might have shared with a human sacrificant.

Such a position locates laboratory animals firmly on the opposite side of an impenetrable divide from humans who fail to recognise any grounds of commensurability with the animal. Drawing on classic (Maussian) definitions of sacrifice, a practice which specifically establishes a connection between the realms of the sacred and profane worlds by means of a victim that is destroyed in the course of a ceremonial process, Reinert (2007) argued that (classical) sacrifice draws at least partially on an enduring affinity between animals and people. This affinity, although it permits the death of the animal victim, also recognises that the animal has the full measure of subjectivity that enables it to be 'sacrificed' rather than simply being killed. Reinert also argued that the term 'sacrifice' works metaphorically, too, to refer to situations in which one thing is given up for another—for instance, 'laboratory animals must die so that humans might live'. The two meanings of sacrifice—one literal, one figurative—combine awkwardly to yield a sacrificial veneer born of the aggregate condition; that is, the thousands of deaths that together compose and bring about the sacrificial benefit for humans are routinized, mundane, banal, and hidden. This yields the condition of 'anti-sacrifice' but a veneer covers it, so that mice, as Leisel suggested, save humans from the ravages of polio. In Leisel's estimation, this calculus, this sacrificial economy, is in the black in terms of its yield for human mammals.

Despite the obvious problem in classical formulations for those people who question the bases upon which human and animal divisions proceed (that animals have to 'come up' to the human category to be eligible for sacrifice at all), Lynch (1988) argued that the termination of animals in laboratory contexts amounts to more than a sacrificial economy of human and nonhuman bodies. For Lynch, scientific 'versions' of sacrifice contain the key basic themes of sacrifice as they might be understood classically: (a) preparing a victim in such a way as to create and sustain an orientation to coordinates in an abstract space, (b) destroying the victim in order to establish a mediating link between the visible and invisible realms, and (c) constituting the victim as a bearer of human attributes (see Lynch, 1988). Although sacrifice is frequently applied to laboratory rats and mice in terms of calculus, whether or not it can be accomplished in classical anthropological terms is quite another question. After all, sacrifice, in anthropological terms, is not reducible to calculus; it requires instead human-animal affinity. Such a sacrifice may be difficult to carry out in the modern laboratory, because only those animals who share human affinity can be sacrificed; everything else is capable only of being killed.

It is by adherence to the three conditions of classical sacrifice that rats and mice transcend the concrete physical limitations to which they are subject, and it is through these conditions that they disclose the ontotheological order of the mathematical. This disclosure occurs as rat and mouse flesh become data. The process of euthanizing laboratory animals connotes the systematic consecration of the animal's body, bringing about its transformation into a bearer of transcendental human significances—into a fully analytic object (data) with generalised and fully realised significance for members of a particular research community. The first of the conditions of sacrifice is met when a rat or mouse victim is prepared in orientation with the analytical, in both temporal and spatial terms. The rat must die on schedule, as opposed to dying outside of schedule, and its bodily extractions must comply with the spatial coordinates that are set out for it. The second condition, which recognises that sacrifice is a mediating act, is met in the moment of the conversion of the naturalistic to the analytic animal. This occasions the organisation of the rat's residues in accordance with an abstracted and purified set of theoretical relations in a scientific world of data sets and publications that exists beyond or invisible to the practical, everyday world of the laboratory.[8]

The third condition—and the one I am most interested in here—is met when the 'analytic' animal becomes a subject of human identification because its anatomical, genetic, and physiological properties are mammalian and therefore human. For Lynch, the rodent's mammalian membership demonstrates that it is commensurate with its human killer. Lynch's assessment of commensurability is based firmly in the recognition that rats and mice are humans' biokin and genekin and that the Great Divide between humans and animals is diminished sufficient that we are commensurate. But, his position equally recognises the poles of the division between animate and inanimate beings in the laboratory.

I have suggested so far that mammalian membership is a central element in both the erosion of the division between humans and animals in the laboratory and in the erection of the division between animate beings and inanimate status. It is the case, though, that speci-ality emerges as an equally key element in establishing the division between humans and animals. Speci-ality emerged at two key moments of laboratory practice to recognise this division: at the moment of the animal's death and when the animals were provided with enrichment, food, and environmental stimuli that were particular to their species. Although their bodily yields (data) might continue to be treated analytically, as Lynch suggested in his second condition of sacrifice, at the moment they are entered into the sacrificial economy, rats and mice are entered precisely as rats and mice. Alan, an immunologist with 20 years of experience in the laboratory, used mouse animal models in his work. When I spoke with him, Alan's mice had come to the end of their research lives. The data generated from their mouse bodies had effectively been collected across the human-animal divide, as it was taken for the purposes of applicability to humans, for whom the mice had stood in at the laboratory; their bodies, in this sense, were human bodies. Alan had been telling me about the ways in which his mouse models were 'ideal models' for the people who would one day reap the benefits of his research work. But now, their commensurability with humans was about to reveal its limits. Alan told me as he was about to dispense with his research mice by gassing them, 'Remember that they're only mice. People kill mice in their houses every single day'. Alan's invocation of the speci-al term 'mouse' here flicks a kind of switch between high mammalian affinity/commensurability and a speci-al distancing/discarding. It reestablishes the division between humans and animals that operates in the laboratory with as much frequency as its erosion.

It is also the case that the mammalian classification of humans, rats, and mice is drawn upon to articulate the division between humans and animals; some mammals can be placed in the service of other mammals as equipment—and moreover, as disposable equipment. Mammalian membership is also, of course, the ground upon which rats, mice, and people are regarded as closely related biokin and genekin—a kinship which diminishes human-animal differences. Articulations of mammalian similarity and speci-al difference do not proceed along straightforward lines that reproduce the human-animal divide; each is used to describe similarity and difference, each is used to maintain and undo hierarchical arrangements of rats and mice and people to one another, and each is used to underscore kinning and killing. Here, then, is yielded an ambiguous terrain in which mice and rats, mammals and species, cross and maintain divisions. But, rats and mice are more than good for biological and gene kinning and good for killing. A rather broader set of understandings and interactions is evident in human-rodent relations as they are conducted in the contingencies of relating in the very thick of lab work, which I turn in chapter 4 to examine.

ENDNOTES

1. Schultz was talking about spontaneous mutations and targeted insertions that cause defects in immunological function in mice.
2. It is possible, of course, that these genes may play an important role in determining species-specific traits and functions.
3. There are, however, some differences; the most significant is not, in fact, the number of genes each species carries but the structure of genes and the activities of their protein products. The cumulative effect of the subtle changes accumulated in each of the 25,000 genes yields different organisms. Additional differences have their genesis in the complex ways in which genes and proteins interact; these complex interactions multiply the functions of each gene. When gene splicing or post-translational modification is added to the mix, a gene can produce more than one protein, and this process might differ between murine and human species. Environmental and developmental conditions and cues can cause a gene to produce more or less protein in different cells at different times, and 'many proteins can express disparate functions in various biological contexts. Thus, subtle distinctions are multiplied by the more than 30,000 estimated genes' (see U.S. Department of Energy Office of Science, Office of Biological and Environmental Research Human Genome Program Website, www.ornl.gov/hgmis).
4. Many species share mammalian body plans and genetic homology with humans (rabbits, cats, monkeys, apes, and rabbits each have comparable DNA content—and the implication is that all mammals have more or less the same number of genes). Where there is a roughly 98% similarity between related genes in humans and apes in general, there is a somewhat lesser similarity between mouse and human genes: an average of 85% similarity. Though the similarities between humans and apes are expressed in ways that are easier for the layperson to appreciate than those between mice and humans, the similarity between mice and humans is privileged in the laboratory in the terms of close mammalian kin because it is this kin relation that will yield the highest beneficial frequency for humans. The most common applications to humans include cancer, heart disease, asthma, Alzheimer's, Down syndrome, deafness, osteoporosis, obesity, diabetes, and mental health research outcomes. However, knockout mice have some limitations which make the use of lab rats a more attractive option. And, rats are more closely related to humans than mice are. 'For example the mouse heart beats 5–10 times faster whilst the heart of a rat is

more in line with our own heart. We also share similar liver enzymes to rats and so eradicate toxins in a similar way. This makes rats a better model for studying the toxicity of potential therapeutics' (see http://www.brighthub.com/science/genetics/articles/46575.aspx#ixzz0qW1yQtxZ).

5. For more than a decade, scientists have worked on the difficult task of transplanting parts of the human immune system into mice.
6. This, of course, stands at odds with Arluke's (1988) insights into the use of the term 'sacrifice'. He took it to be an ambiguous term which suggests both the objectification of an animal that is to be killed and a strong identification with the animal—the term, after all, is one that has its genesis in human-animal or human-human affinity.
7. This position is similar to Agamben's (2002) analysis in *The Open*, in which he argued that 'the decisive political conflict, which governs every other conflict' (p. 80) comes back to the boundary between human and animal and the political circumstances under which this division is worked out.
8. Lynch made an assumption that naturalistic animals inhabit the lab and that they become analytic on their deaths; however, animals in the lab are analytic well prior to their arrival in the lab. Additionally, naturalistic animals also emerge at the point of sacrifice as 'only mice'.

Chapter 4

And Darwin Wept

Introduction

In this chapter, I examine the ways in which the ambivalent location of rats and mice in the laboratory, as simultaneously expressive of opposed qualities—as at once human biokin and wholly unrelated to humans, and as speci-al 'only' mice and generic mammalian units of equipment—is made yet more ambiguous through the crossings that laboratory rats and mice and people make of the great human-animal divide in their interactions in the thick of laboratory work. I turn first to an examination of the notion that rodent research animals may live a 'bare life', in Agamben's (1998) terms, in the context of the laboratory. I will argue in the fifth chapter that the conditions for bare life as Agamben described them are not always met in the context of the laboratory. I introduce the notion of bare life here in order to examine the conditions of detachment from animals that emerge from claims for detachment in the context of the laboratory, according to Acampora (2006). I examine the conditions of detachment and Acampora's attendant claim, that laboratory animals occupy the position of 'ready-to-hand' tools in the laboratory, against the ways in which researchers located animal subjects in the course of scientific research. In this examination, I show that strict detachment and keeping animals under the conditions of bare life are frequently antithetical to the practice of science and that in their stead are a range of attachments and kinships that are critical to scientific knowing.

In the second part of the chapter, I examine the ways in which rodent animal models were located as emotional sites in the laboratory. Emotional relationships with animals were also not damaging to the conduct or outcomes of scientific work; indeed, emotional connections with animals were often incorporated into claims for the greater validity of experimental parameters and the outcomes of scientific investigations. I here examine what constitutes 'good science'.

Finally, I turn again to Agamben's notion of bare life, but not to his original formulation, in which the search for what counts as 'human' is paramount. I turn instead to a latter formulation that he pursued in his *The Open* (2002), in which there appears the germ of an idea which, it is important to note, Agamben may not have intended. What I take to be Agamben's reworking of bare life offers up a conceptual space, a zone of indeterminacy, for the dispensing of the human-animal divide; a space in which a-humanity[1] and a-animality[2] may be conducted. I apply this idea to offer insights into the ways in which relationships between humans and rodent research animals might also be conducted in such a zone of indeterminacy, where fleshy indistinction characterises relationships, kinships, and contacts between humans and animals.

THE BARE LIFE OF THE LABORATORY RAT?

In the preceding chapter, I suggested that the subsumption of rodent animals under the classification of mammal and the emergence of the speci-al, as a lesser variety of mammalian being, combine to qualify rodent animals for entry into the laboratory's sacrificial economy. The entry of animals into the sacrificial economy has led some theoreticians (including Acampora, 2006; Reinert, 2007) to argue that laboratory and other animals that are included in the scientific or industrial coordinates of the lab or the abattoir live a 'bare life', as Agamben described it in his *Homo Sacer* of 1998. Such an argument locates laboratory animals squarely on one side of the animal-human divide, utterly detached from humans and entirely subject to human requirements, including the human requirement for rodents' death. To note that sacrifice undergirds humanist practice in the modern surroundings of the positivist scientific laboratory setting is not new. Critics of humanism have frequently pointed to it and to its consequences; Derrida (2002), for example, considered its main yield—in this case, the simultaneous location of the laboratory animal as both reactive equipment and a saviour—as the ultimate humanist crime against the animal. Just as humans can, in Agamben's (1998) language, become bestialised, animalised, animals can, as Noske (1997) suggested, become deanimalised. As Reinert (2007) put it,

> If animals can indeed be persons in a real, social, interactive and individuated sense—rather than in the merely figurative, symbolic or metaphoric sense all too frequently deployed by social scientists—then this personhood can also be stripped from them, as it can be from humans. In the case of the calf and the patient, the figure of the bare life captures how both bodies are produced and suspended within dedicated social and technical spaces that effectively constitute two distinct but analogous forms of 'death worlds, or 'forms of social existence in which ... populations are subjected to conditions of life conferring upon them the status of the living dead'. (n.p.)

I will come back to bare life in the fifth chapter; I raise the subject here because it is under the conditions of bare life that the coldly detached God-scientists of Bacon's imagining of science appear. In a Judeo-Christian heritage of human supremacy over nature, humanist God-scientists regard the animal as both a biological and genetic mirror for self-reflection and the raw material for self-reproduction in a disease-free, improved form. God-scientists appear as the fulfilment of Bacon's humanist vision of nature made wholly available to the claims and desires of instrumental reason. God-scientists inhabit the ontotheological domain that the union of science and technology has produced; as Heidegger insisted, under the banner of modernity, science itself is arrogated to the place of Plato's Good and the Christian God. God-scientists also represent the fulfilment of Bacon's call to the mastery of nature through its ontological transformation. This is particularly evident in the production of transgenic animals, as God-scientists in this regard claim to have not only omniscience but also the ultimate creative power. Christman (2008) used the same Judeo-Christian language to locate scientific practitioners as masters. In her terms, they are 'the lords of life and death' and 'white-coated priests', whose task is to enact and oversee the migration of the life-force of animals into the 'sanctum of the human body'—a task which is 'divinely mediated' (p. 307).

Instrumental reason incorporates nature and humanity into its calculations and produces a split between animals and human beings; it insists on the fall of animals from the status of gods or as a part of a spiritual world and reallocates animals into a position in nature, as a part of the mass of things and creatures in the external world from which the human order is separated (Adorno & Horkheimer, 2002). As Hudson (2008) noted, reason becomes inextricably intertwined with self-preservation; as human beings become separated from nature, they must dominate it, lest it dominate them. Indeed, in enlightenment perspective, to refuse to participate in these relations of domination is to take up an antihuman, antiprogress stance (as animal rights activists and deep ecologists well know, being frequently accused as they are of being 'anti').

In his *New Ecological Order*, Ferry (1995) suggested that such concerns with nature and the animal, manifesting as environmentalism and animal rights, constitute direct threats to liberal humanist democracy and draw attention and resources away from human social problems. Ferry saw the growing concern with these areas as a continuation of the disillusionment of the political left; ecology and animals had failed to become the bearers of revolutionary meaning. For Ferry, this is at the root of theories of poststructuralism that render all values relative and which identify difference as positive—here emerge cultural relativism, animal rights, and the valuation of ecological diversity. As Hudson (2008) pointed out, this suggests that

> different rules apply to different societies, animals, and environments. Human beings, like animals, become rooted in their environments, with duties to maintain the land that stem from natural laws rather than from human rationality. Human cultures become outgrowths of their natural environments, and animals are accorded their own cultural achievements. Ferry thus launches into a critique of the authoritarian impulses of these 'anti-humanist' movements by invoking the specter of the Nazis. He notes the troubling way in which this shift echoes the Nazi philosophy of 'blood and soil,' and the expulsion of those deemed incapable of being assimilated to the 'biotic community' as alien species. The echoes of Nazism are loudest in the tenets of deep ecology, where biocentrism reduces human claims to bare equality with other animals, even other 'natural entities' such as streams or ecosystems. Ferry reads this reduction of human claims as a thinly veiled hatred of humanity as such. For Ferry, deep ecology, in its veneration of nature, represents the most extreme example of the collusion of threats to liberal democracy from both the right and the left: 'Despite their inherent differences, fascism and communism … share the same wariness of formal democracy, the same repugnance toward the market and the plutocratic society it naturally engenders, the same concern with producing a new man, the same myth, essentially, of uncompromised and uncompromising purity' [Ferry, 1995, p. xxvii] (p. 91)

So, the choice then becomes a terrible one:

> To care about animals is to be linked to the totalitarian forces of Nature, something the Nazis tapped into as the source of their power. To reject the Nazis, however, is to accept that vivisection and torture of animals is part of progress, and that to align oneself with the totalitarian drive of enlightenment as a second nature. There is no escape, and one must choose a side. (Hudson, 2008, p. 116)

In the laboratory, instrumental reason presents animals for human investigation, as nature that must be dominated and as vehicles through which progress might be pursued. As Adorno and Horkheimer (2002) argued, the positions of humans relative to animals are clearly marked:

> In this world liberated from appearance—in which human beings, having forfeited reflection, have become once more the cleverest animals, which subjugate the rest of the universe when they happen not to be tearing themselves apart—to show concern for animals is considered no longer merely sentimental but a betrayal of progress. In the best reactionary tradition Göring linked animal protection to racial hatred, the Lutheran-Germanic joys of the happy murderer with the genteel fair play of the aristocratic hunter. The fronts are clearly drawn; anyone who opposes Hearst and Göring is on the side of Pavlov and vivisection; anyone who hesitates between the two is fair game for both. (p. 211)

These are the conditions under which Acampora presented his caricature of the uncaring, unfeeling, indifferent scientific practitioner, operating within particular coordinates of the scientific research laboratory on wholly subject and detached animal equipment. Acampora (2006) argued, 'Animals in laboratories (most of which are rodents) are not only physically restrained in literal cages but are also ontologically reduced to the status of ready to hand tools' (p. 99).

The world is beginning to question, in a more mainstream way, the claims and desires of instrumental reason. This can be seen in people's concerns about nature, in their attendance to the ways in which nature has been submitted to human progress, and in the debates about genetically modified foods and animal lives in meat production regimes. Consumers demand that the local Woolworths stocks free-range pork, chicken, and eggs. The Human Genome Project, located in the thick of posthuman biopolitics, makes more than claims about human being, rather seeking to arrive at understandings of being as such (see Wolf-Meyer, 2006). In this context, is it reasonable to suggest that instrumental reason continues to hold a death grip on science? Is it possible that science is immune from the concerns in which it is deeply embedded? And, as Shanor and Kanwal (2009) noted, science itself is 'beginning to take us back to nature' (p. 1) as people address these concerns. I think this presents some problems for Ferry's position, where only impasse is possible. It raises problems, likewise, for Acampora's claims about detachment.

One might examine Acampora's (2006) claims by raising this question of whether science remains in the grip of instrumental reason because for Acampora, science remains a domain that has not been penetrated by the questioning of instrumental reason, particularly in its view and location of animals as tools that are wholly submitted to the desire for progress and its mastery of nature in this aim. The claim that laboratory animals are reduced to the ontological status of ready-to-hand tools is one that requires careful examination against the ethnographic circumstances in which rodent research animals are involved. Moreover, Acampora's borrowing of Heideggerian terms requires a careful analysis of Heidegger's own construction of the human-animal division—itself wholly embedded in claims about the arrogated place of science in modernity.

Heidegger (1962) distinguished between three modes of being: *Dasein* (being-there), *Zuhandensein* (readiness-to-hand), and *Vorhandensein* (presence-at-hand). What kind of being is ascribed to animals in such a schema? Unless an animal is ontologically oriented, in the sense that it cares about the meaning of being, as Heidegger understood human beings to do, it can be understood only as present-at-hand or ready-to-hand—as the object of contemplation or study or as merely a tool. For Heidegger, the term 'ready-to-hand' is contrasted with 'present-at-hand'. A tool, such as a hammer, conceals itself when it is ready-to-hand. The tool withdraws from one's explicit attention in the very act of being used; indeed, tools must be absent (otherwise, they are present-at-hand). This is the usual way in which one encounters the world. Presence-at-hand is not the way things in the world are usually encountered, and it is revealed only as a secondary—and often deficient—mode, for example, in the event that the hammer breaks and loses its usefulness. It appears as itself, and it is considered in and of itself. Its beholder—here the person who was just involved in the act of hammering—is now interested in the bare facts of the hammer thing, in order to theorize about it. Where before the hammer (necessarily) disappeared in its determinations (in 'hammering'), it now appears as present-at-hand and stands isolated from any useful set of equipment. The hammer will not stay in such a state for long; it will soon lose its mode of being present-at-hand and become something—for example, that which must be repaired or replaced.

Objects that are present-at-hand are abstractions, in that they are treated as objects for investigation and examination, such as a scientist might make of the mouse-object in the laboratory; in seeing an entity as present-at-hand, the beholder is concerned only with the bare facts of a thing or a concept, as they are present and in order to theorize about it.

Could laboratory mice and rats be reduced to the ontological status of ready-to-hand? What would such a reduction look like? In Acampora's view, as I read it, mice and rats would be reduced to the status of the tool, unexamined in themselves, not themselves held up for examination, except in the event that they were unsatisfactory tools. They are, in such a view, ready for use and involved in projects in which they have no formative role; their role, instead, is equivalent with that of the hammer, which disappears in the broader accomplishment of the experiment.

Acampora's claim is one that acknowledges Heidegger's great emphasis on time and his lesser emphasis on space—Heidegger's attention to the possibility of death-as-mine forced him to pay less attention to the spatial dimension in which embodiment is lived. Acampora noted that Heidegger's ontological framework provides few opportunities for the vitality of an organic animate being to emerge for analytic attention. Acampora indicated that he would normally take Heidegger to task on this, but clearly for him, the lab is one of the few places where Heidegger was right; herein, animate being fails to ever emerge.

It is very difficult indeed to decide that the ontological status of the rat is the same as that of other laboratory tools—the beaker, the pipette. As Czech philosopher Erazim Kohak (1984) once put it, 'Only from a very great conceptual distance could one mistake a porcupine for a boulder and lump them both together under the common label of *l'être-en-soi* [being-in-itself]' (p. 75). Acampora cited Kohak to make the very same point—as long as the point is not being made in the laboratory (see Acampora, 2006, p. 7). How can one be sure that scientists regard animals in the laboratory as such? Acampora was sure, on the basis that science remains a domain of strict nature-culture, animal-human divisions, wherein no somatic relationship between an animal and a human is permitted. Animals remain at abstract distance—and certainly at a sufficient distance to be lumped together with hammers and pipettes.[3] I recall to the reader Acampora's (2006) take on the situation of the laboratory rodent vis-à-vis its human examiner, which is as follows:

> The laboratory research setting dictates parameters of behavioural operation that desensitise the practitioner to the bodily spectacles enacted under his [*sic*] experimental surveillance. Indeed, the 'culture' of modern, positivist scientific practice seeks to disbar the emergence of symphysis or somaesthetic caring in its very methodology. Emphatically, detachment is the watchword of this context. (pp. 97–98)

Acampora's take on the lab and his characterisation of the scientists who inhabit it was shared by most of the students in a semester-long undergraduate course on human-animal relations that I taught on the same campus where I conducted the ethnographic research for this book (and at the same time as I undertook this fieldwork). In that context, I was very often presented with students' thoughts about the practice of science and the lot of the animals that are involved in its production of data and knowledge. When the head of the animal ethics committee at the university where my teaching and research took place made a presentation to the students about the involvement of animals in research at the university, the students' response was by and large one that condemned him to the position of a spin doctor, trying—vainly, in their view—to make the lot of animals in the lab appear better than it was. After I reported this response to the head, he said he was unsurprised and told me that this was generally the view he encountered, on and off campus, from almost everyone who was located outside the domain of science. Many of the scientific researchers I interviewed for the book said the same thing: that people outside the scientific world of the lab conjured readily available images of animals being subjected to the cruellest of treatments, without regard from the cold, Baconian scientist. The scientist was conceived as a figure who was unaffected by and oblivious to animals' pain and suffering and who was devoid of any caring for the hapless animal, even when that animal happened to be a rat that might be reviled in other circumstances external to the laboratory. (Alan's comments, in which he said he was thankful that the mice he was about to dispose of were 'only' the mice that people outside the lab killed every day, clearly reveal this thinking.) Deborah said,

> I don't tell people who don't know the nature of my work really well the ins and outs of what I do here [in the lab] at barbeques and get-togethers. Even though I work with mice, and people [outside the lab] don't seem to have much of an issue with killing mice, they still look at me like I'm evil. The idea that I might be torturing an animal clamped into some kind of apparatus, or injecting them with things that will cause them to die slow and painful deaths, or worse, that I might be using them to test cosmetics (which is what a lot of people think, when they think of laboratory animals)—you can see those images of me being totally detached from an animal's writhing contortions coming straight into their heads.

Is detachment really the watchword of the laboratory context, as Acampora, my undergraduate students, and Deborah's barbeque associates each assumed? Certainly, one might once have assumed this to be the basis of human-animal encounters in the laboratory space. As Johnson (1996) noted, the long and grisly humanist legacy continues to inform how the general public thinks about animals in general and how people assume they are involved in the laboratory culture in particular, and it has done so since Descartes proclaimed that animals were beings without souls.

In 1595, Descartes exaggerated the Christian-centred prevalent humanist attitude of the time into a mechanistic philosophy, labelling animals 'beast-machines', which provided a most convenient ideology for early vivisectionists. During the 17th century, the primary concern issuing from both members of the general public and physiologists was not so much that animal subjects felt pain—the implication of Descartes's claim was that animals in fact did not feel pain—but that experimentation on lesser beings could yield very little benefit, and even less that would lend insight into knowledge of the human body. Criticism of vivisection proceeded primarily on this basis and harked back to St. Thomas Aquinas's declaration in 1260, in his *Summa Theologiae*, that humans were unique. Aquinas opposed the use of data based on vivisection on the grounds that all other animals were too different from humans: They were incapable of rationality because they possessed no mind. But, the idea that animals might experience pain did not escape the physiologists who were working on mammalian subjects, such as dogs. Among the first to record their genuine concern for the welfare of some of their experimental subjects were professional physiologists, including Robert Boyle (1627–1690), Robert Hooke (1635–1703), and Richard Lower (1631–1691) (see Shugg, 1968). Their concerns were based on a moral objection to perceived cruelty that was likely inescapable, given their proximity to those bleeding, tortured subjects (see Oster, 1989). Indeed, Hooke, who served as an experimenter for the Royal Society and was involved in some of the 17th century's most important discoveries about physiology, developed his position on cruelty through direct attendance.

During his long career, he deprived several animals of air in order to observe the outcome; his results indicated that the animals went into convulsions and died. He also conducted an experiment to observe the beating heart and inflating lungs of a dog while the animal was still alive. He was asked by the Royal Society to repeat the experiment, but he refused, citing 'the torture of the creature' (see de Beer, 1955, p. 271) as his reason. He was not alone; Evelyn, a spectator at one of Hooke's oxygen experiments, noted in his diary of the performance, 'This was an experiment of more cruelty than pleased me' (see de Beer, 1955, p. 271). Hooke did not maintain a constant position on cruelty, however; he continued to carry out experiments that deprived dogs of fresh air, which allowed him to make insights into the importance of oxygen (see Egerton, 2005).

Irrespective of Hooke's inconsistent position on animal cruelty, it is worth noting that concerns about animal welfare issued at first from within the scientific and medical fraternities, directly from those people who encountered animal writhing, yelps, howls, moans, cries, and squeals from the vivisection table. Although there is currently a view held by some animal welfare activists and a majority of scientific practitioners, that animal welfare and good science go hand in hand, the more common publicly drawn caricature of the scientist using animal subjects is one of a cold and desensitised practitioner who gains data no matter what the painful cost to the animal may be. That the origins of animal welfare in respect to research animal issues from within the institution itself was an historical fact that was frequently drawn upon by the participants in this study.

Johnson (1996) was of the view that the Cartesian view of animals not only once absolved scientific investigators from consideration of animals—on the basis that animals were merely 'just parts of nature's machines' (p. 59)—but also equally persistently clings to the current public perceptions of scientific and medical investigators. He argued that the history of animal-human relationships is one that science has been instrumental in shifting towards animal welfare—as ironic as such a shift may seem when it issues from the God-scientists of the popular image of the laboratory and its inhabitants—and that scientists do not subscribe to historical ideas about or practices of suffering. Johnson (1996) argued that the close human-animal relationships that are so thoroughly undermined in Cartesian thought are in fact scientifically recognised; that scientists are not somehow excepted from significant turns in the itinerary of thought, particularly when it pertains to their own disciplinary areas; and that scientists themselves make a distinction between those public views that are rooted in the Cartesian past and their own understandings of human-animal relatedness:

> Individuals who have dedicated their careers to science have an underlying motivation to improve the quality of life not only for people, but for animals. ... In laboratory medicine [for example], colony health management is the hallmark of a sound program. Current (lab) viewpoints on the animal/human relationship incorporate modern philosophical interpretations as well as the Darwinist perception, that humans are part of nature. (p. 59)

In this view, scientists understand, in Darwinian and anti-Cartesian terms, that there is relationship between animals and people. On that basis, they have cultivated their abilities to 'interpret animal behaviour and communication with an appreciation of species-differences [and]… clearly there is a relationship between the research staff and its laboratory animals' (p. 59).

In the laboratory I examined, detachment was not understood to be a particularly useful perception to sustain, even and perhaps especially in a context in which an animal is often understood as equipment. The equipment status of animals is not equivalent with scientific detachment from rodent research animals; indeed, their status as mammalian equipment was understood to require specific sorts of entailed involvement on the part of the scientist. Darren described this involvement as entailed evaluation. He explained that 'scientists routinely evaluate pain and distress in research animals—sometimes these responses constitute data'. Of this evaluative practice, he said,

> pain and distress cannot be evaluated easily in animal equipment, and therefore investigators must assume that animals experience pain in a manner similar to humans. So, we have to see the animal equipment we are working on from the same perspective as we would see our very own bodies.

The analysis of analytic rodent animals in the laboratory requires, on the part of the scientist, a series of attunements that begin with the assumption that animals, even when they are equipment, experience pain similarly to humans. The signs of pain and distress and the signs of wellness that scientists are required to interpret in laboratory rodents are ambiguous, in the sense that they are, as Darren also suggested, 'difficult to evaluate'. They issue from nonhuman others—and therefore certain assumptions have to be made about the sharing of pain between humans and animals.

The assumptions that scientists make about animal equipment in this way allow for the interpretation of what Merleau-Ponty described as the ambiguous signs that animal others exhibit. These are not a human's own, but they are nevertheless graspable, interpretable—in this case, to the extent that they form the basis of evaluations of the health and wellness of living rodent equipment in the laboratory. Merleau-Ponty (1964) argued that the practicing of the 'sciences of man' makes it evident that all knowledge that is generated within them requires the scientist to interpret

> as best he can the acts of others, reactivating from ambiguous signs an experience which is not his own, appropriating a structure (e.g., the a priori of the species, the sublinguistic schema ...) of which he forms no distinct concept but which he puts together as an experienced pianist deciphers an unknown piece of music: without himself grasping the motives of each gesture or each operation, without being able to bring to the surface of consciousness all the sediment of knowledge which he is using at that moment. (p. 93)

According to Ruonakoski (2007), these ambiguous signs that issue from 'a priori of the species, or 'specifically, non-human others' (p. 75) are routinely interpreted by scientific researchers. Further, Ruonakoski argued that scientists make these interpretations routinely 'without abandoning the standards of scientific rigour' (p. 75). Ruonakoski's view follows Merleau-Ponty's critical questioning of behaviourism. Behaviourism demands that the scientist be wholly detached from his or her subject of study and that he or she should avoid using terms that might carry his or her own empathies or emotions along with them. This was implied in what many of the scientists in this study called 'outdated lab culture', which, according to them, included keeping one's empathies about how an animal might be feeling in check when it came to interacting with animal research 'equipment'. Merleau-Ponty's line of thought was instead rooted in the view that it was essential to understand and acknowledge that human experience was the only possible starting point for scientific investigations of non-human others and that key scientific questions could only be answered in truly scientific ways through this entailed starting point. The phenomenologist Buytendijk (1974) put it this way:

> If one views without prejudice the structure ... of the relation between an animal and its surroundings as it manifests itself to

> us, then this relation can only be described by … defin[ing] the animal organism as a subject whose life we understand insofar as it demonstrates a relationship with our own [human] life. (p. 17)

In approaching nonhuman others from the only perspective that is available to humans—the human perspective—people try to 'reactivate ourselves in this foreign experience to which we always-already have a connection' (Ruonakoski, 2007, p. 77). This is a perspective which disallows the possibility of true detachment. This 'always-already' connection is, as Toadvine (2007) further noted of Merleau-Ponty's stance on the human interpretation of the animal 'other', born of the simultaneous given-ness of animality and humanity: 'Animality and humanity are given only together … such that we cannot draw a sharp ontological boundary between human and nonhuman animals' (p. 51). Just as such an 'always-already' connection is evident in scientific interpretations about the state of the analytic animal's body and its expressions, the interpretation of these bodies and behaviours requires the assumption that rodents and humans each share a fleshy world—one in which we share pain in the same measure and alleviate it by recourse to the same drugs.

Although it is indubitably true that Merleau-Ponty was principally interested in animality, rather than in animals per se,[4] his lateral redrawing of the traditional hierarchical distinctions between human and nonhuman life provide fruitful grounds for understanding some of the interrelationships between scientists and animals in the context of the laboratory, a context in which hierarchical distinctions appear to be strictly maintained. But, these hierarchies are shot through with the phenomenological consequences of interanimality that Merleau-Ponty described; it is difficult to be detached from those animals that scientists are, in fact, required to make interpretations of. Making them requires an acknowledgement of interanimality for interanimality and the possibility of interpreting animal kin is as crucial to the practice of science as sacrificing the animal other is. The fact that this acknowledgement is made in the laboratory undermines the human-animal divide and indicates that an animal body that is not wholly distinctive from that of humans persists in the lab. This body goes beyond the fixed biology of the animal model, investing it with a broader, fleshier world, which stretches to accommodate humans and rodents in fleshy affiliation. As Merleau-Ponty (1988) conceived of it, 'There is a kinship between the being of the earth and that of my body (*Leib*). ... This kinship extends to others, who appear to me as other bodies, to animals whom I understand as variants of my embodiment' (p. 50).

Affiliations and involvements were present in the assumptions that scientists made about animal welfare on the basis of the shared rodent-human bodily experience, and other registers of connection persisted in the laboratory as well. Merleau-Ponty (1988)[5] suggested that in the course of scientific inquiry, scientists form 'no distinct concept' of the animal's intention, do not grasp 'the motives of each gesture' an animal makes, and are unable to 'bring to the surface of consciousness all the sediment of knowledge which he [*sic*] is using at that moment'(p. 48). However, there are registers of connection that scientists engage in that do seek to form distinct concepts, grasp motives, and bring to the surface sediments of knowledge. In what follows, I take for examination another register of kinship, beyond the one that I have just described—that strange, fleshy variety that emerges when scientists recognise the contingency of species in their animal models across the animal-human and speci-al divides. As I have already suggested, this recognition is precisely of the 'always-already connection' that is evident in scientific interpretations about the state of the animal's body and its expressions. The interpretation of these bodies and behaviours requires the assumption that rodents and humans share a fleshy world. This recognition itself goes beyond biokinship and genekinship. The register of kinship I now turn to examine is one that goes one step further again and recognises animals as related to humans in a kinship of indistinction, from which emotional connections with the animal can and frequently do emerge. This register reconciles the only ostensibly polar positions of animals as sites of emotional investment and animals as analytic data-bearing equipment in the lab (or the positions of the natural animal, with which one might be expected to make relations and anthropomorphic associations outside the laboratory, and the analytic animal, which is routinely deanimalised, in Lynch's (1988) terms, and regarded as equipment in the lab).

Interspecies Kinnings: Rat People, Mouse People

This relating across the speci-al boundary also occurred in the very thick of lab work, not only in cases where mice were kept as pet animals in offices away from the lab proper and certainly not only among animal technicians. Although pet animals were largely kept by animal technicians, scientific researchers reported a variety of interspecies communications and relations between themselves and their research animals that occurred in their interactions with the animals in the course of scientific research. They reported engagements with animals, mostly rats, wherein they felt they were communicating across the species border and that the animals were communicating back. As a result, rats in particular came to be ambiguously located between the terrains of human biokin, as research animals, and interspecies kinship. When this happened, rats and people became indistinctive categories of being and a kind of general contingency between species was recognised.

In his 'thick description' of an immunology lab, Bischur (2008) noted that laboratory animals served as the dual sites of data production and emotional attachments (p. 29). In many cases among the scientists in this study, emotional bonds persisted with laboratory rodent animals. Davis and Balfour (1992) insisted that such bonds inevitably develop between an animal and a researcher. They noted that even under circumstances of what my informants called 'outdated lab practice', in which researchers were trained to minimise or avoid interactions that would result in their connection with their animal subjects, bond formation continued to occur—and occurred with, to use their language, 'unexpected animals' such as chickens, reptiles, and even octopi.

The psychologist Herzog (2002) argued that experiences of affective bonding are not at all unusual in the laboratory—even that they are to be expected. He recounted the experience of his friend and colleague, Ron

Neibor, in his *Ethical Aspects of Relationships Between Humans and Research Animals*. Neibor, a psychobiologist, studied an animal he liked: cats. Herzog recalled of Neibor's experience that his friend's research

> focused on the mammalian visual cortex. His experimental protocol called for the collection of baseline data on the performance of cats in a visual learning task followed by lesions to an area of the occipital lobe. It was then necessary to reassess the animal's learning capabilities after recovery from surgery. The experiments took nearly a year to complete, and Neibor became very attached to his cats. A 'cat person' by temperament, he had arrived at the university with a couple of pet cats in tow. Not surprisingly, his natural affection for them extended to his research subjects. He gave them names and played with them. Nearly every day, he would take them individually from their cages and let them roam around the animal colony. The moral crunch came at the end of the study. Every brain is a little different. In lesion studies, researchers must confirm that the part of the brain they intended to damage really was destroyed. The technical terms—perfusion, microtome, histology—are dry, and they obscure the reality of the procedure: it is necessary to kill each animal, sever the head from the body, and extract the brain from the skull … perfusion … is common and painless and normally entails no greater moral problem … however, to hold in your hand the disconnected head of a cat you have petted every morning for a year is, to say the least, unsettling … the dozen or so perfusions took place over several weeks, during which time he [Neibor] became reclusive and depressed and shaky … Neibor's case is not atypical. (pp. 27–28)

Not only is Neibor's case not atypical in Herzog's experience in and around laboratories, it was also common in the one I studied. Nancy, a neuroscientist with some 30 years of experience, became upset when recalling to me a study she had conducted some 25 years before on aural capacities, also on cats. Like Neibor, she had the animals for more than a year and named them, petted them, and enjoyed them. She then decapitated them and extracted their brains from their skulls, then chemically hardened the neural tissue, sliced it, analysed it, and wrote up her findings in a scientific report. Nancy, like Neibor, was, she said, 'a cat person', and she experienced 'deep personal grief' when the time came to carry out the perfusion on an animal she had come to know and even love.

There can be 'cat people' and there can be 'dog people', and in the laboratory I was exploring, there were also 'rat people' and 'mice people' (something Rader [1998] noted in a study that named murine geneticists working at the Bussey Institution as 'mouse people'). These terms were in frequent use to describe not only the speci-al membership of the animals each scientist was working with but also to describe something of the relationship that might be expected to develop between them. Rat people, according to those scientists who referred to themselves as such, considered rats to be smarter and more interactive than mice; in addition, they believed that rat people could be expected to handle and relate to their animals more than mice people could. Rat people and mouse people were prone to establishing emotional relationships with each speci-al variety of animal equipment.

After Latour (1987), who used the two-headed Janus to introduce ostensibly distinctive and irreconcilable perspectives—Janus talks on the left side like a realist and on the right side like a relativist—I am interested both in how the apparently polar positions that rodents and scientists occupy as animals and humans, respectively, are in some situations reconciled in the laboratory, to yield the ambiguous location of the rodent research animal. I further suggest that both polarity and ambiguity are critical to the production of what my research participants called 'good science'. The scientists in this study insisted that these relationships with research animals, which included affection, were critical to the production of good science and occurred well within the parameters of and standards for scientific rigour. They drew on the legislative bases they knew of to undergird their positions; I was told on numerous occasions that in Europe since the 1980s, affection towards laboratory animals—without exception—was advocated in the European Council Directive (European Economic Community, 1986), and that this model had good purchase in Australia.

Brenda, a neuroscientist, conducted what she called 'good science' by deliberately creating close bonds with her six white rats, which were involved in a neurological study. One morning, Brenda invited me to go with her to visit her rats. Though I was not often allowed to visit animals in the immunology lab for fear I might contaminate the research, I was allowed to visit rats which had physical or neurological problems, including Brenda's rats. When we got to the clear plastic unit that housed six of her white rats, Brenda took the lid off and began to stroke them and talk to them softly, as one might a pet. She greeted them with a 'hello' and asked of the six, 'How are you all today?'

Witnessing her physical and social interactions with the rats and her questions to them about their welfare, I asked Brenda how she felt about these six small white animals. Brenda said she was 'fond' of them and felt she understood them well. 'Rats are intelligent little animals', she told me.

> That's one of the differences between rat people and mouse people: Rat people have a lot more interaction with their animals—probably because of the kind of [neurological] research we are doing, but also because rats are smarter than mice. I really like rats—I have a great affection for them, and I can certainly understand why people keep them as pets.

I asked Brenda about how her fondness and affection for her research rats sat with her use of them as analytic animals. She immediately reconciled these apparently polarised uses of rats through her attention to how her affections and interest in them might have offset some of the impacts of the neurological conditions that were imposed on the rats. She had taken her emotional connection with her laboratory animals into account in her dealings with the rats—and it became entailed in her scientific observations. She told me,

> The way a researcher interacts with animals could, and sometimes does, result in profound behavioural and physiological changes in the animal subject. Things like stress reduction, weight gain—paying attention to them, playing with them—this could be important in understanding how the impacts of some brain disorders could be addressed. You take it into account in your results—certainly,

> rats which were stressed out, say from not being familiar with me, could give a different result.

She went on to say,

> It's not a bad methodological basis to proceed from. I would rather be assured that my rats are relaxed and are used to me, that they know my touch and my ways of approaching them. It would certainly impact my research if my rats were fearful, anxious. … I would also have to account for that in my results.

The rats and equipment and Brenda's affection were not at odds. The tying together of emotional connections with animals, such as affection, and research results is not unusual in the broader literature on research methods involving laboratory animals. (see Davis, 1988, 1996; Reinhardt, 2003). T. Wolfe, in his *How Different Species Affect the Relationship* (1996)—where the 'different' species and their impact refers to how humans treat all kinds of laboratory animals, for instance—noted that the researcher or technician instils in the animal qualities that

> make them better and more reliable research subjects. Stress, on the other hand, leads to profound physiological and behavioural changes that increase the variability of the data and decrease the reliability of the results. Subtle social changes producing these profound effects have been documented in rodents, dogs, chickens, pigs, nonhuman primates, rabbits and people. The effects include … susceptibility to gastric erosions in F-1 generations of mice. … [The researcher] must strive to develop a social bond with all animals … this last statement reflects a change in my attitude. I can remember giving a talk thirty years ago about the fact that laboratory animals are not pets. They have numbers, not names. We treat them as important parts of our environment, but we do not warm up to them. I have come to realise that that attitude is opposed to everything that I now believe about the well-being of animals and the quality of the research. (p. 86)

Like Neibor, Brenda, who handles, grooms, and talks with her rats and works as a neuroscientist, reported that she 'had trouble' entering her rats into the sacrificial economy of the laboratory. She confided that she dreaded the day she had to do so. Although she could have handed the responsibility for the actual deaths of her rats to a technician or another member of her research team, Brenda did not want to. She felt she owed the rats a good death and that she, as the person who had had the most contact with them during their lives, should also be the one to carry out their deaths. But, she approached the day with unease and said that she did not like to do it.

As she had said to me earlier, Brenda had an affection for her rats and was, by her own description, 'a rat person—I enjoy them, I like them; they're interesting and intelligent, good to work with. They come to know a person, and you come to know them, too. You bond with them'. Even though Brenda had effectively worked these bonds into her findings so that the analytic rats that yielded data for her study did not stand at odds with the animals she gave affection to every day, this did not spare her from experiencing feelings of loss when she terminated her rats. Just as Darwin suggested, experiencing an animal's affection in a research setting haunts the scientist when she or he is confronted by the typical requirements of laboratory work—to wound, to cause suffering, and to kill.

Drawing extensively on Levinasian notions of face, Haraway (2008) argued that the discomfort scientists might feel in bringing about the deaths of laboratory animals is attended by a knowledge of the animal as more than reactive equipment and an appreciation that the animal is instead responsive, response-able. Face, as Levinas (2004) conceived of it, describes the abject other—'the stranger, the widow, the orphan' (p. 88) whose corporeal vulnerability is always greater than one's own. It is because this other, in whatever form it appears, is so fragile, so pathetic, that it has the authority to insist on one's compliance with the primordial ethical command, 'Thou shalt not kill'. This compliance, known as ethics, is based on a paradox; it is normally strength which ensures compliance, not relative weakness. The relationship is also asymmetrical—although the vulnerable other must be protected, it owes nothing in return to the relatively strong—and thus, the face-to-face relationship is always asymmetrical (Levinas, 2004, p. 84). Haraway (2008) expanded

Levinas's work to include nonhuman others in the relationship of face and to include the position of the animal as responsive and participatory in a relationship with a human. He argued that

> the animals in the lab ... have face; they are somebody as well as something, just as we humans are both subject and object all the time ... respect is respecere—looking back, holding in regard, understanding that meeting the look of the other is a condition of having face oneself. (p. 88)

And, 'response ... grows with the capacity to respond, this is responsibility' (Haraway, 2008, p. 71).

Taking up Derrida's mantle,[6] Haraway (2008) applied the concept of face to laboratory (and other) animals, arguing that animals are the subjects of an ethical concern as much as they might be located in the laboratory space as tools or objects that can be manipulated to yield the product of data, and that they are so because they are response-able. Though Haraway did not suggest that scientists should fulfil the primordial ethical responsibility, she did indicate that 'meeting the look of the [animal] other is a condition of having face oneself'. Doing so, however, does not indicate equality; just as Levinas's conception of face was asymmetrical, so too is the one that is to be found in the laboratory context. In the laboratory, the appreciation of rat face and mouse face does not lead to the Levinasian compulsion to spare rats and mice (or indeed, other animals) from death. But it did cause scientists significant grief, as it did for Brenda.[7]

The basis for Brenda's grief over her rats' deaths began in the establishment of particular relations with them of an interspeci-al kind, in which a variety of kinship was established. During our visit to her rats while they were alive, Brenda told me, 'Some of my colleagues have taught their animals to jump out of their house and into a bucket, while the cages are being cleaned. Then, they jump back in again'. She added, 'They [the rats] back themselves into the corners of the cage'. This made the rats' tails unavailable to Brenda when she approached them using the proper grasp, which should be applied to the base of the rat's tail, where it is strong and will not be injured. The rats, Brenda explained, knew this move and responded to it. More than this, she thought, the rats were 'telling' her something that she could understand in making themselves ungraspable—'I knew they were refusing me', she said. Brenda very often shares moments like this with rats—this bunch and others. She said, 'We're not that different; there's an enduring relationship between animals and people that most people don't like to acknowledge when it comes to rats. But it's there'. Brenda also spoke about the ways in which her rats communicated to her the particular ways they preferred to be petted: 'They particularly like being scratched on their shoulders, and will present their shoulders for attention', she explained. 'They really can communicate quite plainly about what they want. I've even had some of my rats lick me—that's serious affection', she added.

> They tell you in plain terms what they are feeling, and they know what I want when I go for their tails, as lab protocol requires. The rats have not read the lab protocol; they just say 'no' to me. You might think that just means I have to insist, but it is difficult and potentially damaging to them to just grab them—instead, I have to persuade them by negotiating with them. I might have to give them a treat or pet them for a bit. It's not just that I impose myself on them—there is a space for negotiation.

My field notes are heavily peppered with examples like Brenda's, including Nancy's. Nancy's dog, Judy, had recently had pups, and Nancy called work to say she would not be in because she was witnessing the birth of her 'grandchildren'. Some of Nancy's rats, though they were not the bearers of her other-speci-al generational kin, were not dissimilarly close to her. She explained,

> The rats are not like Judy, who I think of as my daughter. But I am close to them; I know how they feel, as one who has a dog knows that dog's mood, without knowing exactly how they know. I know how my rats are feeling, and what they want, what they do not want. That is because they tell me, and I feel that I can, with some fluency, speak rat.[8]

Brenda's interpretation of her rats' behaviour, and their interpretation of hers, speaks to the simultaneous giveness of animality and humanity that Merleau-Ponty described in the terms of 'strange kinship'—his phrase to capture the sense in which the world is shared among and generally available to the species, despite their evident differences, in the fleshiness of their being. Merleau-Ponty argued that the 'thickness' of flesh, which is constituted by and constituting of the world all animals share, ensures kin-like relations. Brenda's relations with her rats persisted in an indistinctive zone which required neither complete ratness nor complete humanness to operate; each being was strange to the other, yet their sameness emerged sufficient to offer up possible relationships that spanned the animal-human divide. Rats and people became indistinctive categories of being, and a kind of general contingency between species was recognised. This generality was sufficient to allow for an interspecies communication that proceeded without language (with the animals of Merleau-Ponty's sublinguistic schema). It was enough to offer up the possibility of relatedness and relationship and enough to question the strict situation of rats and mice as biological research equipment. It went beyond or preceded ratness and humanness to offer a basal relationship between them; it was enough to be recognised as a kind of kinship that extended to flesh together ratkind and humankind. Such a kinship is constituted by and enacted in the thickness of interaction; as Haraway (2008) put it, 'species of all kinds are consequent on a subject and object shaping dance of encounters' (p. 4). Along with the dance of scientific encounter that produces specific rat research subjects and scientific enquirers was also a dance that produced indistinct partners, in which rat subjects and human scientists diminished as bounded categories of being. Here persisted a 'we' that might trouble the boundary between humans and animals, especially in the laboratory.

As Dillard-Wright (2009) noted, such a relationship might seem unusual only if one is prepared to accept the exceptionalist argument that human communications differ in kind and in practice from those of other animals. Dillard-Wright pointed here not to the flattening of speci-al difference but acknowledged instead the underlying commonalities in animal communication 'that give rise to human culture' (p. 68) through overlap, sufficient that comprehension can take place between the species. 'Communication seizes upon occasions for its enactment and happens at the edge of species; here, the social cannot be delimited to this or that self-enclosed sphere but continually opens to the outside in an unfolding milieu of gestural interplay' (Dillard-Wright, 2009, p. 68).

Other scholars, working in scientific contexts, have also pointed to the commonality of such gestural interspecies communication. Davis (1996), for example, drew on his 15-year-long experience in working with rats to suggest that

> a rat will work simply to be petted by a human—not for food, not for water, and not to avoid shock, but just to have a favoured human reach down and say, 'good girl'. It is a powerful and viable reinforcer, confined to the person involved in the relationship; a rat does not want to be petted by just anyone. Like all animals, it is selective. (p. 70)

Brenda's rats were selective in their preference for her; though they sought out her hand when she offered it to them in the cage, Brenda's rats also nuzzled it and presented their shoulders for petting. They shrank away when they saw me. But, Brenda's rats were not always pleased to see her; they knew when she was going to pick them up, and they made their feelings known about that—by refusing Brenda their tails.

If rats and mice express and make themselves understood across the animal-human divide, as Derrida noted animals could in his *The Animal That Therefore I Am* (2002, pp. 8–9, 51), then the long-standing Cartesian division between animals and humans, which claims that nonhuman animals are automatons capable only of reacting, is undermined in the laboratory space. Brenda's grasp-refusing rats and rats that understand and respond to requests to remove themselves to a temporary bucket space point to crossings of the divide.

Merleau-Ponty's (1994) application of a general behavioural schema to each organism is one in which the animal, at 'each moment of its history is empty of what will follow, an emptiness which will be filled later'

(p. 155). As Deranty (2008) noted of Merleau-Ponty's position, 'This definition of negativity as the absence of meaning to come, which haunts the present and guides it already, characterises organic life. Crucially it has the exact same structure as [human] expression' (p. 179). For Merleau-Ponty, life is expression and expression is life, irrespective of the sophistication or otherwise of the form of life. It follows, as Deranty also suggested, that all living organisms are expressive in terms of their behaviour. Here persists Merleau-Ponty's view of organic life as opening 'a dimension of meaning within the material world [which] enables Merleau-Ponty to develop an immanentist philosophy of nature, where the superior levels actualise potentialities that were already inscribed in the lower ones' (Deranty 2008, p. 179). In humans, the potentialities which lay in other animals are fully realised, and, according to Merleau-Ponty (1994),

> perceived things [become] correlations of a carnal subject, rejoined to its movement and to its sensing; interspersed in its internal circuit—they are made of the same stuff as it … the flesh of the body makes us understand the flesh of the world. (p. 218).

The upshot of this is that the dualism between the human and the animal is no longer required because, for Merleau-Ponty, there is a way of conceiving all life as bios

> since for him [Merleau-Ponty] all life is already expressive, human language and all symbolic institutions more generally are rooted in the meaningful totality of organisms that are symbolically, and even semiotically, linked to their external and social worlds qua integrated forms of behaviour. (Deranty, 2008, p. 181)

The expressive and expressing flesh of animals and persons that allowed Brenda to understand the rats and for the rats to understand her proceeds along the lines of a vitalist ontology of the *Ineinander*[9] 'where things continually step *into* each other' (Deranty, 2008, p. 181), and in which particular openings between the ostensibly firmly closed bounds between humans and animals, specie and specie, are on offer.

These openings are tantalisingly hinted at in Agamben's *The Open* (2002). This might seem an unlikely source for me to turn to. Indeed, for Agamben, 'the Open' is indubitably intended to be read as the reverse of *Dasein*. Agamben's argument, as put forth in his *Homo Sacer*, is that the human is created with and against the animal, a course that proceeds by means of the 'anthropological machine'. The early machine humanised some animals, with the result that biological humans might be considered to belong to the category 'animal'—for instance, kept slaves and racially distinctive 'others' such as barbarians, savages, and foreigners. The more modern machine has not changed significantly in that human life continues to be animalised, relegating people to a lesser category of an animal in human form which may well prove lethal to the members of the category, as it did for Jews in the camp during the Holocaust (the key example that is used in *Homer Sacer*). The Nazi propaganda film *Der Ewige Jude* ('The Eternal Jew', 1940) by Hippler makes the point blatantly. The film includes a montage of images juxtaposing Jewish faces with rat snouts and Jewish crowds with swarming hordes of rats. The accompanying commentary makes the point explicit:

> Whenever rats appear they bring ruin, by destroying mankind's goods and foodstuffs. In this way they spread disease, plague, leprosy, typhoid fever, cholera, dysentery, and so on. They are cunning, cowardly and cruel, and are found mostly in large packs. Among the animals they represent the rudiment of an insidious and underground destruction—just like the Jews among human beings. [Drawing on the success of the rats in flooding the world, the program notes also say], 'We see a parallel in the itinerant routes of rats, which are parasites and bacillus-carriers among animals; the Jews perform this role among mankind'.[10] (*Der Ewige Jude*, 1940)

Agamben's image of the machine allows a certain kind of vision. When a man sees an ape, Agamben (2002) noted, he always sees his own deformed image in its features: 'The machine allows the man to recognise himself in the non man in order to be human' (pp. 26–27). Thus emerges the platform for a poststructural theory of the production of humanity, in which humanity is suspended between nature and culture. The capacity of the machine to produce a state of exception also results. As humanity is always assumed, the machine works to produce the separation of 'man' from 'human'—precisely the task of 19th-century armchair anthropologists, who applied the appropriate language category ('primitive', 'savage') to the level of animality that was present in what was ostensibly human. In its modern form, the anthropological machine divided human from man; the human is in this way dependent upon a category of humanity which can have its very humanness removed (discursively, biopolitically) for the benefit of those who would claim to be civilized. In its premodern operation, the machine worked symmetrically by interpellating the animal to the status of the human. But these 'animals' are the barbarians, slaves, and foreigners that are distinguished from humans, not animals per se. Such a designation locates biological humans in a position of 'bare life' (Agamben, 1998, p. 8), a condition visited upon them that renders them at once subject to unregulated and freely exercised forms of violence and ineligible for sacrifice (p. 102). In the classical world, bare life was distinguished as *zoe* from political life (*bios*). Agamben argued that it is this separation between natural *zoe* and political *bios* that constitutes the fundamental activity of sovereign power and enables bare life to become sacred life—'life that can be killed but not sacrificed, or *homo sacer*' (p. 102).

In *Homo Sacer*, Agamben drew on a long philosophical tradition that defines the human through an opposition to the animal, creating the animal as a category solely to allow what is essential about humans to emerge. This means that one cannot leave aside that bare life, in Agamben's formulation, politically situates the animal—the distinction between the fully human and the human which is more like an animal opens up the possibility of exploiting not only the latter category of (sub) humans but also animals themselves as lesser beings. Further, it creates and sustains the conditions for contemporary biopolitics, in which the biological and animal aspects of human life are increasingly brought under the purview of the state and the judiciary.

Some theoreticians have argued that Agamben's division of humans from animals could be applied to animals per se to describe some of the consequences for, in this instance, laboratory animals as equipment (see Patterson, 2003). Attending to the singular situation of animals as well as to their suffering in his recourse to Holocaust analogy, Derrida (2002) argued that the annihilation of certain species

> is indeed in process, but it is occurring through the organisation and exploitation of an artificial, infernal, virtually interminable survival, in conditions that previous generations would have judged monstrous, outside of every supposed norm of life proper to animals that are thus exterminated by means of their continued existence or overpopulation. As if, for example, instead of throwing people into ovens and gas chambers (let's say Nazi) doctors or geneticists had decided to organise the overproduction and overgeneration of Jews, gypsies and homosexuals by means of artificial insemination so that, being more numerous and better fed, they could be destined in always increasing numbers for the same hell, that of the imposition of genetic experimentation or extermination by gas [as laboratory rodents are] or by fire. In the same abattoirs. (p. 395)

Under Agamben's original conceptualisation of bare life, as he described it in *Homo Sacer* (1998), a human being is given the status of the living dead—it is biologically living, but it does not have human rights. Lacking these, it cannot be sacrificed, and it is necroavailable (to the state) and can be killed without the charge of murder being brought. Many theoreticians of animal rights, including Peter Singer, have argued that animals that are located within the industrial coordinates of the slaughterhouse or the scientific coordinates of the laboratory can be understood as living a bare life. Just as humans can, in Agamben's language, become animalised, animals can become deanimalised.

Despite the fact that rats appear not as sufferers of the conditions of bare life in Hippler's rat/Jew example but as the very representation of how low humans must go in the Nazi view to be placed in the category of 'animal', there are yet several parallels in lab life that invite an analysis of rats and mice living under conditions of bare life. Although pinkie pups are disposed of almost as soon as they are born, their fate is the fate of all lab rats and mice. All of them are enclosed within the coordinates of the scientific space which subjects them to conditions of life that confer upon them the status of the living dead. There are other parallels between the bare life of the camp and the bare life of the lab, which are obvious in the modes of effecting death, including the use in both the laboratory and the camp of the (isoflurane, carbon dioxide–filled) gas chamber.

But, Agamben's work might also point to those tantalising openings I mentioned before. In *The Open* (2002), Agamben (admittedly almost certainly unintentionally) hinted at the undoing of the divide when he suggested that the zone of indistinction of his original conception of bare life might be reconceptualised as a zone of possibility, within which the relation between humans and animals might be reworked. It is certain that throughout his work, Agamben's intention was to find ways of thinking about and speaking to humanist nihilism. However, *The Open* speaks more to the anthropocentrism that is not addressed in his earlier works. Calarco (2008, p. 91) pointed to the presence of this consideration in his analysis of the opening pages of *The Open*, in the section entitled 'Theriomorphous' (literally, 'having the form of an animal'). Here, Agamben considered a 13th-century illustration in the Hebrew Bible (in the Ambrosian Library of Milan), depicting the messianic banquet of the righteous on the last day. The righteous feast on the meat of Leviathan and the Behemoth without concern for whether or not the meat is kosher; they do not concern themselves because the righteous inhabit a time and a space that is outside the law. Agamben was puzzled by the image because the righteous are depicted as having human bodies and animal heads. These righteous figures, it must be remembered, are the conclusion of humanity. Agamben (2002) wondered, 'Why are the representatives of concluded humanity depicted with animal heads?' (p. 2). He answered himself that in attributing an animal head to the righteous who are present for the coming of the Messiah, 'the artist of the manuscript in the Ambrosian intended to suggest that on the last day, the relations between animals and men will take on a new form, and that man himself will be reconciled with his animal nature (p. 3)'.[11]

Calarco (2008) observed that Agamben may have been suggesting that humans will become reconciled with their animal natures and will no longer seek to divide *zoe* from *bios*. This would see humans attending to the production of a human life that is devoid of the division between bare and political life—a task Agamben (1998) set for the coming community in his assessment that such a life remains 'largely to be invented' (p. 11). Such a reading would not depart from Agamben's established line of thought. But, perhaps, as Calarco (2008) suggested, Agamben meant instead to point to a transmutation in the relations between human beings and animals (p. 92). This would, as Calarco suggested, certainly constitute a rupture in Agamben's itinerary of thought, but it is equally certain that it provides fertile grounds upon which to rethink humanimal relations—perhaps it is possible that Agamben meant to suggest that the division between humans and nonhumans might be reworked outside of its current dichotomous and hierarchical arrangement. Calarco (2008) noted of this possibility,

> It is clear given the context that his reading of the illustration is pointing us toward a less violent conception of human-animal relations. Thus, just as Agamben's thought of the coming community is an effort to come to grips with and avert the political failures of our age, his reworking of the human-animal distinction appears to be aimed at creating a space in which human interactions with non-human life can take on a new form and economy that avoids similar disastrous consequences for nonhuman life. (p. 92)

This seems to me to offer a way out of the impasse that is presented by instrumental reason: Humans either dominate nature or are dominated by it. Certainly, Agamben is not the only scholar to suggest a way out; Adorno (2003) suggested the possibility of a new categorical imperative that is based neither in reason nor in nature but somewhere in between. As Hudson (2008) noted,

> the (non)concept of the addendum he introduces seems to stem from the very suspension between human and animal that Agamben calls bare life. The addendum is beyond conceptual, identitarian thinking: it occupies the space of the nonidentity of conceptual thought.

> The addendum is both a somatic impulse and a reflective moment that acts as 'a flash of light between the poles of something long past, something grown all but unrecognizable, and that which some day might come to be' and which offers 'the phantasm of reconciling nature and the mind' [Adorno, 2003, p. 229]. Neither instinct nor concept, the addendum bridges the gap between mind and nature, refusing to be laid open to the probings of reason alone. This non-conceptual concept appears as a flash of an almost forgotten alternative to the dominating drive of instrumental reason, based not in logic but in the bodily experience of compassion. (p. 110)

A bodily experience of some sort of compassion—a fleshy bodily sympathy—is at the basis of the kinship between Brenda and her rats; such a kinship is based not on the biological likeness of bodies or in generation or in descent but rather in the persistence of ambiguous fleshy unspecificity, where, as Haraway (2008) might describe the ambiguous zone, 'no one gets to be Man' (p. 82).[12] In such a zone of unspecificity, Brenda and rats might well be considered indistinct kin. Indistinction preceded ratness and Brenda's humanness to offer a basal relationship between them wherein only the ambiguous bare life that existed prior to these identities being discursively and operationally made persisted. This unspecificity is essentially fleshy, in the sense that the world is shared among and generally available to the species, despite their evident differences, in the fleshiness of their being, in 'we'. This 'we' is at the heart of Merleau-Ponty's (1994) development of 'interanimality', a term by which he meant to point to 'a description of the man-animality intertwining' (p. 274). As fleshy beings each open to *Einfuhlung*, 'what exists are not separate animals, but an interanimality' (p. 248).

Despite her kinship with rats—perhaps a kinship of indistinction, perhaps a kinship of fleshy figuration—Brenda killed her rats and entered them into the sacrificial economy of the lab, where they were destined to go as a result of their biological and genetic kinship with humans. But, she entered them with unease, as she attended this other kinship—of figuration or of indistinction—with the rats. Brenda grieved for her rats on the day they became her data—secretly, because good God-scientists do not openly grieve for equipment. As Darwin (1871) himself noted of the complexities of engaging with animals who could engage back, 'everyone has heard of the dog suffering under vivisection, who licked the hand of the operator: this man, unless he had a heart of stone, must have felt remorse to the last hour of his life' (p. 40). That is, he added, 'unless the operator was fully justified by an increase in our knowledge' (p. 70). But, at some indistinctive or fleshy point before or beyond which she was a scientist and rats were her equipment, Brenda and the rats were some sort of interspecies kin.

The reckoning of rat-human kinship is not as radical a suggestion as it might at first appear. Perhaps it should not be totally unexpected that such an indistinctive unspeci-al 'we' comprised of intercommunicating rats and people should be found in the lab. After all, as Wolf-Meyer (2006) suggested, just this sort of contingency is recognised in the realm of posthuman biopolitics, in which the human genome project is located: An understanding of being—not simply species-specific being—is sought, and it becomes a scientific mandate to arrive at understandings of being as such rather than understandings only of human being. Such a mandate encourages the contingency of species and counters the over-determination of humanity. The recognition of the biological kinship between humans and rodents, along with the recognition of interspecies kinship, demonstrates that 'multiples' of the relations between rodents and humans are played out in the lab; this makes it very difficult to locate the lab neatly in humanist terrain, where it has traditionally lain. This is not, nor should it be regarded as, new. Indeed, as Haraway (2008) observed, it was science which put *Homo sapiens* firmly in the world of animals—Freud's second of the three great wounds dealt to the narcissism of the self-centred human subject specifically picks out the sharply injurious Darwinian blade. As Haraway aptly noted, if any wound was to decentre and undermine man's surety in the world, then surely it would be this one, born in science. Darwin's kinning of people and animals in evolutionary terms, his acknowledgement of their intertwinement, speaks to their entailments in one another. In the ostensibly unlikely setting of the lab, there may well be openings to strange, indistinctive kinship, even as they operate in the shadow of the sacrificial economy.

Endnotes

1. Humanness not defined by membership in the category 'human'.
2. Animality not defined by membership in the category 'animal'.
3. Kohak's (1984) insight implies that the ontological cannot be separated from the practical. In this regard, one cannot leave aside the practical techniques of handling rats and mice. These include that one must retain a wariness of the rat's capacity to turn and bite. Readiness-to-hand cannot be fully assumed of the rat-tool, no matter how the animal is regarded analytically and irrespective of what purpose its physical body is to be used for; a lingering sense of the unpredictable animal necessarily remains. Such a high and—as Karen, an animal technician who had been bitten by a rat, said—necessary consciousness of the animal lurking in the tool indicates that the very last thing rats and mice are in the lab is inanimate tools. An appreciation of the elements of 'natural' animality—mouse fragility, rat reactions, and environmental and enrichment requirements—is not inconsistent whatsoever with the situation of mice and rats as tools in the lab. Animals that are not included in the laboratory space precisely as tools—complete with their natural animal elements—have no place in the laboratory at all. As Reinert observed of the butcher's gaze, a live animal intended for consumption is 'already meat', already equipment, already it is thoroughly integrated with its intended end use. Mice, too, are already thoroughly integrated with the laboratory end goals of using mouse and rat bodies to produce data—that is, to deploy their bodies as tools in the course of acquiring data. But, they remain tools that require the researcher to hold them in inquisitive regard in and of themselves, in their mouseness and ratness, their liveliness, and their capacity to bite, scratch, wriggle, writhe, and escape. The assertion that I am making, that it is difficult to regard rodent animals as ready-to-hand in practical terms, does not mean that the animals involved get an improved deal; they will still suffer the experimental processes to which they are submitted, and they will still die. These brute facts, however, do not in turn indicate detachment between the scientist and the animal, Acampora's other key assertion. Additionally, attachments of various kinds, which I describe later and in the final ethnographic chapter, often mitigate against the uncaring which is characteristic of Acampora's particular view of detachment as it operates in the context of the laboratory.
4. Smyth (2007) noted that Merleau-Ponty used the term 'animality' broadly to refer to human animality (which makes sense of interanimality, which

has general application to the relations between any and all species) because he is, really, a humanist (p. 179). But, in my estimation and Smyth's, he is a nonanthropocentric humanist, if that is possible.

5. These are Merleau-Ponty's "Course Notes" for the course which he gave at the Collège de France in 1959–1960 under the title "Husserl aux limites de la phénoménologie", (Husserl at the limits of phenomenology) together with a revised version of John O'Neill's translation of the summary of this course, which originally appeared in *In Praise of Philosophy and Other Essays*, published by Northwestern University Press in 1988.
6. The notion that animals are understood in Haraway's (2008) work as capable of responding is Derrida's—animals were understood by Haraway as being able to communicate and express. Haraway helped to undermine the Cartesian claim that nonhumans are automatons capable only of reacting (see Calarco, 2008; Derrida, 2002).
7. Haraway (2008) argued that 'to be in response to [the face] is to recognize copresence in relations of use and therefore to remember that no balance sheet of benefit and cost will suffice' (p. 76). Brenda did invoke the balance sheet of benefit to justify the deaths of her rats, saying that their sacrifice, in the broad scheme of things, would be worthy. But it was not sufficient to alleviate her grief, and it was balanced against the calculus of care.
8. As Davis (1996) put it, scientists who work with animal subjects do their best work when they 'learn to speak rat or dog or rhesus' (p. 69).
9. Translated from German, this means 'flowing/stepping in to one another'.
10. The program notes for *Der Ewige Jude* (1940) are at www.holocaust-history.org/der-ewige-jude.
11. Interestingly, the cover of the film *Humanimal*, a production looking closely at the ways in which science is currently producing information about animals that 'proves the border between the two worlds is not quite as impenetrable as once thought' (film jacket notes) also utilises the figure of the human body with the animal head.
12. I am not suggesting that Haraway's (2008) views are the same as Agamben's (2002); indeed, Haraway was unsympathetic to Agamben's view generally and was obviously unwilling to accept that it may present opportunities of the sort I have suggested, writing that 'he [Agamben] is no help at all for figuring out how to get to another kind of opening, the kind feminists and others who never had Heidegger's starting point for *Dasein* of profound boredom can discern' (p. 334, n. 16).

Chapter 5

The Calculus of Care, the Laboratope, and the Relations of Mundane Kinship

Rodent research animals appear in the laboratory that is under study here as units of analytic mammalian equipment, sites of emotional investment, human similars, and beings with whom scientists might make relationships based on their communicative capacities to 'speak rat' with fluency and be understood by knowing rodent partners. As I have argued throughout this book, the multiplicity of possibilities for relating to ambiguously located rodent research animals, which sometimes simultaneously occupy opposed and conflicting positions in the lab, often result in crossings of the human-animal and speci-al borders that are at times invoked in the laboratory. Rats and mice also appear in the laboratory as animals of particular specie requiring specific regimes of care and as generic mammalian models intended for entry into the sacrificial economy of the laboratory. At the moments of their deaths, as I have suggested, mammalian rodent units emerge once again as particularly speci-al—as 'only mice'. In their lives and in their deaths, mice and rats travel through various classifications, from specific speci-al animals to the generalised status of mammals, emerging, once again, at the moment of death, as specifically mouse or rat. In their intercommunicative relationships with those humans who speak rat or mouse with some fluency, mice and rats appear in that ambiguous zone of being that privileges neither ratness, mouseness, or humanness. Indeed, intraspeci-al communication depends on the diminishment of the certain boundaries that otherwise locate mice, rats, and humans as fundamentally different from one another.

As animals which live their lives in the laboratory, mice and rats are ambiguously located between generic mammalian equipment and animals which have particular speci-al needs. In the course of his 'thick description' of an Austrian immunology lab, Bischur (2008) described two animals that persist in a single rat or mouse body: the technological animal that is equipment and the speci-al animal, the rat or mouse. He argued that the persistence of 'both' animals in the context of the laboratory produces relationships between researchers and laboratory animals that are 'highly ambivalent': 'On the one hand animals are reduced to some kind of technological tools, data bearing analytical animals. On the other hand, they certainly remain living natural animals' (p. 29).

That two animals persisted in the one animal body was recognised by researchers and animal technicians in this study. Olivia, an animal technician, told me about how important it was not to forget that laboratory mice were 'still mice' and 'still have needs peculiar to them, even though they are here because they are laboratory equipment'. She said,

> We give them [the mice] toilet roll tunnels. Even though they were not born in the wild—and some of them are altered mice, too—all of them, still, absolutely, want someplace to hide, just as if they were born in the wild, or as if they were normal [unaltered] mice. They're still mice. And toilet rolls are great; they are easily autoclaved, and they are ideal hidey-holes for mice. They enrich the life of the animal, and make it closer to what this species needs to be comfortable and happy.

Olivia went on to explain that to forget that mice were in fact mice, and not only laboratory equipment, was tantamount to abuse and would in practice constitute animal cruelty. Theoreticians of animal lives argue similarly; Dillard-Wright (2009) noted, for instance, that there is no surer way to limit human respect for animals than to flatten speci-al difference to the condition of the generic animal. Shapiro (1989) argued along similar lines. Shapiro's observations of animals' responses to place suggest that the application of a generic membership to animals, such as 'mammalian membership' in the laboratory context, imposes a hierarchical order on nonhuman animals that is expressed in the latter's incapacity to live 'up to their natures' in the laboratory. According to Shapiro, animals respond to place not in terms of access to a home or an approximation of a home that might be provided to them when they are in captivity, but in terms of the peculiarity of speci-al identification—the sense of being speci-al, according to Shapiro, is inextricably intertwined with specific kinds of places and (unhindered) access to those places. Once it is denied access to those places, an animal is, according to Shapiro's line of reasoning, rendered not only homeless but also disembodied, because it is unable to live up to its species identity in its bodily conduct.

Acampora took this observation further, arguing that the distinctive way in which a particular animal lives its species identity is existentially flattened out into the conduct of a generic mammalian laboratory animal model—the very realisation of Olivia's warning about forgetting that mice were, after all, still mice. Lonergan (1978) believed that the biological pattern of existence of animals is concerned not with the immanent aspects of living but rather with external conditions and opportunities. Drawing on this notion as well as on Scheler's (1961) and Agamben's (2002) insights, that the animal lives ecstatically immersed in its environment, Acampora (2006) also argued that animal speci-ality manifests as the specific body-self incorporating, outbound, into its surroundings. This raises existential (and welfare) issues for the containment of animals in the lab (and other circumstances) for Acampora:

> If an animal develops worldhood by appropriating externalities, then the result for an incarcerated lab rat is internalised imprisonment.

> The rat's environment is dominated by bars or walls or fencing—hence the rodent comes to phenomenally assimilate the carceral into the carnal. A clockwork-orange transmogrification, the product of this metamorphosis might better be denominated as a 'jailhouse body'. Indeed, this alteration is reinforced by the treatment of such organisms in testing protocol as 'living laboratory equipment' run through a historical process of greater industrialisation, in which lab animals become standardised and increasingly a production process and part of the apparatus of science itself. (p. 14)

According to Acampora, one result for those laboratory animals that are located as mammalian apparatus is the 'emptying effect', the reduction of the animal's capacity to live a specifically speci-al existence in the openness of space. The essence to be a rat or a mouse is reduced (necessarily for Acampora, because the animal is provided to the lab as equipment and will later be mathematically further reduced as its live ratness is turned into data). Here, the living rat or mouse in the lab cannot live up to its ratness or its mouseness; it is instead offered the opportunity to live only the incarcerated generic mammalian life of the laboratory animal/equipment. Ratness and mouseness cannot be accomplished under the carceral laboratory conditions that accommodate generic mammalian equipment (and emphatically, according to Acampora, not natural, speci-al animals).

That these speci-alities could not be accomplished under carceral laboratory circumstances was the subject of Berdoy's 2001 film exploring the lives of recently released laboratory rats. Berdoy, a zoologist at Oxford University, made a film entitled *The Laboratory Rat—A Natural History*. The film depicts the release of 50 laboratory strains of the domestic brown rat into a controlled wild environment. Berdoy conducted and filmed the release in order to demonstrate that despite their 200-generation-long confinement to the lab environment, brown rats (which were, in this case, white) remained, in their speci-al essence, brown rats. His exploration of key elements of wild rat living—including food selection, group habitation, learning, social organisation, antipredation strategies, olfactory and ultrasonic communication strategies, habitat selection and orientation, mating strategy and sexual selection, neophobia and curiosity, and reproduction—showed that generations of domestication did not remove a rat's natural, speci-al range of behaviours and needs, or its essence to be a rat. The rats immediately displayed a multitude of behavioural instincts that a cage in a laboratory had kept suppressed, and they quickly adapted to their new environment very successfully. Berdoy's film raises questions about what the essence of a laboratory animal might be said to be, both when it is kept under laboratory conditions as a kind of 'repressed' animal and when it has been altered in some way. Weisberg (2009) took the position that

> the genetic engineer may think that the essence of the mouse he is genetically manipulating is to-be-genetically-manipulated, but in truth, its essence is to-be-mouse—to fulfil its natural behaviours and to live amongst its own kind in its natural environment. (p. 55)

In accordance with this belief, Berdoy's film insists that laboratory rats are merely repressed natural animals and that they will slough off the behaviours that their status as mammalian analytic animals thrusts upon them in the confines of the laboratory enclosure. In Berdoy's view, rats are 'animals', and they move naturally back to the place they once occupied as wild beings as soon as the appropriate default environment is encountered. The rat essence is simply a wild one awaiting reversion.[1]

It was not only animal technicians such as Olivia who were mindful never to forget that mice are always mice, despite their location in the laboratory and irrespective of the degree to which they might have been modified. Virologist Mark told me that 'as animals, laboratory mice have particular needs'. Attending to these needs meant, for Marks's mice, providing them with toilet roll tunnels, the company of other mice, and chew blocks. These things came down to the 'natural' needs a mouse might have as a social animal, a predated animal, and a gnawing animal. Mice fared better on all health and well-being counts when they were housed with other mice. According to Mark, they 'needed' toilet roll tunnels to replicate a natural habitat that lab mice would never experience but which was deeply vested in them as speci-al animals which needed to feel safe from predators. Mark told me,

> lab mice—knock-in, knockout, inbred, mutant, are not meant to be outside the lab. They are lab creations, built for a purpose, built for research, ordered up to be here. They don't belong anywhere but here. But still, they are essentially the same animal [as wild/domestic mice]—it's just that laboratory rodents are wholly specialised to this [the laboratory] environment.[2]

For Mark and Olivia, unaltered and transgenic mice both fell into an ambiguous zone between 'natural' rodents with peculiar speci-al needs, including access to tunnels and dark places that appealed to their rat or mouse natures, and animals which were purpose-built or bred for the (cultural) space of the laboratory.[3, 4] Amann (1994) referred to this ambiguous animal as the laboratope, which is meant to indicate that the laboratory space itself produces a 'second nature' of the laboratory animal. This animal is the mouse or rat that meets scientific standards and is subject to particular scientific controls, but which continues to bear the hallmarks of behaviour and needs that are peculiar to its species. In his description of the laboratope as it appeared in his own immunological study, Bischur (2008) argued that the natural animal and analytic animal are reconciled to become 'naturally analytic animals'.

Naturally analytic animals are, according to Bischur, animals which come to be understood by communities of researchers as properly belonging in a context that recognises the duality of such animals, and in which the speci-al needs of animals and the mammalian equipment requirements of science are each met and reconciled.[5] Along similar lines, Haraway (2004) argued that transgenic animals inhabit 'the nature of no nature', and their natural habitat is best understood to be 'the fully artifactual space of technoscience … the lab is its proper niche, its true habitat' (p. 275). Indeed, the laboratory might be considered the habitat which requires and which ushers in particular breeds of rats and mice. Transgenic, knock-in, and knockout animals do not occur as the yield of the 'natural' world; as the laboratory's yield, these animals live in that niche that ushered them in, their 'natural' habitat. But, whether or not the mice and rats which inhabit it are engineered as products designed for laboratory use—whether or not they are engineered transgenic rodents—the cultural space of the laboratory calls forth animals that are themselves nature-culture hybrids, bearing as they do the attributes of mammalian generality that are highly valued within the bounded coordinates of scientific space as well as the attributes of particular species.

Weisberg (2009) linked Haraway's location of laboratory animals in the evolutionary story of the laboratory in which their lives will begin, be lived, and end to Father Solomon's House in Bacon's Utopia; Father Solomon eagerly declares that he has 'places for breeding and generation of those kinds of worms and flies of special use' (Bacon, 1620/1999, p. 264). Weisberg made the linkage to summon the spectre of Baconian inequity that she argued characterises laboratory relations, as well as to point to Haraway's endorsement of vivisection. Where Weisberg connected Haraway's evolutionary claims with Baconian structures of human-animal inequity, it is equally possible, on the basis of ethnographic evidence of attending to speci-al animals in the laboratory space, to say that scientists (and animal technicians) understand that although animals have been issued forth in the context of the laboratory, their lives need not transpire under laboratory evolutionary conditions alone. Instead, they will be amended to reference the speci-al animal that dwells within the laboratory mouse's standardised body: the mouse that must hide in its toilet roll tunnel and nibble, the mouse that must have the company of other mice to be 'happy', the 'natural' mouse that, in its speci-al need, is indistinguishable from its laboratory manifestation.

The attendance to the animal in the laboratope can be described in terms of calculus. Caring for animals in the laboratory reveals another kind of calculus besides that which is made upon the relationship between 'my life and the death of the other' which enables and justifies the scientific exercise of killing: a calculus of care. This calculus of care indicates the cost that the sacrifice of animals exacts on science itself: the provision of specific regimes of care to specific, speci-al animals. The calculus of caring reflects the cost of the death of the mouse or rat other. These two calculi are reconciled in the sense that they form two parts of a whole laboratory economy in which animals are not only worth something to people but are valued in terms of the integrity of their own speci-al worth. They are also reconciled in the sense that one is the genesis for the other—before their deaths, rats and mice are 'compensated', in meaningful speci-al terms, for the loss of their lives in the name of scientific gain.

Johnson (1996) described this calculus in his observation that laboratory rodents

> are recognised as individuals *contributing to the advancement of science thus worthy of the best in care, comfort, concern, compassion and consideration.* Scientists appreciate that laboratory animals contribute greatly to society by furthering science, improving medicine and raising public awareness of our human connection to nature. The field of laboratory animal science provides an expression of the human/animal relationship. As we break new ground in biotechnology and promote the acceptance of this revisionist philosophical view, we are providing leadership in defining human sensitivities and the appreciation of animal awareness and self-awareness. In turn, this will promote a further definition of the human/animal relationship. The traditional three Rs of reduction, replacement and refinement will expand to the six Rs with the addition of: respect, responsibility and relationship. (pp. 56–57; italics added)

Underpinning Johnson's analysis of the current state of laboratory practice and his image of its caring future is the calculus of the sacrificial economy; laboratory animals deserve care because they will sacrifice their lives for the good of science and the good of humans. Also underpinning Johnson's analysis is a calculus of care—a calculation that indicates the cost that the sacrifice of laboratory animals exacts on the laboratory, the cost that taking the life of the rat or the mouse presents for recognition to science. The calculus of caring refers here not to the relationship between 'my life and the death of the other', which enables and justifies the scientific exercise of killing, but instead to the cost of the death of the other. This cost is 'paid' in speci-al terms—in the provision of the animal with its speci-al needs during its life in the laboratory, including 'in housing that meets their specific-species physical and behavioural needs' (Johnson, 1996, p. 56). These are the things, according to Johnson, that the animal deserves because it will die in humans' stead; these things are presented to science for the recognition and the payment of the cost of its sacrifice.

Davis (1996) also referenced this calculus of caring in his observations of Reinhardt's revolutionising of a laboratory regime, in which staff had difficulty in obtaining blood samples from Rhesus monkeys. In this context, Davis noted that the staff were often involved in physical struggles with the monkeys. In contrast, in Reinhardt's new regime, the Rhesus monkeys would 'stick an arm out for blood sampling and receive a treat *in payment* ... the *research transaction is like a contract*' (Davis, 1996, p. 69; italics added).

The attendance to the speci-al animal in the laboratope can also be described in terms of kinship. Though mammalian kinship is at the heart of the calculus of suffering and killing—it is, after all, the basis upon which rats and mice can stand in for humankind in the lab—a mundane kinship is embedded in the calculus of care. I have suggested in the foregoing chapters that the sacrifice of animals in the laboratory is not wholly characterised by the cold detachment of scientific practitioners from rodent research animals. The basis of my claims in this respect lies in the thick of kinship; as much as rodent animals are valuable resources in the quest to stave off human deaths because they are humans' mammalian kin, they also participate with humans in indistinctive kinships which are not based on biological and genetic similarity as well as in kinships that are based on distinctive, speci-al difference. I have argued throughout this book that our mammalian comparability, our genetic and biological kinship, is referenced and attended to in the relations of killing, which draw precisely upon humans' close genetic and biokinship with rodents.

Another register of kinship emerges in the thick of the relations of caring for animals in the laboratory context. This kinship is not based on the recognition of mammalian kinship, in which our biological and genetic similarities are foregrounded. It also is not based on the anthropomorphic kinship that often characterises humans' relationships with pets, as Fox (2006) and others have described, in which human qualities—individuality, emotional capacity, likes, dislikes, and reciprocal sociality—are understood to be present in vertebrate animals (see Sanders, 1993). The register of kinship that is to be found in the laboratory relations of caring is instead at first based on the recognition of profound speci-al difference. In Davis's (1996) view, the recognition of difference that is at the foundation of caring in the laboratory is speci-al. In Haraway's (2008) language, this is a kind of mundane kinship—a kind of kinship that is evident in 'matters of daily life' in the laboratory, matters in which care is shown to be 'intrinsic to the complex felt responsibility … many researchers have for their animals' (p. 90). Mundane kinship—which in her own enquiries, Haraway found extended to snails, corals, and all other laboratory animals irrespective of where they sat on the scale of likeness to humans—is a fundamentally nonanthropomorphic kinship that has its basis in responsibility to different species. The basis of its nonanthropomorphism is born, in fact, in a deep attendance to the distinctive speci-al needs of a variety of animals for which one is responsible. This mundane kinship is founded in the happiness and welfare of the animal—on animal, not human, well-being. I have already hinted at the substantive practices that bear out the notion of mundane kinship: It persists in the provision to mice of toilet roll tunnels, for instance, and it is in the provision to rats of chew blocks, dark places, and particular shale. Here, the inherent value of the rat or mouse as a speci-al entity emerges; it is not valued in hierarchical relationship to humans, but as a species-in-itself—in a rat as a rat, a mouse as a mouse, each with its own peculiar set of needs.

The operation of mundane kinship in the relations of caring does not mean that rodent research animals do not suffer or experience pain in the laboratory. They are there, after all, to suffer and die in humans' stead. But the relations of caring also extend to the alleviation of suffering. I suggest that caring for animals is a practice that is first and for the most part deeply concerned with attendance to the speci-al needs of research rodents and the provision to them of those things that allow them to behave 'up to' their speci-al being. However, it is also the case that caring is given to animals in ways which diminish speci-ality—for instance, when mice and rats are in pain, their pain is assumed to be experienced just as human pain would be, and it is attended to as it would be in a human, with human hospital-grade analgesics and anaesthesia.

The laboratory, of course, is not dedicated solely to providing speci-al care to animals; it also operates to produce data that are applicable to humans. It does both in accordance with the legislatively endorsed ethical protocols that govern the treatment of animals in the laboratory. It should not be surprising that the principles that are applied by the animal ethics committee speak both to the calculus that enables and justifies the scientific exercise of killing and to the calculus of caring which undergirds animal welfare in the laboratory. In so doing, they speak directly to the duality of laboratopes.

The operation of animal ethics in the lab has been a long time in the making. The development of the idea that animals might be anything other than 'beast-machines' was based on the rejection of Cartesian notions of animal being. A slowly emerging empathy, based largely on an ostensibly similar capacity for and set of responses to pain, formed the platform for the accordance of moral status to some animals and moved beyond institutional boundaries into social spaces. English essayists and poets Samuel Johnson (1709–1784) and Alexander Pope (1688–1744) argued that animals may feel pain and that this possibility ought to be taken into consideration. Their contributions were prefaced by those of the writer Richard Steele (1672–1729) (see Centlivre, 1872/1968). In 1710, Steele contributed to the *Tatler*, expressing his disgust at the popularity of the blood sports of cock-throwing, cock- and dog-fighting, bull-baiting, and bear-baiting (see Maehle, 1990). His view was that the pursuit of this bloody entertainment would serve only to make the British appear barbarous in the eyes of other nations. He described three conditions under which he considered it acceptable to kill innocent animals for the purposes of human safety, convenience, and nourishment. All other killing, he insisted, ought be looked on as 'a great piece of cruelty, if not a kind of murder' (Steele, 1710/1970, p. 110). Steele appealed to the British public to abandon these cruel entertainments by invoking the division between reasoned men and brutes, arguing in the *Tatler* that the 'virtues of tenderness, compassion and humanity, are those by which men are distinguished from brutes, as much as by reason itself' (Steele, 1710/1970, p. 110). As Maehle (1990) noted, Steele's attitude towards animals and animal suffering reflected the contemporary educated opinion about 'man's relationship to the animal world':

> On the one hand, his view was traditionally anthropocentric, rooted in the Judeo-Christian belief that man, uniquely endowed with reason, had been given dominion by God over all other creatures [see also Thomas, 1983, pp. 178, 188]. On the other hand, he was indebted to the ideal of a compassionate and benevolent 'Man of Feeling', which at this time had fully emerged from the altruistic teachings of seventeenth-century Latitudinarian clergymen. By now 'General Kindness' was beginning to overflow the borders of human kinship to cover also the irrational 'brute creation' [see also Moore, 1916, p. 298]. Accordingly, in 1709, Steele confessed in the *Tatler* that he was moved to tears of pity by the death of a hunted deer, and, in another issue of the same year, he condemned the 'perverse temper' of a boy tormenting birds. (p. 35)

In 1713, Alexander Pope published his scholarly and humanitarian piece, 'Against Barbarity to Animals', in Steele's periodical *The Guardian* (Pope, 1936). In addition to Steele's objections to the cruelties he saw present in animal entertainment, Pope marshalled what Maehle (1990) called the 'classical authority' against barbarity (p. 36). Pope argued that 'humanity may be extended thro' the whole Order of Creatures, even to the meanest' (see Pope, 1936, pp. 107, 112). He also utilised 'several lines from Ovid's Metamorphoses, in which Pythagoras, out of a belief in metempsychosis, praises vegetarianism and denounces animal slaughtering as leading to homicide' (Maehle, 1990, p. 36; see also Pope, 1936, pp. 107, 112). Pope concluded his essay with the message that humans had the right to destroy only 'noxious' beasts, adding, 'but to the subservient domestic animals, however, man even owes a degree of gratitude, and the life of those animals which were "neither of Advantage or Prejudice to us" should generally be spared' (Maehle, 1990, p. 36).

As I have suggested in this chapter, the notion of gratitude continues to underpin scientific views of animals that are involved in research; I have also suggested that this gratitude (for sacrifice) is practically enacted in the lab in the provision to rodents of specific regimes of speci-al care—these provisions are, I have suggested, presented to science as the cost of sacrifice, paid in meaningful terms to the animal. This is an economy that has been a long time in the making.

In the mid-1700s, at the beginnings of Jeremy Bentham's theory of utilitarianism, there occurred a shift away from the anthropocentric worldview and towards animals' capacity to suffer. In 1776, Humphrey Primatt offered a challenge to Descartes's thesis of the soulless animal. Rejecting humanism, he argued that animals ought to be understood in and on their own terms and protected for their own sake, but that a principle of justice should cover both humans and animals. On the basis that human and animal beings were different yet equally deserving of an applicable justice, Descartes's declaration that animals did not have souls lost its capacity to justify animal experimentation. These ideas gained significant purchase among the scientific fraternity. In 1798, the development of positivism led to the differentiation of empirical investigation and ethical values. Outside the institution, and concerning itself with that differentiation, the U.K. Royal Society for the Prevention of Cruelty to Animals was founded in 1824. From within the institution, British physiologist Marshall Hall pioneered welfare issues and proposed the regulation of physiological procedures that would be designed to take account of and reduce animals' suffering. In 1831, he proposed five principles:

1. An experiment should never be performed if the necessary information could be obtained by observation.
2. No experiment should be performed without a clearly defined, and obtainable, objective.

3. Scientists should be well informed about the work of their predecessors and peers in order to avoid the unnecessary repetition of an experiment.
4. Justifiable experiments should be carried out with the least possible infliction of suffering.
5. Every experiment should be performed under circumstances that would provide the clearest possible results, thereby diminishing the need for the repetition of experiments (see Rupke, 1987).

Hall also proposed the founding of a scientific society to oversee the publication of research results and recommended that the results of experimentation be laid before the public in the simplest, plainest terms (Rupke, 1987). Hall's principles and his notion of the public dissemination of results that were collected by adherence to them certainly met with stiff opposition from those people within and outside of the medical community who disapproved outright of animal experimentation. However, his recommendations endured castigation and indeed, Hall's own death in 1857, to be formally instituted more than a century later in the British Animals (Scientific Procedures) Act and the U.S. Animal Welfare Act.

The publication of Darwin's *The Descent of Man and Selection in Relation to Sex and Expression of the Emotions in Man and Animals* in 1871 also lent strength to the notion that animals and humans were not only similar in terms of a capacity to feel pain but might also be deserving of human consideration in terms of the capacity to feel and act upon emotions. Public opposition to the treatment of animals in experimental situations had grown, but there remained a demand for a regulation-free environment from those researchers who were making gains in knowledge from performing vivisections. Queen Victoria lent her voice to the weight of public opinion, publicly expressing her concern about the treatment of animal subjects in 1874. Subsequently, The U.K. House of Commons was presented with a bill aimed at regulating vivisection and a contrary bill allowing for a regulation-free environment. This resulted in the appointment of a first royal commission of inquiry to investigate laboratory procedures involving animals; it found no instances of animal abuse but recommended that animal experimentation be regulated. The Cruelty to Animals Act received royal assent in 1876. One outcome was that practitioners intending to perform vivisections had to be licensed to do so. By 1906, continuous lobbying by antivivisection societies resulted in the Second Royal Commission on Vivisection. However, due to scientific advances gained through vivisection and the distraction of World War I, which focused the attention of U.K. society in other directions, the public were less keen to condemn all experimentation.

This history is characterised by the way in which the members of scientific and medical institutions made varying responses to the practice of vivisection. Although these members were at the forefront of the objections to vivisection on the basis of their close proximity to the animals which suffered at their hands, they also made significant gains from vivisection; the concern with balancing animal welfare and scientific gain is at the heart of present ethical principles. It is equally characterised by the role that scientists themselves played in recognising cruelty.

In Australia, animal welfare legislation lies with the states and territories. In the lab I explored, the legislation fell under the 1992 ACT Animal Welfare Act. This code of practice has been gazetted into ACT legislation, and the laboratory in which I conducted my ethnographic investigation has a license with the ACT government to carry out research involving animal subjects. Experimentation that is intended to be conducted in the laboratory must proceed through the animal ethics committee, which was established at the university in 1978 (the human ethics committee was established much later, in 1996). The primary responsibility of the Animal Ethics Committee is to ensure that the care for and use of animals is conducted in compliance with the Code of Practice for the Care and Use of Animals for Scientific Purposes and to ensure that the use of animals is justified. The animal ethics committee applies a set of principles that govern the ethical conduct of people whose work involves the use of animals for scientific purposes. These principles begin with the assessment of whether projects intending to use animals are justified. Judgements about justification are made by weighing the predicted scientific or educational value of the project against its impacts on the welfare of research animals. As the head of the committee pointed out to those students who took my animals course in the School of Archaeology and Anthropology, the scientific merit of the planned experimentation sometimes overrules the welfare of the animals who will serve as its subjects. I recall to the reader his examples:

> Would you inject human semen into dogs? Would you allow viper toxin to be injected into cats? Would you allow the injection into rodents of mould originally found growing on unwashed lab glassware? If you said no, you would have aborted the discovery of prostaglandins, the discovery of safe effective antihypertensive acetylcholinesterase inhibitors, the antibacterial properties of penicillin. And you would have denied work that gained two Nobel prizes.

The decisions of the committee are made on the basis of consensus—all of the members must agree before the experimentation can go ahead. Where consensus cannot be reached on the first assessment of a planned project, the committee may explore ways of modifying the project with the project applicant so that it will lead to committee consensus. The membership of the committee is comprised of eight members drawn from four categories (A, B, C, and D), two animal technicians, and a chairperson. The two members from category A are persons holding qualifications in veterinary science. The two members from category B are suitably qualified people with substantial recent experience in the use of animals for scientific and teaching activities. The two members from category C are people with demonstrated commitments to and established experience in furthering the welfare of animals—these members cannot be employed by or otherwise associated with the institution, and they cannot be not involved in the care and use of animals for scientific purposes. Although members from category C cannot serve on the committee as representatives of animal welfare organisations, they are ideally selected on the basis of their active membership in and nomination by such an organisation. The two members from category D are people who are independent of the institution and who have never been involved in the use of animals in scientific or teaching activities, either in their employment or beyond their undergraduate education.

The committee also governs the use of animals in scientific research by the application of the 'three Rs': replacement, reduction, and refinement—the legacy of Marshall Hall's attempts to reduce animal suffering in the name of science. The Medical Advances Without Animals (MAWA) scholarships that are currently on offer at the institution that is under study here were designed to encourage innovative replacement strategies. One scholarship was awarded to a researcher who proposed to study the role of oxytocin in reproductive and social behaviour in humans and its consequent health effects. The usual approach to such a project would call for a population of genetically modified mouse models. Instead, the study proposed the use of DNA from volunteer human donors. A second MAWA scholarship was granted to a researcher who proposed an exploration of the basic mechanisms underlying acute and chronic arthritis triggered by viral infections. Instead of using the usual mouse model, the investigator used a novel human cell culture model to study viral-induced arthritis.

Reduction strategies include the exploration and adoption of methods, including better statistical design, for obtaining comparable levels of information from the use of fewer animals in scientific procedures or for obtaining more information from the same number of animals.[6] Refinement strategies include the development and application of improved anaesthetics and analgesics, better animal housing and species-appropriate environmental enrichment, and improved rodent euthanasia methods and agents. Together, the three Rs provide the ethical backdrop against which animal welfare is judged.

The 'refinement' R is particularly interesting, because it is the one that laboratory staff engage with on a daily basis as they deal in practical terms with laboratory mice and rats. As is evident in the case of refinement, speci-al needs are directly addressed in the provision of housing and enrichment; supplying each of these depends on a close examination of what will count as appropriate housing and environmental enrichment for a given species. Such an investigation and resultant provision is concerned with learning from animals about the daily minutiae and the mundane, repetitive elements of speci-al lives: What does a rat like? What would a mouse want to do? Such considerations mitigate against grand mammalian designs which place organs in the same locations in different animals and against the search for similarity—such as one might seek out in mammalian kin, in a pet dog's smile or its reciprocal sociality—and attends instead to speci-al difference, to mousy life richness, to ratty preference.

As is equally evident in the way in which animal welfare can be trumped by scientific merit—how much more meritorious could an experiment be if it were to deliver prostaglandins, antihypertensive acetylcholinesterase inhibitors, and penicillin?—the ethics environment undergirds the calculus of sacrifice as much as it supports the reduction of animal participants, the replacement of animals with substitutions of various kinds, and the provision of speci-al needs under the 'refinement' R. The 'replacement' R, for instance, may argue for the replacement of mammalian animals that are higher on the scale of human affection precisely with rats and mice. Christman (2008) argued that the 'replacement' R, in particular, reveals the extent to which the laboratory operates in the service of sacrifice, in the sense that nonlethal alternatives to animal experimentation, however efficacious they may be, do not come 'suffused with the ever-alluring elixir of immortality' (p. 308). Commenting on the relatively low rate of replacement compared with the traditional means of conducting research, and locating animal sacrifice firmly in the service of the extension of human control over death, Christman noted that

> the most analytical people ever to have walked the earth, modern scientists, have not lost the ancient conviction that nature is a zero-sum game in which humans are active players, that people can prompt the emergence of new life through the annulment of the old. If anything, researchers have raised the stakes of the game in the sheer magnitude of the scientific sacrifice of animals, erecting a veritable zoological necropolis in the pursuit of their craft. (p. 308)

Such a claim subscribes wholly to the world of warring gods—to that battle between the god who would smite humans and the science-god that humans have created to smite him in the skies above the freshly dug grave pit. For Christman (2008), ethics begins not with the three Rs but instead with the recognition that humans seek to alienate themselves from the frangible conditions of temporal existence: 'In the call to transcend atemporal modes of being by heeding the alterity of all forms of phenomenological discontinuity, the Levinasian copula of transcendence and alterity fosters an ethical outlook that is deconstructive by virtue of its reflexivity' (p. 298). On this basis, it is Christman's hope that there will be a movement of alterity toward alienation from thanatophobic zooicide.

Such gods and battles are readily summonsed in Baconian humanist imaginary, but they are somewhat deflated by ethnographic evidence that suggests that the pursuit of the scientific craft may not rest solely on bloody sacrificial pillars, but equally on caring—in the name of good science. Caring for animals does not seem to fit particularly well with Christman's characterisation of scientific practices involving animals, concerned as he insisted they are with the bloody quest for death transcendence, except in the sense that sacrificed animals are often considered to benefit from having been sacrificed. Brightman's (1993) ethnographic analysis of Rock Cree hunters, who understand animals to receive veneration after their deaths at human hands, is a case in point. But I am concerned here with a less transcendental caring and more with the ways in which caring might be practically embedded in the laboratory.

Caring does have a practical outcome for researchers. As I pointed out in chapter 4 in respect to emotional connections, the delivery of care is not in the least antithetical to scientific practice. I argued in that chapter, in reference to Brenda's emotional relationships with her rats, that the way a researcher interacts with animals can result in profound behavioural and physiological changes in the animal subject. These changes, which were explained by Brenda under the gloss of 'animal happiness', have to be taken into account in the results. As Haraway (2008) noted, practices of care are central to scientific labour; such practices undergird the getting of good data (p. 90). As Davis and Balfour suggested in 1992 in respect to what (unintentional) 'bonding' might positively accomplish for animal physiology and psychology, scientists might become aware of the physiological and psychological impacts that result for animals that have their particular speci-al needs met, who are cared for according to their speci-al requirements. As Heidi, an immunologist, suggested, she, the experimenter, routinely had equally (along with experimentation) in mind an animal's care. 'We're not monsters', she proclaimed, setting her coffee cup back into its saucer so she could emphasise her words with her hands. She said,

> You'll hear the 'greater good' argument a lot—that a lot of mice die so people can live. But the problem with that, for me, is that it isn't just that. It leaves you looking like you don't care for the animals. But suffering, unnecessary suffering, impacts the results, for a start. If mice are cared for properly, they perform properly. Suffering is not the primary or only thing that happens in the lab, but people outside of it usually think that it is.

For Heidi, images of animal suffering were readily available to those people outside the laboratory and could be used to locate her as some kind of monster. Monsters are also at the forefront of Spinelli's (1996) characterisation of the objectification of animals. Spinelli, a director of a large laboratory animal facility, compared animal objectification—for him, the worst outcome for animal subjects and the root of their suffering—with Nazi regimes of objectification:

> the Nazis elevated objectification of human beings to an art … there was a perpetual and deliberate degradation of the inmates at concentration camps … Sabini and Silver (1990) quote a commandant of a concentration camp responding to the question, 'If you were going to kill them anyway, what was the point of all the humiliation, why the cruelty?' The answer was, 'To condition those who actually had to carry out the policies. To make it possible for them to do what they did'. (p. 42)

Though suffering might not actually be the primary experience of rodent research animals, at least according to Heidi and other scientists

I spoke to, it was the primary experience of animals at the beginnings of the history of vivisection. Heidi's lament, that people outside the lab continue to think of animals as subject to research violence, persists in some measure because of the long and grisly history of experimentation on animal bodies and its continued application to contemporary scientists.

The idea that cared-for mice perform properly in their roles as equipment speaks to the ways in which caring and killing are reconciled in the laboratory: An animal that is living under the conditions of imminent death may well be a socially, emotionally, psychologically, and physiologically 'happy' mouse. This possibility calls into some question Reinert's notion that the lab mouse is the mouse living a bare life within the scientific coordinates of the laboratory—those laboratory conditions that are so frequently imagined by nonscientists, which feature the coldly detached scientist and the caged rats and mice living in wretched misery. Such conditions may well be wholly antithetical to good scientific practice—the practice that makes for the good, reliable results that are critical to the production of good science. Acampora (2006) argued that research animals are located in the laboratory purely as ready-to-hand objects or present-at-hand objects of scientific contemplation. Such a position indicates that caring is not present as a principle or a practice—or even as an idea—in the laboratory space. I have argued in the foregoing text that regarding animals as detached objects in the course of scientific enquiry is not necessary for the production of good science, but, as Johnson suggested, it is often assumed to be by people who are located outside of the scientific context.

According to Samantha, the resident veterinarian at one lab I studied, assumptions about how animals fare in a variety of contexts are 'often wrong, and based on misinformation and ideas about how things work, rather than on how things work for the people who work with animals'. Samantha felt that caring was deeply embedded in laboratory practice. She discussed caring at length—the kind of caring that is applied directly to animals and not to the human gains that animals bring. She explained that part of her job was to routinely survey the animals for signs of suffering against a comprehensive list of signs that would indicate its presence in both rats and mice. Occasionally, she was even called in at night to make a judgement about an animal's condition. Samantha had come from private veterinary practice—'you know, pet cats and dogs, mostly'. When I asked her why she had left it, Samantha told me she had become tired of watching animals suffer at the hands of their owners, who did not 'care' sufficiently for the animals but instead cared more for their own feelings. She told me that a vet clinic is a business, and that, for example,

> when someone brings in their dog, and the dog has, say, cancer, and you tell them that the treatment is pretty nasty, they still say, 'Save my dog!', even though there's no way that I can explain to the dog, 'Hey, look, I'm going to put you through some terrible short-term pain so that in the long term you might be able to live'. The dog doesn't understand long-term benefit; it only understands that I am causing it pain. People want their pets to live for their own benefit; they hardly ever stop to think about the animal. And I got tired of that. Here [in the lab], a lot more attention is paid to the animal's condition; it's much more stringent, and you don't have to provide a business service to a demanding customer, even if it means giving a treatment to their dog that won't benefit the dog and will cause it pain. You'd think the opposite would be true, but it isn't. I think we [here in the lab] care much, much more—not about people's feelings about animals, but about the animals themselves. If a mouse is suffering in the course of experimentation, I won't let it go—the mouse either has to be given relief, or be put down. It doesn't matter how much more gain the mouse might give to an experiment.[7]

Even though Samantha is a veterinarian and not a research scientist, she felt that the kind of care she described was delivered to the laboratory animals by everyone who worked in the laboratory, a point of view with which the scientists and animal technicians alike agreed.

The insights of insiders who provide toilet roll tunnels to mice and who feel that animals in the lab fare better than those that are brought into the veterinary practice are interesting to consider against the claims that are made about the kinds and qualities of lives that laboratory animals are permitted to live in the laboratory space. In chapter 4, I suggested that it might be relevant to argue that animals living under conditions of the certainty of death fit Agamben's definition of bare life. But what of the conditions of living in the laboratory, which precede the inevitability of death? These conditions matter; the fate of a battery chicken and that of a free-range bird are equivalent if it is considered only that each bird is destined for death. This much is sure, but the lot of the birds differs greatly in terms of the life each of them might be permitted to lead. Clearly, the life of the battery chicken is maintained in a bare state; it is fed, watered, and sustained to the point that the bird can continue to deliver eggs—the sole purpose for sustaining its life as far as the producers are concerned. These birds live in a zone of indistinction where life persists at the margins of death; calculations are made for sustaining life and eggs and no more. This, too, is the life of Singer's (1975) infamous example of the veal calf, which persists at the minimum of biological activity, kept alive only by and within human technology and only for human benefit:

> The short life of the veal calf is one which is determined strictly within the coordinates of domination. Calculations made around nutritional and fluid intake, lighting levels, stall size and flooring are directed towards the maximization of market profit from the production of the correctly coloured and textured flesh of the animal. But the priority of the life of the veal calf, no matter how short or painful, is apparent in this process. The life of the calf, maintained in a bare, weak state, is maintained scrupulously to prevent a premature death; a death that threatens the profitability of that life for the livestock complex. Thus a 'balance' is struck, where life is held at a point that borders upon death itself. (pp. 129–136; see also Wadiwel, 2002)

Just this sort of life is understood to refer to laboratory animals. Acampora, for instance, characterised the laboratory as the most evident site at which animals are pressed into the service of science and industry. The lives of these animals, he argued, are fundamentally bare.

Just as humans can, in Agamben's language, become animalised, animals can, as Noske (1997) argued, become deanimalised. As Reinert (2007) put it,

> It seems fair to add that the veal calf and other modern livestock animals whose entire lives are now contained within the industrial coordinates of economic profit and human domination—the narrow, scientifically optimized cycles of battery farming, industrial stock-rearing and slaughterhouse disassembly—have effectively been 'de-animalized' (Noske 1997) in ways that reflect and often pre-date the application of analogous techniques and principles to human beings. n.p; cf. Patterson, 2003

But, are the lives of laboratory rodents deanimalised? I am convinced that the conditions for battery chickens and veal calves result in their deanimalisation in the terms Noske (1997) described, and I am equally convinced that these conditions are increasingly recognised by the human consumers of their bodies. Indeed, if the changes in product stocking that have been undertaken by my local Woolworths store are any guide, consumers are now buying free-range pork and free-range eggs and chicken meat, not merely because Woolworths makes them available, but because there has been consumer-driven demand for these products. Can laboratory rodents be regarded as living the same kinds of lives as battery chickens? On the basis of the practices the researchers and animal technicians of lab animals described to me and that I witnessed during my time in the lab, laboratory rats and mice are likely significantly better off than are battery birds. According to Samantha, they might even be better off than some pet animals that are submitted to significant pain and suffering for what she saw as the sole benefit of their human owners.

I indicated in the introductory chapter that mice and rats, though they are indisputably living under the conditions of the certainty of death, are not made killable in the laboratory. I mean in this indication to mirror Haraway (2008) in her advisement of a rejigging of the commandment 'thou shalt not kill':

> The problem is not figuring out to whom such a command applies so that the 'other' killing can go on as usual and reach unprecedented historical proportions. The problem is to learn to live responsibly within the multiplicitous necessity and labour of killing, so as to be in the open, in quest of the capacity to respond in historical, non-teleological, multispecies contingency. Perhaps the commandment should read, 'Thou shalt not make killable'. (p. 80)

If the commandment were to be revised as Haraway suggested, there would not be an end of killing, but there may be an end to the bare lives of battery chickens and veal calves, which are made entirely killable within the industrial coordinates of death in which they barely persist.

The operations of caring, delivered to speci-al animals and mammalian biokin which share with humans an equal capacity for pain and suffering that responsible scientists deliver, contradicts general societal (and most philosophical) views about what happens in labs. Acampora (2006) argued that

> the laboratory is the site that most vividly converts most nonhuman organisms' being into instrumentality or reified objects (what Heidegger called readiness to hand and presence at hand, respectively) … the bioexperimental lab is a place wherein animals are pressed into science's or industry's service; but bluntly, they *become* tools or results/products of science or business (p. 97)

Where Acampora insisted that somaesthetic caring is absent in methodology, I learned from my discussion with researchers, in my observations of laboratory spaces, and in my analysis of the ethical principles and practices that govern the treatment of laboratory animals that shared suffering is at the basis of making judgements about rodent comfort, pain relief, and suffering. The scientists in the lab I examined assumed that rat pain was human pain, and making assumptions on this basis meant that the practitioners had a heightened rather than a lowered or absent sense of how an animal might be feeling, coping, or suffering. This is certainly based on the fact of shared mammalian being. But, more commonly, elements of caring for animals in the laboratory took a fundamentally speci-al form.

I saw many speci-al modifications—a deep consciousness of speci-al need being attended to. I listened to scientists talk about how providing lab mice with a toilet roll tunnel and some toys made the mice 'happy'. They had taken pains to find out about how rats and mice like to live, and they had replicated those conditions in painstaking detail in their provisions to those animals. Such an attendance speaks to those elements of the legislative and institutionally required ethical attendance scientists are required to make that call for a daily immersion in the minutiae of the lives of rats and mice; the ethical guidelines the scientists in this study adhered to required them to give the best reasons for subjecting animals to research practices and to death and to provide the best kind of life the laboratory space could offer. They noted that a mouse was happier with a toilet roll than without one, and they knew what kind of shale a rat preferred, what sort of light would make it most comfortable, and what sorts of toys were played with the most. This articulates directly with the 'refinement' R of the three Rs: to attend to animal happiness in the laboratory. These kinds of attendance, these pains taken over the details of comfort, and these attentions, I think, mitigate against the equipment status and killability of laboratory animals. This mitigation is activated through the idea that is generally accepted among the scientists I worked with: that animals should be made happy.

> Jennifer, a lab technician, talked with me about the rabbits. She said,
>
> We all know that the rabbits here are involved in a neuroscience study. One by one, they will be terminated, and the neuroscientists will look at the relevant elements of the rabbit remains on slides. That's definitely going to happen—it's why the rabbits are here. But the rabbits live a good life before that happens. For example, rabbits love fruit tingles, which are a large kind of fruit-flavoured treat on the market for pet rabbits. They also like toys, particularly those they can pick up, and that make a noise. We give them balls with bells that they can pick up with their teeth, and rings they can also pick up. We make it a rule that the rabbits never have the same toys for more than a week.

According to Mark, the same went for mice, but making mice happy meant providing different things than those rabbits might enjoy: 'Mice like to hide, and have a place to feel safe—that's the crucial thing, that and the company of other mice'.

Both Mark and Jennifer's descriptions of how laboratory animals might be made 'happy', 'safe', or 'comfortable' or how they might otherwise be cared for beyond the provision to them of the basics to sustain life are speci-al fulfilments, and they attend to the essence of the animal that is being cared for. In accordance with Weisberg's (2009) position that 'the genetic engineer may think that the essence of the mouse he is genetically manipulating is to-be-genetically-manipulated, but in truth, its essence is to-be-mouse' (p. 55), Jennifer's provision to rabbits of fruit tingles and Mark's provision to mice of toilet roll hidey-holes and companion mice attend to the essence of rabbit and the essence of mouse. These animals, which were developed and bred for the conditions of the lab, yet retained an essence-to-be-mouse or -rabbit that required expression in a need to have a world—and a particular world, a natural habitat—ready to hand (or paw or tooth). This world, in its naturally occurring manifestations of sunlight and darkness, shale, earthen tunnels, and grassy nests, had never been and would never be seen or touched or felt by them. The laboratory could not supply it; its environment had to be enriched and amended. The toilet roll tunnel was not a part of the evolutionary scene that called forth the laboratory mouse, and it had to be added to approximate the world that should have been—the natural habitat—for the mouse. The mouse, for all its suitability for the syringe, for all its size appropriateness for the hand of the researcher, for all its docility in that hand, and for all its integration with the material dimensions of the laboratory, required something more of the laboratory environs in order that it might attain, in Mark's words, 'a positive state'. As Heinricy (2009) put it, no matter how precisely engineered the laboratory mouse may be, the lived-ness of mouseness remains existentially larger than the analytic category 'mouse' (p. 288). Such a mouse is certainly recognised in the lab as needing a dark tunnel.

Caring and killing might appear at first to be regimes that are fundamentally at odds with one another, as Acampora's analysis readily indicates. In the sense that regimes of killing require the appearance of the mammalian unit of equipment (and at the moment of death, the appearance of mice which are 'only mice') and regimes of caring require the emergence of what is speci-ally specific about rodent research animals, caring and killing regimes allow different qualities of the animal to emerge. But, caring and killing can also be drawn together, either by threads of caring that stretch across both regimes or otherwise by threads of cruelty. As euthanasia proponents argue, giving a person a good death is an extension of a good life and can be constituted as a practice of deep caring. Equally, as Spinelli (1996) suggested, these regimes can be drawn together by a thread of cruelty that is enabled by extreme objectification in each regime, sufficient that the operator (a Nazi, a detached scientist) can do what needs to be done—those people who are in charge of delivering death can remove themselves from any appreciation of corporeal empathy, in life or death, in order to be able to effect death. One might assume that scientists in the laboratory may, as a result of their training and the frequency with which they cause death, practice this kind of extreme objectification. As immunologist Alan explained, a kind of indifference to rodent animals might also persist outside the lab; as he told me, 'They're only mice. People kill mice in their houses every single day'. Having been in the lab and having heard the ways in which the scientists discussed effecting death, it seems that extreme objectification may not be the most prominent way in which practitioners seek to do that which needs to be done. Rather, based on my own ethnographic observations, it seems that some comfort is to be drawn from submitting a rodent animal to death in the knowledge that it has been valued, in and on its own terms, during its life. What kind of value, then, beyond the ostensible value of 'valuing being' in all its forms, might 'killing well'—this being a combination of the happy mouse life with the painless mouse death—present to scientists?

In the laboratory context, 'value' takes many forms; I have already considered the ways in which valuing mouse or rat being as such contributes to the validity and reliability of data. As Brenda's remarks on this topic in chapter 4 readily illustrate, making an animal comfortable has high value for scientists and is not at all at odds with the practice of 'good science'. I have detailed those ways in which the value of recognising the rat life has certain kinds of consequences for science, in that it exacts a cost to science which must be paid: Here is a certain kind of value being recognised. And, of course, there is the value that mouse and rat lives present to human health and wellness. These are all values which pivot on certain kinds of calculation and conversion: How much will this mouse's happiness convert into a reliable model that will generate valid data? How much will it cost in this context? How can taking these lives translate into useful insights into human health? There are other kinds of value, too, including those that are based on affect, reciprocity, and relation, which led Brenda to value her rats as partners in communication, not only as subjects in her quest for knowledge and information. As Skeggs (2010) noted,

> The concept of value … is contingent and situational, circulating through fields (calculation and conversion), and mechanisms (labour, gift, affect) of exchange, carried, inscribed and recognised on [here, rodent and human] bodies. [Both kinds of] bodies move through and enter symbolic templates for exchange—value coding—which are dispersed systems of interlinking the different value chains […] and are not limited to the economic. Value coding now pervades so many areas of life that bodies and the relations they enter into offer ever more possibilities for inscription. (p. 32)

The 'ever more' interests me here, for there may be some other, additional value in treating animals well that scientists gain in terms of making killing easier. Lab killings, after all, are socially difficult to do, even when revolting mice and loathsome rats are the victims; it causes discomfort, as Deborah's barbeque mates suggested, and it causes unsettling images to come to mind. What if it were easier, more socially acceptable, to kill, based on the ways in which animals live and die, when they live and die well? If the consumers who demand that Woolworths stock more free-range chickens and eggs are anything to go by, one might suggest that it is easier to participate in 'good' relations of living and dying than to have a hand in the misery of bare life. It is perhaps the case that scientists reap these kinds of benefits. As I have suggested in the foregoing text, there now exist a range of writings which come from within the institute and which circulate in print and in conferences about the 'new' ways in which scientists can be said to care for research animals. One such text is *The Human/Research Animal Relationship: A Compilation of Presentations from Three Workshops Held on This Subject During 1992–1994*, published by the Scientists Centre for Animal Welfare (Krulisch, Mayer, & Simmons, 1996). Though the lab itself is a research site that is eminently unable to be photographed, carefully managed images do make it into the public domain. This 1996 volume contains images featuring scientists in a range of affectionate poses with typical research animals, including monkeys, dogs, and rabbits (although not rats or mice). It is possible that the entry into the public domain of such images produces a kind of symbolic capital that in its turn produces a sense of good moral relations and positions. The good, responsible, caring scientist, cradling a research animal, is difficult to reconcile with the monster who slaughters; this animal-hugger is, rather, in a research relationship with the animal that will end in the painless death, which will occur after the good life. Scientists are not the only people who are appealing to these kinds of moral relations; one of the largest producers of chicken meat in Australia, which supplies many chicken fast food outlets, recently released a television advertisement that features a worker petting chickens (which are most evidently older than the 6-week slaughter age) that are perched atop hay bales placed in dappled sunlight. No attendant claims are made in the advertisement about any conversion from the industrial coordinates in which these chickens are presently raised; that would require quite different images. The sun-dappled chickens look happy enough; they have had a good life, correct? Here are moral relations in action. Bourdieu (1987) warned his readers to look for misrecognised capital in the thick of what seem to be moral relations. He argued that courtship and marriage are ripe for such misrecognition: 'The conversion of economic capital into symbolic capital … produces relations of dependence that have an economic base but are disguised under a veil of moral relations' (p. 7). Other theoreticians, too, have more recently shown how capital might flow from the appropriation of affect and emotion; Skeggs (2010) did so in her work on reality television, and Bernstein (2007) laid bare the ways in which intimacy and emotion are given financial value in the sex trade.

What is to be made of this possibility? In the case of the laboratory that is under examination here, killing—itself practiced with care, in terms that it is immediate, painless, and generally carried out well prior to the point at which suffering is intolerable by human standards (by which the rodent tolerance for pain is also judged)—is prefaced by the relations of caring, by conditions of life in the laboratory that are attended by speci-al consideration. An attendance to speci-al specificity is, as Dillard-Wright (2009) argued, crucial to the ethical practice of both the philosophical anthropological variety and to any responsible ethical practice involving animals; indeed, to say that all animals are the same, to force them to live their lives in the laboratory as ready-to-hand units of mammalian equipment, would make it impossible for humans—scientists—to treat animals with any respect. Respect for speci-al difference is embedded in the ethical principle of refinement, which requires the provision of a speci-ally suitable habitat, including a place to hide—the enrichments that make it possible for a mouse, a rat, or a rabbit to be happy. In such provision is to be found the attendance to what Dillard-Wright (2009) called the 'immanent logic of other species' and the recognition of 'how other species interact with their environments in ways that have an inner integrity' (p. 67). Dillard-Wright called this attendance a kind of 'attentive wonder', without which

> humans will ride roughshod over the differences that characterise each species, blinding themselves to the depths of meaning inhabiting each vector of the human and extra-human world. Because they potentially ignore the particularities that make each species ... valuable in its own right, the animal rights activist who believes that all animals are equal and the human exceptionalist who believes that humans are inherently more valuable than other species are in the same position. (p. 67)

The kind of interspecies attendance that Dillard-Wright discussed is embedded in the attendance to what Haraway (2008) called 'the mundane and consequential in the little things that make lives' (p. 93), or mundane kinship—that recognition that different species have differently constituted fleshy worlds that make difference out of the relatedness of all species that Merleau-Ponty recognised in his 'strange kinship'. In this lab, attending to the mundane and the consequential means that ethical practice, ethical principle, is not finished, is never finished; the quest for refinement, for betterment, lies always in the provision of the best tunnel, the most effective analgesics, the best ways people have of killing, and the best justifications for it. In these provisions lie evidence of the calculus of care: These things are what must be given to rodent research animals in exchange—perhaps not equal exchange—for their sacrifice. It is not nearly a sufficient payment, but it is a recognition of worth, and one that is paid in meaningful terms to the animal—in the tunnel, the shale, and the provision of speci-al comforts. It is also paid to humans' closely related kin in the provision of those analgesics and anaesthetics that humans would use to diminish their own equivalent pain. This is where I think that the idea that scientists might make some gain, might draw some capital, from making killings easier is, or could be, really consequential. There is no problem with their accrual of such capital on the face of it, but there would be if this capital were to become sufficient, if drawing it became so comfortable that no continuation of the quest for the betterment of animal laboratory lives felt necessary or important anymore.

The kinds of recognitions of speci-al need and the requirement for life-fulfilment that Mark and Jennifer each described are similar in many ways to Brenda's fleshy kinship with rats as well as with mammalian biokinship. They are so because each kinship—mundane, fleshy, and biological—issues from a lived participation in the worlds of rats and mice. The last of these kinships issues from the fact that we inhabit such similar bodies, which each experience pain similarly. Such participation in bodily likeness and such interest in and attendance to rodent lives, as Levinas (1990) noted, are irreducible to (scientific) knowledge or truth, and they occur before any disciplinary worked out ethics are applied:

'Living with' is prior to ethics and involves a 'suspension of rationality' (p. 26). Rationality, in the form of the calculus of sacrifice, though, reasserts itself in the laboratory, in the considerations of the calculations that make rodent animals good to kill and make them subject to suffering in humans' stead.

And here I arrive again at ambiguity: Humans will continue to submit animals into the sacrificial economy and they will continue to submit them to pain. But these scientists will do so with reluctance, with sadness, as Brenda did. They will have an eye to rodent pain as if it were their own, human, pain, in the provision of analgesics that would alleviate pain for a person. And, they will work with caring, with a deep and careful attendance to what makes a rat happy, as Jennifer, Mark, and Olivia did. Nothing could be less straightforward; nothing could be more ambiguous—and not least because Derrida's words pop back up to haunt me here, as do the questions of value I posed earlier. In his invocation of the Holocaust, Derrida (2002) summonsed conditions 'that previous generations would have judged monstrous, outside of every supposed norm of life proper to animals' (p. 395), confronting his readers with the monstrous notion of purposefully creating and keeping in good condition beings that would be submitted to the gas chamber. Does giving a mouse a tunnel or giving a rabbit a fruit tingle make it all acceptable? It does not; humans will still submit rats and mice to the gas chamber, for which they were destined at birth. It is a creepy, grisly notion, but in the same way that I am more comfortable with the thought of buying free-range pork or chicken, I am more comfortable with laboratory rats and mice who get tunnels, and I am hopeful that more and better improvements will be made.

Whether or not doing this makes it all acceptable is not the question I posed in this book; I have been interested in looking at the ways in which rodent research animals and people cross the Great Divide through the operation of kinships that are born of ambiguity. In a way, as much as one has to ask, as Birke (2003) has, 'What are mice and rats in the laboratory?' one also has to ask, 'What are scientists?' If one takes pain, suffering, and death as the only significant moments in the laboratory, one might well conclude that rats and mice and scientists stand on either side of the thick Cartesian divide between humans and animals. But, even in the shadow of death and with the location of mice and rats as mammalian equipment, animals yet stand as kin—and not only as biokin and genekin, but as strangely related kin and as speci-al animals that are attended to in the laboratory space in the relations of mundane kinship. In the thick of different registers of kinship, the recognition of animals as anything but generic mammalian equipment is difficult. In the thick of speci-al indistinction, one finds the operation of fleshy kinship that does not flatten speci-al difference but recognises its intercommunicative possibilities, and in the practicing of mundane kinship, one finds speci-al difference elevated. If one takes the fleshy and mundane operation of kinship as another basis upon which to make an answer, one might say that human gestures, human consciousness even, arise from the broader context of animal communication—a basic connection that places humanity back among the animals. This connection, this 'always-already' thread of continuity, is acknowledged in the laboratory, in things such as the practice of the 'refinement' R, in strange kinship with ratty kind, and in the denial of a self-sustaining, wholly enclosed human world of meaning and being. If these scientists are God-scientists, operating on devalued animals as human exceptionalists, then they do not wholly submit to the principles of their religion—or at least, with Bourdieu's words about misrecognition clamouring in my mind in concert with the sadness that comes from effecting death that I believe the scientists in this study to have felt, at least they do not *seem* to wholly submit to the principles of their religion.

Endnotes

1. The appreciation that a mouse has a requirement of a tunnel goes beyond fulfilling the immediate biological needs of the animal—as Penny said, this is the stuff of enrichment—above and beyond the needs of sustaining the organism; tunnels are for good psychiatric health, for life satisfaction.
2. As Latour argued in his 1987 *Science in Action*, science represents nature.
3. Mark's view—that laboratory rodents were purpose-built for, specialised to, and even in fatal danger outside of the laboratory confines—was a common one in the laboratory I studied. Richard agreed with Mark, saying that 'they [laboratory mice] would not be at all, had we not had requirement for them'. Clearly, Mark considered lab mice to be properly integrated with the laboratory environment and potentially fatally mismatched to the 'natural' environment outside of it.
4. Being naturally derived, pinkie pups, for instance, do not fit the cultural conditions of worth in operation in the laboratory, and they are unproblematically terminated because they cannot conform to the cultural conditions that invest worth in the bodies of research animals.
5. Biochemists are working with what is called 'cell cultures', which actually are cultivated, transformed, nurtured living materials. They are essentially objects as well as tools for biological research and inhabit the refrigerators of biological laboratories. Because they are living materials (cells, antibodies, antigens, enzymes, and so on), they are a part of nature. Because they are kept in cultivation, they are cultural products. The situation works similarly with laboratory animals. The immunologists who were observed in this case study, for instance, use mice models. Mice are bred and transformed into the bearers of immune responses. Thereby, the mouse as a scientific model itself serves as a kind of representation: It represents the natural processes of immune response. The construction of the model allows the scientist to study certain natural phenomena under the more or less controllable conditions of the specific cultural setting of the laboratory.
6. Of course, this may not bode well for rodents—in some cases, they may in fact be the reductions which stand in for dogs, cats, or other animals that are located higher on the ladder of human affection.
7. This is not to suggest that all veterinarians hold such a view or practice in ways they feel to be detrimental to animals; this is Samantha's personal view.

Chapter 6

Ambiguity

Indistinctive Kinship in the Shadow of the Sacrificial Economy

It has not been my intention in this book to push science's barrow when it comes to researching on animals. It is very clear to me, even after all that I have said about making mice happy and even after describing the ways in which scientists know that rats are asking to be petted about the shoulders, that animals located within the confines of the modern research laboratory are animals that will in many cases suffer and will in all cases die. They will suffer and die for the benefit of humans and for the purposes of allaying humans' thanatophobia, and in their deaths, they will articulate the hierarchy of mammals and the differences between a mouse and a person, even as their kinship with humans on biological and genetic levels bridges the human-animal division. There is no getting away from this sacrificial calculus to which humans submit their closely related genekin and biokin. Throughout this book, I have traced several kinds of kinships—kinships made on the basis of biological and genetic relatedness, kinships that are indistinct and de-privilege the positions of 'human' and 'animal', and mundane kinships that are forged through the relations of caring and responsible killing. These kinships always articulate human-animal relatedness, but their conduct does not always bode well in terms of animal treatment in the laboratory—after all, it is because mice are humans' kin that they die in their stead.

I have not intended this book as one that apologises for animal suffering, but I am asking a question in writing it: Is the laboratory treatment of experimental animals as cruel and as welfare-deficient as other contexts in which animals are raised for the benefit of humans? I have suggested in this book that it is not. I do not think that the lives of battery chickens or veal calves are attended by a calculus of care while they are situated within the industrial coordinates that are in the service of the calculus of killing. In contrast, I do think that mice, rats, and other experimental animals are, at least in the laboratories I have focused on here, offered opportunities to live up to their speci-al identities. I believe that human scientists attend to their pain (even as they inflict it) with an eye to how similarly their kinned bodies might suffer, and I believe that efforts are routinely made to make animals happy—efforts that are institutionally endorsed. Although I am not an apologist for animal suffering, I am also unprepared to relegate scientists to the category of unfeeling, uncaring, detached practitioners who cannot forge relationships and participate in kinships with the animals with whom they share laboratory space. There is no practical prohibition on caring or on kinship in the laboratory—as I have pointed out in each of the chapters, none of the kinships, biological and genetic, indistinctive, and mundane—is antithetical to scientific inquiry or to its aims, its outcomes, and certainly not to its conduct. As I demonstrated in chapter 3, biological and genetic kinship with rats and mice is utterly critical to the practice of science that seeks to apply the results from experimentation on nonhuman animal bodies to human mammals. As I argued in chapter 4, emotional kinships that are forged in the zone of indistinction are far from antithetical to scientific orientation, inquiry, or outcome; often, emotional relationships with animals resulted in what the scientists themselves regarded as the more reliable outcomes of their enquiry. Milton (2002) submitted that emotion is a driving motivation for scientific inquiry and cannot be validly regarded as antithetical to it; I add to this insight that emotional relationships with animals are equally embedded in and incorporated into the conduct of good science and into the interacting bodies of rats and people. Mundane kinships between scientists and animals, forged in the ambiguous terrain of caring for and killing animals and undergirded by ethical rules and practices that speak to ambiguity, also resulted in the upgrading of animal conditions. This was a result of the concern that was taken over the minutiae of rat and mouse lives and how they might be best lived in the laboratory space—itself an ambiguous zone where the cultural conditions of laboratory life met the speci-al needs of the animals dwelling in it in the provision of tunnel, shale, and block. The high regard for the welfare of the animal subjects also resulted in better outcomes for laboratory animals. Kinships of various kinds are eminently possible in the laboratory, and they are to be found in the presence of good science.

As I have argued throughout this book, each of these relationships of kinship proceeds upon the ambiguous location of the laboratory rat and the laboratory mouse. It is the ambiguous location of the rodent animal model that makes it such a suitable animal for scientific explorations of the human body in the laboratory in the first place. Its biological and genetic homology with humans brings it into the realm of kinship with humans. A mammalian bridge, constructed out of our gene and biological sameness, is built across the human-animal divide in the subsumption of rodent speci-ality. In this sense, mice and rats appear as humans' close kin in the laboratory.

As I pointed out in chapter 3, this mammalian bridge is a sloping one—it is unevenly built and is perched upon pylons that are much, much higher at the human end of the bridge. Across the divide, at the animal terminus of the bridge, the pylons are significantly shorter. Rats and mice are revealed to be 'lesser' mammals, even as their speci-al characteristics are subsumed to yield a biological and genetic collinearity with human mammals. The primary consequence of the subsumption of speci-ality to pan-mammalian membership is the relegation of the speci-ally reduced mouse or rat to the position of a mammalian unit of equipment. After all, the rodent mammal is in the laboratory only because it can yield data will be directly applicable to the human mammal. Out of the very terms of biological and genetic kinship is yielded a hierarchy of bodies, wherein one mammalian embodiment is in the service of another, considerably more valued, embodiment. As Lynch (1988) argued, the animal is effectively deanimalised to yield the mammalian equipment that will bear fruit for the human mammals at the far end of the tilted bridge of mammalian kinship. The death of the mammalian other, made other to the human 'us' even as it is recognised in the laboratory as humans' close kin, is balanced against humans' lives, thanatophobia, and quest to vanquish the spectre of death. Just as the mammalian bridge is unbalanced, so too is the calculus of the scientific war on death, which ironically consumes lesser mammalian lives in order to save greater human ones. One defiance of death comes precisely through the death of the other, as, in Christman's (2008) terms, one animal vitality is transferred into the sanctified flesh of the human mammal. But is this a 'primal', sacrificial economy, based firmly in the bloody quest for death transcendence, based in a fascination for the properties of animal lifeblood? Do Christman's white-coated priests oversee bloody rituals as they transfer sanguinary vitality from a lesser to a higher body?

In chapter 3, I began to draw out the ways in which scientists attended to the speci-al qualities of rats and mice and the ways in which this attendance simultaneously articulated the limits of biological and genetic kinship and served to reanimalise mammalian units of equipment as the needs that are peculiar to rats and mice were attended to in the laboratory. At the point of entry into the sacrificial economy, the speci-al characteristics of rats and mice emerge; they are, at this point, as Alan said, 'only mice'. But the speci-al characteristics of mice and rats emerge with greater frequency in the course of laboratory attendances to the speci-al needs of rats and mice; the provision of a toilet roll tunnel or a chew block speaks directly to those 'natural' needs that dwell in the animal that is produced for the cultural space of the laboratory, that fully artifactual space that is, in Haraway's terms, the natural niche of the laboratory animal.

The emergence of speci-al animals out of mammalian equipment boded both well and ill for laboratory animals; their mouseness articulated the point at which their mammalian kinship with humans ended, and it articulated the point at which they were supplied with those tunnels and blocks that would make a natural, speci-al mouse happy.

Speci-ality was again diminished in the fleshy kinships of indistinction I described in chapter 4. In the zone of indistinction, ratness, mouseness, and the scientist disappear in fleshy interaction, in communications that are based on mutual understanding and on repetitive, unstated, corporeally enacted proclamations of kinship through actions, gestures, and mutually understood responses. One need not be a rat or a person to understand this gestural interplay between the species. Here persists a 'bare life' of sorts—not Agamben's formulation, in which *zoe* is separated from *bios* and animal from human, but an ambiguous life that persists prior to the naming of each position. This exists before the political, hierarchical relations of scientists and animals are arrayed, which will see mouse and rat kin entered into the sacrificial economy, where they are all, after all, destined to go.

Speci-ality also emerged in the ambiguous ethical terrain that oversees caring and killing in the laboratory space. I have argued that a mammalian membership that encompasses rat, mouse, and humankind is at the basis of the sacrificial economy and that speci-ality equally emerges at the bounds of this kinship to articulate its limits. Speci-ality also emerges to articulate the differences from human mammals in the regimes of caring for laboratory animals—indeed, caring for laboratory animals is based largely in the recognition of speci-al difference. The recognition of peculiar, speci-al needs forms the basis, for example, of the third of the three Rs that guide ethical practice in the lab: the 'refinement' R. This R guides laboratory staff, including research scientists, to attend to animal happiness in the laboratory. These are the attendances to speci-al concerns and the pains that are taken over the details of comfort and happiness—the most mundane of the kinships I have described herein.

Taken together, these speci-al and mammalian forged kinships yield a pattern of ambiguity. This ambiguity is sufficiently elastic to allow for caring and killing, for rats to be regarded as equipment and for rats to be regarded as kin. It is also sufficient for scientists to be located at once as white-coated priests who preside over the sacrificial economy and as the companions of rats and mice, as those who might grieve the deaths of their kin. Such are the ambiguous coordinates of the scientific research laboratory, in which scientists and laboratory rodents dwell in fleshy, indistinctive kinship and in the shadow of the sacrificial economy. And so, I close this book as I began it—with ambiguity.

References

Acampora, R. (2006). *Corporal compassion: Animal ethics and philosophy of the body*. Pittsburgh, PA: University of Pittsburgh Press.

Adorno, T. (2003). *Negative dialectics* (E. B. Ashton, Trans.). New York: Continuum.

Adorno, T., & Horkheimer, M. (2002). *Dialectic of enlightenment: Philosophical fragments* (Edmund Jephcott, Trans.; Gunzelin Schmid Norr, Ed.). Stanford, CA: Stanford University Press.

Agamben, G. (1998). *Homo sacer: Sovereign power and bare life* (Danile Heller-Roazen, Trans.). Stanford, CA: Stanford University Press.

Agamben, G. (2002). *The open: Man and animal* (Kevin Attell, Trans.). Stanford, CA: Stanford University Press.

Amann, K. (1994). Men, mice and flies. *Journal for Sociology*, *23*, 22–40.

Arluke, A. (1988). Sacrificial symbolism in animal experimentation: Object or pet? *Anthrozoos*, *2*, 97–116.

Arluke, A. (1994). We build a better beagle: Fantastic creatures in lab animal ads. *Qualitative Sociology*, *17*, 143–158.

Arluke, A., & Sanders, C. (1996). *Regarding animals*. Philadelphia: Temple University Press.

Bacon, F. (1999). *Francis Bacon: Selected philosophical works* (Rose-Mary Sargent, Ed.). Cambridge: Indianapolis. (Original work published 1620).

Barnett, S. (2002). *The story of rats: Their impact on us, and our impact on them*. Crows Nest, New South Wales: Allen & Unwin.

Becker, E. (1973). *The denial of death*. New York: Free Press.

Berdoy. M. (2001). *The laboratory rat—A natural history*. Oxford University. Retrieved June 26, 2010, from http://video.google.com/videoplay?docid=-7746085357822333003#

Bernstein, E. (2007). *Temporarily yours: Intimacy, authenticity and the commerce of sex*. Chicago: University of Chicago Press.

Bhan, A., Singer, P., & Daar, A. (2010). Human-animal chimeras for vaccine development: An endangered species or opportunity for the developing world? *BioMed Central International Health and Human Rights*, *10*(8). Retrieved May 20, 2010, from http://www.ncbi.nlm.nih.gov/pmc/articles/PMC2890684/

Birke, L. (2003). Who—or what—are the rats (and mice) in the laboratory? *Society and Animals*, *11*(3), 207–224.

Bischur, D. (2008). Working with mice in immunological research: Attachment, emotion and care. *Electronic Journal of Communication, information and Innovation in Health*, *2*(1), 29–37.

Bourdieu, P. (1987). What makes a social class? On the theoretical and practical existence of groups. *Berkeley Journal of Sociology*, *32*, 1–17.

Bowd, A. (1980). Ethics and animal experimentation. *American Psychologist*, *35*, 224–225.

Brightman, R. (1993). *Grateful prey: Rock Cree human-animal relationships*. Berkeley: University of California Press.

Burke, K. (2009, September 6). Free range egg claims don't add up. *The Sydney Morning Herald*. Retrieved 18 July 2010 from http://www.smh.com.au/national/freerange-egg-claims-dont-add-up-20090905-fc4b.html

Butler, J. (2000). *Antigone's claim: Kinship between life and death*. New York: Columbia University Press.

Buytendijk, F. (1974). *Prolegomena to an anthropological physiology* (A. Giorgi et al., Trans.). Pittsburgh, PA: Duquesne University Press.

Calarco, M. (2008). *Zoographies: The question of the animal from Heidegger to Derrida*. New York: Columbia University Press.

Carsten, J. (2000). Introduction. In J. Carsten (Ed.), *Cultures of relatedness: New approaches to the study of kinship* (pp. 1–36). Cambridge: Cambridge University Press.

Castree, N. (2003). Environmental issues: Relational ontologies and hybrid politics. *Progress in Human Geography*, *27*, 203–211.

Centlivre, S. (1968). *The dramatic works of the celebrated Mrs. Centlivre*. New York: AMS Press. (Original work published 1872)

Christman, J. (2008). The Gilgamesh complex: The quest for death transcendence and the killing of animals. *Society and Animals*, *16*, 297–315.

Crist, E. (2004). Against the social construction of nature and wilderness. *Environmental Ethics*, *26*, 5–24.

Darwin, C. (1871). *The descent of man and selection in relation to sex*. London: Murray.

Davis, H. (1988). Human based social interaction can reward a rat's behaviour. *Animal Learning Behaviour*, *16*, 89–92.

Davis, H. (1996). How human/animal bonding affects the animal. In L. Krulisch, S. Mayer, & R. Simmons (Eds.), *The human/research animal relationship* (pp. 67–76). Greenbelt, MD: Scientists Centre for Animal Welfare.

Davis, H., & Balfour, D. (1992). *The inevitable bond: Examining scientist-animal interactions*. Cambridge: Cambridge University Press.

de Beer, E. S. (Ed.). (1955). *The diary of John Evelyn*. Oxford: Clarendon Press.

Deleuze, G., & Guattari, F. (1987). *A thousand plateaus: Capitalism and schizophrenia* (Brian Massumi, Trans.). Minneapolis: University of Minnesota Press.

Deranty, J. (2008). Witnessing the inhuman: Agamben or Merleau-Ponty. *South Atlantic Quarterly, 107*(1), 165–186.

Der Ewige Jude. (1940). Program notes. [Motion picture]. Retrieved June 10, 2010, from www.holocaust-history.org/der-ewige-jude

Derrida, J. (2002). The animal that therefore I am (more to follow). *Critical Inquiry, 28*, 369–418.

Derrida, J. (2004). Violence against animals. In J. Derrida & E. Roudinesco (Eds), *For what tomorrow?* (Jeff Fort, Trans.), (pp. 62–67). Stanford, CA: Stanford University Press.

Descola, P. (2005). *Pare delà nature et culture*. Paris: Editions Gallimard.

Despret, V. (2008). The becomings of subjectivity in animal worlds. *Subjectivity, 23*, 123–139.

Dickens, C. (1860). *The uncommercial traveller*. London: Chapman and Hall.

Dillard-Wright, D. (2009). Thinking across species boundaries: General sociality and embodied meaning. *Society and Animals, 17*, 53–71.

Douglas, M. (1957). Animals in Lele religious symbolism. *Africa, 27*(1), 46–58.

Douglas, M. (1966). *Purity and danger: An analysis of concepts of pollution and taboo*. London: Routledge and Kegan Paul.

Douglas, M. (1990). The pangolin revisited: A new approach to animal symbolism. In R. Willis (Ed.), *Signifying animals: Human meaning in the natural world* (pp. 25–36). London: Routledge.

Edelman, B. (2002). 'Rats are people, too!': Rat-human relations rerated. *Anthropology Today, 18*(3), 3–8.

Egerton, F. (2005). Robert Hooke and the Royal Society of London. *Bulletin of the Ecological Society of America, 86*(2), 93–101.

Ellmann, M. (2004). Writing like a rat. *Critical Quarterly, 46*(4), 59–76.

European Economic Community. (1986). Council Directive 86/609 on the approximation of laws, regulations, and administrative provisions regarding the protection of animals used for experimental purpose: Annex II guidelines for accommodation and care of animals. *Official Journal of the European Communities*, *L358*, 7–28.

Feeley-Harnik, G. (2001). The ethnography of creation: Lewis Henry Morgan and the American beaver. In S. Franklin & S. McKinnon (Eds.), *Relative values: Reconfiguring kinship studies* (pp. 54–84). Durham, NC: Duke University Press.

Ferry, L. (1995). *The new ecological order* (Carol Volk, Trans.). Chicago: University of Chicago Press.

Finkler, K. (2000). The kin in the gene: The medicalization of family and kinship in American society. *Current Anthropology*, *42*(2), 235–263.

Fissell, M. (1999). Imagining vermin in early modern England. *History Workshop Journal*, *47*, 1–29.

Foote, A., & Crystal, J. (2007). Metacognition in the rat. *Current Biology*, *17*(6), 551–555.

Foucault, M. (2004). *Society must be defended.* London: Penguin Books.

Fox, R. (2006). Animal behaviours, post-human lives: Everyday negotiations of the animal-human divide in pet-keeping. *Social and Cultural Geography*, *7*(4), 525–537.

Franklin, J. (2007). Killing and replacing animals. *Journal of Animal Law and Ethics*, *77*, 77–89.

Franklin, S. (2001). Biologization revisited: Kinship theory in the context of the new biologies. In Sarah Franklin & Susan McKinnon (Eds.), *Relative values* (pp. 302–325). Durham, NC: Duke University Press.

Franklin, S., & McKinnon, S. (2001). Introduction. In S. Franklin & S. McKinnon (Eds.), *Relative values: Reconfiguring kinship studies* (pp. 1–25). Durham, NC: Duke University Press.

Frazer, J. (1951). *The golden bough: A study in magic and religion: Vol. 3. Taboo and the perils of the soul.* New York: Macmillan Company. (Original work published 1919)

Freud, S. (2003). *The uncanny*. London: Penguin. (Original work published 1919)

GenOway.Retrieved June 10, 2010, from http: //www.genoway.com

Golding, C. (1990). *Rats: The new plague*. London: Weidenfeld & Nicholson.

Guerrini, A. (1989). The ethics of animal experimentation in seventeenth century England. *Journal of the History of Ideas*, *50*(3), 187–223.

Guthrie, R. (1976). *Even the rat was white: A historical view of psychology*. New York: Harper & Row.

Haraway, D. (1991). *Simians, cyborgs and women: The reinvention of nature*. New York: Routledge.

Haraway, D. (1997). *Modest_witness@Second_millenuium. FemaleMan©_Meets OncoMouuse™*. New York: Routledge.

Haraway, D. (2003). *The companion species manifesto—Dogs, people and significant otherness*. Chicago: Prickly Paradigm Press.

Haraway, D. (2004). Race: Universal donors in a vampire culture. It's all in the family: Biological kinship categories in the twentieth century United States. In *The Haraway Reader* (pp. 251–294). New York: Routledge.

Haraway, D. (2008). *When species meet*. Minneapolis: University of Minnesota Press.

Harris, M. (1974). *Cows, pigs, wars and witches*. New York: Vintage.

Heidegger, M. (1962). *Being and time* (John Macquarie & Edward Robinson, Trans.). New York: Harper and Row.

Heidegger, M. (1998). Letter on Humanism (Frank A. Capuzzi, Trans.). In W. McNeill (Ed.), *Pathmarks* (pp. 239–276). Chicago: Chicago University Press.

Heinricy, S. (2009). [Review of the book *When species meet*]. *Journal of Communication Inquiry, 33*, 287–289.

Hendrickson, R. (1983). *More cunning than man: A complete history of the rat and its role in civilization*. London: Kensington Books.

Herbert, C. (1988). Rat worship and taboo in Mayhew's London. *Representations, 23*, 1–24.

Herzog, H. (2002). Ethical aspects of relationships between humans and research animals. *Institute for Laboratory Animal Research Journal, 43*(1), 27–32.

Hudson, L. (2008). The political animal: Species-being and bare life. *Mediations, 23*(2), 88–117.

Ingold, T. (1988). *What is an animal?* New York: Routledge.

Ingold, T. (1994). *Companion encyclopaedia of anthropology*. London: Routledge.

Instone, L. (1998). The coyote's at the door: Revisioning human-environment relations in the Australian context. *Ecumene, 5*, 452–467.

Johnson, D. (1996). Human/research animal relationships: Research staff perspectives. In L. Krulisch, S. Mayer, & R. Simmons (Eds.), *The human/research animal relationship* (pp. 57–60). Greenbelt, MD: Scientists Centre for Animal Welfare.

Joyce, J. (1922). *Ulysses* (Hans Walter Gabler, Ed.). London: Bodley Head.

Knutson, B., Burgdorf, J., & Panksepp, J. (1998). The prospect of play elicits high-frequency ultrasonic vocalizations in young rats. *Journal of Comparative Psychology, 112*, 65–83.

Kohak, E. (1984). *The embers and the stars: A philosophical inquiry into the moral sense of nature*. Chicago: Chicago University Press.

Kristeva, J. (1982). *Powers of horror: An essay on abjection* (L. S. Roudiez, Trans.). New York: Columbia University Press.

Krulisch, L., Mayer, S.; & Simmons, R. (Eds.). (1996). *The Human/Research Animal Relationship: A Compilation of Presentations from Three Workshops Held on This Subject During 1992–1994*. Greenbelt, MD: Scientists Centre for Animal Welfare.

Lasseter, J. & Stanton, A. (Producers). (2007). *Ratatouille* [Motion Picture]. United States: Walt Disney Company.

Latham, C. (1878). Some West Sussex superstitions lingering in 1868. *Folk-Lore Record*, 1, 1–67.

Latour, B. (1987). *Science in action—How to follow scientists and engineers through society*. Cambridge, MA: Harvard University Press.

Latour, B. (2004). *The politics of nature: How to bring the sciences into democracy*. Cambridge, MA: Harvard University Press.

Latour, B., & Weibel, P. (2005). *Making things public: Atmospheres of democracy*. Cambridge, MA: MIT Press.

Leach, E. (1964). Anthropological aspects of language: Animal categories and verbal abuse. In E. Lennenberg (Ed.), *New directions in the study of language* (pp. 23–63). Cambridge: Cambridge University Press.

Levinas, E. (1969). *Totality and infinity: An essay on exteriority* (Alphonso Lingis, Trans.). Pittsburgh, PA: Duquesne University Press.

Levinas, E. (1990). The name of a dog, or natural rights. In *Difficult freedom: Essays on Judaism* (Sean Hand, Trans.), (pp. 151–153). Baltimore: John Hopkins University Press.

Levinas, E. (2004). Ethics as first philosophy. In Sean Hand (Ed.), *The Levinas reader* (pp. 75–87). Oxford: Blackwell Publishing.

Lloyd, N., & Mulcock, J. (2007). Guest editors' introduction: Human-animal studies in Australia: current directions. *Society and Animals*, *15*, 1–5.

Lonergan, B. (1978). *Insight: A study of human understanding*. San Francisco: Harper and Row.

Lovecraft, H. P. (1924). The rats in the walls. *Weird Tales*, *3*(3), 25–31.

Lynch, M. (1988). Sacrifice and the transformation of the animal body into a scientific object: Laboratory culture and ritual practice in the neurosciences. *Social Studies of Science*, *18*(2), 265–289.

Maehle, A. (1990). Literary responses to animal experimentation in seventeenth and eighteenth century Britain. *Medical History*, *34*, 27–51.

Marcuse, H. (1964). *One dimensional man: Studies in the ideology of advanced industrial society*. Boston: Beacon Press.

Martin, E. (1994). *Flexible bodies: Tracking immunity in American culture*. Boston: Beacon Press.

Masefield, J. (1927). *The midnight folk*. London: Heinemann.

Matthews, I. (1898). *Full revelations of a professional rat-catcher, after 25 years' experience*. Manchester: Friendly Societies Printing Co.

Mayhew, H. (1851). *London labour and the London poor: Volume 3*. London: Griffen, Bohn and Company, Stationer's Hall Court.

Merleau-Ponty, M. (1963). *The structure of behavior* (Alden L. Fisher, Trans.). Boston: Beacon Press.

Merleau-Ponty, M. (1964). *Sens and non-sens*. Evanston, IL: Northwestern University Press.

Merleau-Ponty, M. (1968). *The visible and the invisible*. Evanston, IL: Northwestern University Press.

Merleau-Ponty, M. (1988). Husserl at the limits of phenomenology. In *In praise of philosophy and other essays* (J. O'Neill, Trans.). Evanston, IL: Northwestern University Press.

Merleau-Ponty, M. (1994). *La nature: Notes, cours du College de France* (Dominique Seglard, Ed.). Paris: Seuil.

Michael, M., & Birke, L. (1994). Science and morality in animal experiments: Demarcating the core set. *Social Studies of Science*, *24*, 81–95.

Milmo, C. (2007, February 19). Organic farming no better for the environment. *The Independent Sunday*. Retrieved 20 February 2010 from http://www.independent.co.uk/environment/green-living/organic-farming-no-better-for-the-environment-436949.html

Milton, K. (2002). *Loving nature: Towards an ecology of emotion*. New York: Routledge.

Moore, C. (1916). *Shaftesbury and the ethical poets in England, 1700–1760*. Modern Language Association, *24*, 264–325.

Morris, B. (2000). *The power of animals*. New York: Berg.

Mullin, M. (1999). Mirrors and windows: Sociocultural studies of human-animal relationships. *Annual Review of Anthropology*, *28*, 201–224.

Mullin, M. (2002). Animals and anthropology. *Society and Animals*, *10*(4), 387–393.

National Human Genome Research Institute. Retrieved August 2010 from http://www.genome.gov/10005834

Noske, B. (1997). *Beyond borders*. London: Black Rose Books.

Oliver, K. (2007). Stopping the anthropological machine: Agamben with Heidegger and Merleau-Ponty. *PhaenEx*, *2*(2), 1–23.

Oster, M. (1989). The 'Beame of Diuinity': Animal suffering in the early thought of Robert Boyle. *British Journal for the History of Science*, *22*, 151–180.

Paigen, K. (1995). A miracle enough: The power of mice. *Nature Medicine*, *1*, 215–217.

Painter, C., & Lotz, C. (Eds.). (2007). Introduction: Phenomenology and the question of the non-human animal. In *Phenomenology and the non-human animal: At the limits of experience* (1–13). Dordrecht: Springer.

Paton, W. (1993). *Man and mouse: Animals in medical research*. Oxford: Oxford University Press.

Patterson, C. (2003).*Eternal Treblinka: Our treatment of animals and the Holocaust*. New York: Lantern.

Philo, C., & Wilbert, C. (2000). *Animal spaces, beastly places: New geographies of human-animal relationships*. London: Routledge.

Plumwood, V. (2002). *Environmental culture: The ecological crisis of reason*. London: Routledge.

Poe, E. A. (1842). *The gift: A Christmas and New Year's present for 1843*. Philadelphia: Carey and Hart.

Pope, A. (1936). Against barbarity to animals—The Guardian No. 61, May 21, 1713. In Norman Ault (Ed.), *The prose works of Alexander Pope: Vol. 1. The earlier works, 1711–1720* (pp. 107–114). Oxford: Basil Blackwell.

Porter, W. (2000). *Laboratory animal medicine and science series II. Rats and mice: Introduction and use in research*. Washington, DC: Health Sciences Center for Educational Resources University of Washington.

Rabinow, P. (1992). Artificiality and enlightenment: From sociobiology to biosociality. In Jonathan Crary & Sanford Kwinter (Eds.), *Incorporations* (pp. 234–252). New York: Zone Books.

Rackham, M. (2001). Carrier becoming symborg. *Culture Machine*, *3*, 1–7.

Rader, K. (1998). The mouse people: Murine genetics work at the Bussey Institution, 1909–1936. *Journal of the History of Biology*, *31*(2), 327–354.

Regan, T. (1983). *The case for animal rights*. Berkeley: University of California Press.

Reinert, H. (2007). The pertinence of sacrifice—Some notes on Larry the Luckiest Lamb. *Borderlands* 6(3). http://www.borderlands.net.au/

Reinhardt, V. (1996). Letter to the editor. *Lab Animal*, *25*(5), 42.

Reinhardt, V. (2003). Compassion for animals in the laboratory: Impairment or refinement of research methodology? *Journal of Applied Animal Welfare Science*, *6*(2), 123–130.

Ruonakoski, E. (2007). Phenomenology and the study of human behaviour. In C. Painter & C. Lotz (Eds.), *Phenomenology and the non-human animal: At the limits of experience* (pp. 75–84). Dordrecht: Springer.

Rupke, N. (Ed.) (1987). *Vivisection in historical perspective*. London: Croom Helm.

Russell, S. (2002, December 5). Of mice and men: Striking similarities at the DNA level could aid research. *San Francisco Chronicle*. Retrieved May 23, 2010, from http://articles.sfgate.com/2002-12-05/news/17575344_1_human-genome-eric-lander-director-mouse-genes

Sabini, J., & Silver, M. (1990). Destroying the innocent with a clear conscience: A sociopsychology of the Holocaust. In J. Dimsdale (Ed.), *Survivors, victims and perpetrators* (pp. 329–358). Washington, DC: Hemisphere Publications Corporation.

Salamone, J., Correa, M., Mingote, S., Weber, S., & Farrar, M. (2006). Nucleus accumbens dopamine and the forebrain circuitry involved in behavioral activation and effort-related decision making: Implications for understanding anergia and psychomotor slowing in depression. *Current Psychiatry Reviews*, *2*(2), 267–280.

Sanders, C. (1993). Understanding dogs: Caretakers' attributions of mindedness in canine-human relationships. *Journal of Contemporary Ethnography*, *22*, 205–226.

Scheler, M. (1961). *Man's place in nature* (H. Meyerhoff, Trans.). Boston: Beacon Press.

Seager, J. (2003). Pepperoni or broccoli? On the cutting wedge of feminist environmentalism. *Gender, Place and Culture*, *10*, 195–214.

Serres, M. (1982). *The parasite* (L. Schehr, Trans.). Baltimore: John Hopkins University Press.

Shanklin, E. (1985). Sustenance and symbol: Anthropological studies of domesticated animals. *Annual Review of Anthropology, 14*, 375–403.

Shanor, K., & Kanwal, J. (2009). *Bats sing, mice giggle: Revealing the secret lives of animals*. London: Icon Books.

Shapiro, K. (1989). The death of the animal: Ontological vulnerability. *Between the Species, 5*, 183–193.

Shugg, W. (1968). Humanitarian attitudes in the early animal experiments of the Royal Society. *Annals of Science, 24*, 227–238.

Singer, P. (1975). *Animal liberation*. New York: Avon.

Skeggs, B. (2010). The value of relationships: Affective scenes and emotional performances. *Feminist Legal Studies, 18*, 29–51.

Smyth, B. (2007). Merleau-Ponty and the generation of animals. *PhanEx, 2*, 170–215.

Spinelli, J. (1996). Human/research animal relationships: Research staff perspectives. In L. Krulisch, S. Mayer, & R. Simmons (Eds.), *The human/research animal relationship* (pp. 35–56). Greenbelt, MD: Scientists Centre for Animal Welfare.

Steele, R. (1970). The Tatler No. 134, February 16, 1709–10. In George A. Aitken (Ed.), *The Tatler* (pp. 110–113). New York: Olms Hildesheim. (Original work published 1710)

Strathern, M. (1992a). *After nature: English kinship in the late twentieth century*. Cambridge: Cambridge University Press.

Strathern, M. (1992b). *Reproducing the future: Anthropology, kinship and the new reproductive technologies*. New York: Routledge.

Strong, T. (2001). Kinship between Judith Butler and anthropology? A Review Essay. *Ethnos, 67*(3), 401–418.

Tambiah, S. (1969). Animals are good to think and good to prohibit. *Ethnology, 8*(4), 423–459.

Turning Point Project. (1999, October 11). This is an actual photo of a genetically engineered mouse with a human ear on its back. *New York Times*, p. 11.

Thomas, K. (1983). *Man and the natural world–a history of the modern sensibility*. New York: Pantheon Books.

Toadvine, T. (2007). How not to be a jellyfish: Human exceptionalism and the ontology of reflection. In C. Painer & C. Lotz (Eds.), *Phenomenology and the non-human animal: At the limits of experience* (pp. 39–56). Dordrecht: Springer.

U.S. Department of Energy Office of Science. Office of Biological and Environmental Research Human Genome Program. Retrieved June 20, 2010, from http://www.ornl.gov/hgmis

van den Bos, R., van der Harst, J., Jonkman, S., Schilders, M, & Spruijt, B. (2006). Rats assess costs and benefits according to an internal standard. *Behavioural Brain Research, 171*(2), 350–354.

Vint, S. (2005). Becoming other: Animals, kinship, and Butler's 'clay ark'. *Science Fiction Studies, 32*(2), 281–300.

Wadiwel, D. (2002). Cows and sovereignty: Biopower and animal life. *Borderlands*, 1(2). http://www.borderlands.net.au/

Weisberg, Z. (2009). The broken promises of monsters: Haraway, animals and the humanist legacy. *Journal for Critical Animal Studies, 2*(2), 22–62.

Westwood, J., & Simpson, J. (2005). *The lore of the land:Guide to England's legends, from Spring-heeled Jack to the witches of Warboys*. London: Penguin.

Whatmore, S. (2002). *Hybrid geographies—Natures, cultures, spaces*. London: Sage.

White, E. B. (1945). *Stuart Little*. New York: Harper Collins Publishers.

White, E. B. (1952). *Charlotte's web*. New York: Harper Collins Publishers.

Wick, D. (Producer), & Minkoff, R. (Director). (2002). *Stuart Little* [Motion picture]. United States: Columbia Pictures.

Wolch, J., & Emel, J. (1998). *Animal geographies—Place, politics and identity in the nature-culture borderlands*. London: Verso.

Wolfe, C. (2003). *Animal rites: American culture, the discourse of species and posthumanist theory*. Chicago: Chicago University Press.

Wolfe, T. (1996). How different species affect the relationship. In L. Krulisch, S. Mayer, & R. Simmons (Eds.), *The human/research animal relationship* (pp. 85–92). Greenbelt, MD: Scientists Centre for Animal Welfare.

Wolf-Meyer, M. (2006). Review essay: Agamben's *The Open Reconstruction: Studies in Contemporary Culture*, *6*(1). Retrieved May 17, 2010, from http://reconstruction.eserver.org/BReviews/revTheOpen.htm,

Yeo, E. (1971). Mayhew as a social investigator. In E. Thompson & E. Yeo (Eds.), *The unknown Mayhew: Selections from the Morning Chronicle, 1849–1850* (pp. 51–97). Harmondsworth: Penguin. New York: Harper & Row.

Zinsser, H. (1963). *Rats, lice and history*. Boston: The Atlantic Monthly Press. (Original work published 1934)

Index

www.ingramcontent.com/pod-product-compliance
Lightning Source LLC
Chambersburg PA
CBHW031415220926
51612CB00004B/43